Fodor's

D0107951

MOSCOW & ST. PETERSBURG

9th Edition

Where to Stay and Eat for All Budgets

Must-See Sights and Local Secrets

Ratings You Can Trust

Fodor's Travel Publications   New York, Toronto, London, Sydney, Auckland
www.fodors.com

FODOR'S MOSCOW & ST. PETERSBURG

Editor: Salwa Jabado

Editorial Contributor: John Rambow
Writers: Sabra Ayres, Anna Coppola, Tom Parfitt, Ezekiel Pfeifer, Galina Stolyarova, Irina Titova

Production Editor: Jennifer DePrima
Maps & Illustrations: David Lindroth and Mark Stroud, *cartographers;* Bob Blake, Rebecca Baer, *map editors;* William Wu, *information graphics*
Design: Fabrizio La Rocca, *creative director;* Guido Caroti, Siobhan O'Hare, *art directors;* Tina Malaney, Chie Ushio, Nora Rosansky, *designers;* Melanie Marin, *senior picture editor*
Cover Photo: (The Assumption Cathedral, Kremlin, Moscow): SIME/eStock Photo
Production Manager: Angela L. McLean

COPYRIGHT

Copyright © 2011 by Fodor's Travel, a division of Random House, Inc.

Fodor's is a registered trademark of Random House, Inc.

9th Edition

ISBN 978-0-307-48061-3

ISSN 1538-6082

SPECIAL SALES

This book is available at special discounts for bulk purchases for sales promotions or premiums. Special editions, including personalized covers, excerpts of existing books, and corporate imprints, can be created in large quantities for special needs. For more information, write to Special Markets/Premium Sales, 1745 Broadway, MD 6-2, New York, NY 10019, or e-mail specialmarkets@randomhouse.com.

AN IMPORTANT TIP & AN INVITATION

Although all prices, opening times, and other details in this book are based on information supplied to us at press time, changes occur all the time in the travel world, and Fodor's cannot accept responsibility for facts that become outdated or for inadvertent errors or omissions. So **always confirm information when it matters,** especially if you're making a detour to visit a specific place. Your experiences—positive and negative—matter to us. If we have missed or misstated something, **please write to us.** Share your opinion instantly through our online feedback center at fodors.com/contact-us.

PRINTED IN THE UNITED STATES OF AMERICA

10 9 8 7 6 5 4 3 2 1

Eugene Fodor:
The Spy Who Loved Travel

As Fodor's celebrates our 75th anniversary, we are honoring the colorful and adventurous life of Eugene Fodor, who revolutionized guidebook publishing in 1936 with his first book, *On the Continent, The Entertaining Travel Annual*.

Eugene Fodor's life seemed to leap off the pages of a great spy novel. Born in Hungary, he spoke six languages and graduated from the Sorbonne and the London School of Economics. During World War II he joined the Office of Strategic Services, the budding spy agency for the United States. He commanded the team that went behind enemy lines to liberate Prague, and recommended to Generals Eisenhower, Bradley, and Patton that Allied troops move to the capital city. After the war, Fodor worked as a spy in Austria, posing as a U.S. diplomat.

In 1949 Eugene Fodor—with the help of the CIA—established Fodor's Modern Guides. He was passionate about travel and wanted to bring his insider's knowledge of Europe to a new generation of sophisticated Americans who wanted to explore and seek out experiences beyond their borders. Among his innovations were annual updates, consulting local experts, and including cultural and historical perspectives and an emphasis on people—not just sites. As Fodor described it, "The main interest and enjoyment of foreign travel lies not only in 'the sites,' . . . but in contact with people whose customs, habits, and general outlook are different from your own."

Eugene Fodor died in 1991, but his legacy, Fodor's Travel, continues. It is now one of the world's largest and most trusted brands in travel information, covering more than 600 destinations worldwide in guidebooks, on Fodors.com, and in ebooks and iPhone apps. Technology and the accessibility of travel may be changing, but Eugene Fodor's unique storytelling skills and reporting style are behind every word of today's Fodor's guides.

Our editors and writers continue to embrace Eugene Fodor's vision of building personal relationships through travel. We invite you to join the Fodor's community at fodors.com/community and share your experiences with like-minded travelers. Tell us when we're right. Tell us when we're wrong. And share fantastic travel secrets that aren't yet in Fodor's. Together, we will continue to deepen our understanding of our world.

Happy 75th Anniversary, Fodor's! Here's to many more.

Tim Jarrell, Publisher

CONTENTS

MAPS

ABOUT THIS BOOK

Our Ratings

At Fodor's, we spend considerable time choosing the best places in a destination so you don't have to. By default, anything we recommend in this book is worth visiting. But some sights, properties, and experiences are so great that we've recognized them with additional accolades. Orange **Fodor's Choice** stars indicate our top recommendations; black stars highlight places we deem **Highly Recommended**; and **Best Bets** call attention to top properties in various categories. Disagree with any of our choices? Care to nominate a new place? Visit our feedback center at www.fodors.com/feedback.

Hotels

Hotels have private bath, phone, TV, and air-conditioning, and do not offer meals unless we specify that in the review. We always list facilities but not whether you'll be charged an extra fee to use them.

For expanded hotel reviews, visit **Fodors.com**

Restaurants

Unless we state otherwise, restaurants are open for lunch and dinner daily. We mention dress only when there's a specific requirement and reservations only when they're essential or not accepted—it's always best to book ahead.

Credit Cards

We assume that restaurants and hotels accept credit cards. If not, we'll note it in the review.

Budget Well

Hotel and restaurant price categories from ¢ to $$$$ are defined in the opening pages of the respective chapters. For attractions, we always give standard adult admission fees; reductions are usually available for children, students, and senior citizens.

Listings
* ★ Fodor's Choice
* ★ Highly recommended
* ⊠ Physical address
* ✛ Directions or Map coordinates
* ⌂ Mailing address
* ☎ Telephone
* 🖷 Fax
* ⊕ On the Web

* ✍ E-mail
* 🎫 Admission fee
* ☉ Open/closed times
* Ⓜ Metro stations
* ▭ No credit cards

Hotels & Restaurants
* ☷ Hotel
* ⌁ Number of rooms
* ♿ Facilities
* ⏁Ⓞ| Meal plans
* ✕ Restaurant
* ⌯ Reservations
* 🏛 Dress code
* ↘ Smoking

Outdoors
* 🏌 Golf
* ⛺ Camping

Other
* ♨ Family-friendly
* ⇨ See also
* ⊠ Branch address
* ☞ Take note

1

Experience Moscow and St. Petersburg

WORD OF MOUTH

"I highly recommend learning the Cyrillic alphabet at the very least. It will help to navigate in train stations, find restaurants and for me, read many of the cards next to artwork in museums that weren't in English. So many times I wanted to know who the artist was and I was able to sound it out!"

— amyb

"In late August–early September, the weather was much cooler than we anticipated, so next time I would pack warmer clothes. I would also pack more stylish clothes; the Russians were beautifully dressed, and we stood out like the tourists that we are."

— fluffnfold

MOSCOW AND ST. PETERSBURG TODAY

Russia has come a long way since the break up of the Soviet Union in 1991, allowing visitors more access to what makes the country so enticing—its rich history, vast expanses of land, and hospitable people. The country is at once exciting, overwhelming, and inviting. Perhaps Winston Churchill said it the best when in 1939 he described Russia as "a riddle, wrapped in a mystery, inside an enigma."

Economy

Moscow and St. Petersburg are not budget travel destinations. There is unimaginable wealth in the two cities, despite unnerving poverty in some of the farther regions of Russia's vast expanse. In Russia, oil and gas are still the biggest games in town, and economic development is directly dependent upon their prices. Despite several economic crises during the past 15 years, Russia's economy has bounced back and remains fairly stable, meaning the rich do indeed keep getting richer. The infamous business oligarchs who made their money during the post-Soviet privatization of Russia are still around, but the next generation, too, have acquired multimillionaire and billionaire status. In the summer, Moscow hosts the annual Millionaire Fair, where yacht makers, luxury brands, and international real estate brokers come to woo Russia's nouveau riche. All this opulent wealth can't hide the persistent poverty of these cities. Central Asian immigrants, in particular, come seeking economic stability and a better life only to find they can barely survive on the low wages of street cleaners and construction workers. The Kremlin's attempts and promises to diversify the economy have, so far, been slow to bring significant results. However, there has been some trickle down and Russia's middle class continues to grow. And as their incomes continue to rise, so, too, do the prices in Moscow and St. Petersburg.

Politics

If you can't remember whether Vladimir Putin is president or prime minister, don't worry. Neither can many Russians. Prime Minister Putin's political strength and influence are still highly regarded in Russia, even after he exhausted his two-term limit as president in 2008. A recent poll indicated that more than half of all Russians believed Putin was still calling the shots, despite President Dmitri Medvedev's efforts to show he's in charge. Western pundits criticize Putin's erosion of Russia's young democracy, but ask most Russians about how they feel about the president, er, Putin, and they are likely to tell you they admire him and what he's done for the country. The population seems to like Medvedev, too, and will likely continue to for as long as Putin favors him. Russians won't hesitate to complain about the bureaucracy and poor state of much of the cities' infrastructure, however. This harks back to an old Russian custom of praising the tsar but blaming the bureaucrats. Still, the praise for Putin and Medvedev doesn't mean that the whole population is swooning. Critical voices do exist, although their dissent is usually quashed when it gets too loud. Russia continues to be one of the most dangerous places for practicing journalists.

Olympic Fever

The Olympic committee surprised the world when it chose the southern Russian city of Sochi to host the 2014 Winter Games. Russians greeted the news with less surprise, however. Sochi was a favorite winter sports mecca during Soviet times, and was repopularized when

Putin's ski trips there were broadcast on state news channels. The remaking of Sochi and its surroundings continues with much to-do about controversial government spending and questionable project tenders. Some estimates put a $15 billion price tag on the project of turning Sochi into a smooth-running Olympic operation. But in Moscow and St. Petersburg, Olympic pride is beginning to take hold. Bosco Sports, a Russian sports clothing line and one of the official sponsors of the events, has opened stores around the country to sell some of the Team Russia paraphernalia. You'll see Bosco Sport's mascot bear pop up around both cities as part of the event's promotion.

Religion

The Russian Orthodox Church is experiencing a new surge in believers after having an on-again, off-again relationship with its congregation for decades. During the years of the Soviet Union, the church—and religion in general—was forbidden at times and used to manipulate nationalist sentiment during others. This was particularly true during World War II, when the Communist Party pulled on the heartstrings of god-fearing Russians to go fight against the fascists on the front line. Today, many previously destroyed churches have been reconstructed, most notable of these being the sparkling Cathedral of Christ the Savior in Moscow. Ethnic Russians make up about 80% of the country's 142 million population, and polls show that some 90% of them say they are part of the Orthodox Church. This holds true even with the younger crowd. It's not uncommon to see hip, twentysomethings standing in line at the Kazan Cathedral in St. Petersburg to kiss an icon, or trying to squeeze a place inside a golden-domed church in Moscow during a crowded Easter service. Religion can still get political in Russia. State-run news channels don't hesitate to show Putin in photo ops with heads of the church.

Tearing Down the Past

To the visitor's naked eye, it may not be apparent that there is a vicious war raging being the massive amounts of construction happening in both St. Petersburg and Moscow. What some see as progress, others see as the destruction of Russian architectural heritage. Preservationists in St. Petersburg accuse the local government of giving the go-ahead to big investors—particularly Gazprom—to build modern office buildings that will ruin Peter the Great's European feel. In Moscow, the fight has been particularly contentious as the city's skyline continues to be dominated by massive construction cranes. Former Mayor Yuri Luzhkov, who lost his job in late 2010 after falling out of favor with President Medvedev, was in office during the destruction of what critics say was some 400 architecturally significant buildings in the capitol. Lushkov's billionaire wife, Elena Baturina, and her construction company, Inteco, contributed to the lucrative build up of the city, adding to accusations of corruption on the part of the former mayor. In both cities, activists groups have formed to try to put a stop to the great teardown.

WHAT'S WHERE

1 Moscow. Cosmopolitan in flavor, Russia's capital exudes prosperity and vigor. From Stalin's carved-marble metro stations to the sprawl of modern business complexes, Moscow flaunts its ambition with a penchant for going over the top. It is an all-night-party town whose days offer endless opportunities for those who can keep up. A merchant capital by birth, Moscow was fashioned for big spenders, and money has always made the wheels go 'round here. Now counted as one of the world's most expensive cities, the only possible limit is the size of your wallet.

2 Moscow Environs and the Golden Ring. In the 12th to 14th centuries, the Golden Ring cities were the most important political, religious, and commercial centers in Russia before Moscow usurped all power. Nowadays these ancient enclaves are perfect destinations for rolling back the centuries. A visit to their medieval convents, ancient trade chambers, and kremlins is like stepping into a living encyclopedia of Russian culture, complete with picture-postcard views of onion-domed churches set on the banks of the Volga River.

3 St. Petersburg. Serenity and reflection reign in this city. Tsars don't rush—it would

KEY

⊢—∙—∙— Rail lines

be undignified. St. Petersburg was founded as the new capital of the Russian Empire in 1703 by Peter the Great and still carries itself with austere regal grace. The city build on the marshy banks of the Neva River today attracts more tourists than anywhere else in Russia. A brilliant fusion created by Italian and French architects, St. Petersburg invites comparisons with Amsterdam, Venice, and Stockholm. The big attractions here are the pastimes of the nobility—artwork, classical concerts, ballet, and idyllic promenading in the 19th-century landscape.

4 Summer Palaces and Historic Islands. Several of St. Petersburg's imperial summer residences have been meticulously restored to their original splendor, and the sheer opulence is stunning. Peterhof's (Petrodvorets) park is Russia's answer to Versailles, while Pushkin's (Tsarskoye Selo) Catherine Palace houses the legendary Amber Room. Lomonosov (Oranienbaum), a UNESCO World Heritage Site, and the Konstantine Palace, which hosted the G8 summit in 2006, have both undergone restoration and are great places for a summer stroll or picnic.

TOP ATTRACTIONS

Red Square, Moscow
No matter how many times you walk on the uneven cobblestones of Red Square, the view is awe-inspiring and the experience monumental. Stand in the center and let your mind wander as centuries of Russian history unfold in the architecture. Tsars were crowned and traitors beheaded just outside of St. Basil's Cathedral's colorful domes. Soviet tanks once rolled ceremoniously across as Stalin surveyed from the sidelines, and Lenin's mausoleum is still guarded by stern-faced soldiers.

The Kremlin and Armory Palace, Moscow
The first walls of the Kremlin were erected more than 850 years ago and continue to symbolize Russian power today. Don't miss the Tomb of the Unknown Soldier in Alexander Gardens, a popular place for newly weds to have their first photo taken. The Armory Palace is the jewel of the Kremlin and contains one of the richest collections of Russian silver, gold, diamonds and Fabergé eggs in the country. Several halls display more than 4,000 artifacts dating back to the 12th century, including diamond-encrusted coronation thrones and extravagant Russian armor.

Bolshoi Theater, Moscow
Moscow's oldest—and most famous—theater recently reopened after a complete renovation. Watching a ballet performance of a Russian classic, such as Tchaikovsky's Nutcracker, on the main stage is unforgettable.

Tretyakov Gallery, Moscow
Wander through the rooms of Old Tretyakov's extraordinary collection of famous Russian icons, landscapes, and portraits housed in an early-20th-century building that feels more like a castle. The museum boasts one of the largest and most renowned collections of work from the prerevolutionary Russian realists known as the Wanderers.

Palace Square and the State Hermitage Museum, St. Petersburg
Russia's other historic square is the heart of its imperial past, as well as the host to pivotal moments in Tsarist Russia's demise. On Bloody Sunday in 1905, palace guards shot dead hundreds of peaceful protestors here, sparking the first of Russia's revolutions. Housed in the pastel green and white Winter Palace, the Hermitage museum contains one of the world's most important art collections. On par with the Louvre, the collection is housed in what was once the tsars' family residence.

Peter and Paul Fortress, St. Petersburg
Peter the Great built the fortress in 1703 to defend Russia from the Swedes, making it the oldest building in the city. Inside the fortress walls, the cathedral's gilded 400-foot spire one of the city's most recognizable landmarks.

St. Isaac's Cathedral, St. Petersburg
It took more than 40 years to complete the world's third-largest domed cathedral, now the dominant feature of St Petersburg's skyline. Climb up the 262 steps of the colonnade to get a spectacular panoramic view of the city.

Peterhof and Pushkin summer palaces, St. Petersburg
A hydrofoil cruise on the Gulf of Finland to Peterhof's cascading fountains and lavish gardens gets you in an imperial mood. The ornate, golden interiors and recently reconstructed Amber Room of the 18th-century Catherine's Palace at Pushkin (Tsarskoye Selo) offer a look into the extravagance of the Russian royal family.

FLAVORS OF MOSCOW AND ST. PETERSBURG

The variety of international cuisine in Moscow and St. Petersburg might make you think traditional Russian fare ended with the Soviet Union. Luckily, sushi and ostrich burgers haven't completely replaced the hearty classic dishes that have satisfied everyone from the tsars to the Soviet collective farm workers. Russians know how to do comfort food right, and most meals consist of meats, potatoes, and a variety of typically Eastern European vegetables such as cabbage, beets, carrots, and onions. These days there are more choices for vegetarians, but don't expect a large variety. Russians don't tend to go overboard with spices, but do expect garlic, onions, dill, and mayonnaise to play a large part in your flavor palate. What Russian dishes lack in exotic ingredients they make up for in satisfying taste.

Zakuski

If you are lucky enough to be invited to a Russian's house for a meal, you'll be greeted by a tableful of *zakuski,* or appetizers. They are usually eaten before the main meal or soup, and preferably accompanied with vodka. A few typical zakuski you might find on the menu of Russian restaurants are *olivie* salad—think potato salad with pickles, boiled eggs, green peas, and lots of mayonnaise. Another staple salad is *shuba*, a layered combination of herring, boiled eggs, beets, carrots, potatoes, and, of course, mayonnaise. This is sometimes called herring in shuba, or *selyodka pod shuboy*, which roughly translates as "herring under a fur coat." On special occasions, you might be offered some *salo*, which is cured pork fat. Russians say the best salo comes from Ukraine. It looks like lard, but tastes like bacon and is the perfect chaser after a shot of peppered vodka.

Pelmeni

Every Eastern European nation seems to have its own form of the dumpling. Russians call them *pelmeni*, and they are sometimes referred to as Siberian pelmeni. The flour-based dough is stuffed with a mixture of meat (usually beef and pork mixed together) and onions, and then boiled. They are generally served with a dollop or *smetana*, or sour cream, on top. Don't confuse pelmeni with Ukrainian *vareniki*, which can be stuffed with potatoes and mushrooms, cabbage, cottage cheese, or cherries. It's not unusual to see both vareniki and pelmeni on the same menu.

Borsch

The beet-based soup is packed with carrots, onions, potatoes, meat, and sometimes beans. It's not as thick as stew, but it's nonetheless a good remedy for tired legs after a long walk around the city, particularly in winter. Borsch is usually followed by a main course, although a large bowl is sometimes filling enough on its own. Whisk in a heaping spoonful of sour cream and slurp it down with a slice of brown bread.

Georgian Cuisine

Russia and Georgia may have heated territorial disputes, but there is one thing they can agree on—Georgian cuisine is delicious and a favorite of most Russians. Both Moscow and St. Petersburg have plenty of Georgian restaurants. Be sure to try *khachapuri* (a baked bread stuffed with salty cheese) and the eggplant slices stuffed with walnuts, followed by succulent pieces of kababs. Georgia also makes good wines, but you won't readily find them in Russia unless a 2006 ban on their import is lifted.

TOP EXPERIENCES

Ride the Moscow metro

The efficiency of Stalin's metro system contradicts the standstill of Russian bureaucracy. The vast system transports about 9 million passengers a day, and the frequency and regularity of the trains put New York's and London's underground systems to shame. You could spend hours just riding the rails as a sight-seeing visitor, stopping to gaze up at the mosaic ceilings Komsomolskaya or to ogle Ploshchad Revolyutsii's bronzed statues of beefy Soviet workers, farmers, and soldiers.

See and be seen at a Moscow café

European style coffee joints and, yes, Starbucks have taken over downtown Moscow. It seems endless spouts of caffeine are energizing the whole city. Cafés now provide space for high-powered business meetings as well as hangout spots for the younger blogging set. Coffee Mania on Bolshoi Nikitskaya was one of the first European-style cafés to burst onto the scene and remains one of the favorites of Moscow's trendsetters and arty elite.

Take a walk

Muscovites know how to take advantage of the city's green spaces and parks in a city rushed with ambition and development. Russians old or young see a good, long stroll with friends as the best way to dive into the day's gossip or spend time with aging grandparents. Slowly cruise down the Boulevard Ring's green walkways and you'll pass young lovers kissing on benches and pairs of babushkas discussing the latest price increases at neighborhood shops.

Shop'til you drop

A touristy market that's often full of Muscovites as well, Ismailovsky is a one-stop spot for souvenirs, antiques, and Russian kitsch. Wander through the aisles of wooden stalls to find everything from old Soviet posters, samovars, and fur hats to Central Asian carpets.

Celebrate winter

Muscovites love the cold and thrive in it. One of the best ways to celebrate a crisp winter day or evening is to get on the ice and show off your inner Irina Slutskaya (who hails from Moscow, by the way). Several city parks have rinks where you can rent a pair of skates for a few dollars. Gorky Park and Patriarch's Pond (*Patriashy Prudi*) are some of the best in the center. Grab your partner's hand and skate around the rink, or try and join in on a pickup game of ice hockey.

Party all night long

If partying is your pastime, Moscow is sure to satisfy. This is an all-night party town with enough energy to keep the beat going for as long as your dancing shoes can hold up. Party with the elite and wanna-be elite at one of the city's thumping nightclubs, many of which boast brand-name DJs and serious face control. Or relax with friends in a small, smoky student café with blaring Russified reggae. But don't be surprised if you end up out on the town until the sun comes up.

Get out of town

Russians who live outside Moscow love to criticize the capital for being out of touch with the real Russia. Test out their theory by taking a breather in one of the picturesque cities along the Volga River. Even if your Russian language skills are limited to spacibo (thank you), you'll find the culture and people of the Golden Ring cities

to be notably more open and friendly and the delicately painted golden domes and colorful wooden houses are worth a look.

Celebrate White Nights

The end of June's long daylight hours breathes festive energy into St. Petersburg after months of bitter cold. During these days, the sun sets only long enough to leave a dim glow and St. Petersburg stays up all night, too. These are the peak tourist weeks, and festivals and parties abound. There's even a marathon that has recently attracted runners from around the world because of its historic path and late start—5 pm. A fireworks show on the last night of the White Nights festival lights up the sky.

Cruise St. Petersburg's canals

Peter the Great intended for St. Petersburg to be one of the leading cities of Europe. One of the best ways to see his Venice-like creation is via the waterways of the city's man-made canals. Most cruises pass by the city's top attractions, while giving you time to pick up on the little details of the city's grand and ornate buildings and bridges. Guided tours in English will lead you as you inch by the former residents of nobility, artists, and writers.

Soak up some sun

St. Petersburg knows how to take advantage of the generous daylight granted to it in the short summer months. Generations of expert sunbathers have perfected the art of the even tan by soaking in the sun along the sandy beach on the Neva just outside the walls of Peter and Paul Fortress. But you won't find them flipping around on beach towels. Locals will tell you that standing is the only way to an even tan when you only have a few months of summer. And small bikinis are the norm, so don't be surprised to see grandfathers catching rays in Speedos.

Attend world-class performances at reasonable prices

For opera and ballet lovers, seeing a performance by the world-renowned Kirov Ballet and Opera companies is a must. The companies, which are called the Mariinsky companies at home in Russia, perform in the imperially grand and sparkling Mariinsky Theater. The green and white theater, built in the mid-19th century, has been the cultural hub of Russia since tsarist times. Tickets can be bought online, usually at half the price of one of their traveling performances.

Get caught on the wrong side of the bridge

Commerce on the Neva River is a prime source of revenue for St. Petersburg. During the warmer months, from the end of April to November, the bridge's roads are closed to traffic and the drawbridges are raised to let large ships pass through. Each year there is a published schedule, which consistently has started around 1:30 am. Night owls and pub crawlers who miss the cutoff get stuck on the other side until the bridges are lowered and they can head home. Boat tours during the bridge openings offer a unique perspective on the process.

QUINTESSENTIAL MOSCOW & ST. PETERSBURG

Festivals

Rio and Venice may have their colorful carnivals, but Russians have something no less amazing up their sleeves—Maslenitsa, or Shrovetide, celebrated on the last week before Lent on the Julian calendar.

Today Shrovetide is a rambunctious outdoor spring festival where Russians indulge in dressing up and wild singing and dancing. Russian *blini* (pancakes), golden and round to symbolize the sun, are served in virtually every eatery across the nation during this week.

The White Nights Festival, which takes place in St. Petersburg at the end of June. Named in honor of the remarkably long days around the summer solstice, the festival features performances by Russia's top ballet, opera, and musical ensembles, as well as a massive fireworks display once the sun finally does set.

Epic Food

In Russian folk tales, amorous admirers ply their sweethearts with *pryaniki pechatnie* (printed gingerbreads). This ancient Russian culinary delight is a baked sweet pastry filled with honey or jam and flavored with spices; try it at any bakery.

While gingerbread might have done the trick in the olden days, caviar is one of the preferred methods of impressing your darling in modern Russia. It's sold everywhere, from grocery stores to local markets called *rynoks*. The best caviar comes from the beluga variety of sturgeon. It is silvery gray, uniform in size and shape, and tastes like a million bucks.

Another favorite is *kvas,* a refreshing nonalcoholic drink. Kvas, which literally translates as "sour drink," is made with fermented rye bread and is a renowned hangover remedy.

Experience Russia with all your senses and discover what "Russianness" means. We guide you through some of the most exciting pursuits, basic rituals, and beloved symbols of this country.

Vodka

Social lubricant and vice of choice for centuries, the national drink is produced by hundreds of brands and comes in many flavor varieties. A few of the best labels are Flagman, Russky Standart, Beluga, and Beloye Zoloto. If straight shots aren't your thing, flavored vodkas can help take the edge off. *Limonnaya*, slightly sweet lemon-flavor vodka, is particularly tasty, as is spicy *pertsovka*, infused with peppercorns and chilies.

At the bar, toasts such as *Vashe zdorovie!* (To your health!) and clinking glasses accompany every shot as do *zakuski* (appetizers) chasers, which vary from humble pickles to fine caviar. For reasons shrouded in the mists of time, empty bottles are considered bad luck and are immediately discarded or put on the floor, so watch your step and mind your manners.

Banya

Sweaty people whipping themselves with wet bundles of birch twigs in a room full of steam may sound like purgatory or sadomasochism. But for Russians the *banya* experience is the way to nirvana and longevity. Most people in Russia believe the excruciating wet heat of the banya makes you shed toxins ultrafast, through heavy sweating, and that it rejuvenates the internal organs. If you're willing to give it a try, Moscow's ornate Sandunovskiye bani is the gold standard.

The banya also appears in an ancient Russian legend. In the year 945, Olga, widow of Kievan prince Igor, lured his murderers—the elite corps of an East Slavic tribe of Drevlyane—into a banya and set the bathhouse on fire. Meet Russia's first saint.

IF YOU LIKE

Palaces and Estates

Lovers of all things beautiful and luxurious should not miss Russia's imperial estates and palaces. Far from frugal, the tsars truly went all out when it came to their residences. Hiring the world's best architects and using literally tons of gold, marble, and semiprecious stones was only the beginning—these palaces and estates are truly Russian in size as well. Most were built close to Moscow and St. Petersburg as the tsars' summer residences and are therefore just a day trip away from the major cities.

Peterhof (Petrodvorets). Nicknamed the "Russian Versailles," the elaborate interiors, formal gardens, and beautiful fountains of Peter the Great's summer palace live up to their moniker. This is St. Petersburg's most famous imperial residence, located in the suburbs about 40 minutes away.

Pushkin (Tsarskoye Selo). This St. Petersburg palace, with its richly decorated baroque facade, was the favorite residence of the last Russian tsar, Nicholas II. It's main draw is the turquoise and gold Catherine Palace, home to the sumptuous Amber Room.

Romanov Palace Chambers in Zaryadye. Located in Moscow's historic Kitai Gorod neighborhood, this palace-museum gives a taste of the luxurious boyar lifestyle, including period costume, furniture, and household items.

Kuskovo. Pastel pink and neoclassical in style, this estate just outside of Moscow was once the summer residence of the Sheremetyevs, one of Russia's wealthiest and most distinguished families. It also houses the celebrated Kuskovo State Ceramics museum.

Ballet

Classical ballet is the only art form that never really went dissident in Russia. Russia's last tsar, Nicholas II, fell for the charms of ballerina Matilda Kshessinskaya, and from then on, through the Communist era and into the Putin years, ballet and especially ballerinas have been beyond criticism and free from oppression. As ballet has continued to thrive under state sponsorship, it has become an essential part of any official visit, as much a part of protocol as a trip to the war memorials.

Russian ballet is known for its exquisite blend of expressiveness, technique, and ethereal flair. Visiting ballet professionals envy both coordination and torso, the two strongest elements of Russian ballet training. Russian classical ballet, with its antique poetic charm, has preserved its precious legacy without becoming old-fashioned. New stars, such as the amazing Nikolai Tsiskaridze, inject new life into one of Russia's oldest and most respected arts.

Swan Lake. See this signature ballet at the Bolshoi (Moscow) or Mariinsky (St. Petersburg) theaters.

Sleeping Beauty. This marvel of 19th-century choreography has been meticulously restored in its original form at the Mariinsky Theatre in St. Petersburg.

The Nutcracker. The Bolshoi, Mariinsky, and other companies perform this Christmas classic year-round.

Vaganova Ballet Academy in St. Petersburg. Russia's most prestigious classical ballet academy is alma mater to Anna Pavlova, George Balanchine, and Mikhail Baryshnikov. It has a wonderful museum.

Exploring the Communist Legacy

Attitudes toward Soviet times are complex, with many people of all ages regarding them as "the good old days." Soviet themes and symbols are everywhere, from old monuments and inscriptions on buildings to the red star, which is still the symbol of the Russian armed forces.

KGB Museum, Moscow. Housed in the infamous Lubyanka Square building that served as KGB headquarters since the days of Felix Dzerzhinsky (aka "Iron Felix"), who founded its first incarnation, the CHEKA, in 1917, the KGB museum is a chilling reminder of Russia's often repressive past.

Gulag Museum, Moscow. The small museum provides a harrowing look into one of Russia's most brutal histories. Tens of millions of Soviet citizens were subjected to the harsh life of these labor camps, which played a major role in the USSR's political oppression.

Lenin's Mausoleum, Moscow. Vladimir Lenin has lain in state here since his death in 1924.

Museum of the Contemporary History of Russia, Moscow. If you're a Soviet history buff, you'll enjoy this museum and its collection of USSR propaganda posters, velvet flags, and socialist worker's medals. It often hosts special exhibits.

The Seven Sisters, Moscow. The seven legendary skyscrapers which dominate Moscow's skyline were constructed just after World War II by Stalin and intended as a symbol of Soviet power at the beginning of the Cold War.

Russian Political History Museum, St. Petersburg. The museum documents all aspects of the Communist past, from the paraphernalia of spying to propaganda.

Porcelain and Folk Art

When Catherine the Great ordered her elaborate dinner service from the renowned Imperial Porcelain Manufacturer, porcelain was the exclusive preserve of aristocrats. But since then it has become almost every Russian's favorite gift.

In addition to porcelain, Russia also has a large number of other folk handicrafts, such as Gzhel ceramics, Palekh boxes, and, of course, the ubiquitous *matryoshka* doll.

Lomonosov Porcelain Factory. Arguably the most famous porcelain manufacturer in Russia, this St. Petersburg gem was founded in 1744 and owned for a time by the Romanovs. Its patented and instantly recognizable cobalt-blue pattern lends a distinctly Russian flavor to any event.

Palekh Boxes. These beautiful hand-painted lacquer boxes are handicrafts of the Golden Ring towns. Typically a fairy-tale scene adorns the box top, but images of landscapes, battle scenes, or even poetry can be found. They require about two months to create and the finer details are drawn using a special brush made from a squirrel's tail.

Gzhel Ceramics. First manufactured in the village of Gzhel outside Moscow in the 6th century, this famous white-and-blue pottery may be Russia's oldest folk art.

Matryoshka. Dating from 1890, these nesting dolls are a relatively new Russian handicraft. The largest wooden doll opens to reveal ever-smaller wooden figures inside. They usually depict red-cheeked, brightly dressed peasant women, although matryoshkas can be purchased featuring everyone from Soviet leaders to *Star Wars* characters.

BANYA

Of all Russia's traditions, perhaps none is more steeped in ritual than a trip to the steamy banya, a sauna-style bathhouse where the steam is produced by throwing a steady supply of water over heated rocks. In fact, for many banya lovers a trip to the bathhouse is almost a religious experience, complete with birch twigs for self-flagellation (to open pores and promote circulation). There's even a traditional garment—a peaked woolen hat (sold at numerous shops and sometimes at the banyas themselves) to keep the tips of your ears from burning and prevent heat from escaping through the top of your head. Manicures, pedicures, and massages are also often available, and some banyas are even attached to fitness centers.

The banya, or bathhouse, is a cultural tradition that became popular in the 17th century, when attending a communal bath was the only way for many Russians to stay clean. Today, it is still believed to have therapeutic benefits and is also valued as a place to relax, socialize, and even do business.

BANYA BASICS

Though visiting a banya can be one of the highlights of a trip to Moscow or St. Petersburg, it can also be a confusing experience and there are a few ground rules you should know, like men and women are separated in general sections, although families and couples can hire a private bath for use together, and soap is strictly forbidden (the steam is supposed to clean you).

Here are a few easy steps that will help you get the best steam possible:

1. Check Yourself: If you have low or high blood pressure, a heart ailment, or some other health issue, you may want to stay away. Pregnant women and asthma sufferers are advised to do the same.

2. Check In: After paying the entrance fee, your valuables are handed to a special attendant who puts them in a locker and watches over them. Theft is rare, but you may be better off leaving valuables in a hotel safe. Tipping is customary, generally 50R–150R for the attendant, 300R–500R for a good masseur. You will then be given a towel and assigned a locker for your clothes. Bring a pair of flip-flops to walk around in.

3. Sweat It Out: Champions of the Russian banya believe that steaming helps combat respiratory problems, aids in circulation, and opens the pores to help rid you of all the nasty toxins in your body—that's why the steam room is kept hotter than the fires of hell—a toasty 90°C (194°F) to be exact. Have a seat on one of the benches lining the walls (the higher up you sit, the hotter you'll be). You can wrap yourself in a towel but most bathers in gender-segregated rooms go nude. Towels are, however, very useful for sitting on. Are the tips of your ears burning? That means it's working. Don't overdo it: 10–15 minutes is more than enough for your first time.

4. Cool Down: Once you feel sufficiently steamed, dunk yourself in the pool, barrel, or bucket of icy water provided. This is an essential part of the process—if you don't get your body temperature down, your next trip to the steam room won't be much fun.

5. Relax: The banya will probably have a relaxation zone that provides everything from couches and cold drinks to meals. While the ultra-Russian ambience might seem ideal for doing a shot or two of vodka, keep in mind that you will be

dehydrated. Stick to beer, juice, or best of all, water.

6. Repeat Steps 3–5: Once you're rested, reenter the steam room. You'll likely sweat more profusely this go round. This is an ideal time to engage in some self-flagellation with a bunch of soaked *veniki*, or birch twigs. Repeat the process as many times as you see fit, and when you're done, give your neighbors the traditional post-banya salutation: *s lyokhim parom*—may your steam be light!

VISIT A BANYA

Unless otherwise indicated, the banyas listed here are open daily. Note that over the summer, most banyas close for two or three weeks when hot water is turned off for a few weeks at a time in different parts of the city.

Moscow's Banyas

With a gym, salon, bar, pool, and massage, **Bani na Presne** (⊠ *7 Stolyarny per., Presnensky* ☎ *495/609–3550* ⊕ *banina-presne.ru/index.php* Ⓜ *Ulitsa 1905 Goda*) is a popular, casual banya. It's 750R to 850R for a two-hour visit. **Russkie Bani** (⊠ *25A Bolshoy Strochenovsky per., Zamoskvoreche* ☎ *495/236–3171* Ⓜ *Dobrinskaya or Serpukhovskaya*) is part of a fitness center across the street from the South African embassy. Two-hour sessions cost around 350R.

Fodor's Choice ★ Dating to the late 1800s, the impeccably clean **Sandunovskiye Bani** (⊠ *Neglinnaya ul. 14., Kitai Gorod* ☎ *495/ 625–4631 or 495/628–4633* ⊕ *www. sanduny.ru* ⊙ *Daily 8 am–11 pm* Ⓜ *Kuznetsky Most*) is probably the city's most elegant bathhouse, with a lavish interior. Prices depend on your gender and which section you visit, but range from 1,000R to 1,800R. On-site facilities

include a beauty parlor and, of course, massage. They are closed on Tuesday for cleaning.

One of the better banya bargains in town, **Seleznyovskiye Bani** (⊠ *15 Seleznyovsky ul., Tverskoi* ☎ *499/978–8491* Ⓜ *Novoslobodskaya*) combines quality service with low prices. Two hours cost around 400R, depending on what section you go into and the day of the week. Prices range from 300R to 700R. It's closed Monday.

St. Petersburg Banyas

For the best experience, consider sticking to the places we recommend and opt for a private cabin, rather than the general section.

Kazachi Bani (⊠ *11 Kazachii per.* ☎ *812/ 315–0734* Ⓜ *Pushkinskaya*) is located in a somewhat dilapidated building, but is still a good place to try. It has a private banya for 10 people. **Yamskie Bani** (⊠ *9 ul. Dostoyevskovo* ☎ *812/713–3580* ⊕ *www. yamskie.ru* Ⓜ *Vladimirskaya*) has individual rooms as well as a sauna, tanning, and a fitness center.

Banya Accoutrements

A few stores around Moscow sell banya goods, including hats, chamomile-soaked towels, and herb-enriched lotions. **Perekryostok Supermarket** (⊠ *1 Tishinskaya Pl., Presnensky* ☎ *495/662–8888* ⊕ *www. perekrestok.ru* Ⓜ *Belorusskaya*) stocks hats, aromatic oils, and ready-packed birch twigs at more than 50 branches around the city. **Novaya Zarya** (⊠ *4 Ilinka ul., in Gostiny Dvor, Kitai Gorod* ☎ *495/298–0752* Ⓜ *Ploshchad Revolutsii*) is one of Russia's oldest perfume manufacturers, which makes its own line of fragrant essences that you can add to banya water (you can get your own tub even at a public banya).

MOSCOW AND ST. PETERSBURG MADE EASY

Airports and Visas

All foreigners, except citizens of some former Soviet republics, need a visa to visit Russia. An official invitation is required to apply for a visa. The invitation can be issued by a Russian citizen, or, more commonly, from an official tour agency or company. Processing fees, times, and additional visa application needs vary according to the issuing consulate or embassy. ⇨ *See Travel Smart Moscow and St. Petersburg for more details.*

Flying into Russia has gotten remarkably easier, thanks to several major U.S. and European carriers that now have direct flights from hub cities like New York, Atlanta, Washington, D.C., London, and Frankfurt. Moscow's airports make international travel even easier with airport trains that whisk you to the center of the city within 30-40 minutes. St. Petersburg's Pulkovo airport has yet to catch up with the number of international carriers flying in. Some travelers opt to fly into Helsinki and then travel by connecting flight (about 1 hour) or by bus, car, or train to St. Petersburg (about 3–4 hours) when the price brings a significant savings. Either way, flying in and out of Russia's biggest cities is now as easy as flying to London or Paris.

Customs of the Country

Russians, particularly Muscovites, have a reputation for being cold and unfriendly, but extremely hospitable to guests invited into their homes. This is indeed the case, and should you be invited to a meal at a Russian friend's house be sure to say yes; you're likely to make friends for life. Russians tend to dress more formally than in the West. You won't see super baggy jeans even on teenagers. Men don't always wear a coat and tie, but they will usually wear a jacket to upscale restaurants. Women dress femininely, and rarely adopt the casual, tomboyish look popular in the West. They take great pride in how they appear, even in winter when the attire is heavy coats, hats, scarves and gloves.

Eating Out

While only the wealthy dine out in the Russian provinces, in Moscow and St. Petersburg you'll likely need a reservation for many restaurants. Most restaurants are open from noon to 11 pm, and Russians tend to dine around 8 pm or later. Your choices of cuisine are plentiful, but sushi has been all the rage for several years. It's not uncommon to see a separate sushi menu, even at an Italian restaurant. Business lunches are popular in the cities, and you can often get good deals on set menus that include a soup, salad, and main dish, as well as coffee or tea. Breakfasts tend to be smaller, except in some hotels that offer "American-style" breakfast. Otherwise, simple omelets, fried eggs, yogurt or pastries are common menu items. Cafés are springing up everywhere and can easily provide a quick snack or simple meal.

Greetings

Russian men shake hands for business, and may throw one hand around the back of a friend for a brotherly, quick hug. Some Russian men have adopted the European habit of kissing a woman's cheeks, but it's not that common on the first meeting. Russians consider it bad luck to shake hands or pass anything across a threshold, so be sure to step inside first. And if you are presenting flowers to a Russian, remember that an even number of flowers in a bouquet is for funerals only, so skip the dozen roses.

Language

Russian is the national language. Outside of Moscow and St. Petersburg, you'll have a hard time getting by without knowing a little more than the basics. In the cities, however, many people, particularly those under 40, use English in their daily lives. In hotels and more popular restaurants, you're not likely to have a problem communicating the essentials. But public transportation and smaller museums and shops will be a challenge. While the Cyrillic alphabet looks daunting, it's actually not that difficult to learn enough to find your way around, particularly in the Metro. Russians know their language is difficult and appreciate foreigners' efforts to try to speak it. In both cities, you are likely to run into people who are more than happy to practice their English with you.

Money and Shopping

The Russian ruble has had its up and downs over the last decade, but is—for now—stable at about 30R to the $1. Moscow and St. Petersburg are expensive, and it's easy to run up high restaurant bills. Other things, like public transportation, are extremely affordable. Russian law dictates that all prices be quoted in rubles. However, in places such as airports, you'll see "conditional units" (*uslovnye yedinitsy*, often using the symbol *YE*). This is a euphemism for the dollar (or in some cases the euro). Even when it's marked as this, Russian law requires all transactions to be made in rubles. Tip in rubles; smaller dollar bills are harder to exchange so most Russians would rather have their own currency. Using ATMs to withdraw cash from your bank account back home is preferable to using traveler's checks, which are not always accepted outside of the larger hotels. You'll pay an 18% VAT on hotels and services, and Moscow tacks on an additional 1% to that rate. ⇨ *See Travel Smart Moscow and St. Petersburg for more details.*

Safety

Use caution in Moscow and St. Petersburg just as you would in any major metropolitan or urban center. Avoid walking alone on empty streets at night, particularly if you are a woman. As a foreigner, you will be targeted at tourist spots by pickpockets and scam artists. Use common sense, and keep a close eye on your belongings, particularly in crowds. Moscow has been the scene of several terrorist bombings, so you should heed any warnings from public announcements about avoiding crowded, public spaces during these times, including the metro. However, the days of violent outbreaks between rival gangs in downtown Moscow are long over.

When to Go

The climate in Russia changes dramatically with the seasons. Both Moscow and St. Petersburg are best visited in May or late August. In Moscow, summers tend to be hot, and thunderstorms and heavy rainfall are common in July and August. In St. Petersburg, on the other hand, it rarely gets very hot, even at the height of summer, though you will likely need an umbrella. Try to visit St. Petersburg during the White Nights (June to early July), when the northern day is virtually endless. In winter months both cities are covered in an attractive blanket of snow, but only the hardiest travelers should visit between late November and early February when the days are short, dark, and bitterly cold.

GREAT ITINERARIES

Russia may span 11 time zones and two continents, but it's still possible to take in the sights of two major cities and a bit of countryside in just a few days.

MOSCOW ITINERARY

Day 1: The Kremlin, Moscow

Devote this day to exploration of the Kremlin museums and cathedrals. Stroll through Red Square, St. Basil's Cathedral, and the shopping arcades of GUM. Admire the crowns of the Russian tsars at the Armory Palace. If you're into treasures, don't miss the notorious 190-carat Orlov Diamond at the Diamond Fund. Lenin's Mausoleum is entirely optional. Take a ride on the world's most opulent and ornate metro, with its marble columns, mosaic panoramas, elaborate chandeliers, and quirky Soviet-era monuments. If you have any energy left, spend the evening at the Bolshoi Theatre.

Logistics: The most fascinating metro stations are on the brown circle line (#5). Mayakovskaya and Ploshchad Revolutsii are also exciting. The Armory is closed on Thursday, and the Mausoleum, open Tuesday through Sunday, closes at 1 pm.

Day 2: Old Moscow

Discover old Moscow: wander through the winding narrow streets and visit the ancient churches of Kitai Gorod and pass through the cheerful Old Arbat. Make a pilgrimage to the sad and stately 1524 New Maiden's Convent, a refuge for exiled noble women in the tsarist era. Be sure to see the Romanov Palace Chambers in Zaryadye, the impressive 16th-century palace of the Romanov boyars, and the home of the Romanov family before they made it to the throne. End your day with a steam at a banya—the palatial, venerable Sandunovskiye bani has been considered the best in Russia since the 19th century.

Logistics: The Romanov palace is open to groups with reservations during the week and Saturday; Sunday is the best day for individual visitors. It costs from 800 to 1,000 rubles per person to visit Sandunovskiye bani.

Day 3: Tretyakov Gallery and Cathedral of Christ Our Savior

Spend the morning at the Tretyakov Gallery, which has one of the finest collections of Russian art. To feel the vigor of the new Moscow, head to the resurrected Cathedral of Christ Our Savior, demolished in 1931 and rebuilt from scratch. Travel to St. Petersburg on the stylish Nikolayevsky Express, fashioned to resemble an early-20th-century train and named after Russia's last tsar, Nicholas II.

Logistics: Nikolayevsky Express leaves from Moscow daily at 11:30 pm, and gets to St. Petersburg at 7:40 am. A second train departs from St. Petersburg at 11:30 pm and arrives in Moscow at 7:40 am.

ST. PETERSBURG ITINERARY

Day 1: St. Petersburg from Above and the Hermitage

For an invigorating start, climb the 260 steps to the colonnade of St. Isaac's Cathedral for a fabulous all-around panorama of the historical center. Then head to the State Hermitage Museum. But don't try to rush through this huge place all in one go. Make a list of your favorite things and return when you can. In the evening attend a performance at the Mariinsky Theatre, and take a short detour before the start of the show to visit the magnifi-

cent 18th-century St. Nicholas (patron saint of sailors) Cathedral.

Logistics: The Hermitage is free on the first Thursday of every month.

Day 2: Icons, Onion Domes, and Peter and Paul Fortress

Culture vultures should begin the day at the State Museum of Russian Art, home to the world's largest collection of Russian art, from icons to avant-garde to socialist realism. The brightly colored onion domes of the Church of the Savior on Spilled Blood are just around the corner. In good weather, spend an hour observing the city from the water on one of the many boat trips. Visit the Peter and Paul Fortress in the late afternoon. Sightseeing can be continued even during a meal. The Bessonnitsa ("Insomnia") restaurant next to the fortress overlooks the Hermitage, Admiralty, and the Strelka.

Logistics: The quickest way to get to the Peter and Paul Fortress from Nevsky Prospect is to travel one stop by metro and get off at Gorkovskaya. When you get out of the station, turn right and walk through a little park until you reach the fortress.

Day 3: A Palace Visit

Devote the day to a trip to one of the former royal residences. Choose Pushkin (Tsarskoye Selo) in winter and Peterhof (Petrodvorets) in summer.

Logistics: It takes 30 minutes to get to Peterhof by hydrofoils departing from several quays along Dvortsovaya embankment, near the Hermitage and the Bronze Horseman.

TIPS

■ All top tourist sights and central metro stations in both cities are notorious for pickpockets. Be extra careful.

■ To save time and money, buy tickets for Moscow's Bolshoi and St. Petersburg's Mariinsky theaters online at ⊕ www.bolshoi.ru and ⊕ www.mariinsky.ru.

■ To prepare best for the Russian banya, go to the Sandunovskiye bani's Web site (⊕ www.sanduny.ru) and read the expertly written "secrets" section (available in English).

■ Be sure to bring an umbrella. According to the latest research, St. Petersburg boasts a pathetic 30–40 cloudless days a year.

■ Consider staying in one of St. Petersburg's more than 200 mini-hotels—small, 8- to 10-room guesthouses that offer an intimate alternative to the city's major hotels. Most are centrally located, reasonably priced, and if you travel in a group, you could have the property all to yourselves.

■ Alcohol counterfeiting, which can lead to alcohol poisoning, is a problem, so try to purchase vodka from a reputable-looking store or, if buying from a kiosk, check to see that the seal has not been broken.

■ In some museums, galleries, and palaces, such as the Tretyakov Gallery, you may be asked to put on plastic booties, similar to the kind surgeons wear, over your shoes before entering the gallery. When entering a Russian home, always remove your shoes at the entryway.

A WALK THROUGH MOSCOW'S HISTORIC CENTER

Moscow can at once overwhelm and awe. The city's sights are somewhat spread out, meaning you'll need a few days to see them. The outlined walk is designed to weave you around the city center for an introduction to the city, allowing you to pick and choose where to spend more time later.

Tverskaya ulitsa: Moscow's Main Drag

The **statue** of Russia's most beloved poet, Pushkin, is a popular meeting spot for Muscovites and a great starting point. **Tverskaya ulitsa**, in various forms, has been the main drag of Moscow for centuries. Shops and government buildings line the sides of its wide street, which is often blocked with Moscow's worst inhabitant—traffic. Stroll south, making sure to stop and browse in **Yeliseyevsky Grocery** at No. 14. Despite its ornate chandeliers and stained glass, the store's prices are reasonable making it a favorite of Muscovites.

The **mayor's office** is just another block down, housed in a red building with white Corinthian columns across the street from a commanding **statue** of Moscow's founder, Yuri Dolgoruky.

Kamergersky pereulok to Kuznetsky Most

You can while away a day sitting at one of this pedestrian street's sidewalk cafés. Making your way east, Kuznetsky Most is chock-full of interesting, prerevolutionary architecture, such as the art-nouveau apartment building at **3 Kuznetsky Most**. Look up at the colorful mosaics on the facade. The intersection at **Petrovka ulitsa** is the heart of Moscow's high-end shopping. Take note of the Central Department Store, or **TsUM**, which has been completely remolded and now serves as a hub for expensive Russian and foreign labels. Continue on Kuznetsky most as it winds up past more high-end shops, cafés, and student hangouts. **Secreti Bulochka** at Ploshchad Vorovskovo is a cozy café with cakes and sandwiches if you need a break.

Lubyanskaya Ploshchad to Teatralnaya Ploshchad

On the northeast side of Lubyanskaya Ploschad, the yellow stone building was once the **KGB headquarters** and notorious **Lubyanka prison**. It remains the offices of Russia's security services, as well as the starting point for exploring Kitai Gorod's windy streets and trendy bars and restaurants. Down the Teatralny proyezd, you'll pass **Destky Mir** (*Children's World*), a store dear to every Soviet childhood, as well as the luxury-shopping lane, **Tretyakovsky pereulok,** on your left. The 19th-century remodeled archway bumps up against 16th-century walls that once fortified the ancient Kitai Gorod. Further down, the **Metropol Hotel** stands across from Teatralnaya Ploshchad and the pink **Bolshoi Theater**.

Teatralnaya Ploshchad to Red Square

You are now entering some of the oldest parts of Moscow. Facing Zhukov atop his horse, you can enter **Red Square** from the right or left of the red **State Historical Museum**. Either way, coming onto the square is breathtaking. The walls of the **Kremlin, St. Basil's Cathedral, Lenin's Mausoleum,** and **GUM** surround you as you absorb the centuries of history that have unfolded here.

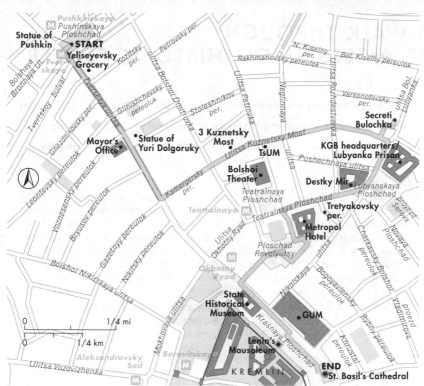

Highlights:	Posh shopping streets, people-watching from sidewalk cafés, prerevolutionary architecture, the former KGB headquarters, Bolshoi Theater, and Red Square.
Where to Start:	Take the metro to either Pushkinskaya, Tverskaya, or Chekovskaya Station and follow the signs to Pushkinskaya Ploshchad (Pushkin Square) on Tverskaya ulitsa.
Length:	Between 2 and 4 hours, depending on shopping. About 2.5 mi in all.
Where to Stop:	Red Square
Best Time to Go:	Midday during the week for best people-watching.
Worst Time to Go:	Shops can get crowded on the weekends.
Best Views:	After the walk, get an impressive view of Red Square and Tverskaya ulitsa from the **O2 Lounge** (⊠ 3/5 Tverskaya ulitsa) at the top of the Ritz Carlton.

A WALK THROUGH ST. PETERSBURG'S HISTORIC CENTER

Many of St. Petersburg's top attractions are located in the historical center of the city and within walking distance of each other. The following walk is designed to get you oriented in Peter the Great's "Window to the West."

Palace Square to the Church of the Savior on Spilled Blood

Visitors and locals use picturesque **Palace Square** and the central Alexander Column as a meeting point. The green and white **Winter Palace** occupies the north side of the square. Take a romantic stroll through the arch of the **General Staff Building** on the southern side of the square. Leave the square on the northeast corner via Millionnaya ulitsa. Be sure to get a shot taken with one of the muscular Atlases holding up the columns of the pink **State Hermitage Museum** here. The delicate bridge here is another good photo opportunity if you get the Neva River in the background through the arch. This area of the Moika River has seen the residents change over the centuries from wealthy nobles to beloved poets (don't miss **Pushkin's Apartment Museum**) and eventually Soviet-era communal flats, many of which have been redeveloped into luxurious apartments. The run-down pink **Imperial Stables** once housed the imperial horses. Wander around the colorful and impressive **Church of the Savior on Spilled Blood**.

Square of the Arts to Kazan Cathedral

Continue to the **Square of the Arts** *(Iskusstv Ploshchad)*. St. Petersburgers use the park in front of the **State Museum of Russian Art** for a peaceful lunch break. International and Russian bankers and movers-and-shakers frequent the über-luxurious **Grand Hotel Europe** for fine dining. The intersection with Nevsky prospect is a good starting point for taking in the pulse of St. Petersburg's main drag. The street has a wide range of shopping and dining, as well as several historical churches and buildings, such as the **Kazan Cathedral**. Don't miss the stunning facade of the former Singer building, which now holds **Dom Knigi** *(House of Books)*.

Along the Moika River to St. Isaac's Cathedral

Turn left onto Naberezhnaya moika past the **Stroganov Palace**, walk alongside the canal, and cross over **Krasny Most** *(red bridge)*. The buildings on Bolshaya Morskaya once housed the city's banking and insurance industries. The golden dome of **St. Isaac's Cathedral** dominates the scene, but be sure to notice the **Siniy Most** *(blue bridge)* to the south of the square. It's the widest bridge in the city. North of the cathedral is the green area that makes up **Decembrists' Square** and the **Admiralty** gardens. Newlyweds often have their first photos taken in front of the **Bronze Horseman statue** depicting Peter the Great.

Neva riverbank to Strelka

Take advantage of nice weather with a stroll along the Admiralty embankment. Crossing over the bridge, you'll come onto **Vasilievsky Island**. Standing on the **Strelka** with its red columns behind you, you'll get a city view that includes the **Winter Palace** and the **Peter and Paul Fortress**.

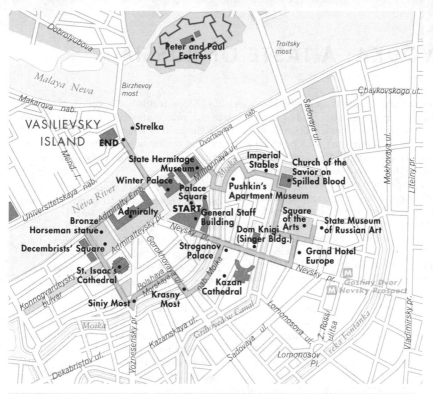

Highlights:	Palace Square, the nobilities' houses along the Moika River, St. Isaac's Cathedral's golden dome, and the golden spire of the Admiralty, Kazan Cathedral, and Nevsky prospect.
Where to Start:	Take the metro to Nevsky prospect and walk west. Palace Square will be on your right.
Length:	This 2.5-mi walk will take from 2 to 4 hours, depending on your pace and refueling stops.
Where to Stop:	Strelka on the tip of Vasilievsky Island.
Best Time to Go:	If it's summer, anytime since there's plenty of daylight.
Worst Time to Go:	A late evening stroll is not optimal because stores and sites will be closed.
Best place to Refuel:	Sip cappuccinos and watch the world go by on Nevsky prospect at **Café Singer** (⊠ 28 Nevsky pr.) in the old Singer building.

VODKA: A TASTE OF RUSSIA

The national drink is an inseparable part of Russian social life. Vodka is drunk everywhere, with the intention of breaking down inhibitions and producing a state of conviviality Russians refer to as *dusha-dushe* (soul-to-soul). When a Russian taps the side of his throat, beware: it's impossible to refuse this invitation to friendship. If you have a cold, sore throat, or any such minor ailment, don't be surprised if someone prescribes a shot of vodka—even for a hangover. Russians' belief in the curative and preventative powers of this drink is almost limitless.

Choosing Vodka

There are hundreds of brands of vodka in Russia, as a glance into any store will show. Some of these are rough and best left alone; three of the best are Flagman, Beluga, and Russky Standart, although there are many acceptable cheaper brands. Alcohol counterfeiting, which can lead to alcohol poisoning, is a big problem, so you should always purchase vodka from a reputable-looking store, and never from a kiosk.

The Vodka Procedure

When you're drinking vodka, there is some etiquette involved. In North America and Great Britain, vodka is generally associated with cocktails and martinis. In Russia, mixing vodka with anything else is considered a waste, unless the mixer is beer, which produces a fearsome beverage known as *yorsh*. Vodka is meant to be gulped down in one go, not sipped. Since this can give you a bit of a kick, Russians always have some zakuski, or snacks (including pickles, herring, boiled potatoes, and black bread), to chase the shot. You may witness something called the "vodka procedure," which, if you want to try it yourself, goes roughly as follows.

Prepare a forkful of food or chunk of bread. Inhale and exhale quickly, bringing the food to your nose. Breathe in and tip the vodka down your throat. Now breathe out again, and eat your food.

A Toast

Vodka shots (unlike beer and wine) are downed collectively, and always preceded by a toast. You'll score points if you propose toasts—it doesn't matter if they are in English, particularly if you wax long and eloquent. Drinking before a toast is considered a faux pas of the first order. Although you're expected to gulp down the first couple of shots, no one will mind if you take it a little easier after that— saying *choot'-choot', pozhaluista* (just a little, please) is a polite way of asking for a smaller refill. Vodka is also considered predominantly a man's drink, so it's more acceptable for women to take things easier.

If all this sounds like an ordeal, rest assured that vodka drinking can be an extremely pleasurable experience, involving good food, great company, and a unique sense of mild inebriation that can last for hours. It's a memorable taste of Russia in more ways than one.

Exploring
Moscow

Updated by
Ezekiel Pfeifer

Moscow is a city of tremendous power and energy. Hulking gothic towers loom over its broad skyline. Massive avenues form a sprawled web around the Kremlin and course with traffic day and night. The city has drawn religious pilgrims for centuries, and today Moscow continues to be a magnet across the region and the world.

Founded in the 12th century as the center of one of several competing principalities, Moscow eventually emerged as the heart of a unified Russian state in the 15th century. One hundred years later it had grown into the capital of a strong and prosperous realm, one of the largest in the world. But under Peter the Great (1672–1725), the city was demoted. Influenced by his exposure to the West, Peter deliberately turned his back on the old traditions and established his own capital—St. Petersburg—on the shores of the Baltic Sea. Yet Moscow continued to thrive as an economic and cultural center, and more than 200 years later, within a year of the Bolshevik Revolution in 1917, the young Soviet government restored its status as the nation's capital.

The city became the undisputed political and ideological center of the vast Soviet empire. And even though it has been nearly two decades since that empire broke apart, the city retains its political, industrial, and cultural sway as Russia's capital. With a population of more than 10 million, Moscow is Russia's largest city and the site of some of the country's most renowned cultural institutions, theaters, and film studios. It's also the country's most important transportation hub—even today many flights to the former Soviet republics are routed through Moscow's airports.

To fortify and spur forward Russia's giant economy, the government and city's business communities actively court outside investments and set ambitious economic agendas. For visitors, this translates into a modern, fast-paced city with increased availability of Western-style services and products. But even as Moscow becomes a hub of international business activity, it is determinedly holding onto its Russian roots. Restaurant kitchens, many of which strove to satisfy Russians' thirst for foreign tastes in the '90s, are turning back to the country's native cuisine, serving gourmet borscht and delicious *pelmeni* (bite-sized dumplings). Business deals may no longer be made over a banquet table and sealed with a shot of vodka, but Muscovites take hospitality seriously, as a visit to any private home will show you. This tradition of welcoming with open arms has persisted alongside a less generous Soviet mentality, however: stubborn indifference remains the default attitude of staff at some hotels, restaurants, and stores. This is gradually fading, but you might still face with surly ticket sellers or even ungracious hotel employees, especially if trying to communicate strictly in spoken English.

TOP REASONS TO GO

Red Square at Night: The heart of Russia is transformed at night by the glowing red stars atop the Kremlin towers and the lit-up fairy-tale onion domes of St. Basil's Cathedral.

Chekhov to Tchaikovsky: Tapping into the thriving arts scene in Moscow is easy; choosing from among your many options is the hard part. Be it a play at the Moscow Art Theater, opera or ballet at the Bolshoi, or classical music at the Conservatory, don't leave Moscow without a bit of culture.

Hidden City: If you can conquer your fear of getting lost, wandering through the intricate side streets can be a rewarding experience. You may accidentally bump into architectural wonders, like the Melnikov House,

hidden away on Krivoarbatsky pereulok, or find a quiet square or park you can call your own.

Eating Well: Whether sharing drinks and zakuski (appetizers) with friends, grabbing a blini on the run, or sitting down to a bowl of borscht and pelmeni (meat dumplings), dining in Moscow is a heart-warming experience.

Church Choirs: Although you can often hear a choir sing in the three cathedrals of the Kremlin, don't let that stop you from visiting the dozens of churches in the city center, such as the Church of the Resurrection on Bryusov pereulok, which can be an oasis of serenity in the bustling city.

As Russia enters its third decade of post-Soviet life, development and reconstruction are at an all-time high. Parts of Moscow, especially within the Boulevard Ring (Bulvarnoye Koltso), are now sparkling clean and well kept. Although the Russians are protecting some of their architectural heritage, they're also creating a new, often controversial legacy, in the form of soaring skyscrapers, shopping malls, and churches. Many of these buildings are designed to be harmonious with the ancient Russian style, but there are a growing number of shockingly modern steel-and-glass office towers, particularly in central Moscow. The decades ahead promise more change and hurdles to overcome. But this city has survived devastating fires, an invasion by Napoléon, and more than half a century of alternating demolition and breakneck construction by the Soviets. Moscow is ready for anything.

ORIENTATION AND PLANNING

GETTING ORIENTED

The best way to orient yourself in Moscow is via the city's efficient and highly ornate metro system. ■ TIP→ **Most of the sights in this chapter are located on or within the metro's brown line (#5) which circles the old historic center.** Learning the Cyrillic alphabet will prove infinitely useful in helping you to distinguish between metro stops. When asking locals for directions, it's often more fruitful to discuss locations by the nearest metro stop than by neighborhood names.

Moscow is laid out in a series of concentric circles that emanate from its heart—the Kremlin/Red Square area. This epicenter, encircled by the tree-lined Boulevard Ring (*Bulvarnoye Koltso*), is rich with palaces and churches. Although the individual streets that make up the Boulevard Ring have different names, most of them have the word for boulevard, *bulvar*, in their names. The Boulevard Ring passes by stations Arbatskaya, Pushkinskaya, and Chistye Prudy on its way around the city. Much of your time is likely to be spent near metro stop Pushkinskaya, a few hundred yards up Tverskaya ulitsa, the city's main street, which goes north directly from the Kremlin.

Marking the outer edge of the city center is the Garden Ring (*Sadovoe Koltso*), a wide boulevard which has lost all the trees it was once famous for. The metro's brown number 5 line almost follows the route of the Garden Ring. Metro stations Smolenskaya, Barrikadnaya, Mayakovskaya, Sukharevskaya, Krasniye Vorota, Taganskaya, Paveletskaya, Oktyabrskaya, and Park Kultury are all located on the Garden Ring road.

The Kremlin and Red Square. The ancient heart of the city stands out for its grand palaces, towers, and some of the country's most sacred churches, including St. Basil's and Assumption Cathedral. In addition to the historical sights, there are also modern shopping centers and a lively atmosphere in this most central area.

Kitai Gorod. North and east of the Kremlin/Red Square area and within the Boulevard Ring, this neighborhood began as an outgrowth of the Kremlin. Its sights include the Bolshoi Theatre and Sandunovskiye Bani, as well as some of the city's best restaurants.

Tverskaya Ulitsa. North of the Kremlin is the famous northern road to St. Petersburg, Tverskaya ulitsa, which extends from the Kremlin through the Boulevard Ring and out to the Garden Ring. This is Moscow's main shopping street. The Museum of the Contemporary History of Russia just north of the Boulevard Ring provides an interesting look at Moscow's evolution.

Bolshaya Nikitskaya Ulitsa. Bolshaya Nikitskaya ulitsa is another main thoroughfare and home to stunning old mansions and the Tchaikovsky Conservatory.

The Arbat. Two streets radiating out of the Kremlin to the west are the Stary Arbat (Old Arbat) and the Novy Arbat (New Arbat). The Stary Arbat is referred to by Russians simply as "the Arbat" and is a cobblestone pedestrian street with cafés, street performers, and all manner of souvenir shops. Novy Arbat is a modern thoroughfare with shopping malls and upscale restaurants.

The Kropotkinsky District. Southwest of the Kremlin, the Kropotkinsky District is home to the monumental Church of Christ Our Savior, where the Russian Patriarch leads mass on the most important holidays. Also here are the venerable Pushkin Museum of Fine Arts and the Tolstoy Memorial Museum.

Zamoskvoreche. This area is best known for its many churches, especially along the long north–south street Bolshaya Ordynka. Also here is the Tretyakov Gallery, the country's best art museum.

Southern Outskirts. Four magnificent monasteries are the main points of interest south of the city center. The can't-miss among them is New Maiden's Monastery, with its colorful battle towers and peaceful pond.

Moscow Excursions. Parks and former estates outside the city give you a glimpse of the verdant Russian countryside. Perfect for a visit on a day with fine weather, these spots draw masses of picnicking Muscovites all summer long. For those on a tight schedule, the sprawling Victory Park takes just a quick trip on the Moscow metro.

PLANNING

WHEN TO GO

Far and away the best time to visit Moscow is in the late spring or summer. During the months of May to September, the weather is usually balmy, with averages in the 70s. It should be said that in recent years, it has also become uncomfortably and even dangerously hot at stretches. In the summer of 2010, high temperatures and a two-month-long drought led to the outbreak of wildfires all over Russia, with smoke wafting into Moscow for a few weeks in early August. That was, however, a first in the city's history. From October to April, the weather is unpredictable and typically high in rain and snow, making it inconvenient for touring the city on foot. In contrast, the warm temperatures and long days of summer bring out some of the best aspects of cultural life in Moscow, such as outdoor terraces at restaurants, music festivals at countryside estates, and nonstop grilling in the city's parks.

GETTING HERE AND AROUND
AIR TRAVEL

As the most important transportation hub in the Commonwealth of Independent States (CIS, a quasi-confederation of states that includes most of the former Soviet Union), Moscow has several airports. Most international flights arrive at Sheremetyevo II, north of the city center. The Russian carrier Aeroflot operates flights from Moscow to just about every capital of Europe, as well as to Canada and the United States. The airline also serves numerous domestic destinations. Skyexpress, another Russian carrier, runs a popular shuttle flight from Moscow to St. Petersburg that takes only an hour and can cost as little as 2,200R round-trip.

Domodedovo, one of the largest airports in the world (and perhaps the nicest in Russia), is some 48 km (30 mi) southeast of Moscow. British Airways, Swiss, and United fly out of Domodedovo. Flights also depart from Domodedovo to the republics of Central Asia. After a terrorist bombing in the one of the airport's waiting areas in early 2011, additional security checkpoints were put into place, including metal detectors and bag scanners at the airport's entrances. As a result, you should budget extra time when flying from here, as the lines to enter the building can be long. (The same measures were taken at Moscow's other major airports, Sheremetyevo and Vnukovo.)

One of the most modern airports in Russia when it was built in 1979, Sheremetyevo is now inadequate and old-fashioned in places, though the opening of two sparkling terminals in 2010 shows the airport is serious about upgrading its facilities. There are five passenger terminals, known by letters B through F; most international flights are served by terminals E and F. (There is a terminal A as well, used for business air traffic.) At every terminal, be prepared for lines everywhere and a wait of up to an hour at passport control. Beyond the baggage area is customs, past which you'll be greeted by mobs of eager gypsy cab drivers shouting, "Taksi! Taksi!"

> ## STALIN'S EIGHTH SISTER?
>
> You may notice a new stepsister to the Seven Gothic Sisters on the drive in from Sheremetyevo II airport. Triumph Palace, near the Sokol metro station, is a modern copy of the original skyscrapers. This expensive block of apartments, the tallest residential building in Europe at 866 feet (264 meters), has been criticized by architects, but its huge size and similarity to the original buildings that Stalin built will likely make it another city symbol.

Vnukovo, 29 km (18 mi) southwest of the city center, services flights to Georgia, the southern republics, and Ukraine. Bykovo, the smallest of the domestic terminals, generally handles flights within Russia and some flights to Ukraine.

For general information on arriving international flights, call the airline directly. Calling the airports usually takes longer and fewer people speak English.

Airport Information Bykovo (☎ *495/558–4738*). **Domodedovo** (☎ *495/933–6666*). **Sheremetyevo Airport** (☎ *495/232–6565 or 800/100–6565*). **Vnukovo** (☎ *495/937–5555*).

TRANSFERS   You can make arrival a lot easier by arranging in advance for your transfer from the airport. Most hotels will provide airport transfers (for a fee, usually about 1,500R) upon advance request by a phone call or fax (which you should confirm).

If you don't have many bags and feel comfortable navigating public transport straight off the plane, consider using the airports' newly spiffed-up Aeroexpress trains to get into the city. You will see arrows pointing to the small stations from which they leave when you exit customs at each airport. A regular ticket (320R) takes you to one of the city's central train stations—Belorussky Station from Sheremetyevo, Paveletsky Station from Domodedovo, and Kievsky Station from Vnukovo—from which you can take a cab or the metro to wherever you're staying. When heading to the airport on these trains, you can sometimes check into your flight at the train station (it depends on which airline you're using) and even hand off any baggage you want to check.

There are plenty of unofficial gypsy cabs available at the airports, but there's always a risk of being swindled. (If you do take one, be sure to bargain, bargain, bargain.) It's better to use the services offered on the airports' ground floors. These private firms are less risky, they can provide you with a receipt, and you may find their prices more reasonable than those of the gypsy cabs. The prices are still not cheap, however, ranging from 1,500–2,000R depending on your destination. Traveling to the airport from the city is cheaper. It's best to book a taxi in advance to do this. The rate is typically 1,000R–1,500R.

The cheapest option for getting to and from the city's airports is buses and *marshrutka* (minibuses), which shuttle back and forth from various outlying metro stations. Those going to Sheremetyevo leave from metro station Rechnoy Vokzal (at the northern end of the green line); to Domodedovo from metro station Domodedovskaya (also on the green line but in the south). Those headed to Vnukovo leave from metro station Yugo-Zapadnaya, a name that translates as South-West, as it is at the southwestern end of the red metro line. It can be confusing trying to find the next bus leaving, but you can usually just follow someone else carrying luggage once you are outside the metro station. Oddly enough, the buses each take about 30 minutes to get to the different airports. Traffic is unpredictable, though, and it can take longer, sometimes significantly so. The road to Sheremetyevo is particularly notorious, often becoming gridlocked for hours during the commuter rushes in morning and early evening.

To get to Bykovo airport, you can take a train from Kazansky train station.

BUS, TRAM, AND TROLLEY TRAVEL

You're unlikely to want to travel by long-distance bus in Russia, since trains are frequent, cheap, and reliable. Most bus services go to provincial towns that lack good rail links.

For travel within Moscow, the municipal buses, trams, and trolleys all use the same tickets (25R), which you can buy in special kiosks, usually near metro stations. The tickets come in various denominations, ranging from one to 60. You can also buy tickets from the driver, but then they cost 28R. You don't need exact change, but drivers always appreciate it when you have it. You have to get on at the entrance next to the driver and put the ticket through an electronic turnstile, frontside down. Single-ride tickets are valid for a ride on one bus only; if you transfer to another bus or to a tram or trolley, you must pay another fare. Buses, trams, and trolleys operate from 5:30 am to 1 am, although service in the late-evening hours and on Sunday tends to be unreliable. Trolleys are connected to overhead power lines, trams to metal rails.

Local bus and tram routes tend to be mysterious, since bus stops don't provide information and the vehicles only carry a terse lists of destinations, often referring to factories or landmarks and the like that may or may not still exist. Newspaper kiosks sell a map that shows all of Moscow's transport routes: it's called *karta Moskvy so vsem transportom*.

The tram can be a fun way to take in part of the city while also resting your legs. A nice tram ride is the 39, which goes from Universitet metro station, on the red line in the southwest of the city, to Chistiye Prudy metro station, past Donskoy Monastery and Danilovsky Market. The B trolley bus runs around the Garden Ring and can be a pleasant way to see the Ring when the traffic's not heavy.

Bus, Tram, and Trolley Contacts Moskovsky Avtovokzal (*Moscow Bus Station*✉ *75/2 Shchelkovskoe shosse, Eastern Outskirts* ☎ *495/468–0400* Ⓜ *Shchelkovskaya*). **Mosgortrans** (☎ *495/953–0061* ⊕ *www.mosgortrans.com*) runs all the city's surface transport.

CAR TRAVEL

You can reach Moscow from Finland and St. Petersburg by taking the Helsinki–St. Petersburg Highway through Vyborg and St. Petersburg and continuing from there on the Moscow–St. Petersburg Highway. Using a car for getting around Moscow is not advised, though, as driving in Russia is invariably more of a hassle than a pleasure. Roads are very poorly maintained, and many streets in the city center are one-way. Renting a car can also be much more expensive than in the U.S. To top it all off, Moscow traffic police are famous for seeking out bribes, especially from foreigners, and they will often demand that you pay a "shtraf" (fine) whether you have all the proper documents or not.

METRO TRAVEL

The Moscow metro, which opened in 1935, ranks among the world's finest public transportation systems. With more than 300 km (186 mi) of track, the Moscow metro carries an estimated 8 million passengers daily. Even though it scrapes by with inadequate state subsidies, the system continues to run efficiently, with trains every 50 seconds during rush hour. It leaves New Yorkers green with envy.

If you're not traveling with a tour group or if you haven't hired your own driver, taking the metro is the best way to get around the Russian capital. You'll be doing yourself a big favor and saving yourself a lot of frustration if you learn the Russian (Cyrillic) alphabet well enough to be able to transliterate the names of the stations. This will come in especially handy at transfer points, where signs with long lists of the names of metro stations lead you from one major metro line to another. You should also be able to recognize the entrance and exit signs (⇨ *English–Russian Vocabulary, at the end of this book*).

Pocket maps of the system are available at newspaper kiosks and sometimes from individual vendors at metro stations. Be sure that you obtain a map with English transliterations in addition to Cyrillic. If you can't find one, try any of the major hotels. (Even if you're not a guest of the hotel they'll probably give you a map.) Plan your route beforehand and have your destination written in Russian and its English transliteration to help you spot the station. As the train approaches each station, the station name will be announced over the train's public-address system; the name of the next station is given before the train starts off. Reminders of interchanges and transfers are also given. All trains have the transliterated names of stations on line maps, and newer trains have electronic displays next to the doors that show the names of all the stations on the line and the train's progress.

Stations are built deep underground (they were built to double as bomb shelters); the escalators are steep and run fast, so watch your step. If you use the metro during rush hour (8:30–10 am, 5–7 pm), be prepared for some pushing and shoving. In a crowded train, just before a station, you're likely to be asked, *"Vy vykhódíte?"* or whether you're getting off at the next station. If not, you're expected to move out of the way. Riders are expected to give up seats for senior citizens and small children.

FARES AND
SCHEDULES The metro is easy to use and amazingly inexpensive. Stations are marked with a large illuminated "M" sign and are open daily 5:30 am to 1 am. The fare is the same regardless of distance traveled, and there are many stations where lines connect and you may transfer for free. You purchase a magnetic card (available at all stations) for 1, 5, 10, 20, or more journeys and hold it near the yellow circle on the right side of the entry gate. Wait until you see the red light replaced by a green one, signaling that your card has registered, then walk through. At old-style entry gates without doors, make sure to wait until you see that your card has registered, as walking through the gate prematurely will cause barriers to burst out from both sides to block your way, delivering a painful blow to the hip if you end up in their path. (You will often see teenagers without tickets hopping high over the gates to avoid them.) A single ride costs 28R, and discounts are available for multiple-journey cards. A card for 10 trips costs 265R.

TAXI TRAVEL

Exercise caution when using taxis. There are standard taxis of various makes and colors, but professional ones all have taxi lights on top. Official taxis also have a "T" and checkered emblem on the doors (but there are not many of them). When you enter a cab, check to see if the meter is working; if it is not, agree on a price beforehand. Professional taxis cannot always be easily hailed in the city center, though, because Muscovites generally flag down unmarked cars operating as taxis. Everyone with a car is a potential taxi driver in Moscow, and there are huge masses of people who make extra money or even their entire livelihood driving people in their private vehicles (often beat-up Soviet models), so you never have to wait long for someone to stop. This is generally a safe practice, but it's best to avoid it, particularly if you don't speak Russian, as most drivers will try to swindle you. Some private drivers also don't know the city very well and may not be able to reach your destination without directions from you. If you do choose to take a ride in an ordinary car, take some precautions: Never get in a car with more than one person inside, and if the driver wants to stop for another fare, say no or get out of the car.

The easiest thing to do if you want a cab is to order one by phone or through your hotel. Moscow has numerous cab companies, most with 24-hour service. There is sometimes a delay, but a cab usually arrives within the hour. If you order a cab in this way, you usually pay a set rate for the first 20–40 minutes (around 350R–500R) and then a set rate per minute (usually around 10R per minute) after that. Always ask for an approximate price when you telephone for a cab. Unfortunately, most operators don't speak English, so when possible ask your hotel concierge (or a restaurant's maître d') to order one for you. Formula Taxi provides city cabs (typically silver Renault sedans) as well as airport service from hotels or private residences. Novoye Zhyoltoye Taksi (New Yellow Taxi) is a cab firm with a good reputation.

Taxi Contacts Novoye Zhyoltoye Taksi (☎ 495/940–8888). Formula Taxi (☎ 495/777–5777).

TRAIN TRAVEL

Moscow is the hub of the Russian railway system, and the city's several railway stations handle nearly half a billion passengers annually. There are several trains daily to St. Petersburg, and overnight service is available to Helsinki, Riga, and Tallinn. All the major train stations have a connecting metro stop, so they're easily reached by public transportation. Note that although there are phone numbers for each station, it's all but impossible to get through to them. If you have limited time, it's best to ask your hotel service bureau or a travel agent for railway information and schedules. If you want to check schedules and ticket prices ahead of time, you can use the booking function on the Russian Trains Web site (⊕ *www.russianrails.com*). The most important stations are Belorussky station, for trains to Belarus, Lithuania, Poland, Germany, and France; Kazansky station, for points south, Central Asia, and Siberia; Kievsky station, for Kiev and western Ukraine, Moldova, Slovakia, the Czech Republic, and Hungary; Kursky station, for eastern Ukraine, the Crimea, and southern Russia; Leningradsky station, for St. Petersburg, northern Russia, Estonia, and Finland; Paveletsky station, for eastern Ukraine and points south; Rizhsky station, for Latvia; and Yaroslavsky station, for points east, including Mongolia and China. Trains to Vladivostok on the Trans-Siberian Railway depart from Yaroslavsky station thrice daily, at 12:35 am, 5:38 am and 9:25 pm.

Both overnight trains and high-speed day trains depart from Leningradsky and Kursky stations for St. Petersburg. The daytime high-speed Sapsan trains take four hours and leave at various times throughout the day. Those departing from Leningradsky station leave at 6:45 am, 1:30 pm, 4:30 pm, 4:45 pm, and 7:45 pm, while one evening Sapsan leaves from Kursky station at 7:20 pm. Of the numerous overnight trains, the most popular is the *Krasnaya Strela* (Red Arrow), which leaves Moscow at 11:55 pm and arrives the next day in St. Petersburg at 7:55 am. The *Grand Express* has a similar schedule, departing Moscow at 11:40 pm and arriving in St. Petersburg at 8:35 am. There are half a dozen categories of accommodation; the higher-class compartments have showers, first class and above have satellite TV and other amenities.

FARES AND SCHEDULES For information on train schedules, reservations, and ticket delivery, call the Moscow Railways Agency. You can also purchase tickets at the railway stations, but expect long lines and brusque clerks, most of whom have little patience for those who speak no Russian. The easier route is to ask your hotel for help, as they typically have a connection with a travel agency who can arrange tickets for you. In either case, have your passport or a photocopy with you. You need it to buy tickets (they print your name and your passport number on the ticket), and you'll need to show your passport to the attendant on the train.

Train Information Russian Railways (✉ 2 Novaya Basmannaya ul., Chistiye Prudy Ⓜ Krasniye Vorota ☎ 499/262–9901 ⊕ www.rzd.ru).

Train Station Information Belorussia station (*Belorussky Vokzal*✉ Northern Outskirts ☎ 495/266–0300 Ⓜ Belorusskaya). Kazan station (*Kazansky*

Vokzal✉ *Northern Outskirts* ☎ *495/266–2300* Ⓜ *Komsomolskaya*). **Kiev station** (*Kievsky Vokzal*✉ *Krasnaya Presnya* ☎ *499/240–7071* Ⓜ *Kievskaya*). **Kursk station** (*Kursky Vokzal*✉ *Eastern Oustkirts* ☎ *495/266–5310* Ⓜ *Kurskaya*). **Leningrad station** (*Leningradsky Vokzal*✉ *Northern Outskirts* ☎ *495/262–9143*). **Pavelets station** (*Paveletsky Vokzal*✉ *Southern Outskirts* ☎ *495/950–3700* Ⓜ *Paveletskaya*). **Riga station** (*Rizhsky Vokzal*✉ *Northern Outskirts* ☎ *495/266–8512* Ⓜ *Rizhskaya*). **Yaroslav station** (*Yaroslavsky Vokzal*✉ *Northern Outskirts* ☎ *495/266–6300* Ⓜ *Komsomolskaya*).

TOUR OPTIONS

Every major hotel maintains a tourist bureau that books individual and group tours to Moscow's main sights. In addition, there are numerous private agencies that can help with your sightseeing plans.

Patriarshy Dom Tours conducts unusual day and overnight tours in and around Moscow and St. Petersburg for groups or individuals. Among the tours are Novodevichy Convent and Cemetary and the Andrei Sakharov Museum, literature and architectural walks, and the space-flight command center. They also have a daily hop-on, hop-off bus tour around the city and day trips out of town. You can check their Web site or call for schedules. Capital Tours handles group and individual tours in Moscow, including a guided trip through the most interesting metro stations and a tour of a former Soviet nuclear command bunker. They can also arrange custom tours or even whole itineraries through Russia.

Contacts Patriarshy Dom Tours (✉ *6 Vspolny per., Bolshaya Nikitskaya* ☎ *495/795–0927; 650/678–7076 in U.S.* ⊕ *www.russiatravel-pdtours.netfirms.com* Ⓜ *Barrikadnaya.* **Capital Tours** (✉ *4 Ilyinka ul., Kremlin/Red Square* ☎ *495/232–2442* ⊕ *www.capitaltours.ru* Ⓜ *Kitai-Gorod*).

VISITOR INFORMATION

Travel agents in all the major hotels offer their guests (and anyone else willing to pay their fees) various tourist services, including help in booking group or individual excursions, making a restaurant reservation, or purchasing theater or ballet tickets. The Moscow city government offers very little assistance to tourists, in part because the established Soviet travel service monopoly, Intourist, was sold off by the government during the '90s privatization spree. However, there is an official Moscow tourist office that runs a hotline you can call to ask questions and obtain information regarding museums, tour agencies, emergency services, and other tourist activities. The operators speak English. There used to be an office where you could consult with someone in person, but it is out of operation at this writing.

Contact Tourist Hotline (☎ *495/690–1301*).

EXPLORING MOSCOW

Moscow is an in-your-face metropolis that can overwhelm you with monstrous-size avenues, unbearable traffic jams, and a 24-hour lifestyle that seems to exclude any peace and harmony. But behind that brash facade is a city that also allows for quiet moments of serenity and beauty.

GREAT ITINERARIES

You can get a decent introduction to the capital in just a few days, leaving time to travel to St. Petersburg.

IF YOU HAVE 3 DAYS

Start with a stroll across Red Square, a tour of St. Basil's Cathedral, the shopping arcades of GUM, and, if you're a devoted student of Soviet history and/or embalming techniques, the Lenin Mausoleum. Then walk through Alexander Garden to reach the tourist entrance to the Kremlin. Plan on spending the better part of your first day exploring the churches, monuments, and exhibits within the grounds of this most famous of Russian fortresses. On the second day, spend the morning sightseeing and shopping on Tverskaya ulitsa. In the afternoon, head to Kitai Gorod; this neighborhood has churches and historic buildings on Varvarka ulitsa, which extends from the eastern edge of Red Square, just behind St. Basil's. Try also, toward the end of the day, to squeeze in a stroll across Teatralnaya Ploshchad to see the Bolshoi and Maly theaters. Devote the third morning to the Tretyakov Gallery, which has the finest collection of Russian art in the country. In the afternoon stroll down the Arbat, where you can find plenty of options for haggling over Russian souvenirs.

IF YOU HAVE 7 DAYS

Follow the three-day itinerary above. On the fourth day explore Bolshaya Nikitskaya ulitsa, with its enchanting mansions. Devote the fifth day to the Pushkin Museum of Fine Arts and an exploration of some of the streets in the surrounding Kropotkinsky District. Come back the next day and walk from the Russian State Library to the Kropotkinsky District. Be sure to include the Pushkin Memorial Museum and a walk along the Kremlyovskaya naberezhnaya (the embankment of the Moskva River) in the late afternoon for the spectacular views of the cupolas and towers of the Kremlin. Depending on whether your interests tend toward the religious or the secular, you could spend your last day visiting either the New Maiden's Convent and the adjoining cemetery or Gorky Park and the Tolstoy House Estate Museum, where Tolstoy once lived.

Even Muscovites often find themselves in new corners of the city that they have never before seen. Don't be afraid to wander off the beaten track, for the city, despite its disorganized and chaotic edge, is organized in a clear manner. Russians often call Moscow a *bolshaya derevnya*, or "big village," and the center itself is more compact and vital than many other world capitals.

THE KREMLIN AND RED SQUARE
КРЕМЛЬ КРАСНАЯ ПЛОЩАДЬ

Fodor's Choice ★ Few places in the world possess the historic resonance of the Kremlin, the walled ancient heart of Moscow and the oldest part of the city. The first wooden structure was erected on this site sometime in the 12th century. As Moscow grew, the city followed the traditional pattern of Russian cities, developing in concentric circles around the elevated fortress at its center (*kreml* means "citadel" or "fortress"). After Moscow emerged as the center of a vast empire in the late 15th century, the Kremlin came to symbolize the mystery and power of Russia, as it has ever since. Before the black-suited men of the Bolshevik Revolution took over, tsars were ceremoniously crowned and buried here. In the 20th century the Kremlin became synonymous with the Soviet government, and "Kremlinologists," Western specialists who studied the movements of the politicians in and around the fortress, made careers out of trying to decipher Soviet Russian policies. Much has changed since the Soviet Union broke up, but the Kremlin itself remains mysteriously alluring. A visit to the ancient Kremlin grounds reveals many signs of the old—and new—Russian enigma.

You can buy tickets for the Kremlin grounds and cathedrals at the two kiosks on either side of the Kutafya Tower. Tickets, which cost 300R, grant you access to all the churches and temporary exhibits within the Kremlin. Tickets to the Armory Palace (Oruzheynaya Palata) and Diamond Fund (Almazny Fond) cost extra (350R each); you can buy them at the kiosks or at the entrances to these buildings. Tickets for the Diamond Fund are limited in number and are sold 1½ hours before the four showings each day. Between April and October tickets are also available for a changing-of-the-guard ceremony, which takes place on Saturday at noon. Tickets cost 1,000R and include entry to all the churches and temporary exhibits. Ignore scalpers selling tickets. Keep in mind that you need to buy a 50R ticket if you wish to take pictures with your camera, and that video cameras are not allowed. All heavy bags must be checked for about 60R at the *kamera khraneniya*, which is in Aleksandrovsky Sad (Alexander Garden), to the right down and behind the stairs from the ticket kiosks.

GETTING HERE AND AROUND

If you're staying outside the Boulevard Ring, the best way to get to the Kremlin/Red Square area is to take the metro to one of the following stations: Ploschad Revolyutsii, Alexsandrovsky Sad, Borovitskaya, or Teatralnaya. If you're closer in, it's a pleasant walk to this central circle of the city, especially if you're coming from the north (you have to cross traffic-heavy bridges if walking up from the south). Many of the surrounding neighborhoods are easily walked to from here as well; the metro is advisable only if you are traveling more than a few stops.

TIMING Plan to spend a half a day, at the very least, touring the Kremlin; budget a full day or more if you want to linger at the museums. The Kremlin grounds and cathedrals are open 10 to 5 every day except Thursday. The Armory Palace and Diamond Fund are also closed on Thursday. Note that the Kremlin occasionally closes on other days for official functions. Check with your hotel concierge.

If you don't want to tackle all of this solo, you should consider a tour of the Kremlin grounds, which includes the Armory Palace, available from virtually any tour service in Moscow. A tour is particularly helpful because there are no signs, in any language, explaining the displays.

Plan to come back in the evening, when Red Square and its surrounding buildings are beautifully illuminated.

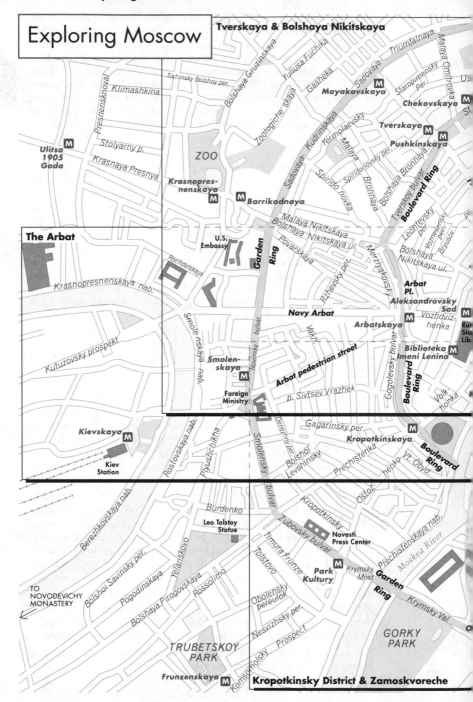

Exploring Moscow

Tverskaya & Bolshaya Nikitskaya

The Arbat

Kropotkinsky District & Zamoskvoreche

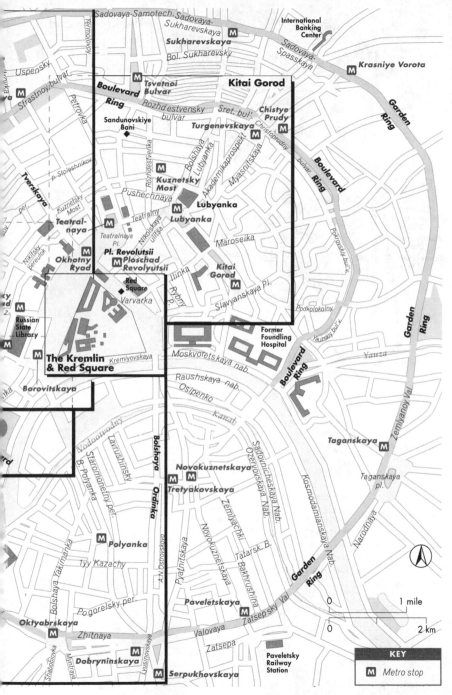

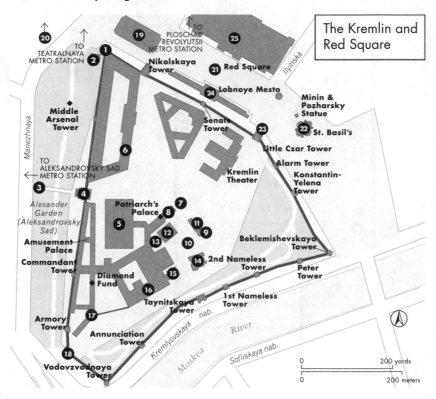

The Kremlin and Red Square

2

TOP ATTRACTIONS

Annunciation Cathedral (*Blagoveshchensky Sobor*, Благовещенский Собор). This remarkable monument of Russian architecture, linking three centuries of art and religion, was the private chapel of the royal family. Its foundations were laid in the 14th century, and in the 15th century a triangular brick church in the early Moscow style was erected on the site. Partially destroyed by fire, it was rebuilt in the 16th century during the reign of Ivan the Terrible, when six gilded cupolas were added. Tsar Ivan would enter the church by the southeast-side porch entrance, built especially for him. He was married three times too many (for a total of six wives) and was therefore, under the bylaws of the Orthodox religion, not allowed to enter the church through its main entrance. The interior is decorated by brilliant frescoes painted in 1508 by the Russian artist Feodosy. The polished tiles of agate jasper covering the floor are said to be a gift from the Shah of Persia. Most striking of all is the chapel's iconostasis. The fine icons of the second and third tiers were painted by some of Russia's greatest masters—Andrei Rublyov, Theophanes the Greek, and Prokhor of Gorodets. ✉ *Kremlin, Kremlin/Red Square* ☎ *No phone* 💵 *350R Kremlin ticket* ◷ *Fri.–Wed. 10–5* Ⓜ *Aleksandrovsky Sad or Borovitskaya.*

Fodor's Choice ★ **Armory Palace** (*Oruzheynaya Palata*, Оружейная Палата). The Armory Palace is the oldest and richest museum in the Kremlin. It was originally founded in 1806 as the Imperial Court Museum, which was created out of three royal treasuries: the Court Treasury, where the regalia of the tsars and ambassadorial gifts were kept; the Stable Treasury, which contained the royal harnesses and carriages used by the tsars during state ceremonies; and the Armory, a collection of arms, armor, and other valuable objects gathered from the country's chief armories and storehouses. The Imperial Court Museum was moved to the present building in 1851. It was further enhanced and expanded after the Bolshevik Revolution with valuables taken from wealthy noble families as well as from the Patriarchal Sacristy of the Moscow Kremlin. The roughly 4,000 artifacts here date from the 12th century to 1917, and include a rare collection of 17th-century silver. You can visit the museum only by a tour, which begins on the second floor. Halls (*zal*) VI–IX are on the first floor, Halls I–V on the second.

Hall I displays the works of goldsmiths and silversmiths of the 12th through 19th centuries, and **Hall II** contains a collection of 18th- to 20th-century jewelry. One of the most astounding exhibits is the collection of Fabergé eggs on

FABERGÉ EGGS

Intricate, playful, and exuberantly luxurious, Fabergé eggs were created by the 19th-century jeweler Carl Fabergé for the tsarist family. Alexander III began the tradition by ordering a bejeweled egg as an Easter present for his wife. Sixty-eight eggs in all were created before the Bolshevik Revolution; each one is unique and contains an Easter surprise inside. On display in the Armory Palace are two eggs, one with a train dedicated to the Trans-Siberian Railway, the other with a cruiser ship to commemorate a sea journey made by the Royal Family in 1890.

display in Hall II (Case 23). Among them is a silver egg whose surface is engraved with a map of the Trans-Siberian Railway. The "surprise" inside the egg, which is also on display, was a golden clockwork model of a train with a platinum engine, windows of crystal, and a headlight made of a tiny ruby. ■ TIP→ Feeling overwhelmed by everything to see at the Armory Palace? If nothing else, be sure to see the Fabergé eggs. If the weather is too good to spend all day indoors, check out the splendor of the Cathedral Square and come back to see the Armory another day.

Hall III contains Asian and Western European arms and armor, including heavy Western European suits of armor from the 15th to 17th centuries, pistols, and firearms.

Hall IV showcases a large collection of Russian arms and armor from the 12th to early 17th centuries, with a striking display of helmets. The earliest helmet here dates from the 13th century. Here, too, is the helmet of Prince Ivan, the son of Ivan the Terrible. The prince was killed by his father at the age of 28, an accidental victim of the tsar's unpredictable rage. The tragic event has been memorialized in a famous painting by Ilya Repin now in the Tretyakov Gallery, showing the frightened tsar holding his mortally wounded son.

Hall V is filled with foreign gold and silver objects, mostly ambassadorial presents to the tsars. Among the displays is the "Olympic Service" of china presented to Alexander I by Napoléon after the signing of the Treaty of Tilsit in 1807.

Hall VI holds vestments of silk, velvet, and brocade, embroidered with gold and encrusted with jewels and pearls.

Hall VII contains regalia and the imperial thrones. The oldest throne, veneered with carved ivory, belonged to Ivan the Terrible. The throne of the first years of Peter the Great's reign, when he shared power with his older brother Ivan, has two seats in front and one hidden in the back. The boys' older sister, Sophia (1657–1704), who ruled as regent from 1682 to 1689, sat in the back, prompting the young rulers to give the right answers to the queries of ambassadors and others. Among the crowns, the oldest is the sable-trimmed Cap of Monomakh, which dates to the 13th century. Also on display in this section are several coronation dresses, including the one Catherine the Great wore in 1762.

Hall VIII contains dress harnesses of the 16th through 18th centuries.

Hall IX has a marvelous collection of court carriages. Here you'll find the Winter Coach that carried Elizaveta Petrovna (daughter of Peter the Great and someone who clearly liked her carriages; 1709–62) from St. Petersburg to Moscow for her coronation. ⊠ *Kremlin, Kremlin/Red Square* ☎ *495/695–4631* 🎫 *350R, tickets sold one hour before each tour* 🕐 *Fri.–Wed. tours at 10, noon, 2:30, and 4:30* Ⓜ *Aleksandrovsky Sad.*

Assumption Cathedral (*Uspensky Sobor, Успенский Собор*). This dominating structure is one of the oldest edifices of the Kremlin. Designed after the Uspensky Sobor of Vladimir, it was built in 1475–79 by the Italian architect Aristotle Fiorovanti, who had spent many years in Russia studying traditional Russian architecture. Topped by five gilded domes, the cathedral is both austere and solemn. The ceremonial entrance faces Cathedral Square; the visitor entrance is on the west side (to the left). After visiting the Archangel and Annunciation cathedrals, you may be struck by the spacious interior here, unusual for a medieval church. Light pours in through two rows of narrow windows. The cathedral contains rare ancient paintings, including the icon of the Virgin of Vladimir (the work of an 11th-century Byzantine artist), the 12th-century icon of St. George, and the 14th-century Trinity icon. The carved throne in the right-hand corner belonged to Ivan the Terrible, and the gilt wood throne to the far left was the seat of the tsarina. Between the two is the patriarch's throne. Until the 1917 revolution, Uspensky Sobor was Russia's principal church. This is where the crowning ceremonies of the tsars took place, a tradition that continued even after the capital was transferred to St. Petersburg. Patriarchs and metropolitans were enthroned and buried here. After the revolution the church was turned into a museum, but in 1989 religious services were resumed here on major church holidays. ✉ *Kremlin, Kremlin/ Red Square* ☎ *495/697–0349* 🎫 *350R Kremlin ticket* ☉ *Fri.–Wed. 10–5* Ⓜ *Aleksandrovsky Sad.*

Cathedral of the Archangel (*Arkhangelsky Sobor,* Архангельский Собор). This five-dome cathedral was commissioned by Ivan the Great (1440– 1505), whose reign witnessed much new construction in Moscow and in the Kremlin in particular. The cathedral was built in 1505–09 to replace an earlier church of the same name. The architect was the Italian Aleviso Novi, who came to Moscow at the invitation of the tsar; note the distinct elements of the Italian Renaissance in the cathedral's ornate decoration, particularly in the scallop-shaped gables on its facade. Until 1712, when the Russian capital was moved to St. Petersburg, the cathedral was the burial place of Russian princes and tsars. Inside there are 46 tombs, including that of Ivan Kalita (Ivan "Moneybags"; circa 1304–40), who was buried in the earlier cathedral in 1340. The tomb of Ivan the Terrible (1530–84) is hidden behind the altar; that of his young son, Dmitry, is under the stone canopy to your right as you enter the cathedral. Dmitry's death at the age of seven is one of the many unsolved mysteries in Russian history. He was the last descendant of Ivan the Terrible, and many believe he was murdered because he posed a threat to the ill-fated Boris Godunov (circa 1551–1605), who at the time ruled as regent. A government commission set up to investigate Dmitry's death concluded that he was playing with a knife and "accidentally" slit his own throat. The only tsar to be buried here after 1712 was Peter II (Peter the Great's grandson; 1715–30), who died of smallpox while visiting Moscow.

The walls and pillars of the cathedral are covered in frescoes that tell the story of ancient Russian history. The original frescoes, painted right after the church was built, were repainted in the 17th century by a team of more than 50 leading artists from several Russian towns. Restoration work in the 1950s uncovered some of the original medieval frescoes, fragments of which can be seen in the altar area. The pillars are decorated with figures of warriors; Byzantine emperors; the early princes of Kievan Rus' (the predecessor of modern-day Russia and Ukraine), Vladimir and Novgorod; as well as the princes of Moscow, including

Vasily III, the son of Ivan the Great. The frescoes on the walls depict religious scenes, including the deeds of Archangel Michael. The carved baroque iconostasis is 43 feet high and dates from the 19th century. The icons themselves are mostly 17th century, although the revered icon of Archangel Michael is believed to date to the 14th century. ⊠ *Kremlin, Kremlin/Red Square* ☎ *495/697–0349* ☒ *350R Kremlin ticket* ☉ *Fri.– Wed. 10–5* Ⓜ *Aleksandrovsky Sad.*

QUICK BITES

There are plenty of outdoor cafés along the side of the Manezh closest to the Kremlin—many of them Western chains—but if it's sunny, head up to 5 Kamergersky ulitsa, the second street on your right as you go up ulitsa Tverskaya and grab a bite from the sandwich shop Prime Star. You can sit outside here or return to Aleksandrovsky Sad and picnic on the lawn.

Cathedral Square (*Sobornaya Ploshchad,* Соборная Площадь). This paved square, the ancient center of the Kremlin complex, is framed by three large cathedrals in the old Russian style, the imposing Ivan the Great Bell Tower, and the Palace of Facets. A changing-of-the-guard ceremony takes place in the square every Saturday at noon in the summer months. ⊠ *Kremlin, Kremlin/Red Square* ☎ *No phone* Ⓜ *Aleksandrovsky Sad.*

★ **Diamond Fund** (*Almazny Fond,* Алмазный Фонд). In 1922 the fledgling Soviet government established this amazing collection of diamonds, jewelry, and precious minerals. The items on display within the Armory Palace date from the 18th century to the present. Highlights of the collection are the Orlov Diamond, a present from Count Orlov to his mistress, Catherine the Great (1729–96); and the Shah Diamond, which was given to Tsar Nicholas I (1796–1855) by the Shah of Persia as a gesture of condolence after the assassination in 1829 of Alexander Griboyedov, the Russian ambassador to Persia and a well-known poet. Tickets to view the exhibit are sold for specific times, and viewings begin every 20 minutes. They are sold at the entrance to the Fund (inside the Kremlin), not at Kutafya Tower, where tickets for other Kremlin museums can be bought. ⊠ *Armory Palace, Kremlin/Red Square* ☎ *495/629– 2036* ☒ *500R* ☉ *Fri.–Wed. 10–1, 2–5* Ⓜ *Aleksandrovsky Sad.*

Great Kremlin Palace (*Bolshoi Kremlyovsky Dvorets,* Большой Кремлевский Дворец). The palace actually consists of a group of buildings. The main section is the newest, built between 1838 and 1849. Its 375-foot-long facade faces south, overlooking the Moskva River. This was for centuries the site of the palace of the grand dukes and tsars, but the immediate predecessor of the present building was badly damaged in the major fire of 1812. It's currently closed to the general public.

The other buildings of the Great Kremlin Palace include the 17th-century **Terem** (Tower Chamber), where the tsarina received visitors, and the 15th-century **Granovitaya Palata** (Palace of Facets). Both of these buildings are also closed to the public. ⊠ *Kremlin, Kremlin/Red Square* ☎ *495/697–0349* Ⓜ *Aleksandrovsky Sad.*

GUM (ГУМ). Pronounced "goom," the initials are short for Gosudarstvenny Universalny Magazin, or State Department Store. This staggeringly enormous emporium, formerly called the Upper Trading Rows, was built in 1889–93 and has long been one of the more famous sights of Moscow. Three long passages with three stories of shops run the length of the building. A glass roof covers each passage, and there are balconies and bridges on the second and third tiers. Another series of passages runs perpendicular to the three main lines, creating a maze-like mall. It all feels like a cavernous turn-of-the-20th-century European train station. There are shops (both Western and Russian) aplenty here now, with all the world's big-name boutique brands crowding the first floor, and a saunter down one of the halls is enjoyable. One can't-miss spot is the newly restored Gastronom No. 1, which runs the length of one side of the ground floor. It's a nostalgic supermarket with pricey caviar and champagne, as well as lowbrow canned meats that Russian World War II vets would recognize. In the adjacent hall, the store also runs a row of small cafés that serve affordable and tasty eclectic fare. Back across the ground floor from the market is the elegant Bosco restaurant, which has a small summer terrace that looks out onto Red Square. ✉ *3 Red Sq., Kremlin/Red Square* ☎ *495/788–4343* ⏱ *Mon.– Sun. 10–10* ⊕ *www.gum.ru* Ⓜ *Ploshchad Revolutsii.*

Historical Museum (*Istorichesky Muzey,* Исторический Музей). This redbrick museum was built in 1874–83 in the pseudo-Russian style, which combined a variety of backward-looking architectural styles. You may recognize the building's twin towers if you've ever caught clips of Soviet military parades on television. Against the backdrop of the towers' pointed spires, the tanks and missiles rolling through Red Square seemed to acquire even more potency. The museum's extensive archaeological and historical collections and interesting temporary exhibits outline the development of Russia, from the Stone Age to the Romanovs and beyond. ✉ *1 Red Sq., Kremlin/Red Square* ☎ *495/692– 4019* ▧ *250R* ⏱ *Wed., Fri.–Mon. 10–6, Thurs. 11–8. Closed 1st Mon. of the month* ⊕ *www.shm.ru* Ⓜ *Ploshchad Revolutsii.*

Ivan the Great Bell Tower (*Kolokolnya Ivana Velikovo,* Колокольня Ивана Великого). The octagonal main tower of this, the tallest structure in the Kremlin, rises 263 feet. According to a tradition established by Boris Godunov, no building in Moscow is allowed to rise higher than the bell tower. The first bell tower was erected on this site in 1329. It was replaced in the early 16th century, during the reign of Ivan the Great (hence the bell tower's name). But it was during the reign of Boris Godunov that the tower received its present appearance. In 1600 the main tower was rebuilt, crowned by an onion-shaped dome and covered with gilded copper. For many years it served as a watchtower; Moscow and its environs could be observed for a radius of 32 km (20 mi). Altogether, the towers have 52 bells, the largest weighing 70 tons. The annex of the bell tower is used for temporary exhibits of items from the Kremlin collection; tickets may be purchased at the entrance. ✉ *Kremlin, Kremlin/Red Square* ☎ *495/697–0349* ▧ *350R Kremlin ticket* ⏱ *Fri.–Wed. 10–5* Ⓜ *Aleksandrovsky Sad.*

Kutafya Tower (*Kutafya Bashnya,* Кутафья Башня). This white bastion, erected in 1516, once defended the approach to the drawbridge that linked Aleksandrovsky Sad to the Kremlin. In Old Slavonic, *kutafya* means "clumsy" or "confused"; this adjective was applied to the tower because it so differs in shape and size from the other towers of the Kremlin. Kutafya Tower marks the main public entrance to the Kremlin, which opens promptly at 10 am every day except Thursday. You can buy tickets to the Kremlin grounds and cathedrals at the kiosks on either side of the tower. The guards may ask where you're from and check inside your bags; there's a small security checkpoint to walk through, similar to those at airports. ⊠ *Manezhnaya ul., Kremlin/Red Square* ☎ *No phone* 🎫 *350R Kremlin ticket* ⊙ *Fri.–Wed. 10–5* Ⓜ *Aleksandrovsky Sad.*

Lenin Mausoleum (*Mavzolei Lenina,* Мавзолей Ленина). Except for a brief interval during World War II, when his body was evacuated to the Urals, Vladimir Ilyich Lenin (1870–1924) has lain in state here since his death. His body is said to be immersed in a chemical bath of glycerol and potassium acetate every 18 months to preserve it. Whether it's really Lenin or a wax look-alike is probably one of those Russian mysteries that will go down in history unanswered. From 1924 to 1930 there was a temporary wooden mausoleum, which has been replaced by the pyramid-shaped mausoleum you see now. It's made of red, black, and gray granite, with a strip of black granite near the top level symbolizing a band of mourning. Both versions of the mausoleum were designed by one of Russia's most prominent architects, Alexei Shchusev, who also designed the grand Kazansky train station near Komsomolskaya metro station.

In the Soviet past, there were notoriously endless lines of people waiting to view Lenin's body, but this is now rarely the case, although if a large tourist group has just encamped the wait may be long. Now only the curious tourist or the ardent Communist among Russians visits the mausoleum. A visit to the mausoleum, however, is still treated as a serious affair. The surrounding area is cordoned off during visiting hours, and all those entering are observed by uniformed police officers. It's forbidden to carry a camera or any large bag. Inside the mausoleum it's cold and dark. It's considered disrespectful to put your hands inside your pockets (the same applies when you visit an Orthodox church).

Outside the mausoleum you can look at the Kremlin's burial grounds. When Stalin died in 1953, he was placed inside the mausoleum alongside Lenin, but in the early 1960s, during Khrushchev's tenure, the body was removed and buried here, some say encased in heavy concrete. There is discussion almost every year of finally burying Lenin as well, and though this would still be a controversial move in today's Russia, momentum has steadily been gaining for the mausoleum to be closed. Also buried here are such Communist leaders as Zhdanov, Dzerzhinsky, Brezhnev, Chernenko, and Andropov. The American journalist John Reed, friend of Lenin and author of *Ten Days That Shook the World,* an account of the October revolution, is buried alongside the Kremlin wall. Urns set inside the wall contain ashes of the Soviet writer Maxim Gorky; Lenin's wife and collaborator, Nadezhda Krupskaya; Sergei Kirov, the Leningrad Party leader whose assassination in 1934 (believed to have been arranged by Stalin) was followed by enormous purges; the first Soviet cosmonaut, Yury Gagarin; and other

Soviet eminences. ✉ *Red Sq., Kremlin/Red Square* ☎ *No phone* ✆ *Free* ⊙ *Tues.–Thurs. and weekends 10–1* Ⓜ *Ploshchad Revolutsii.*

Lobnoye Mesto (Лобное Место). The name of the strange, round, white-stone dais in front of St. Basil's Cathedral literally means "place of the brow," but it has come to mean "execution site," for it is next to the spot where public executions were once carried out. Built in 1534, the dais was used by the tsars as a podium for public speeches and the proclamation of imperial *ukazy* (decrees). When the heir apparent reached the age of 16, he was presented to the people from this platform. ✉ *Red Sq., Kremlin/Red Square* Ⓜ *Ploshchad Revolutsii.*

Minin and Pozharsky statue (Памятник Минину и Пожарскому). In 1818 sculptor Ivan Martos built this statue, which honors Kuzma Minin (a wealthy Nizhni-Novgorod butcher) and Prince Dmitry Pozharsky, who drove Polish invaders out of Moscow in 1612 during the Time of Troubles. This period of internal strife and foreign intervention began in approximately 1598 with the death of Tsar Fyodor I and lasted until 1613, when the first Romanov was elected to the throne. This was the first monument of patriotism funded by the public. The inscription on the pedestal reads, "To citizen Minin and Prince Pozharsky from a thankful Russia 1818." The statue originally stood in the center of the square, but was later moved to its current spot in front of St. Basil's. In 2005, November 4 was named a new public holiday in honor of Minin and Pozharsky, replacing the old Communist November 7 holiday, which celebrated the anniversary of the Bolshevik Revolution. ✉ *Red Sq., Kremlin/Red Square* Ⓜ *Ploshchad Revolutsii.*

Fodor's Choice ★ **Red Square (***Krasnaya Ploshchad,* **Красная Площадь).** World famous for the grand military parades staged here during the Soviet era, this was originally called the Torg, the Slavonic word for marketplace. Many suppose that the name "Red Square" has something to do with Communism or the Bolshevik Revolution. In fact, however, the name dates to the 17th century. The adjective *krasny* originally meant "beautiful," but over the centuries the meaning of the word changed to "red," hence the square's present name. The square is most beautiful and impressive at night, when it's entirely illuminated by floodlights, with the ruby-red stars atop the Kremlin towers glowing against the dark sky. There are five stars in all, one for each of the tallest towers. They made their appearance in 1937 to replace the double-headed eagle, a tsarist symbol that is again an emblem of Russia. The glass stars, which are lighted from inside and designed to turn with the wind, are far from dainty: the smallest weighs a ton. ✉ *Red Sq., Kremlin/Red Square* ☎ *No phone* Ⓜ *Ploshchad Revolutsii.*

Resurrection Gates (*Voskresenskiye Vorota*, Воскресенские Ворота). These gates, which formed part of the Kitai Gorod defensive wall, were named for the icon of the Resurrection of Christ that hangs above them. However, the gates are truly "resurrection" gates; they have been reconstructed many times since they were first built in 1534. In 1680 the gates were rebuilt and a chapel honoring the Iberian Virgin Mary was added. In 1931 they were destroyed by the Soviets. Stalin ordered their demolition partly so that tanks could easily make their way onto Red Square during parades. They were most recently rebuilt in 1994–95. Today the redbrick gates with the bright-green-and-blue chapel are truly a magnificent sight and a fitting entrance to Red Square. The bronze compass inlaid in the ground in front of the chapel marks Kilometer Zero on the Russian highway system. ⊠ *Red Sq., Kremlin/Red Square* ☎ *No phone* ☉ *Chapel daily 8 am–10 pm* Ⓜ *Ploshchad Revolutsii.*

> ## HISTORY OF THE ONION DOME
>
> Historians argue over the origin of the onion dome commonly associated with Russian churches. One theory for the dome shape is that it was simply a way to ensure the snow slid off the church in the winter. Others say that the style was borrowed from the Mongols. St. Basil's Cathedral is home to the most famous onion domes in the world.

Fodor's Choice
★

St. Basil's Cathedral (*Pokrovsky Sobor*, Покровский Собор). Although it's popularly known as St. Basil's Cathedral, the proper name of this whimsical structure is Church of the Intercession. It was commissioned by Ivan the Terrible to celebrate his conquest of the Tatar city of Kazan on October 1, 1552, the day of the feast of the Intercession. The central chapel, which rises 107 feet, is surrounded by eight towerlike chapels linked by an elevated gallery. Each chapel is topped by an onion dome carved with its own distinct pattern and dedicated to a saint on whose day the Russian army won battles against the Tatars. The cathedral was built between 1555 and 1560 on the site of the earlier Trinity Church, where the Holy Fool Vasily (Basil) had been buried in 1552. Basil was an adversary of the tsar, publicly reprimanding Ivan the Terrible for his cruel and bloodthirsty ways. He was protected, however, from the tsar by his status as a Holy Fool, for he was considered by the Church to be an emissary of God. Ironically, Ivan the Terrible's greatest creation has come to be known by the name of his greatest adversary. In 1558 an additional chapel was built in the northeast corner over Basil's remains, and from that time on the cathedral has been called St. Basil's.

Very little is known about the architect who built the cathedral. It may have been the work of two men—Barma and Postnik—but now it seems more likely that there was just one architect, Postnik Yakovlyev, who went by the nickname Barma. Legend has it that upon completion of the cathedral, the mad tsar had the architect blinded to ensure that he would never create such a masterpiece again.

After the Bolshevik Revolution, the cathedral was closed and in 1929 turned into a museum dedicated to the Russian conquest of Kazan. Although services are held here on Sunday at 10 am, the museum is still open. The antechamber houses displays outlining the various stages of the Russian conquest of Kazan as well as examples of 16th-century Russian and Tatar weaponry. Another section details the history of the cathedral's construction, with displays of the building materials used. After viewing the museum

2

exhibits, you're free to wander through the cathedral. Compared with the exotic exterior, the dark and simple interiors are somewhat disappointing. The brick walls are decorated with faded flower frescoes. The most interesting chapel is the main one, which contains a 19th-century baroque iconostasis. ⊠ *Red Sq., Kremlin/Red Square* ☎ *495/698–3304* 🖃 *150R* ☉ *Daily 11–5* Ⓜ *Ploshchad Revolutsii.*

Tomb of the Unknown Soldier (*Mogila Neizvestnovo Soldata,* **Могила Неизвестного Солдата**). Dedicated on May 9, 1967, the 22nd anniversary of the Russian victory over Germany in World War II, this red-granite monument within Alexander Garden contains the body of an unidentified Soviet soldier, one of those who, in autumn 1941, stopped the German attack at the village of Kryukovo, just outside Moscow. To the right of the grave there are six urns holding soil from the six "heroic cities" that so stubbornly resisted the German onslaught: Odessa, Sevastopol, Stalingrad (the current Volgograd), Kiev, Brest, and Leningrad (now St. Petersburg). Very likely, no matter what time of year you are visiting, you'll see at least one wedding party. The young couple in full wedding regalia, along with friends and family, customarily stops here after getting married, leaving behind flowers and snapping photographs along the way. The gray obelisk just beyond the Tomb of the Unknown Soldier was erected in 1918 to commemorate the Marxist theoreticians who contributed to the Bolshevik Revolution. It was created out of an obelisk that had been put up three years earlier, in honor of the 300th anniversary of the Romanov dynasty. ⊠ *Manezhnaya ul., Kremlin/Red Square* 🖃 *No phone* Ⓜ *Ploshchad Revolutsii.*

Tsar Bell (*Tsar Kolokol,* **Царь-Колокол**). The world's largest bell is also the world's most silent: it has never rung once. Commissioned in the 1730s, the bell was damaged when it was still in its cast. It weighs more than 200 tons and is 20 feet high. The bas-reliefs on the outside show Tsar Alexei Mikhailovich and Tsarina Anna Ivanovna. ⊠ *Kremlin, Kremlin/Red Square* 🖃 *No phone* Ⓜ *Aleksandrovsky Sad.*

Tsar Cannon (*Tsar Pushka,* **Царь-Пушка**). This huge piece of artillery (*pushka*) has the largest caliber of any gun in the world, but like the Tsar Bell that has never been rung, it has never fired a single shot. Cast in bronze in 1586 by Andrei Chokhov, it weighs 40 tons and is 17½ feet long. Its present carriage was cast in 1835, purely for display purposes. ⊠ *Kremlin, Kremlin/Red Square* 🖃 *No phone* Ⓜ *Aleksandrovsky Sad.*

WORTH NOTING

Alexander Garden (*Aleksandrovsky Sad,* Александровский Сад). Laid out in the 19th century by the Russian architect Osip Bove, this garden named after Alexander I stretches along the northwest wall of the Kremlin, where the Neglinnaya River once flowed. The river now runs beneath the garden, through an underground pipe. Bove added the classical columns topped with an arc of chipped bricks; in the 19th century such "romantic" imitation ruins were popular in gardens. Today this mock ruin is blocked by a gate, but in eras past it was a famous place for winter sledding. A few pleasant outdoor cafés opposite the garden on the side of the Manezh building provide a nice place to rest after a tour of the Kremlin. ⊠ *Manezhnaya ul., Kremlin/Red Square* 🕾 *No phone* ☉ *Fri.–Wed. 10–5* Ⓜ *Aleksandrovsky Sad.*

Amusement Palace (*Poteshny Dvorets,* Потешный Дворец). Behind the State Kremlin Palace stands the Amusement Palace—so called because it was used by *boyarin* (nobleman) Alexei in the 17th century as a venue for theatrical productions. Later, both Stalin and Trotsky had apartments here. ⊠ *Kremlin, Kremlin/Red Square* 🕾 *495/697–0349* 💷 *350R Kremlin ticket* ☉ *Fri.–Wed. 10–5* Ⓜ *Aleksandrovsky Sad.*

Arsenal (Арсенал). Commissioned in 1701 by Peter the Great, the weapons arsenal was partially destroyed by the fire that greeted Napoléon as he stormed the city in 1812 (some say the Russian army set fire to the city intentionally). Its present form dates from the early 19th century, when it was given its yellow color and simple, but impressive shape by Osip Bove (the same architect who designed the Alexander Garden). Notable on the building's facade are arched windows framed in white granite and statuettes built into the walls flanking the main entrance. Once planned to be the site of a museum dedicated to the Napoleonic wars, today it houses government offices and is closed to the public. ⊠ *Kremlin, Kremlin/Red Square* 🕾 *495/697–0349* Ⓜ *Aleksandrovsky Sad.*

Borovitskaya Tower (*Borovitskaya Bashnya,* Боровицкая Башня). The main entrance to the Kremlin rises to more than 150 feet (46 meters). At its base a gate pierces its thick walls, and you can still see the slits for the chains of the former drawbridge. Formerly black Volgas and, now, top-of-the-line Mercedes and BMWs whiz through the vehicular entrance, carrying government employees to work. ⊠ *Manezhnaya ul., Kremlin/Red Square* 🕾 *No phone* Ⓜ *Borovitskaya.*

Cathedral of the Twelve Apostles (*Sobor Dvenadtsati Apostolov,* Собор Двенадцати Апостолов). Built in 1655–56 by Patriarch Nikon, this was used as his private church. An exhibit here displays icons removed from other Kremlin churches destroyed by the Soviets. The silver containers and stoves were used to make holy oil. Next door to the church is the Patriarch's Palace. ⊠ *Kremlin, Kremlin/Red Square* 🕾 *495/697–0349* 💷 *350R Kremlin ticket* ☉ *Fri.–Wed. 10–5* Ⓜ *Aleksandrovsky Sad.*

Church of the Deposition of the Virgin's Robe (*Tserkov Rizopolozheniya,* Церковь Ризоположения). This single-dome church was built in 1484–86 by masters from Pskov. It was rebuilt several times and restored to its 15th-century appearance by Soviet experts in the 1950s. Brilliant frescoes dating to the mid-17th century cover the church's walls, pillars, and vaults. The most precious treasure is the iconostasis by Nazary Istomin. On display inside the church is an exhibit of ancient Russian wooden sculpture from the Kremlin collection. ⊠ *Kremlin, Kremlin/ Red Square* ☎ *495/697–0349* 💷 *350R Kremlin ticket* ☉ *Fri.–Wed. 10–5* Ⓜ *Aleksandrovsky Sad.*

Patriarch's Palace (*Patriarshy Dvorets,* Патриарший Дворец). Adjoining the Cathedral of the Twelve Apostles, the Patriarch's Palace has housed the **Museum of 17th-Century Applied Art** since 1963. The exhibits here were taken from the surplus of the Armory Palace and include books, tableware, clothing, and household linen. ⊠ *Kremlin, Kremlin/Red Square* ☎ *495/697–0349* 💷 *350R Kremlin ticket* ☉ *Fri.– Wed. 10–5* Ⓜ *Aleksandrovsky Sad or Borovitskaya.*

Sobakina Tower (*Sobakina Bashnya,* Собакина Башня). More than 180 feet high, the Sobakina (formerly Arsenal) Tower at the northernmost part of the thick battlements that encircle the Kremlin was an important part of the Kremlin's defenses. It was built in 1492 and its thick walls concealed a secret well, which was of vital importance during times of siege. It isn't open for touring. ⊠ *Manezhnaya ul., Kremlin/Red Square* ☎ *No phone* 💷 *350R Kremlin ticket* Ⓜ *Ploshchad Revolutsii.*

State Kremlin Palace (*Gosudarstvenny Kremlyovsky Dvorets,* Государственный Кремлевский Дворец). In 1961 this rectangular structure of glass and aluminum was built as the Dvorets Syezdov (Palace of Congresses) to accommodate meetings of Communist Party delegates from across the Soviet Union. Today it's affiliated with the Bolshoi Theater and is used for concerts, fashion shows, and ballets. Big names such as Tom Jones, Elton John, and Rod Stewart have played here. A sizable portion of the palace is underground: the architect designed the structure this way so that it wouldn't be higher than any of the other Kremlin buildings. Apart from attending a concert, the building is of no real interest. ⊠ *Kremlin, Kremlin/Red Square* ☎ *495/620–7831* Ⓜ *Aleksandrovsky Sad.*

Tower of the Savior (*Spasskaya Bashnya,* Спасская Башня). Until Boris Yeltsin's presidency (1991–99) this 1491 tower served as the main entrance to the Kremlin. Indeed, in the centuries before Communist rule, all who passed through it were required to doff their hats and bow before the icon of the Savior that hung on the front of the tower. The icon was removed, but you can see the outline of where it was. The embellished roof and the first clock were added in 1625. President Vladimir Putin uncharacteristically used the Spasskaya Tower exit in May 2003 when hurrying to the Paul McCartney concert on Red Square. ⊠ *Red Sq., Kremlin/Red Square* ☎ *495/697–0349* Ⓜ *Ploshchad Revolutsii.*

Troitskaya Tower (*Troitskaya Bashnya,* Троицкая Башня). Rising 240 feet above the garden, this is the tallest *bashnya* (tower) in the Kremlin wall and is the passage to the Kremlin territory. This tower is linked to the Kutafya Tower by a bridge that once spanned a moat. Its deep, subterranean chambers were once used as prison cells. Napoléon supposedly lost his hat when he entered the Kremlin through this gate in 1812. ⊠ *Aleksandrovsky Sad, Kremlin/Red Square* ☎ *495/697–0349* 🖭 *350R Kremlin ticket* ⊗ *Fri.–Wed. 10–5* Ⓜ *Aleksandrovsky Sad.*

KITAI GOROD КИТАЙ-ГОРОД

Kitai Gorod, with its winding streets, is the oldest section of Moscow outside the Kremlin. The literal translation of Kitai Gorod is "China Town," but there has never been a Chinese settlement here. The origin of the word *kitai* is disputed; it may come from the Tatar word for fortress, but most likely it derives from the Russian word *kita,* in reference to the bundles of twigs that were used to reinforce the earthen wall that once surrounded the area.

Kitai Gorod begins to the east of where Red Square ends. Settlement of this area began in the 12th century, around the time that the fortified city of Moscow was founded on Borovitsky Hill (the site of the present-day Kremlin). By the 14th century Kitai Gorod was a thriving trade district, full of shops and markets. At that time it was surrounded by earthen ramparts, which were replaced in the 16th century by a fortified wall, remnants of which still remain. As Moscow grew, so did Kitai Gorod. At the time of the Bolshevik Revolution it was the city's most important financial and commercial district, with major banks, warehouses, and trading companies concentrated here. These days the multitude of shops, restaurants, and banks demonstrates the area's reasserted role as an energized commercial center.

GETTING HERE AND AROUND

Kitai Gorod can be reached by the Kitai Gorod, Lubyanka, Kuznetsky Most, Turgenevskaya, Chistiye Prudy, and Tsvetnoi Bulvar metro stations. The central street in the neighborhood, ulitsa Maroseika, originates in the west at Staraya Ploschad, sloping gently uphill and east. It becomes ulitsa Pokrovka after the intersection with the Boulevard Ring and runs all the way to the Garden Ring. The only way to get around the side streets here is on foot, but tram number 39 and a few others run the length of the boulevard that goes north to metro station Chistiye Prudy and south across the Moskva River.

TOP ATTRACTIONS

ⓒ
Fodor's Choice
★

Bolshoi Theatre (Большой Театр). Moscow's "big" (*bolshoi* means "big") and oldest theater, formerly known as the Great Imperial Theater, was completely rebuilt after a fire in 1854. Lenin made his last public speech here, in 1922. Its main building, closed for many years for renovation, is expected to reopen in 2011. Even if the Old Stage remains closed when you go, you can still see performances at the Novaya Tsena (New Stage) to the left of it. Renovation on the front of the exterior was already complete at the time of this writing, with the building's stately colonnade and chariot of Apollo atop it once again in full view on Teatralnaya Square. The interior is dressed in crimson and gold and is similarly grand. All this splendor is matched by the quality of the resident opera and ballet troupes, two of the most famous performing-arts companies in the world. If you want to see a performance at the Bolshoi, be sure to book one of its 2,155 seats as far ahead as

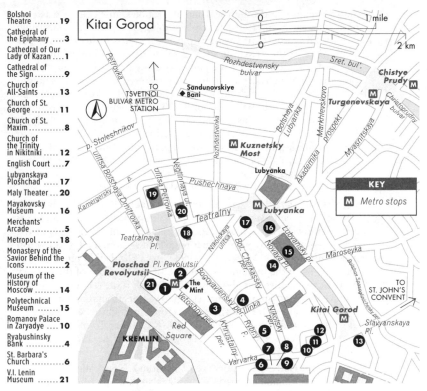

possible on it Web site, because performances can sell out quickly. To the left of the Bolshoi is the **RAMT** (Russian Academic Youth Theater), which puts on performances with a talented group of young actors. This is where you'll find the Bolshoi's main ticket office. The plaza, with fountains and fine wooden benches, is a nice spot for a relaxing look at the theater. ⊠ *1 Teatralnaya Pl., Kitai Gorod* ☎ *499/250–7317 tickets* ⊕ *www.bolshoi.ru* Ⓜ *Teatralnaya.*

QUICK BITES

The small café-bar at the **Metropol** (⊠ *4 Teatralny proyezd, Kitai Gorod* ☎ *495/927–6010* Ⓜ *Teatralnaya*) is a sophisticated spot for tea, coffee, and a selection of delicious cakes and pastries. In this busy part of town its expense is worth the calming effect of comfy, padded seats and intimate service provide. The hotel also has a famous (and even pricier) restaurant with an enormous dining hall in art nouveau style. The entrance to the café is on the right-hand side of the hotel.**Coffeemania** (⊠ *6/9 Rozhdestvenka ul., Kitai Gorod* ☎ *495/624–0075* Ⓜ *Kuznetsky Most*) is just around the corner from the Bolshoi Theater. Good coffee and food make it a favorite spot with theatergoers.

Cathedral of Our Lady of Kazan (*Kazansky Sobor,* Казанский Собор). Built between 1633 and 1636 to commemorate Russia's liberation from

Polish occupation during the Time of Troubles, this church was purposely blown up in 1936, at the beginning of a planned remodeling of all Kitai Gorod that was to help usher in a new industrial era. The centerpiece of the area was to be a monumental House of Industry, but neither the House nor the plan ever came to fruition. The current cathedral is a replica, rebuilt and fully restored in 1993. Its salmon-and-cream–painted brick and gleaming gold cupolas are now a colorful magnet at the northeast corner of Red Square, between the Historical Museum and GUM. Inside and outside hang icons of Our Lady of Kazan; every inch of the impressive interior is covered in frescoes and whorled floral patterns. Many worshippers visit throughout the day. ⊠ *8 Nikolskaya ul., at Red Sq., Kitai Gorod* ☎ *495/698–2726* 🎫 *Free* ⊙ *Daily 8–7, except Mon., when it closes at end of 5 pm vespers service. Sun. services at 7 and 9:30 am* Ⓜ *Ploshchad Revolutsii.*

English Court (*Anglisky Dvor,* **Английский Двор**). Built in the mid-16th century, this white-stone building with a steep shingled roof and narrow windows became known as the English Court because Ivan the Terrible—wanting to encourage foreign trade—presented it to English merchants trading in Moscow. In 1994 Queen Elizabeth II presided over the opening of the building as a branch of the Museum of the History of Moscow. Its displays about Russian–British trade relations over the centuries are probably most interesting to visitors from the United Kingdom. Phone ahead for information on tours in English. ⊠ *4a Varvarka ul., Kitai Gorod* ☎ *495/698–3952* 🎫 *45R* ⊙ *Tues., Thurs., and weekends 10–6, Wed. noon–8, Fri. 11–7* Ⓜ *Ploshchad Revolutsii or Kitai Gorod.*

Lubyanskaya Ploshchad (**Лубянская Площадь**). Now called by its prerevolutionary name again, this circular "square" had been renamed Dzerzhinsky Square in 1926 in honor of Felix Dzerzhinsky, a Soviet revolutionary and founder of the infamous CHEKA, the forerunner of the KGB. His statue once stood in the center of the square but was toppled in August 1991, along with the old regime. It now resides in the sculpture garden next to the Central House of Artists in the Kropotkinsky District. Instead, a slab of stone stands in the middle of the square now, as a tribute to those who were oppressed by the Soviet government. The stone comes from the Solovetsky Islands, once home to an infamous prison camp. The large yellow building facing the square, with bars on the ground-floor windows, was once the notorious Lubyanka Prison and KGB headquarters. The **KGB Museum,** which chronicles the history of espionage in Russia, is in an annex of this building. However, it is currently closed, fittingly, for an undisclosed reason. ⊠ *Kitai Gorod* Ⓜ *Lubyanka.*

Mayakovsky Museum (*Muzey Mayakovskovo,* **Музей Маяковского**). The museum for one of Russia's great revolutionary poets is suitably among the most imaginative and revolutionary installations in the city. The museum, which is housed in the building the poet inhabited opposite the headquarters of the KGB, relies on symbols to explain Vladimir Mayakovsky's (1893–1930) life. The entrance gate is shaped like a rib cage. Emblems of the life and loves of the poet hang everywhere inside, tracing his early revolutionary activities, complicated love affairs, and death. The collection includes archival documents, photos, manuscripts, paintings, and posters of and by the poet, including his handwritten suicide note. ✉ *3/6 Lyubansky proyezd, bldg. 4, Kitai Gorod* ☎ *495/621–6591* ⊕ *www.mayakovsky.info* 💳 *90R* ☉ *Mon., Tues., and Fri.–Sun. 10–5, Thurs. 1–8. Closed last Fri. of month* Ⓜ *Lubyanka.*

Merchants' Arcade (*Gostinny Dvor,* Гостиный Двор). This former market,

which takes up an entire block between ulitsa Ilinka and Varvarka ulitsa, just east of Red Square, is made up of two imposing buildings. Running the length of Khrustalny pereulok is the Old Merchant Arcade, erected by the Italian architect Quarenghi between 1791 and 1805; on the other side of the block, bordering Rybny pereulok, is the New Merchant Arcade, built between 1838 and 1840 on the site of the old fish market. The entire complex has been renovated and is now an expo center with a number of restaurants and shops, though none of them are worth making a special trip to visit. Besides the facade, the only parts of the building of historical interest are the capacious glass-topped arcade inside and a small exhibition of the structure's old molding and other features, displayed simply in a set of rooms on the western side of the complex. ✉ *4 ul. Ilinka, Kitai Gorod* ⊕ *www.mosgd.ru* Ⓜ *Ploshchad Revolutsii or Kitai Gorod.*

Metropol (Метрополь). Built at the turn of the 20th century in preparation for the celebrations commemorating 300 years of the Romanov dynasty, the Metropol underwent reconstruction in the late 1980s to restore its brilliant art nouveau facade to its original colorful guise. The ceramic mosaics are especially arresting, as the sun bounces off the tiles. Look for the Princess "Greza" panel made by Mikhail Vrubel, as inspired by the plays of the French writer Edmond Rostand. On the main facade of the building is a mosaic depicting the four seasons. The hotel was the focus of heavy fighting during the revolution, and it was also the venue of many historic speeches, including a few by Lenin. For some time the Central Committee of the Russian Soviet Federal Republic met here under its first chairman, Yakov Sverdlov. ✉ *1/4 Teatralny proyezd, Kitai Gorod* ☎ *499/501–7800* ⊕ *www.metropol-moscow.ru* Ⓜ *Ploshchad Revolutsii or Teatralnaya.*

Museum of the History of Moscow (*Muzey Istorii Goroda Moskvy,* Музей Истории Города Москвы). This small, manageable museum, housed in the former Church of St. John the Baptist (1825), presents Moscow's architectural and cultural history through paintings, artifacts, and amusing life-size dioramas. It's worth stopping in for a brief visit to get a fuller view of the Moscow history only hinted at in older neighborhoods, though unfortunately there is no written information in English, making it difficult to glean much from the exhibits unless you read Russian or have a guide. ✉ *12 Novaya Pl., Kitai Gorod* ☎ *495/624–8490*

⊕ *www.mosmuseum.ru* ✉ *50R* ⊙ *Tues., Thurs., and weekends 10–6, Wed. and Fri. 11–7. Closed last Friday of month* Ⓜ *Lubyanka.*

St. John's Convent (*Ivanovsky Monastyr*, **Ивановский Монастырь**). This convent, which was built in the 16th century and restored in the 19th century, was used as a prison in the Stalinist era and was in shambles for many years after that. The convent is open for services. Among the noblewomen who were forced to take the veil here were Empress Elizabeth's illegitimate daughter, Princess Augusta Tarakanova, and the countess Dariya Saltykova, who was imprisoned here after she murdered 138 of her serfs, most of them young women. ✉ *4 Zabelina ul., Kitai Gorod* ☎ *495/624–7521* ✉ *Free* ⊙ *Services weekdays at 7:30 am, weekends at 8:30 am and 5 pm* Ⓜ *Kitai Gorod.*

Fodor's Choice ★ **Sandunovskiye Bani** (**Сандуновские Бани**). Dating to the early 1800s, this impeccably clean banya, known also simply as "Sanduny," is probably the city's most elegant bathhouse, with a lavish blue-and-gold-painted interior. The entrance is marked by wrought-iron lamps and a circular marble staircase. Prices range from 1,000R to 1,800R—the cost depends on your sex and which section you visit. The VIP section has a pool surrounded by marble columns and a lounge with leather booths. Note that the banya essentials of a towel and a sheet to sit on in the steam room cost extra; you can also bring your own. You can also purchase birch branches, which you may be able to convince a fellow bather to beat you with (or you can hire a trained masseuse there to do it). This is a classic Russian banya procedure that's supposedly good for the skin. There is a thorough list of rules and recommendations printed in English at the ticket booth. On-site facilities include a beauty parlor and, of course, more traditional massage. ✉ *Neglinnaya ul. 14, Kitai Gorod* ☎ *495/625–4631* ⊕ *www.sanduny.ru* ✉ *1,000R–1,800R* ⊙ *Daily 8 am–11 pm* Ⓜ *Kuznetsky Most.*

V.I. Lenin Museum (*Muzey V.I. Lenina*, **Музей В.И. Ленина**). Although during the time of Soviet Russia this was a solemn and sacred place, the museum is now closed—all its holdings went to the Historical museum, next door. The magnificent redbrick exterior is well worth a look, however. Former disciples of Lenin usually congregate outside the building selling pamphlets, books, and old badges. ✉ *2/3 Ploshchad Revolutsii, Kitai Gorod* Ⓜ *Teatralnaya.*

WORTH NOTING

Cathedral of the Epiphany (*Sobor Bogoyavleniya*, **Собор Богоявления**). This church is all that remains of the monastery that was founded on this site in the 13th century by Prince Daniil of Moscow. A good example of the Moscow baroque style, the imposing late-17th-century cathedral sits among former mansions and current government buildings near Red Square. One exit of the Ploshchad Revolutsii metro station is directly across the street. The entire church, both inside and out, has been restored in recent years, though the rather plain interior pales in comparison to the bright pink bell tower and walls of the facade. ✉ *2/4 Bogoyavlensky per., Kitai Gorod* ☎ *495/698–3771* ✉ *Free* ⊙ *Daily 8–8* Ⓜ *Ploshchad Revolutsii.*

Cathedral of the Sign (*Znamensky Sobor*, Знаменский Собор). This solid redbrick church, topped with one gold and four green onion domes, was part of the monastery of the same name, built on the estate of the Romanovs in the 17th century (right after the establishment of the Romanov dynasty). After the death of the last heir to Ivan the Terrible, a dark period set in, marked by internal strife and foreign intervention. That period, commonly known as the Time of Troubles, ended in 1613, when the Boyar Council elected the young Mikhail Romanov tsar. At this writing the cathedral is closed for renovation and isn't expected to reopen until 2012 at the earliest. ✉ *8a Varvarka ul., Kitai Gorod* ☎ *495/698–3398* Ⓜ *Kitai Gorod.*

Church of All-Saints in Kulishki (*Tserkov Vsekh Svyatykh na Kulishkakh*, Церковь Всех Святых на Кулишках). This fine example of 17th-century religious architecture was built in honor of the Russian forces who won the decisive Battle of Kulikovo three centuries earlier, between Muscovy and the Tatar Golden Horde. Standing at the southern end of Slavyanskaya Square below a sloping park, the graceful church is one of the few survivors of the Soviet reconstruction of the area. Inside it's rather dark and the walls highly gilded; every inch of the ceilings are covered in frescoes. Both morning and evening services are held daily. ✉ *2 Slavyansky Pl., Kitai Gorod* ☎ *495/623–7566* Ⓜ *Kitai Gorod.*

Church of St. George on Pskov Hill (*Tserkov Georgiya na Pskovskoy Gorke*, Церковь Георгия на Псковской Горке). This majestic five-dome church with blue cupolas studded by gold stars, built in 1657 by merchants from Pskov, stands right next to the Romanov Palace Chambers in Zaryadye. The bell tower is an addition from the 19th century. The interior of the church is somewhat bare, though there are a few impressive old icons and frescoes. ✉ *12 Varvarka ul., Kitai Gorod* ☎ *No phone* Ⓜ *Kitai Gorod.*

Church of St. Maxim the Blessed (*Tserkov Maksima Blazhennovo*, Церковь Максима Блаженного). In 1698 this white-stone church was built on the site where the Holy Fool Maxim was buried. It's between St. Barbara's and the Cathedral of the Sign (in front of the northern side of the bare field where the Hotel Rossiya once stood). The church's exterior is in a sad state, dingy with exhaust from the cars that speed by on ulitsa Varvarka, and the interior is currently closed to visitors. ✉ *4 Varvarka ul., Kitai Gorod* ☎ *No phone* Ⓜ *Kitai Gorod.*

Church of the Trinity in Nikitniki (*Tserkov Troitsy v Nikitnikakh*, Церковь Троицы в Никитниках). Painted with white trim and topped by five green cupolas, this lovely redbrick creation—one of the most striking churches in the city—mixes baroque decoration with the principles of ancient Russian church architecture. Its handsome semblance is unfortunately hidden from view at the nearby Staraya Ploshchad, tucked away as it is among presidential administration buildings. The church was built between 1628 and 1634 for the merchant Grigory Nikitnikov; the private chapel on the south side was the family vault. The murals and iconostasis were the work of Simon Ushakov, a famous icon painter whose workshop was nearby in the brick building across the courtyard. The church has two areas for worship, one on the ground floor and the other up a set of stairs; the upper one is used only on holidays. The lower area is open daily. ⊠ *3 Nikitnikov per., Kitai Gorod* ☎ *495/698–5018* Ⓜ *Kitai Gorod.*

Gulag Museum (*Muzei Istorii Gulaga*, **Музей истории Гулага**). After being yanked from their beds in the middle of the night and loaded onto cattle cars, many of those purged by Stalin were shipped off to the

WORD OF MOUTH

"We had no trouble getting around on foot or by metro because we had a good set of maps. Also it was fun to study the Cyrillic alphabet while learning our way around the metro and elsewhere."　　　—tatersalad

camps of the infamous Gulag. The Soviet Union's network of prison camps is the focus of this small but moving museum. The entrance to the museum is through a simulated gauntlet with metal gates, barbed wire, and a guard tower. Inside the crumbling building are six rooms with paintings of camp scenes with titles like "A Failed Escape" and "In the Dining Hall" many of which were done by former prisoners. Glass cases hold prisoners' personal effects, including handicrafts made by them like walrus-tusk cups and a metal cigarette case, and other Gulag-related documents and pictures. The bottom floor has a life-size diorama of typical camp bunks and an isolation cell. There are often excellent temporary exhibits here as well. Guided tours are available in English. ⊠ *16 ul. Petrovka, Kitai Gorod* ☎ *495/621–7346* ⊠ *100R* ☉ *Fri.–Wed. 11–7, Thu. 12–8* Ⓜ *Teatralnaya.*

Maly Theater (**Малый Театр**). Writer Maxim Gorky (1868–1936), known as the father of Soviet socialist realism, once called this theater famous for its productions of Russian classics "the Russian people's university." It opened in 1824 and was originally known as the Little Imperial Theater (*maly* means "little"). Out front stands a statue of a beloved and prolific playwright whose works are often performed here, the 19th-century satirist Alexander Ostrovsky. ⊠ *1 Teatralnaya Pl., bldg. 1, Kitai Gorod* ☎ *495/623–2621* Ⓜ *Teatralnaya.*

The Mint (*Monetny Dvor*, **Монетный Двор**). Built in 1697, the former mint, near the Cathedral of Our Lady of Kazan, is an excellent example of old baroque architecture. Its facade can be seen through the courtyard of an 18th-century building immediately next to the cathedral. It is not currently open to visitors, but the outside is worth a look. ⊠ *5 Nikolskaya ul., at Red Sq., Kitai Gorod* ☎ *No phone* Ⓜ *Ploshchad Revolutsii.*

Monastery of the Savior Behind the Icons (*Zaikonospassky Monastyr*, **Заиконоспасский Монастырь**). The monastery was founded at the beginning of the 17th century by Boris Godunov. Russia's first institution of higher learning, the Slavonic-Greco-Latin Academy, was opened in this building in 1687. Many an illustrious scholar studied here, including scientist and poet Mikhail Lomonosov (1711–65) from 1731 to 1735. Hidden inside the courtyard is the monastery's cathedral, **Spassky Sobor,** built in 1600–61 in the Moscow baroque style. The tower of the church is under ongoing renovation, but the interior is intact, and services are held daily. ⊠ *7 Nikolskaya ul., Kitai Gorod* ☎ *No phone* Ⓜ *Ploshchad Revolutsii.*

Ⓒ **Polytechnical Museum** (*Politekhnichesky Muzey,* **Политехнический Музей**). The achievements of science and technology, including an awesome collection of early-20th-century Russian cars, fill an entire Moscow block. The monumental building that houses the museum was built in 1875 by Ippolit Monigetti, a Russian of Italian birth whose day job was designing annexes on the royal family's country estates. The endless series of exhibits—miners' lamps, Soviet televisions, even a full-scale replica of the USSR's first atomic bomb—can be overwhelming and esoteric, but kids love it. There are also many good temporary exhibits, as well as a small planetarium at the southern entrance. ⊠ *3/4 Novaya Pl., Kitai Gorod* ☎ *495/623–0756* ⊕ *www.polymus.ru* ☜ *100R* ⊙ *Tues.–Sun. 10–6. Closed last Fri. of month* Ⓜ *Lubyanka.*

Romanov Palace Chambers in Zaryadye (*Palaty Romanovykh v Zaryadye,* **Палаты Романовых в Зарядье**). It's believed that Mikhail Romanov (1596–1645), the first tsar of the Romanov dynasty, was born in this house. Today the mansion houses a lovely museum devoted to the boyar lifestyle of the 16th and 17th centuries. Period clothing, furniture, and household items furnish the rooms, illustrating how the boyars lived. During the week the museum is generally open only to groups with advance reservations—these are typically throngs of school children—but if you ask, you may be allowed to join one of the groups. On Sunday the museum is open to the general public. Tours are available in English, but you must make reservations. The entrance is downstairs. ⊠ *10 Varvarka ul., Kitai Gorod* ☎ *495/698–1256* ☜ *150R* ⊙ *Mon. and Thurs.–Sun. 10–6, Wed. 11–7. Closed 1st Mon. of month* Ⓜ *Kitai Gorod.*

Ryabushinsky Bank (**Рябушинский Банк**). Fyodor Shekhtel designed this turn-of-the-20th-century art nouveau masterpiece for the rich merchant Ryabushinsky. The pale-orange building on the opposite side of the street, built in the classical style at the end of the 19th century, is the former Birzha (Stock Exchange); it now houses the Russia Chamber of Commerce and Industry. ⊠ *Birzhevaya Pl. at ul. Ilinka, Kitai Gorod* Ⓜ *Ploshchad Revolutsii.*

St. Barbara's Church (*Tserkov Velikomuchenitsy Varvary,* **Церковь Великомученицы Варвары**). This peach-and-white church, built in the classical style at the end of the 18th century, lends its name to the street. Like most Orthodox churches in the city, it is open to the public all day, though the interior is less impressive than those of its many neighbors. ⊠ *Varvarka ul. off Red Sq., Kitai Gorod* Ⓜ *Ploshchad Revolutsii.*

TVERSKAYA ULITSA ТВЕРСКАЯ УЛИЦА

As the line of the road that led from the northern tip of the Kremlin to the ancient town of Tver, Tverskaya ulitsa had been an important route for centuries. Later that road was extended all the way to the new capital on the Baltic Sea, St. Petersburg. Tverskaya ulitsa is Moscow's main shopping artery, attracting shoppers hungry for the latest trends. The lovely, wide boulevard is lined with perfumeries, banks and exchanges, eateries, and bookshops. Some of the city's best and biggest stores are on the ground floors of massive apartment buildings, some quite attractive and graced by a fine art nouveau style. On a sunny day, Tverskaya is an especially pleasant walk. Tverskaya ulitsa was given its present form in the mid-1930s, and from 1932 to 1990 the road was known as Gorky Street, in honor of the writer Maxim Gorky, the father of Soviet socialist realism. In 1990 the first section of the street, leading from the heart of town to Triumfalnaya Ploshchad, was given back its prerevolutionary name of Tverskaya ulitsa. A year later, the second section, ending at the Belorussian Railway Station, was also returned to its old name of Tverskaya-Yamskaya. Until the rebuilding in the 1930s, Tverskaya ulitsa was narrow and twisting, lined in places with wooden houses. Today it's a broad, busy avenue, a tribute to the grandiose reconstruction projects of the Stalinist era.

GETTING HERE AND AROUND
The area around Tverskaya ulitsa can be reached through the Tverskaya, Pushkinskaya, Chekhovskaya, Mayakovskaya, and Okhotny Ryad metro stations. Once here, unless you're traveling north all the way to Belorusskaya metro station, which sits at the north end of Tverskaya-Yamskaya ulitsa past the Garden Ring, you're best off walking the web of streets in this neighborhood. The distances can be long at times, but other transportation options—with the exception of a car—are not convenient for moving around here.

TIMING If you stay in Moscow for more than a few days you will always end up on or near Tverskaya ulitsa. Consider spending half a day if you'd like to visit the museums in this neighborhood.

TOP ATTRACTIONS
Church of the Resurrection (*Tserkov Voskreseniya*, Церковь Воскресения). Built in 1629, this is one of the few lucky churches to have stayed open throughout the years of Soviet rule. As a survivor, the church was the recipient of many priceless icons from less fortunate churches destroyed or closed by the Soviets. Services are still held here daily. Be sure to look at the beautiful frescoes on the ceilings in the chapels on either side of you as you enter. Two famous icons, depicting the Coronation of the Virgin Mary and the Assumption of the Blessed Virgin Mary, hang in the vaults on either side of the vestibule. ⊠ *15/2 Bryusov per., Tverskaya* 🕾 *495/629–6616* Ⓜ *Tverskaya.*

Moscow Art Theater (*MKhAT*, Московский Художественный Театр). One of Moscow's most historically important theaters, this performance space is renowned for its productions of the Russian classics, especially those of Anton Chekhov (1860–1904). Founded in 1898 by the celebrated actor and director Konstantin Stanislavsky (1863–1938) and playwright and producer Vladimir Nemirovich-Danchenko (1858–1943), the theater staged the first productions of Chekhov's and Maxim Gorky's (1868–1936) plays. It was here that Stanislavsky developed the Stanislavsky Method, based on the realism in traditional Russian theater. After the successful production of Chekhov's *The Seagull* (the first staging in St. Petersburg had bombed), the bird was chosen as the theater's emblem. An affiliated, more modern theater, with a seating

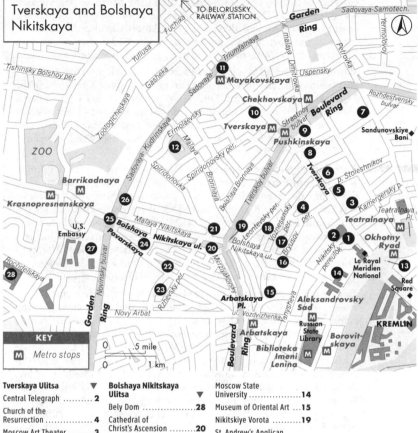

Tverskaya and Bolshaya Nikitskaya

KEY

🅼 Metro stops

capacity of 2,000, also confusingly called the Moscow Art Theater, was opened in 1972 on Tverskoi bulvar, near Stanislavsky's home. The mural opposite the old theater depicts Anton Chekhov, as does the statue at the start of Kamergersky pereulok. ☒ *3 Kamergersky per., Tverskaya* ☎ *495/692–6748* ⊕ *www.art.theatre.ru* Ⓜ *Okhotny Ryad.*

Moscow City Council (*Mossoviet*, Моссовет). This impressive structure was built at the end of the 18th century by Matvey Kazakov for the Moscow governor-general. During the reconstruction of Tverskaya ulitsa in the 1930s, the building was moved back about 45 feet in order to widen the street. The top two stories—a mirror image of the mansion's original two stories—were added at that time. ☒ *22 Tverskaya ul., Tverskaya* Ⓜ *Tverskaya.*

OFF THE
BEATEN
PATH

Dostoyevsky Memorial Apartment (*Muzey-Kvartira Dostoevskovo*, Музей-квартира Достоевского). This museum is devoted to the great Russian novelist. It's on the grounds of the hospital where he was born and where his father, Mikhail Andreevich, resided and worked as a doctor. Fyodor Dostoyevsky (1821–81) lived here until he was 16. The museum has kept things much as they were, from family pictures to the neat, middle-class furniture. ☒ *2 ul. Dostoevskovo, Northern Outskirts* ☎ *495/681–1085* ☎ *50R* ⊘ *Wed. and Fri. 2–7, Thurs. and weekends 11–6. Closed last day of month* Ⓜ *Dostoyevskaya.*

Museum of the Contemporary History of Russia (*Muzey Sovremennoi Istorii Rossii*, Музей Современной Истории России). The onetime social center of the Moscow aristocracy has an entrance flanked by two smirking lions. Originally built by Giliardi in 1787, the mansion was rebuilt in the classical style after the Moscow Fire of 1812. The building housed the Museum of the Revolution from 1926 to the late 20th century, at which time the museum was converted to its present purpose. Although it retains many of its former exhibits—heavily imbued with Soviet propaganda—the museum has been updated to reflect the changing political climate in Russia and exhibits cover events up to 2000. The permanent exhibit, on the second floor, begins with a review of the first workers' organizations in the 19th century. The exhibits outlining the 1905 and 1917 revolutions include the horse-drawn machine-gun cart of the First Cavalry Army, the texts of the first decrees of the Soviet government on peace and land, dioramas and paintings portraying revolutionary battles, and thousands of other relics. The next rooms outline the history of Soviet rule, with extensive material devoted to Stalin's rise to power before whizzing through the short post-Soviet history.

With a huge archive and the country's best collection of political posters and medals, the museum has a reputation for hosting excellent temporary exhibits. Explanations are only in Russian, but you can arrange a tour in English by calling ahead. The fine gift shop sells Russian souvenirs (including some beautiful amber) and great vintage items like flags and political-rally posters. ☒ *21 Tverskaya ul., Tverskaya* ☎ *495/699–6724* ⊕ *www.sovr.ru* ☎ *150R* ⊘ *Tues., Wed., and Fri. 10–6; Thurs. and Sat. 11–7; Sun. 10–5. Closed last Fri. of month* Ⓜ *Tverskaya.*

Patriarch's Pond (*Patriarshy Prudy*, Патриаршие Пруды). The beginning of Russian satirist and novelist Mikhail Bulgakov's (1891–1940) novel *The Master and Margarita* is set in this small park. Bulgakov is most famous for this novel and his satirical novel *Heart of a Dog*. The park and pond were named after the patriarch of the Orthodox Church, who once owned the area. Shaded by trees and with plenty of benches, it's a nice spot for a break, and there are several good restaurants nearby, including the paradoxical Pavilion at one end where they serve kitschy Soviet cuisine in an opulent setting. In winter the pond is used as a skating rink. ✉ *ul. Malaya Bronnaya, Tverskaya* ☎ *No phone* Ⓜ *Mayakovskaya.*

> ## METRO 2
>
> Moscow's metro is one of the deepest in the world, but below it, if you believe the Soviet legend, is a second even deeper metro system, Metro 2. This metro was purportedly built for Stalin as a private line for top party officials. One of the lines supposedly led from the Kremlin to the Lubyanka, the home of the feared KGB.

Pushkin Square (*Pushkinskaya Ploshchad*, **Пушкинская Площадь**). Located at the intersection of Tverskaya ulitsa and the Boulevard Ring, Pushkin Square is most popular meeting place in town. Every evening in good weather you will see dozens of people waiting by the bronze statue of Alexander Pushkin (1799–1837), which stands at the top of a small park. It's the work of Alexander Opekushin and was erected by public subscription in 1880. It is impossible to underestimate Russia's love for the poet who is credited with founding modern Russian literature. One of his most famous lines, from his novel in verse *Eugene Onegin* (1823) is about Moscow: "Moscow, how many strains are fusing / in that one sound, for Russian hearts! / what store of riches it imparts!" Summer and winter, fresh flowers on the pedestal prove that the poet's admirers are still ardent and numerous. The city claims to have big plans for the constantly packed underpass that links the square's four corners, with a large shopping center seemingly in the cards, but it's unclear when work will begin. Also at this site is the country's first McDonald's, once the busiest in the world, and a recently opened restaurant and shop called Armenia, which sells that country's famed Ararat brandy and other delicacies. ✉ *Junction between Tverskaya and Boulevard Ring, Tverskaya* ☎ *No phone* Ⓜ *Pushkinskaya.*

Le Royal Meridien National (**Гостиница Националь**). The ornate art nouveau splendor of the National, built in 1903, belies its revolutionary function as the pre-Kremlin residence for Lenin, and subsequent home for Communist Party operatives and fellow travelers, such as author John Reed. Beautiful mosaics adorn the hotel facade; inside, the luxurious rooms and restaurants conjure up the National's prerevolutionary dominance in elegance. ✉ *15/1 Mokhovaya ul., Tverskaya* ☎ *495/258–7000* ⊕ *www.national.ru* Ⓜ *Okhotny Ryad.*

Triumphal Square (*Triumfalnaya Ploshchad*, **Триумфальная Площадь**). This major intersection is where the grand boulevard of Moscow, the Garden Ring, crosses Tverskaya ulitsa. Traffic here also passes through a tunnel running below Tverskaya ulitsa, and there's an underpass for pedestrians. A statue of the revolutionary poet Vladimir Mayakovsky (1893–1930) stands in the center of the square. It's generally believed that Mayakovsky committed suicide after he became disillusioned with the revolution he had so passionately supported.

The square is a center of Moscow's cultural life—and lately it's also become the political opposition's preferred site for anti-Putin rallies. (In order to prevent the latter, city authorities occasionally cordon off much of the square, supposedly to undertake emergency construction work.) The **Tchaikovsky Concert Hall,** which opened in 1940, stands on one corner. In its foyer are various food outlets, including tasty croissants and coffee at the dependable Brioche. The **Satire Theater** is next door, on the Garden Ring. **Mossoviet Theater,** which shares space in the Aquarium Garden with the popular expat hangout **Starlite Diner,** is also nearby, at 16 Bolshaya Sadovaya. To your far left is the multitiered tower of the elegant **Peking Hotel,** opened in 1956 as a mark of Sino-Soviet friendship.

While you're here, it's worth riding the escalator down for a peek at the spectacular interior of the **Mayakovskaya metro station,** which, like many early stations, lies deep underground (it doubled as a bomb shelter during World War II). Stalin made a famous speech here on the 24th anniversary of the Bolshevik Revolution, at the height of the Siege of Moscow. Colorful, pastel mosaics depicting Soviet achievements in outer space decorate the ceiling. ⊠ *Junction between Tverskaya and the Garden Ring, Tverskaya* Ⓜ *Mayakovskaya.*

Yeliseyevsky's (Елисеевский). Of all the stores and boutiques on Tverskaya ulitsa, this grocery store at No. 14, in a Matvei Kazakov–designed, late-18th-century classical mansion, has the most dazzling interior, with chandeliers, stained glass, and gilt wall decorations. Under Communist administration, the store had the official, generic title Gastronom No. 1, but it once again carries the name that most people continued to call it even then—Yeliseyevsky's, after the rich merchant from St. Petersburg who owned the store before the revolution. The large alcohol and souvenir section in the back room includes a number of vodkas, some in bottles shaped as eagles (in reference to the double-headed one on Russia's coat of arms) and matryoshka dolls. Also available are replica Fabergé eggs, filled with vodka and costing a steep 62,000R. Coffee beans, caviar, and candy, as well as a standard array of fresh foods, are for sale here as well. One of the few grocery stores in the city center, and open 24 hours, it's a good place to stock up on snacks and drinks. ⊠ *14 Tverskaya ul., Tverskaya* ☎ *495/650–4643* ☉ *Daily, 24 hrs* Ⓜ *Tverskaya or Pushkinskaya.*

WORTH NOTING

Moscow Museum of Modern Art (Moskovsky Muzei Sovremennovo Iskusstvo, Московский Музей Современного Искусства). Though dwarfed in both size and prominence by New York's MOMA (and bearing no relation to that museum), the Moscow Museum of Modern Art has gained respect in a city suddenly busy with contemporary art galleries. It was founded in 1999 by sculptor Zurab Tsereteli, a magnet for controversy best known (and mostly disdained) for his enormous statue of Peter the Great on the Moskva River. At that time, his collection of works by the likes of Picasso and Dalí and, especially,

Moscow's Magnificent Metro

Even if you don't plan on using the metro to get around Moscow, it's still worth taking a peek at this wonder of the urban world. The first line opened in 1935, and the earliest stations—in the city center and along the ring line—were built as public palaces. Many of the millions of commuters using the system each day bustle past chandeliers, sculptures, stained-glass windows, beautiful mosaics, and pink, white, and black marble. With its rich collection of decorative materials, the metro has often been called a museum; it's even been said that no geological museum in the world has such a peculiar stone library.

Mayakovskaya station, opened in 1938, may well be the jewel in the crown of the Moscow metro. The vaulted ceiling of the grand central hall has 33 mosaic panels, based on the theme "One Day of Soviet Skies,"

by Russian artist Alexander Deineka. **Novoslobodskaya,** opened in 1952, sparkles, thanks to its light-backed stained glass. Several other stations—such as **Ploshchad Revolutsii,** with its bronze figures from the socialist world order (farmers, soliders, and such)—are tourist attractions in their own right.

In the past, Moscow's metro architects won international architecture awards for their designs. Designs of new stations, however, have departed from these grand old stations; they lack brass sculptures and intricate stained glass, for example. But with indirect lighting, exquisite marble, and an open, airy feeling, these new stations reflect modern life in a way that the monumental Soviet displays of past glories do not. Moscow's metro is one of the top three most heavily used metro systems in the world.

artists from the Russian avant-garde movement formed the core of the museum's holdings. There are no permanent exhibits, however, so you should check the Web site or call to see what's currently showing. Exhibits rotate in and out every few months and range in content from retrospectives of eminent Russian émigrés to debut collections to experimental video art to interactive exhibitions. The museum's main building is a restored 18th-century mansion, but there are three other branches that are also in the city center. ✉ *25 Petrovka ul., Kitai Gorod* ☎ *495/694–6660* 🖳 *150R* ☉ *Mon.–Wed. and Fri.–Sun. noon–8, Thurs. 1–9. Closed last Mon. of month* ⊕ *www.mmoma.ru* Ⓜ *Pushkinskaya.*

Tverskaya Square (*Tverskaya Ploshchad,* Тверская Площадь). This square, which dates to 1792, was named for the street, but in 1918 it was renamed Sovetskaya (Soviet) Ploshchad. In 1994 its historical name, Tverskaya, was reinstated. In the small park here stands a statue of Prince Yuri Dolgoruky, the founder of Moscow in 1147. The equestrian statue was erected in 1954, shortly after the celebrations marking Moscow's 800th anniversary. One of the city's most popular bookstores, called simply Moskva, is just north of the square, on the east side of Tverskaya ulitsa. ✉ *Tverskaya* ☎ *No phone* Ⓜ *Tverskaya.*

Tverskaya-Yamskaya ulitsa (Тверская-Ямская улица). This last section of Tverskaya ulitsa leads to Belorussky railway station, which also has two interconnecting metro stations. The entrances to all three stations are spread along the edge of sprawling Tverskaya Zastava Square, known for its gnarled traffic patterns caused by construction projects that have occupied it for years. Lately, the area surrounding the square has become home to a number of popular restaurants, including the gastropub favorite Ragout and a mid-range steakhouse called Torro Grill. Belorussky station is where trains roll in from Western Europe and is the site of the former Triumphal Gates, built in the 19th century by the architect Osip Bove to commemorate the Russian victory in the war with Napoléon. The gates were demolished in a typical fit of destruction in the 1930s. A replica of the original gates was erected in 1968 near Poklonnaya Hill, at the end of Kutuzovsky prospekt. ⊠ *Tverskaya* ☏ *No phone* Ⓜ *Mayakovskaya.*

Yermolova Theater (*Teatr imeni Yermolovoi,* Театр имени Ермоловой). The theater housed in this short building with an arched entrance was founded in 1937 and named after the Russian actress Maria Yermolova (1853–1928). ⊠ *5/6 Tverskaya ul., Tverskaya* ☏ *495/629–0031* Ⓜ *Okhotny Ryad.*

BOLSHAYA NIKITSKAYA ULITSA
БОЛЬШАЯ НИКИТСКАЯ УЛИЦА

Bolshaya Nikitskaya ulitsa is one of the many old streets radiating from the Kremlin, spokelike, just like Tverskaya ulitsa to the northeast and Novy Arbat to the southwest. The street was laid out along the former road to Novgorod, an ancient town northwest of Moscow, and is divided into two sections. The first part is lined with 18th- and 19th-century mansions and also includes the Tchaikovsky Conservatory and Moscow State University buildings; it begins at Manezhnaya Ploshchad, across from the fortification walls of the Kremlin. The second section, notable for its enchanting art nouveau mansions, starts at Nikitskiye Vorota Square, where Bolshaya Nikitskaya ulitsa intersects with Bulvarnoye Koltso (the Boulevard Ring).

GETTING HERE AND AROUND
Bolshaya Nikitskaya is served by the Krasnopresnenskaya, Barrikadnaya, Okhotny Ryad, Arbatskaya, and Biblioteka Imeni Lenina metro stations. You can approach the street from Pushkin Square walking south along the Boulevard Ring, from metro station Arbatskaya walking north, also on a boulevard, or from Manezhnaya Ploshchad, where the eastern end of the street is. It's a bit of a trek to get to the street from any metro station except Biblioteka Imeni Lenina, so plan accordingly.

TIMING This neighborhood is spread over quite a bit of territory and includes detours down crooked streets, so it's best to allow a full day to see everything at a leisurely pace. If you start out at the Okhotny Ryad metro station and walk through the sights to end at the Barrikadnaya station, you'll have walked roughly 3 km (2 mi).

TOP ATTRACTIONS
Bely Dom (*White House,* Белый Дом). This large, white, modern building perched along the riverbank is the headquarters of the Russian government and the prime minister. Before the August 1991 coup, the "White House" was the headquarters of the Russian Republic of the

USSR. In October 1993 the building was shelled in response to the rioting and near-coup by Vice President Alexander Rutskoi and parliamentarians. They had barricaded themselves in the White House after Yeltsin's decision to dissolve parliament and hold new elections. Today the building is also known as the Dom Pravitelstvo, or Government House. It sits directly across the Moskva River from the Radisson Royal hotel, once the Ukraina, one of the seven "Stalin Gothic" skyscrapers built in Moscow in the mid-20th century. ⊠ *2 Krasnopresnenskaya nab., Bolshaya Nikitskaya* ☎ *495/605–5329* Ⓜ *Krasnopresnenskaya.*

Cathedral of Christ's Ascension in Storozhakh (*Hram Vozneseniya Gospodnya v Storozhakh,* Храм Вознесения Господня в Сторожах). Like Moscow State University, this classical church was designed by Matvei Kazakov and built in the 1820s. For years it stood empty and abandoned, but after major repair, religious services have resumed here. The church is most famous as the site where the Russian poet Alexander Pushkin married the younger Natalya Goncharova; Pushkin died six years later, in a duel defending her honor. There is a kitschy and much despised statue of the couple on the square outside the church. (History has judged Natalya harshly; she was probably not guilty of adultery, although she did enjoy flirting.) The statue in the park to the left of the church as you face it is of Alexey Tolstoy, a relative of Leo's and a well-known Soviet writer of historical novels. A house museum dedicated to him is next to the Ryabushinsky Mansion. ⊠ *36 Bolshaya Nikitskaya ul., Bolshaya Nikitskaya* ☎ *No phone* Ⓜ *Arbatskaya.*

CDL: Central House of Writers (*Tsentralny Dom Literatorov,* Центральный Дом Литераторов). The CDL is an exclusive club for members of the Writers' Union, now run as an independent nonprofit. The club (at 53 Bolshaya Nikitskaya; it's the same building, but the club entrance is on another street) is off-limits, but the dining room is open to the public and is now one of the city's best and most elegant restaurants. Next door (No. 52) is a large mansion, enclosed by a courtyard, that houses the administrative offices of the Writers' Union. It's commonly believed that Leo Tolstoy (1828–1910) used this mansion as a model for his description of the Rostov home in *War and Peace.* A statue of Tolstoy stands in the courtyard. Mikhail Bulgakov (1891–1940) set part of his satire of Soviet life, *The Master and Margarita,* here. ⊠ *50 Povarskaya ul., Bolshaya Nikitskaya* ☎ *495/691–1515* Ⓜ *Barrikadnaya.*

Chaliapin House Museum (*Dom-muzey Chaliapina,* Дом-музей Шаляпина). Fyodor Chaliapin (1873–1938), one of the world's greatest opera singers, lived in this beautifully restored manor house from 1910 to 1922. Chaliapin was stripped of his Soviet citizenship while on tour in France in 1922; he never returned to Russia again. The Soviets turned his home into an apartment building, and until restorations in the 1980s, the building contained 60 communal apartments. With help from Chaliapin's family in France, the rooms have again been arranged and furnished as they were when the singer lived here. The walls are covered with works of art given to Chaliapin by talented friends, such as the artists Mikhail Vrubel and Isaac Levitan. Also on display are Chaliapin's colorful costumes, which were donated to the museum by his son. When you reach the piano room, you'll hear original recordings

The Seven Gothic Sisters

With their spookily lit cornices dominating the skyline since the mid-20th century, the "Seven Sisters" (also known as the "Stalin Gothics") are as much a part of the Moscow experience as the Empire State Building is in New York. The neo-Gothic buildings are often called "wedding cake" skyscrapers because their tiered construction creates a sense of upward movement and grandeur, like a rocket on standby.

The seven buildings—the White House (Bely Dom) at the end of the Arbat; the Ukraina and Leningradskaya hotels; the residential buildings at Kudrinskaya Ploshchad (Kudrinsky Square), Kotelnicheskaya naberezhnaya (Kotelnicheskaya Embankment), and Krasniye Vorota; and the imposing Moscow State University on Sparrow Hills—were constructed when the country lay in ruins, just after World War II. Stalin ordered the skyscrapers to be built in 1947, on the 800th anniversary of Moscow's founding, as a symbol of Soviet power. German prisoners of war were forced to work on several of the buildings.

An eighth skyscraper was planned (before the others were started) but never built: this was the grandiose Palace of Soviets, which was meant to replace the Kremlin as the seat of government power. It was intended to be the tallest building in the world, with a height of 1,378 feet topped by a 300-foot statue of Lenin. The site of the Cathedral of Christ Our Savior on the Moskva River was chosen, and the church was demolished in 1931. Only later did builders realize that the ground was too wet to support such an enormous structure. The plans were abandoned, and the area was turned into a swimming pool until the cathedral was rebuilt in 1997.

According to the Soviet propaganda of the time, most of the new buildings were part of the government's drive to replace slums with better housing. In truth, residents were mainly party members, actors, writers, and other members of the elite. With few ordinary people living in or having access to the buildings, legendary stories developed around the Seven Sisters. The Ukraina's spire was said to hide a nuclear-rocket launcher, while Moscow State University was rumored to have a secret tunnel leading to Stalin's dacha. The university was also said to run as deep underground as it did above, concealing secret study centers and a metro connection. The building at Kudrinskaya Ploshchad overlooks the U.S. embassy. It was said that KGB spies kept an eye on the embassy compound from certain windows.

Today you can easily visit most of the skyscrapers, particularly the Ukraina and Leningradskaya hotels, now the Radisson Royal and Hilton Moscow hotels, respectively.

---

of Chaliapin singing his favorite roles. Entrance is from inside the courtyard. English-language tours are available and should be reserved ahead of time. ⊠ *25 Novinsky bulvar, Bolshaya Nikitskaya* ☎ *495/605–6236* ⊕ *www.shalyapin-museum.org* ⊠ *150R* ⊘ *Wed.–Sun. 11–6. Closed last day of month* Ⓜ *Barrikadnaya.*

Chekhov House Museum (*Dom-muzey Chekhova*, Дом-музей Чехова). The sign "Dr. Chekhov" still hangs from the door of this home where

Chekhov resided from 1886 to 1890. The rooms are arranged as they were when he lived here, and some of the furniture, such as two sturdy desks covered in green felt, belonged to the author's family. One room showcases photos and memorabilia from Chekhov's trek to the island of Sakhalin in the Russian Far East. Overall, the materials on display at the museum are not particularly enthralling, so unless you are a Chekhov diehard, this is far from an essential stop. ⊠ *6 Sadovaya-Kudrinskaya ul., Bolshaya Nikitskaya* ☎ *495/691–6154* 🎫 *100R* ☉ *Tues., Thurs., and Sat. 10–6; Wed. and Fri. 2–8* Ⓜ *Barrikadnaya.*

Cook Street (*Povarskaya ulitsa,* Поварская улица). This is where the tsars' cooks lived. After the revolution the street was renamed Vorovskovo, in honor of a Soviet diplomat who was assassinated by a Russian, but it has returned to its prerevolutionary name. Povarskaya ulitsa is an important center of the Moscow artistic community, with the film actors' studio, the Russian Academy of Music (the Gnesin Institute), and the Tsentralny Dom Literatorov (Central House of Writers) all located here. Many of the old mansions have been preserved, and the street retains its prerevolutionary tranquillity and charm. In the first flush days of summer your walk is likely to be accompanied by a rousing drum set or tinkling piano sonata issuing from the open windows of the music school. ⊠ *Bolshaya Nikitskaya* Ⓜ *Arbatskaya.*

Gorky House Museum (*Dom Ryabushinskovo,* Дом Рябушинского). This marvelous and wonderfully preserved example of Moscow art nouveau was the home of Maxim Gorky from 1931 to 1936. Sometimes called the Ryabushinsky Mansion, it was built in 1901 for the wealthy banker of that name and designed by the architect Fyodor Shektel. (If you arrived in Moscow by train, you may have noticed the fanciful Yaroslav station, another of his masterpieces, just opposite the Leningrad railway station.) Although Gorky was a champion of the proletariat, his home was rather lavish. Gorky himself apparently hated the *style moderne,* as art nouveau was termed back then. Those who don't, however, are charmed by this building of ecru brick and stone painted pink and mauve atop gray foundations. On the exterior, a mosaic of irises forms a border around the top of most of the house, and a fanciful yet utilitarian iron fence matches the unusual design of the window frames. The spectacular interior includes a stained-glass roof and a twisting marble staircase that looks like a wave of gushing water. Tours in English are available; call ahead for more information. ⊠ *6/2 Malaya Nikitskaya ul., Bolshaya Nikitskaya* ☎ *495/690–0535* 🎫 *Free* ☉ *Wed.–Sun. 11–5:30. Closed last Thurs. of month* Ⓜ *Arbatskaya.*

Kudrinskaya Ploshchad (*Kudrinsky Square,* Кудринская Площадь). Along one side of this square, cars race along the Garden Ring, the major circular road surrounding Moscow. If you approach the ring from Bolshaya Nikitskaya ulitsa or Povarskaya ulitsa, the first thing to catch your eye will be the 22-story skyscraper directly across Novinsky bulvar. One of the seven Stalin Gothics, this one is 525 feet high. The ground floor, home to a grand supermarket in Soviet times, is now occupied by clothing stores and a cafeteria called Central Restaurant House—this is worth peeking into to admire the towering ceilings and stained-glass windows inside. The rest of the building contains apartments. This area saw heavy fighting during the uprisings of 1905 and 1917 (the plaza was previously called Ploshchad Vosstaniya, or Insurrection Square). The Barrikadnaya (Barricade) metro station is very close by. Cross the ulitsa Barrikadnaya and bear right and down the hill; you'll see people streaming into the station to your right. ✉ *Bolshaya Nikitskaya* ☏ *No phone* Ⓜ *Barrikadnaya.*

Manezhnaya Ploshchad (*Manezh Square,* Манежная Площадь). When the Soviets razed this square in 1938, many of the area's old buildings were lost. The plan, which never came to pass, was to build a superhighway through the area. In 1967 the square was renamed "50th Anniversary of the October Revolution Square." In the 1990s the square reverted to its original name and construction of an underground shopping mall began. Construction was halted in 1993 to let archaeologists excavate the area. The team found a plethora of artifacts dating as far back as the 13th century. In 1997 the Manezh shopping mall was finally opened, much to the chagrin of most Muscovites, who saw it as an eyesore. The present (and prerevolutionary) name comes from the Imperial Riding School, or Manezh, that stands on the opposite side of the square from the Moskva Hotel. The 1817 structure was gutted by a fire in early 2004, but has since been restored.

Opened in 1935, the **Moskva Hotel** was one of the first buildings erected as part of Stalin's reconstruction plan for Moscow. Despite protests, the hotel that's featured on Stolichnaya vodka labels was demolished in late 2003 to make way for a new Moskva, which replicates the facade of the original structure; the new hotel is complete but not yet open to the public as of this writing. (If you look carefully at the facade, you'll notice that the design on the west side doesn't match the design on the east side. Legend has it that Stalin was given a preliminary draft that showed two possible versions for the hotel. He was supposed to sign under the one he liked best, but instead he signed his name right across the middle. The story goes that the architects, too timid to go back to Stalin a second time, went ahead and built the hotel with the asymmetrical facade.)

Nikitskiye Vorota (Никитские Ворота). This square was named after the *vorota* (gates) of the white-stone fortification walls that once stood here. On one side of the square is a modern building with square windows; this is the office of ITAR-TASS, once the official news agency of the Soviet Union and the mouthpiece of the Kremlin. In the park in the center of the square stands a monument to Kliment Timiryazev, a famous botanist.

The busy road intersecting Bolshaya Nikitskaya ulitsa is the **Bulvarnoye Koltso** (Boulevard Ring), which forms a semicircle around the city center. It begins at the banks of the Moskva River, just south of the Kremlin, running in a northeastern direction. After curving eastward, and then south, it finally reaches the riverbank again after several miles, near the mouth of the Yauza River, northeast of the Kremlin. Its path follows the lines of the 16th-century white-stone fortification wall that gave Moscow the name "White City." The privilege of living within its walls was reserved for the court nobility and craftsmen serving the tsar. The wall was torn down in 1775, on orders from Catherine the Great, and was replaced by the current Boulevard Ring. The perfect way to get a good view of the inner city is to slowly walk along the ring—this is best done on the weekend or late at night to avoid traffic on the boulevard. Running along its center is a broad strip of trees and flowers, dotted with playgrounds and benches. Summer brings out a burst of outdoor cafés, ice-cream vendors, and strolling lovers along the boulevard. ✉ *Bolshaya Nikitskaya* Ⓜ *Arbatskaya.*

Stanislavsky Museum (*Muzey Stanislavskovo,* **Музей Станиславского**). Konstantin Stanislavsky was a Russian actor, director, and producer, as well as the founder of the Stanislavsky Method, the catalyst for method acting. He was also one of the founders of the Moscow Art Theater. Stanislavsky lived and worked in this house, an elegant 19th-century building with stunning painted ceilings, during the last 17 years of his life. The house has been kept as it was while he lived here, showcasing a small practice theater, the various leather chairs he preferred, a few of his old theater costumes, and other memorabilia. The entrance to the museum is through the courtyard. ✉ *6 Leontyevsky per., Bolshaya Nikitskaya* ☎ *495/629–9088 or 495/629–2442* ✎ *120R* ☉ *Wed. and Fri. 12–7, Thurs. and weekends 11–6. Closed last Thurs. of month* Ⓜ *Pushkinskaya.*

Tchaikovsky Conservatory (*Konservatoriya imeni Chaykovskovo,* **Консерватория имени Чайковского**). The famous Tchaikovsky Music Competition takes place every four years in this prestigious music school's grand performance space. The main hall is currently closed due to renovation being done on the facade but is scheduled to reopen in time for the start of the next Competition, in June 2011. There are almost daily concerts in the school's various performance spaces, which include the smaller Rachmaninovsky and Maly Halls. Both of these host chamber music concerts. Tickets, almost always affordable, are sold at a small window directly on the sidewalk on Bolshaya Nikitskaya ulitsa east of the main hall. The conservatory was founded in 1866 and moved to its current location in 1870. Rachmaninoff, Scriabin, and Tchaikovsky are among the famous composers who worked here. There's a statue of Tchaikovsky designed by Vera Mukhina, a famous Soviet sculptor, in the semicircular park outside the main entrance. If you'd rather not attend a performance, can also just sit back with a coffee and listen to rehearsals and concerts from the summer garden of the Coffeemania here, near the Tchaikovsky statue. ✉ *13/6 Bolshaya Nikitskaya ul., Bolshaya Nikitskaya* ☎ *495/629–9401 or 495/629–0225* ⊕ *www.mosconsv.ru* Ⓜ *Okhotny Ryad or Arbatskaya.*

WORTH NOTING

St. Andrew's Anglican Church. Moscow's only Anglican church is inside this attractive red-sandstone building. Built in 1884, it served the British-expatriate community for more than 40 years, including a mass for Queen Victoria after her death in 1901. No bells were rung then, however, because only Orthodox churches were allowed to have them in the city. Instead the tower was used as a strong room for rich British merchants. The 1917 revolution ended both spiritual and secular functions, however, and the church was closed. The pews are believed to have been burned in the harsh winters of the early 1920s, and the stained glass was replaced when the building was converted into a recording studio. Today the Church of England has reacquired the property, and it's again a vibrant, working church and a gathering place for the community. ⊠ *8 Voznesensky per., Bolshaya Nikitskaya* ☎ *495/629–9889* ⊕ *www. standrewsmoscow.org* Ⓜ *Okhotny Ryad.*

Gorky Literary Museum (*Literaturny Muzey Gorkovo,* Литературный Музей Горького). For Gorky buffs only, this museum is packed with the letters, manuscripts, and pictures of the great proletarian writer. There are also portraits of him by Nesterov and Serov and a remarkable photograph of him playing chess with Lenin in Capri, Italy, where Gorky made his home for many years both before and after the Soviets took power in Russia. Gorky never lived here, but there is a miniature wooden reproduction of his childhood home, complete with village yard and outbuildings. Phone ahead for individual or group tours in English. ⊠ *25a Povarskaya ul., Bolshaya Nikitskaya* ☎ *495/690–5130* 🖃 *Free* ☉ *Mon., Tues., and Thurs. 10–5, Wed. and Fri. noon–7. Closed 1st Thurs. of month* Ⓜ *Barrikadnaya.*

Museum of Oriental Art (*Muzey Iskusstva Narodov Vostoka,* Музей Искусства Народов Востока). Glass cases filled to capacity with artwork and clothing from the Central Asian republics, China, Japan, and Korea make up the museum's large permanent collection. The museum itself is a cool and calm place to take a leisurely stroll. Most of the placards in the museum are in Russian, but there are a few annotations in English. ⊠ *12a Nikitsky bulvar, Bolshaya Nikitskaya* ☎ *495/691–0212* ⊕ *www.orientmuseum.ru* 🖃 *150R* ☉ *Tues.–Sun. 11–8* Ⓜ *Arbatskaya.*

Tsvetaeva House Museum (*Dom-muzey Tsvetaevoy,* Дом-музей Цветаевой). Marina Tsvetaeva (1892–1941), the renowned poet, lived in an apartment on the second floor of this building from 1914 to 1922. Today the building houses not only a museum dedicated to her but also a cultural center that arranges international literary evenings, musical events, and annual conferences covering the poet and the Silver Age (1890s–1917) in general. You must ring the bell to enter the museum, which begins on the second floor. Although the rooms are decorated in the style of the early 1900s, they are not as they were when Tsvetaeva lived here. The poetry written on the wall in her bedroom has been re-created. The children's room has some stuffed animals in place of the real animals— a dog, a squirrel, and a turtle, to name a few—Tsvetaeva kept in her home. ⊠ *6 per. Borisoglebski, Bolshaya Nikitskaya* ☎ *495/695–3543* 🖃 *50R* ☉ *Mon.–Wed. and Fri. noon–6, Thurs. noon–8, Sun. noon–5. Closed last Fri. of month* Ⓜ *Arbatskaya.*

THE ARBAT АРБАТ

Two of downtown Moscow's most important avenues are the Arbat (also known as the Stary Arbat, or Old Arbat) and Novy Arbat (New Arbat), which are two more spokelike routes leading away from the Kremlin. The pedestrian-only Stary Arbat is revered by many Muscovites, who usually refer to it simply as "the Arbat." The area is an attractive, cobbled pedestrian precinct lined with gift shops and cafés; it used to be packed with souvenir stands as well, but they have all been moved indoors. It's a carnival of portrait artists, poets, and musicians, as well as the enthusiastic admirers of their work. One of the oldest sections of Moscow, the Arbat dates from the 16th century, when it was the beginning of the road that led from the Kremlin to the city of Smolensk. At that time it was also the quarter where court artisans lived, and several of the surrounding streets still recall this in such names as Plotnikov (Carpenter), Serebryany (Silversmith), and Kalashny (Pastry Cook). Early in the 19th century the Arbat became a favorite district of the aristocracy, and a century later it became a shopping street.

Novy Arbat has both a different history and spirit. For almost 30 years it was named Kalinin prospekt, in honor of Mikhail Kalinin, an old Bolshevik whose prestige plummeted after 1991. The stretch from the Kremlin to Arbatskaya Ploshchad has been given back its prerevolutionary name of ulitsa Vozdvizhenka. The second section—which begins where Vozdvizhenka ends and runs west for about a mile to the Moskva River—is now called Novy Arbat. In contrast to ulitsa Vozdvizhenka, which has retained some of its prerevolutionary charm, and the Arbat, which is actively re-creating the look of its past, Novy Arbat is a modern thoroughfare. It is now something of an entertainment area, with flashy shopping malls and lots of decent restaurants.

GETTING HERE AND AROUND

You can reach the Arbat via the Arbatskaya, Smolenskaya, and Biblioteka Imeni Lenina metro stations. The Novy Arbat is an enormous avenue packed with traffic and therefore not very pleasant to walk along; it's best to have a specific destination in mind if going there. The side streets off the Stary Arbat are easy to get lost in, but you inevitably make your way to a recognizable major thoroughfare, whether it's back to Stary Arbat, to Novy Arbat to the north, the Garden Ring on the western edge, or ulitsa Prechistinka to the south, which is another spoke heading southwest from the Kremlin.

TIMING   You can easily spend a whole day exploring the Arbat, especially if you go souvenir shopping at the shops and street kiosks you'll see along the way. There are the numerous charming side streets just off the Old Arbat and plenty of cafés to stop off for a break. If you want to avoid crowds, check this neighborhood out on a weekday; the pedestrian zone on the Old Arbat, in particular, draws big crowds on the weekends. The museums in this neighborhood are all fairly small; you'll need no more than an hour for each of them.

TOP ATTRACTIONS

Arbatskaya Ploshchad (*Arbat Square,* **Арбатская Площадь**). At this busy intersection, ulitsa Vozdvizhenka crosses the Boulevard Ring. On the southeastern corner is one of Russia's oldest movie theaters, the Kinoteatr Khudozhestvenny, which was opened in 1912. The pedestrian underpass in front of the movie theater was once a bustling marketplace as well as an unsanctioned concert space, though lately it has turned into just another row of vendors. When you emerge on the other side, you will be in front of a neoclassical building that was long the home

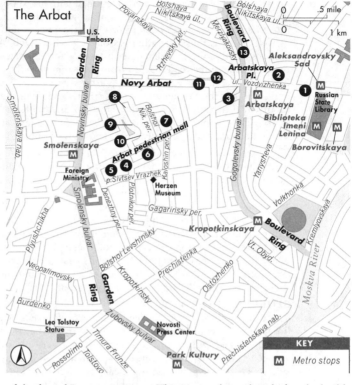

of the famed Praga restaurant. This is set to be replaced after the build-ing was sold (in 2010) for the umpteenth time. ⊠ *Arbat* ☎ *No phone* Ⓜ *Arbatskaya.*

Church of St. Simon the Stylite (*Tserkov Simeona Stolpnika,* Церковь Симеона Столпника). This bright white 17th-century church stands out in stark contrast to the modern architecture that dominates the area. During the reconstruction of Novy Arbat in the 1960s, many old churches and buildings were destroyed, but this one was left purposely standing as a reminder of the past. For years it housed a conservation museum, but now it's been returned to the Orthodox Church and is active. Nothing remains, however, of the original interiors. ⊠ *4 ul. Novy Arbat, Arbat* ☎ *No phone* Ⓜ *Arbatskaya.*

Church of the Transfiguration on the Sands (*Khram Spasa Preobrazheniya na Peskakh,* Храм Спаса Преображения на Песках). Built in the 17th century, this elegant church was closed after the 1917 revolution and

turned into a cartoon-production studio. Like many churches throughout Russia, however, it has been returned to its original purpose. The church is depicted in Vasily Polenov's well-known canvas *Moskovsky Dvornik (Moscow Courtyard)*, which now hangs in the Tretyakov Gallery. Services are at 8 am on weekdays and at 10 am on Sundays. ✉ *4a Spasopeskovsky per., Arbat* ☎ *495/241–6203* 🎫 *Free* 🕙 *Daily 8–8* Ⓜ *Smolenskaya.*

Dom Druzhby Narodov (*Friendship of Nations House,* Дом Дружбы Народов). One of Moscow's most interesting buildings—it looks like a Moorish castle—was built in the late 19th century by the architect V. A. Mazyrin for the wealthy (and eccentric) industrialist Savva Morozov (Tolstoy mentions this home in his novel *Resurrection*). The building's name is a holdover from the Soviet days, when Russians and foreigners were supposed to meet only in officially sanctioned places. Today its rooms are used by the federal government for meetings and conferences and are not open to the public. ✉ *16 Vozdvizhenka ul., Arbat* ☎ *No phone* Ⓜ *Arbatskaya.*

Dom Knigi (*House of Books,* Дом Книги). One of the country's largest bookstores has an English-language section on the second floor. ✉ *8 Novy Arbat, Arbat* ☎ *495/789–3591* 🕙 *Weekdays 9 am–11 pm, weekends 10 am–11 pm* Ⓜ *Arbatskaya.*

Melnikov House (*Dom Melnikova,* Дом Мельникова). This cylindrical concrete building was designed by the famous Constructivist architect Konstantin Melnikov in the late 1920s. The house is currently in a state of major disrepair but remains remarkable for its wall-length windows and spiral staircases inside that link the three floors. Plans to open it as a museum have been in motion for years but look nowhere near completion, as arcane issues regarding the house's ownership are still being settled. The architect's granddaughter lives in the house. ✉ *10 Krivoarbatsky per., Arbat* ☎ *No phone* 🌐 *www.melnikovhouse. org* Ⓜ *Smolenskaya.*

Pushkin Apartment Museum (*Muzey-kvartira Pushkina,* Музей-квартира Пушкина). The poet Alexander Pushkin lived here with his bride, Natalya Goncharova, for several months in 1831, right after they were married. Experts have re-created the original layout of the rooms and interior decoration. The first floor presents various trinkets and poems, plus information on Pushkin's relationship with Moscow; the second floor is a reconstruction of a typical early-19th-century room. ✉ *53 Arbat, Arbat* ☎ *499/241–9295* 🎫 *80R* 🕙 *Wed.–Sun. 10–6. Closed last Fri. of the month* Ⓜ *Smolenskaya.*

Scriabin Museum (*Muzey Scriabina,* Музей Скрябина). This charming, dusty house-museum is in the composer Alexander Scriabin's (1872–1915) last apartment, where he died of blood poisoning in 1915. Visitors are scarce because foreign tourist groups are not usually brought here. The rooms are arranged and furnished just as they were when Scriabin lived here. Downstairs there's a concert hall where accomplished young musicians perform his music, usually on Tuesday and Wednesday evenings. Call for more information. ✉ *11 Bolshoi Nikolopeskovsk per., Arbat* ☎ *499/241–1901* 🎫 *150R* 🕙 *Wed. 1–9, Thurs. and Sa*

11–6, Fri. 12–7, Sun. 11–5. Closed Mondays, Tuesdays, and last Fri. of month Ⓜ *Smolenskaya.*

Shchusev Architecture Museum (*Muzey Arkhitektury imeni Shchuseva,* **Музей Архитектуры имени Щусева**). This museum, in an 18th-century neoclassical mansion, has a good reputation for displaying works by some of the best and most controversial architects in Russia and from around the world. The temporary exhibits cover Moscow architecture from ancient through contemporary times. ✉ *5 Vozdvizhenka ul., Arbat* ☎ *495/691–2109* ⊕ *www.muar.ru* 🎟 *100R* ☉ *Tues.–Sun. 11–7* Ⓜ *Biblioteka Imeni Lenina.*

WORTH NOTING

Andrei Bely Apartment Museum (*Muzey-kvartira Andreya Belovo,* **Музей-квартира Андрея Белого**). On display are artifacts from the life of the writer Andrei Bely (1880–1934), considered to be one of the great Russian Symbolists—he's most famous for his novel *Petersburg*. As of this writing, the museum was undergoing renovation, though it is still possible to tour the exhibits. The "Lines of Life" drawing on the wall of the first room shows the "energy" of Bely's life (the blue line in the middle) marked by dates and names of people he knew during specific times. The keepers of the museum offer exhaustive tours of the apartment, but they are in Russian only. The general entrance to the museum is through the souvenir shop. ✉ *55 Arbat, Arbat* ☎ *499/241–7702* 🎟 *80R* ☉ *Wed.–Sun. 10–6. Closed last Fri. of the month* Ⓜ *Smolenskaya.*

Gogol statue (Pamyatnik Gogolyu, **Памятник Гоголю**. This statue of a melancholy Nikolai Gogol (1809–52) originally stood at the start of Gogolevsky bulvar but was replaced by a more "upbeat" Gogol. The statue now stands inside a courtyard near the apartment building where the writer spent the last months of his life. The statue actually captures Gogol's sad disposition perfectly. He gazes downward, with his long, flowing cape draped over his shoulder, protecting him from the world. Gogol is perhaps best known in the West for his short stories, his novel Dead Souls, and for his satirical drama *Revizor (The Inspector General)*, about the unannounced visit of a government official to a provincial town. Characters from his works are engraved on the pedestal. ✉ *7 Nikitsky bulvar, Arbat* ☎ *No phone* Ⓜ *Arbatskaya.*

Spaso House (**Спасо-Хаус**). The yellow neoclassical mansion behind the iron gate is the residence of the American ambassador. It was built in the early 20th century for a wealthy merchant. The building's front looks on a small square between Arbat and Novy Arbat that features an undersized statue of Pushkin in the center. It's a pleasant place to take a break. ✉ *Spasopeskovskaya Pl., Arbat* Ⓜ *Smolenskaya.*

Vakhtangov Theater (*Teatr imeni Vakhtangova,* **Театр имени Вахтангова**). An excellent traditional theater is housed within this impressive structure named after Stanislavsky's pupil Evgeny Vakhtangov (1883–1922). The gold statue of Princess Turandot and stone fountain to the right of the theater were created in honor of the 850th anniversary of Moscow in 1997; they are loved and hated by an equal proportion of Muscovites. ✉ *26 Arbat, Arbat* ☎ *499/241–1679* Ⓜ *Arbatskaya.*

THE KROPOTKINSKY DISTRICT РАЙОН КРОПОТКИНСКОЙ

This picturesque old neighborhood is known as the Kropotkinsky District after the famous Russian anarchist Prince Pyotr Kropotkin. Heading out of the district's metro station, which is also named in honor of him, you will find yourself at the intersection of the Boulevard Ring and the area's main street, ulitsa Prechistenka, which leads southwest out to the Garden Ring. It's yet another ancient section of Moscow whose history dates back nearly to the foundation of the city itself. Almost none of its earliest architecture has survived; the area suffered badly during the 1812 conflagration of Moscow, so most of its current buildings date to the postwar period of reconstruction, when neoclassicism and the so-called Moscow Empire style were in vogue. Before the revolution, the area was the favored residence of Moscow's old nobility, and it's along its thoroughfares that you'll find many of their mansions and homes, often called "nests of the gentry." It was also the heart of the literary and artistic community, and there were several famous literary salons here. Prince Kropotkin compared it to the Saint-Germain quarter of Paris.

GETTING HERE AND AROUND

The Kropotkinsky District is served by the Kropotkinskaya, Borovitskaya, Biblioteka Imeni Lenina, and Park Kultury metro stations. The central landmark in the area is Cathedral of Christ the Savior, its imposing white corpus rising up along the Moscow River next to the southwestern end of the Boulevard Ring. The Kropotkinsky District is about a 20-minute walk from the Kremlin; the easiest way to reach it from there is either along the river embankment or on ulitsa Volkhonka, which runs directly from Aleksandrovsky Sad to the Kropotkinskaya metro station.

TIMING   Taken at a leisurely pace, you could cover the neighborhood in three to four hours but the area is worth spending at least half a day on and, with stops at any of the various museums here, your exploration could easily expand to two days (the Pushkin Museum of Fine Arts alone is worth a day). If you're definitely interested in visiting some of the museums in this district, do *not* head out on a Monday, as most of the museums are closed that day.

TOP ATTRACTIONS

Cathedral of Christ Our Savior (*Khram Khrista Spasitelya*, **Храм Христа Спасителя**). This cathedral carries an amazing tale of destruction and reconstruction. Built between 1839 and 1883 as a memorial to the Russian troops who fell fighting Napoléon's forces in 1812, the cathedral was the largest single structure in Moscow, and it dominated the city's skyline. It took almost 50 years to build what only a few hours would destroy. On December 5, 1931, the cathedral was blown up. Under Stalin, the site had been designated for a mammoth new "Palace of Soviets," intended to replace the Kremlin as the seat of the Soviet government. Plans called for topping the 1,378-foot structure with a 300-foot statue of Lenin that would have spent more time above the clouds than in plain view if the plans had ever materialized. World War II delayed construction, and the entire project was scrapped when

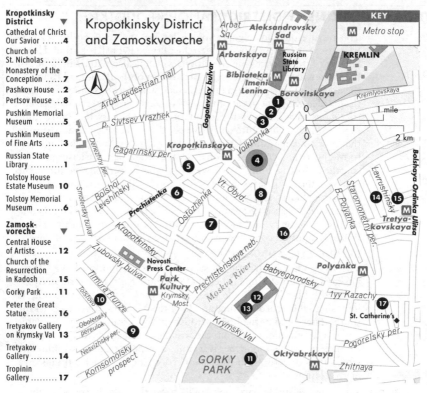

it was discovered that the land along the embankment was too damp to support such a heavy structure.

The site lay empty and abandoned until 1958, when the Moscow Pool, one of the world's largest outdoor swimming pools, was built. Divided into several sections, for training, competition, diving, and public swimming, it was heated and kept open all year long, even in the coldest days of winter. The pool was connected to the locker rooms by covered tunnels, and you could reach it by swimming through them. The pool was dismantled in 1994. Then—in perhaps one of architectural history's stranger twists—the cathedral was resurrected in 1997 from the ruins at a cost of more than $150 million.

Today the giant cathedral is complete, with a stunning interior. You enter into a hallway lined with writing that surrounds the central chamber. These marble panels covered in prerevolution Russian script describe the Napoleonic invasion of Russia in 1812. Hundreds of battles are detailed, beginning with the French army's first steps into Russian territory and ending with Napoleon's downfall in Paris and the reinstatement of peace in Europe. The immense main hall is covered in frescoes. Look straight up into the central cupola to see a dramatic painting of the Holy Father with baby Jesus in his hands. Across from the figures is the word "elohim" (meaning "God") written in Hebrew. Off to one side are two thrones behind a short fence. These are symbolic seats for Saint Nicholas the Miracle-Maker and the legendary Russian war hero Prince Alexander Nevsky, who has been honored as a saint by the Orthodox Church since his death in 1243.

There are tours offered by the church in which you can learn about other details of the interior and tour the entire complex. Call for more information or ask your hotel concierge. ⊠ *15 ul. Volkhonka, on the bank of the Moskva river, Kropotkinsky District* ☎ *495/637–1276* ☉ *Tues.–Sun. 8–7:30* ⊕ *www.xxc.ru* Ⓜ *Kropotkinskaya.*

> ### CATHEDRAL OF CHRIST OUR SAVIOUR
>
> On your way to the Cathedral of Christ Our Savior, stop in the Kropotkinskaya metro station to see what is left of the original cathedral, which was bombed by the Bolsheviks in 1931. The interior of the station is decorated using marble stripped from the old cathedral before it was destroyed.

Monastery of the Conception (*Zachatievsky Monastyr,* **Зачатьевский Монастырь**). Founded in the 16th century, this working monastery is the oldest complex in the district, though only the redbrick Gate Church remains of the original buildings. In 2010, however, on the grounds rose a sparkling new church, with star-spangled silver domes and gold-rimmed eaves. It does not imitate the design of the cathedral that once stood here. The monastery was established by the last surviving son of Ivan the Terrible, in what amounted to a plea to God for an heir (hence its name). He and his wife failed to have a son, however, and Boris Godunov became the next Russian leader. ⊠ *2 2nd Zachatievsky per., Kropotkinsky District* Ⓜ *Kropotkinskaya.*

Pashkov House (*Dom Pashkova,* **Дом Пашкова**). Designed by Vasily Bazhenov, one of Russia's greatest architects, this mansion was erected between 1784 and 1786 for the wealthy Pashkov family. The central building is topped by a round belvedere and flanked by two service wings. In the 19th century it housed the Rumyantsev collection of art and rare manuscripts. Following the 1917 revolution, the museum was closed and the art collection was transferred to the Hermitage in St. Petersburg and the Pushkin Museum of Fine Art. The manuscripts were donated to the Russian State Library which now owns this building. Now, after 20 years of restoration, Pashkov House is open to anyone with a State Library card. Unfortunately, they turn away anyone who just wants a peek inside. ⊠ *Mokhovaya ul. and ul. Znamenka, Kropotkinsky District* Ⓜ *Borovitskaya.*

Pertsov House (*Dom Pertsova,* **Дом Перцова**). One of the finest examples of Moscow art nouveau was built in 1905–07 by the architects Schnaubert and Zhukov. The facade of the steep-roofed and angled building, which is closed to the public, is covered in colorful mosaics. Walk all the way to the end of Soymonovsky pereulok, coming out at the river, and straight across you'll see a large, redbrick compound. This is the **Krasny Oktyabr (Red October) candy factory,** which used to fill the neighborhood with the smell of chocolate early in the morning. Now, the former factory complex is full of restaurants, clubs, art galleries, and a boutique hotel. To your left, the buildings of the Kremlin line the distance, the golden cupolas of its churches gleaming. To the right you can see the behemoth Peter the Great statue. ⊠ *Soymonovsky proyezd and Prechistenskaya nab., Kropotkinsky District* 🚇 *No phone* Ⓜ *Kropotkinskaya.*

Fodor's Choice ★   **Pushkin Museum of Fine Arts** (*Muzey Izobrazitelnykh Iskusstv imeni Push-kina,* Музей Изобразительных Искусств имени Пушкина). One of the finest art museums in Russia, the Pushkin is famous for its Gauguin, Cézanne, and Picasso paintings, among other masterpieces. Founded by Ivan Vladimirovich Tsvetayev (1847–1913) of Moscow State University, father of poet Marina Tsvetaeva, the museum was originally established as a teaching aid for art students, which explains why a large part of its collection is made up of copies. The original building dates from 1895 to 1912 and was first known as the Alexander III Museum. It was renamed for Pushkin in 1937, on the centennial of the Russian poet's death. Next door, the **Musey Chastnykh Kollektsiy** (Museum of Private Collections) hosts some of the museum's most famous works and has separate hours and a small entrance fee.

The first-floor exhibit halls in the original building contain a fine collection of ancient Egyptian art (Hall 1); Greece and Rome are well represented, though mostly by copies (Room 7). The Italian school from the 15th century (Room 5) is represented by Botticelli's *The Annunciation,* Tomaso's *The Assassination of Caesar,* Guardi's *Alexander the Great at the Body of the Persian King Darius,* and Sano di Pietro's *The Beheading of John the Baptist,* among others. When you reach the Dutch School of the 17th Century (Hall 10), look for Rembrandt's *Portrait of an Old Woman,* whose subject may have been the artist's sister-in-law. Flemish and Spanish art from the 17th century are also well represented, with paintings by Murillo, Rubens, and Van Dyck (Hall 11). There are also frequent exhibits of collections on loan from other prominent European art museums. Check the museum Web site to find out what's showing currently.

The Museum of Private Collections (🚇 *495/697–1610* 💵 *50R* ☼ *Wed.– Sun. noon–6*) houses a stunning assortment of impressionist, postimpressionist, and modern art. There are many fine canvases by Picasso (Hall 17), including several from his "blue" period. The same hall contains fascinating works by Henri Rousseau, including *Jaguar Attacking a Horse.* There are 10 works by Gauguin, mainly in Hall 18, which also houses Cézanne's *Pierrot and Harlequin.* The museum owns several works by Matisse (Hall 21), although they're not all on display. In the same hall hangs the poignant *Landscape at Auvers After the Rain* by Vincent van Gogh. The collection ends at Hall 23, which has works by Degas, Renoir, and Monet, including Monet's *Rouen Cathedral at Sunset.* ⊠ *12 and 14 ul. Volkhonka, Kropotkinsky District* 🚇 *495/697– 7998 or 495/697–9578* ⊕ *www.museum.ru/gmii* 💵 *300R* ☼ *Tues.–Sun. 10–7* Ⓜ *Kropotinskaya.*

Russian State Library (*Rossiyskaya Gosudarstvennaya Biblioteka,* Российская Государственная Библиотека). Once called Biblioteka Imeni Lenina, or the Lenin Library, this is Russia's largest library, with more than 30 million books and manuscripts. The modern building was built between 1928 and 1940. Bronze busts of famous writers and scientists adorn the main facade. The portico, supported by square black pillars, is approached by a wide ceremonial staircase. A 12-foot statue of Dostoyevsky was erected in front of the library in 1997 in honor of the 850th anniversary of Moscow. The great novelist, sculpted by Alexander Rukavishnikov, sits where the Soviets once considered erecting a giant Lenin head. In theory, anyone can visit the library as a day visitor, but you need some persistence to fill in forms and deal with the bureaucracy (bring your passport). It's arguably worth it, though, to see the grand main hall. ✉ *3/5 ul. Vozdvizhenka, Kropotkinsky District* ☎ *495/695–5790* ⊕ *www.rsl.ru* ⊗ *Mon.–Fri. 9–7, Sat. 9–6* Ⓜ *Biblioteki Imeni Lenina.*

Tolstoy House Estate Museum (*Muzey-usadba Tolstovo,* Музей-усадьба Толстого). Tolstoy bought this house in 1882, at the age of 54, and spent nine winters here with his family. In summer he preferred his country estate in Yasnaya Polyana. The years here were not particularly happy ones. By this time Tolstoy had already experienced a religious conversion that prompted him to disown his earlier great novels, including *War and Peace* and *Anna Karenina.* His conversion sparked a feud among his own family members, which manifested itself even at the dining table: Tolstoy's wife, Sofia Andreevna, would sit at one end with their sons, while the writer would sit with their daughters at the opposite end.

The ground floor has several of the children's bedrooms and the nursery where Tolstoy's seven-year-old son died of scarlet fever in 1895, a tragedy that haunted the writer for the rest of his life. Also here are the dining rooms and kitchen, as well as the Tolstoys' bedroom, in which you can see the small desk used by his wife to meticulously copy all of her husband's manuscripts by hand.

Upstairs you'll find the Tolstoys' receiving room, where they held small parties and entertained guests, who included most of the leading figures of their day. The grand piano in the corner was played by such greats as Rachmaninoff and Rimsky-Korsakov. When in this room, you should ask the attendant to play the enchanting recording of Tolstoy greeting a group of schoolchildren, followed by a piano composition written and played by him. Also on this floor is an Asian-style den and Tolstoy's study, where he wrote his last novel, *Resurrection.*

Although electric lighting and running water were available at the time to even the lesser nobility, Count Tolstoy chose to forgo both, believing it better to live simply. The museum honors his desire and shows the house as it was when he lived there. Tickets to the museum are sold in the administrative building to the far back left. Inside the museum, each room has signs in English explaining its significance and contents, but you might want to consider a guided tour (which must be booked in advance). You can also arrange a tour of the museum's attractive gardens, which include a number of trees from Tolstoy's time. ✉ *21 ul. Lva Tolstovo, Kropotkinsky District* ☎ *499/246–9444* 🎫 *200R* ⊗ *Tues.,*

Wed., and Fri. 10–6; Thurs. 1–8; weekends 11–6. Closed last Fri. of month Ⓜ *Park Kultury.*

Tolstoy Memorial Museum (*Muzey Tolstovo,* Музей Толстого). Architect Afanasy Grigoriev designed this mansion, a fine example of the Moscow Empire style (1822–24). The minor poet Lopukhin, a distant relative of Tolstoy's, lived here, and the mansion was converted into a museum in 1920. The exhibit halls contain a rich collection of manuscripts and photographs of Tolstoy and his family, as well as pictures and paintings of Tolstoy's Moscow. Even if you don't know Russian, you can learn about the writer's life through the photographs, and in each room there's a typed handout in English to help explain its holdings. Note the picture of 19th-century Moscow in the second hall (on the left-hand wall). The huge cathedral taking up more than half the photograph is the Cathedral of Christ Our Savior—the original 19th-century structure that was torn down and subsequently re-created. ✉ *11/8 ul. Prechistenka, Kropotkinsky District* ☎ *499/766–9328* ⊕ *www. tolstoymuseum.ru* ✉ *200R* ⊙ *Tues., Wed., and Fri. 10–6; Thurs. 1–8; weekends 11–6. Closed last Fri. of month* Ⓜ *Kropotkinskaya.*

QUICK BITES

Baguette sandwiches and a large selection of wines by the glass can be found at **Gavroche** (✉ *11 ul. Timura Frunze, bldg. 19, wing 8 Kropotkinsky District* ☎ *495/558-0838* ⊕ *www.thewinebar.ru* Ⓜ *Park Kultury*), an affordable French place favored by Moscow's burgeoning foodie community. Its covered summer terrace is a pleasant place to rest your legs. The café is at the very end of an enormous business complex, but it's right on the street, not in any of the many alleys or courtyards that appear on both sides every few yards.

WORTH NOTING

Church of St. Nicholas in Khamovniki (*Tserkov Nikoly v Khamovnikakh,* Церковь Николы в Хамовниках). This church, which was built between 1679 and 1682 and remained open throughout the years of Communist rule, has been well preserved, and its elegant bell tower is particularly impressive. Five gilded domes top the church, and the tangerine and forest-green trim against a white facade makes it look like a frosted gingerbread house. In fact, the design was meant to suggest a festive piece of woven cloth, for it was a group of weavers, who settled in considerable numbers in this quarter in the 17th century, who commissioned the building of this church. Morning and evening services are held daily, and the church's interior, containing a wealth of icons, is one of the most ornate in the city. ✉ *Komsomolsky pr. and ul. Lva Tolstovo, Kropotkinsky District* ☎ *No phone* Ⓜ *Park Kultury.*

Pushkin Memorial Museum (*Muzey Pushkina,* Музей Пушкина). Aleksandr Pushkin (1799–1837) never lived here and probably never even visited this fine yellow mansion built in the 19th century by architect Afanasy Grigoriev, but don't let that put you off. A redesign in 1999 that coincided with the 200th anniversary of Pushkin's birth made this one of the smartest museums in town and an increasingly popular place for conferences and business bashes. Upon first entering the museum

you'll step into a beautiful atrium that floods the building with light. Beyond the atrium are several rooms showcasing Pushkin's sketches, letters, and personal effects. ⊠ *12/2 ul. Prechistenka, Kropotkinsky District* ☎ *495/637–5674* ⊕ *www.pushkinmuseum.ru* ⊠ *80R* ☼ *Tues.–Sun. 10–6. Closed last Fri. of the month* Ⓜ *Kropotinskaya.*

ZAMOSKVORECHE ЗАМОСКВОРЕЧЬЕ

Zamoskvoreche ("beyond the Moskva River") applies to the southern area of the old city opposite the Kremlin. Until modern times Zamoskvoreche had a sleepy rural feel—even today the old twisting streets give it a character all but obliterated in other parts of the city. By the 17th century Zamoskvoreche was well settled by artisans serving the court; it was also the first line of defense against the Tatars. In the 19th century members of the most distinctive of classes, the Moscow merchants, built their homes here. They also sponsored artists and after time created Russia's first art museum, Tretyakov Gallery.

Gorky Park, popularized by Martin Cruz Smith's Cold War novel of the same name, is situated along the right bank of the Moskva River, just beyond Krymsky Most (Crimea Bridge). Aside from the park and the Tretyakov Gallery, Bolshaya Ordinka ulitsa is a draw for its Russian Orthodox churches.

GETTING HERE AND AROUND
Zamoskvoreche is served by the Tretyakovskaya, Polyanka, and Oktyabrskaya metro stations. It's better to take the metro or other transportation to this neighborhood, as opposed to walking, because the only way across the Moskva River at most points is over a large, traffic-filled bridge. The main exception to this is the pleasant pedestrian bridge on one side of the Cathedral of Christ the Savior. Once in the area, it's most efficient to walk between sights, though you should give yourself plenty of time for doing so, as Zamoskvoreche covers a large area.

TIMING There is a lot to see in this area so it might be worth spending a day or even two on the sights. To truly enjoy the Tretyakov Gallery, it's probably best to plan a separate visit. A full exploration of Gorky Park could also easily take an afternoon. Note that many of the sights are closed on Monday.

TOP ATTRACTIONS
Bolshaya Ordinka ulitsa. Russian Orthodox churches, many recently restored, line this north–south street that runs for more than a mile. Near the Dobrininskaya metro, the white classical-style **St. Catherine's Church** (*Tserkov Ekaterini* Церковь Екатерины⊠ *No. 60, Zamoskvoreche* ☎ *No phone*) sits on the corner of Pogorelsky pereulok. It was commissioned by Catherine the Great in 1763 and designed by Karl Blank. The freshly restored interior is rather modest compared to some other churches in the city, but the central dome has some impressive A-shaped frescoes painted around the windows. Across from the entrance is a shop that sells icons, vivid cloth, and small clothing items (such as scarves) for low prices. Walk farther north to reach **Martha and Mary Convent** (*Marfo-Mariinskaya Obitel* Марфо-Мариинская Обитель⊠ *No. 34, Zamoskvoreche* ☎ *No phone*), which opened in 1909 and is most noted

for its white Church of the Intercession of the Virgin Mary. It has been recently restored, with intricate floral patterns woven through the religious imagery, and is open for services daily at 8 am. The religious order of the convent is now across the street. A few doors from the convent is **Church of St. Nicholas in Pyzhi** (*Tserkov Nikoly v Pyzhakh* **Церковь Николы в Пыжах**⊠ *No. 27a, Zamoskvoreche* ☎ *495/231–3742* ⊘ *Mon., Tues., and Thurs. noon–6:30; weekends 10–6:30* Ⓜ *Dobrininskaya*), an ornate, bright-white building with one gold and four dark gray cupolas, dating from 1670. Continue up Bolshaya Ordinka ulitsa and take a right on Klimentovsky pereulok. Push your way through the throngs exiting the metro to the middle of the small alleyway to view the baroque **St. Clement's Church** (*Tservkov Klimenta* **Церковь Климента**⊠ *26 Klimentovsky per., Zamoskvoreche* ☎ *No phone* Ⓜ *Tretyakovskaya*). The construction of this church, begun in 1743 and designed by Pietro Antonio Trezzini, took three decades. Today the interior is undergoing renovation, though its impressive star-studded cupolas and redbrick baroque walls remain worth a stop. Retrace your steps to Bolshaya Ordinka ulitsa and cross the street and take a right. A few steps away is the yellow **Church of the Virgin of All Sorrows** (*Tserkov Bogomateri Vsekh Skorbyashchikh Radostei*⊠ *No. 20, Zamoskvoreche* ☎ *No phone* Ⓜ *Tretyakovskaya*). Designed by Osip Bove and built between 1828 and 1835, the neoclassical-era church is an excellent example of the Empire style popular in the early 19th century. It replaced one that had burned down in the fire of 1812. The interior, filled with icons and gold, is nothing earth-shattering, but it's good for getting the feel of a typical working church. Sunday services are often at 10 am, but the church is usually open daily. From here, you're not far from the famous Tretyakov Gallery. ⊠ *Bolshaya Ordinka ul., Zamoskvoreche* Ⓜ *Oktyabrskaya or Dobrininskaya.*

Central House of Artists (*TsDKh; Tsentralny Dom Khudozhnikov,* **Центральный Дом Художников**). The street entrance of this huge, modern building leads to the exhibit halls of the Artists' Union, where members display their work on three floors. This is a great place to find a sketch or watercolor to take home with you. There's also a tiny movie theater that shows old international cinema as well as a concert hall with pop and rock performances almost nightly. Massive exhibitions on everything from books to fur coats to architecture take over the building periodically, and some are worth checking out. If you look hard enough, you can find info about what's currently showing on the organization's chaotic Web site. The cavernous space also has room enough to house the modern branch of the Tretyakov Gallery. Next door is the **Art Park**, where contemporary sculpture and old statues of Soviet dignitaries stand side by side. It's a pleasant place for a stroll. ⊠ *10 Krymsky Val, Zamoskvoreche* ☎ *495/238–9843 or 495/238–9634* ⊕ *www.cha.ru* 🎫 *200R* ⊘ *Tues.–Sun. 11–8* Ⓜ *Park Kultury or Oktyabrskaya.*

Church of the Resurrection in Kadosh (*Tserkov Voskreseniya v Kadashakh,* **Церковь Воскресения в Кадашах**). Because a high fence surrounds it, this colorful church is best viewed from far away. Look for a red-and-white brick bell tower and a large gold onion dome surrounded by three smaller ones. Built in 1687, the church is an excellent example of the

Moscow baroque style. If you're with a group, you can arrange to tour the bell tower and get a more detailed look at the rest of the grounds. ✉ *7 Vtoroi (2nd) Kadashevksy per., Zamoskvoreche* ☎ *495/953–1319* ⊕ *www.kadashi.ru* Ⓜ *Tretyakovskaya.*

Fodor'sChoice **Tretyakov Gallery** (*Tretyakovskaya Galereya,* Третьяковская Галерея).
★ The Tretyakov Gallery—now often called the "Old Tretyakov" in light of the annex, the New Tretyakov—is the repository of some of the world's greatest masterpieces of Russian art. Spanning the 11th through the 20th centuries, the works include sacred icons, stunning portrait and landscape art, the famous Russian Realists' paintings that culminated in the Wanderers' Group, and the splendid creations of Russian Symbolism, impressionism, and art nouveau.

The Tretyakov was officially opened in 1892 as a public state museum, but its origins predate that time by more than 35 years. In the mid-1800s, a successful young Moscow industrialist, Pavel Mikhailovich Tretyakov, was determined to amass a collection of national art that would be worthy of a museum of fine arts for the entire country. In pursuit of this high-minded goal, he began to purchase paintings, drawings, and sculpture, adjudged both on high artistic merit and on their place within the various important canons of their time. For the most part undeterred by critics' disapproval and arbiters of popular taste, he became one of the—if not *the*—era's most valued patrons of the arts, with honor and gratitude conferred upon him still to this day.

Up until six years before his death, Tretyakov maintained his enormous collection as a private one, but allowed virtually unlimited free access to the public. In 1892 he donated his collection to the Moscow city government, along with a small inheritance of other fine works collected by his brother Sergei. The holdings have been continually increased by subsequent state acquisitions, including the seizure of privately owned pieces after the Communist revolution.

There are no English-language translations on the plaques here, but you can rent an audio guide or buy an English-language guidebook.

It may be the rich collection of works completed after 1850, however, that pleases museumgoers the most, for it comprises a selection of pieces from each of the Russian masters, sometimes of their best works. Hanging in the gallery are paintings by Nikolai Ge (*Peter the Great Interrogating the Tsarevich Alexei*), Vasily Perov (*Portrait of Fyodor Dostoyevsky*), Vasily Polenov (*Grandmother's Garden*), Viktor Vasnetsov (*After Prince Igor's Battle with the Polovtsy*), and many others. Several canvases of the beloved Ivan Shishkin, with their depictions of Russian fields and forests—including *Morning in the Pine Forest,* of three bear cubs cavorting—fill one room. There are also several paintings by the equally popular Ilya Repin, whose most famous painting, *The Volga Boatmen,* also bedecks the walls. Later works, from the end of the 19th century, include an entire room devoted to the Symbolist Mikhail Vrubel (*The Princess Bride, Demon Seated*); Nestorov's glowing *Vision of the Youth Bartholomew,* the boy who would become St. Sergius, founder of the monastery at Sergeyev-Posad; and the magical pieces by Valentin Serov (*Girl with Peaches, Girl in Sunlight*). You'll also see turn-of-the-20th-century paintings by Nikolai Konstantinov-ich Roerich (1874–1947), whose New York City home is a museum.

The first floor houses the icon collection. Among the many delights here are icons painted in the late 14th and early 15th centuries by the master Andrei Rublyov, including his celebrated *Holy Trinity.* Also on display are icons of his disciples, Daniel Chorny among them, as well as some of the earliest icons to reach ancient Kievan Rus', such as the 12th-century *Virgin of Vladimir,* brought from Byzantium.

The second floor holds 18th-, 19th-, and 20th-century paintings and sculpture and is where indefatigable Russian art lovers satisfy their aesthetic longings. A series of halls of 18th-century portraits, including particularly fine works by Dmitry Levitsky, acts as a time machine into the country's noble past. Other rooms are filled with works of the 19th century, embodying the burgeoning movements of romanticism and naturalism in such gems of landscape painting as Silvester Shchedrin's *Aqueduct at Tivoli* and Mikhail Lebedev's *Path in Albano* and *In the Park.* Other favorite pieces to look for are Karl Bryullov's *The Last Day of Pompeii,* Alexander Ivanov's *Appearance of Christ to the People,* and Orest Kiprensky's well-known *Portrait of the Poet Alexander Pushkin.*

When you leave the gallery, pause a moment to look back on the fanciful art nouveau building itself, which is quite compelling. Tretyakov's original home, where the first collection was kept, still forms a part of the gallery. As the demands of a growing collection required additional space, the house was continually enlarged, until finally an entire annex was built to function as the gallery. In 1900, when there was no longer a family living in the house, the artist Viktor Vasnetsov undertook to create the wonderful facade the gallery now carries, and more space was later added. Keep in mind that the ticket office closes at 6:30 pm. ⊠ *10 Lavrushinsky per., Zamoskvoreche* ☎ *499/238–1378 or 499/951–1362* ⊕ *www.tretyakovgallery.ru* 🖃*360R* ☉ *Tues.–Sun. 10–7:30* Ⓜ *Tretyakovskaya.*

Tretyakov Gallery on Krymsky Val (*Tretyakovskaya Galereya na Krymskom Valu,* Третьяковская Галерея на Крымском Валу). Reached through a side entrance, this branch of the Tretyakov Gallery shares a building with the Tsentralny Dom Khudozhnikov (Central House of Artists) across from Gorky Park. Often called the "New Branch," it has a permanent exhibit titled "Art of the 20th Century" that spans from prerevolutionary work by Chagall, Malevich, and Kandinsky to the Socialist Realist, Modern, and Postmodern periods. ⊠ *10 Krymsky Val, through sculpture-garden side entrance, Zamoskvoreche* ☎ *499/238–1378 or 499/951–1362* ⊕ *www.tretyakovgallery.ru* 🖃*360R* ☉ *Tues.–Sun. 10–7:30* Ⓜ *Park Kultury.*

QUICK BITES

Convivial service and a laidback atmosphere await at **Coffee Bean** (✉ *5 Pyatnitskaya ul., Zamoskvoreche* ☎ *495/953–6726* Ⓜ *Novokuznetskaya*), north of Novokuznetskaya metro station heading toward the river. Their cases hold a large spread of well-prepared tarts and cakes, and some say their coffee is among the best in the city.

WORTH NOTING

Gorky Park (Парк Горького). Muscovites usually refer to this park made famous by Martin Cruz Smith's Cold War novel *Gorky Park* as Park Kultury (Park of Culture); its official title is actually the Central Park of Culture and Leisure. The park was laid out in 1928 and covers an area of 275 acres. It's an all-around recreation center, and in summer, especially on weekends, it's crowded with children and adults partaking of its many attractions. The grounds have seen better days, though; the rides are rather rundown and the landscaping unkempt. At night, the lighting is dim and festivities are dominated by a row of lowbrow outdoor bars and dancehalls, so go during the day if you're with kids. A giant Ferris wheel dominates the park's green; if you're brave enough to ride it, you'll be rewarded with great views of the city. Note that the park's admission price does not include individual rides. The park also has a boating pond, a fairground, sports grounds, and numerous cafés. In summer, boats leave from the pier for excursions along the Moskva River, and in winter the ponds are transformed into skating rinks. ✉ *9 Krymsky Val, Zamoskvoreche* ☎ *No phone* 💰 *100R in summer, free in winter* ☉ *Daily 11–10* ⊕ *www.propark.ru* Ⓜ *Oktyabrskaya*.

Peter the Great statue (Памятник Петру Великому). The enormous statue of the tsar stands atop a base made in the form of a miniature ship. He's holding the steering wheel of a ship, symbolizing his role as the founder of the Russian naval force in the 1700s. The statue, measuring 90 feet high, has been a source of controversy since construction started on it in 1996. Most Muscovites agree that the statue, made by former Moscow mayor Yuri Luzhkov's favorite sculptor, Zurab Tsereteli, is not only an eyesore but also has no place in Moscow—it was Peter the Great, after all, who moved the capital of Russia from Moscow to St. Petersburg. Citizens complained, a board of art experts was formed to decide if the statue would stay. They decided to keep it. In 2010, after Luzhkov was ousted from power, another campaign to remove the statue gained traction but ultimately failed. The decision both times was made mostly in light of the fact that erecting the statue cost $20 million and dismantling it would cost half that amount. When you finally set eyes on the statue you'll probably understand why common nicknames for it are "Cyclops" and "Gulliver." The colossal statue is so tall that a red light had to be put on its head to warn planes. ✉ *Krymskaya nab., Zamoskvoreche* Ⓜ *Park Kultury*.

SOUTHERN OUTSKIRTS

Southwest and southeast of the city center are some of Moscow's most notable holy sites. Especially of interest are Donskoy Monastery and New Maiden's Convent in the east and, in the west, the monasteries across the river from the Kremlin built to defend the capital.

DONSKOY MONASTERY AND NEW MAIDEN'S CONVENT
ДОНСКОЙ МОНАСТЫРЬ И НОВОДЕВИЧИЙ МОНАСТЫРЬ

The New Maiden's Convent, southwest of the city center, is one of Moscow's finest and best-preserved ensembles of 16th- and 17th-century Russian architecture. It's interesting not only for its impressive cathedral and charming churches but also for the dramatic chapters of Russian history that have been played out within its walls. It stands in a wooded section bordering a small pond, making this a particularly pleasant place for an afternoon stroll. After the Bolshevik Revolution, the convent was made into a museum. One of the convent's churches is open for services. Attached to the convent is a fascinating cemetery where some of Russia's greatest literary, military, and political figures are buried. A few metro stops away is another fabled religious institution, Donskoy Monastery, founded in the 16th century by Boris Godunov, with a cathedral commissioned a century later by the regent Sophia, Peter the Great's half-sister.

GETTING HERE AND AROUND
These sights can be reached via the Sportivnaya and Shabolovskaya metro stations. It will take you about 45 minutes' travel to reach the area from downtown Moscow.

Fodor'sChoice
★
Donskoy Monastery (*Donskoy Monastyr*, **Донской Монастырь**). The 16th-century Donskoy Monastery, situated in a secluded, wooded area in the southwest section of Moscow, is a fascinating memorial to Russian architecture and art. From 1934 to 1992, a branch of the Shchusev Architecture Museum, keeping architectural details of churches, monasteries, and public buildings destroyed under the Soviets, was located—more or less secretly—inside its walls. Today the monastery is once again functioning as a religious institution. But the bits and pieces of demolished churches and monuments remain, forming a graveyard of destroyed architecture from Russia's past.

The monastery grounds are surrounded by a high defensive wall with 12 towers, the last of the defense fortifications to be built around Moscow. The monastery was built on the site where, in 1591, the Russian army stood waiting for an impending attack from Tatar troops grouped on the opposite side of the river. According to legend, the Russians awoke one morning to find the Tatars gone. Their sudden retreat was considered a miracle, and Boris Godunov ordered a monastery built to commemorate the miraculous victory. Of course, it didn't happen quite like that, but historians confirm that the Tatars did retreat after only minor skirmishes, which is difficult to explain. Never again would they come so close to Moscow. The victory was attributed to the icon of the Virgin of the Don that Prince Dimitry Donskoy had supposedly carried previously, during his campaign in 1380 (in which the Russians won their first decisive victory against the Tatars). The monastery was named in honor of the wonder-working icon.

When you enter the grounds through the western gates, an icon of the Virgin of the Don looks down on you from above the entrance to the imposing **New Cathedral.** The brick cathedral was built in the late 17th century by Peter the Great's half-sister, the regent Sophia. It has been under restoration for decades; services are held in the gallery surrounding the church, where the architectural exhibits were once housed. The smaller **Old Cathedral** stands to the right of the New Cathedral. The attractive red church with white trim was built between 1591 and 1593, during the reign of Boris Godunov. It's open for services.

The graveyard here contains many fine examples of memorial art. After the plague swept through Moscow in 1771, Catherine the Great forbade any more burials in the city center. The Donskoy Monastery, at that time on the city's outskirts, became a fashionable burial place for the well-to-do. The small **Church of the Archangel** built against the fortification wall on the far right was the private chapel and crypt of the prominent Golitsyn family (original owners of the Arkhangelskoye estate). Many leading intellectuals, politicians, and aristocrats were buried here in the 18th, 19th, and 20th centuries. ✉ *1 Donskaya Pl., Southern Outskirts* ☎ *495/952–1481* 🎟 *Free* 🕐 *Daily 7:20–6* Ⓜ *Shabolovskaya.*

Novodevichy cemetery (Новодевичье кладбище). The Novodevichy cemetery (*kladbishche*) contains a fascinating collection of graves, tombstones, and other memorials, but it's difficult for non-Russian speakers to identify the graves. For more than a generation, the cemetery was closed to the general public in large part because Nikita Khrushchev (1894–1971) is buried here, rather than on Red Square, like other Soviet leaders. Thanks to glasnost, the cemetery was reopened in 1987, and now anyone is welcome to visit its grounds.

Khrushchev's grave is near the rear of the cemetery, at the end of a long tree-lined walkway. If you can't find it, any of the *babushki* (a colloquial term, which means "grandmothers," used throughout Russia to refer to museum caretakers, often hearty grandmothers who wear babushka head coverings of the same name) will point out the way. Krushchev was deposed in 1964 and lived his next and last seven years in disgrace, under virtual house arrest. The memorial consists of a stark black-and-white slab, with a curvilinear border marking the separation of the two colors. The contrast of black and white symbolizes the contradictions of his reign. The memorial caused a great furor of objection among the Soviet hierarchy when it was unveiled. It was designed by the artist Ernst Neizvestny, himself a controversial figure. In the 1960s Khrushchev visited an exhibit of contemporary art that included some of Neizvestny's works. Khrushchev dismissed Neizvestny's contributions as "filth," and asked the name of their artist. When Neizvestny (which means "Unknown") answered, Khrushchev scornfully said that the USSR had no need for artists with such names. To this the artist replied, "In front of my work, I am the premier." Considering the times, it was a brave thing to say to the leader of the Soviet Union. Neizvestny eventually joined the ranks of the émigré artists; he now lives in the United States.

Many of those buried in the cemetery were war casualties in 1941 and 1942. Among the memorials you might want to look for are those to the composers Prokofiev and Scriabin and the writers Chekhov, Gogol, Bulgakov, and Mayakovsky. Chekhov's grave is decorated with the trademark seagull of the Moscow Art Theater, the first to successfully produce his plays (including, naturally, *The Seagull*). Recent burials include Russia's first president Boris Yeltsin and cellist and conductor Mstislav Rostropovich. You can request a tour in English from the cemetery's excursion bureau; call and reserve ahead as they usually need advance warning. In light of the bountiful history and scant English translations, these tours can be very rewarding. ⊠ *Luzhnetsky proyezd, Southern Outskirts* ☎ *499/246–6614* ⤳ *Free* ☉ *Daily 9–5* Ⓜ *Sportivnaya.*

Fodor's Choice **New Maiden's Convent** (*Novodevichy Monastyr,* Новодевичий
★   Монастырь). Enclosed by a crenellated wall with 12 colorful battle towers, the convent comprises several groups of buildings. Tsar Vasily III (1479–1533) founded the convent in 1524 on the road to Smolensk and Lithuania—a strategic way to commemorate Moscow's capture of Smolensk from Lithuania. Due to the tsar's initiative, it enjoyed an elevated position among the many monasteries and convents of Moscow and became a convent primarily for noblewomen. Little remains of the original structure. The convent suffered severely during the Time of Troubles (approximately 1598–1613), concluding when the first Romanov was elected to the throne. Its current appearance dates largely from the 17th century, when the convent was significantly rebuilt and enhanced.

Among the first of the famous women to take the veil here was Irina, wife of the feebleminded Tsar Fyodor and the sister of Boris Godunov, in the 16th century. Opera fans may be familiar with the story of Boris Godunov through the well-known work by Mussorgsky. Godunov was a powerful nobleman who exerted much influence over the tsar. When Fyodor died, Godunov was the logical successor to the throne, but rather than proclaim himself tsar, he followed his sister to Novodevichy. Biding his time, Godunov waited until the clergy and townspeople begged him to become tsar. His election took place at the convent, inside the Cathedral of Smolensk. But his rule was ill-fated, touching off the Time of Troubles.

In the next century, Novodevichy became the residence of yet another royal: Sophia, the half-sister of Peter the Great, who ruled as his regent from 1682 through 1689, while he was still a boy. She did not wish to give up her position when the time came for Peter's rule and was deposed by him. He then kept her prisoner inside Novodevichy. Even that was not enough to restrain the ambitious sister, and from her cell at the convent she organized a revolt of the *streltsy* (Russian militia). The revolt was summarily put down, and to punish Sophia, Peter had the bodies of the dead streltsy hung up along the walls of the convent and outside Sophia's window. He left the decaying bodies hanging for more than a year. Yet another of the convent's later "inmates" was Yevdokiya Lopukhina, Peter's first wife. Peter considered her a pest and rid himself of her by sending her to a convent in faraway Suzdal. She outlived him, though, and eventually returned to Moscow. She spent her final years at Novodevichy, where she is buried.

You enter the convent through the arched passageway topped by the **Preobrazhensky Tserkov** (Gate Church of the Transfiguration), widely considered one of the best examples of Moscow baroque. To your left as you enter is the ticket booth, where tickets are sold to the various exhibits housed in the convent. Exhibits include rare and ancient Russian paintings, both ecclesiastical and secular; woodwork and ceramics; and fabrics and embroidery. There's also a large collection of illuminated and illustrated books, decorated with gold, silver, and jewels. The building to your right is the Lophukin House, where Yevdokiya lived from 1727 to 1731. Sophia's prison, now a guardhouse, is to your far right, in a corner of the northern wall.

The predominant structure inside the convent is the huge five-dome **Sobor Smolenskoy Bogomateri** (Cathedral of the Virgin of Smolensk), dedicated in 1525 and built by Alexei Fryazin. It was closely modeled after the Kremlin's Assumption Cathedral. Inside, there's a spectacular iconostasis with 84 wooden columns and icons dating from the 16th and 17th centuries. Simon Ushakov, a leader in 17th-century icon art, was among the outstanding Moscow artists who participated in the creation of the icons. Also here are the tombs of Sophia and Yevdokiya. Yet another historic tale connected to the convent tells how the cathedral was slated for destruction during the War of 1812. Napoléon had ordered the cathedral dynamited, but a brave nun managed to extinguish the fuse just in time, and the cathedral was spared.

To the right of the cathedral is the **Uspensky Tserkov** (Church of the Assumption) and **Refectory,** originally built in 1687 and then rebuilt after a fire in 1796. It was here that the blue-blooded nuns took their meals.

A landmark feature of Novodevichy is the ornate belfry towering above its eastern wall. It rises 236 feet and consists of six ornately decorated tiers. The structure is topped by a gilded dome that can be seen from miles away. ⊠ *1 Novodevichy proyezd, Southern Outskirts* ☎ *499/246–8526* 🖼 *150R* ⊙ *Museum Wed.–Mon. 10–5:30, convent daily 10–7. Closed first Mon. of month* Ⓜ *Sportivnaya.*

QUICK BITES

U Pirosmani (⊠ *4 Novodevichy proyezd, Southern Outskirts* ☎ *499/255–7926* Ⓜ *Sportivnaya*), a well-known restaurant specializing in the spicy cuisine of Georgia, is across the pond from the convent. If you're visiting on a weekend, you may want to book ahead.

THE MONASTERIES OF SOUTHEAST MOSCOW
МОНАСТЫРИ ЮГО-ЗАПАДА МОСКВЫ

There are three ancient monasteries along the banks of the Moskva River, in the southeast section of Moscow. Their history dates to Moscow's earliest days, when it was the center of a fledgling principality and constantly under threat of enemy attack. A series of monasteries was built across the river from the Kremlin to form a ring of defense fortifications. Two of the monasteries here were once part of that fortification ring.

Formerly suburban, this area did not fare well as the city grew. Beginning in the 19th century, factories were built along the banks of the river, including the famous Hammer and Sickle metallurgical plant. In the midst of the long-gone industrial center are the quaint monasteries of Moscow's past, being slowly restored.

GETTING HERE AND AROUND

These sights can be reached via the Proletarskaya and Taganskaya metro stations.

Andronik Monastery (*Andronikov Monastyr,* Андроников Монастырь). A stroll inside the heavy stone fortifications of this monastery, which is in far better condition than Novospassky Monastyr or Krutitskoye Podvorye, is an excursion into Moscow's past. The loud crowing of birds overhead drowns out the rumble of the city. Even the air seems purer here, perhaps because of the old birch trees growing on the monastery grounds and just outside its walls. The monastery was founded in 1360 by Metropolitan Alexei and named in honor of its first abbot, St. Andronik. The site was chosen not only for its strategic importance—on the steep banks of the Moskva River—but also because, according to legend, it was from this hill that Metropolitan Alexei got his first glimpse of the Kremlin.

The dominating structure on the monastery grounds is the **Spassky Sobor** (Cathedral of the Savior), Moscow's oldest stone structure. Erected in 1420–27 on the site of an earlier, wooden church, it rests on the mass grave of Russian soldiers who fought in the Battle of Kulikovo (1380), the decisive Russian victory that eventually led to the end of Mongol rule in Russia. Unfortunately, the original interiors, which were painted by Andrei Rublyov and another famous icon painter, Danil Chorny, were lost in a fire in 1812. Fragments of their frescoes have been restored, however. The cathedral is open for services at 5:30 pm on Saturday and 9 am on Sunday.

The building to your immediate left as you enter the monastery is the former abbot's residence. It now houses a permanent exhibit titled "Masterpieces of Ancient Russian Art," with works from the 13th through 16th centuries. The exhibit includes icons from the Novgorod, Tver, Rostov, and Moscow schools. A highlight of the collection is the early-16th-century *St. George Smiting the Dragon,* from the Novgorod School.

The next building, to the left and across the pathway from the Cathedral of the Savior, is the **Refectory.** Like the Novospassky Monastyr, it was built during the reign of Ivan the Great, between 1504 and 1506. Today it houses an exhibit of the monastery's newer acquisitions, primarily icons from the 19th to 20th centuries. Attached to the Refectory is the **Tserkov Archangela Mikhaila** (Church of St. Michael the Archangel), another example of the style known as Moscow baroque. It was commissioned by the Lopukhin family—relatives of Yevdokiya Lopukhina, the first, unloved wife of Peter the Great—as the family crypt in 1694. But there are no Lopukhins buried here, as Peter had Yevdokiya banished to a monastery in faraway Suzdal before the church was even finished, and her family was exiled to Siberia.

The last exhibit is in the former monks' residence, the redbrick building just beyond the Tserkov Archangela Mikhaila. The exhibit is devoted to 3rd-century saint Nikolai the Miracle Worker (270–343), better known in the West as St. Nicholas, the inspiration for Santa Claus. Icons here depict his life and work. From Ploshchad Ilyicha, follow Sergiya Radonezhskovo until you come out onto a square with tramlines. On your right you will find the monastery. ⊠ *10 Andronevskaya Pl., Southern Outskirts* ☎ *495/678–1467* 🖾 *Free* ☉ *Daily 8–8* Ⓜ *Ploshchad Ilyicha.*

Church of St. Martin the Confessor (*Tserkov Svyatitelya Martina Ispovednika*, Церковь Святителя Мартина Исповедника). This lovely church dates from the late 18th century and is in need of a restoration, but it remains a working church. Down the street, to the left at the fork in front of St. Martin, is another set of buildings with historical significance: the estate owned by the Stanislavsky family, among whom the best known is the theater director and actor Konstantin. The biggest piece of the complex is a long building that was once a factory owned by the wealthy family of industrialists. It is now an office complex. ⊠ *15 Ul. Alexandra Solzhenitsyna, Southern Outskirts* Ⓜ *Taganskaya.*

Krutitskoye Ecclesiastical Residence (*Krutitskoye Podvorye*, Крутицкое Подворье). The first cathedral on this hill was erected sometime in the 13th century. Its name comes from the word *kruta*, meaning "hill." This was originally a small monastery, a site of defense in the 14th century against the Tatar-Mongol invaders. At the end of the 16th century the monastery's prestige grew when it became the suburban residence of the Moscow metropolitan. The church and grounds were completely rebuilt, and the current structures date from this period. As monasteries go, Krutitskoye's period of flowering was short-lived; it was closed in 1788 on orders from Catherine the Great, who secularized many church buildings. In the 19th century it was used as army barracks, and it's said that the Russians accused of setting the Moscow fire of 1812 were tortured here by Napoléon's forces. In the 20th century, the Soviets turned the barracks into a military prison. Although the buildings have been returned to the Orthodox Church, the prison, now closed, remains on the monastery grounds.

To your left as you enter the monastery grounds is the five-dome, redbrick **Uspensky Sobor** (Assumption Cathedral), erected at the end of the 16th century on the site of several previous churches. It's a working church, undergoing restoration like many of its counterparts throughout the city. Still very attractive inside, it has an assemblage of icons, lovely frescoes, and an impressive all-white altar and iconostasis. The cathedral is attached to a gallery leading to the **Teremok** (Gate Tower), a splendid example of Moscow baroque. It was built between 1688 and 1694, and its exterior decoration is the work of Osip Startsev. The gallery and Teremok originally served as the passageway for the metropolitan as he walked from his residence (to the right of the Teremok) to the cathedral. Passing through the gate tower, you will see the military prison, including its lookout towers, on the opposite side of the Teremok gates. Film crews often come to shoot inside the now-defunct prison.

You should go through the gate tower to take a full walk around the tranquil grounds. From this side, you can enter the bell tower, which dates from 1680. Taking the stairs inside, through the door off its first level, you'll have access to the gallery itself and can walk along the walls. To get here from Proletarskaya station, take only lefts out of the station to emerge on Sarinsky proyezd. With your back to the metro, walk toward Trety (3rd) Krutitsky pereulok, the busy street a short distance ahead. Turn right to reach the older, tree-lined street leading up an incline. This is Chetvyorty (4th) Krutitsky pereulok. Climb to the top of the hill and you'll see the five-dome Uspensky Sobor. ⊠ *11–13 Kruititskaya ul., Southern Outskirts* ☎ *495/676–3093* ⊙ *Daily 8–8. Closed 1st Mon. of month* Ⓜ *Proletarskaya.*

New Savior Monastery (*Novospassky Monastyr,* **Новоспасский Монастырь**). The monastery was built in 1462, but its history dates to the 13th century, when it was inside the Kremlin. The current site on the banks of the Moskva River is "new" because it was a transfer ordered by Ivan III, also known as Ivan the Great, who wanted to free up space in the Kremlin for other construction. Ivan was the first Russian leader to categorically (and successfully) renounce Russia's allegiance to the khan of the Golden Horde. It was during his reign that a unified Russian state was formed under Moscow's rule. This monastery was just one of the numerous churches and monasteries built during the prosperous time of Ivan's reign. None of the monastery's original 15th-century structures has survived. The present fortification wall and most of the churches and residential buildings on the grounds date from the 17th century. In more modern times, a site just outside the monastery's walls was one of the mass graves for those executed during Stalin's purges.

You enter the monastery at the nearest entrance to the left of the **Bell Tower Gate**, which was erected in 1786. The first thing you see as you enter the grounds is the massive white **Sobor Spasa Preobrazheniya** (Transfiguration Cathedral). You may notice a resemblance, particularly in the domes, to the Kremlin's Assumption Cathedral, which served as this cathedral's model. The structure was built between 1642 and 1649 by the Romanov family, commissioned by the tsar as the Romanov family crypt. The gallery leading to the central nave is decorated with beautiful frescoes depicting the history of Christianity in Kievan Rus'. It's worth timing your visit with a church service (weekdays at 8 am and 5 pm, Saturday at 8 am, Sunday at 7 and 9 am) to see the interior. Even if the church is closed, the doors may be unlocked. No one will stop you from taking a quick peek at the gallery walls.

In front of the cathedral, on the right-hand side, is the small red **Nadmo-gilnaya Chasovnya** (Memorial Chapel), marking the grave of Princess Augusta Tarakanova, the illegitimate daughter of Empress Elizabeth and Count Razumovsky. The princess lived most of her life as a nun in Moscow's St. John's Convent, forced to take the veil by Catherine the Great. During her lifetime her identity was concealed, and she was known only as Sister Dofiya. The chapel over her grave was added in 1900, almost a century after her death. In an odd twist, Princess Tara-kanova had an imposter who played a more visible role in Russian history. The imposter princess appeared in Rome in 1775, to the alarm of Catherine, who dispatched Count Alexei Orlov to lure the imposter back to Russia. Orlov was successful, and the imposter Tarakanova was imprisoned in St. Petersburg's Petropavlovskaya Krepost (Peter and Paul Fortress). A mysterious character of European origin, the imposter never revealed her true identity. The false Princess Tarakanova died of consumption in 1775. Her death in her flooded, rat-infested cell was depicted in a famous painting by Konstantin Flavitsky in 1864.

To the right as you face Transfiguration Cathedral stands the tiny **Pok-rovsky Tserkov** (Church of the Intercession). Directly behind the cathe-dral is the **Tserkov Znamenia** (Church of the Sign). Painted in the dark yellow popular in its time, with a four-column facade, the church was built between 1791 and 1808 by the wealthy Sheremetyev family and contains the Sheremetyev crypt. In the rear right-hand corner of the grounds, running along the fortification walls, are the former monks' residences.

Proletarskaya station is the closest metro stop. Take only lefts to get out of the station, and you will emerge on Sarinsky proyezd. With your back to the metro, walk toward Trety (3rd) Krutitsky pereulok, the busy street a short distance ahead. This will take you in the direc-tion of the Moskva River, and as you head to where the streets inter-sect, the yellow belfry of the monastery gate church will appear in the distance to your right (southwest). When you reach the intersection, use the underground passageway to cross to the other side. From here it's just a short walk up a slight incline to the monastery's entrance. ✉ *10 Krestyanskaya Pl., Southern Outskirts* ☎ *495/676–9570* 💰 *Free* 🕐 *Daily 7–7* Ⓜ *Proletarskaya.*

MOSCOW EXCURSIONS

Within easy reach of half-day excursions from the city await majestic old palaces, estates, and former noble residences, all set in emblematic Russian countryside. To see them to the best advantage you should try to make your visits in spring or summer. ■ TIP→ All of these sights can be accessed by metro, though you may have to take a connecting bus or trolley.

ARKHANGELSKOYE АРХАНГЕЛЬСКОЕ

26 km (16 mi) northwest of Moscow via Volokolamskoye shosse.

In addition to its fine location on the banks of the Moskva River, the town of Arkhangelskoye holds a beautiful example of a noble country palace of the late tsarist era, the imposing estate of Prince Yusupov.

GETTING HERE AND AROUND

The Arkhangelskoye Estate Museum can be reached by bus or car. To go by public transit, take Bus 541 or 549 from the Moscow metro station Tushinskaya to the "Arkhangelskoye" stop, or minibus 151 to the "Sanatory" stop. To get there by car, go west on Novorizhskoye shosse and look for the signs for the estate.

Yusupov's neoclassical palace forms the centerpiece of a striking group of 18th- and 19th-century buildings that make up the **Arkhangelskoye Estate Museum.** The main palace has been closed due to restoration work for many years, and although a few rooms have recently opened once again to visitors, the completion date for the rest of the building continues to be pushed back. Check with your hotel's concierge or your tour agency for the latest information.

The main palace complex was built at the end of the 18th century for Prince Golitsyn by the French architect Chevalier de Huerne. In 1810 the family fell upon hard times and sold the estate to a rich landlord, Yusupov, the onetime director of the imperial theaters and St. Petersburg's Hermitage Museum, and ambassador to several European lands.

The estate became home to Prince Yusupov's extraordinary art collection. The collection includes paintings by Boucher, Vigée-Lebrun, Hubert Robert, Roslin, Tiepolo, Van Dyck, and many others, as well as antique statues, furniture, mirrors, chandeliers, glassware, and china. Much of the priceless furniture once belonged to Marie Antoinette and Madame de Pompadour. There are also samples of fabrics, china, and glassware that were produced on the estate itself.

Allées and strolling lanes wind through the **French Park,** which is populated with statues and monuments commemorating royal visits. There's also a monument to Pushkin, whose favorite retreat was Arkhangelskoye. In the western part of the park is an interesting small pavilion, known as the Temple to the Memory of Catherine the Great, that depicts the empress as Themis, goddess of justice. Supposedly Yusupov turned the head of Russia's empress, renowned herself for having legions of lovers. This "temple" was built to complement a painting she had previously commissioned—one in which she was depicted as Venus, with Yusupov as Apollo.

Back outside the estate grounds on the right-hand side of the main road stands the **Estate (Serf) Theater,** built in 1817 by the serf architect Ivanov. Currently a museum, the theater originally seated 400 and was the home of the biggest and best-known company of serf actors in Russia. Serf theaters first appeared in Russia in the mid-18th century and disappeared after 1861, when Tsar Alexander II freed the serfs. Although serf theaters existed even in the most remote rural parts of Russia, the most prominent was housed by the Sheremetyev family at their Kuskovo estate (the theater was later moved to the Ostankino estate to the north of Moscow). The star of the troupe was the actress Praskovya Kovalyova-Zhemchugova (1768–1803), who played more than 50 opera roles during her short stage career. By 1798, when Count Nikolai Sheremetyev freed her from serfdom, she was already suffering from the tuberculosis that would later take her life. The actress and the count married in secret in 1801; she died two years later, shortly after giving birth to their son. In his summer serf theater in Arkhangelskoye, Prince Nikolai Yusupov also favored weekly opera performances as well as dance shows with rich stage decorations. The well-preserved stage decorations are by the Venetian artist Pietrodi Gonzaga. ⊠ *Arkhangelskoye* ☎ *495/363–1375* ⊕ *www.arkhangelskoe.ru* ⌦ *80R* ☉ *Park Wed.–Sun. 10–8, exhibits Wed.–Fri. 10–5, weekends 10–6. Closed last Wed. of month*

WHERE TO EAT

$$ ✕ **Russkaya Izba.** This wooden restaurant's rustic decor is patterned on
EASTERN the *izba,* a Russian country home. Caviar, blini, and other Russian
EUROPEAN dishes are served here. The place can get quite filled up; reservations are recommended. ⊠ *Ilyinskoye village, on road to Arkhangelskoye, near Moskva River* ☎ *495/561–4244* ▭ No *credit cards.*

VICTORY PARK ПАРК ПОБЕДЫ

10 km (6 mi) west of Moscow city center via Kutuzovsky pr.

GETTING HERE AND AROUND
The park is near the Park Pobedy metro station, on the dark-blue line. The Park Pobedy stop is only one away from the brown circle line, and is therefore not a long trip from the city center.

EXPLORING
The 335-acre park **Victory Park** (Park Pobedy) near the landmark Triumphal Arch, on the western edge of the city, is historically linked to the defense of Moscow against invaders. Poklonnaya Gora, as the hill that used to be here is known, was supposedly the vantage from which Napoléon waited in vain for the keys to Moscow in 1812. Once the highest hill in Moscow, Poklonnaya Gora was razed in the 1970s to build Triumphal Arch, a World War II memorial, which was unveiled in 1995 in time for the 50th anniversary of the victory over Nazi Germany. Packed with all sorts of documentary evidence of the Soviet Army's victory, the memorial is the centerpiece of the park, but also

here are a World War II museum, a chapel, and an outdoor display of vintage weaponry. Victory Park is a popular spot for festivities on public holidays, including Victory Day, Orthodox Easter, and Christmas. On a warm day, expect to see strolling couples and hordes of rollerbladers, including whole families rollerblading together. ⊠ *7 Ul. Bratyev Fonchenko, Poklonnaya Gora* ☎ *499/142–4911* ☒ *Free* Ⓜ *Park Pobedy.*

KOLOMENSKOYE КОЛОМЕНСКОЕ

17 km (10½ mi) south of Moscow city center via Kashirskoye shosse, on west bank of Moskva River.

GETTING HERE AND AROUND

To get to Kolomenskoye take the metro to Kolomenskaya station; a walk of about 10 minutes up a slight hill brings you to the park's entrance.

EXPLORING

★ If you want to spend an afternoon in the great Russian outdoors without actually leaving the city, **Kolomenskoye,** on a high bluff overlooking the Moskva River, is just the right destination. The estate was once a favorite summer residence of Moscow's grand dukes and tsars. Today it's a popular public park with museums, a functioning church, old Russian cottages, and other attractions. It's also the site of the city's main celebration of the holiday Maslenitsa, or Butter Week, which usually falls at the end of February or beginning of March. Traditional Russian amusements such as mock fistfights, bag races, and tug-of-war are held on the park's grounds, with heaps of hot blini served as round reminders of the spring sun.

As you approach Kolomenskoye, the first sights you see are the striking blue domes of the **Church of Our Lady of Kazan,** a functioning church that is open for worship. It was completed in 1671. Opposite the church there once stood a wooden palace built by Tsar Alexei, Peter the Great's father. Peter spent much time here when he was growing up. Nothing remains of the huge wooden structure (Catherine the Great ordered it destroyed in 1767), but there's a scale model at the **museum,** which is devoted to Russian timber architecture and folk crafts. The museum lies inside the front gates of the park, at the end of the tree-lined path leading from the main entrance of the park.

The most remarkable sight within the park is the **Church of the Ascension,** which sits on the bluff overlooking the river. The church dates from the 1530s and was restored in the late 1800s. Its skyscraping tower is an example of the tent or pyramid-type structure that was popular in Russian architecture in the 16th century. The view from the bluff is impressive in its contrasts: from the 16th-century backdrop you can look north across the river to the 20th-century concrete apartment houses that dominate the contemporary Moscow skyline. In summer you'll see Muscovites bathing in the river below the church, and in winter the area abounds with cross-country skiers.

Examples of wooden architecture from other parts of Russia have been transferred to Kolomenskoye, turning the estate into an open-air museum. In the wooded area near the site of the former wooden palace you'll find a 17th-century prison tower from Siberia, a defense tower from the White Sea, and a 17th-century mead brewery from the village of Preobrazhenskaya. One of the most attractive original buildings on the site is the wooden cottage where Peter the Great lived while supervising the building of the Russian fleet in Arkhangelskoye. The cottage was relocated here in 1934. ⊠ *39 Andropova pr.* ☎ *499/612–5217 or 499/612–1155* ⊕ *www.mgomz.com* ✉ *Free* ⊙ *Exhibits Tues.–Sun. 10–6, Park Nov.–Mar. 8–9, Apr.–Oct. 8–10*

TSARITSYNO ЦАРИЦЫНО

21 km (13 mi) south of Moscow city center via Kashirskoye shosse.

GETTING HERE AND AROUND
Tsaritsyno is close to the metro station of the same name, which is three metro stops south of Kolomenskoye.

EXPLORING
This popular boating and picnicking spot is the site of the 18th-century summer palace that was started but never completed for Catherine the Great. **Tsaritsyno** was always an ill-favored estate. The empress pulled down the work of her first architect; the second building phase was never completed, probably for financial reasons. Her heirs took no interest in Tsaritsyno, so the estate served all sorts of functions, from a wine factory to a testing ground for rock climbers. In 1984 the long-needed reconstruction began, and a museum was founded 10 years later. By that time some buildings had been so neglected that tall trees grew inside the walls. In 2004, this most neglected of the Moscow estates was transferred to the control of the Moscow city government. Mayor Yury Luzhkov announced a plan to spend 410 million rubles ($14.38 million) on the ruins and surrounding park. Restoration of the bread house (kitchen), Main Palace, and the grounds was completed in 2007. The Gothic Revival architectural ensemble is worth checking out, along with a collection of porcelain, paintings, and sculptures on display at the Opera House. ⊠ *1 ul. Dolskaya* ☎ *495/321–0743* ⊕ *www.tsaritsyno-museum.ru* ✉ *Park is free; ticket for entry to museum complex 200R* ⊙ *Park: 6–midnight. Museum: Wed.–Fri. 11–6, Sat. 11–8, Sun. 11–7*

KUSKOVO ESTATE AND PALACE MUSEUM
ДВОРЕЦ-УСАДЬБА КУСКОВО

18 km (11 mi) southeast of Moscow city center via Ryazansky pr.

GETTING HERE AND AROUND
Kuskovo is just outside the ring road marking the city boundary (known by the acronym MKAD, pronounced em-KAT) You can reach it by public transportation. Take the metro to Ryazansky Prospekt station and then Bus 208 or 133 six stops to Kuskovo Park. You may find it more convenient to book a tour that includes transportation. Whatever you do, be sure to phone ahead before making the trek, because the estate often closes when the weather is very humid or very cold.

EXPLORING

In the 18th and 19th centuries the country estate of **Kuskovo** was a summer playground for the Moscow aristocracy. It belonged to the Sheremetyevs, one of Russia's wealthiest and most distinguished families, whose holdings numbered in the millions of acres. (Today, Moscow's international airport, built on land that once belonged to one of their many estates, takes their family name.)

The Sheremetyevs acquired the land of Kuskovo in the early 17th century, but the estate, often called a Russian Versailles, took on its current appearance in the late 18th century. Most of the work on it was commissioned by Prince Pyotr Sheremetyev, who sought a suitable place for entertaining guests in the summer. The park was created by Russian landscape artists who had spent much time in Europe studying the art. The French-style gardens are dotted with buildings representing the major architectural trends of Europe: the Dutch cottage, the Italian villa, the grotto, and the exquisite hermitage, where, as was the showoffy fashion at that time, dinner tables were raised mechanically from the ground floor to the second-floor dining room, as if they were in a dumbwaiter. The centerpiece of the estate is the **Kuskovo Palace**, built in the early Russian classical style by the serf architects Alexei Mironov and Fedor Argunov. Fronted by a grand horseshoe staircase and Greek-temple portico, this building exemplifies Russian neoclassical elegance. The palace, which is made of timber on a white-stone foundation, overlooks a man-made lake. It has been a house museum since 1918, and its interior decorations, including fine parquet floors and silk wall coverings, have been well preserved. The bedroom, with its lovely canopy bed, was merely for show: the Sheremetyevs used the palace exclusively for entertainment and did not live here. The parquet floors, gilt wall decorations, and crystal chandeliers of the marvelous White Hall testify to the grandeur of the ballroom extravaganzas that once took place here. On display in the inner rooms are paintings by French, Italian, and Flemish artists; Chinese porcelain; furniture; and other articles of everyday life from the 18th and 19th centuries. The palace also houses a collection of 18th-century Russian art and a celebrated ceramics museum with a rich collection of Russian, Soviet, and foreign ceramics.

Pyotr Sheremetyev had more than 150,000 serfs, many of whom received architectural training and participated in the building of his estate. The serfs also constituted a theater troupe that gave weekly open-air performances, a common practice on nobles' estates—the cream of Moscow society made a point of attending the Sheremetyev showings. Today, of course, only the setting for this spectacular lifestyle remains, but the dreamlike park and palace persist as vivid evidence of a royalty long vanished. ⊠ *2 ul. Yunosti* ☎ *495/375–3131* ⊕ *www.kuskovo.ru* ⊟ *100R–250R* ☾ *Nov.–Mar., Wed.–Sun. 10–4; Apr.–Oct., Wed.–Sun. 10–6. Closed last Wed. of month.*

Moscow
Where to Eat

WORD OF MOUTH

"Yolki Palki, a chain . . . that my guide said had decent Russian food, was really pretty good. I had stewed beef with cranberry sauce and honeyed chili potatoes, both of which were filling and tasty."

—amyb

Updated by
Ezekiel Pfeifer

Even though the Soviet Era ended back in 1991, the Moscow restaurant scene is still going through growing pains. Still, there are more signs all the time that the changes are for the better and that great things will come. For much of the post-Soviet era, the city was overrun with glittering showplaces where the food was an afterthought, but now gastropubs such as Ragout and Delicatessan abound, and a new generation of Russian diners is demanding more from the city's cadre of chefs.

Culinary competitions are in vogue among the country's young cooking talent, who exhibit more ambition and knowledge than many of their predecessors. And local restaurateurs are beginning to tap into international trends, importing "locavorism" and the tenets of molecular cuisine.

There are many ways in which the scene is still isolated. Not literally, of course—Moscow sits in the center of the sweeping East European Plain. However, this location means that ocean fish must travel a long way to reach restaurant coolers; because of poor local infrastructure, much meat and even a lot of produce are imported from distant lands as well. As a result, standards of freshness are generally lower than they are in the U.S. and Western Europe.

Most Moscow restaurants have more positive characteristics, too. In contrast to the hurried, quick-turnover system of seating that many American restaurants employ, those in Moscow let diners embrace a slower pace. It's common for people to linger at their tables long after finishing dessert, and you're almost never handed the bill until you ask for it.

There's a new breed of restaurants that serves Russian fare, and occasionally gives it a twist, as the fad for Western food has lost some of its glamour. One European cuisine to invade the city anew, however, is Italian, with scores of dark-haired chefs from the Mediterranean braving the cold to bring Muscovites minestrone and carbonara. Ethnic restaurants have long since arrived as well, and you can sample Tibetan, Indian, Chinese, Latin American, or Turkish any night of the week. But be warned: chef turnover is high in Moscow, and a restaurant can swiftly go downhill.

PRICES

Prices at top restaurants are higher than what you'd expect to pay in the United States, and even then service at them can have hiccups. As in many metropolises, the hefty bill in some sorts of restaurants here isn't so much the price for skilled cooking and service as much as it's a fee for admiring the thousand-crystal chandeliers and the models stalking the bar. If it's a gourmet experience you're after, head to one of the city's expensive hotels for a Sunday brunch, when you can enjoy their haute cuisine and elegant surroundings at greatly reduced prices, usually 750R–2,250R. (The Baltschug-Kempinski, a luxury hotel just south of the Kremlin, has a particularly popular one, beloved for its weekly changing themes and mellow atmosphere.)

There is fantastic low-cost food to be had all over the city as well. Just as a few thousand rubles may not deliver you gastronomic rapture, as little as a few hundred rubles may end up buying you your favorite meal of the trip.

3

WHAT IT COSTS IN RUSSIAN RUBLES				
¢	$	$$	$$$	$$$$
AT DINNER	under 250R	250R–450R	451R–650R	651R–850R	over 850R

Prices are per person for a main course at dinner.

RESTAURANT REVIEWS

Use the coordinate (✛ B2) at the end of each review to locate a site on the Where to Eat in Moscow map.

KREMLIN/RED SQUARE

$$
ITALIAN
✗ **Academiya.** This reliable Italian chain may not whisk you away to a Roman piazza or the Tuscan countryside, but you can expect a well-cooked risotto and efficient if unenthusiastic service. There's a very popular terrace that looks on Tverskaya Street: it's great for sipping a beer and watching the crowds in summer. Upper-mid prices and slick interiors keep the tables filled with tieless businessmen and high-heeled women with large purses. Portions can be a bit small—an entrée may not fill you up if you're famished—but everything is very fresh. ⊠ *2, bld. 1, Kamergerkiy per., Kremlin/Red Square* ☎ *495/692–9649* ⊕ *www. academiya.ru* ▤ *MC, V* Ⓜ *Teatralnaya* ✛ *E2.*

$$
ITALIAN
✗ **Bosco Café.** On the first floor of the GUM department store, this Italian restaurant has the enviable advantage of being one of the very few places in Moscow with a terrace on Red Square. Bosco charges for the view by making its prices quite high, but it's tasty, and you can always just order a coffee. The terrace closes once it gets cold. ⊠ *3 Red Sq., Kremlin/Red Square* ☎ *495/929–3182* ⊕ *www.bosco.ru/restoration/ bosco_cafe* ▤ *AE, DC, MC, V* Ⓜ *Ploshchad Revolutsii* ✛ *F3.*

$$$$
ASIAN
✗ **Gingko by Seiji.** The Moscow Ritz-Carlton's flagship restaurant, Gingko, is a cool and collected pan-Asian place with an emphasis on Japanese cuisine. With a floor-to-ceiling web of windowpanes that angles out like a flying saucer, some say Gingko feels like an airport lounge, but the marble floors give it a touch of luxury. The kitchen is led by one of the city's leading culinary lights, Japanese chef Seiji Kusano. He surrounds his country's traditional flavors with an often creative mix of Thai, Chinese, and Indonesian dishes, so that Thai curries and Peking duck can be ordered alongside immaculately fresh sashimi and

BEST BETS FOR DINING IN MOSCOW

With hundreds of restaurants to choose from, how will you decide where to eat? Fodor's writers and editors have selected their favorite restaurants by price, cuisine, and experience in the Best Bets lists below. In the first column, Fodor's Choice properties represent the "best of the best" in every price category. You can also search by neighborhood for excellent eats—just peruse our reviews on the following pages.

Fodor'sChoice ★

CDL, p. 120
Gusyatnikoff, p. 126
Hachapuri, p. 117
Ragout, p. 118

By Price

¢

Dukhan Chito-Ra, p. 125
Lyudi Kak Lyudi, p. 115
Mu-mu, p. 115
Prime Star, p. 121

$

Filial, p. 114
Glamur, p. 114
Hachapuri, p. 117
Kvartira 44, p. 120
Volkonsky, p. 115, 120

$$

Coffeemania, p. 114, 120
Delicatessen, p. 117
Ragout, p. 118

$$$

Staraya Ploshchad, p. 111
U Pirosmani, p. 125

$$$$

CDL, p. 120
L'Albero, p. 124
Les Menus Par Pierre Gagnaire, p. 121
Shinok, p. 126

By Cuisine

RUSSIAN

Café Pushkin, p. 116
CDL, p. 120
Gusyatnikoff, p. 126
Yolki Palki, p. 116

ITALIAN

L'Albero, p. 124
Coffeemania, p. 114, 120

ASIAN

Gingko by Seiji, p. 109
Uryuk, p. 119

FRENCH

Carré Blanc, p. 124
The Most, p. 111

GEORGIAN

Dukhan Chito-Ra, p. 125
Hachapuri, p. 117
U Pirosmani, p. 125

By Experience

GREAT VIEWS

Bosco Café, p. 109
Buono, p. 126
Strelka Bar, p. 123

CREATIVE CUISINE

Delicatessen, p. 117
Gusyatnikoff, p. 126
Ragout, p. 118

HOT SPOTS

Café Pushkin, p. 116
Galereya, p. 117
Strelka Bar, p. 123
Vogue Café, p. 115

MOST ROMANTIC

Gogol-Mogol, p. 122
The Most, p. 111
Staraya Ploshchad, p. 111

OUTDOOR SEATING

Café Pushkin, p. 116
Coffeemania, p. 114, 120
L'Albero, p. 124
Strelka Bar, p. 123

sushi. Diners are a mix of hotel guests and upper-crust epicures. ✉ *Ritz-Carlton Hotel, 3 Tverskaya ul., Kremlin/Red Square* ☎ *495/662–8190* 🌐 *www.ritzcarlton.com/en/properties/moscow/dining/ginkgobyseiji* ✍ *Reservations essential* ▭ *AE, MC, V* Ⓜ *Okhotny Ryad* ✥ *E3.*

$$$$ CONTINENTAL ✕ **Metropol.** Recalling the splendor of prerevolutionary Russia, the opulent interiors of the Metropol hotel's grand dining hall are a stunning memorial to Russian art nouveau. The nearly three-story-high dining room is replete with stained-glass windows, marble pillars, and a leaded-glass roof. Among the famous guests to come here are George Bernard Shaw, Vladimir Lenin, and Michael Jackson. French and Russian delicacies are served here, such as the popular fried duck with wild-cherry sauce and a baked apple. Cap your meal off with wine from the extensive list and cheese. There is also live music at breakfast and in the evenings. ✉ *Metropol Hotel,1/4 Teatralny proyezd, Kremlin/Red Square* ☎ *499/270–1061* 🌐 *www.metropol-moscow.ru* ✍ *Reservations essential* 👔 *Jacket and tie* ▭ *AE, DC, MC, V* Ⓜ *Ploshchad Revolutsii or Teatralnaya* ✥ *F3.*

$$$$ FRENCH ✕ **The Most.** Set off by red velvet curtains, with lush furniture and intricately gilded walls, The Most feels like a royal drawing room. And indeed, it is a hangout of sorts for Moscow's modern-day *boyars* (aristocrats)—the kind who wear Armani suits—who you can spot swooping in for espresso and a croissant in the morning, then returning for oysters and champagne when the sun goes down. Follow their lead, or reserve a candlelit corner table for a romantic evening. The menu transports you to Burgundy, Alsace, and the Riviera, offering frequent sights of fois gras and truffles. Despite the regal setting, the waitstaff is not stiff or white-gloved, but instead quite personable. ✉ *6/3 Kuznetsky Most ul., Kremlin/Red Square* ☎ *495/660–0706* 🌐 *www.themost.ru* ▭ *AE, MC, V* Ⓜ *Teatralnaya* ✥ *E2.*

¢ ECLECTIC ✕ **Prime Star.** This citywide chain is one of the few trustworthy spots to get fresh, tasty food on the fly. With many shelves of low-cost wraps, salads, soups, and even sushi (Moscow's love affair with raw fish is in full swing), there's a lot to choose from. There's also a pastry case with surprisingly good fresh-baked cinnamon rolls, and even a worthy chocolate mousse. When it's warm, sit under a patio umbrella here, on a pedestrian street near Red Square, and watch every class of Muscovite go by. ✉ *7/5, bld. 1 Bolshaya Dmitrovka ul., Kremlin/Red Square* ☎ *495/692–5011* 🌐 *www.prime-star.ru* ▭ *No credit cards* Ⓜ *Okhotny Ryad or Teatralnaya* ✥ *E2.*

$$–$$$ ECLECTIC ✕ **Staraya Ploshchad.** On a side street near Red Square, this elegant café pays homage to old Moscow. Photographs of candelabra-filled imperial-era restaurants greet you in the foyer; candlestick sconces line the upper dining room. Despite the nostalgic theme, the sturdy tables and upholstered chairs look just-bought. The bottom floor is completely covered in red velvet. Deferential white-shirted waiters file up and down the stairs between the two levels, placing silver before businessmen at lunch and, later, date-night couples. The menu features Continental, Russian, and touches of Asian cuisines, with classics like salade Olivier (a mayonnaise-dressed salad of meat, potatoes, and lettuce) as well as originals that include a sumptuous crab gratin. As for dessert, the hot cherry pie

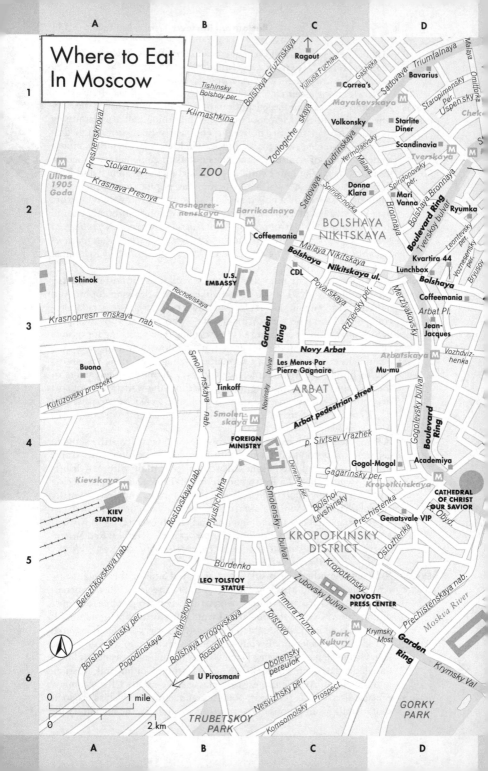

Where to Eat
In Moscow

A   **B**   **C**   **D**

1

Tishinsky
Bolshoy per.

Klimashkina

Bolshaya Gruzinskaya

Yuliusa Fuchika

Ragout

Gasheka

Sadovaya- Triumfalnaya

Correa's

Bavarius

Staropimensky Per.

Uspensky
Chek

Mayakovskaya

Volkonsky

Starlite Diner

Scandinavia

Presnenskoval

Stolyarny p.

Krasnaya Presnya

**Ulitsa
1905
Goda**

ZOO

Zoologiche
skaya

Sadovaya- Kudrinskaya

Yermolaevsky

Malaya

Spirdo-novka

Tverskaya

2

Krasnopres-
nenskaya

Barrikadnaya

Donna
Klara

Spiridonovka
per.

Mari
Vanna

Bolshaya Bronnaya

Tverskoy bulvar

Boulevard Ring

Ryumka

Coffeemania

**BOLSHAYA
NIKITSKAYA**

Malaya Nikitskaya

Bolshaya

Bolshaya Bronnaya

Kvartira 44

Lunchbox

Leontevsky
per.

voznesensky
per.

Bryusov

Shinok

U.S.
EMBASSY

CDL

Nikitskaya ul.

Povarskaya

Merzlyakovsky

Coffeemania

Arbat Pl.

Rochdelskaya

Bolshaya

3

Krasnopresn enskaya nab.

Smole nskaya nab.

Garden

Ring

Rzhevsky per.

Jean-
Jacques

Vozhdvi-
zhenka

Novy Arbat

Arbatskaya

Buono

Tinkoff

Novinsky bulvar

Les Menus Par
Pierre Gagnaire

Mu-mu

Kutuzovsky prospekt

**Smolen-
skaya**

ARBAT

Arbat pedestrian street

Gogolevsky bulvar

**Boulevard
Ring**

4

Kievskaya

Rostovskaya nab.

**FOREIGN
MINISTRY**

Denezhny per.

p. Sivtsev Vrazhek

Gagarinsky per.

Gogol-Mogol

Academiya

Kropotkinskaya

**KIEV
STATION**

Plyushchikha

Smolensky- bulvar

Bolshoi
Levshinsky

Prechistenka

Genatsvale VIP

**CATHEDRAL
OF CHRIST
OUR SAVIOR**

Ostozhenka

Obyd.

5

Berezhkovskaya nab.

Bolshoi Savinsky per.

Yelanskovo

Burdenko

**LEO TOLSTOY
STATUE**

Zubovsky bulvar

**KROPOTKINSKY
DISTRICT**

Kropotkinsky

**NOVOSTI
PRESS CENTER**

Prechistenskaya nab.

Moskva River

Pogodinskaya

Bolshaya Pirogovskaya

Rossolimo

Tolstovo

Timura Frunze

**Park
Kultury**

Krymsky
Most

Garden

Ring

Krymsky Val

6

U Pirosmani

Obolensky
pereulok

Nesvizhsky per.

Komsomolsky Prospect

**TRUBETSKOY
PARK**

**GORKY
PARK**

0   1 mile

0   2 km

A   **B**   **C**   **D**

here is highly memorable. ⊠ *8 Bolshoy Cherkassky per., Kremlin/Red Square* ☎ *495/698–4688* ▭ *AE, DC, MC, V* Ⓜ *Lubyanka* ✛ *F3.*

KITAI GOROD

$$$
ASIAN

✕ **Beloye Solntse Pustyni.** Named after a legendary Soviet film from 1970, *White Sun of the Desert,* this theme restaurant specializes in Uzbek food, which incorporates Russian, Persian, and Chinese elements. The restaurant's sun-bleached walls instantly sweep you down to Central Asia. Inside, the illusion continues: a diorama with a ship marooned in the desert, waitresses dressed as Uzbek maidens, and intricately carved wooden doors. Make sure you try the salad bar's mouthwatering vegetables. The Dastarkhan, a set meal, overwhelms you with food—unlimited access to the salad bar, a main course such as mutton kebabs and *manty* (large mutton ravioli), *plov* (a Central Asian rice pilaf), and numerous desserts. ⊠ *29/14 Neglinnaya ul., Kitai Gorod* ☎ *495/625–2596* ⊕ *www.bsp-rest.ru* ≋ *Reservations essential* ▭ *MC, V* Ⓜ *Sretenskiy bulvar* ✛ *F1.*

¢
CAFÉ

✕ **Coffee Bean.** This is one of the first and best of the many Starbucks-style coffee chains that have opened in Moscow. Giant cappuccinos and some of the best coffee in town are brewed here and served with a smile. There's a sparse selection of sandwiches and lots for dessert, though the latter aren't very good. This is one of a small but growing number of no-smoking cafés in Moscow. ⊠ *21 Pokrovka ul., Kitai Gorod* ☎ *925/006–4224* ⊕ *www.coffeebean.ru* ▭ *MC, V* Ⓜ *Kitay-Gorod* ✛ *F2.*

$$
CAFÉ

✕ **Coffeemania.** With a seamless plate-glass facade and crystal chandeliers, this is a coffee place for the glam crowd. Fittingly, the brew is quite pricey (a cappuccino runs 235R), but it's also considered by many to be the best in the city. They also have excellent cakes and pastries and a large menu of well-prepared Italian, Russian, and Japanese dishes. There are other branches all over the city, including one with a nice terrace near Belorussky Station and their flagship location in the same building as the Tchaikovsky Conservatory on Bolshaya Nikitskaya ulitsa. *18/18 Pokrovka ul., bldg. 3, Kitai Gorod* ☎ *495/623–9793* ⊕ *coffeemania.ru* ▭ *AE, DC, MC, V* Ⓜ *Kitai Gorod* ✛ *G6.*

$
ECLECTIC

✕ **Filial.** In this reliable and friendly place, student waiters speed around serving highly affordable food to fellow students, as well as to a sizeable portion of the local office-worker population—the cafe's lunch special (three courses for 260R) is famous. In the evening, the low lighting, curved lines, and soft wood tones make the cafe warm and intimate. It's hard to go wrong when ordering from the eclectic menu, whose influences veer from the Alps to the Andes, but special consideration should be given to the salade niçoise and the steak with peppercorn sauce, the latter an unbelievable deal at 400R. ⊠ *3, bld. 1 Bolshoy Krivokolenny per., Kitai Gorod* ☎ *495/621–2143* ⊕ *www.filialmoscow.com* ▭ *No credit cards* Ⓜ *Lubyanka* ✛ *G2.*

$
GEORGIAN

✕ **Glamur.** Café Glamur is nothing like the name suggests—instead of being posh, it is humble and homey, with a perpetually laughing host, lively keyboard music, and country-style Georgian fare. Between the stone walls decorated with swirling metal disks, big-bellied men sip vodka and cut into kebab meat next to family banquets and groups of friends. A word of warning: The music is loud, so conversing can be a challenge, although the musicians do take breaks. The traditional way to order at a Georgian restaurant is family-style; if you do that here, make sure to make plenty of selections, as the portions aren't large. Try the bubbling *hachapuri po-adzharski*—cheese bread topped with an egg—and the savory *lobio,* a bean soup. Reservations are essential to get a table near the band, but there's no extra charge. ⊠ *15 Neglinnaya ul., Kitai Gorod* ☎ *495/276–1500* ⊕ *www.glamurkhinkalnaya.ru* ⊟ *No credit cards* Ⓜ *Kuznetsky Most* ⚓ *F2.*

3

¢–$ **✗ Lyudi kak lyudi.** Some of the New Russian elite undoubtedly have
CAFÉ closets bigger than this hole-in-the-wall student hangout. But what it lacks in size it makes up in hipster-bohemian charm. The menu is populated by options ideal for a 2 am mid-clubbing snack or a late-morning pick-me-up—salmon-and-spinach pie, Russian-style sweet-cheese pancakes, and fruit smoothies. The café's perpetual fullness can make service inconsistent and hectic, but the teenage waitstaff always get you your order—eventually. ⊠ *1/4 Solyansky tupik, Kitai Gorod* ☎ *495/621–1201* ⊕ *www.ludikakludi.com* ⊟ *No credit cards* Ⓜ *Kitai Gorod* ⚓ *G3.*

¢ **✗ Mu-Mu.** Join the masses for pancakes and kebabs at this popular cafe-
RUSSIAN teria-style chain. This location is just a block away from the Lubyanka, once the home of the KGB, and still the main building of that notorious agency's successor. There are a number of other worthy restaurants on either side of this Mu-Mu, but here you'll end up with the smallest bill by far. ⊠ *14 Myasnitskaya ul., Kitai Gorod* ☎ *495/623–4503* ⊕ *www. cafemumu.ru* ⊟ *No credit cards* Ⓜ *Lubyanka* ⚓ *G2.*

$ **✗ Propaganda.** This may be one of Moscow's most popular clubs, but
ECLECTIC before it opens up the dance floor, it lays out the tables for its own hearty, delicious food, for some of the most reasonable prices in the city center. The cuisine ranges over all the continents, from Indian to Thai to Russian, but the dishes are kept simple, and service is quick. The filling sandwiches and pastas, with such accompaniments as curried chicken and porcini mushrooms, are particularly good values. ⊠ *7 Bolshoi Zlatoustinsky per., Kitai Gorod* ☎ *495/624–5732* ⊕ *www. propagandamoscow.com* ⊟ *No credit cards* Ⓜ *Kitai Gorod* ⚓ *G2.*

$$$$ **✗ Vogue Café.** Drawing models and the well-heeled, the aptly named
ECLECTIC Vogue is one of the most fashionable restaurants in town, and it does it in a distinctly Russian way. The interior is sophisticated and under-stated, with gold and black suede booths and photos of fashion mod-els on the walls. However, the menu is partly a throwback to Soviet times, with items such as Russian cured sausage (a kind of less spicy salami) and kefir, a sour-milk drink. It's cool to consume these retro dishes here. The rest of the menu is a mix of Russian, Italian, and French dishes. ⊠ *7/9 Kuznetsky Most ul., Kitai Gorod* ☎ *495/623–1701* ⊕ *www.novikovgroup.ru* ⊟ *AE, DC, MC, V* Ⓜ *Kuznetsky Most* ⚓ *F2.*

$–$$ **✗ Volkonsky.** Moscow has waited years for a place like this to arrive.
CAFÉ Volkonsky is a sophisticated French bakery with lines out the door at all three of its Moscow locations. Leaving aside its mouthwatering choice of pastries, biscuits, and cakes, it's also an ideal place to pick up a sand-wich or a freshly prepared salad to go. This branch has a seating area

and a range of quiches and pastas for a sit-down lunch. ✉ *4/2 Maroseika ul., Kitai Gorod* ☎ *903/185–3291* ⊕ *www.wolkonsky.ru* ▤ *DC, MC, V* Ⓜ *Kitai Gorod* ✛ *G3.*

¢   ✗ **Yolki Palki.** For a gentle introduc-
RUSSIAN   tion to Russian cooking, there is no better value than this, one of the first chain restaurants in Russia.

WORD OF MOUTH

"[R]ed caviar is a good bet. I recommend it on warm blinis, covered with a generous layer of butter, and red caviar on top."
                                    —echnaton

With stuffed chickens and waitresses dressed in national costume, the decor is more kitsch than traditional Russian. Don't miss the salad bar where you can also try numerous types of marinated vegetables. There is a good selection of blini as well as another delicious pancake variety called *olady,* which is often made with potatoes. If you overhear "yolki palki" being muttered by a Russian, he's not talking about the restaurant—it's a light curse akin to "gee whiz." ✉ *1/2 bld. 1 Solyanka ul., Kitai Gorod* ☎ *495/628–5539* ⊕ *www.elki-palki.ru* ▤ *MC, V* Ⓜ *Kitai Gorod* ✛ *F2.*

TVERSKAYA

$$ ✗ **Bavarius.** In this restaurant that could have come straight from
GERMAN   Munich's Oktoberfest, oompah music plays in the background, dirndl-clad waitresses carry fistfuls of liter-size mugs, and the smell of sauerkraut lingers in the air. Whether you fancy a snack of knockwurst (a mild pork sausage) or just want to sample German and Czech beers, this is the place. Instead of sitting indoors, head through the arch to the left of the main entrance to reach the quiet courtyard that holds the biggest beer garden in Moscow. Food is served in both areas, but credit cards are accepted only in the restaurant. ✉ *2/30 Sadovaya-Triumfalnaya ul., Tverskaya* ☎ *495/699–4211* ⊕ *www.bavarius.ru* ▤ *MC, V* Ⓜ *Mayakovskaya* ✛ *D1.*

$$$$ ✗ **Café Pushkin.** Imagine traveling back in time to when Pushkin strolled
RUSSIAN   the boulevards of 19th-century Moscow. That's what the designers of this high-class Russian restaurant intended when they created a replica mansion not far from the statue of Pushkin. Staff members dress like 19th-century servants; the menu resembles an old newspaper, with letters no longer used in the Russian alphabet; and the food is fit for a tsar. All the favorites can be found here—blini, caviar, pelmeni (meat dumplings)—and there's a fine wine list. Prices rise with each floor (there are three) of the restaurant. Open daily, 24 hours, Pushkin is popular among the business elite and rich kids, who come for breakfast after a night of clubbing. In summer you can dine on the rooftop patio. ✉ *26a Tverskoi bulvar, Tverskaya* ☎ *495/739–0033* ⊕ *www.cafe-pushkin.ru* ⌂ *Reservations essential* ▤ *AE, DC, MC, V* Ⓜ *Pushkinskaya* ✛ *E2.*

$$ ✗ **Correa's.** An expat from the United States, chef Isaac Correa has
ITALIAN   stood out throughout his long Moscow career. This, his first major independent venture in the city, is an intimate family restaurant that has become a favorite, though Correa himself has recently left it to work on other projects. The great pizzas and other simple, good Italian food with contemporary touches come in large portions and are served

by friendly waitstaff. ⊠ *7 Gasheka ul., Tverskaya* ☎ *495/789–9654* ⊕ *www.correas.ru* ⊟ *AE, DC, MC, V* Ⓜ *Mayakovskaya* ⊹ *C1.*

$–$$ ✕ **Delicatessen.** Going to basement foodie haven Delicatessen is like vis-
ECLECTIC   iting the apartment of a quirky friend, where people you've never met
treat you like family. Greetings come first from the pirate-moustached
owner, then from the team of goofy and gregarious bartenders, who
will soon cajole you into trying one of the house-made liquors. As if to
reward your locating the place (it's hidden in a courtyard with a front
sign that's subtitled "Thanks for finding us"), the staff seems driven to
make you join in their revelry. Fresh flowers brighten the windowless
space; menus on clipboards and the drink list written in chalk across
a wall lend a funky schoolhouse theme. Sample one of their well-prepared pizzas or pastas, or select from the list of juicy burgers—the
one with bacon jam is popular. ⊠ *20, bld. 1 Sadovaya-Karetnaya ul.,
Tverskaya* ☎ *495/699–3952* ⊕ *www.newdeli.ru* ⊟ *MC, V* Ⓜ *Tstvetnoi
Bulvar* ⊹ *E1.*

$$ ✕ **Donna Klara.** Comfy window seats, a laid-back staff, and a selection
CAFÉ   of sticky cakes make this a cozy place to eat. The menu consists mostly
of classic Continental salads, sandwiches, and other light fare, though
the real attraction is the pastry case, which holds house-made cakes
and other sweets that pair perfectly with a steaming cup of coffee. It's
often busy with quiet pairs sipping coffee and businessmen speaking
in low voices, making for a tranquil atmosphere ideal for a break from
sightseeing or for whiling away a rainy afternoon. It's a few minutes
away from Patriarch's Pond. ⊠ *21/13 Malaya Bronnaya ul., Tverskaya*
☎ *495/690–6974* ⊟ *AE, DC, MC, V* ⊕ *www.donnaklara.com* Ⓜ *Maya-
kovskaya* ⊹ *D2.*

$$$$ ✕ **Galereya.** Most nights of the week, large Mercedes, Hummers, and
CONTINENTAL   Bentleys are parked outside of Galereya, one of Moscow's hippest res-
taurants. Owned by Moscow restaurant magnate Arkady Novikov,
Galereya has slick leather upholstery and sophisticated contemporary
food that rarely hits a false note. The lamb dishes are always tender, for
instance. The restaurant's name is the Russian word for "gallery" and
the walls are lined with edgy contemporary art. All that said, people
mostly come here to be seen and to watch the crowds of beautiful
people who cram the restaurant. ⊠ *27 Petrovka ul., Tverskaya* ⊕ *www.
gallerycafe.ru* ☎ *495/937–4504* ⊟ *AE, DC, MC, V* Ⓜ *Pushkinskaya*
⊹ *E1.*

$ ✕ **Hachapuri.** This modern café shares a name with Georgia's most
GEORGIAN   beloved culinary export, a crispy pie filled with a creamy, tangy cheese
Fodor's Choice   (six varieties of this Caucasus pizza are on the menu). The brick walls
★   and track lighting create a bright and airy space, one that stands in
contrast to many of the more traditional, oak-laden Georgian restau-
rants in the city. The cooking also displays a refreshing contemporary
sensibility, with the always luscious *chanakhi* (a lamb stew, light with
fragrant cilantro) and the *hinkali* (large dumplings you eat with your
hands), available with salmon or pumpkin in addition to the traditional
ground beef. Go for lunch to get the best value. ⊠ *10 Bolshoi Gnezd-
nikovsky per., Tverskaya* ☎ *495/629–6656* ⊕ *www.hacha.ru* ⊟ *DC,
MC, V* Ⓜ *Tverskaya* ⊹ *D2.*

$$ ✗ **Mari Vanna.** Find the unmarked entrance, ring the right doorbell, and
RUSSIAN   you will be taken back half a century at Mari Vanna, to a somewhat
idealized Soviet home. In this dining room near Patriarch's Ponds, it
could be New Year's or Red Army Day, the way the tables are gar-
nished with white cloth and water goblets—and the flour-and-water
baranki crackers on the table evoke bygone scarcity. Stolid, apron-clad
waitresses glide from table to table delivering beet salads, mushroom
soup, and other nostalgic fare. Wooden shelves and the bric-a-brac on
them—glass cookie jars, an old radio, a deer figurine—make it feel truly
homey. ⊠ *10a Spiridonevsk per., Tverskaya* ☎ *495/650–6500* ⊕ *www.
marivanna.ru* ⊟ *DC, MC, V* Ⓜ *Pushkinskaya* ✛ *D2.*

¢   ✗ **Mu-mu.** Join the masses for pancakes and kebabs at this popular cafe-
RUSSIAN   teria-style chain. This location, like most in the chain, is discreetly cav-
ernous, with extensive basement seating to accommodate the throngs
of office workers, families, and students who congregate here. Portions
here are plentiful, and the food is also quite fresh, with a dozen or so
salads to choose from—the cabbage one is refreshing—in addition to all
manner of stuffed and fried cutlets and dumplings, grilled meat and fish,
and classic Russian soups, including borsch and shi, a cabbage soup.
The staff doesn't speak much English, but you can generally get by fine
with gestures. The café is one long block away from Pushkin Square.
⊠ *9, bld. 1 Maly Gnezdnikovsky per., Tverskaya* ☎ *495/629–0346*
⊕ *www.cafemumu.ru* ⊟ *No credit cards* Ⓜ *Tverskaya* ✛ *D2.*

$$ ✗ **Ragout.** A favorite among the city's growing crowd of foodies, Ragout
CONTINENTAL   spurns Moscow trends with a menu that's only one page, rather than
Fodor's Choice   being novella-length, and features mostly original dishes instead of clas-
★   sics. Located on the ground floor of a business center, the café has an
unobtrusive metal-and-wood interior and indie-rock sound track that
let the food play the leading role. Elements of Continental and Eastern
European traditions get equal time in the spotlight, and the constantly
changing menu often include sausages and pâtés, gratins and pies, and
confit and tartare. The restaurant always comes up with a superb lamb
dish, and it frequently features fried zander, a Russian perch served
with an addictive mint-and-green-pea puree. The mid-range prices
make it one of the best values in the city. ⊠ *69 Bolshaya Gruzinskaya
ul., Tverskaya* ☎ *495/662–6458* ⊕ *www.caferagout.ru* ⊟ *AE, MC, V*
Ⓜ *Belorusskaya* ✛ *C1.*

$$$$ ✗ **Scandinavia.** Cozy and relaxing, this is one of the most serene din-
SCANDINAVIAN   ing rooms in the city, with comfortable wooden chairs, upholstered
benches, and dried-flower arrangements on deep window ledges. The
Swedish chef mixes modern European and Scandinavian cooking. If
you're out for a purely Scandinavian selection, try the herring with
boiled potatoes, which comes with a shot of aquavit. The burgers are
the highest ranked in Moscow. Despite being near the bustle of Tverskaya ulitsa, Scandinavia's balcony and summer beer garden are the
city's most laid-back and popular places for outdoor dining. There's a
slightly cheaper menu for the summer garden. ⊠ *7 Maly Palashevsky
per., Tverskaya* ☎ *495/937–5630* ⊕ *www.scandinavia.ru* ⊟ *AE, DC,
MC, V* Ⓜ *Pushkinskaya* ✛ *D1.*

RUSSIAN STEAK HOUSES

The word "steak" has only recently entered the Russian language and culture, as Soviet farmers couldn't pamper their steers enough to produce suitable meat for the dish, but the term is widely known now. The now-crowded steak-house category was launched in large part by the mid-priced **Goodman** chain, whose flagship location is next to the Museum of Modern Russian History on Tverskaya ulitsa. Another chain by the name of **Torro Grill** soon popped up; their most central location is outside the Belorusskaya circle-line metro station. A long procession of followers have since joined those two, including **Goodbeef**, a café with great steak and low prices near Red Square; **21 Prime**, a pricey Americana-and-leather-filled place on Novy Arbat ulitsa; **Chicago Prime**, an even pricier, slightly more formal spot near Pushkin Square; and the reigning choice of the city's elite, **Myasnoi Club**, where a rib eye for two will run you a steep 7,200R.

$$ ✕ **Starlite Diner.** All the branches of this round-the-clock diner are identical to those back in the United States, with brightly lit 1950s design and large portions of sandwiches and burgers. In Moscow these spots are popular with late-night workers, exhausted early-morning partygoers, and old friends getting together for a weekend brunch. It's always full of boisterous first-timers to Russia and expats looking for a taste of home. This location is busier, because of its city-center location and its secluded summertime patio. Waiters are young and friendly, speak English, and serve fast. ✉ *16 Bolshaya Sadovaya ul., in garden by Mossoviet Theater, Tverskaya* ☎ *495/650–0246* ⊕ *www.starlite.ru* ▭ *AE, DC, MC, V* Ⓜ *Mayakovskaya* ✢ *D1.*

AMERICAN

$ ✕ **Uryuk.** While Russian food is still undergoing de-Sovietization, the cuisines of the parts of the former USSR largely escaped the grasp of the food scientists. Through it all, tangy and savory Uzbek cuisine has remained one of the best, and that's what's served here, in an over-the-top but comfortable setting. The palatial dining room appears decorated by a particularly extravagant sultan, its walls and booths swathed in Persian rugs, transparent curtains, embroidered pillows, and turquoise-and-white tile. The food here is also quite profuse, with a selection of more than 20 extremely fresh salads, plus grilled meat and tandoori breads. This is a great place to try plov, the Central Asian take on rice pilaf, served with lamb and dried fruit, or one of the filling Uzbek soups, such as the hearty lamb-and-noodle lagman. Servers are friendly but also a bit pushy, so be firm if they offer something you don't want. ✉ *30, bld. 1 Tsvetnoi bulvar, Tverskaya* ☎ *495/694–2450* ⊕ *www.urukcafe. ru* ▭ *MC, V* Ⓜ *Tsvetnoi Bulvar* ✢ *F1.*

ASIAN

$$$$ ✕ **Varvary.** Baroque and theatrical, this highly gastronomic restaurant is a product of the grandiose imagination of its founder, Anatoly Komm, who is famous for being the only Russian chef to receive a Michelin star (it was at a restaurant in Geneva). Around the gray velvet armchairs and crimson trim, however, peek dabs of festive Russian folk patterns; and the intricate cuisine fuses molecular cooking techniques with down-home ingredients, all of which come from within Russia. Although

RUSSIAN

the foams and jellies may leave you bewildered at times, certain items, such as the two-bite borscht and the "salade Olivier" ice cream, might make you smile, as at a magic trick. Nothing's à la carte here but there are many prix-fixe options, including "History of Kamchatka Crab" and "Beet Evolution." ✉ *8a Strastnoi bulvar, Tverskaya* ☎ *495/229–2800* ⊕ *www.anatolykomm.ru* ⚄ *Reservations essential* 🖃 *AE, MC, V* Ⓜ *Pushkinskaya* ✢ *E1.*

$　✕ **Volkonsky.** This sophisticated French bakery chain has lines out the
CAFÉ　door at all three of its Moscow locations. If you're looking for somewhere to eat around Patriarch's Pond, this branch is just a short walk away. The dining room here is cramped, the only seating being on a dozen bar stools around a collective table, and it's often busy, so taking out is best here. If the weather's decent, you can grab a sandwich or salad and head to the Pond, which is lined with benches. ✉ *2/46 Bolshaya Sadovaya ul., Tverskaya* ☎ *495/699–3620* ⊕ *www.wolkonsky. com* 🖃 *D, MC, V* Ⓜ *Mayakovskaya* ✢ *D1.*

BOLSHAYA NIKITSKAYA

$$$$　✕ **CDL.** Inside this elegant mansion is one of the city's most beautiful
RUSSIAN　dining rooms—and one of the best places to sample authentic Rus-
Fodor's Choice　sian cuisine. In the 19th century the house served as the headquarters
★　for Moscow's Freemasons; more recently it was a meeting place for members of the Soviet Writers' Union. Crystal chandeliers, rich wood paneling, fireplaces, and antique balustrades make CDL among the warmest and most lavish eateries in Moscow. The food is extremely well prepared; try the *ukha* (fish soup) or pelmeni for starters, and move on to one of the menu's many duck dishes. If you're feeling adventurous, cleanse your palate between courses with *kvas* (mildly alcoholic beer made from bread). ✉ *50 Povarskaya ul., Bolshaya Nikitskaya* ☎ *495/691–1515* ⊕ *www.cdlrest.ru* 🖃 *AE, DC, MC, V* Ⓜ *Barrikadnaya* ✢ *C2.*

$$　✕ **Coffeemania.** Tucked into the side of the Tchaikovsky Conservatory,
CAFÉ　this is the perfect place to come for a snack before or after a concert, or just to eavesdrop on the musicians rehearsing during the day. There's a huge indoor area, excellent coffee, and one of the city's best summer gardens, which overlooks a statue of Tchaikovsky. Apart from the usual coffee drinks, Coffeemania has a large menu with well-prepared Italian, Russian, and Japanese dishes. There are other branches all over the city, including one with a nice terrace near Belorussy Station. ✉ *13 Bolshaya Nikitskaya ul., Bldg. 1, Bolshaya Nikitskaya* ☎ *495/229–3901* ⊕ *www.coffeemania.ru* 🖃 *AE, DC, MC, V* Ⓜ *Biblioteka Imeni Lenina* ✢ *C2.*

$　✕ **Kvartira 44.** Paper-shaded lamps and mounted bookshelves line this
CAFÉ　two-floor café; it's popular with students and intellectuals, both of whom come to take advantage of the budget prices. Personal space is at a minimum here, but no one seems to mind. The menu offers a reliable bistro-like range of salads and braised and grilled meat and vegetable dishes, including prosciutto-wrapped chicken breast, beef braised in red wine, and grilled salmon, as well as seasonal selections, such as roasted pumpkin in fall and gazpacho come June. If you're headed here

for beers, as many people do, be sure to order some of the scrumptious garlic bread. It's a smoky atmosphere but there is one small nonsmoking area; there is also free Wi-Fi. ⊠ *22/2 Bolshaya Nikitskaya ul., Bolshaya Nikitskaya* ☏ *495/291–7503* ⊕ *www.kv44.ru* ▭ *DC, MC, V* Ⓜ *Arbatskaya, Pushkinskaya, or Okhotny Ryad* ✛ *D2.*

$ | ✕ **Lunchbox.** Perhaps just like it was when you were a kid, this Lunchbox has a sleek design and occasionally zany food that is only sometimes what you were hoping for. Chocolate-colored leather booths hug the walls downstairs and one corner of the snug upper mezzanine; coffee-table cookbooks lie strewn in front of the floor-to-ceiling glass facade. The food is, as you could guess, ideal for taking as a to-go lunch—pre-packaged soups, grain salads, sandwiches of all sorts. And while certain combinations seem questionable, such as meat ravioli with sun-dried tomatoes, mint, and dill, there are so many options that you're likely to find something that suits your mood. ⊠ *24, bld. 1 Bolshaya Nikitskaya ul., Bolshaya Nikitskaya* ☏ *495/697–6088* ⊕ *www.lunchboxcafe. ru* ▭ *MC, V* Ⓜ *Tverskaya, Arbatskaya or Okhotny Ryad* ✛ *D3.*

ECLECTIC

ARBAT

$$ | ✕ **Jean-Jacques.** You may not be able to smoke in restaurants in Paris anymore, but Jean Jacques, a cheap and cheerful 24-hour French bistro, is a copy of the old smoky Parisian classic. The café is nearly always busy and has one of the best selections of reasonably priced wines by the glass in Moscow. The daily lunch special, with a small range of soups, salads and mains, is also a great value. ⊠ *12 Nikitsky bulvar, Arbat* ☏ *495/690–3886* ⊕ *www.jan-jak.com* ▭ *MC, V* Ⓜ *Arbatskaya* ✛ *D3.*

FRENCH

$$$$ | ✕ **Les Menus Par Pierre Gagnaire.** This is the only restaurant in Moscow to be set up by an international culinary heavyweight—in this case, French Michelin-star holder Pierre Gagnaire. Here he has helped create dishes that are evanescent and fairy-tale-like—lobster with mango sorbet; a "molecular" borscht—but only for those who can spend freely. The richly upholstered furniture, in tones from cream to beige to dark slate, is laced with gold trim; the luxury of the place, inside the lavish Lotte Hotel, is palpable. Oenophiles will be happy with the wine list, and unlike at many other high-end places in the city, the sommelier here is French-trained and really knows his stuff. ⊠ *Lotte Hotel, 8, bld. 2 Novinsky bulvar, Arbat* ☏ *495/745–1000* ⊕ *www.lottehotel.ru* ▭ *AE, MC, V* Ⓜ *Smolenskaya* ✛ *C3.*

CONTINENTAL

¢ | ✕ **Mu-mu.** Join masses of office workers and families for home-style Russian food at this popular cafeteria-style chain. This location at the eastern end of the Arbat is easy to spot, as it features a ceramic version of Mu-Mu's mascot, a classically mottled black-and-white cow, outside the entrance. The kitschy café offers the best quality for the price among the chain eateries congregated at this spot. ⊠ *4, bld. 1 ul. Arbat, Arbat* ☏ *495/691–8588* ⊕ *www.cafemumu.ru* ▭ *No credit cards* Ⓜ *Arbatskaya* ✛ *D3.*

RUSSIAN

¢ | ✕ **Prime Star.** This citywide chain is one of the few trustworthy spots to get fresh, tasty food on the fly. Located at the eastern end of the Arbat, this is a good place to grab a snack, such as one of their diverse wraps or a pasta salad, before strolling the pedestrian-only street. ⊠ *9, bld.*

ECLECTIC

1 ul. Arbat, Arbat ☎ *495/663–7233* ⊕ *www.prime-star.ru* ▤ *MC, V* Ⓜ *Arbatskaya* ⊹ *F4.*

$$$ ✗ **Tinkoff.** A few yards from the glassy British-embassy building is a
ECLECTIC   plain brick building that holds this stylish Russian microbrewery. The
series of bars and rooms has a brick-and-glass design. Although there
are four cuisines on offer in different areas of the brewery—Japanese,
German, Italian, and modern European—people come for the beer,
not the food. Ten very different beers are brewed on the premises, with
prices starting at less than 179R for a half liter. ✉ *11 Protochny per.,
Arbat* ☎ *495/780–5888* ⊕ *www.tinkof.ru* ▤ *AE, DC, MC, V* Ⓜ *Smolenskaya* ⊹ *B4.*

KROPOTKINSKY DISTRICT

$$ ✗ **Academiya.** This reliable Italian chain may not whisk you away to a
ITALIAN   Roman piazza or the Tuscan countryside, but you can expect a well-
cooked risotto and efficient if unenthusiastic service. This outlet is right
in front of the Christ the Savior cathedral, with tables on the back
side offering views of the monumental marble building. ✉ *15/17 Volkhonka ul., Kropotkinsky District* ☎ *495/771–7446* ⊕ *www.academiya.
ru* ▤ *MC, V* Ⓜ *Kropotkinskaya* ⊹ *D4.*

$ ✗ **Dome.** Dome is one of the still-growing contingent of bars and restau-
ECLECTIC   rants installed in the buildings of the former Krasny Oktyabr chocolate
factory, on the sliver of an island south of Christ the Savior cathedral.
In the capacious exposed-brick hall, pre-partying hipsters sip whis-
key at the bar while dining couples recline in purple velvet egg chairs;
speakers fill the air with everything from soul to retro rock. The mood
is decidedly down-tempo, but it's worth rousing yourself to eat, as the
eclectic cuisine is a cut above typical bar food. The salads are fresh
and well prepared, and some of the small plates go beyond the call
of duty; the harissa-spiked chicken wings, for instance, are a revela-
tion. Drinks are overpriced, but the food is a good value. ✉ *3/10, bld.
7 Bersenevsky per., Kroporkinsky District* ☎ *495/788–6524* ⊕ *www.
domebar.ru* ▤ *AE, MC, V* Ⓜ *Kropotkinskaya* ⊹ *E4.*

$ ✗ **Genatsvale VIP.** An offshoot of its neighbor Genatsvale, the VIP branch
GEORGIAN   is designed to look like an old Georgian country house. After entering
through a tunnel of vine leaves, you're seated at oak tables in a somewhat Disneyfied version of Georgia (the country). The food is genuine,
however, and in the evenings you can enjoy an authentic Georgian
choir and traditional dancing. If you come in a group, you may want to
share the special kebab combination. Unfortunately, at this writing you
cannot pair this with one of the famed Georgian wines because of an
embargo. Service can be brusque, but the food is often praised. ✉ *14/2
Ostozhenka ul., Kropotkinsky District* ☎ *495/695–0393* ⊕ *www.
restoran-genatsvale.ru* ▤ *MC, V* Ⓜ *Kropotkinskaya* ⊹ *D5.*

$$ ✗ **Gogol-Mogol.** Sink into folds of burgundy velour with a plate of choc-
CONTINENTAL   olates and a cappuccino at this indulgent dessert spot off the Boule-
vard Ring. Unapologetically frilly and romantic, the two-room café is
adorned with pink ribbons on gauzy white curtains and floral-patterned
cushions atop wrought-iron chairs; gold-framed still lifes line the walls.
The menu is about two-thirds sweets—truffles, praline, mille-feuille,

FROM FACTORY TO FOOD HALL

Fittingly, the former **Krasny Oktyabr** chocolate factory has turned into a food mecca of sorts, with almost a dozen restaurants and cafés installing kitchens where conveyor belts once whirled. The top performers in this new class of food providers are the sleek **Strelka** and the cushioned **Dome**, both reviewed here, but also worth noting are **Bon Tempi**, a cozy mid-range Italian; **Koloniya**, a hip one-room coffee shop; **Mao**, a pan-Asian place up an industrial elevator; and

Art-Academiya, another mid-range Italian, which distinguishes itself with an enormous bar and two-story canvases on its exposed-brick walls. Meander through the large complex, remembering to turn your gaze in all directions, and you'll find lots more as well.

cookies, cakes, pies—but it also includes a weekday lunch selection of soups, pastas, and pancakes, and a handful of dinner items. Service is genial as well as assiduous, and almost even courtly. ⊠ *6 Gagarinsky per., Kroporkinsky District* ☎ *495/695–1131* ⊕ *www.gogol-mogol.ru* ⊟ *MC, V* Ⓜ *Kropotkinskaya* ✛ *D4.*

\$\$
ECLECTIC
✕ **Strelka Bar.** A trendy bar-restaurant with a spectacular view, Strelka could easily coast on its location but thankfully does not, instead relying on a reliable menu (an interesting mix of salads, pastas, and grilled items) and solicitous service as much as its breezy rooftop terrace. However, the view does remain the main draw, and understandably so. A row of windows and the blond-wood patio provide you with a panorama of the Moskva River, the Kremlin, and the white marble monolith that is Christ the Savior cathedral. But the place also buzzes with hipster youth from a neighboring design institute. A velvet rope appears on Friday and Saturday nights after 10 pm, but, as at many Moscow clubs, foreigners don't usually have a problem getting in. ⊠ *14, bld. 5 Bersenevskaya nab, Kroporkinsky District* ☎ *495/771–7416* ⊕ *www.barstrelka.com* ⊟ *AE, DC, MC, V* Ⓜ *Kropotkinskaya* ✛ *E4.*

ZAMOSKVORECHE

¢
CAFÉ
✕ **Coffee Bean.** This is one of the first and best of the many Seattle-style coffee chains that have opened in Moscow. Service is friendly, the coffee high quality, and some of the baked goods are tasty, though most of them are overpriced. (If you want a light meal, you're better off going next door to Prime Star.) There is a wide range of free English-language periodicals here, also. ⊠ *5 Pyatnitskaya ul., Zamoskvoreche* ☎ *495/953–6726* ⊕ *www.coffeebean.ru* ⊟ *MC, V* Ⓜ *Novokuznetskaya* ✛ *F5.*

\$
ECLECTIC
✕ **Kvartira 44.** Paper-shaded lamps and mounted bookshelves line this two-floor café popular among students and intellectuals, both of whom come to take advantage of its budget prices. On weekends at this location, you can take in live jazz and rock right in the small first-floor

dining room. This is one of only a handful of affordable cafés with well-prepared food in this upscale neighborhood south of the city center. ✉ *24/8 Malaya Yakimanka ul., Zamoskvoreche* ☎ *499/238–8234* ⊕ *kv44.ru* ☐ *DC, MC, V* Ⓜ *Polyanka* ✛ *E5.*

¢–$ ╳ **Ossetinskiye Pirogi.** Many of the ethnic groups scattered throughout

RUSSIAN   Russia have culinary outposts in Moscow, and this relaxed cafeteria-style café is the territory of bakers of savory pies from the Caucasus republic of North Ossetia. Half a dozen varieties of these filling, doughy treats sit steaming on shelves behind the counter (varieties include those with spinach and cheese, ground beef, and cabbage). The food, which also includes fried *pirozhki* (filled pastries) and mayo-dressed salads, is not for those with sensitive stomachs—but it's a great value if you're famished. The friendly female cashiers speak no English but are happy to interpret your gestures in order to pack a tray with food. Everything but the pies is prepackaged, making ordering to-go a cinch. ✉ *19, bld. 1 Malaya Ordynka ul., Zamoskvoreche* ☎ *495/225–8316* ⊕ *www. vkusnee.ru* ☐ *No credit cards* Ⓜ *Tretyakovskaya* ✛ *F5.*

¢ ╳ **Prime Star.** This city-wide chain is one of the few trustworthy spots to

ECLECTIC   get fresh, tasty food on the fly. This location just north of metro station Novokuznetskaya is perfect for stopping by for a pick-me-up before or after admiring the masterpieces at the nearby Tretyakov Gallery. It is also not far from the banks of the Moscow River and the Big Moscow River Bridge, which leads to the Kremlin and the Red Square from the south. ✉ *5, bld. 1 Pyatnitskaya ul., Zamoskvoreche* ☎ *495/664–2363* ⊕ *www.prime-star.ru* ☐ *MC, V* Ⓜ *Novokuznetskaya* ✛ *F4.*

NORTHERN OUTSKIRTS

$$$$ ╳ **L'Albero.** This is one of the few truly excellent Italian restaurants in

ITALIAN   a city full of pretenders. Head chef Nicola Canuti is a pupil of French great Alain Ducasse, and his creative Mediterranean cuisine has an artistic flair hard to find in Moscow. The menu is surprisingly large given its haute style, with standouts that include foie gras with a sangria sauce and a signature 36-hour braised lamb. Potted plants dot the sumptuous glassed-in dining room, making it feel like a modern noble's playhouse/greenhouse. Prices are high, but on a par with those of other restaurants in its class here, and the food's better than at many of its peers. ✉ *7 Delegatskaya ul., Northern Outskirts* ☎ *495/650–1674* ⊕ *www.albero. su* ☐ *AE, DC, MC, V* Ⓜ *Novosloboskaya* ✛ *E1.*

$$$ ╳ **Carré Blanc.** A much-praised restaurant, Carré Blanc has captured the

FRENCH   hearts of Moscow gourmets. A group of expats established the place, which magically combines exquisite French cooking; one of Moscow's best wine collections; and a relaxed, convivial atmosphere. Sample the exotic roasted duck with celeriac cappuccino, or slurp down a few of the delectable Bélon oysters, which are flown in from France. Also here are a bar and a bistro with somewhat, if not significantly, lower prices. ✉ *19/2 Seleznyovskaya ul., Northern Outskirts* ☎ *495/258–4403* ⊕ *www.carreblanc.ru* ☐ *AE, DC, MC, V* Ⓜ *Novoslobodskaya* ✛ *F1.*

$$ ╳ **Coffeemania.** With a plate-glass facade and crystal chandeliers, this

CAFÉ   is a coffee place for the glam crowd. This location sits on the bottom floor of a gleaming new business center, which towers incongruously

MOSCOW'S OPEN-AIR MARKETS

Real estate in central Moscow is so expensive that convenience stores and gargantuan supermarket chains have come to dominate food sales there, and the authorities don't allow the already congested roads to close for open-air markets, even on weekends. Instead, most markets have retreated to the outskirts; there are prominent clusters of vegetable vendors along almost every spoke of the metro system. Two of the best are upscale **Dorogomilovsky Rynok** ("rynok" is the Russian word for "market"), near the Kievskaya metro station, and lively **Danilovsky Rynok,** across from the Tulskaya metro. Both have alternately pushy and charming hawkers selling exotic produce, such as apricots from the mountains of Tajikistan and bulbous tomatoes from Azerbaijan, as well as fish, meat, dried fruit and nuts, and locally made cheeses—perhaps most notably, the tangy Georgian suluguni. If you want foodstuffs grown closer to Moscow and prepared for you, head to **Lavka** (⊕ *lavkalavka.ru*), a fledgling farm-to-city company that also serves prix-fixe lunches near metro station Kurskaya from 2 to 4 pm on weekdays by reservation only; call Liliya at ☎ *+7-967/290-7693* to reserve a table.

over a beautiful old domed church in the same square. The popular summer patio here gives a great view of the newly renovated cathedral. As for the menu, there are excellent cakes and pastries and a large menu of well-prepared Italian, Russian, and Japanese dishes, as well as highly regarded coffee. There are other branches all over the city, including their flagship location in the same building as the Tchaikovsky Conservatory on Bolshaya Nikitskaya ulitsa. *5 Lesnaya ul., Northern Outskirts* ☎ *495/290–0141* ⊕ *coffeemania.ru* ⊟ *AE, DC, MC, V* Ⓜ *Belorusskaya* ✛ *D3.*

SOUTHERN OUTSKIRTS

$$$ ✕ **U Pirosmani.** Whitewashed walls and wood-panel ceilings inside this
GEORGIAN   popular restaurant named for Georgian artist Niko Pirosmani re-create the aura of an artist's studio. Copies of Pirosmani's naive art decorate the walls. Try to sit by the window in the main hall or on the balcony so you can enjoy beautiful views of New Maiden's Convent, across the pond from the restaurant. The menu reads like a Georgian cookbook. Some complain that the food can be a bit hit-or-miss but order the *khachipuri,* or Georgian cheese pies, and some shish kebab and you can't go wrong. ✉ *4 Novodevichy proyezd, Southern Outskirts* ☎ *495/247–1926* ⊕ *www.upirosmani.ru* ⊟ *MC, V* Ⓜ *Sportivnaya* ✛ *B6.*

EASTERN OUTSKIRTS

¢–$ ✕ **Dukhan Chito-Ra.** This one-room café has home-style Georgian food so
GEORGIAN   good that the staff doesn't need to serve you quickly, be nice, or generally do anything other than get the plates to you for it to be worth a visit. This is fortunate, because Chito-Ra has about as many frills as a tavern deep in the Caucasus hinterlands. Menus are on plastic stands

on rough-hewn picnic tables that line the walls; typical Georgian-restaurant kitsch, such as fake grape vines and wine jugs, festoon a tiny bar. The house specialty is succulent *hinkali*, fist-sized dumplings filled with ground meat and broth that you eat with your hands; the variety with herbs is best. Add a crisp-crusted hachapuri (cheese bread), if your stomach enjoys abundance. Go only if someone in your party has a moderate knowledge of Russian, or ordering will be difficult. ⊠ *10 Kazakova ul., Eastern Outskirts* ☎ *495/265–7876* ⊟ *No credit cards* Ⓜ *Kurskaya* ✛ *H2.*

$$$$
RUSSIAN
Fodor's Choice
★

✕ **Gusyatnikoff.** Feast on exquisite traditional Russian fare here, in what was once (and still feels like) a private mansion. In the four-level building, there are spaces to fit every mood: a Middle Eastern room with hookahs; a billiard room; intimate, plush dining rooms; and a chandeliered main hall with lots of natural light, a refreshing contrast with the dimness of many places with old-style cuisine. Try the *ukha*, a fish soup, and a basket of their excellent pirozhki, savory filled pastries; the beef Stroganoff is also outstanding. The clientele—suited businessmen out to lunch and pairs of wealthy women in designer labels—can be a bit haughty, but the lightning-quick waitstaff is unassuming and attentive. Gusyatnikoff is a worthy, more laidback competitor to the famed Café Pushkin, and the prices are less outrageous, too. ⊠ *2a Aleksandra Solzhenitsyna ul., Eastern Outskirts* ☎ *495/632–7558* ⊕ *www.gusyatnikoff.ru* ⊟ *DC, MC, V* Ⓜ *Taganskaya* ✛ *H4.*

WESTERN OUTSKIRTS

$$$$
ITALIAN

✕ **Buono.** It's all about the view at this expensive Italian option. Atop the Stalin-era skyscraper that also houses the Radisson Royal hotel, Buono has a 360-degree prospect that makes it a great spot to get a sense of the city and admire Moscow's diverse architecture. The cuisine takes few chances, hewing to classics, such as a lemony octopus salad and sea bream with tomato and fennel. You can sometimes spot local celebrities among the women with collagen-filled lips and men in Dolce & Gabbana tees filling many of the tables. ⊠ *2/1, bld. 1 Kutuzovsky pr., Western Outskirts* ☎ *495/221–5555* ⊕ *www.ginzaproject.ru* ⊟ *MC, V* Ⓜ *Kievskaya* ✛ *A3.*

$$$$
EASTERN
EUROPEAN

✕ **Shinok.** In this high-priced and gourmet theme restaurant—the kind of oddball combination of qualities Moscow restaurants are known for—there's a faux-Ukrainian farmyard with goats, a cow, hens, and a knitting granny. The enclosure is completely sound- and smell-proof, and the animals don't really impinge on the meal. Ukrainian cuisine doesn't differ that much from Russian—they both have in common such dishes as borscht, *vareniki* (Ukrainian-style pelmeni stuffed with cottage cheese), and *solyanka* (a spicy, thick stew made with vegetables and meat or fish). Everything is exquisite, but the borscht really stands out. For an unusual taste from Ukraine, try *salo* (thin slices of salted pork fat) and the Ukrainian beer Starokiyevskoye. The helpful servers can give advice, although not all speak English. Go on an empty stomach, because the food can be very filling. ⊠ *2a 1905 Goda ul., Western Outskirts* ☎ *495/651–8101* ⊕ *www.shinok.ru* ⊟ *AE, MC, V* Ⓜ *Ulitsa 1905 Goda* ✛ *A3.*

Moscow Where to Stay

WORD OF MOUTH

"For something more traditional, there is the Soviet-sky Hotel. Moscow Renaissance is another option, near to Prospect Mira metro and near to the . . . VDNKh, which has interesting pavilions, each named after a former Soviet Republic."

—Odin

"I was pleasantly surprised at how big the singles were [in Moscow] compared to singles I've had in, say, Venice or Paris!"

—amyb

Updated by
Ezekiel Pfeifer

For years, Moscow hotels were plagued by the same Soviet-bequeathed deficiencies the city's other service industries had: poor value; inconsistent service; and a limited selection. These days, the situation is improved over what it was five or even three years ago, but progress is still slow. Four- and five-star luxury behemoths still dominate, although there is also a growing number of unfrilly, steel-and-Plexiglas business hotels that fill their rooms with exhibition-goers and salespeople. Unfortunately, only a handful of places in the center could be called both intimate and affordable.

That said, the glitzy affairs that crowd Tverskaya ulitsa and other boulevards downtown are world-class, with soaring marble foyers, celestial spas, and increasingly gracious and well-trained staff. One new arrival, the magnificent Radisson Royal, which spread red carpets over the remains of the former Hotel Ukraine, has already leapfrogged its peers and been named the best luxury hotel in the city by the World Travel Awards. The Moscow Ritz, steps from the Kremlin and still the gold standard for opulence and fine service in the city, is one of the plushest in the chain. Across the street, a replica of the old Hotel Moskva, famous for having its image on the label of Stolichnaya vodka, has risen on Manezh Square. It is scheduled to open to the public in early 2012.

A major shortage of worthy choices remains in the mid-range segment, especially inside the Garden Ring. Within those bounds, you might have to scour every side street to find a room for under 6,000R a night, and for that price, you typically won't get the hearty breakfast spread and heated pool you could expect at a typical chain place in the U.S. However, amenities are improving rapidly. Once the norm was plywood furniture and tarnished polyester upholstery, but now cabinets and desks are sturdier, and you will often find leather chairs and softer linens on beds. (Plenty of hotels still haven't gutted that mouse-brown carpet, though.)

The more glaring Soviet carryover is in the area of service. The customer is not always right at many mid-range hotels, so it helps to treat the staff with extra care when making requests and even when asking questions. And ask questions you should; because standards vary widely, it's advisable to ask about everything you might want—including turndown service, assistance with concert tickets, and no-smoking rooms—before booking.

At hotels in Moscow, someone on staff speaks English, so you can almost always find someone who can help you. However, the English-speakers typically are not fluent, so be patient when explaining anything complicated. You can also charm people by at least trying to say a few

Russian words here and there, even those as simple as *spasibo* (thank you) and *do svidaniya* (good-bye). In general, very few people will be offended if you speak English with them—in fact, many are eager for the practice—but do ask whether someone knows the language first (*Vi gavaritye pa-angliisky?*).

If you're a confident traveler, you should consider renting a short-term apartment like those provided by Four Squares Apartments in Tverskaya, as they often provide the best value. You might even be able to find living quarters near the Red Square that dwarf the suites of a luxury hotel next door. But if you want to be central, expect to pay a hefty sum no matter where you stay; for now, that's what Moscow demands.

4

WHAT IT COSTS IN RUSSIAN RUBLES				
	¢	$	$$	$$$	$$$$
FOR TWO PEOPLE	under 5,000R	5,000R–7,500R	7,501R–10,000R	10,001R–12,500R	over 12,500R

Prices are for a standard double room in high season, excluding taxes and service charge.

LODGING REVIEWS

Hotel reviews have been abbreviated in this book. For expanded reviews, please visit Fodors.com. Use the coordinate (✛ B2) at the end of each review to locate a property on the Where to Stay in Moscow map.

KREMLIN/RED SQUARE

$$$$ 🏨 **Ararat Park Hyatt.** One of the most luxurious of Moscow's hotels combines the traditional and modern. **Pros:** central location; great city view from rooftop café; plush linens; free fruit in rooms every day. **Cons:** restaurants are overpriced; room rates are among highest in the city. ⊠ *4 Neglinnaya ul., Kremlin/Red Square* ☎ *495/783–1234* ⊕ *www.moscow. park.hyatt.com* ➳ *216 rooms, 21 suites* ⚭ *In-room: a/c, Wi-Fi. In-hotel: restaurants, room service, bars, gym, spa* ▭ *DC, MC, V* Ⓜ *Okhotny Ryad or Teatralnaya* ✛ *E2.*

$$$$ 🏨 **Metropol.** Originally built between 1899 and 1903, this first-class hotel has been the stage for some fabled events: Lenin spoke frequently in the assembly hall of the building, and David Lean filmed part of *Doctor Zhivago* in the restaurant. **Pros:** superb location; beautiful interiors; great buffet breakfast. **Cons:** some guest rooms need updating. ⊠ *1/4 Teatralny proyezd, Kremlin/Red Square* ☎ *499/501–7800* ⊕ *www. metropol-moscow.ru* ➳ *362 rooms, 72 suites* ⚭ *In-room: a/c, no safe, Wi-Fi (some). In-hotel: restaurants, room service, bars, pool, gym, business center* ▭ *AE, MC, V* Ⓜ *Ploshchad Revolutsii or Teatralnaya* ✛ *E3.*

$$$$ 🏨 **Savoy.** The Savoy opened in 1913 in connection with celebrations commemorating the 300th anniversary of the Romanov dynasty; interiors of gilded chandeliers, ceiling paintings, and polished paneling invoke the spirit of prerevolutionary Russia. **Pros:** great location;

BEST BETS FOR MOSCOW LODGING

Fodor's offers a selective listing of quality lodging experiences in every price range, from the city's best budget beds to its most sophisticated luxury hotels. Here, we've compiled our top recommendations by price and experience. The very best properties—in other words, those that provide a particularly remarkable experience in their price range—are designated in the listings with the Fodor's Choice logo.

Fodor's Choice ★

Danilovskaya, p. 138
Hotel National, p. 134
Radisson Royal, p. 139

By Price

¢

Gamma-Delta Izmailovo, p. 138

$

Danilovskaya, p. 138
Krasnaya Zarya, p. 136
Ozerkovskaya, p. 137
Sovietsky Historical, p. 138

$$

Mamaison Pokrovka, p. 131
Medea, p. 136
Melody Hotel, p. 136

$$$

Courtyard Marriott, p. 135
Katerina–City, p. 136

$$$$

Baltschug Kempinski, p. 136
Golden Apple, p. 131
Lotte Hotel, p. 135
Metropol, p. 129
Savoy, p. 129

By Experience

BEST SPA

Lotte Hotel $$$$, p. 135
Ritz-Carlton Moscow $$$$, p. 135

HISTORICAL INTEREST

Hotel National $$$$, p. 134
Metropol $$$$, p. 129
Savoy $$$$, p. 129

Sovietsky Historical $, p. 138

BUILDING ARCHITECTURE

Hotel National $$$$, p. 134
Peking $$, p. 134
Radisson Royal $$$$, p. 139

BEST VALUE

Danilovskaya $, p. 138
Four Squares Apartments $, p. 131
Melody Hotel, p. 136

COOL BARS

Ritz-Carlton Moscow $$$$, p. 135
Swissôtel Krasnye Holmy $$$$, p. 137

BUSINESS HOTELS

Katerina–City $$$, p. 136
Novotel Moscow Center $$$, p. 137

Sheraton Palace $$, p. 138

SPACIOUS ROOMS

Mamaison Pokrovka $$, p. 131
Medea $$, p. 136
Peking $$, p. 134

TOP-FLIGHT FOOD

Lotte Hotel $$$$, p. 135
Sheraton Palace $$, p. 138
Swissôtel Krasnye Holmy $$$$, p. 137

SMALL AND INTIMATE

Kebur Palace $$$, p. 136
Krasnaya Zarya $, p. 136
Medea $$, p. 136
Ozerkovskaya $, p. 137

BEST VIEWS

Baltschug Kempinski $$$$, p. 136
Gamma-Delta Izmailovo ¢, p. 138
Hotel National $$$$, p. 134
Peking $$, p. 134
Radisson Royal $$$$, p. 139

beautiful interiors; swimming pool open 24 hours. **Cons:** some rooms are small, especially given the price; can be overrun by business people and bureaucrats on weekdays. ✉ *3/6, bldg. 1 Rozhdestvenka ul., Kremlin/Red Square* ☎ *495/620–8500* ⊕ *www.savoy.ru* ⬎ *67 rooms, 11 suites* ⚄ *In-room: a/c, Wi-Fi. In-hotel: restaurant, room service, bar, pool* ⊟ *AE, DC, MC, V* Ⓜ *Kuznetsky Most* ✤ *F2.*

KITAI GOROD

$$ ⛏ **Mamaison Pokrovka.** This puzzling place at the end of winding Pokrovka ulitsa has some but not all the hallmarks of a boutique hotel, with striking design decisions and lavish rooms but also an inert atmosphere and service that can occasionally stumble. **Pros:** stylish, comfortable rooms; close to many restaurants and metro stations. **Cons:** poor views; impersonal service. ✉ *40 Pokrovka, bldg. 2, Kitai Gorod* ☎ *495/229–5757* ⊕ *www.mamaison.com/moscow-pokrovka.html* ⬎ *84 suites* ⚄ *In-room: a/c, kitchen (some), Wi-Fi. In-hotel: restaurant, room service, bar, pool, gym, spa* ⊟ *AE, DC, MC, V* Ⓜ *Krasniye Vorota* ✤ *H2.*

$$$$ ⛏ **Marriott Royal Aurora.** On the corner of ulitsa Petrovka and the cobblestoned Stoleshnikov pereulok, the Marriott Royal Aurora is close to the Kremlin, Tverskaya ulitsa, and the Bolshoi Theater, which is only a three-minute walk away. **Pros:** perfect location; helpful concierge staff. **Cons:** overpriced Internet access and breakfast. ✉ *11/20 ul. Petrovka, Kitai Gorod* ☎ *495/937–1000* ⊕ *www.marriott.com* ⬎ *227 rooms, 36 suites* ⚄ *In-room: a/c In-hotel: restaurants, bar, pool, gym, spa, parking, some pets allowed* ⊟ *AE, DC, MC, V* Ⓜ *Okhotny Ryad or Kuznetsky Most* ✤ *E2.*

$$$$ ⛏ **Sretenskaya.** Surround yourself in the atmosphere of an old Russian fairy tale: there's massive carved oak furniture, stained-glass windows, and wall paintings depicting popular tales like "Little Scarlet Flower" (the Russian version of "Beauty and the Beast"). **Pros:** helpful staff; excellent restaurant. **Cons:** long walk to Red Square; small rooms; very expensive. ✉ *15 ul. Sretenka, Kitai Gorod* ☎ *495/933–5544* ⊕ *www. hotel-sretenskaya.ru* ⬎ *38 rooms* ⚄ *In-room: a/c, Wi-Fi. In-hotel: restaurant, bar, gym, parking* ⊟ *AE, DC, MC, V* Ⓜ *Sukharevskaya, Kitai Gorod* ✤ *F1.*

TVERSKAYA

$–$$ ⛏ **Four Squares Apartments.** If you're up to the task of navigating the maze-like courtyards of Moscow's residential buildings, you'll definitely want to a consider a serviced apartment, as they're in many ways a better value than other accommodations in the city. **Pros:** spacious, modern accommodations; full kitchens. **Cons:** lack of on-site service staff. ✉ *32 Bolshaya Dmitrovka, bldg. 7, 3rd fl., Tverskaya* ☎ *495/937–5572* ⊕ *www.foursquares.com* ⬎ *26 apartments* ⚄ *In-room: a/c (some), no safe, kitchen, Internet, Wi-Fi (some)* ⊟ *AE, DC, MC, V* Ⓜ *Chekhovskaya.*

$$$$ ⛏ **Golden Apple.** Catching up with the global obsession, this was Moscow's first boutique hotel, and this cozy, stylish, quirky, and upmarket entry is still the city's best example of the genre. **Pros:** chocolate appears

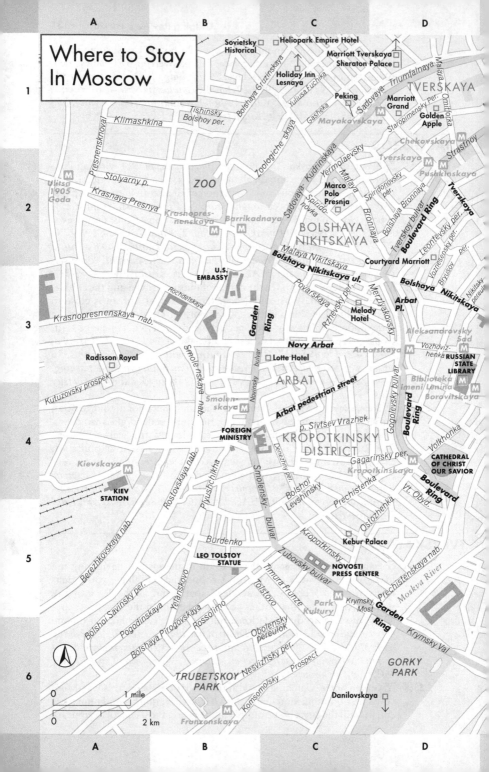

Where to Stay
In Moscow

A   **B**   **C**   **D**

Sovietsky Historical
Heliopark Empire Hotel
Marriott Tverskaya
Sheraton Palace
Holiday Inn Lesnaya
TVERSKAYA
Malaya Triumfalnaya
Peking
Marriott Grand
Golden Apple
Ornitorka per.
Staroplimensky
Yuliusa Fuchika
Gasheka
Mayakovskaya
Sadovaya-
Chekovskaya
Strastnoy

Tishinsky Bolshoy per.
Bolshaya Gruzinskaya
Zoologiche skaya
Yermolaevsky
Tverskaya
Pushkinskaya
Presnenskaya
Klimashkina

Stolyarny p.
ZOO
Sadovaya- Kudrinskaya
Malaya Bronnaya
Spiridonovsky per.
Bolshaya Bronnaya
Tverskoy bulvar
Boulevard Ring
Tverskaya

Ulitsa 1905 Goda
Krasnaya Presnya
Krasnopresnenskaya
Barrikadnaya
Marco Polo Presnja
Spiridonka
BOLSHAYA
NIKITSKAYA
Bolshaya Bronnaya
Leontevsky per.

Rochdetskaya
U.S. EMBASSY
Malaya Nikitskaya
Bolshaya Nikitskaya ul.
Courtyard Marriott
Bolshaya Nikitskaya
Nikitsky pereulok
Voznesensky per.
Bryusov

Krasnopresnenskaya nab.
Garden Ring
Smolenskaya nab.
Povarskaya per.
Rzhevsky per.
Melody Hotel
Merzlyakovsky
Arbat Pl.
Aleksandrovsky Sad
Vozhdvizhenka

Radisson Royal
Novy Arbat
Arbatskaya
RUSSIAN STATE LIBRARY

Kutuzovsky prospekt
Smolenskaya
Lotte Hotel
ARBAT
Biblioteka Imeni Lenina
Borovitskaya

Kievskaya
Noviinsky bulvar
Arbat pedestrian street
p. Sivtsev Vrazhek
KROPOTKINSKY DISTRICT
Gogolevsky bulvar
Boulevard Ring
Volkhonka

FOREIGN MINISTRY
Denezhny per.
Gagarinsky per.
Kropotkinskaya
CATHEDRAL OF CHRIST OUR SAVIOR
Boulevard Ring

KIEV STATION
Rostovskaya nab.
Plyushchikha
Bolshoi Levshinsky
Prechistenka
Ostozhenka
Ul. Obyd.

Berezhkovskaya nab.
Burdenko
Smolensky bulvar
Kebur Palace

Bolshoi Savinsky per.
LEO TOLSTOY STATUE
Zubovsky bulvar
Kropotkinsky
NOVOSTI PRESS CENTER
Prechistenskaya nab.
Moskva River

Pogodinskaya
Usranskovo
Timura Frunze
Tolstovo
Park Kultury
Krymsky Most
Garden Ring
GORKY PARK

Bolshaya Pirogovskaya
Rossolimo
Obolensky pereulok
Komsomolsky Prospect
Krymsky Val

TRUBETSKOY PARK
Nesvizhsky per.
Danilovskaya

0   1 mile
0   2 km
Frunzenskaya

A   **B**   **C**   **D**

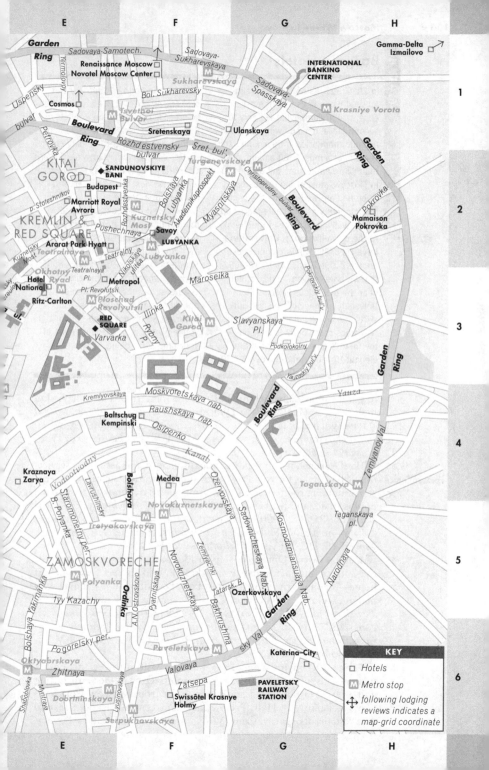

CLOSE UP

Bargain Hotels

In 2010, Russia's hotel sector relinquished its dubious title of most expensive in Europe, but fell only to second place, behind Switzerland; the average room price in the country still came in at almost $200 a night, or roughly an entire suite full of kopecks. In Moscow, most of the real bargains to be had are well outside the center, though plenty of affordable places are within walking distance of the metro. At the dorm-like **Hotel Universitetskaya** (✉ 8/29 Michurinsky prospekt, Southern Outskirts ☎ 499/147–2062 ⊕ www.hotel-universitet.ru), located near the prestigious Moscow State University in the southwestern outskirts, rooms even have refrigerators. Two stops south of the center on the metro's green line is the rather elegant **Hotel Kolomenskoye** (✉ 39

Prospekt Andropova, Southern Outskirts ☎ 499/725–1174 ⊕ www.hotel-kolomenskoye.ru), on the grounds of the sprawling park of the same name. In the east, **Hotel Lefortovsky Most** (✉ 9/23 2nd Baumanskaya ul., Eastern Outskirts ☎ 495/777–9451 ⊕ www.lefortovskymost.ru), which takes its name from a bridge over the River Yauza that it overlooks, has small rooms but modern furnishings. Very small surroundings await at **Nanotel** (✉ 4 Sharikopodshipnikovskaya ul., Southern Outskirts ☎ 495/675–8595 ⊕ www.nanotel.org) in the city's southeast, but there are Internet hookups and the location isn't too removed, so it's not a bad option if you're planning on spending most of your time sightseeing.

---

in guest rooms daily; helpful staff. **Cons:** some rooms are small; sky-high rates. ✉ 11 ul. Malaya Dmitrovka, Tverskaya ☎ 495/980–7000 ⊕ www.goldenapple.ru ⟲ 92 rooms, 2 suites ⟳ In-room: a/c, Wi-Fi. In-hotel: restaurant, bar, gym ⊟ AE, MC, V Ⓜ Chekhovskaya or Pushkinskaya ✛ D1.

$$$$ 🖼 **Hotel National.** If you seek historical splendor and assiduous service, **Fodor's Choice** this 1903 hotel is for you. **Pros:** outstanding location; helpful concierge ★ staff; stunning room decor. **Cons:** some rooms overlook nearby roofs; pool is small, and the health club's dull. ✉ 15/1 Mochovaya ul., Tverskaya ☎ 495/258–7000 ⊕ www.national.ru ⟲ 206 rooms, 56 suites ⟳ In-room: a/c, Wi-Fi. In-hotel: restaurants, room service, bars, pool, gym ⊟ AE, DC, MC, V Ⓜ Okhotny Ryad ✛ E3.

$$ 🖼 **Marriott Grand.** Once you step inside, past the renovated turn-of-the-20th-century art nouveau facade, you'll likely feel very much at home—if home is the United States. **Pros:** beautiful lobby bar area with piano; excellent fitness center. **Cons:** overpriced food and drink. ✉ 26 Tverskaya ul., bldg. 1 Tverskaya ☎ 495/937–0000 ⊕ www.marriott. com ⟲ 377 rooms, 13 suites ⟳ In-room: a/c, Wi-Fi. In-hotel: restaurants, room service, bars, pool, gym, spa ⊟ AE, DC, MC, V Ⓜ Mayakovskaya or Tverskaya ✛ D1.

$$ 🖼 **Peking.** Occupying a tall 1955 building with a tower, this hotel's main asset is its superb location, at the intersection of the Garden Ring and Tverskaya ulitsa and across the street from Moscow Conservatory's Tchaikovsky Hall. **Pros:** convenient central location; several nice restaurants nearby. **Cons:** Wi-Fi costs extra; beds can be bouncy.

✉ *5 Bolshaya Sadovaya ul., Tverskaya* ☎ *495/234–2467* ⊕ *www. hotelpekin.ru* ⤳ *135 rooms, 23 suites* ⏃ *In-room: a/c, Wi-Fi. In-hotel: restaurants, room service, bar, gym, spa* ⊟ *AE, MC, V* Ⓜ *Mayakovskaya* ✛ *C1.*

$$$$ ⚑ **Ritz-Carlton Moscow.** Considered by many to be the city's finest luxury hotel—and with rooms rates hovering around $1,000 a night, it ought to be—the flashy Moscow Ritz does its best to dazzle guests at every turn. **Pros:** prime location;

excellent service. **Cons:** too expensive for anyone but the über rich. ✉ *3 Tverskaya ul., Tverskaya* ☎ *495/225–8888* ⊕ *www.ritzcarlton.com* ⤳ *334 rooms, 35 suites* ⏃ *In-room: a/c, Internet. In-hotel: restaurants, bars, pool, spa* ⊟ *AE, DC, MC, V* Ⓜ *Okhotny Ryad* ✛ *E3.*

$ ⚑ **Ulanskaya.** At the undersized Hotel Ulanskaya, you pay a premium for an excellent location and get a discount for rooms that are strictly efficient. **Pros:** lots of dining options and bars nearby; steps from the metro; cheerful service. **Cons:** standard rooms are small; bouncy beds; drab decor. ✉ *16, bldg. 1A, Ulansky per., Tverskaya* ☎ *495/607–1010* ⊕ *www.ulanskaya.com* ⤳ *61 rooms* ⏃ *In-room: a/c, no safe, Internet. In-hotel: restaurant, bar, parking* ⊟ *MC, V* ✛ *F1.*

BOLSHAYA NIKITSKAYA AND ARBAT

$$$ ⚑ **Courtyard Marriott.** The location of this hotel is probably the best of any in its class. **Pros:** wide selection of restaurants and coffee shops in the area; very comfortable beds. **Cons:** small fitness room and no pool. ✉ *7 Voznesensky per., Bolshaya Nikitskaya* ☎ *495/981–3300* ⊕ *www. marriott.com* ⤳ *208 rooms, 10 suites* ⏃ *In-room: a/c, Internet. In-hotel: restaurants, gym, spa* ⊟ *AE, DC, MC, V* Ⓜ *Pushkinskaya or Tverskaya* ✛ *D2.*

$$$$ ⚑ **Lotte Hotel.** With its foyer's towering black marble columns, a spiky crystal chandelier, and asymmetrical (but plush) armchairs, the Lotte Hotel feels like the palace of a fashionable but villainous monarch. **Pros:** impressive restaurants; unique spa; luxurious marble bathrooms. **Cons:** standard rooms are on the small side; so-so views; service can be somewhat aloof. ✉ *8, bldg. 2 Novinsky bulvar, Arbat* ☎ *495/745–1000; 495/287–0500 for reservations* ⊕ *www.lottehotel.ru* ⤳ *304 rooms, 38 suites* ⏃ *In-room: a/c, Wi-Fi. In-hotel: restaurants, room service, bar, pool, gym, spa, parking* ⊟ *AE, DC, MC, V* ✛ *C3.*

$$$$ ⚑ **Marco Polo Presnja.** Opened in 1904 as a residence for English teachers and then later the exclusive domain of the Communist Party, this hotel is an intriguing choice for those interested in the Soviet era. **Pros:** art-lined halls and rooms; close to Patriarch's Pond with cafés and bars. **Cons:** some unfriendly staff; guest rooms are small; room rates rather high. ✉ *9 Spiridonevsky per., Bolshaya Nikitskaya* ☎ *495/660-0606, 499/244-3631* ⊕ *www.presnja.ru* ⤳ *70 rooms, 16 suites* ⏃ *In-room:*

a/c, Wi-Fi. In-hotel: restaurant, room service, bar, gym ▤ *AE, DC, MC, V* Ⓜ *Mayakovskaya or Pushkinskaya* ✛ *C2.*

$$ 🖵 **Melody Hotel.** The Melody (Melodiya) is one of the best deals in the center, with a great location and functional rooms, though also a few off notes. **Pros:** excellent location; spacious rooms; attractive restaurant. **Cons:** odd atmosphere and decor; negligible views. ✉ *13 Skatertny per., Bolshaya Nikitskaya* ☏ *495/660–7178* ⊕ *www.melody-hotel.com* ⌨ *75 rooms, 3 suites* ♿ *In-room: a/c, no safe, Wi-Fi. In-hotel: restaurant, room service, bar* ▤ *DC, MC, V* ✛ *C3.*

KROPOTKINSKY DISTRICT AND ZAMOSKVORECHE

$$$$ 🖵 **Baltschug Kempinski.** On the banks of the Moskva River opposite the
ⓒ Kremlin and Red Square, this deluxe hotel has extraordinary views and gracious service. **Pros:** close to Red Square; best breakfast in town; kid friendly. **Cons:** some rooms need updating; far from metro. ✉ *1 Baltchug ul., Zamoskvoreche* ☏ *495/287–2000* ⊕ *www.kempinski-moscow.com* ⌨ *190 rooms, 40 suites* ♿ *In-room: Wi-Fi. In-hotel: restaurants, room service, bars, pool, gym, spa, children's programs* ▤ *AE, DC, MC, V* Ⓜ *Novokuznetskaya or Tretyakovskaya* ✛ *F4.*

$$$ 🖵 **Katerina–City.** Near the river and Riverside Towers, one of the city's main business centers, this small Swedish-run hotel is popular with European business travelers. **Pros:** tasty breakfast; fast Internet; great views. **Cons:** during rush hour, the walk to the metro station and the metro itself may be unpleasantly congested with people. ✉ *6 Shlyuzovaya nab., Zamoskvoreche* ☏ *495/795–2444* ⊕ *www.katerinahotels.com* ⌨ *120 rooms, 10 suites* ♿ *In-room: a/c, no safe, Wi-Fi. In-hotel: restaurant, room service, bar, gym* ▤ *AE, DC, MC, V* Ⓜ *Paveletskaya* ✛ *G6.*

$$$ 🖵 **Kebur Palace.** Formerly known as Tiflis, this small, attractive hotel is built in the style of an old Tbilisi town house. **Pros:** excellent location. **Cons:** some rooms are noisy due to a Georgian restaurant attached to the hotel; the concierge does not have great tourist information. ✉ *32 ul. Ostozhenka, Kropotkinskaya* ☏ *495/733–9070* ⊕ *www.keburpalace.ru* ⌨ *79 rooms, 7 suites* ♿ *In-room: a/c, no safe, Wi-Fi. In-hotel: restaurant, room service, bar, pool* ▤ *MC, V* Ⓜ *Kropotkinskaya* ✛ *C5.*

$ 🖵 **Krasnaya Zarya.** With its factory facade and location in a labyrinthine complex of clubs, galleries, and restaurants, this tiny hotel is for those seeking something hip. **Pros:** surrounded by trendy bars and restaurants; spacious, comfortable rooms; central location. **Cons:** minimal support staff; interiors are rather bare. ✉ *3/10, Bersenevsky per., bld. 8, Kropotkinsky District* ☏ *495/980–4774* ⊕ *www.red-zarya.ru* ⌨ *8 rooms* ♿ *In-room: a/c, no safe, Wi-Fi. In-hotel: restaurant, bar, parking* ▤ *MC, V* ✛ *E4.*

$$ 🖵 **Medea.** If you are looking for privacy and quiet in the very heart of the city, this is the place for you. **Pros:** steps from the metro; helpful staff; kitchens in most rooms. **Cons:** on a grungy side street; negligible views; Wi-Fi is extra. ✉ *4 Pyatnitsky per., bldg. 1, Zamoskvoreche* ☏ *495/232–4898* ⊕ *www.medea-hotel.ru* ⌨ *21 rooms, 15 suites* ♿ *In-room: a/c, kitchen (some), Wi-Fi. In-hotel: restaurant, room service, bar* ▤ *MC, V* Ⓜ *Tretyakovskaya or Novokuznetskaya* ✛ *F4.*

$ ⊡**Ozerkovskaya.** In a city whose hotels tend toward the gargantuan and impersonal, the Ozerkovskaya is a refreshing contrast, with fewer than 30 rooms inside its square brick frame and a staff that strives to make it feel like a home. **Pros:** helpful staff; decent location; great views from some rooms. **Cons:** small common areas; unexciting decor; linens could use an update. ✉ *50 Ozerkovskaya nab., bldg. 2, Zamoskvoreche* ☎ *495/951–9582* ⊕ *www.ozerkhotel.ru* ⇗ *27 rooms* ⇘ *In-room: a/c (some), Wi-Fi. In-hotel: room service, bar, gym, spa, parking* ▭ *MC, V* ✥ *G5.*

$$$$ ⊡**Swissôtel Krasnye Holmy.** Rising 34 stories above the city, this sleek glass-and-metal cylinder is the tallest luxury hotel in town, as well as a conspicuous addition to a skyline dominated by Stalin's seven towers. **Pros:** stunning view of Moscow from top-floor City Space bar; caviar and champagne for breakfast. **Cons:** expensive everything. ✉ *52 Kosmodamianskaya nab., bldg. 6, Zamoskvoreche* ☎ *495/787–9800* ⊕ *www.swissotel.com* ⇗ *233 rooms, 27 suites* ⇘ *In-room: a/c, Wi-Fi. In-hotel: restaurants, bars, pool, gym, spa* ▭ *AE, DC, MC, V* Ⓜ *Paveletskaya or Taganskaya* ✥ *F6.*

NORTHERN OUTSKIRTS

$ ⊡**Cosmos.** This huge, 26-story hotel built by the French for the 1980 Olympics is popular with tour groups, for good reason: it's one of the city's best bargains. **Pros:** bargain prices. **Cons:** Soviet-style service. ✉ *150 Prospekt Mira, Northern Outskirts* ☎ *495/234–1000, 495/234–1206* ⊕ *www.hotel-cosmos.ru* ⇗ *1,777 rooms* ⇘ *In-room: a/c, no safe, Wi-Fi (some). In-hotel: restaurants, room service, bars, pools, gym, spa, business center, parking* ▭ *AE, DC, MC, V* Ⓜ *VDNKh* ✥ *E1.*

$$ ⊡**Heliopark Empire Hotel.** This modern hotel is in a rapidly developing quarter near Belorussky Station that's becoming known as a dining destination. ✉ *60/1 Pervaya (1st) Brestskaya ul., Northern Outskirts* ☎ *499/251–6413* ⊕ *www.heliopark.ru* ⇗ *33 rooms, 1 junior suite, 1 deluxe room* ⇘ *In-room: a/c, no safe, Wi-Fi. In-hotel: restaurant, room service* ▭ *AE, MC, V* Ⓜ *Belorusskaya* ✥ *C1.*

$$$ ⊡**Marriott Tverskaya.** After a stroll from Red Square along bustling Tverskaya ulitsa, you may find comfort in the coziness of this eight-story art nouveau building. **Pros:** spacious rooms; comfortable beds; 24-hour health club. **Cons:** far from Red Square and the Kremlin. ✉ *34 Pervaya (1st) Tverskaya-Yamskaya ul., Northern Outskirts* ☎ *495/258–3000; 800/228–9290 outside Russia* ⊕ *www.marriotthotels.com* ⇗ *119 rooms, 43 suites* ⇘ *In-room: a/c, Internet, Wi-Fi. In-hotel: restaurant, room service, bar, gym, business center, some pets allowed* ▭ *AE, DC, MC, V* Ⓜ *Belorusskaya* ✥ *D1.*

$$$ ⊡**Novotel Moscow Center.** This 18-floor hotel just a few metro stops from the Kremlin is a favorite mid-price option for business travelers. **Pros:** lots of cafés and bars in the area; reasonably priced. **Cons:** staff are not well-versed in tourist information. ✉ *23 Novoslobodskaya ul., Northern Outskirts* ☎ *495/780–4000* ⊕ *www.novotel.com* ⇗ *255 rooms, 1 suite* ⇘ *In-room: a/c, Wi-Fi. In-hotel: restaurant, bar, gym, Wi-Fi hotspot* ▭ *AE, DC, MC, V* Ⓜ *Mendeleyevskaya* ✥ *F1.*

4

$$ ⬚ **Renaissance Moscow.** Rooms are large and equipped with every amenity at this hotel, a busy place for conferences and meetings. **Pros:** attentive staff; comfortable beds; shuttle bus service to city center every hour. **Cons:** far from Kremlin; no restaurants nearby. ✉ *18/1 Olympisky pr., Northern Outskirts* ☎ *495/931–9000* ⊕ *www.marriott.com* ✈ *471 rooms, 10 suites* ⚅ *In-room: a/c, Wi-Fi. In-hotel: restaurants, room service, bar, pool, gym* ⊟ *AE, DC, MC, V* Ⓜ *Prospekt Mira* ✛ *F1.*

$$ ⬚ **Sheraton Palace.** The European business community loves this place, thanks to amenities that include a chauffeur-driven fleet of cars. **Pros:** well-organized transportation from airports; delicious breakfast; helpful staff. **Cons:** a long walk from the Kremlin. ✉ *19 Pervaya (1st) Tverskaya-Yamskaya ul., Northern Outskirts* ☎ *495/931–9700; 7502/256–3000 outside Russia* ⊕ *www.starwood.com/sheraton* ✈ *221 rooms, 18 suites* ⚅ *In-room: a/c, Wi-Fi. In-hotel: restaurants, room service, bars, gym, parking* ⊟ *AE, DC, MC, V* Ⓜ *Belorusskaya* ✛ *D1.*

$ ⬚ **Sovietsky Historical.** Plunge into Soviet-era grandeur at this historic hotel, which upgraded its facilities a few years ago but still has its nostalgic atmosphere. **Pros:** very spacious, clean, and well-lit rooms; gracious service; famous Russian restaurant (Yar) on premises. **Cons:** a 15-minute walk to the metro and 10- to 15-minute ride to the Kremlin. ✉ *32/2, Leningradsky pr., Northern Outskirts* ☎ *495/960–2000* ⊕ *www.sovietsky.ru* ✈ *106 rooms, 24 suites* ⚅ *In-room: a/c, no safe, Wi-Fi. In-hotel: restaurant, room service, bar, business center, parking, some pets allowed* ⊟ *MC, V* Ⓜ *Dinamo or Belorusskaya* ✛ *B1.*

SOUTHERN OUTSKIRTS

$ ⬚ **Danilovskaya.** This hotel is serene and lovely, with fountains, religious-themed paintings, and domed monastery buildings—it's inside the walls of the Danilovsky (St. Daniel) Monastery—the official residence of Patriarch Kirill I of Moscow and All Russia. **Pros:** nice hotel grounds; clean rooms; excellent pirozhki (traditional Russian pastries). **Cons:** remote location; staff can be a bit stern. ✉ *5 Bolshoi Starodanilovsky per., Southern Outskirts* ☎ *495/954–0503* ⊕ *www.danilovsky.ru* ✈ *131 rooms, 25 suites* ⚅ *In-room: a/c, no safe, Wi-Fi. In-hotel: restaurant, room service, bar, pool, business center* ⊟ *MC, V* Ⓜ *Tulskaya* ✛ *D6.*

FodorsChoice ★

EASTERN OUTSKIRTS

¢ ⬚ **Gamma-Delta Izmailovo.** At one time this mammoth complex included five buildings, making it Europe's largest hotel, with thousands of rooms. **Pros:** excellent views of the city and the neighboring pond from upper floors; bargain prices. **Cons:** far away from the center and most tourist sights; standard rooms are small. ✉ *71 Izmailovskoye shosse, Eastern Outskirts* ☎ *495/166–4490 or 495/737–7000* 🖷 *495/166–7486* ⊕ *www.izmailovo.ru* ✈ *2,000 rooms, 28 suites* ⚅ *In-room: a/c (some), no safe, Wi-Fi. In-hotel: restaurants, room service, bars, parking* ⊟ *AE, DC, V* Ⓜ *Partizanskaya* ✛ *H1.*

WESTERN OUTSKIRTS

$$$$
Fodor'sChoice
★

⌖ **Radisson Royal.** This elegant, impressive hotel along the Moscow River keeps its luxurious accoutrements inside a historical facade, one of the famed Seven Sisters skyscrapers commissioned by Stalin in the 1950s. **Pros:** friendly service; great views; diverse dining options. **Cons:** far from metro and the Kremlin; expensive. ⊠ *2/1 Kutuzovsky pr., bldg. 1 Western Outskirts* ☎ *495/221–5555* ⊕ *www.radisson.ru/royalhotel-moscow* ⇌ *505 rooms* ♿ *In-room: a/c, Wi-Fi. In-hotel: restaurants, room service, bars, pool, gym, spa* ⊟ *AE, DC, MC, V* Ⓜ *Kievskaya* ✛ *A3.*

4

Moscow Nightlife and the Arts

WORD OF MOUTH

"A ballet performance is a mandatory experience wherever you are in Russia. Attending a Moscow ballet is . . . a stylish event. People dress up, and in the pauses, you consume drinks and snacks, some of them of outstanding quality."

—Echnaton

Updated by
Tom Parfitt

A city of classical culture, Moscow also offers plenty of glamour and glitz. Ballet at the Bolshoi, concerts at the Tchaikovsky Conservatory, and theaters packed for Chekhov plays are among the highlights of the intense arts scene, while the nightlife takes in cozy cellar bars and glittering clubs for the elite.

Ticket booths on city streets testify to Muscovites' love of theater, and low prices ensure that high culture remains a mass pursuit. This enthusiasm means that the most popular shows can sell out weeks ahead, but smaller arts events, such as the regular free concerts at the Conservatory, are often equally rewarding. Although the Bolshoi's famous columned theater has been closed for repairs, the troupe still performs in a newly built venue whose elaborate interior rivals the original. On a much smaller scale, the Helikon Opera's innovative productions of classics such as *Carmen*, mounted on its tiny stage, gain critical raves.

The ranks of Mercedes cars outside certain city clubs make it clear that Moscow is a city for big spenders. But you don't have to be one to have a good time. A more bohemian crowd gathers at bars and clubs that offer live concerts by local bands, cheap beers, and tasty eats. Although in the past Moscow was too far off the beaten track to attract top-name Western stars, in the last year the city has seen performances by everyone from U2 to Sting and Elton John, so it's a good idea to check the bulletins a few weeks in advance—you never know who might be in town. Also, be sure to catch the many talented Russian musicians playing jazz and blues, as well as ethnic folk acts from other regions in Russia, such as the Tuvan throat singers, who frequently appear at festivals.

THE ARTS

St. Petersburg may be known as Russia's cultural capital, but Moscow easily rivals its northern neighbor. Estimates differ, but the city has anywhere from 60 to 200 theaters, not to mention several prestigious acting schools and the increasingly popular Chekhov International Theater Festival, which usually takes place late August through early September. Every Thursday the free English-language newspaper, the *Moscow Times* (⊕ *www.themoscowtimes.com*), publishes a schedule of cultural events for the coming week. Pick up a copy at the airport when you arrive or at a hotel, restaurant, or bar in the city center.

Most theaters' tickets can be obtained at the theaters themselves or at the box offices (*teatralnaya kassa*) scattered throughout the city. Note that some theaters charge different prices for Russians and foreigners. If you're intimidated by the language barrier, ask your hotel's concierge for help. The prices are inflated, but a concierge can often get you tickets to otherwise sold-out performances. Scalpers usually can be found selling tickets outside theaters immediately prior to performances, but they have been known to rip off tourists, either charging exorbitant prices or selling fake tickets.

Numerous private galleries sell Russian artwork, a nice alternative to the kitsch available at most of the tourist and riverside markets. The Friday edition of the *Moscow Times* carries a review of current exhibits. At group shows and festivals, keep an eye peeled for the one-man Coat Gallery (aka Alexander Petrelli), who has paintings hidden inside his overcoat. Just go up to him and ask and he'll open up and show you his wares. For opening hours, check with the galleries themselves; some are open only by appointment, and most are closed on Sunday and Monday.

Moscow's musical life has always been particularly rich; the city has several symphony orchestras as well as song-and-dance ensembles. Moiseyev's Folk Dance Ensemble is well known in Europe and America, but the troupe is on tour so much of the year that when it performs in Moscow (generally at the Tchaikovsky Concert Hall), tickets are very difficult to obtain. Other renowned companies include the State Symphony Orchestra and the Armed Forces Song and Dance Ensemble. With the exception of special performances, tickets are usually easily available and inexpensive.

Even if you don't speak Russian, you might want to explore the intense world of Russian dramatic theater. Unfortunately, headphones providing English translations are virtually unheard of, so it's best to stick to something you already know in English (Shakespeare is, of course, widely performed, as are many plays based on classic works that would be familiar to readers of Russian literature, such as *The Master and Margarita* and *Brothers Karamazov*). Note that evening performances begin at 7 pm *sharp*.

KREMLIN/RED SQUARE

OPERA AND BALLET

State Kremlin Palace. Formerly the hall where Soviet Communist Party congresses were held, this modern concert venue now hosts regular performances by opera and ballet troupes, including those from the Bolshoi. Of late it also has become the stage for international stars such as Elton John, Bryan Adams, Cher, and Mariah Carey. Entrance is through the whitewashed Kutafya Gate. ⊠ *1 ul. Vozdvizhenka, in Kremlin, Kremlin/Red Square* ☎ *495/620–7831 or 495/917–2336* Ⓜ *Aleksandrovsky Sad.*

KITAI GOROD

ART GALLERIES

Dom Nashchokina Gallery. A mixture of classic Russian art and crowd-pulling exhibitions by celebrity artists can be found at this established space. ⊠ *12 Vorotnikovsky per., Kitai Gorod* ☎ *495/699–1178 or 495/699–4774* ⊕ *www.domnaschokina.ru* Ⓜ *Mayakovskaya.*

MOVIES

35mm. An artsy crowd frequents this simple theater with top-quality projection and sound. The films are always shown in their original language, usually with Russian subtitles. ✉ *47/24 Pokrovka, Kitai Gorod* ☎ *495/917–5492 or 495/917–1883* ⊕ *www.kino35mm.ru* Ⓜ *Krasniye Vorota or Kurskaya.*

OPERA AND BALLET

Fodor's Choice
★

Bolshoi Opera and Ballet Theatre. The landmark building of this world-renowned theater is closed for restoration until late 2011. Until then, performances are held either on a second stage next to the main theater, or at the Kremlin State Palace. The quality of the Bolshoi's productions has been uneven at times, but recent guest foreign directors have made for more innovative shows. The Russian flair for set and costume design alone can often be enough to keep an audience enthralled. Performances sell out quickly, so order tickets far in advance. ✉ *1 Teatralnaya pl., Kitai Gorod* ☎ *495/692–9986; 495/250–7317 tickets* ⊕ *www.bolshoi. ru* Ⓜ *Teatralnaya.*

THEATER

Maly Theater. Moscow's first dramatic theater, opened in 1824, the Maly is famous for its staging of Russian classics, especially those of the 19th-century satirist Alexander Ostrovsky—his statue stands outside the building. ✉ *1/1 Teatralny proyezd, Kitai Gorod* ☎ *495/624–4083 or 623–2621* ⊕ *www.maly.ru* Ⓜ *Teatralnaya.*

Operetta Theater. The Operetta stages lighthearted, and much humbler, versions of Western musicals, as well as the latest Russian musicals. ✉ *ul. 6 Bolshaya Dmitrovka, Kitai Gorod* ☎ *495/692–1237* ⊕ *www. mosoperetta.ru* Ⓜ *Teatralnaya.*

Sovremennik Theater. This well-respected theater stages a mix of Russian classics and foreign adaptations. ✉ *19 Chistoprudny bulvar, Kitai Gorod* ☎ *495/621–6473 or 495/621–1790* ⊕ *www.sovremennik.ru* Ⓜ *Chistiye Prudy.*

TVERSKAYA ULITSA

ART GALLERIES

Fine Art. This was one of the first private galleries in post-Soviet Russia. Today it displays contemporary art from the best of the previous generation's nonconformists to current names. ✉ *3/10 Bolshaya Sadovaya, Bldg. 10, Tverskaya* ☎ *499/251–7649* ⊕ *www.galleryfineart.ru* Ⓜ *Mayakovskaya.*

MUSIC

Glinka Music Museum Hall. This is one of many small concert halls scattered throughout the city. ✉ *4 ul. Fadeyeva, Tverskaya* ☎ *495/739–6226* ⊕ *www.glinka.museum* Ⓜ *Mayakovskaya.*

Tchaikovsky Concert Hall. With seating for more than 1,600, this huge hall is home to the State Symphony Orchestra. ✉ *4/31 Triumfalnaya pl., Tverskaya* ☎ *495/232–0400, 495/699–2262, or 495/232–5353* ⊕ *www. classicalmusic.ru* Ⓜ *Mayakovskaya.*

OPERA AND BALLET

Kolobov Novaya Opera. After opening in 1992, the *Novaya* ("new") opera house, opened in 1991 quickly established itself as one of the best and most innovative in the city. The surrounding Hermitage Garden is perfect for a pre- or post-theater stroll. The choir is ranked as the best in the city. ⊠ *3 Karetny Ryad, Tverskaya* 🕿 *495/694–0868* ⊕ *www. novayaopera.ru* Ⓜ *Tverskaya.*

THEATER

LenKom Theater. Good, often flashy productions are on the playbill here. Tickets are frequently very hard to get. ⊠ *6 Malaya Dmitrovka ul., Tverskaya* 🕿 *495/699–0708 or 495/699–9668* ⊕ *www.lenkom.ru* Ⓜ *Pushkinskaya.*

Fodor's Choice
★ **Moscow Art Theater** *(MKhAT).* Founded in 1898, the MKhAT is the heart of the Moscow theater scene. The theater is famous for its productions of the Russian classics, but it also stages plenty of modern and foreign performances. The American Studio at the Chekhov Art Theater presents performances, typically Russian classics, in English a few times a year. ⊠ *3 Kamergersky per., Tverskaya* 🕿 *495/629–8760 or 495/692–6748* ⊕ *www.art.theatre.ru* Ⓜ *Okhotny Ryad.*

★ **Moscow Theater for Young Viewers.** Despite its name, this acclaimed theater mainly stages adult productions. It's famed for its dramatizations of Chekhov short stories, staged by director Kama Ginkas. ⊠ *10 Mamonovsky per., Tverskaya* 🕿 *495/699–9917 or 495/699–5360* ⊕ *www.moscowtyz.ru* Ⓜ *Pushkinskaya.*

Mossoviet Theater. Contemporary drama shares the stage with comedies and musicals here. ⊠ *16 Bolshaya Sadovaya, Tverskaya* 🕿 *495/699–2035* ⊕ *www.mossoveta.ru* Ⓜ *Mayakovskaya.*

BOLSHAYA NIKITSKAYA ULITSA

ART GALLERIES

★ **Stella Art.** Works by top names such as Andy Warhol are exhibited at this commercial gallery, which opened in 2003. ⊠ *7 Skaryatinksy per., Bolshaya Nikitskaya* 🕿 *495/691–3407* ⊕ *www.safmuseum.org* Ⓜ *Krasnopresnenskaya or Barrikadnaya.*

MUSIC

Fodor's Choice
★ **Tchaikovsky Conservatory.** Rachmaninoff, Scriabin, and Tchaikovsky are among the famous composers who have worked here. The acoustics of the magnificent Great Hall are superb, and portraits of the world's great composers hang above the high balcony. The adjacent Small Hall is usually reserved for chamber-music concerts. ⊠ *13/16 Bolshaya Nikitskaya ul., Bolshaya Nikitskaya* 🕿 *495/629–0225 or 495/629–9401* ⊕ *www. mosconsv.ru* Ⓜ *Okhotny Ryad or Arbatskaya.*

THE ARBAT

MUSIC

Scriabin Museum Hall. Performances are held usually on Wednesday in a small concert hall in the apartment building where the composer Alexander Scriabin lived. ✉ *11 Bolshoi Nikolopeskovsky per., Arbat* ☎ *499/241–1901 or 499/241–5156* Ⓜ *Smolenskaya.*

OPERA AND BALLET

★ **Helikon Opera.** In addition to delivering consistently appealing and critically acclaimed opera performances, the Helikon troupe is equally talented in space management: even the grandest of classics are fitted with ease onto the small stage. ✉ *11 Novy Arbat, Arbat* ☎ *495/695–6584 or 495/690–6592* ⊕ *www.helikon.ru* Ⓜ *Arbatskaya.*

KROPOTKINSKY DISTRICT

ART GALLERIES

NB Gallery. In the unlikely event that none of the contemporary landscape paintings displayed here catches your eye, proprietor Natalya Bykova, a friendly English-speaking art lover, is happy to offer advice on other top art venues in Moscow. The gallery is within an apartment, so it's best to call ahead. ✉ *6/2 Sivtsev Vrazhek, Apartment 2, Kropotkinsky District* ☎ *495/203–4006 or 495/737–5298* ⊕ *www.nbgallery. com* Ⓜ *Kropotkinskaya.*

ZAMOSKVORECHE

ART GALLERIES

Baibakov Art Projects. Founded by Maria Baibakova—the daughter of metals magnate Oleg Baibakov—this huge gallery is housed in a former Soviet Palace of Culture on the embankment of the Moskva River. Exhibitions can be intermittent, so check out the Web site or call ahead of time. ✉ *2 Paveletskaya nab, Bldg. 18, Zamoskvoreche* ☎ *495/663–3722* ⊕ *www.baibakovartprojects.com* Ⓜ *Paveletskaya.*

Krokin Gallery. There's a focus on modern art here, particularly photography and graphic art. ✉ *15 Bolshaya Polyanka, Zamoskvoreche* ☎ *495/959–0141* ⊕ *www.krokingallery.com* Ⓜ *Polyanka.*

Tsentralny Dom Khudozhnika (*TsDKh*). Many different galleries are housed within this vast exhibition center, the Central House of Artists, and if you wander long enough you're likely to find something to fit your taste, from traditional landscapes to the latest avant-garde outrage. In front of TsDKh a huge painting market snakes its way along the river. Among the piles of kitsch and banal landscapes you can find some real gems. Be prepared to bargain. ✉ *10 Krymsky Val, Zamoskvoreche* ☎ *499/238–9843 or 499/230–1782* ⊕ *www.cha.ru* Ⓜ *Park Kultury or Oktyabrskaya.*

MUSIC

Moscow International Performing Arts Center (*Moscow International House of Music*). Opened in 2002, this architecturally striking center stages major classical concerts in its Svetlanov Hall, which contains Russia's largest organ. ⊠ *52 Kosmodamianskaya nab., Bldg. 8, Zamoskvoreche* ☎ *495/730–1011* ⊕ *www.mmdm.ru* Ⓜ *Paveletskaya.*

THEATER

Estrada Theater. The curtain goes up here for comedies starring some of Russia's best-known actors, along with a number of variety shows. ⊠ *20/2 Bersenyovskaya nab., Zamoskvoreche* ☎ *495/959–0550* ⊕ *www.teatr-estrada.ru* Ⓜ *Kropotkinskaya.*

NORTHERN OUTSKIRTS

ART GALLERIES

Ⓒ **Garage Center for Contemporary Culture.** Buoyed with funding from oligarchs like Chelsea Football Club owner Roman Abramovich, the center has become one of Moscow's hottest venues for international and Russian contemporary art since it opened in 2008. It's worth a visit just to see the building itself: it's in the former Bakhmetevsky bus garage, a masterpiece of constructivism built by architect Konstantin Melnikov during a brief flourishing of utopian arts in the late 1920s. There's a good café here, too. ⊠ *19A Obraztsova Ul., Northern Outskirts* ☎ *495/645–0520* ⊕ *www.garageccc.ru* Ⓜ *Novoslobodskaya or Dostoyevskaya.*

Fodor's Choice ★

5

MUSIC

Russian Army Theater. The Armed Forces Song and Dance Ensemble calls this venue home. ⊠ *2 Suvorovskaya Pl., Northern Outskirts* ☎ *495/681–2110 or 495/681–5120* Ⓜ *Dostoyevskaya.*

SOUTHERN OUTSKIRTS

ART GALLERIES

★ **Stella Art Russian.** Veteran Russian conceptual artists are featured at this gallery branch. In 2004 it invited prominent, New York–based artist Ilya Kabakov for his first Moscow exhibition since emigrating. ⊠ *62 Mytnaya ul., Southern Outskirts* ☎ *495/954–0253* ⊕ *www.safmuseum.org* Ⓜ *Tulskaya.*

MUSIC

Tsaritsyno Museum. A music hall at Catherine the Great's restored Moscow palace regularly holds classical-music concerts. ⊠ *1 ul. Dolskaya, Southern Outskirts* ☎ *495/321–0743* ⊕ *www.tsaritsyno-museum.ru* Ⓜ *Orekhovo or Tsaritsyno.*

THEATER

Ⓒ **Tereza Durova Clown Theater.** Attracting children and adults, the shows here, based on the commedia dell'arte, are filled with music, dance, and acrobatics. ⊠ *6 Pavlovskaya ul., inside DK Zavoda Ilyicha, Southern Outskirts* ☎ *499/637–1689* ⊕ *www.durova.org* Ⓜ *Serpukhovskaya or Dobryninskaya.*

EASTERN OUTSKIRTS

ART GALLERIES

★ **Winzavod.** In Soviet times, it was a massive wine factory. Today, Winzavod is the epicenter of Moscow's burgeoning contemporary arts scene, housing more than a half-dozen galleries, as well as a café, a bookstore, and a clothing boutique called Cara & Co. ✉ *1 4th Syromantichesky per., Bldg. 6, Eastern Outskirts* ☎ *495/917–4646* ⊕ *www.winzavod. com* Ⓜ *Kurskaya or Chkalovskaya.*

Aidan Gallery. The artists displayed in this seasoned gallery—founded in 1992—are young, little known, and very stylish. ✉ *Winzavod, 1 4th Syromantichesky per., Bldg. 6, Eastern Outskirts* ☎ *495/228–1158* ⊕ *www.aidangallery.ru* Ⓜ *Kurskaya or Chkalovskaya.*

Guelman Gallery. One of Moscow's first galleries, this is also one of its most controversial, due to the attention-loving nature of owner Marat Guelman. There's a definite shock value to many of the modern and avant-garde exhibits. It's a good bet for performance art. ✉ *Winzavod, 1 4th Syromantichesky per., Bldg. 6, Eastern Outskirts* ☎ *495/229–1339* ⊕ *www.guelman.ru* Ⓜ *Kurskaya or Chkalovskaya.*

XL-Gallery. Russia's most renowned conceptual artists exhibit drawings, photographs, and installations, and occasionally put on performances in this intimate space. ✉ *Winzavod, 1 4th Syromantichesky per., Bldg. 6, Eastern Outskirts* ☎ *495/775–8373 or 916/125–0995* ⊕ *xlgallery. artinfo.ru* Ⓜ *Kurskaya or Chkalovskaya.*

MOVIES

Dome Cinema. A hotel movie house, Dome Cinema caters to the expatriate community with recent Hollywood releases. ✉ *Renaissance Moscow hotel, 18/1 Olympiisky pr., Eastern Outskirts* ☎ *495/931–9873* ⊕ *www. domecinema.ru* Ⓜ *Prospekt Mira.*

THEATER

★ **Taganka Theater.** Run by the legendary Yuri Lyubimov, the Taganka is one of the world's most famous theaters. The troupe's most famed dramatization is of Mikhail Bulgakov's novel *The Master and Margarita*. Performances sell out far in advance. ✉ *76/21 Zemlyanoy Val, Eastern Outskirts* ☎ *495/915–1015* ⊕ *www.taganka.theatre.ru* Ⓜ *Taganskaya.*

NIGHTLIFE

From raucous, boho joints like Kitaisky Lyotchik to sophisticated "minigarch" (wannabe oligarch) hangouts, Moscow's bar scene has a little bit of something for everyone.

Almost all the major hotels have upscale bars: those at the Baltschug Kempinski, Ararat Park Hyatt, and Golden Ring are elegant and have majestic views of the city. But you'll likely have more fun if you head out on the town and taste a little Russian hedonism, be it smoking cigars and sipping cognac at the GQ Bar, carousing at Real McCoy's, or jumping about to a guitar band at Krizis Zhanra. For those after something calmer, there are several English-style pubs like Sixteen Tons that are great for a quiet pint and a bite to eat. Unless there's live music, there's no cover charge for most bars.

Moscow's vibrant clubbing scene means there are plenty of great places to go. However, *feis kontrol* (face control, or a velvet-rope mentality) is common at most high-end clubs. Most clubs don't get busy until between midnight and 2 am. Live music is popular, and some larger clubs put on shows by famous foreign DJs and musicians. At some of the high-end places, there's a fee to be seated at a table.

No other part of Moscow's clubbing scene is more subject to closings than the tiny gay circuit, so these listings are far from definitive. A good way to keep up with the scene is by checking ⊕ *www.gay.ru*, which has regular updates in English. Note that the club Propaganda has a popular gay night on Sundays.

The *Moscow Times* (⊕ *www.themoscowtimes.com*), *Element* (⊕ *www. elementmoscow.ru*), *Passport* (⊕ *www.passportmagazine.ru*), and *Life-Style,* available for free at hotels, bars, and restaurants, publish up-to-date calendars of events in English.

⚠ **Foreigners make easy crime targets: take special precautions at night. You're safest venturing out with other people. Do not drive under any circumstances after drinking; Russia has a zero-tolerance drunk-driving law, and traffic police can and do stop cars at will.**

KITAI GOROD

BARS

Annushka. Housed on a tram that makes a constant and short loop around the picturesque Chistiye Prudy area, Annushka is a cozy bar and restaurant. Wait outside the metro station, where it stops every 10 to 15 minutes. ✉ *Stops outside Chistiye Prudy metro station, Kitai Gorod* ☎ *495/507–5770* Ⓜ *Chistiye Prudy.*

Bilingua. Young, creative types frequent this smoky bar-club-bookshop, which also has inexpensive food. ✉ *10 Krivokolenny per, Bldg. 5, Kitai Gorod* ☎ *495/623–9660* ⊕ *www.bilinguaclub.ru* Ⓜ *Chistiye Prudy or Lubyanka.*

Glavpivtorg. Live musicians perform songs from the Soviet era at this enormous retro eatery. It has a big choice of beers, including its own brand. The traditional Russian dishes are expensive but served up with style. Book ahead, as it gets busy even on weeknights. ✉ *5 Bolshaya Lubyanka ul., Kitai Gorod* ☎ *495/628–2591 or 495/624–1996* ⊕ *www. glavpivtorg.ru* Ⓜ *Lubyanka.*

Kitaiysky Lyotchik Jao Da. Live music and tasty, affordable food draw a bohemian crowd to this cellar bar, whose name translates to "Chinese Pilot." ✉ *25 Lubyansky proyezd, Bldg. 1, Kitai Gorod* ☎ *495/624–5611 or 495/623–2896* ⊕ *www.jao-da.ru* Ⓜ *Kitai Gorod.*

Krizis Zhanra. An easygoing but stylish clientele fills this café-bar. In the evenings, staff push away the tables to create a small dance floor. Live music on the weekends is mostly indie-rock, but DJs through the week play an eclectic mix of pop, rock, reggae, and funk. ✉ *16/16 Pokrovka*

GETTING PAST THE VELVET ROPES

Although clubs the world over reserve the right to be choosy about who gets in and who gets left out in the cold, few doormen have a reputation for being as stringent—or as sadistic—as the ones working Moscow's nightspots. The truth is, many of the places listed here can easily be called *demokratichny*, meaning that they maintain an egalitarian door policy. If you do find yourself in a run-in with the face-control goons, however, there are a few strategies that can help you skip the velvet rope:

Dress to impress: Try to find out the type of crowd your club attracts, and wear the right clothes. Keep in mind, however, that "right" and "formal" are two different things. A pair of Prada jeans may get you a lot farther than a three-piece suit.

Speak English: Although foreigners seldom create the impression that they did, say, 10 years ago, many clubs consider it desirable to have an international clientele. Speaking some English, flashing your passport, and saying you'll tell everybody back in Boise how cool the club is might be enough for you to waltz right in.

Let your money do the talking: If you really want to get in and are still getting the cold shoulder, call the club's PR manager over and ask to buy a club card. The card makes you face-control proof and may also get you a discount on drinks and food, but it won't come cheap. Club cards cost from a few hundred to a few thousand dollars.

ul., Bldg. 2, Chistiye Prudy ☎ *495/623–2594* ⊕ *www.kriziszhanra.ru* Ⓜ *Chistiye Prudy.*

Proyekt O.G.I. This was one of the city's first bohemian clubs, complete with a bookstore and live music. It has since evolved into an increasingly commercial, expanding chain of cheap restaurants. The original, however, is still a good time. ✉ *8/12 Potapovsky per., Kitai Gorod* ☎ *495/627–5366* ⊕ *www.proektogi.ru* Ⓜ *Chistiye Prudy.*

CLUBS

Club Che. This is a vibrant Latin American–theme club staffed by Cuban waiters. Drink service can be slow at night, when the staff often dances with the crowd. Show up early or you'll never get in. ✉ *10/2 Nikolskaya ul., Kitai Gorod* ☎ *495/621–0668* ⊕ *www.clubche.ru* Ⓜ *Lubyanka.*

Karma Bar. Top 40 hits and a crew of die-hard regulars mean that hardly a weekend goes by without Karma's dance floor being packed wall to wall. Lenient face control also helps bring in the crowds. ✉ *3 Pushechnaya ul., Kitai Gorod* ☎ *495/649–1797* ⊕ *www.karma-bar.ru* Ⓜ *Kuznetsky Most.*

Papa's Place. Nights at Papa's are all about strip egg-and-spoon races, wet T-shirt contests, or any other silly games the management can think of. Dirt-cheap happy-hour drinks are a big draw for students. ✉ *22 Myasnitskaya ul., Kitai Gorod* ☎ *495/755–9554* ⊕ *www.papas. ru* Ⓜ *Chistiye Prudy.*

★ **Propaganda.** This is probably the city's most reliable club for trendy, yet laid-back crowds and good DJs. It's *the* place to be on Thursday night. On Sunday night it turns into one of the city's most popular gay clubs. ✉ *7 Bolshoi Zlatoustinsky per., Kitai Gorod* ☎ *495/624–5732* ⊕ *www.propagandamoscow.com* Ⓜ *Kitai Gorod.*

> **IN THE LIMELIGHT**
>
> Opened by the renowned Russian designer of the same name, the **Denis Simachev Bar** (✉ *12 Stoleshnikov per., Bldg. 2, Tsverskaya* ☎ *495/629–8085 or 495/629–5702* ⊕ *denissimachev. blogspot.com* Ⓜ *Teatralnaya*) combines kitsch, elegance, and a hot crowd for a unique bar experience that can be a treat for those keen on people-watching. Here's where Moscow's "Zolotoy Molodyozh," or "Gilded Youth," go for their pre-party drinks.

TVERSKAYA ULITSA

BARS

Silvers. This is the place to go for those desperate for authentic Irish pub atmosphere and a pint of Guinness. Wood-paneled walls, shamrocks, and tons of expatriates are enough to make even the weariest traveler feel at home. ✉ *5/6 Nikitsky per., Tverskaya* ☎ *495/690–4222* Ⓜ *Okhotny Ryad.*

CLUBS

B-2. One of the best places in Moscow for live rock performances, B-2 is an enormous five-story club that includes a sushi bar, a big-screen TV, a dance club, and several bars. ✉ *8 Bolshaya Sadovaya, Tsverskaya* ☎ *495/650–9918 or 495/650–9909* ⊕ *www.b2club.ru* Ⓜ *Mayakovskaya.*

Garazh. Getting into this popular nightclub on the weekend isn't always easy, but if you make it you'll be among Moscow's most dedicated clubbers. Wednesday is R & B and hip-hop night. ✉ *8 Brodnikov per., Bldg. 2/2, Tsverskaya* ☎ *499/238–7075* ⊕ *www.garageclub.ru* Ⓜ *Polyanka.*

GAY AND LESBIAN CLUBS

12 Volt. This club for both men and women is tricky to find, but has a welcoming atmosphere. It has DJs, film screenings, karaoke, and cheap drink deals. ✉ *12 Tverskaya ul., Bldg. 2, entrance in yard off Kozitsky per., Tsverskaya* ☎ *495/933–2815* ⊕ *12voltclub.ru* Ⓜ *Tverskaya.*

BOLSHAYA NIKITSKAYA ULITSA

BARS

Real McCoy's. A speakeasy theme pervades this bar. Weekend nights, the place explodes into an alcohol-fueled party that includes customers dancing on the bar. ✉ *1 Kudrinskaya Pl., Bolshaya Nikitskaya* ☎ *499/255–4144* ⊕ *www.mccoy.ru* Ⓜ *Barrikadnaya.*

5

THE ARBAT

BARS

Hard Rock Cafe. It may be an international chain, but somehow the Moscow branch manages to maintain its own flavor. Locals come for the pop-music classics, and Westerners stop by for a taste of home. ✉ *44 Arbat, Bldg. 3, Arbat* ☎ *499/241–9853 or 499/241–4342* ⊕ *www. hardrockcafe.ru* Ⓜ *Smolenskaya.*

Tinkoff. A futuristically styled beer restaurant run by Tinkoff brewery, this spot is popular with diplomats working in nearby embassies. ✉ *11 Protochny per., Arbat* ☎ *495/780–5888* ⊕ *www.tinkoff.ru* Ⓜ *Smolenskaya.*

JAZZ AND BLUES

★ **Roadhouse.** Fanatically unpretentious, this friendly joint has cheap food, pool tables, and excellent live blues almost every night, along with an occasional blast of rock and roll. There's a charge of about 200R if you stay for the music. ✉ *19 Starovagankovsky per., Bldg. 2, Arbat* ☎ *903/145–3716* ⊕ *www.roadhouse.ru* mBiblioteka im. Lenina.

KROPOTKINSKY DISTRICT

CLUBS

Keks. Housed in a former factory, this retro-theme café turns into a club at night with guest DJs and a small dance floor. ✉ *11/34 Timura Frunze ul., Kropotkinsky District* ☎ *495/472–7469* ⊕ *www.cafekeks. ru* Ⓜ *Park Kultury.*

ZAMOSKVORECHE

BARS

Bar Strelka. The superbly positioned summer terrace overlooking the Moscow River and the Cathedral of Christ Our Savior is the main attraction of this upscale bar, which has laid-back DJs and piano recitals inside. ✉ *14 Bersenevskaya nab., Bldg. 5 Zamoskvoreche* ☎ *495/771–7417* ⊕ *www.barstrelka.com* Ⓜ *Kropotkinskaya.*

GQ Bar. It's not cheap, and the face control gets strict from time to time, but if you're looking for an elite bar scene, it's hard to beat. This is where Moscow's upper crust—everyone from upwardly mobile execs to almost-oligarchs—comes to grab its after-work drink, or a bite in one of the three lavishly appointed dining halls. ✉ *5 ul. Baltchug, Zamoskvoreche* ☎ *495/956–7775* ⊕ *bar.gq.ru* Ⓜ *Novokuznetskaya.*

> **VODKA SHOTS**
>
> For a true Russian vodka-drinking experience, head to **Ryumochnaya** (✉ *22/2 Bolshaya Nikitskaya ul., Bldg. 1, Bolshaya Nikitskaya* ☎ *495/691–5474* Ⓜ *Okhotny Ryad*), a 125-year-old tavern whose name literally translates as "shot bar." Drinks are affordable at 60R per shot and there's a large variety of zakuski, tasty bites that help the booze go down, like salmon sandwiches, boiled prawns, and fried potatoes.

Sally O'Brien's. Despite the country music often played here, this is a pub with a definite Irish feel. It's also a good place to meet other foreigners. ✉ *1/3 Polyanka ul., Zamoskvoreche* ☎ *495/959–0175* ⊕ *www.sallyobriens.ru* Ⓜ *Polyanka.*

CLUBS

Fabrique. Popular with expats and students, this two-story club features tasty food and sessions by top guest DJs. ✉ *2 Kosmodamianskaya nab., Zamoskvoreche* ☎ *495/951–1313* or *495/953–6576* ⊕ *www.fabrique.ru* Ⓜ *Novokuznetskaya* or *Paveletskaya.*

Rai. For those seeking the full-on Moscow clubbing experience, with pink mirrored ceilings, stunning podium dancers, and top international DJs, Rai (Paradise) is the place to go. Be warned: the face control is the toughest in the city, and prices for drinks border on gouging. ✉ *9 Bolotnaya nab., Zamoskvoreche* ☎ *495/364–0101* or *495/767–1474* ⊕ *www.raiclub.ru* Ⓜ *Kropotkinskaya.*

Vermel. Cheap drinks and affordable concerts have made Vermel a big hit with students and other young clubbers. ✉ *4/5 Raushskaya nab., Zamoskvoreche* ☎ *495/238–3303* ⊕ *www.vermel.ru* Ⓜ *Tretyakovskaya.*

> ### COCKTAILS . . . NOT THE MOLOTOV KIND
>
> As much progress as the Moscow bar scene has made in recent years, many of the capital's bartenders have not yet mastered the art of mixology, resulting in the occasional mangled Martini (though nothing explosive yet). **Help** (✉ *27 [1st] Tverskaya-Yamskaya ul., Bldg. 1, Northern Ouskirts* ☎ *495/995-5395* ⊕ *www.helpbar.ru* Ⓜ *Belorusskaya*) is on the way, however, at this bar which offers more than 200 drink options, from classics like the Long Island Iced Tea to more exotic but well-made local creations.

NORTHERN OUTSKIRTS

CLUBS

Arena. With the biggest club stage in Moscow and a dance floor capacity of 3,500 people, this live music venue is a prime spot to see big and up-and-coming Russian groups, as well as foreign acts and DJs. ✉ *31 Leningradsky pr., Bldg. 4, Northern Outskirts* ☎ *495/940–6755* ⊕ *www.arenamoscow.ru* Ⓜ *Dinamo.*

GAY AND LESBIAN CLUBS

Central Station. This gay club, a popular spot with students, is one of the most well established in town, with a regular rotation of good DJs. Mostly men come here, but women are welcome. ✉ *4 Yuzhny proyezd, Northern Outskirts* ☎ *495/988–3585* ⊕ *www.centralclub.ru* Ⓜ *Komsomolskaya.*

JAZZ AND BLUES

BB King Blues Club. The man himself came for the opening, and visiting Western stars have continued to make appearances here, often for post-concert jams. ✉ *4 Sadovaya-Samotyochnaya ul., Bldg. 2, Northern Outskirts* ☎ *495/699–8206* ⊕ *www.bbkingclub.ru* Ⓜ *Tsvetnoy Bulvar.*

EASTERN OUTSKIRTS

JAZZ AND BLUES

Jazz Town. Lit up like a Christmas tree year-round, this relative new-comer to Moscow's live music scene features bands performing nearly every night, as well as the occasional DJ. ✉ *12 Taganskaya Pl., Eastern Outskirts* ☎ *495/363–4223* ⊕ *www.jazztown.ru* Ⓜ *Taganskaya.*

WESTERN OUTSKIRTS

BARS

Sixteen Tons. A popular pub with a club upstairs, this spot serves its own home-brewed beer. ✉ *6 Presnensky Val, Western Outskirts* ☎ *499/253–5300* ⊕ *www.16tons.ru* Ⓜ *Ulitsa 1905 Goda.*

CLUBS

Crocus City Hall. Sting and Bryan Ferry have played at this huge complex on the Moscow ring road with a 6,200-seat auditorium. Check ahead and you might catch your favorite group from home. ✉ *65–66 km Moscow Ring Road (MKhAD), Crocus City, Crocus Expo, Pavilion 3, Western Outskirts* ☎ *495/223–4020* ⊕ *www.crocus-hall.ru* Ⓜ *Myakinino.*

Moscow Shopping

WORD OF MOUTH

"No, you do not need a guide if you are willing to invest a couple of hours in learning the Cyrillic alphabet and maybe a couple of key phrases before going on holiday. Buy a good guidebook and decide from home what you want to see. I suggest spending at least one day around the Red Square, GUM, Lenin's tomb, Saint Basil's Cathedral and the Kremlin. If you like churches and monasteries, do visit the Cathedral of Christ the Savior, the Kazan Cathedral, and Novodevichy Convent and Monastery. Also, you don't want to miss the Moscow metro (cheap, efficient, and beautifully decorated), the Arbat shopping street, and the VDNKh exhibition center."

—Westcoast8

Updated by
Anna Coppola

These days, shopping is a national sport in Moscow. Locals shop in brand new mega-malls, revamped department stores, designer boutiques, and busy food markets. However, it hasn't been this way for very long.

It was in the mid-2000s that the word *lukshery* (luxury) first became popular in Russia, along with a vast expansion of goods and services catering to Russia's new upper class. Parts of historical shopping districts in downtown Moscow, such as Stoleshnikov pereulok, Kuznetsky Most, and Tretyakovsky proyezd, are filled with brands like Hermès, Louis Vuitton, Dior, Burberry, Prada, and Fendi. For more mid-range Western brands like Levi's and Nike, visit shopping malls such as GUM and Evropeisky. However, the prices will be much higher than in the United States. Instead, take a look at the stores of Russian designers, which sell clothes at prices ranging from reasonable to outrageous. A few fashion names to look out for include Sultanna Frantsuzova, Igor Chapurin, and Denis Symachev.

For good souvenir hunting, head straight to the Arbat. Stores here cater to tourists and Moscow's expatriate community, so you can expect good selection and service, but prices are on the high end. The Arbat's individual outdoor vendors invariably charge much more than they should, so stick to the stores.

Hours of operation can be unpredictable in the case of smaller stores, but stores are generally open Monday through Saturday 10 to 7. Food stores may open an hour earlier, and department stores may remain open later, with additional hours on Sunday (typically 11 to 6). Some specialty stores and many supermarkets may operate 24/7, but most of the newer shopping malls stay open daily from 10 or 11 in the morning to 9 or 10 at night.

KREMLIN/RED SQUARE

DEPARTMENT STORES AND MALLS

★ **GUM.** A series of shops and boutiques inside a 19th-century arcade, this shopping emporium sits on Red Square, across from the Kremlin. GUM, which stands for Gosudarstvenny Universalny Magazin, or State Department Store, now stocks only a handful of Russian brands in the upper-level stores. On the first floor you will find an arcade of upscale boutiques, including MaxMara, Hugo Boss, and La Perla. Also here is the elegant Bosco restaurant, which overlooks Red Square and has a summer terrace. Cheaper eats are available at fast-food outlets on the top floor. ⊠ *3 Red Sq., Kremlin/Red Square* ☎ *495/788–4343* ⊕ *www. gum.ru* Ⓜ *Ploshchad Revolutsii.*

Okhotny Ryad. Some call this underground shopping mall Manezh for the square on which it sits. Department-store standards like Aldo, Benetton, Tommy Hilfiger, BeeFree, Motivi, and MEXX along with gift items are the strong point of this shopping showcase. Set under the main square adjacent to the Kremlin, the Manezh attracts crowds of Russian out-of-towners, who stroll, photograph the intricate cupola that extends aboveground, and window-shop. ✉ *Trade Center Okhotny Ryad, 1 Manezhnaya Pl., Kremlin/Red Square* Ⓜ *Okhotny Ryad.*

SPECIALTY STORES
ARTS AND CRAFTS
Ikonnaya Lavka. The Cathedral of Our Lady of Kazan, near Russian Museum World, houses this icon shop. In addition to icons, you can purchase religious books, silver crosses, and other Orthodox religious items. ✉ *3 Nikolskaya ul., at Red Sq., Kremlin/Red Square* ☎ *No phone* Ⓜ *Ploshchad Revolutsii.*

Russian Museum World. The Historical Museum's art shop deals in many sorts of souvenirs, including jewelry, T-shirts, handmade crafts, replicas of museum pieces, and Russian- and Ukrainian-style embroidered shirts, Gzhel ceramics, and more. Wooden bowls and spoons decorated in *khokhloma* style—with bright oils painted on a black-and-golden background—fill the shelves. The store is on the right-hand side of the museum as you enter Red Square through the Resurrection Gates. ✉ *1/2 Red Sq., Kremlin/Red Square* ☎ *495/692–1320* Ⓜ *Ploshchad Revolutsii.*

> **BUYING ANTIQUES**
>
> Keep in mind that you're forbidden to take some items out of the country. The law basically disallows the export of anything of "cultural value to the Russian nation." In practical terms, this means that art and craft items older than 30 to 40 years are not allowed out without special permission from the Ministry of Culture or its local agent; the item may be confiscated at the border if you lack the necessary papers. If you're buying paintings or art objects, it's important to consult with the seller regarding the proper documentation of sale for export. Keep receipts of your purchases.

KITAI GOROD

DEPARTMENT STORES AND MALLS
Petrovsky Passazh. MaxMara, Nina Ricci, Givenchy, Kenzo, and Bally boutiques and an antiques store are in this chic, glass-roof space, the most luxurious shopping *passazh* (arcade) in town. ✉ *10 ul. Petrovka, Kitai Gorod* ☎ *495/928–5012* Ⓜ *Kuznetsky Most.*

TsUM. TsUM (Central Department Store), a historical rival of GUM, has upgraded itself to an expensive store with collections of nearly all the top European designers. Although the architecture is nothing like the stunning Red Square's arcade, TsUM usually has the larger choice. It's a two-minute walk down ulitsa Petrovka from Petrovsky Passazh. ✉ *2 ul. Petrovka, Kitai Gorod* ☎ *495/933–7300* ⊕ *www.tsum. ru* Ⓜ *Kuznetsky Most.*

SPECIALTY STORES
ARTS AND CRAFTS
Art boutiques of the Varvarka ulitsa churches. These boutiques are inside the Church of St. Maxim the Blessed, open daily 11–6, and the Church of St. George on Pskov Hill, open daily 11–7. Both carry a fine selection

of handicrafts, jewelry, ceramics, and other types of native-Russian art. ✉ *6 Varvarka ul., Kitai Gorod* Ⓜ *Kitai Gorod* ✉ *12 Varvarka ul., Kitai Gorod* Ⓜ *Kitai Gorod.*

FOOD

Korkunov. This is an upscale store selling individual chocolates and boxed candies produced in Russia. ✉ *13/16 Bolshaya Lubyanka ul., Kitai Gorod* ☎ *495/625–6411* ☉ *Mon.–Sat. 10–8* Ⓜ *Lubyanka.*

TVERSKAYA

DEPARTMENT STORES AND MALLS

Gallery Aktyor. Next door to the high-end Yeliseyevsky's grocery, this mall is smaller, more elegant, and often less crowded than GUM or Okhotny Ryad. Popular brands like Naf Naf, Levi's, Chevignon, and Lacoste are for sale. The first floor houses a Swatch outlet and a Clinique cosmetics store. ✉ *16/2 Tverskaya ul., Tverskaya* ☎ *495/290–9832* ⊕ *www.galleryactor.ru* Ⓜ *Tverskaya or Pushkinskaya.*

SPECIALTY STORES

ARTS AND CRAFTS

Novodel. This small store sells quirky contemporary crafts from local artists, including unique felt jewelry, toys, clocks, greetings cards, and T-shirts. ✉ *9 Bolshoi Palashevsky pereulok, Tverskaya* ☎ *495/926–4538* ⊕ *www.novodel.net* Ⓜ *Mayakovskaya or Tverskaya.*

CLOTHING

Denis Simachev Shop & Bar. This trendy Russian designer is known for his humorous reinventions of traditional Russian fashion—enormous fur accessories and enlarged folk art patterns. The outside of the store is decorated with designs based on red-and-gold *khokhloma* bowls. At night, the tiny bar and nightclub within the store is one of the hottest spots in town. ✉ *12 Stoleshnikov per., Bldg. 1, Tverskaya* ☎ *495/629–5702* ☉ *24 hrs* Ⓜ *Teatralnaya.*

FOOD

Volkonsky. This French-owned chain now has three branches in Moscow, where you can buy freshly baked cookies, pastries, and bread, and also drink coffee in a small café. This branch is perfect to combine with a walk around Patriarch's Pond. ✉ *2/46 Bolshaya Sadovaya, Tverskaya* ☎ *495/699–3620* Ⓜ *Tverskaya.*

Fodor's Choice
★
Yeliseyevsky. Historic, sumptuous, upscale—this turn-of-the-20th-century grocery store is the star of Tverskaya ulitsa, and even if you're not feeling hungry, the spectacle makes it well worth a visit. A late-18th-century classical mansion houses the store, and the art nouveau interior sparkles with chandeliers, stained glass, and gilt wall decorations. The fine products here include cognac, Armenian berry juices, Russian chocolate, and candy of all sorts. This is one of the best places to buy freshly baked goods, caviar, and deli fish. You'll find traditional favorite Russian rye breads such as *borodinsky* and *stolichny*, wheat *nareznoi*, as well as a wide variety of croissants (including dark and multigrain), brioches, and seven-grain loaves that were virtually unknown to Mus-

CLOSE UP

Russian Food and Spirits

CAVIAR

Caviar in Russia? Who can resist? Unfortunately, since the end of 2007 it has only been possible to find the cheaper red caviar in city stores, due to restrictions on black caviar that were put in place to save sturgeon stocks. Black caviar is slowly making its way back into stores, albeit at exorbitant prices (2,900R per 100-gram jar).

LIQUOR

Buying liquor—especially vodka—in Russia is a de rigueur activity fraught with danger. Alcohol counterfeiting is a big problem; according to various estimates, illegally produced vodka accounts for 40% to 70% of what is available on the market. If you don't follow safe buying practices, you could end up with a severe case of alcohol poisoning. Your best bet on price and safety is to buy well-known brands such as Kristall and Russky Standart at reputable supermarkets. Note that every bottle of vodka sold in Russia must bear a white excise stamp, glued over the cap, and those sold in Moscow must also bear a bar-code stamp.

BAKED GOODS

Western-style supermarkets are rapidly squeezing the poorly designed Soviet-style bakeries and other food stores out of business. Though there are still some of the stand-alone bakers in operation, supermarket bakery counters are a good option, selling Russian bread for less than 20R a loaf. *Podmoskovny* and *nareznoi* sell for about 16R and are lighter than the black bread generally associated with Russia. Varieties of black rye bread (*borodinsky* and *khamovnichesky*) are the tastiest, and they still won't put you out more than 30R. Branches of Perekryostok, often open 24 hours, have proliferated like underbrush below the high-rise canopies of Moscow's suburbs. This supermarket offers good freshly baked bread including round *stolichny* loaves with a crisp crust. The delicious and hugely popular Armenian lavash—soft, thin flatbread—is made with flour and water. Perhaps the best bread in the city is baked at Volkonsky, a small French-owned chain that sells expensive but great quality loaves baked on-site as well as cookies and pastries that you can enjoy in the store's café.

6

covites until 2000 or so. Another plus: the store is open 24 hours. ✉ *14 Tverskaya ul., Tverskaya* ☎ *495/650–4643* Ⓜ *Pushkinskaya.*

ARBAT

SPECIALTY STORES
ARTS AND CRAFTS

Arbatskaya Kollektsia. This pleasant souvenir shop sells the best of locally produced folk art, including *palekh* (colorful, lacquered wood with folklore designs) chess sets, cocktail glasses, and coffee sets made of amber. ✉ *12 Arbat, Arbat* ☎ *495/291–9300* Ⓜ *Arbatskaya or Smolenskaya.*

Arbatskaya Lavitsa. In this large, old-fashioned store you can find Gzhel china, linen tablecloths, nesting dolls, and wooden toys at reasonable prices and without the hard sell. ⊠ *27 Arbat, Arbat* ☎ *495/290–5689* Ⓜ *Arbatskaya or Smolenskaya.*

Russkaya Vyshivka. Specializing in Russian linen, this store stocks beautiful embroidered christening gowns as well as table linens and rag rugs. ⊠ *31 Arbat, Arbat* ☎ *495/241–2841* Ⓜ *Arbatskaya or Smolenskaya.*

CLOTHING

Moskvichka. Although poorly laid out (a side effect of its age), this store has a good selection of merchandise, including popular clothing brands like Guess, Sisley, Esprit, SoFrench, and MEXX, and also stocks Russian brands Sultanna Frantsuzova, Yevgeniya Ostrovskaya, and Sunie Li, popular with the city's office girls. It's a few doors down Novy Arbat from Novoarbatsky Gastronom. ⊠ *15 Novy Arbat, Arbat* ☎ *495/202– 5250* Ⓜ *Arbatskaya.*

SOUVENIRS

Art. Lebedev Shop and Café. Artemiy Lebedev is probably the most successful graphic designer, style guru, and blogger in Russia. At his outlet you can find wittily designed apparel, accessories, and office supplies that make great gifts. They're also a revealing look into the concerns and obsessions of Russian intellectuals. ⊠ *35 B. Nikitskaya ul., Arbat* ☎ *495/697–2635* ⊕ *store.artlebedev.com* ⊙ *Daily 9 am–11 pm* Ⓜ *Arbatskaya or Biblioteka im. Lenina.*

KRASNAYA PRESNYA

SPECIALTY STORES

FOOD

Krasny Oktyabr chocolate factory. Russian-made chocolates make a great, unexpected souvenir from Russia. Chocolates from Moscow's Krasny Oktyabr (Red October) factory are the best; most of them retain Soviet-style wrappers. You can buy various kinds of individually wrapped candies—*Krasnaya Shapochka* (Little Red Riding Hood), *Mishka Kosolapy* (Little Clumsy Bear), *Alyonka* (whose wrapper features a girl wearing a scarf), and *Yuzhnaya Noch* (Southern Night). As box of *Slivochnaya Pomadka* (Cream Fudge) sells for just over 60R; a gift tin of chocolate Mishka Kosolapy sells for about 350R. The chocolates are also widely available in supermarkets and kiosks, but the best assortment, including gift boxes and chocolate animal figures, is at the main store. ⊠ *29/36 Povarskaya ul., Krasnaya Presnya District* ☎ *495/691–0937* ⊙ *Daily 10 am–9 pm* Ⓜ *Krasnopresnenskaya or Barricadnaya.*

ZAMOSKVORECHE

SPECIALTY STORES

FOOD AND SPIRITS

Globus Gourmet. Picky eaters will like this 24-hour grocery store, which since 2005 has been supplying Moscow with high-quality imported foodstuffs. Among the wide array of deli foods, Globus offers Italian raspberry-flavor balsamic vinegar, priced at 815R for a 250-milliliter jar. Also lining the shelves and cases are chocolates from Belgium, fish from Norway, ham from Spain, and special local cheeses. The store's cheese department in general here has to be seen to be believed. ✉ *22 Bolshaya Yakimanka, Gimenei trade center Zamoskvoreche* ☎ *495/995–2170* Ⓜ *Oktyabrskaya and Polyanka* ✉ *19 Novy Arbat, basement of Vesna shopping center, Arbat* ☎ *495/775–0918 or 495/775–0923* Ⓜ *Arbat.*

Konditersky. This cozy, old-fashioned candy store, which will weigh out chocolates for you, has a good choice of Russian brands, including Krasny Oktyabr. ✉ *22 Pyatnitskaya ul., Zamoskvoreche* ☎ *495/951–3764* ◔ *Weekdays 9–8, Sat. 10–6. Closed Sun.* Ⓜ *Tretyakovskaya.*

CLOTHING

Mir Shersti. Tucked away in a side street, this store specializes in Russian-made felt boots, or valenki, which it stocks in children's and adult sizes. You can also buy ribbon-trimmed felt slippers and fleece-lined clothing. A small valenki museum is next door. ✉ *12 (2nd) Kozhevnichesky per., Zamoskvoreche* ☎ *495/775–2577* Ⓜ *Paveletskaya.*

> **UGG, MEET VALENKI**
>
> Perfect for a cold climate, *valenki* are traditional (and bulky) boots made of wool felt. They come in gray, black, or white with detachable rubber galoshes to keep out the snow. While they're not Moscow high fashion—you'd get funny looks if you wore these on the metro—Russians wear them at their *dachas* (country cottages) and traffic police pull them on for winter shifts. You can buy them at Moscow markets and stores including Mir Shersti. You should purchase a pair two sizes larger than normal because the wool shrinks when it gets wet.

NORTHERN OUTSKIRTS

DEPARTMENT STORES AND MALLS

Kalinka-Stockmann. This major Finnish chain store occupies three floors of the Metropolis Mall, combining several departments: men's, women's, and kids' clothing, houseware, linens, electronics, and footwear—all of notable quality. ✉ *16, bldg. 4 Leningradskoye Shosse (inside Metropolis mall), Northern Outskirts* ◔ *Daily 10 am–11 pm* Ⓜ *Voikovskaya.*

SPECIALTY STORES

ARTS AND CRAFTS

Culture Pavilion. Part of the Soviet showpiece that's now called the All-Russian Exhibition Center, the elegant white Pavilion No. 66 stocks a huge range of crafts, including Turkmen embroidery, earthenware pots from Suzdal, and carved stone animals from Perm. ✉ *Prospect Mira, All-Russian Exhibition Center, Northern Outskirts* ☎ *495/544–3400* Ⓜ *VDNKh.*

FARMERS' MARKETS

Preobrazhensky Rynok. This historic market is worth visiting more for its picturesque setting than its produce. It stands next to the Old Believers' church and cemetery and is surrounded by high walls topped with towers. Stalls sell household goods, such as saucepans and blankets, as well as food. You can also buy felt boots, or valenki, here in winter. The

Russian Markets

Rynoks (outdoor markets) are places to find some strange and delicious foods. Look for lumpy red *churchkhela*, a kind of Georgian candy made from walnuts and grape juice. Stalls sell piles of bright-pink pickled garlic and strings of dried wild mushrooms. In fall, the berry selection might include rose hips; orange *oblepikha*, or sea buckthorn; and *brusnika*, or cowberry. You can also sample unfamiliar fruits including the small red plum, *kizil*, or Cornelian cherry, and aromatic green fruit *feikhua* (feijoa), a citrus fruit with an interior that tastes like strawberry.

■ TIP→ Bargaining often takes place at food stalls since usually no price is shown for goods. Ask *SkOlko stOit?* or "how much is it?" If the price sounds too high, say the number of rubles you think is reasonable. If the offer is refused, and you don't like the price, say *Nyet, dOrogo,* or "no, it's expensive," and turn away. The trader may then tell you, *Dlya vas skidka,* or "you get a discount." You'll likely receive a realistic price then.

Moscow's fresh-food markets may be popular with consumers, but not all of their owners have been on the correct side of the city's tightly knit political and business establishment, leading to forced closings in some cases.

covered section of the market is rather dingy and lacking in atmosphere. ✉ *Preobrazhensky val 17, Northern Outskirts* Ⓜ *Preobrazhenskaya.*

FOOD
Bulochka Brioche. A much cheaper alternative for bread than Volkonsky, the Bulochka Brioche chain sells crusty olive bread and baguettes in kiosks outside metro stations. ✉ *Gruzinsky Val, outside the Circle Line exit of Belorusskaya metro station, Northern Outskirts* Ⓜ *Belorusskaya* ☏ *No phone* ✉ *36 Propect Mira, Northern Outskirts* ☏ *No phone* Ⓜ *Prospect Mira.*

SOUTHERN OUTSKIRTS

SPECIALTY STORES
FARMERS' MARKETS
Danilovsky Rynok. A bustling outdoor market surrounds a covered hall where you can buy meat in all its shapes and forms (including halal meat); many kinds of pickles and spices; and even blue, white, and gold Uzbek tea sets. Outside, fruits and vegetables for sale are stacked up in pyramids. In fall, you can buy berries and mushrooms. Also on sale are flowers, woven baskets, and hand-knit wool socks. ✉ *74 Mytnaya, Southern Outskirts* ☏ *495/958–1725 or 495/958–5319* ⊙ *Sat.–Mon. 8–7, Sun. 8–6* Ⓜ *Tulskaya.*

EASTERN OUTSKIRTS

DEPARTMENT STORES AND MALLS

Atrium. A giant shopping mall in front of the Kursk station, Atrium is yet another symbol of modern Moscow. With everything under one roof, including numerous clothing stores (2010's opening of Japanese clothing outlet UNIQLO was a particular hit), a perfume "supermarket," a huge grocery store, a casino, and the Formula Kino movie theater. There are also a trendy Italian café and a sushi bar. ⊠ *33 Zemlyanoi Val, Eastern Outskirts* ☎ *495/970–1555* Ⓜ *Kurskaya.*

SPECIALTY STORES

SOUVENIRS

Izmailovsky Flea Market. This market is a part of Izmailovsky Vernisazh— an arts-and-crafts shopping arcade that opened in the early '90s, when private business became legal again, and artists from Moscow and nearby cities were able to put their works on sale. You could easily spend a whole day at Moscow's Izmailovo (flea market), with its reasonably priced souvenirs, handicrafts, used books, and Soviet memorabilia (such as authentic army belts and gas masks). *Matryoshki* (nesting dolls) come in both classic and updated styles: some bear likenesses of Soviet and Russian leaders; others depict American basketball stars and Barack Obama. Nearby is the former royal residence of Izmailovo, inside an old hunting preserve. The flea market is open daily 9–6, but many stalls are only open on weekends. It's best to go early. ⊠ *Izmailovskoe shosse, building 73-G (take the metro to Partizanskaya station and follow crowds as you exit), Eastern Outskirts* ⊕ *www.moscow-vernisage.com.*

WESTERN OUTSKIRTS

SPECIALTY STORES

CLOTHING

Valentin Yudashkin Trading House. Make an appearance at Valentin Yudashkin for the latest in Russian women's haute couture. Many Russian celebrities prefer Yudashkin's clothes to those of Western designers. Look for extravagant evening dresses, jeans embellished with Swarowski crystals, and golden accessories, all tailored to attract the eye of Russia's rich and fabulous. ⊠ *19 Kutuzovsky pr., Western Outskirts* ☎ *495/240–1189* Ⓜ *Kievskaya or Kutuzovskaya.*

Evropeisky. This huge, well-laid-out mall has a European theme (note the name) that is expressed through decor that includes a conspicuous sculpture of a euro sign in the front of a department store. You'll find branches of Britain's Marks & Spencer and Topshop as well as Spain's Bershka and Zara. The romantic and feminine Russian brands Sultanna Frantsuzova and Sunie Li both have stores here. Another possible reason to visit Evropeysky is the T-shirt vending machine on the third floor: that's the way young Russian designer Antonina Shapovalova markets her designs, which have provocative pro-Russian slogans such as "Yura, thank you, the space is ours" (a reference to Yuri Gagarin, the first man in space) and "The Russians are coming." ⊠ *2 Ploshchad Kievskogo Vokzala, Western Outskirts* ☎ *495/925–3444* Ⓜ *Kievskaya.*

MATRYOSHKI

Perhaps surprisingly, nesting dolls, or *matryoshki*, date only to the 19th century; they are said to be based on a Japanese tradition. The center for matryoshka-making is Sergiyev Posad outside Moscow. In Soviet times, a matryoshka was used as the symbol of the state-owned travel agency, Intourist, which had a monopoly on organizing trips for foreigners (its name is short for *inostranny*, or foreign) and ran its own hotels. It still exists as a travel agency, but the hotels have all closed down. Consequently, Russians came to think of the dolls chiefly as gifts for foreign visitors. In many Russian homes, you will find a simple matryoshka doll wearing a head scarf, but the elaborately decorated dolls on sale at the Arbat are strictly for export.

Imperial Porcelain. Get yourself some fine Russian porcelain at this factory's chain store. Founded in the 18th century by the order of Queen Elizaveta, daughter of Peter the Great, Imperial (also known as Lomonosov) sold porcelain to the Russian royal families before the revolution. Dining tableware and collectible sculptures come in styles that include a classic cobalt fishnet design as well as prints inspired by Malevich, Kandinsky, and other members of the Russian avant-garde. Many of the items here would make tasteful and truly authentic gifts. ⊠ *9 Kutuzovsky, Western Outskirts* ☏ *499/243–7501 or 499/243–1752* ⊕ *www.ipm.ru/enstart* ☼ *Daily 10–10* Ⓜ *Kievskaya.*

FARMERS' MARKETS

Dorogomilovsky Rynok. This large covered hall is beyond the outdoor Veshchevoy Rynok (literally, "Market of Things," which is certainly an apt name). Inside are rows of vendors hawking homemade cheese and milk products, honey, flowers, and produce of all kinds. Against one wall are sellers of pickled goods, an understandably popular form of conservation in this land of long winters; you may want to sample some of their cabbage and carrot slaws, salted cucumbers, or spiced eggplant or garlic. Many Moscow chefs buy ingredients here. ⊠ *10 Mozhaisky Val ul., near Kiev station, Western Outskirts* ☏ *No phone* ☼ *Daily 7 am–8 pm* Ⓜ *Kievskaya.*

Side Trips from Moscow

WORD OF MOUTH

"The attractions in the Golden Ring are not so much the urban architecture but the towns' kremlins and monasteries, which are superb. Suzdal is small, more village than town, and is quite delightful."

—wasleys

Updated by
Tom Parfitt

The river valleys east and north of Moscow hold a unique realm you might call Russia's Capital-That-Might-Have-Been—Suzdalia, the region that encompassed the historic centers of Rostov, Vladimir, Suzdal, and Yaroslavl. These small towns, all within easy striking distance of Moscow, were where the Russian nation was born nearly a millennium ago and, consequently, are home to some of the country's most beautiful churches and monasteries, romantic kremlins (fortresses), and famous works of art, such as Andrei Rublyov's frescoes in the cathedral at Vladimir.

Many of these towns and districts have more than 10 centuries of history to share, but their story really begins early in the 12th century, when Prince Yuri Dolgoruky, son of Vladimir Monomakh, the Grand Prince of Kiev, was given control over the northeastern outpost of what was then Kievan Rus' (the early predecessor of modern-day Russia and Ukraine). Dolgoruky established his power and authority, and founded the towns that would become Pereslavl-Zalessky and Kostroma. He also built frontier outposts to guard against his neighbors, including one on the southwest border, called Moscow.

Yuri Dolgoruky's son, Andrei Bogolyubsky, amassed considerable power within Kievan Rus', centered on his inherited lands of Suzdalia. He made Vladimir his capital and built up its churches and monasteries to rival those of Kiev, the capital of Kievan Rus'. In 1169, unhappy with the pattern of dynastic succession in Kiev, Bogolyubsky sent his and allied troops to sack Kiev and placed his son on the throne as grand prince. From that point forward, political and ecclesiastical power began to flow toward the northeastern region of Rus'.

If a Mongol invasion hadn't arrived a century later in 1237, Vladimir might have continued to grow in power and be the capital of Russia today. But invade the Mongols did, and within three years every town in the region was nearly destroyed; the region remained subjugated for more than 200 years. Moscow, meanwhile, with the cunning it's still known for today, slowly rose to prominence by becoming tax (or tribute) collector for the Mongols. Ivan Kalita ("Ivan Moneybags") was a particularly proficient go-between, and, as Mongol power receded in the 14th century, he began gathering together the lands surrounding Moscow, beginning with Vladimir.

The ancient Russian towns north and east of Moscow that make up what is most commonly called the "Golden Ring" seem quite unassuming now in comparison to the sprawling, bustling capital. Before the Mongol invasion, Rostov, Vladimir, Suzdal, and Yaroslavl were the centers of Russian political, cultural, and economic life. Although they

TOP REASONS TO GO

Architecture: These towns are home to some of the finest examples of Russian architecture; the oldest, most beautiful kremlins; and religious buildings decorated with ancient frescoes.

Experience the "Real" Russia: A visit to a quiet provincial town like Vladimir or Rostov is markedly different from the bustle of Moscow's city. The towns' proximity to Moscow makes them easy for day or overnight trips.

Onion Domes: The Troitse-Sergieva Lavra's Cathedral of the Assumption has some of the most beautiful and most photographed blue and gold onion domes, and is also the main pilgrimage site for all of Russia.

Tchaikovsky and Tolstoy's Homes: Visit the home in Klin where Russia's best-known classical music composer wrote *The Nutcracker* and *Sleeping Beauty*. See the desk where Tolstoy penned *Anna Karenina* and *War and Peace* in his home in Yasnaya Polyana.

Heritage: Steep yourself in the history of this land of princes: it's one of the birthplaces of modern Russia and a cradle of the Russian Orthodox religion.

may lack some of the amenities you can easily find in Moscow, they have a provincial charm and aura of history that make them an important stop for anyone seeking to become acquainted with Mother Russia.

7

ORIENTATION AND PLANNING

GETTING ORIENTED

With some exceptions, what you'll be traveling to see are churches and monasteries—the statement-making structures that princes, metropolitans (leaders of the Orthodox church), and merchants in old Russia built to display their largesse and power. Because most civil and residential buildings until the 18th century were constructed from wood, these religious buildings, constructed of stone, have best survived the ravages of time, invading armies, and fire. Today, many are being returned to their original, ecclesiastical purposes, but most are still museums. In either instance, neglect and funding shortages have taken their toll on preservation and restoration efforts, and at times it can be difficult to imagine these historic monuments in their original glory.

Moscow Environs. Don't worry if your schedule's tight. Day trips from Moscow bring spectacular sites within reach. At Sergiev Posad, a working monastery, you can see how Russian Orthodoxy has clawed back a place for itself in post-Soviet society. Tolstoy admirers will get a better measure of the man with a visit to his peaceful estate at Yasnaya Polyana.

The Northern Golden Ring. Here lies a scattering of ancient towns—Pereslavl-Zalessky, Rostov, and Yaroslavl. The first two are pretty and small, and the third is a lively city where the centuries of sights can be rooted out among all the trappings of modern, urban Russia.

The Eastern Golden Ring. Rich in stunningly varied churches and monasteries, Suzdal (population 12,000) is a strong contender for most beautiful town in Russia. Vladimir is a worthy neighbor, especially given the presence of the Church of the Intercession on the Nerl, a few miles away.

PLANNING

WHEN TO GO

To see the monasteries, churches, and kremlins of the region to the best advantage you should try to make your visits in spring or summer. Winter visits to the Golden Ring can be magical, but in December and January it gets dark not long after 3 pm. Avoid late March, when the snow turns into slush.

PLANNING YOUR TIME

A few of the attractions of the Moscow Environs section, such as the Abramtsevo Estate Museum and Sergiev-Posad, can be combined in one visit, but most of the sights of this region will require individual day trips. The towns of the Golden Ring lie on two main routes that most visitors travel as two separate excursions—north of Moscow to Sergiev-Posad, Pereslavl-Zalessky, Rostov, and Yaroslavl; and east of Moscow to Vladimir and Suzdal.

GETTING HERE AND AROUND
BOAT TRAVEL

Cruises from Moscow to St. Petersburg, along the Moscow-Volga canal, visit just one city of the Golden Ring, Yaroslavl.

BUS TRAVEL

Though it's not as comfortable as traveling by train, the bus can be a decent way to travel as long as it's not the height of summer, when the vehicles can be very stuffy. Buses run on direct routes to all the towns of the Golden Ring. And, to get to two towns—Pereslavl-Zalessky and Suzdal—by public transport, you'll need to travel by bus at least part of the way.

For short-distance travel between towns, buses can't be beat. But buses are the most unreliable form of long-distance transport. Be sure to check schedules before you leave Moscow to make sure that there are plenty of return buses if you need one.

FARES & SCHEDULES Pereslavl-Zalessky is a three-hour journey from Moscow's Central Bus Station (Tsentralny Avtovokzal). There are four buses daily that run between the capital and Pereslavl-Zalessky; many other buses travel farther on and simply stop here. There are also four buses each day between Pereslavl-Zalessky and Sergiev-Posad (about a one-hour ride).

From Moscow it's a five-hour trip to Rostov and a 1- or 1½-hour trip to Sergiev-Posad. Vladimir is four hours and Yaroslavl is six hours from Moscow. Just one daily bus goes directly to Suzdal from Moscow, departing at 5 pm and taking five hours. It's best to take the train or bus to Vladimir and then change to a bus (running nearly every hour) between Vladimir and Suzdal.

Bus Contacts Central Bus Station (✉ *2 ul. Uralskaya, Moscow* ☎ *499/748–8029 or 499/748–8964* ⊕ *www.mostransavto.ru/?page=avshelk*).

CAR TRAVEL

For the towns of the Golden Ring, which lie relatively close to one another and are connected by some of Russia's best paved roads, travel by car is by far the most flexible option. There's no problem getting gas in these towns.

TAXI TRAVEL

You'll usually have no trouble getting a taxi at a train or bus station in these towns, which is important, because the stations are often far from the town center. Most of the towns are small enough to be navigated easily on foot, but a taxi may be a desirable alternative to short bus trips (e.g., from Vladimir out to Bogolyubovo, from Vladimir to Suzdal, or from Tula to Yasnaya Polyana).

TRAIN TRAVEL

The easiest way to get to the towns of the Golden Ring is by train. Trains going from Moscow's Yaroslavsky train station will take you to Yaroslavl and Rostov. Trains from Moscow's Kursky train station run to Vladimir several times a day, while trains for Nizhny Novgorod always stop in Vladimir. Unless you speak some Russian you might find it easier to ask a hotel concierge to check the train schedule for you; buying the tickets at a train station is hardly ever a problem even for foreigners.

There are plenty of trains running on the main routes (Moscow–Yaroslavl and Moscow–Nizhny Novgorod) on which most all the towns in this region lie, so it's quite easy to travel between towns here, as well as to and from Moscow. Two types of trains will get you to most of these towns: *elektrichkas* (suburban commuter trains) and normal long-distance trains. In addition to being cheaper, elektrichkas run more frequently. But they are also a bit less comfortable, and there's no reserved seating. Check with a local travel agent in Moscow or at the station itself for train schedules. With the exception of traveling by elektrichka at busy times (Friday evenings and weekends), you should not have trouble getting a ticket the same day you wish to travel.

TRAIN FARES AND SCHEDULES

Most elektrichkas will stop in all the towns listed here; it's best to double-check, however, which stops your long-distance train makes.

Commuter trains to Klin, site of Tchaikovsky's House Museum, depart from Moscow's Leningrad station. For the New Jerusalem Monastery, take an elektrichka from Moscow's Rizhsky station and get off at Istra. From there take any local bus to the Muzey (museum) stop. Rostov is four hours by long-distance train from Yaroslavsky station in Moscow, and five hours by elektrichka (changing in Aleksandrov). Elektrichkas also run regularly between Rostov and Yaroslavl (originating in Moscow's Yaroslav station); the trip lasts 1–1½ hours. Sergiev-Posad is 1½ hours by elektrichka from Yaroslavsky station. Vladimir is a three- to four-hour train ride by long-distance train from Moscow's Kursky station. There is no train directly to Suzdal. To get there, take the train to Vladimir, then catch one of the frequent buses to Suzdal that run every hour from Vladimir bus station. Although there's a train station near

Yasnaya Polyana, the commuter trains departing from Moscow's Kursky station run only to Tula. The trip takes about three hours. Yaroslavl is five hours by long-distance train from Moscow's Yaroslavsky station.

RESTAURANTS

There are still few private restaurants in many of these town, largely because Russians themselves do not dine out that frequently. The most reliable restaurants are in hotels catering to tourists or, occasionally, in downtown locations near main tourist sights. This is slowly changing, and some of the restaurants outside hotels can be quite cozy. Happily, restaurant prices here are considerably lower than in Moscow *as reflected in the What It Costs chart, below.*

HOTELS

None of the towns covered in this section has a long list of hotels, let alone good, tourist-class options, although basic amenities are not usually a problem. The one exception is Suzdal, which has almost a dozen small private guesthouses. As with restaurants, these hotels' prices are far below Moscow levels.

Hotel reviews have been abbreviated in this book. For expanded reviews, visit Fodors.com.

WHAT IT COSTS IN RUBLES					
	¢	$	$$	$$$	$$$$
Restaurants	under 125R	125R–250R	251R–375R	376R–500R	over 500R
Hotels	under 1,500R	1,500R–2,000R	2,001R–2,500R	2,501R–3,000R	over 3,000R

Restaurant prices are for a main course at dinner. Hotel prices are for two people in a standard double room in high season, excluding tax.

TOURS

There are several local and international travel agents who specialize in tours to the Golden Ring and Moscow environs. Seattle-based Mir Corporation is particularly good for individual travelers and also conducts regular tours to Russia that include the Golden Ring. Moscow-based Patriarshy Dom Tours offers a variety of one-day and multiday tours throughout the Golden Ring at very reasonable rates.

Tour Contacts Mir Corporation (☎ *800/424–7289* ⊕ *www.mircorp.com*).
Patriarshy Dom Tours (☎ *495/795–0927 in Moscow; 650/678–7076 in the U.S.* ⊕ *www.russiatravel-pdtours.netfirms.com*).

VISITOR INFORMATION

There's no regional tourist office dealing with the Golden Ring region. Any questions should be directed to travel agencies and guided tour companies in Moscow. The State Historical Architecture and Art Vladimir-Suzdal Museum-Reserve Web site (⊕ *www.museum.vladimir.ru*) has some interesting information on Vladimir and Suzdal.

GREAT ITINERARIES

IF YOU HAVE 1 OR 2 DAYS
The **Tchaikovsky's House Museum in Klin, Leo Tolstoy's Museum in Yasnaya Polyana, Sergiev-Posad,** and **Abramtsevo Estate Museum** can all be easily visited as separate day trips from Moscow.

If you have two days to explore the towns of the Golden Ring, drive or take a morning train to **Vladimir.** Explore the town, being sure to take in the Church of the Intercession on the Nerl, then travel on to **Suzdal,** where you can stay overnight and spend a day tackling its delight-ful—and walkable—sights. Return to Moscow via Vladimir late in the day.

Alternatively, take a morning train to **Yaroslavl** and spend the day and night there. The next morning catch a return train on the same route, stopping off in **Rostov** (1½ hours from Yaroslavl) to spend the day before catching a late-afternoon train back to Moscow.

IF YOU HAVE 3 OR 4 DAYS
Follow any of the itineraries above. But for the Vladimir and Suzdal trip, devote another full day to Suzdal. For the Yaroslavl and Rostov trip, overnight in **Rostov** and then stop for several hours in **Pereslavl-Zalessky** before returning to Moscow.

MOSCOW ENVIRONS

7

Within easy distance of Moscow are several sights of interest, including two monasteries: the New Jerusalem Monastery near Istra and the Troitse-Sergieva Lavra in Sergiev-Posad. Russian-culture buffs may want to explore Tchaikovsky's former home in Klin, Tolstoy's estate in Yasnaya Polyana, and the Abramtsevo Estate Museum, a beacon for Russian artists in the 19th century.

TCHAIKOVSKY'S HOUSE MUSEUM IN KLIN
ДОМ-МУЗЕЙ ЧАЙКОВСКОГО В КЛИНУ

84 km (52 mi) northwest of Moscow via Leningradskoye shosse and M10.

GETTING HERE AND AROUND
To get here from Moscow, take Bus 437 from the Rechnoy Vokzal metro stop, or a commuter train from Leningradsky railway station to Klin.

From Klin railway station, you can take Bus 5, 30, 37, or 40 to Tchaikovsky's House Museum.

EXPLORING
Visiting **Tchaikovsky's House Museum in Klin** is a must for classical-music lovers, despite the town's relatively remote location. Pyotr Tchaikovsky (1840–93) spent a total of eight years in Klin, where he wrote Symphony No. 6 (*Pathétique*) and two of his three ballets, *Sleeping Beauty* and *The Nutcracker*. He resided at a series of addresses, but this was his last home. It's a typical, wooden residential building of the late 19th century, eclectic in style. Its standout features are the lantern-shaped balcony with stained-glass windows and a tower-shaped roof.

Russia's best-known composer left this house for the last time on October 7, 1893, for St. Petersburg, where he performed his last concert before his death on November 6 of that year. Less than a year after his death, the composer's brother, Modest Tchaikovsky, transformed the house into a museum. A gifted playwright and translator, Modest also played an outstanding role in preserving his brother's heritage. He preserved the original appearance of the second-floor rooms, and secured personal belongings, photographs, and a unique library of some 2,000 volumes. Some of the original scores, drafts, and letters that Modest collected are now displayed in Klin. The centerpiece of the museum is Tchaikovsky's Becker piano, on which only renowned musicians are permitted to play on special occasions. During World War II the house suffered major damage when the Nazis turned the first floor into a bike garage, and the second-floor rooms into soldiers' barracks. In the late 1940s the museum underwent major renovations, and a brick building with a concert hall was constructed next to the composer's house. The finalists of the annual Tchaikovsky International Competition of Young Musicians (held in May or June) perform in this Soviet-era hall. Additionally, on the anniversary of the composer's birth (May 7) and death (November 6) memorial concerts are held in the hall. Tchaikovsky's music plays continuously in the museum. ■**TIP**➜ **The museum cafeteria serves a traditional Russian tea service from a samovar.** ✉ *48 ul. Tchaikovskovo, Klin* ☎ *49624/5–8196* ⊕ *www.cbook.ru/tchaikovsky* ✉ *280R* ☾ *Mon., Tues., and Fri.–Sun. 10–6, ticket office closes at 5. Closed last Mon. of month.*

NEW JERUSALEM MONASTERY
НОВО-ИЕРУСАЛИМСКИЙ МОНАСТЫРЬ

65 km (40 mi) northwest of Moscow via Volokolamskoye shosse and the M9.

GETTING HERE AND AROUND
The monastery is near the town of Istra, at a bend in the river of the same name. This is not the most visited locale in Russia, and it's included in the standard offerings of tourist agencies only in summer. If you can't book a tour and are feeling adventurous, you can reach the monastery by commuter train—take one from the Rizhsky railway station to Istra or Novy Ierusalim station. From there, it's a 20-minute walk.

Trains leave from Riga station and take about an hour and a half. Or, you could ask your concierge to arrange for a car and driver to drive you there. Be sure to pack your lunch—the best you'll find in Istra is an occasional cafeteria or outdoor café.

EXPLORING
Far from the crowds, the captivating Russian countryside surrounding the **New Jerusalem Monastery** (Novoierusalimsky Monastyr) is a marvelous setting for walks and excursions. The monastery was founded in 1652 by Nikon (1605–81), patriarch of the Russian Orthodox Church. It lies on roughly the same longitude as Jerusalem, and its main cathedral, **Voskresensky Sobor** (Resurrection Cathedral), is modeled after the Church of the Holy Sepulchre in Jerusalem. Nikon's objective in

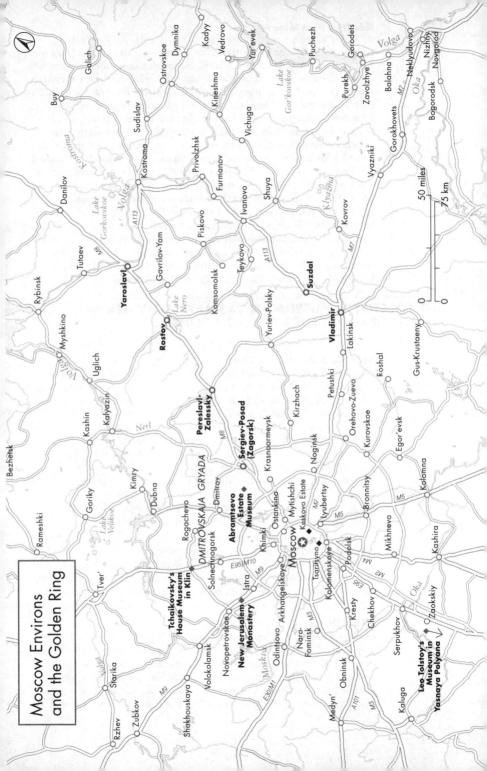

re-creating the original Jerusalem in Russia was to glorify the power of the Russian Orthodox Church and at the same time elevate his own position as its head. It was Nikon who initiated the great church reforms in the 17th century that eventually led to the *raskol* (schism) that launched the Old Believer sects of the Russian Orthodox faith. As a reformer he was progressive and enlightened, but his lust for power was his undoing. In 1658, before the monastery was even finished, the patriarch quarreled with Tsar Alexei Mikhailovich, claiming that the Church was ultimately superior to the State. Nikon was ultimately defrocked and banished to faraway Ferapontov Monastery, in the Vologda region, some 400 km (246 mi) north of Moscow. He died in virtual exile in 1681, and was then buried in the monastery that was supposed to have glorified his power. You can find his crypt in the Church of St. John the Baptist, which is actually inside the Resurrection Cathedral. Ironically, the same church commission that defrocked Patriarch Nikon later voted to institute his reforms. ⊠ *On the banks of the river Istra, 2 ul. Sovetskaya, Istra* ☎ *495/994–5643* ⊠ *Monastery grounds free; small fees for exhibits* ⊙ *Tues.–Sun. 10–5. Closed last Fri. of month.*

LEO TOLSTOY'S MUSEUM IN YASNAYA POLYANA
МУЗЕЙ ЛЬВА ТОЛСТОГО В ЯСНОЙ ПОЛЯНЕ

190 km (118 mi) south of Moscow via Simferopolskoye shosse and M2.

GETTING HERE AND AROUND

A visit to the estate requires the whole day, because the trip from Moscow takes 2½ to 3 hours. First head to the industrial town of Tula, some 170 km (105 mi) south of Moscow along Simferopolskoye shosse. After you pass through Tula's southern outskirts, Tolstoy's estate, 14 km (9 mi) away, is easy to find if you're taking a car, thanks to clear signs in Russian and English; the roads, however, are notoriously bad. If you are traveling in the summer, avoid driving on Saturday morning as there is often heavy traffic due to hordes of Muscovites traveling to their *dachas* (summer cottages). You can also get to Tula by commuter train from Moscow's Kursk station, or by bus from metro stations Domodedovskaya, Prazhskaya, or ul. Akademika Yangelya; once in Tula, take a bus traveling to Shchyokino from the station at prospekt Lenina.

If you plan to explore the grounds of Yasnaya Polyana independently you should strive to arrive there as early in the morning as possible, especially on Friday and weekends, to avoid busloads of tourists and crowds of newlyweds who flock to places such as this on their wedding day. A guided tour of the museums and the grounds, however, does give a better idea of all the important sights and Tolstoy's favorite spots.

EXPLORING

Leo Tolstoy's Museum in Yasnaya Polyana. More than 50 years of Leo Tolstoy's life (1828–1910) was spent at Yasnaya Polyana, where he was born, wrote his most significant works, undertook social experiments, and was buried. Here he freed his serfs and taught peasant children at a school that he opened, attempting to transfer his ideal of a perfect world of universal equality to reality. Disappointed with his way of life and nobleman status, he decided at the age of 82 to depart from home forever, venturing out shortly before his death in October 1910.

In his home's upstairs dining room, you're greeted by numerous portraits of the Tolstoy aristocratic dynasty. Under their eyes, Tolstoy held significant social discussions with his family and his many visitors. Next-door is the study where Tolstoy wrote *Anna Karenina* and *War and Peace* at his father's Persian desk. Tolstoy seemed to prefer moving around his house to work on different books, however: another room downstairs was also used as a study. This is usually the last room on a visit to the main house. In November 1910, the writer's body lay here in state as some 5,000 mourners passed to pay their last respects.

The far wing of the building houses a literary museum dedicated to Tolstoy's writing career. Drawings and prints produced by Tolstoy's contemporaries, derived from the plots and characters of his novels, as well as Tolstoy's original manuscripts are displayed in the six halls. A path from the main house into the forest leads to Tolstoy's simple, unadorned grave. On the edge of a ravine in the Stary Zakaz forest, the site was a favorite place of Tolstoy's and is now a popular pilgrimage destination for wedding parties. The walk to the grave takes about 20 minutes.

The estate-turned-museum is run by Tolstoy's great-great-grandson Vladimir Tolstoy, who is striving to turn it into a major cultural center. His concept is to purge the great author's home of modern technology (not that there's much modern technology there now) and turn the area back into a working 19th-century estate. Around this "living museum," Tolstoy plans to construct a tourist complex with a hotel, restaurants, and parking lots—none of which now exist.

The cafeteria and the bookstore are directly opposite the main entrance. ⊠ *Near Tula Yasnaya Polyana* ☎ *4872/39–3599 or 4872/47–6712* ⊕ *www.yasnayapolyana.ru* 🖼 *20R, foreign-language guided tours 2,400R (3,600R at weekends) for a group of up to 8 people. Lower prices apply for bigger groups. Tours run throughout the day, until 3:30 pm* ⊙ *Tues.–Sun. 10–4. Closed last Wed. of month.*

WHERE TO EAT AND STAY

$ ✕ **Voronka Cafe.** Only 1½ km (1 mi) from Yasnaya Polyana on the way to Tula, Voronka is a good way to end a trip to Tolstoy's estate. The menu has an extensive selection of Russian dishes, including *solyanka* (a sharp-tasting soup of vegetables and meat or fish), borscht, *shashlyk* (kebabs), blini, and *ikra* (caviar). ⊠ *152 Orlovskoye shosse* ☎ *4872/23–014* 🖃 *No credit cards.*

$$$$ 🏨 **Premiera.** The first Western-style hotel in Tula opened in 2004; the petite hotel, close to the center, has seven rooms and two suites. ⊠ *3 ul. Maksimovskovo, Tula* ☎ *4872/49–0262 or 4872/49–0368* ⊕ *www.premieratula.ru* 🛏 *7 rooms, 2 suites* ⚑ *In-room: a/c, no safe. In-hotel: bar.*

EASTERN EUROPEAN (left margin label for Voronka Cafe)

SERGIEV-POSAD (ZAGORSK) СЕРГИЕВ ПОСАД (ЗАГОРСК)

Fodor's Choice
★

75 km (47 mi) northeast of Moscow via Yaroslavskoye shosse and the M8.

GETTING HERE AND AROUND

The best way to visit the town is to join an organized tour, because it's a full-day affair out of Moscow. The cost usually includes lunch in addition to a guided tour and transportation. You can also visit on your own by taking the commuter train from Moscow's Yaroslavsky station. The ride takes about two hours. This is much less expensive than an organized tour, but far from hassle-free. You can also take bus 388 from VDNKh metro station. If you choose either of these options, be sure to pack your own lunch, because Sergiev-Posad's few restaurants fill up fast with prebooked tourist groups, especially in summer.

EXPLORING

Sergiev-Posad is a comfortable and popular day trip from Moscow. The town's chief attraction is the Troitse-Sergieva Lavra, which for 500 years has been the most important center of pilgrimage in Russia and remains one of the most beautiful of all monasteries—the fairy-tale gold and azure onion domes of its Cathedral of the Assumption are among the most photographed in the country. Until 1930 the town was known as Sergiev, after the monastery's founder, and in 1991 it was officially renamed Sergiev-Posad. But the Soviet name of Zagorsk—in honor of a Bolshevik who was assassinated in 1919—has stuck, and you're as likely to hear the town and the monastery itself called one as the other.

The ride to Sergiev-Posad takes you through a lovely stretch of Russian countryside, dotted with colorful wooden cottages. As you approach the town, you see the sad and monolithic apartment buildings of more recent times. Then, peeking out above the hills, the monastery's golden cupolas and soft-blue bell tower come into view.

■ TIP→ Be sure to dress appropriately for your visit to the functioning monastery: men are expected to remove their hats, and women are required to wear below-knee-length skirts or slacks (never shorts) and bring something to cover their heads.

The **Troitse-Sergieva Lavra** (*Trinity Monastery of St. Sergius*) was founded in 1340 by Sergius of Radonezh (1314–92), who would later become Russia's patron saint. The site rapidly became the nucleus of a small medieval settlement, and in 1550 the imposing white walls were built to enclose the complex of buildings, whose towers and gilded domes make it a smaller, but still spectacular, version of Moscow's Kremlin. The monastery was a Russian stronghold during the Time of Troubles (the Polish assault on Moscow in the early 17th century), and, less than a century later, Peter the Great (1672–1725) took refuge here during a bloody revolt of the *streltsy* (Russian militia), which took the lives of some of his closest relatives and advisers. It remained the heart of Holy Russia until 1920, when the Bolsheviks closed down most monasteries and shipped many monks to Siberia. Troitse-Sergieva Lavra itself became a museum. During World War II, however, in an attempt to mobilize the country and stir up patriotism, the Soviet government

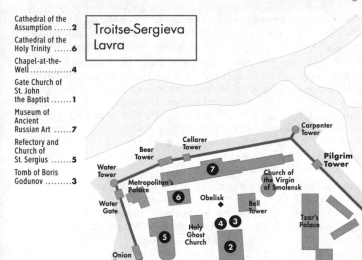

Troitse-Sergieva Lavra

gained the support of the Orthodox Church by returning to religious purposes some of the Church property that had been confiscated earlier, including the Troitse-Sergieva Lavra. Today the churches are again open for worship, and there's a flourishing theological college here. Until the reopening in 1988 of the Danilovsky (St. Daniel) Monastery in Moscow, this monastery was the residence of the patriarch and administrative center of the Russian Orthodox Church.

You enter the monastery through the archway of the **Gate Church of St. John the Baptist,** which was erected in the late 17th century and is decorated with frescoes telling the life story of St. Sergius. One of the most important historic events in his life occurred prior to 1380, when the decisive Russian victory in the Battle of Kulikovo led to the end of Mongol rule in Russia. Before leading his troops off to battle, Prince Dmitri Donskoy sought the blessing of the peace-loving monk Sergius, a move that is generally thought to have greatly aided the Russian victory.

Although all of the monastery's cathedrals vie for your attention, the dominating structure is the massive, blue-domed, and gold-starred, **Cathedral of the Assumption** (Uspensky Sobor) in the center. Built between 1554 and 1585 with money donated by Tsar Ivan the Terrible (1530–84)—purportedly in an attempt to atone for killing his own son in a fit of rage—it was modeled after the Kremlin's Uspensky Sobor. Its interior contains frescoes and an 18th-century iconostasis. Among the artists to work on it was Simon Ushakov, a well-known icon painter from Moscow. The cathedral is open for morning services.

The small building just outside the Cathedral of the Assumption (near the northwest corner) is the **tomb of Boris Godunov and his family.** Boris Godunov, who ruled as regent after Ivan the Terrible's death, died suddenly in 1605 of natural causes. This was during the Polish attack on Moscow led by the False Dmitri, the first of many impostors to claim he was the son of Ivan. The death of Godunov facilitated the invaders' victory, after which his family was promptly murdered. This explains why Godunov was not bestowed the honor of burial in the Kremlin normally granted to tsars.

Opposite Boris Godunov's tomb is a tiny and colorful chapel, the **Chapel-at-the-Well,** built in 1644 above a fountain that is said to work miracles. According to legend, the spring here appeared during the Polish Siege (1608–10), when the monastery bravely held out for 16 months against the foreign invaders (this time led by the second False Dmitri). You can make a wish by washing your face and hands in its charmed waters. Towering 86 meters (285 feet) next to the chapel is the five-tier baroque belfry. It was built in the 18th century to a design by the master of St. Petersburg baroque, Bartolomeo Rastrelli.

Along the southern wall of the monastery, to your far left as you enter, is the 17th-century **Refectory and Church of St. Sergius.** The church is at the eastern end, topped by a single gilt dome. The long building of the refectory, whose colorful facade adds to the vivid richness of the monastery's architecture, is where, in times past, pilgrims from near and far gathered to eat on feast days. The pink building just beyond the refectory is the metropolitan's residence.

Across the path from the residence is the white-stone **Cathedral of the Holy Trinity** (Troitsky Sobor), built in the 15th century over the tomb of St. Sergius. Over the centuries it has received many precious gifts from the powerful and wealthy rulers who have made the pilgrimage to the church of Russia's patron saint. The icons inside were created by famous master Andrei Rublyov and one of his disciples, Danil Chorny. Rublyov's celebrated *Holy Trinity,* now on display at the Tretyakov Gallery in Moscow, originally hung here; the church's version is a copy. The interior's beauty is mainly due to its 17th-century gilded iconostasis (which separates the sanctuary from the altar and body of the church). The upper tier of the church was once used by monks as a manuscript library. A continual service in memoriam to St. Sergius is held all day, every day.

The vestry, the building behind the Cathedral of the Holy Trinity, houses the monastery's **Museum of Ancient Russian Art.** It's often closed for no apparent reason or open only to groups, which is yet another reason to visit Sergiev-Posad on a guided tour. The museum contains a spectacular collection of gifts presented to the monastery over the centuries. On display are precious jewels, jewel-encrusted embroideries, chalices, and censers. Next door to the vestry are two more museums, which are open to individual tourists. The first museum contains icons and icon covers, portrait art, and furniture. The other museum (on the second floor) is devoted to Russian folk art, with wooden items, toys, porcelain, and jewelry. There's also a gift shop here. ⊠ *Sergiev-Posad* 🕾 *496/540–5334* ⊕ *www.stsl.ru* 🎟 *Lavra free; museum 60R* ☉ *Lavra daily 5 am–9 pm; museum daily 10–5.*

DID YOU KNOW?

The world's first *matryoshka* (that colorful, wooden nesting doll) was designed in Sergiev-Posad at the beginning of the 20th century, and most of the matryoshkas you see for sale in Moscow and St. Petersburg are made here. The **Toy Museum** (*Muzey Igrushki*) is evidence of Sergiev-Posad's claim to fame as a center for toy making. Although it is rarely included on organized tours, it is well worth an hour of your time and is within walking distance of the Troitse-Sergieva Lavra monastery. Its toys have amused, educated, and illuminated the lives of Russian children for generations. ⊠ *136 pr. Krasnoy Armii* 🕾 *496/540–4101* 🎟 *300R* ☉ *Wed.–Sun. 10–5. Closed last Fri. of month.*

WHERE TO EAT AND STAY

$$$
CAFÉ

✕ **Russky Dvorik.** A pleasant downtown café popular with tourist groups, this spot is right across from the Lavra. Be prepared for slow service. ⊠ *134/2 ul. Krasnoy Armii, Sergiev-Posad* 🕾 *496/540–5114* ⊕ *www. russky-dvorik-restaurant.ru.*

$
EASTERN EUROPEAN

✕ **Zolotoye Koltso.** The "Golden Ring" is considered the best restaurant in town. It caters to tour groups and has a good service record for preparing basic Russian fare: a selection of salads, soups, and (mostly) meat dishes. ⊠ *121 ul. Krasnoy Armii, Sergiev-Posad* 🕾 *496/544–6517* ▭ *No credit cards.*

$$

⛺ **Hotel Aristokrat.** This redbrick hotel is in the town center on Blinnaya Gora (Pancake Hill), a five-minute walk from the Lavra. **Pros:** great views of the Lavra. **Cons:** in summer, rooms must be booked in advance. ⊠ *1A ul. Sergiyevskaya, Sergiev-Posad* 🕾 *496/547–2594 or 546–0259* ⇗ *18 rooms* ⚑ *In-room: a/c, no safe, refrigerator. In-hotel: restaurant, pool* ▭ *No credit cards.*

7

ABRAMTSEVO ESTATE MUSEUM МУЗЕЙ-УСАДЬБА АБРАМЦЕВО

61 km (38 mi) northeast of Moscow via Yaroslavskoye shosse and the M8.

GETTING HERE AND AROUND

The estate can easily be visited on the way back from Sergiev-Posad. For Russian art aficionados, however, it may be worth making it a single one-day trip. You can visit the estate on a tour or head there yourself by commuter train; take the train from Yaroslavsky station to Sergiev-Posad or Alexandrov and get off at the Abramtsevo station.

EXPLORING

The 18th-century, wooden **Abramtsevo Estate** served as the center of Russia's cultural life in two different periods of the 19th century. Its guest list from different years includes writers Nikolai Gogol and Ivan

Turgenev, opera singer Fyodor Chaliapin, and theater director Konstantin Stanislavsky. The artists Valentin Serov, Mikhail Vrubel, Ilya Repin, Viktor Vasnetsov, and Vasily Polenov were just a few of the luminaries who frequented the estate. It's easier to name those cultural figures of the 19th and early 20th centuries who have not visited Abramtsevo than all of those who have.

Until 1870 Abramtsevo belonged to Sergei Aksakov, a Slavophile who advocated the exportation of Orthodox Christianity to the West. A very religious man, Aksakov chose Abramtsevo as his residence because it was close to the Troitse-Sergieva Lavra. He opened his home to sympathetic writers and intellectuals of the 1840s. Nowadays only two rooms in the main house—Aksakov's dining room and study with his memorabilia—recall his presence. The rest of the house is dedicated to famed Abramtsevo guests and the next (and final) private owner.

After Aksakov's death, railway tycoon Savva Mamontov purchased the estate in 1870 and turned it into an artists' colony. Here Mamontov and a community of resident artists tried to revive traditional Russian arts, crafts, and architecture to stimulate interest in Russian culture and make arts more accessible to the people.

In the 1880s half a dozen resident artists participated in the construction of the prettiest structure on Abramtsevo's grounds, the diminutive **Tserkov Ikony Spasa Nerukotvornovo** (Church of the Icon of the Savior Not Made by Hands). The idea to build a church was born when a flood prevented the local community from attending the festive Easter church service. The artist Polenov chose a 12th-century church outside Novgorod as a model. He and fellow artists Repin and Nesterov painted the gilt iconostasis; Vasnetsov laid the mosaic floor he had designed in the shape of a giant blooming flower. Some of the resident artists created their finest works in Abramtsevo. Serov painted his *Girl with Peaches,* an 1870 portrait of Mamontov's daughter, Vera, which now decorates Mamontov's dining room. Vasnetsov worked on his 1898 *Bogatyri* (Russian epic heroes) in Abramtsevo as well. Other structures on Abramtsevo's grounds include the wooden Izbushka Na Kuryikh Nozhkakh (House on Chicken Legs), a rendering of the residence of the witch Baba-Yaga from Russian fairy tales; Polenov's dacha; and an artists' workshop. In 1889 the troubled artist Mikhail Vrubel joined the Abramtsevo colony to participate in the ceramics workshop, where his provocative grotesque designs are still evident in the tile stoves, ceramic inlay, and furniture. The estate has been a museum since 1918, when it was nationalized. ✉ *Sergiev-Posad district, Abramtsevo station,1 Muzeunaya ul.* ☎ *496/543–2470* ⊕ *www.abramtsevo.net* 🖃*255R* ☽ *Wed.–Sun. 10–6. Closed last Thurs. of month.*

WHERE TO EAT

$$$$ ✕ **Galereya**. The extensive menu of traditional Russian food served at
EASTERN   this restaurant makes it a solid lunch option, and so does the fact
EUROPEAN   that it's right across the street from the central gate of the Abramtsevo
estate. If you don't feel like dining in, order a few *pirozhki* (small pies of cabbage, apple, or potatoes) to go. They're particularly delicious

with *mors*, a traditional Russian cranberry drink. ⊠ *3 Muzeynaya ul.* ☎ *495/725–3195* ⊕ *www.galereya.name* ▭ *No credit cards.*

THE NORTHERN GOLDEN RING

Within this historic region northeast of Moscow are ancient towns, venerable churches, and the magnificent Rostov kremlin and Monastery of St. Ipaty. There are plenty of guided-tour options, ranging from one-day outings to 1,000-km (620-mi) bus tours. And if you want to visit this region on your own, you're in luck: these towns are tourist-friendly.

PERESLAVL-ZALESSKY ПЕРЕСЛАВЛЬ-ЗАЛЕССКИЙ

127 km (79 mi) northeast of Moscow via the M8.

Pereslavl-Zalessky was founded in 1157 by Yuri Dolgoruky for two very important reasons. The first was political: he sought to draw parallels between the power base he was building in the Rus' region and the center of power in Kiev, to the southeast. So he named this town Pereyaslavl (meaning "to achieve glory"; the "ya" was later dropped) after a town outside of Kiev, and he named the river alongside the town Trubezh, just as in the Kievan Pereyaslavl. The "Zalessky" appellation, added in the 15th century, means "beyond the forests" and was used to distinguish the town from many other Pereyaslavls (not least the one near Kiev).

The second reason was economic. The location of the town on the southern shore of Lake Pleshcheyevo was ideal for defending the western approaches to vital trade routes along the Nerl River to the Klyazma, Oka, and Volga rivers. The topography only accentuates this role. From the hills, the impressive Danilovsky and Goritsky monasteries peer down on the low wooden and stone buildings of the town.

As the birthplace of Alexander Nevsky (1220–63), Pereslavl-Zalessky has yet another claim to fame. Nevsky entered the pantheon of Russia's great heroes when, as Prince of Novgorod, he beat back invading Swedes in 1240 at the Battle of the Neva (thus his last name). For his victory, the Mongol Khan awarded Nevsky the title of Grand Prince of Vladimir. There's a small church in town honoring Nevsky.

GETTING HERE AND AROUND

■ TIP➔ Note that the town can be reached by bus or car, but not by train.

A bus leaves from Moscow's Shchelkovskaya metro station and reaches Pereslavl-Zalessky in two and a half to three hours.

EXPLORING

The fortresslike **Goritsky Monastyr**, high on a hill south of the town center, was founded in the first half of the 14th century and is now an art and history museum. It displays ancient manuscripts and books found in this area, jewelry, and sculptures. An impressive collection of icons includes the 15th-century treasure, *Peter and Paul Apostles*, the oldest icon in the region, and a small collection of paintings with works of Konstantin Korovin. Outside the entrance to the museum is a proud monument to the T-34 tank, which was the tank that saved

Russia from the Germans in World War II. Inside is the large Uspensky Sobor (Cathedral of the Assumption), built in 1544. ⊠ *4 Muzeyny per* ☎ *48535/381–00* 🎫 *15R* ☼ *Wed.–Mon. 10–4:30. Closed last Mon. of month.*

In the center of town, along Sovetskaya ulitsa, is the 12th-century lime-stone **Cathedral of the Transfiguration** (*Spaso-Preobrazhensky Sobor*). Construction began on this church in the same year as the Church of Saints Boris and Gleb in Kideksha, near Suzdal, making it one of the oldest stone buildings standing in Russia. ⊠ *Krasnaya pl.* ☎ *48535/381–00* 🎫 *Free* ☼ *May–Oct., Wed.–Mon. 10–6.*

Pereslavl-Zalessky was the birthplace of the Russian navy. The **Botik museum**, 3 km (2 mi) outside of town, houses the only remaining boat of the more than 100 Peter the Great built for the fleet he sailed on Lake Pleshcheyevo. The *botik*, a small sailboat, usually single-mast, is often called the grandfather of the Russian fleet. The museum also displays several naval guns, a triumphal arch, and a monument to Peter the Great. To get to the museum, take a narrow-gauge train running south and west along the lake from the bus station, which is on ulitsa Kardovskovo, just below the Goritsky Monastery. It departs the bus station at 9 am, 1 pm, and 4:30 pm and returns from the museum at 12:30 pm, 4 pm, and 8:30 pm. ⊠ *Near Veslevo village* ☎ *48535/22–788 or 48535/23–124.* 🎫 *70R* ☼ *Tues.–Sun. 10–5. Closed last Thurs. of month.*

WHERE TO EAT AND STAY

$$ 🍴**Botik Tourist Complex.** A café and six pretty wooden houses that accommodate two people each are down the path from the Botik museum, on the bank of Pleshcheyevo Lake. **Pros:** great views of the lake; beachfront location. **Cons:** rooms look a bit shabby and must be booked in advance. ⊠ *Near Veslevo village* ☎ *48535/98–085* 🖨 *08535/98–865* ⚓ *6 houses* ⚒ *In-room: a/c, no safe. In-hotel: bar, beach* ⊟ *No credit cards.*

$$ 🏨**Hotel Pereslavl.** The Pereslavl is a Soviet-era hotel with a convenient downtown location. **Pros:** convenient location. **Cons:** bar can get loud on weekends. ⊠ *27 Rostovskaya ul., Pereslavl-Zalessky* ☎ *08535/21–788 hotel; 48535/31–788 restaurant* ⊕ *www.hotelpereslavl.ru* ⚓ *59 rooms* ⚒ *In-room: a/c, no safe. In-hotel: restaurant, bar* ⊟ *No credit cards.*

$$$ 🏨**Hotel Zapadnaya.** On the bank of the Trubezh River, this hotel has a superb, picturesque location in the historical center of town. **Pros:** great location; helpful staff. **Cons:** a bit overpriced. ⊠ *1-A Pleshcheyevskaya ul., Pereslavl-Zalessky* ☎ *48535/34–378 or 48535/34–395* ⊕ *www.westhotel.ru* ⚓ *11 rooms* ⚒ *In-room: a/c, no safe, Internet. In-hotel: restaurant* ⊟ *No credit cards.*

ROSTOV РОСТОВ

225 km (140 mi) northeast of Moscow via the M8, 58 km (36 mi) southwest of Yaroslavl.

Rostov, also known as Rostov-Veliky ("the Great") so as not to confuse it with Rostov-on-the-Don, is one of the oldest towns in Russia.

Founded even before Riurik, a semi-legendary Viking prince, came to rule Russia in the 9th century, Rostov is first mentioned in historical chronicles in 862. It became an independent principality at the beginning of the 13th century and soon became one of the most prosperous and influential political centers of ancient Russia. However, the city was destroyed when the Mongols invaded in 1238. In the 15th century Rostov ultimately lost its political independence but retained its influence as a major religious center. It became the seat of the metropolitan, the leader of the Orthodox Church, in the late 16th century.

The town, with a population of 36,000, is on the edge of Lake Nero, with earthen ramparts and radial streets.

GETTING HERE AND AROUND

From Moscow you can take a three-hour "express" train from Yaroslavsky station or get a bus from the Shchelkovskaya or Komsomolskaya metro stations. The bus takes about four hours.

EXPLORING

Fodor'sChoice
★

At the center of Rostov is the incomparable **Rostov kremlin**, a fortress with 6-foot-thick white-stone walls and 11 circular towers topped with wood-shingle cupolas. The kremlin dates from 1631, but it was built to its current glory between 1670 and 1690 by Rostov Metropolitan Jonah. Its main purpose was to serve as court and residence for the metropolitan, though Jonah saw himself as creating an ideal type of self-enclosed city focused on spiritual matters. As such, it was Russia's first planned city.

The huge, blue-dome **Cathedral of the Assumption** (Uspensky Sobor) stands just outside the walls of the kremlin. Inside are frescoes dating to 1675. But the truly memorable site is the adjacent four-tower **belfry**. The famous 13 bells of Rostov chime on the half hour and full hour and can play four tunes. It's said that the largest of the bells, which weighs 32 tons and is named Sysoi, for Jonah's father, can be heard from 19 km (12 mi) away.

You enter the kremlin through the richly decorated northern entrance, past the **Gate Church of the Resurrection** (Nadvratnaya Voskresenskaya Tserkov). Well-groomed pathways and a pleasant, tree-lined pond lend themselves to a contemplative walk. Just to the right of the entrance into the kremlin is the **Church of the Mother of God Hodegetria** (Tserkov Bogomateri Odigitrii), whose faceted baroque exterior rises to a single onion dome.

The **Church of John the Theologian** (Tserkov Ioanna Bogoslova), another gate church, is on the west side of the kremlin. Adjacent to this church is the two-story **Red Palace** (Krasnaya Palata), once known as the Chamber for Great Sovereigns. Built first for Ivan the Terrible for his visits to the town, it was later used by Peter the Great and Catherine the Great.

Adjacent is the **White Palace** (*Belaya Palata* ☎ *No phone* ☉ *May–Oct., daily 10–5*)—the metropolitan's residence—most notable for its large hall (3,000 square feet) supported by a single column. Connected to the residence is the private church of the metropolitan, the Church of the Savior on the Stores, which was built over a food-storage shelter. This church has the most beautiful wall paintings in the entire complex, as well as gilded columns and handsome brass doors. The metropolitan's residence now houses a museum of icons and Rostov enamel (*finift*), a craft the town is famous for throughout Russia. The southern portion of the kremlin features the tall **Church of Grigory the Theologian** (Tserkov Grigoria Bogoslova). ☎ *48536/61–717* ⊕ *www.rostmuseum.ru* 🖾 *140R for all churches and palaces inside the kremlin* ☉ *Daily 10–5, except Jan. 1. Churches: May–Oct., daily 10–5.*

On your way out of the kremlin complex, be sure to explore the shop arcade called **Torgoviye Ryady** (*trade rows*), across the square from Uspensky Sobor. In the early 19th century, after Rostov had lost its metropolitanate to nearby Yaroslavl, it became an extremely important trading center. Rostov's annual market was the third largest in Russia.

Along the lakefront and southwest of the kremlin is the rather eclectic **Yakovlevsky (Jacob) Monastery**. Dominating the ensemble is the huge, Romanesque Dmitriyev Church, crowned by a large spherical central dome and four smaller corner domes. The monastery was founded in 1389. Take the guided tour for access to the premises of the working monastery. ☎ *48536/743–69 or 48536/770–04* 🖾 *Monastery grounds free, guided tours 150R* ☉ *Daily 9–5.*

Avraamiyev (Abraham) Monastery was founded at the end of the 11th century. Now the oldest monastery in Russia, it was erected on the site of a former pagan temple to Veles, god of cattle. The five-dome Epiphany Cathedral in the monastery complex dates from 1553 and is the oldest standing building in Rostov. The nuns' cloister, which is still working, is on the lakefront, northeast of the kremlin. ☎ *48536/637–12 or 48536/740–05* 🖾 *Free* ☉ *Daily 9–5.*

WHERE TO EAT AND STAY

$
EASTERN
EUROPEAN
✕**Teremok**. Borscht, solyanka, and blini with caviar are among the good Russian dishes served at this cozy restaurant in front of the kremlin. ✉ *1 ul. Moravskovo* ☎ *48536/61–648* ➖ *No credit cards.*

$$$
🏠**Boyarsky Dvor**. Just 50 meters away from the kremlin, this 18th-century, two-story historic mansion-turned-hotel has all the amenities you could ask for from a provincial hotel. **Pros:** great location; comfortable beds. **Cons:** advance booking required in summer. ✉ *4 Kammeny Most ul.* ☎ *48536/6–0446 or 48536/6–4800* ⊕ *www.reinkap-hotel.ru* ⤴ *53 rooms* ⚬ *In-room: a/c, no safe. In-hotel: restaurant* ➖ *No credit cards.*

$$
🏠**Dom na Pogrebakh**. If you've ever wanted to stay overnight in a kremlin, here's your chance. ✉ *Rostov kremlin, in Red Palace* ☎ *48536/61–244* ⊕ *www.rostmuseum.ru/hotel/hotel.html* ⤴ *13 rooms with shared bath* ⚬ *In-room: a/c, no safe. In-hotel: restaurant* ➖ *No credit cards.*

YAROSLAVL ЯРОСЛАВЛЬ

282 km (175 mi) northeast of Moscow on the M8.

Yaroslavl has a very storied history, beginning with an apocryphal founding. It's said that local inhabitants set loose a bear to chase away Prince Yaroslav the Wise (978–1054). Yaroslav wrestled and killed the bear and founded the town on the spot. If true, these events happened early in the 11th century; Yaroslav decreed the town's founding as a fortress on the Volga in 1010. About 600 years later, in 1612, during the Time of Troubles, the town was the center of national resistance against the invading Poles, under the leadership of Kuzma Minin and Dmitri Pozharsky.

The town rests at the confluence of the Volga and Kotorosl rivers, which made it a major commercial center from the 13th century until 1937, when the Moscow-Volga canal was completed, allowing river traffic to proceed directly to the capital. This commercial heritage bequeathed the city a rich legacy that offers a glimpse of some of the finest church architecture in Russia.

In the town center, proceed northwest along Pervomaiskaya ulitsa, a favorite pedestrian route that follows the semicircular path of the town's former earthen ramparts. Peruse the impressive, colonnaded **trade rows** and walk on to the Znamenskaya watchtower, which in the middle of the 17th century marked the western edge of the town—another watchtower stands on the Volga embankment. The yellow building directly across the square is the **Volkov Theater.** The theater and square are named for Fyodor Volkov, who founded Russia's first professional drama theater here in 1750—the theater was the first to stage *Hamlet* in Russia. Continue along Pervomaiskaya and it will take you to the banks of the Volga, which is 1 km (½ mi) wide at this point. Look for the monument to the great Russian poet Nikolai Nekrasov, who came from nearby Karabikha.

GETTING HERE AND AROUND

You can take a train from Moscow's Yaroslavsky train station to Yaroslavsky Glavny. It takes four hours.

EXPLORING

The mid-17th-century **Church of Elijah the Prophet** (*Tserkov Ilyi Proroka*) stands at the center of town on Sovetskaya Ploshchad (Soviet Square), some say on the site of Yaroslav's alleged wrestling match with the bear (though a monument down by the Volga commemorates the spot of the town's founding). Its tall, octagonal belfry and faceted green onion domes make the church the focal point of the town. Inside the ornamental church are some of the best-preserved frescoes (1680) by Gury Nikitin and Sila Savin, whose works also adorn Moscow Kremlin cathedrals, as well as churches throughout the region. The frescoes depict scenes from the Gospels and the life of Elijah and his disciple Elisha. ⊠ 7 *Sovetskaya pl.* ☎ *4852/3040–72* 💰 *70R* ☉ *May–Oct., daily 10–1 and 2–6.*

The **Monastery of the Transfiguration of the Savior** (*Spaso-Preobrazhensky Monastyr*), surrounded by white, 10-foot-thick walls, was the site of northern Russia's first school of higher education, dating to the 13th century. It houses several magnificent churches and is where Ivan the Terrible took refuge in 1571, when the Mongols were threatening Moscow. Dating to 1516, the **Holy Gates** entrance to the monastery, on the side facing the Kotorosl River, is the oldest extant structure in the compound. A six-story **belfry** rises high above the round-dome Cathedral of the Transfiguration of the Savior. Climb to the top of the belfry for a panoramic view of the city. The clock in the belfry hung in the famous Spasskaya Tower of the Moscow Kremlin until 1624, when it was purchased by the merchants of Yaroslavl. ⊠ *25 Bogoyavlenskaya Pl.* 🕾 *4852/3040–72* 🖾 *Free, small fee for individual churches and belfry within monastery* ⊘ *Tues.–Sun. 10–5. Closed 1st Wed. of month.*

A **statue of Yaroslav the Wise**, unveiled in 1993 by Russian president Boris Yeltsin and Ukrainian president Leonid Kravchuk, stands not far from the monastery. Yaroslav is depicted holding a piece of the kremlin and staring off in the direction of Moscow. To see the statue, walk away from the river down ulitsa Nakhimsona toward the monastery.

The large, redbrick, blue-cupola **Church of the Epiphany** (*Tserkov Bogoyavleniya*) is renowned for its fine proportions, enhanced by splendid decorative ceramic tiles and unusually tall windows. Inside are eight levels of wall paintings in the realistic style that began to hold sway in the late 1600s. The church is directly west of the Monastery of the Transfiguration of the Savior. ⊠ *Bogoyavlenskaya Pl.* 🕾 *4852/3034–29 or 4852/7256–23* 🖾 *Free* ⊘ *Wed.–Sun 9–4.*

The 100-foot-tall "**candle of Yaroslavl**" is actually a belfry for two churches, Ioann Zlatoust (St. John Chrysostom, 1649) and the miniature Tserkov Vladimirskoi Bogomateri (Church of the Vladimir Virgin, 1678). The former is a larger summer church, ornately decorated with colorful tiles; the latter is the more modest and easy-to-heat winter church. From the Monastery of the Transfiguration of the Savior, it's a 1-km (½-mi) walk (or two stops on Bus 4) across the bridge and along the mouth of the Kotorosl to the churches and belfry.

Although it looks as though it's made from wood, the 17th-century five-dome **Church of St. John the Baptist** (*Tserkov Ioanna Predtechi*) is actually fashioned from carved red brick. The church is on the same side of the Kotorosl River as the candle of Yaroslavl, but it's west of the bridge by about 1 km (½ mi). ⊠ *69 Kotoroslnaya nab.* 🕾 *No phone.*

WHERE TO EAT AND STAY

$ ✕ **Golden Bear Café.** In this pleasant café you'll find tasty Russian cook-
EASTERN ing, good service, and a modern interior. If the *salat* (salad) selection
EUROPEAN doesn't appeal, try the *buterbrod* (open-face sandwich), a dependable choice. ⊠ *3 Pervomaiskaya ul.* 🕾 *4852/328–532* 🖃 *No credit cards.*

$$$ ✕ **Skver.** St. Petersburg–brewed Baltika beer accompanies the moder-
EASTERN ately priced traditional Russian dishes served at this café behind the
EUROPEAN Volkov Theater. ⊠ *5 Pervomaiskaya bulvar* 🕾 *4852/20–2010* 🖃 *No credit cards.*

$$$$ 🏨 **Ring Premier Hotel.** Five minutes by foot from the Transfiguration monastery and just steps from Shinnik soccer stadium, this four-star hotel has the most luxurious accommodations in town. **Pros:** staff speaks excellent English; great sauna and pool. **Con:** hotel bar and restaurant are a bit overpriced. ⊠ *55 ul. Svobody* 🕾 *4852/5811–58 or 4852/5808–58* ⊕ *www.ringpremier-hotel.ru* ⇋ *122 rooms* ⟁ *In-room: a/c, no safe. In-hotel: restaurant, bar, pool.*

$$ 🏨 **Kotorosl.** This decent tourist-class hotel is not far from the city center, near the railway station. **Pros:** close to train station. **Cons:** standard rooms are overpriced, given that bathrooms are shared between

two rooms. ✉ *87 Bolshaya Oktyabrskaya ul.* ☎ *4852/211–581 or 4852/212–415* ⊕ *www.kotorosl.yaroslavl.ru* ⊷ *184 rooms* ☾ *In-room: a/c, no safe: In-hotel: restaurant, bar, gym* ⊟ *No credit cards.*

$$$$ 🖭 **Yubileynaya.** Located near the monastery, the Yubileynaya overlooks the Kotorosl River and the historic town. **Pros:** central location on the riverbank; Wi-Fi; nice buffet breakfast. **Con:** a bit overpriced. ✉ *26 Kotoroslnaya nab., Yaroslavl* ☎ *4852/309–259* ⊕ *www.yubil.yar.ru* ⊷ *220 rooms* ☾ *In-room: a/c, no safe. In-hotel: restaurant, bar* ⊟ *No credit cards.*

THE EASTERN GOLDEN RING

Vladimir and Suzdal, which together make up a World Heritage Site, hold some of Russia's most beautiful medieval kremlins, churches, and monasteries. The towns lie to the east of Moscow.

VLADIMIR ВЛАДИМИР

190 km (118 mi) east of Moscow via the M7.

Although this city of 350,000 seems unassuming today, half a millennium ago it was the cultural and religious capital of northeastern Rus'. Several of the monuments to this time of prosperity and prestige remain, and a visit to this city, and nearby Suzdal, is vital to understanding the contemporary Russia's roots.

Vladimir was founded in 1108 on the banks of the Klyazma by Vladimir Monomakh, grandson of Yaroslav the Wise and father of Yuri Dolgoruky. Yuri, as he increased his power en route to taking the throne in Kiev, preferred Suzdal, however, and made that town his de facto capital in 1152. Upon Yuri's death five years later, his son, Andrei Bogolyubsky, moved the capital of Suzdalia to Vladimir and began a massive building campaign.

GETTING HERE AND AROUND

From Moscow, take the express train from Kursky train station or a bus from Shchelkovskaya metro station. Onece you're in Vladimir you can get bus number 18 or 152 to visit Bogolyubovo village.

EXPLORING

Cathedral of the Assumption (*Uspensky Sobor*) is an important city landmark from Andrei Bogolyubsky's time, completed in 1160. Still a working church in the center of town, the cathedral has a huge, boxy outline and golden domes that rise high above the Klyazma River. After a fire in 1185, the cathedral was rebuilt, only to burn down again in 1237 when the Mongols attacked the city. The town's residents took refuge in the church, hoping for mercy. Instead, the invaders burned them alive. The cathedral was again restored, and in 1408 the famous medieval painter Andrei Rublyov repainted the frescoes of the Last Judgment, which in themselves make this impressive monument worth a visit. Ivan the Great (1440–1505) had his architects use this cathedral as a model to build the Assumption Cathedral in the Moscow Kremlin. The cathedral also houses a replica of Russia's most revered icon, the Virgin of

Vladimir; the original was moved from here to Moscow in 1390. Andrei Bogolyubsky is entombed here. ⊠ *Sobornaya Pl.* ☎ *4922/3242–63 or 4922/3252–01* ⊑ *100R* ☉ *Tues.–Sun. 1–4:45.*

Andrei Bogolyubsky was succeeded by Vsevolod III, also known as "the Great Nest" because of the great number of his progeny. Although he focused much of his energy in the neighboring regions of Ryazan and Murom, he was instrumental in rebuilding Vladimir's town center in 1185 after a fire caused much damage. He also built the remarkable **Cathedral of St. Dmitri** (*Dmitriyevsky Sobor*), finished in 1197. The cathedral stands adjacent to Vladimir's much larger Cathedral of the Assumption, where he is buried, and is covered in ornate carvings with both secular and religious images. The lower images are quite precise and detailed; the upper ones have fewer details but deeper grooves for better visibility. ⊠ *Sobornaya Pl.* ☎ *4922/3242–63* ⊑ *80R* ☉ *Mon. and Wed.–Sun. 11–5. Closed last Wed. of month.*

Originally, Vladimir had four gates guarding the main approaches to the town. The 12th-century **Golden Gates** (*Zolotye Vorota*), which stand in the middle of Moskovskaya ulitsa, a few hundred yards west of the Cathedral of the Assumption, guarded the western approach. The main road from Moscow to Siberia passed through these gates, which, starting in the 1800s, became a significant monument on the infamous Vladimirka—the road prisoners took east to Siberia.

Most of Andrei Bogolyubsky's construction projects were built in **Bogolyubovo**, 10 km (6 mi) east of Vladimir. Near the convergence of the Nerl and Klyazma rivers, he built an impressive fort and living compound. The dominant building in the compound today is the richly decorated **Cathedral of the Assumption** (Uspensky Sobor), rebuilt in the 19th century. Remnants of his quarters—a tower and an archway—still stand. It was on the stairs of this tower that Andrei, despised by many for his authoritarian rule, was stabbed to death by several members of his inner circle. In the 13th century, Bogolyubovo became a convent, which it remains today. In 1702 Andrei was canonized. ⊠ *Bogolyubovo village* ☎ *4922/3242–63 tour reservations* ⊑ *Free, fee for tour* ☉ *Daily 10–5.*

★ Andrei's greatest creation and arguably the most perfect medieval Russian church ever built, is the 1165 **Church of the Intercession on the Nerl** (*Khram Pokrova Na Nerli*), less than 2 km (1 mi) from Bogolyubovo. On a massive limestone foundation covered with earth, the church sits near the confluence of the Nerl and Klyazma rivers and appears to be rising out of the water that surrounds it. Andrei built the church in memory of his son Izyslav, who was killed in a victorious battle with the Bulgars. Look for the unique carvings of King David on the exterior, the earliest such iconographic carvings in this region. Inside, the high, narrow arches give an impressive feeling of space and light. To get to the church from Bogolyubovo, walk a few hundred yards west of the monastery, down ulitsa Frunze and under a railway bridge; then follow the path through a field to the church.

WHERE TO EAT AND STAY

$ ✕ **Stary Gorod.** This "Old Town" restaurant serving Russian and Euro-
pean cuisine is a good option for a meal, in part because it's just steps
away from Sobornaya Ploschad. The place is quiet, and the staff is
friendly. The summer terrace is open May through September. ⊠ *41 Bolshaya Moskovskaya ul., Vladimir* ☎ *4922/3251–01* ⊕ *www.oldcity33.
ru* ⊟ *No credit cards.*

EASTERN
EUROPEAN

$$$ ⊞ **Monomah Hotel.** This mini-hotel with 16 rooms offers one of the
best accommodations in the city, though it's a bit on the pricey side.
Pros: central location; slippers in each room. **Con:** a bit overpriced.
⊠ *20 ul. Gogolya, Vladimir* ☎ *4922/4404–44* ⊕ *www.monomahhotel.
ru* ➶ *16 rooms* ♿ *In-room: a/c, no safe, refrigerator, Wi-Fi. In-hotel:
restaurant, bar.*

$$$ ⊞ **U Zolotykh Vorot.** This elegant hotel is in a recently renovated 19th-
century building, next to the Golden Gates, as its name suggests. **Pros:**
central location; great breakfast. **Con:** rooms with a street view can
be noisy. ⊠ *17 Bolshaya Moskovskaya ul., Vladimir* ☎ *4922/4208–23*
⊕ *www.golden-gate.ru* ➶ *13 rooms, 1 suite* ♿ *In-room: a/c, no safe.
In-hotel: restaurant, bar.*

$$$ ⊞ **Vladimir Hotel.** Although somewhat Soviet in atmosphere, this hotel
offers decent service and standard amenities. **Pros:** central location.
Cons: uninspiring restaurant. ⊠ *74 ul. Bolshaya Moskovskaya, Vladi-
mir* ☎ *4922/3230–42* ⊕ *www.vladimir-hotel.ru* ➶ *45 rooms* ♿ *In-
room: a/c, no safe, refrigerator. In-hotel: restaurant, bar.*

SUZDAL СУЗДАЛЬ

★ *190 km (118 mi) east of Moscow on the M7 via Vladimir, then 26 km
(16 mi) north on the A113.*

Suzdal is the crown jewel of the Golden Ring, with more than 200 his-
toric monuments and some of the most striking churches in Russia. This
quiet tourist town of 12,000 on the Kamenka River is compact enough
to be explored entirely on foot, but to do it justice, give it two days.

One of the earliest settlements in central Russia, Suzdal has been inhab-
ited since the 9th century and was first mentioned in the *Russian Chron-
icle* (Russia's ancient historical record) in 1024. In 1152 Yuri Dolgoruky
made Suzdal the capital of his growing fiefdom in northeastern Russia.
He built a fortress in nearby Kideksha—that town, 4 km (2½ mi) to
the east, is the site of the oldest stone church in northeastern Russia,
the Church of Saints Boris and Gleb, built in 1152. His son, Andrei
Bogolyubsky, preferred nearby Vladimir and focused much of his build-
ing efforts there. Still, Suzdal remained a rich town, largely because of
donations to the many local monasteries and church building commis-
sions. Indeed, medieval Suzdal had only about 400 families, but some
40 churches.

GETTING HERE AND AROUND

Buses to Suzdal go from Moscow's Shchelkovskaya metro station. Or
you can get the Moscow–Vladimir express from Kursky train station
and then catch a bus to Suzdal.

EXPLORING

The **Suzdal kremlin**, which may have first been built in the 10th century, sits on an earthen rampart, with the Kamenka River flowing around all but the east side (demarcated by ulitsa Lenina). The dominant monument in the kremlin (and indeed the town) is the mid-13th-century **Sobor Rozhdestva Bogorodnitsy** (Cathedral of the Nativity of the Virgin), topped by deep-blue cupolas festooned with golden stars.

Original limestone carvings can still be found on its corners and on its facade. Its exquisite bronze entry doors are the oldest such doors in Russia, having survived since the 13th century. Inside, the brilliant and colorful frescoes dating from the 1230s and 1630s are without compare.

The long, white, L-shaped three-story building that the cathedral towers over is the **Archbishop's Chambers.** Behind its broad windows you'll find the superb "cross chamber" (named for its shape), which is a large hall without any supporting pillars—the first hall of its type in all Russia. The kremlin also holds museums of antique books and art. ⊠ *Kremlevskaya ul., Suzdal* ☎ *49231/20–937* ☒ *200R for entire kremlin* ◔ *Wed.–Sun. 10–6. Closed last Fri. of month.*

The **Museum of Wooden Architecture** (*Muzey Derevyannovo Zodchestva*) contains interesting wooden buildings moved here from around the region. Of particular interest is the ornate **Church of the Transfiguration,** dating from 1756; it was moved here from the village of Kozlyatievo. The buildings can be viewed from the outside any time of year, but from the inside only from May to October. The museum is just below the kremlin and across the river to the south; to get here you'll need to go south on ulitsa Lenina, cross the river, and turn right on Pushkarskaya ulitsa. ⊠ *Pushkarskaya ul.* ☎ *49231/207–84* ☒ *150R* ◔ *May–Oct., Thurs.–Tues. 9–7; Nov.–Apr., daily 9–4.*

Walking north from the kremlin on ulitsa Lenina, you'll pass several churches on your left and the pillared trading arcades. Just beyond the arcades are the beautiful **Churches of St. Lazarus and St. Antipy** (*Tserkov Svyatovo Lazarya and Tserkov Svyatovo Antipiya*), their colorful bell tower topping the unique, concave tent-roof design. This ensemble is a good example of Russian church architecture, where a summer church (St. Lazarus, with the shapely onion domes, built in 1667) adjoins a smaller, easier-to-heat, and more modest winter church (St. Antipy, built in 1745). ⊠ *Ul. Lenina* ☎ *No phone* ☒ *Free.*

Rising 236 feet high, the bell tower in the **Monastery of the Feast of the Deposition of the Robe** (*Rizopolozhensky Monastyr*) complex is the tallest building in Suzdal. It was built by local residents in 1819 to commemorate Russia's victory over Napoléon. The monastery is on ulitsa Lenina, opposite the post office.

Fodor's Choice ★ The impressive **Monastery of St. Yefim** (*Spaso-Yefimsky Monastyr*) dates from 1350. The tall brick walls and 12 towers of the monastery have often been the cinematic stand-in for the Moscow Kremlin. The main church in the monastery, the 16th-century **Church of the Transfiguration of the Savior,** is distinctive for its extremely pointed onion domes and its New Testament frescoes by Gury Nikitin and Sila Slavin, 17th-century painters from the city of Kostroma. A museum in the monastery is devoted to their lives and work. The church also houses the tomb containing the remains of Dmitri Pozharsky, one of the resistance leaders against the Polish invaders in the Time of Troubles. Adjoining the church is a single-dome nave church, which is actually the original Church of the Transfiguration; it was built in 1509, constructed over the grave of St. Yefim, the monastery's founder. Every hour on the hour there's a wonderful chiming of the church's bells. The 16th-century **Church of the Assumption** (Uspenskaya Tserkov), next door to the larger Church of the Transfiguration of the Savior, is one of the earliest examples of tent-roof architecture in Russia.

In the middle of the 18th century, part of the monastery became a place for "deranged criminals," many of whom were actually political prisoners. The prison and hospital are along the north wall and closed to visitors. ⊠ *Ul. Lenina* ☎ *No phone* 🖃 *Monastery grounds 60R, for grounds and all museums 300R* ◔ *Tues.–Sun. 10–6. Closed last Thurs. of month.*

In addition to being a religious institution, the **Convent of the Intercession** (*Pokrovsky Monastyr*) was also a place for political incarcerations. Basil III divorced his wife Solomonia in 1525 and banished her here when she failed to produce a male heir. Basil may have chosen this monastery because, in 1514, he had commissioned the splendid octagonal, three-dome Cathedral of the Intercession here, as supplication for a male heir. Interestingly, local legend has it that Solomonia subsequently gave birth to a boy and then staged the child's death to hide him from Basil. Basil subsequently married Yelena Glinskaya, who did give him an heir: Ivan IV, who would be known as "the Terrible." Ivan, in turn, banished his wife Anna here. And when Peter the Great, after returning from Europe in 1698, finally decided that he wanted to rid himself of his wife, Yevdokia, he forced her to take the veil and live out the rest of her life in this convent. A fine view of the monastery can be had from across the river, from the sparse remains of the Alexander Nevsky monastery. The convent sits across the Kamenka River from Spaso Yefimsky, in an oxbow bend of the river. To get here, turn east off ulitsa Lenina onto ulitsa Stromynka, and then go north on Pokrovskaya ulitsa. ☎ *49231/2–0609* 🖃 *50R* ◔ *Fri.–Tues. 10–6. Closed last Fri. of month.*

WHERE TO EAT AND STAY
Suzdal has a wider range of hotels that other towns of the Golden Ring. For a more comprehensive list of Suzdal accommodations, see ⊕ *www. suzdal.org.ru.*

$$$
EASTERN
EUROPEAN

✕ **Trapeznaya Kremlya.** Arguably the best restaurant in town, and not to be confused with the restaurant of the same name in the Convent of the Intercession (which now serves only pilgrims), this is a pleasant Russian-style eatery within the Suzdal kremlin. The quality of your meals may depend on the day of the week you visit; it's likely to be better on weekdays, when the crowds are thinned out. If you don't want to order a full meal, consider trying some tea and *keks* (cakes) or *pirozhnoye* (pastry), all-day selections in Russia. ⊠ *Archbishop's Chambers, Suzdal kremlin* ☎ *49231/21–763* ▤ *No credit cards.*

$$$ 🏨 **Sokol Hotel.** This hotel's location in the historic part of the town makes it a pleasant 10-minute walk to the kremlin. **Pros:** hearty breakfast

included. **Cons:** some staff may not speak English. ⊠ *2A Torgovaya Pl.* ☎ *49231/20–987* ⊕ *www.hotel-sokol.ru* ➥ *39 rooms* ᐈ *In-room: a/c, no safe, Wi-Fi. In-hotel: restaurant* ⊟ *No credit cards.*

$ ⚏ **Tatyana's House.** A good alternative to a hotel, this guesthouse in a white-brick two-story building is a five-minute walk to the Museum of Wooden Architecture and the kremlin. *6B Lenina ul.* ☎ *905/057–7453* ➢ *ann.05@mail.ru* ➥ *5 rooms with shared bath* ᐈ *In-room: a/c, no safe* ⊟ *No credit cards.*

$$ ⚏ **Tourcenter.** A large former Soviet complex, Tourcenter includes the Hotel Suzdal, which offers 200 double rooms and winning personal service. **Pros:** nice pool; bowling alley in hotel. **Con:** the huge complex can get crowded with tour groups on some weekends and public holidays. ⊠ *7 ul. Korovniki* ☎ *49231/21–530 or 49231/20–908* 🖶 *49231/207–66* ⊕ *www.suzdaltour.ru* ➥ *430 rooms* ᐈ *In-room: a/c, no safe. In-hotel: restaurant, pool.*

Exploring
St. Petersburg

WORD OF MOUTH

"Maybe the comparison is not fair, but if you have a choice between Moscow and St. Petersburg, the answer is quick and easy: St. Petersburg. Frankly, I consider it one of the most beautiful cities on the planet if not THE most beautiful one. [There's] an incredible wealth of palaces, museums, churches and, furthermore, [it] has a stunning architectural cohesiveness, with over 3,000 listed historical buildings."

—Echnaton

Updated by
Irina Titova

Commissioned by Tsar Peter the Great (1672–1725) as "a window looking into Europe," St. Petersburg is a planned city whose elegance is reminiscent of Europe's most alluring capitals. Little wonder it's the darling of fashion photographers and travel essayists today: built on more than a hundred islands in the Neva Delta linked by canals and arched bridges, it was called the "Venice of the North" by Goethe, and its stately embankments are reminiscent of those in Paris. A city of golden spires and gilded domes, of pastel palaces and candlelit cathedrals, this city conceived by a visionary emperor is filled with pleasures and tantalizing treasures.

With its strict geometric lines and perfectly planned architecture, so unlike the Russian cities that came before it, St. Petersburg is almost too European to be Russian. And yet it's too Russian to be European. The city is a powerful combination of both East and West, springing from the will and passion of its founder, Tsar Peter the Great (1672–1725), to guide a resistant Russia into the greater fold of Europe, and consequently into the mainstream of history. That he accomplished, and more.

With a population of nearly 5 million, St. Petersburg is the fourth largest city in Europe after Paris, Moscow, and London. Without as many of the fashionably modern buildings that a business center like Moscow acquires, the city has managed to preserve much more of its history. Here, you can imagine yourself back in the time of the tsars and Dostoyevsky. Although it's a close race, it's safe to say that most visitors prefer St. Petersburg's culture, history, and beauty to Moscow's glamour and power.

That said, St. Petersburg has begun to play a more active role in politics in recent years, as if it were the country's northern capital. It may be because of the affection the city holds in the heart of the country's political elite, many of whom are natives of the city. In recent years St. Petersburg has hosted a number of significant national and international events, such as the G8 summit in 2006 and the International Tiger Forum in 2010. The city's infrastructure has also been developed, with new high-speed trains now traveling between Moscow and St. Petersburg, construction begun on a new international airport, new metro stations opening, and some crumbling parts of the city undergoing reconstruction.

TOP REASONS TO GO

The State Hermitage Museum: In one of the world's premier historical and art collections, you can see works by Monet, Picasso, and Matisse, the opulence of tsarist Russia, Egyptian mummies, and Scythian gold.

St. Isaac's Cathedral: The third largest cathedral in the world dominates St. Petersburg's skyline, with a gilded dome covered in 100 kilograms (220 pounds) of pure gold. Climb the colonnade for a great panoramic view of the city.

White Nights: If you are planning to visit in May through July you'll be witness to this unusual phenomenon: the city is aglow in daylight throughout the night. Enjoy the romance and the beauty of the illuminated nights on the banks of the Neva River.

Mariinsky Opera and Ballet Theatre: Ballet stars such as Anna Pavlova, Vaslav Nijinsky, Rudolf Nureyev, and Mikhail Baryshnikov once graced this theater's stage; now it also turns out great modern ballet as well as opera performances by the likes of Anna Netrebko.

Peter and Paul Fortress: St. Petersburg was founded at this citadel, built by Peter the Great. It never saw battle, and instead became a political prison for Peter's rebellious son, Alexei. It later held Dostoyevsky, Gorky, and Trotsky to name a few. The dynasty of Russian tsars is buried within the fortress.

ORIENTATION AND PLANNING

GETTING ORIENTED

8

It's easy to find your way around St. Petersburg's center. The major sights, such as the Hermitage Museum, Palace Square, Peter and Paul's Fortress, St. Isaac's Cathedral, the Admiralty, and Strelka, are all mainly along or near the Neva River, and within sight of each other. The city's main avenue, Nevesky prospekt, leads directly to the river and to the Dvortsovyi, one of its major bridges. Most streets run straight, except in places where they curve along canals or small rivers. It's helpful to keep in mind that addresses on street that begin at the Neva go higher as they go away from the river. The smaller the number, the closer the address is to the river and to most of the major sights.

One of the city's weak points for foreign tourists is the rarity of signs in general as well as signs in English (an exception is the metro, however, where stops are identified in English). The names of the streets are written in Cyrillic, so it's well worth spending some time familiarizing yourself with its letters before you arrive. In any case, don't forget your city map. Finally, although a lot fewer people in St. Petersburg speak English compared to cities in Western Europe, there are still more and more of those who do. It's always worth asking a passerby for directions (the young or middle-aged are most likely to understand).

City Center. The City Center embraces Palace Square, the Hermitage, and the northern end of Nevsky prospekt, with the Fontanka River as its southeastern border. Most of St. Petersburg's major attractions are within this area.

Admiralteisky and Vasilievsky Island. To the west of the City Center is the smaller neighborhood of the Admiralteisky, surrounding the Admiralty building. Second in number of sights, including the Chamber of Art and the Rostral Columns, is Vasilievsky Island, opposite the Admiralty and set off from the City Center by the Little and Great Neva rivers.

The Petrograd Side. North of the City Center and the Neva River is the Petrograd Side, which holds Peter and Paul Fortress and the sights of Petrograd Island.

Upper Nevsky Prospekt and Vladimirskaya (Lower Nevsky Prospekt). On the mainland, Vladimirskaya is an area south of the Fontanka, taking in the lower part of Nevsky prospekt and bordered by the Obvodny Canal.

Smolny. This region lies to the northeast of Vladimirskaya and includes the Smolny cathedral. The Kirov Islands (north of the city), the Southern Suburbs, and the Vyborg Side (in the northeast corner of the city) have just a few sights.

PLANNING

WHEN TO GO
St. Petersburg's weather is the most pleasant from early May through August. May and June brings the White Nights, when the city never gets darker than a couple hours of twilight. It's an incredibly romantic time to visit, although the high hotel rates can also make it a costly time.

GETTING HERE AND AROUND
Although St. Petersburg is spread out over 650 square km (250 square mi), most of its historic sites are concentrated in the downtown section and are best explored on foot. These sites are often not well served by the extensive public transportation system, so be prepared to do a lot of walking. Bilingual city maps with bus routes marked on them are sold at the bookstore **Dom Knigi** (⊠ 62 *Nevsky prospekt*), while *St. Petersburg In Your Pocket* prints valuable info about *marshrutki* (minibus) routes in every issue.

AIR TRAVEL
St. Petersburg is served by two airports, Pulkovo I (domestic) and Pulkovo II (international), just 2 km (1 mi) apart and 17 km (11 mi) south of central St. Petersburg. The runways of the two Pulkovos interconnect, so it's possible you could land at Pulkovo I and taxi over to Pulkovo II. Compared with Moscow's Sheremetyevo II, Pulkovo II is a breeze. It's compact and well lit, with signs in both Russian and English.

However, the airport's small size—there are only eight gates—prevents it from receiving more airlines and developing into a venue fit for a large European city. In 2010 an international consortium began construction of a big and modern international hub that would unite Pulkovo's domestic and international sections. The first stage of the terminal is to be completed by 2013. The new facility will make Pulkovo one of the biggest airports in the Baltic region and double the number of passengers it can handle.

Remember that on departure you'll need to fill out a final customs declaration (available at all the long tables) before proceeding through the first checkpoint. If you have nothing to declare, just head through the "green channel" of the customs area. Try to arrive at the airport at least two hours in advance. Bear in mind that check-in stops 40 minutes before departure, so don't count on making the plane at the last minute without some frantic pleading.

Both domestic and foreign airlines offer regular flights from Pulkovo to 45 countries. St. Petersburg air carrier Rossiya, Russia's second-largest airline after Aeroflot, offers direct flights to 27 countries out of Pulkovo II. Aeroflot only flies from St. Petersburg to Moscow, where passengers must take connecting flight to other destinations. Its tough competitor Transaero schedules flights both within Russia's and to countries that include Egypt, Thailand, Japan, the Dominican Republic, and India.

Airport Information Pulkovo I Airport (☎ 812/704-3822 ⊕ www. pulkovoairport.ru). **Pulkovo II Airport** (☎ 812/704-3444 ⊕ www.pulkovoairport.ru)

TRANSFERS

From Pulkovo I, municipal bus 39 (in Russian, the word to look for is "avtobus") or minibus ("marshrutka") 39 will take you to the Moskovskaya metro stop on Moskovsky prospekt; the stop at the airport is right outside the terminal. Tickets are sold on the bus, which runs every 20 minutes during the day. From Pulkovo II you can take municipal bus 13 or minibus 3, 13, 113, or 213. The bus ride costs about 27R. If you are traveling with a tour package, all transfers will have been arranged. If you're traveling alone, you're strongly advised to make advance arrangements with your hotel. There are plenty of taxis available, but you would be ill-advised to pick up a cab on your own if you don't speak Russian. Foreign tourists, especially passengers arriving at train stations and airports, are prime targets for scams, so be skeptical about offers.

If you want to take a cab, look for a desk with a "TAXI" sign at the exit from the airports. A clerk there will tell you the price you need to pay for your destination in the city. He or she will also give you two pieces of paper, one for you and one for a taxi driver, on which the price is stated. Therefore the driver won't be able to charge you more than that. A taxi from Pulkovo II to the city center will cost 700R–1000R. As you exit the airport, look for a person in a reflective yellow vest, who will direct you to a vacant taxi driver. The airport is about a 40-minute ride from the city center. When you return to the airport, a regular cab that you order by phone will cost you between 750R and 1,250R. The operator for Taxi Million tells you the fare in advance.

To take a bus back to Pulkovo II, take bus No. 13 from outside the Moskovskaya metro stop (you may have to buy an extra ticket for your luggage if it takes up what the conductor considers to be too much room). There are also marshrutki outside the metro stop; these are clearly marked, but difficult to squeeze your suitcases into. Marshrutki 213 and K-3 go along Moskovsky prospekt down to Sennaya Ploshchad in the city center, and a single fare costs 25R. Marshrutka 350 follows the same route until Sennaya Ploshchad, and then continues up to Primorskaya metro station via Teatralnaya Ploshchad. Full fare costs 30R.

Taxi Contacts Central Taxi (*Tsentralnoye Taksi* ☎ 812/312–0022). **Petersburg Taxi** (*Petersburgskoye Taxi* ☎ 068). **Taxi Million** (☎ 812/700–0000).

BOAT AND FERRY TRAVEL

In summer, you can enjoy a lovely one- or two-hour boat trip along the city's Neva River, seeing all the major sights from the water. Boats leave from piers in front of the Hermitage Museum, the Medny Vsadnik (Bronze Horseman) monument, and Peter and Paul Fortress. The pier at the Hermitage also docks hydrofoils that go to Peterhof, one of St. Petersburg's most attractive suburbs, which is famous for its fountains. A hydrofoil, which leaves every 15–30 minutes, takes you there in half an hour. You can take a hydrofoil to Kronshtadt, a suburb famous for its navel history, as well as Lomonosov. Both trips depart from Finland Station. Tours to the latter are rare, so expect a long wait in line. To take the ferry Princess Maria, which travels between St. Petersburg and Helsinki, make arrangements at the sea passenger terminal, which is on Vasilievsky Island at Ploshchad Morskoi Slavy. The trips takes a day to reach Helsinki and gives you a day to explore before returning. For inland trips to places such as Valaam Island, Kizhi Island, the popular Russian tourist village of Verkhniye Mandrogi, or Moscow, boats depart from the river passenger terminal from the end of April through early November.

Boat and Ferry Contacts River passenger terminal (✉ 195 pr. Obukhovskoi Oborony, Vladimirskaya ☎ 812/362–0239 or 812/362–5101 Ⓜ Proletarskaya). **Sea passenger terminal** (✉ Pl. Morskoi Slavy, 1, Vasilievsky Island ☎ 812/322–6052; St. Petersburg line for ferry tickets 812/702–0799).

BUS, TRAM, AND TROLLEY TRAVEL

Several firms operate bus routes between St. Petersburg and central Europe. A bus trip can be a reasonably comfortable way to connect with the Baltic states, Scandinavia, and Germany, although as with train travel in and out of the country, it entails a two- to three-hour wait at the border for everyone to clear customs. The Gorodskoi Avtobusny Vokzal (City Bus Station), open from 6:30 am until 11:30 pm, sells tickets for international and domestic routes. It takes about 15 minutes to walk to the station from Ligovsky prospekt metro station, but you are better off targeting the representative offices of the company you wish to use or going through a travel agent.

Among the most reliable of the bus companies is Eurolines, which runs coaches to Tallinn and Riga (and from these cities to destinations all over Europe). The Finnish bus company Finnord runs coaches between Helsinki and St. Petersburg via the border town of Vyborg. The service runs twice daily, leaving from Finnord's offices at 37 Italyanskaya ulitsa, and then at half a dozen Finnish towns before reaching Helsinki.

When traveling by bus, tram, or trolley, you must purchase a ticket from the conductor. At this writing, a ticket valid for one ride costs 21R, regardless of the distance you intend to travel; if you change buses, you must pay another fare. Buses, trams, and trolleys operate from 5:30 am to midnight, although service in the late evening hours and on Sunday tends to be unreliable.

Note that all public transportation vehicles tend to be extremely over-crowded during rush hours. It's very much the Russian philosophy that there's always room for one more passenger. Make sure you position yourself near the exits well before the point at which you want to disembark, or risk missing your stop. Buses tend to be newer and reasonably comfortable. Trolleys and trams, on the other hand, sometimes give the impression that they're held together with Scotch tape and effort of will, and can be extremely drafty. In winter the windows tend to ice up to the point where it's impossible to see where you are, so ask the conductor to tell you if in doubt.

Bus, Tram, and Trolley Contacts The City Bus Station (✉ *36 Obvodnovo kanala nab., Vladimirskaya* ☎ *812/766–5777* Ⓜ *Ligovsky Prospekt*). **Eurolines** (☎ *812/441–3757* ⊕ *www.eurolines.ru*). **Finnord** (✉ *37 Italyanskaya ul.* ☎ *812/314–8951* Ⓜ *Nevsky Prospekt*).

CAR TRAVEL

You can reach St. Petersburg from Finland via the Helsinki–St. Petersburg Highway through the border town of Vyborg; the main street into and out of town for Finland is Kamennoostrovsky prospekt. To reach Moscow, take Moskovsky prospekt; at the hotel Pulkovskaya round-about, take Mosvoskoye shosse (M–10/E–95), slightly to the left of the road to the airport. Bear in mind that it will take at least two hours to clear customs and immigration at the border, and at busy times (e.g., Friday night and weekends) it may take much longer.

METRO TRAVEL

St. Petersburg's metro is straightforward, efficient, and inexpensive, but its stops tend to be far apart.

Stations are deep underground—the city's metro is the deepest in the world—necessitating long escalator rides.

All central stations are infamous for theft and rank high in the city's list of pickpocket hot spots. Although the city police regularly trumpet successes and report arrests of more gangs, it doesn't seem to get any safer.

FARES AND SCHEDULES

To use the metro, you must purchase a token or a magnetic card (available at stations). The fare (25R) is the same regardless of distance. Alternatively, you may purchase a pass valid for an entire month (600R) and good for transport on all modes of city transportation. You can also opt for a two-week all-inclusive pass (300R), well worth the convenience if you plan to use the metro often.

There's a monthly pass for the metro only (460R), The price for tokens and passes has, in the last few years, been raised by a ruble or two each New Year. The metro operates from 5:30 am to 12.30 am, but is best avoided during rush hours. The nicer hotels often give out metro maps printed in English.

St. Petersburg History

"The most abstract and intentional city on earth"—to quote Fyodor Dostoyevsky—became the birthplace of Russian literature, the setting for his *Crime and Punishment* and Pushkin's *Eugene Onegin*. From here, Tchaikovsky, Rachmaninov, Prokofiev, and Rimsky-Korsakov went forth to conquer the world of the senses with unmistakably Russian music. It was in St. Petersburg that Petipa invented— and Pavlova, Nijinsky, and Ulanova perfected—the ballet. Later, at the start of the 20th century, Diaghilev enthralled the Western world with the performances of his Ballets Russes. Great architects were summoned to the city by 18th-century empresses to build palaces of marble, malachite, and gold. A century later it was here that Fabergé craftsmen created those priceless objects of beauty that have crowned the collections of royalty and billionaires ever since.

The grand, new capital of the budding Russian empire was built in 1703, its face to Europe, its back to reactionary Moscow, which had until this time been the country's capital. It was forcibly constructed, stone by stone, under the might and direction of Peter the Great, for whose patron saint the city is named. Building this city on such marshy ground was nearly an impossible achievement—so many men, forced into labor, died laying the foundations of this city that it was said to have been built on bones, not log posts. As one of 19th-century France's leading lights, the writer Madame de Staël, put it: "The founding of St. Petersburg is the greatest proof of that ardor of the Russian will that does not know anything is impossible." But if Peter's exacting plans called for his capital to be the

equal of Europe's great cities, they always took into account the city's unique attributes. Peter knew that his city's source of life was water, and whether building palace, fortress, or trading post, he never failed to make his creations serve it. Being almost at sea level (there is a constant threat of flooding), the city appears to rise straight up from its embracing waters. Half of the River Neva lies within the city's boundaries. As it flows into the Gulf of Finland, the river subdivides into the Great and Little Neva and the Great and Little Nevka. Together with numerous tributaries, they combine to form an intricate delta. Water weaves its way through the city's streets as well. Incorporating more than 100 islands and crisscrossed by more than 60 rivers and canals, the much more northerly St. Petersburg is often compared to that other great maritime city, Venice.

St. Petersburg's gleaming imperial palaces emphasize the city's regal bearing, even more so in the cold light of the Russian winter. The colorful facades of riverside estates glow gently throughout the long days of summer, contrasting with the dark blue of the Neva's waters. Between June and July, the city falls under the spell of the White Nights, or *Belye Nochy*. During this time following the summer solstice (from June to early July), night is banished, replaced by a twilight that usually lasts no more than 30 to 40 minutes. To honor this magical phenomenon, music festivals and gala events adorn the city's cultural calendar.

St. Petersburg is not just about its fairy-tale setting, however, for its history is integrally bound up in Russia's dark side, too—a centuries-long procession of wars and revolutions. In the 19th century, the city witnessed the struggle against tsarist oppression. Here the early fires of revolution were kindled, first in 1825 by a small band of starry-eyed aristocratic officers—the Decembrists—and then by organized workers' movements in 1905. The full-scale revolutions of 1917 led to the demise of the Romanov dynasty, the foundation of the Soviet Union, and the end of St. Petersburg's role as the nation's capital, as Moscow reclaimed that title. But the worst ordeal by far came during World War II, when the city—then known as Leningrad—withstood a 900-day siege and blockade by Nazi forces. Nearly 1.1 million civilians were killed in air raids, as a result of indiscriminate shelling, or died of starvation and disease.

St. Petersburg has had its name changed three times during its brief history. With the outbreak of World War I, it became the more Russian-sounding Petrograd. After Lenin's death in 1924, it was renamed Leningrad in the Soviet leader's honor. Following the failed coup d'etat of August 1991, which hastened the demise of the Soviet Union and amounted to another Russian revolution, the city reverted to its original name—it was restored by popular vote, the first time the city's residents were given a choice in the matter. There were some who opposed the change, primarily because memories of the siege of Leningrad and World War II had become an indelible part of the city's identity. But for all the controversy surrounding the name, residents have generally referred to the city simply—and affectionately—as Piter.

In honor of the city's 300th anniversary in May 2003, the government spent more than $1 billion restoring St. Petersburg to its prerevolutionary splendor. Some of that hastily applied gloss has begun to fade, but with St. Petersburg's most famous son, Vladimir Putin, having shone a light on his hometown, revamping for prestige events continues in fits and starts. More than ever, busloads of tourists come to feast their eyes on pastel palaces, glittering churches, and that great repository of artwork, the Hermitage.

8

TAXI TRAVEL

Although taxis roam the city quite frequently, it's far easier—and certainly safer—to order a cab through your hotel. Fares vary according to the driver's whim; you're expected to negotiate. Foreigners can often be charged much more than Russians, and oblivious tourists tend to be gouged. Make sure that you agree on a price before getting into the car, and try to have the correct money handy. ■TIP→ **If you speak Russian, you can order a cab by dialing one of the numbers listed below.**

There's sometimes a delay, but usually the cab arrives within 20–30 minutes; the company will phone you back when the driver is nearby. If you order a cab this way, you pay the official state fare, which turns out to be reasonable in dollars, plus a fee for the reservation. No tip is expected beyond rounding up the amount on the meter. If you hail a cab or a private car on the street, expect to pay the ruble equivalent of $8–$10 (around 250R) for most usual trips.

> ### SAFETY TIP
>
> St. Petersburg is a large city of almost 5 million inhabitants, and petty crime is a problem here. As a foreigner, you're an even more likely target for pickpockets and the like, especially in the metro and in and around Nevsky prospekt. Watch belongings carefully in such areas, and be careful when using your phone. Thieves have been known to grab mobiles and similar devices while their owners are distracted.

Taxi Contacts Central Taxi (*Tsentralnoye Taksi* ☎ 812/312-0022). **Petersburg Taxi** (*Peterburgskoye Taxi* ☎ 068). **Taxi Million** (☎ 812/700-0000).

TRAIN TRAVEL

St. Petersburg has several train stations, the most important of which are Baltic station (Baltiysky Vokzal), for trains to the Baltic countries; Finland station (Finlandsky Vokzal), for trains to Finland; Moscow station (Moskovsky Vokzal), at Ploshchad Vosstania, off Nevsky prospekt, for trains to Moscow and points east; and Vitebsk station (Vitebsky Vokzal), for trains to Ukraine and points south. Trains for Karelia and points north depart from the Finland station. All the major train stations have a connecting metro stop.

Train tickets may be purchased through the tourist bureau in your hotel or at the Central Railway Agency Office (Tsentralnoye Zheleznodorozhnoye Agenstvo) off Nevsky prospekt, adjacent to the Kazan Cathedral. The agency is open 8–8 Monday through Saturday and 8–4 on Sunday. The office has three information points that can point you in the direction of the correct desks. Even better is the Central Airline Ticket Agency on Nevsky, which has two train-ticket desks and is a far quieter option. It's possible to buy tickets at the stations themselves, but this is best attempted only by the brave or bilingual. You can also buy electronic tickets online.

FARES AND SCHEDULES

Several trains run daily between Moscow and St. Petersburg, including the *Krasnaya Strela* (Red Arrow), a night train that departs from one end at 11:55 pm and arrives at the other at 8:25 am the next day. Its Empire-style rival, *Nikolayevsky Express*, departs the city at 11:24

am and gets to Moscow at 7:10 pm. Designed to resemble a typical early-20th-century train and named after Russia's last tsar, Nicholas II, this romantic train has staff dressed in turn-of-the-20th-century costumes, oak settings in its restaurant, and brass details in compartments. You pay roughly 7,500R round-trip for a berth in a four-person compartment. The most popular trains between St. Petersburg and Moscow are the high-speed Sapsan trains. At least five trips are scheduled each day, traveling the 800 km

> ### WORD OF MOUTH
>
> "We were very glad we hired a private tour guide. We could have done it on our own, but she saved us a lot of time and provided excellent commentary in English (she, too, spoke better English than ours!) everywhere we went.... We communicated often prior to our trip, and she was invaluable in helping us plan our time." —Djkbooks

(500 mi) between the two cities in 3½ to 4¼ hours. The price ranges from 1,800R–4,900R. The Sapsans let you leave St. Peterburg as early as 6:45 am and arrive in Moscow by 10:30 am, or leave Moscow at 7:45 pm and arrive to St. Petersburg at 11:30 pm. The trains are modern, with amenities that include TV, food service, and the ability to order a taxi ahead of time. Check ⊕ *www.trainsrussia.com* for availability and pricing with an easy-to-use, budget-airline style online booking system in English for all trains between St. Petersburg and Moscow. Another good Web site is ⊕ *www.rzd.ru*, although it is easier to use if you know some Russian. There is also a train that travels twice daily to and from Helsinki; the trip, which leaves from Finland Station, takes 3½ hours; it costs from €84–€134.

Train Contacts **Central Airline Ticket Agency** (✉ *7/9 Nevsky pr., City Center* ☎ *812/315–0072 or 812/314–6959* Ⓜ *Nevsky Prospekt*). **Central Railway Agency Office** (✉ *24 Kanal Griboyedova, City Center* ☎ *812/710–6616* Ⓜ *Nevsky prospekt*). **Train information** (☎ *812/768–3344* ⊕ *www.trainsrussia.com*).

TOUR OPTIONS
TRAVEL AGENCIES
In addition to the private agencies, every major hotel has a tourist bureau through which individual and group tours can be booked. The Favorit travel agency can arrange many kinds of English-language tours around the city, including canal and river cruises. Reisebuero-Welt travel company has a similar range of services, including excursions around St. Petersburg and its suburbs in Russian, English, German, French, Italian, and other languages. Mir Travel Agency provides group and special themed tours.

Tour Contacts **Favorit** (✉ *10 ul. Marata, Vladimirskaya* ☎ *812/327–7163* ⊕ *www.favorit-travel.com* Ⓜ *Mayakovskaya*). **Mir Travel Agency** (✉ *1½ ul. Marata, Liteiny/Smolny* ☎ *812/325–7122 or 812/325–2595* ⊕ *mir-travel.com* Ⓜ *Mayakovskaya*). **Reisebuero-Welt** (✉ *Northern Capital business center, office 602h, 6th fl., 36 Naberezhnaya Moika River, City Center* ☎ *812/449–4564* ⊕ *www.reisebuero-welt.com* Ⓜ *Nevsky Prospekt*).

8

BOAT TOURS

A float down the Neva or through the city's twisting canals—*Exkursii na katere po rekam i kanalam*—is always a pleasant way to spend a summer afternoon or a White Night. For trips through the canals, take one of the boats at the pier near Anichkov Bridge on Nevsky prospekt. Boats cruising the Neva leave from the pier outside the State Hermitage Museum. Both boat trips have departures early morning to late afternoon from mid-May through mid-September. In warmer months, typically May through October, you can find many boats offering such trips along the Neva, and travel agents can help with booking. One of the biggest boat-tour companies is Vodohod.

Boat Tour Contacts Vodohod (✉ *39 Dvortsovaya Naberezhnaya, in front of the Hermitage Museum, Admiralteisky* ☎ *812/335–1717* ⊕ *www.vodohodneva.ru* Ⓜ *Nevsky Prospekt*).

PRIVATE TOUR GUIDES

There are many private tour guides who can provide detailed tours in English on the many sights within and outside of St. Petersburg. They can prove very helpful, especially in places like the Hermitage. Many of them are highly educated in history and art, and they must also go through a rigorous training process before becoming licensed. Rates can cost $20 an hour or higher. *Below is a sampling of a few trusted names.*

Private Tour Contacts Ksenia Belous (☎ *905/229–1907* ✎ *bel-ksenia@ yandex.ru*). **Taisiya Ivanova** (☎ *904/644–5550* ✎ *encc.ru@gmail.com* ⊕ *www. enjoypetersburg.com*). **Natalia Velikaya** (☎ *905/277–5394* ✎ *natour@mail.ru*). **Irina Yaschenko** (☎ *981/734–8639* ✎ *rina_yashl@mail.ru*).

WALKING TOURS

If you prefer to plunge into city life instead of observing it from the window of your tour bus, the best bet is to take an excursion (from 600R) with one of the city's best-known walking tour companies, Peter's Walking Tours. Founded by inveterate local backpacker Peter Kozyrev, the company turns walks and pub crawls into a real experience. The guides masterfully interweave history, current affairs, mystery, and gossip. The most popular walk is the five-hour-long Original Walking Tour: express your wishes and the guide tailors the route. Check the schedule on the company's Web site, choose a walk, and book it by email. There's no telephone number for the company, and all private tours have to be made via email.

Walking Tour Contacts Peter's Walking Tours (⊕ *www.peterswalk.com*).

GREAT ITINERARIES

IF YOU HAVE 3 DAYS

If you have only three days, begin your visit of the city on Vasilievsky Island and the Left Bank. Most of the city's historic sites are here, including the Rostral Columns, the Admiralty (Admiralteistvo), and the elegant St. Isaac's Cathedral. If you have the energy after lunch, dedicate some time to the State Museum of Russian Art, one of the country's most important art galleries. On your second day, rise early to tackle the gargantuan Hermitage, one of the world's richest repositories of art. Don't try to see it all in one visit; instead, cross the river to the Petrograd Side and have lunch by the Peter and Paul Fortress. After lunch spend the afternoon touring the Peter and Paul Fortress. On your third day, consider an excursion to Pushkin (formerly Tsarskoye Selo), south of St. Petersburg, once the summer residence of the Imperial family and a popular summer resort for the Russian

aristocracy. The main attraction here is the Catherine Palace, with its magnificent treasures, including the famed Amber Room. If you have the energy, take in a performance at the Mariinsky Theatre.

IF YOU HAVE 5 DAYS

Follow the three-day itinerary described above. Devote your fourth day to St. Petersburg's inner streets, squares, and gardens. Begin with the grandeur of Ploshchad Iskusstv, or Square of the Arts. Here you can visit the Ethnography Museum before moving on to the colorful Church of the Savior on Spilled Blood. Finish your walk at the Summer Garden with its famous railing designed by Yuri Felten in 1779. After lunch, visit the Kazan Cathedral. On the fifth day, if it's summer season, head west of St. Petersburg to Peterhof (*Petrodvorets*), accessible by hydrofoil. The fountains, lush parks, and the magnificent Great Palace are at their best in the summer.

8

VISITOR INFORMATION

The staff members of the City Tourist Information Center (Gorodskoi Turistichesky Tsentr Informatsii ot Soveta po Turismu) are generally friendly, although they have a tendency to thrust maps and booklets at you in the absence of any great ideas themselves. The center has a database on cultural and sports events, hotels, major tourist attractions, and so on. The center also runs information booths in the most-visited spots of the city, including Palace Square, St. Isaac's Square, Pulkovo I and Pulkovo II airports, in front of Gostinyi Dvor metro station, and at at Moskovsky Railway Station. At these booths, which have a big letter "I" on top, you can ask for help with directions, hours, and the like. Booth operators speak English, German, French, and Spanish. The booths are open daily 10–7. The center's tourist help line, staffed daily 9–11, can be quite useful. The English-speaking operators can help with typical tourist questions, but they can also call police or an ambulance and help translate in case of emergency. They can also book hotels, get you a table in a restaurant, or even order flowers upon your request. The center also runs the Angels Service (Sluzhba Angelov), in which young Russian students help visitors from Gostinyi Dvor metro station, the Moskovsky railway station, and other busy locations. The "angels" are dressed in a uniform that includes a red jacket, a white baseball cap with letter "I" on it, and blue bags. In summer they work 10–10 and in winter noon–6. Another good source for information and assistance is your hotel, because virtually all of the hotels have established tourist offices for their guests. These offices, which provide many services, can help you book individual and group tours, make restaurant reservations, or purchase theater tickets. Even if you're not a hotel guest, you're usually welcome to use these facilities, provided you are willing to pay the hefty fees for their services.

If you plan on spending a great deal of time in the city, it might be worthwhile to invest about 125R in the *Traveller's Yellow Pages for Saint Petersburg* (⊕ *www.infoservices.com*), a compact telephone book and handbook written in English, with maps as well as indexes in several languages, including English. You can pick one up at most of the bookstores that carry English-language books.

Visitor Information **City Tourist Information Center** (✉ *14/52 Sadovaya ul., City Center* ☏ *Information 812/310–2822 or 812/310–223; tourist help line 812/300–3333* ⊕ *eng.ispb.info* ⊘ *Weekdays 10–6* Ⓜ *Sennaya Ploshchad*).

EXPLORING ST. PETERSBURG

The city's focal point is the Admiralteistvo, or Admiralty, a spire-top golden-yellow building; a stone's throw away is the Winter Palace, the city's most visited attraction (it houses the Hermitage). Three major avenues radiate outward from the Admiralty: Nevsky prospekt (St. Petersburg's main shopping street), Gorokhovaya ulitsa, and Voznesensky prospekt. Most visitors begin at Palace Square, site of the fabled Hermitage. The square housed not only the center of power—the tsar's residence and the great offices of state—but also the splendid art collections of the imperial family. In the twilight of the tsar's empire, it was here that troops were ordered to disperse a workers' demonstration on Bloody Sunday in 1905—a decision that may have made the the Revolution of 1917 inevitable.

Wherever you go exploring in the city, remember that an umbrella can come in handy. In winter be prepared for rather cold days that alternate with warmer temperatures, often resulting in the famous Russian snowfalls. One note: as with most Russian museums, you will find that St. Petersburg's museums charge a small extra fee to entitle you to use your camera or video camera within their walls.

In Russia prices are officially listed in rubles. However, you may still see some prices listed in "conditional units." The "unit" is basically that day's dollar rate, or increasingly in St. Petersburg, that day's euro rate.

CITY CENTER: PALACE SQUARE AND THE HERMITAGE
ДВОРЦОВАЯ ПЛОЩАДЬ И ЭРМИТАЖ

The best place to get acquainted with St. Petersburg is the elegant Dvortsovaya Ploshchad, or Palace Square. Its scale alone can hardly fail to impress—the square's great Winter Palace was constructed to clearly out-Versailles Versailles—and within the palace is the best reason to come to St. Petersburg, the Hermitage. Renowned as one of the world's leading art museums, it also served as a residence of the Russian Imperial family, and provides a setting of unparalleled opulence for its dazzling collections, which include some of the greatest old master paintings in the world. As a relief from all this impressive glitz and grandeur, tucked away in the shadows of the great Imperial complex is the moving apartment museum of Alexander Pushkin, that most Russian of writers, set in a neighborhood that still conjures up early-19th-century Russia.

GETTING HERE AND AROUND

You can get close to the area by taking the metro to the Nevsky Prospekt station, exiting at the Kanal Griboyedova end. However, you'll still have to walk for 10–15 minutes along noisy Nevsky prospekt to reach the quiet of Palace Square. (It's not worth taking the bus for this distance, though—just walk.) Once you've reached the area, you'll find that the sites are all quite close to each other.

TIMING

Strolling through the Palace Square and taking in the sights from the outside may only take an hour or so, but it is a great introduction to St. Petersburg. The entire Hermitage cannot be seen in one day; you'll want to devote anywhere from a morning to two days to wander through it.

TOP ATTRACTIONS

Alexander Column (*Aleksandrovskaya Kolonna,* **Александровская Колонна**). The 156-foot-tall centerpiece of Palace Square is a memorial to Russia's victory over Napoléon. It was commissioned in 1830 by Nicholas I in memory of his brother, Tsar Alexander I, and was designed by Auguste Ricard de Montferrand. The column was cut from a single piece of granite and, together with its pedestal, weighs more than 650 tons. It stands in place by the sheer force of its own weight; there are no attachments fixing the column to the pedestal. When the memorial was erected in 1832, the entire operation took only an hour and 45 minutes, but 2,000 soldiers and 400 workmen were required, along with an elaborate system of pulleys and ropes. Crowning the column is an angel (symbolizing peace in Europe) crushing a snake, an allegorical depiction of Russia's defeat of Napoléon. ⌧ *Dvortsovaya Pl., City Center* Ⓜ *Nevsky Prospekt.*

Dvortsovaya Ploshchad (*Palace Square,* **Дворцовая Площадь**). One of the world's most magnificent plazas, the square is a stunning ensemble of buildings and open space, a combination of several seemingly incongruous architectural styles in perfect harmony. It's where the city's imperial past has been preserved in all its glorious splendor, but it also resonates with the history of the revolution that followed. Here, the fate of the last Russian tsar was effectively sealed, on Bloody Sunday in 1905, when palace troops opened fire on peaceful demonstrators, killing scores of women and children. It was across Palace Square in October 1917 that Bolshevik revolutionaries stormed the Winter Palace and overthrew Kerensky's Provisional Government, an event that led to the birth of the Soviet Union. Almost 75 years later, during tense days,

8

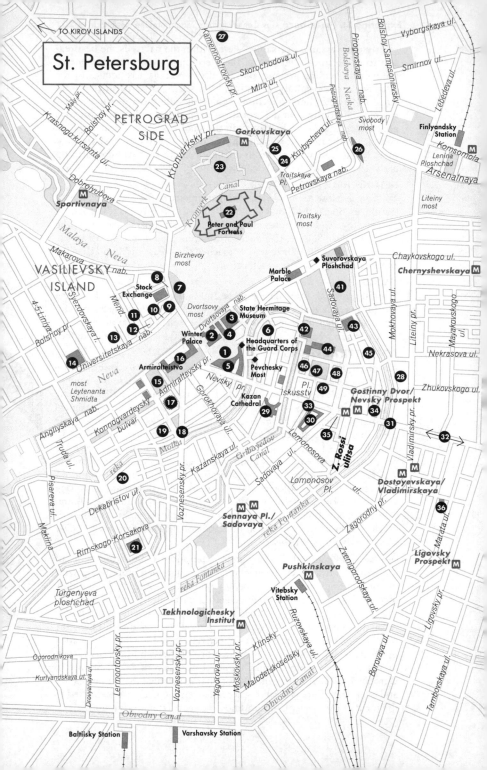

VYBORG
SIDE

Mineralnaya ul.

Zhukova ul.

Arsenalnaya

Kondratyevsky pr.

Sverdlovskaya nab.

Ploshchad
Lenina

ul.

Neva

nab.

Shpalernaya ul.

37 **38**

Tavricheskaya ul.

Tavrichesky
Park

Saltykova-Shchedrina ul.

Bolsheokhtinsky
most

Tulskaya ul.

LITEINY
SMOLNY

Suvorovski pr.

Moiseyenko ul.

Novgorodskaya ul.

Vosstaniya ul.

Grecheskiy pr.

8 Sovetskaya ul.

Mytninskaya ul.

Neva

Ploshchad
Vosstaniya/
Mayakovskaya

39

Bakunina

M Moskovsky
Station

Stary

VLADIMIRSKAYA

Nevsky pr.

A. Nevsky
Pl.

most
A. Nevsky

Ploshchad
Aleksandra Nevskovo

M

Alexander
Nevsky Lavra

40

Obuchovsky pr.

Glinyanaya ul.

KEY

M   Metro stops

8

A Walk Through the Historic District

Begin at **Dvortsovaya Ploshchad** (Palace Square). Extending the length of the western side of the square, with its back to the river, is the **Winter Palace,** which houses the legendary **State Hermitage Museum.** In the center of the square is the **Alexander Column,** commemorating the Russian victory over Napoléon in 1812. Dominating the eastern side of the square is the **General Staff Building,** formerly the army's general staff headquarters and now part of the Hermitage. Next to it is the **Headquarters of the Guard Corps;** leave by its right-hand side and cross the Pevchesky most, or Singing Bridge, to enter one of the most charming parts of the city, enchantingly threaded by the Zimnaya Kanavka, or the Little Winter Canal. On the opposite side of the Moika River, head for the moving museum honoring the great Pushkin, the **Alexander Pushkin Apartment Museum,** a short walk from the corner of Nevsky prospekt and naberezhnaya Moiki.

huge crowds rallied on Palace Square in support of perestroika and democracy. Today, the beautiful square is a bustling hubbub of tourist and marketing activity, lively yet seemingly imperturbable as ever. Horseback and carriage rides are available for hire here. A carriage ride around the square costs about 200R per person. A 20-minute tour of the city in the direction of your choosing costs about 2,000R, for up to six people. ⊠ *City Center* Ⓜ *Nevsky Prospekt.*

Fodor's Choice **State Hermitage Museum** (*Gosudarstvenny Ermitazh Muzey,* ★ Государственный Эрмитаж). Leonardo's *Benois Madonna* . . . Rembrandt's *Danaë* . . . Matisse's *The Dance* . . . you get the picture. As the former private art collection of the tsars, this is one of the world's most famous museums, virtually wallpapered with celebrated paintings. In addition, the walls are works of art themselves, for this collection is housed in the lavish Winter Palace, one of the most outstanding examples of Russian baroque magnificence. The museum takes its name from Catherine the Great (1729–96), who used it for her private apartments, intending them to be a place of retreat and seclusion. "Only the mice and I can admire all this," the empress once declared.

Between 1764 and 1775, the empress undertook, in competition with rulers whose storehouses of art greatly surpassed Russia's, to acquire some of the world's finest works of art. Sometimes acquiring entire private collections outright, she quickly filled her gallery with masterpieces from all over the world. This original gallery section of the Hermitage, completed in 1770 by Vallin de la Mothe, is now known as the Maly (Little) Hermitage. It's attached to the Stary (Old) Hermitage, which was built in 1783 by Yuri Felten to house the overflow of art (it also contained conference chambers for the tsarina's ministers). Attached to the Hermitage by an arch straddling the Winter Canal is the **Hermitage Theater,** built between 1783 and 1787 by the Italian architect Giacomo Quarenghi. Yet another addition, the New Hermitage, was built between 1839 and 1852 under Catherine's grandson,

Nicholas I; it became Russia's first public museum, although admission was by royal invitation only until 1866. Its facade is particularly striking, with 10 male figures cut from monolithic gray granite supporting the portico. Today's Hermitage is one of the world's richest repositories of art; it was continually enlarged with tsarist treasures and acquisitions, all later confiscated and nationalized, along with numerous private collections, by the Soviet government after the 1917 Bolshevik Revolution.

The entrance to the museum is through the main gates on Palace Square. When you first enter the Hermitage, you'll see a *kassa* (ticket window) on both the right and left. Once you buy tickets, you can check your belongings and then return to enter the hall that was to your left as you entered the museum. Note that ticket-takers are strict about oversize bags and about foreigners trying to enter on Russian-rate tickets.

> **WORD OF MOUTH**
>
> "I spent one entire day, from open to close, in the Hermitage.... Good god, what is there to say. It far, far, far exceeded my expectations. I saw more than I thought I would, I liked more than I thought I would.... Then the Michelangelo, oh good lord, hurt me now, just sublime with the back and leg muscles just perfect. And just when you start to get the feeling that life can't be any better than four Velázquez, three El Grecos, and an exquisite Goya, [there's] Rembrandt's *Danaë*.... This painting is just absolutely breathtaking."　　—Amyb

With more than 400 exhibit halls and gilded salons, it's impossible to see everything here in a single day. Since you probably only have a few hours, be sure to take in the major attractions, which include Egyptian mummies and Scythian gold; the splendid halls of Russian tsars; the Peacock Clock; the great paintings of Leonardo, Rembrandt, Van Dyck, and Velázquez; and the outstanding collection of Impressionists and Postimpressionists.

Official guided tours (in English) tend to be rushed and you may want to return on your own. Consider hiring a private guide from outside the museum instead—their licensing requires a year of study and training and they'll take their time explaining the artwork to you. During peak tourist season, or when there's a special exhibition, you may encounter long lines at the museum entrance. Note that the Hermitage is closed on Monday.

The museum's eight sections are not clearly marked, and the floor plans available are not very useful, though they are in English as well as Russian. To orient yourself before your trip, you can go on a virtual tour of the museum on the Web site (⊕ *www.hermitagemuseum.org*). Just after you have your ticket checked at the front entrance, head straight to the computer consoles in front of you—the plans shown here are similarly short on information, but you can print them out, complete with instructions on how to get to various rooms. Enjoy your wander, and don't be shy about asking the guards to point you in the right direction.

There's also a helpful information desk in the main hall, before you go into the museum, where you can ask specific questions.

There are three floors to wander through: the ground, first, and second. The **ground floor** covers prehistoric times, displaying discoveries made on former Soviet territory, including Scythian relics and artifacts; art from the Asian republics, the Caucasus, and their peoples; and Greek, Roman, and Egyptian art and antiquities. On the ground floor, head for the Hall of Ancient Egypt, the Pazyryk exhibition, and the Hall of the Big Vase. The first contains the remains of a mummified priest; the second, a mummified Scythian tsar and his horses as well as the most ancient carpet in the world; the third, a magnificent example of Russian stone-carving—the huge Kolyvan vase in the center of the hall. It's 2.57 meters (2.81 yards) high and weighs 19 tons.

Possibly the most prized section of the Hermitage—and definitely the most difficult to get into—is the ground floor's **Treasure Gallery**, also referred to as the Zolotaya Kladovaya (Golden Room). This spectacular collection of gold, silver, and royal jewels is well worth the hassle and additional entrance fee. The collection is divided into two sections. The first section, covering prehistoric times, includes Scythian gold and silver treasures of striking simplicity and refinement recovered from the Crimea, Ukraine, and Caucasus. The second section contains a dizzying display of precious stones, jewelry, and such extravagances as jewel-encrusted pillboxes and miniature clocks, all from the 16th through the 20th centuries.

You'll find the Pavilion Hall on the **first floor**, which is known for the wondrous Peacock Clock. The hall itself, with 28 crystal chandeliers, is impressive in its own right. The Knights' Room is also on this floor, with armor on display that includes a child-size version and one made for a horse. The first floor also has many rooms that have been left as they were when the imperial family lived in the Winter Palace. Through the entrance hall you can reach the first-floor galleries by way of the Jordan Staircase, a dazzling 18th-century creation of marble, granite, and gold. One of the first rooms you pass through on the first floor is the Malachite Room, with its displays of personal items from the imperial family. In the White Dining Room the Bolsheviks seized power from the Provisional Government in 1917. Balls were staged in the Great Hall and in the smaller Concert Hall (which now also holds the silver coffin—but not the body—of the hero Alexander Nevsky).

A wealth of Russian and European art is also on this floor: Florentine, Venetian, and other Italian art through the 18th century, including Leonardo's *Benois Madonna* and *Madonna Litta* (Room 214), Michelangelo's *Crouching Boy* (Room 229), two Raphaels, eight Titians, and works by Tintoretto, Lippi, Caravaggio, and Canaletto. The Hermitage also houses a superb collection of Spanish art, including works by El Greco, Velázquez, Murillo, and Goya. Its spectacular presentation of Flemish and Dutch art contains roomfuls of Van Dycks, including portraits done in England when he was court painter to Charles I. Also here are more than 40 canvasses by Rubens (Room 247) and an equally impressive number of Rembrandts, including *Flora, Abraham's*

CLOSE UP

The Fate of Rembrandt's Danaë

One of the most celebrated of Rembrandt's works, and among the most beautiful examples of European painting, the *Danaë* was almost irreparably damaged in 1985 when a mentally deranged man twice knifed and then splashed sulfuric acid on the painting in front of a stunned tour group. Acquired by Catherine the Great in 1772, it was one of the jewels of her collection. After the shocking act of vandalism the canvas, completed by the Dutch master in 1636, was a mess of brown spots and splashes. The process of restoration began the same day, when after consulting chemists, the Hermitage restorers washed the canvas with water to stop the chemical reaction. It then took 12 years to reconstruct the picture, which was finally placed on view again in 1997. It's now covered with armored glass to prevent any further damage. The painting is not 100% Rembrandt anymore, but the original spirit of the work remains intact.

Sacrifice, and *The Prodigal Son* (Room 254). His famous *Danaë*, which was mutilated by a knife- and acid-wielding lunatic in 1985, was put back on display in 1997. A smattering of excellent British paintings, extending also to the next floor, includes works by Joshua Reynolds, Thomas Gainsborough, and George Morland.

Reflecting the Francophilia of the empresses Elizabeth and Catherine, the museum is second only to the Louvre in its collection of French art. The scope is so extraordinary that the collection must be housed on both the first and second floors. Along with masterpieces by Lorrain, Watteau, and Poussin—including Poussin's *Tancrède et Herminie* (Room 279)—there are also early French art and handicrafts, including some celebrated tapestries.

On the **second floor,** you can start with the French art of the 19th century, where you'll find Delacroix, Ingres, Corot, and Courbet. You then come to a stunning collection of Impressionists and Postimpressionists, originally gathered mainly by two prerevolutionary industrialists and art collectors, Sergei Shchukin and Ivan Morozov. They include Monet's deeply affecting *A Lady in the Garden,* Degas's *Woman at Her Toilette* and *After the Bath,* and works by Sisley, Pissarro, and Renoir. Sculptures by Auguste Rodin and a host of pictures by Cézanne, Gauguin, and van Gogh are followed by Picasso and a lovely room of Matisse, including one of the amazing *Joys.* Somewhat later paintings—by the Fauvist André Derain and by Cubist Fernand Léger, for example—are also here. Rounding out this floor is the museum's collection of Asian and Middle and Near Eastern art, a small American collection, and two halls of medals and coins.

■ **TIP→** The best deal is to buy a two-day combined-entrance ticket, which allows you to visit the State Hermitage Museum and three other museums: the original, wooden Winter Palace of Peter the Great, accessible through a tunnel from the museum (historians believe this tunnel is the site where Peter died); the General Staff Building; and Menshikov Palace.

CLOSE UP

The Peacock Clock

The Peacock Clock (*Tchasy Pavlin*), one of the most delightful pieces on display at the State Hermitage Museum, is in the Pavilion Hall, on the first floor. The clock consists of a gilded peacock on a branch, a rooster, and an owl in a cage. Designed by the famous London jeweler and goldsmith James Cox and brought in pieces to St. Petersburg for Russian empress Catherine the Great in 1781, the clock is still in working order. Over the past decades it has been wound once a week to activate the moving pieces—the peacock spreads its wings and turns in a circle, the rooster crows, and the owl opens and closes its eyes—but recently the museum has cancelled this weekly ritual to save the aging mechanisms. Even without motion the clock is still a must-see. If you have kids with you, ask them to count all the creatures on the clock. There are more than just the three birds: for instance, there's a dragonfly that acts as the tiny second hand on the mushroom dial.

Tours in English (of several sections of the museum or just the Trea-sure Gallery) are available and highly recommended. Tours are nor-mally given once or twice a day around noon, 1, or 2 pm, but make sure to call a day before to figure out the exact time. An exchange bureau, Internet café, and theater ticket office are on the premises. ⊠ *2 Dvortsovaya Pl., City Center* ☎ *812/710–9625 recorded informa-tion in Russian; 812/710–9079 information desk; 812/571–8446 tours* ⊕ *www.hermitagemuseum.org* ✉ *State Hermitage Museum 400R (free 1st Thurs. of month), two-day combined-entrance ticket 780R (this can only be purchased through the Web site), personal excursion guide 7,000R for groups up to seven people, Treasure Gallery 300R in addi-tion to the entrance ticket price (check the schedule for the tours to the Gallery a day before your visit by calling the tour service phone)* ⊙ *Tues.–Sat. 10:30–6, Sun. 10:30–5; kassa (ticket window) open Tues.– Sat. until 5, Sun. until 4* Ⓜ *Nevsky Prospekt.*

Fodor's Choice
★
Winter Palace (*Zimny Dvorets*, Зимний Дворец). With its 1,001 rooms swathed in malachite, jasper, agate, and gilded mirrors, this famous pal-ace—the residence of Russia's rulers from Catherine the Great (1762) to Nicholas II (1917)—is the focal point of Palace Square. The palace, now the site of the State Hermitage Museum, is the grandest monument of Russian rococo, that eye-popping mix of the old-fashioned 17th-century baroque and the newfangled 18th-century neoclassical style (at the time of the palace's construction a chic import from France). Now "Rus-sianized," the palace's neoclassic ornament lost its early gracefulness and Greek sense of proportion and evolved toward the heavier, more monumental, Imperial style. Still, the exterior—adorned with rows of columns and outfitted with 2,000 heavily decorated windows—is par-ticularly successful and pleasing; note the way its enormous horizontal expanses of outer wall are broken up by vertical lines and variations of lines, pediments, and porches, all topped with a roof balustrade of statues and vases.

The palace, which was created by the Italian architect Bartolomeo Francesco Rastrelli, stretches from Palace Square to the Neva River embankment. It was the fourth royal residence on this site, the first having been a wooden palace for Peter the Great (today, a remnant of this palace exists and has been restored; it can be visited separately within the State Hermitage Museum). Oddly enough, the all-powerful tsar had to observe some bureaucratic fine print himself. Because it was forbidden to grant land from this site to anyone not bearing naval rank, Peter had to obtain a shipbuilder's license before building his palace. The current palace was commissioned in 1754 by Peter the Great's daughter Elizabeth. By the time it was completed,

> ## PUSHKIN: RUSSIA'S POETIC LOVE
>
> Alexander Pushkin is undoubtedly the most beloved poet in Russia, and most any citizen can quote from his poetry the way Westerners may quote Shakespeare. *"Moroz I solntse! Den chudesnyi!"* ("Snow, frost and sunshine. Lovely morning!") Russians exclaim on a clear winter day, reciting lines from "Winter Morning" ("Zimneye Utro"). Though he only lived to be 37, he had many loves, was exiled by Tsar Alexander I for his criticism of the monarchy, and married one of the most beautiful women of his time, Natalya Goncharova.

in 1762, Elizabeth had died and the craze for the Russian rococo style had waned. Catherine the Great left the exterior unaltered but had the interiors redesigned in the neoclassical style of her day. In 1837, after the palace was gutted by fire, the interiors were revamped once again. Three of the most celebrated rooms are the Gallery of the 1812 War, where portraits of Russian commanders who served against Napoléon are on display; the Great Throne Room, richly decorated in marble and bronze; and the Malachite Room, designed by the architect Alexander Bryullov and decorated with columns and pilasters of malachite. These rooms and parts of the Winter Palace that encompass the State Hermitage Museum are the only bits of the palace on view to the public. When touring the museum, you must therefore think of portions of it as the imperial residence it once was. ✉ *34 Dvortsovaya Pl., City Center* ☎ *812/710–9625 recorded information in Russian or 812/710–9079 directory service in Russian and English* ⊕ *www.hermitagemuseum. org* ✉ *400R; 2-day combined-entrance ticket 780R (this can only be purchased through the Web site* ☉ *Tues.–Sat. 10:30–6, Sun. 10:30–5 kassa open Tues.–Sat. until 5, on Sun. until 4* Ⓜ *Nevsky Prospekt.*

WORTH NOTING

★ **Alexander Pushkin Apartment Museum** (*Muzey Kvartira Alexandra Pushkina,* Музей-квартира Александра Пушкина). After fighting a duel to defend his wife's honor, the beloved Russian poet Alexander Pushkin died in a rented apartment in this building on January 27, 1837. The poet lived out the last act of his illustrious career here, and what a life it was. Pushkin (b. 1799) occupies in Russian literature the position enjoyed by Shakespeare and Goethe in the respective literatures of England and Germany. He is most famous as the author of *Eugene Onegin,* the ultimate tale of unrequited love, whose Byronic hero is seen more as the victim than as the arbiter of his own fate (a new sort of "hero" who cleared the path for the later achievements of Tolstoy and Chekhov). At the heart of this story—which involves a young genteel girl who falls in love with Onegin only to be rejected, then years later winds up rejecting Onegin when he falls in love with her—is a sense of despair, which colored much of Pushkin's own life and death. The poet was killed by a dashing count who had openly made a play for Pushkin's wife, Natalya Goncharova, reputedly "the most beautiful woman in Russia."

BEST BETS

■ **For Architecture**: Dvortsovaya Ploshchad, St. Isaac's Cathedral

■ **For Art**: State Hermitage Museum

■ **For Romance**: Strelka

■ **For Kids**: Zoological Museum

■ **For Military Sights**: *Avrora* cruiser ship

■ **For History**: Peter and Paul Fortress

Pushkin actually lived at this address less than a year (and could afford it only because of the palace owners, the noble Volkhonsky family, co-sympathizers with the poet for the Decembrist cause). The apartment museum has been restored to give it the appearance of an upper-middle-class dwelling typical of the beginning of the 19th century. (Pushkin had to support a family of six with his writing, so his apartment was less luxurious than it looks now.) Although few of the furnishings are authentic, his personal effects (including the waistcoat he wore during the duel) and those of his wife are on display. Recently, St. Petersburg forensic experts verified that the bloodstains on the sofa here were indeed left by the poet's gunshot wound. The library, where Pushkin actually expired, has been rebuilt according to sketches made by his friend and fellow poet Vasily Zhukovsky, who was holding vigil in his last hours. A moving tape-recorded account leads you through the apartment and retells the events leading up to the poet's death. ⊠ *12 nab. Moika, City Center* ☎ *812/314–0006* ⊕ *www.museumpushkin. ru* ⊠*100R; audioguide in English, German, French, or Italian 100R* ☉ *Wed.–Mon. 10:30–5. Closed last Fri. of month* Ⓜ *Nevsky Prospekt.*

QUICK BITES

The Pushka Inn (⊠ *14 nab. Moika, City Center* ☎ *812/312–0957* Ⓜ *Nevsky Prospekt*), a business-class hotel and bar-restaurant next to the Alexander Pushkin Apartment Museum and a short walk from the Hermitage and Palace Square, is a great place to grab a refreshing drink and something to eat at any time of the day. The extensive menu includes *blini* (pancakes) with caviar, homemade *pelmeni* (meat dumplings), borscht, and *vareniki* (a Ukrainian dish—dumplings filled with all kinds of stuffing, such as cabbage, cherries, and mushrooms). The name is both a play on Pushkin's name and the Russian word for cannon—which explains the military-theme paintings and the miniature cannon near the entrance. The spot is popular with expats.

General Staff Building (*Glavny Shtab,* **Главный Штаб**). The eastern side of Palace Square is formed by the huge arc of this building; its form and size give the square its unusual shape. During tsarist rule this was the site of the army headquarters and the ministries of foreign affairs and finance. Created by the architect Carlo Giovanni Rossi in the neoclassical style and built between 1819 and 1829, the General Staff Building is actually two structures connected by a monumental archway. Together they form the longest building in Europe. The arch itself is another commemoration of Russia's victory over Napoléon. Topping it is an impressive 33-foot-tall bronze of Victory driving a six-horse chariot, created by the artists Vasily Demut-Malinovsky and Stepan Pimenov. The passageway created by the arch leads from Palace Square to St. Petersburg's most important boulevard, Nevsky prospekt. Part of the Hermitage, the building has a permanent display on its history and architecture, plus temporary exhibits of local and international artwork. ⊠ *Dvortsovaya Pl., City Center* ☎ *812/311–3420* ⊕ *www. hermitagemuseum.org* 🎫 *200R, 700R for multi-access ticket to several branches of State Hermitage Museum* ☉ *Tues.–Sun. 10:30–6, kassa open until 5* Ⓜ *Nevsky Prospekt.*

THE ADMIRALTEISKY AND VASILIEVSKY ISLAND
АДМИРАЛТЕЙСТВО И ВАСИЛЬЕВСКИЙ

The Admiralteisky is the area just west of the City Center. It is centered around the famous golden-yellow Admiralteistvo, or Admiralty building. This neighborhood is also home to Decembrists' Square, the site where roughly 3,000 army officers revolted on December 14, 1825. One of the city's most famous monuments, the Bronze Horseman is located in the middle of the square—it's dedicated to Peter the Great. Across the Neva river is Vasilievsky Ostrov (Vasilievsky Island), the largest island in the Neva Delta and one of the city's oldest developed sections. Peter the Great wanted his city center there, and his original plans for the island called for a network of canals for the transport of goods from the main sea terminal to the city's commercial center at the opposite end of the island. These plans to re-create Venice never materialized, although some of the smaller canals were actually dug (and later filled in). These would-be canals are now streets, and are called "lines" (*liniya*). Instead of names they bear numbers, and they run parallel to the island's three main thoroughfares: the Great (Bolshoi), Middle (Sredny), and Small (Maly) prospekts. Now the island is a popular residential area, with most of its historic sites concentrated on its eastern edge. The island's western tip, facing the Gulf of Finland, houses the city's main sea terminals.

GETTING HERE AND AROUND

To get to the Admiralteisky, take a metro to Nevsky prospekt station and leave it through the Canal Griboyedova exit. After a 15-minute walk down Nevsky prospekt, you'll reach the golden-spired Admiralty. You can take a 1 or 7 trolley from any stop on Nevsky prospect. You can also take a taxi there or drive if you're far away. To reach Vasilievsky Island, from the Admiralty, cross Dvortsovy most (Palace

8

St. Petersburg in Literature

"On an exceptionally hot evening early in July, a young man came out of the garret in which he lodged in S. Place and walked slowly, as though in hesitation, towards K. Bridge." Thus opens Fyodor Dostoyevsky's *Crime and Punishment,* one of the greatest crime stories ever written, with the protagonist Rodion Raskolnikov making his way through 19th-century St. Petersburg. Both the grand landmarks and miserable details of St. Petersburg were so powerfully inspiring to the giants of Russian literature that the city became as much an inseparable part of their writing as it was of their lives.

The beloved Russian poet Alexander Pushkin (1799–1837) lived and died in St. Petersburg, and he honored the mighty capital in his works. In his epic *Bronze Horseman,* he immortalized the equestrian statue of Peter the Great on Decembrists' Square. In the poem, a poor clerk imagines that the rearing statue—which evokes the creative energy and ruthlessness of Peter—comes to life and chases him though the streets. In his poetic novel *Eugene Onegin,* Pushkin writes of St. Petersburg's early-19th-century high society—of balls, receptions, theaters, and ballets.

In contrast, Dostoyevsky's St. Petersburg is a place of catastrophes, strange events, crimes, and dramas. His heroes live desperate lives in a dank city of slums, poverty, and hopelessness. Fyodor Dostoyevsky (1821–81) was born in Moscow but spent much of his life in St. Petersburg, and was so scrupulous about describing the city that you can find many of the places where his "brain-children"—as he called his characters—lived. Dostoyevsky lived at 19 ulitsa Grazhdanskaya for a time, and many believe this is the apartment he used as a model for Raskolnikov's home. Dostoyevsky wrote that on his way to murder the elderly pawnbroker, Raskolnikov took 730 steps from his lodgings to the victim's lodging at 104 Kanal Griboyedova/25 ulitsa Rimskovo-Korsakova. You can re-create this walk, though it requires more than 730 steps.

Nikolai Gogol (1809–52) also portrayed a shadowy St. Petersburg— a city of nonsensical businesslike character and ridiculous bureaucratic fuss. In Gogol's short story "The Nose," the protagonist, low-rank civil servant Kovalyov, loses his nose and must search through St. Petersburg to find it. The nose starts boosting its own bureaucratic career, obtains a higher rank than its owner, and ignores the desperate Kovalyov. To mark Gogol's satirical story, a bas-relief nose is displayed at the corner of Voznesenskii prospekt and ulitsa Rimskogo-Korsakova. The "memorial" regularly gets stolen.

The poetry of Anna Akhmatova (1889–1966) reflects the changing face of St. Petersburg during her lifetime. Born in the St. Petersburg suburb of Tsarskoye Selo, Akhmatova wrote romantic and nostalgic verse about her beloved city at the beginning of her career. As the city changed, so did her poetry, based in part on her firsthand experience of Stalin's repression. Her son was imprisoned, and her works were harshly denounced by government officials. Her poem "Requiem" describes the horrors of those times. During the siege of Leningrad, Akhmatova read on the city radio her poems of support for the hungry and dying city residents.

Bridge), which starts between the Admiralty and the Hermitage. The bridge takes you to the island's end, and you'll get right to the island's easternmost tip, called Strelka ("arrow"). It's here that the Neva River splits into two parts, on either side of the island. As you stand in Birzhevaya Ploshchad, as the park on the Strelka is called, you'll be between two thick, brick-red columns, known as the Rostral Columns, and have a magnificent view of the city's major sights.

TOP ATTRACTIONS

Admiralty (*Admiralteistvo*, **Адмиралтейство**). The Admiralty is considered the city's architectural center, and its flashing spire—visible at various points throughout the city—is one of St. Petersburg's most renowned emblems. To get the picture-perfect first impression, walk around to the front of this lovely golden-yellow building.

A series of earlier constructions, all related to the naval industry, were once on this site. The first was a shipyard of Peter the Great's, followed by an earthen fortress that guarded the port; after these came the first Admiralty, made of stone and topped by the famous spire that has endured to grace each successive structure.

Used as a shipbuilding center through the 1840s, it has belonged to the Higher Naval Academy since 1925 and is closed to the public.

An Admiralty Lawn once adorned its front expanse, but in Tsar Alexander I's time it was turned into a small park bearing his name (to which it has been returned, after having been named for Maxim Gorky under the Communists). As you walk through the park, you'll see various statues, mostly of artists such as the composer Mikhail Glinka and the writer Mikhail Lermontov; the one accompanied by the delightful camel is of Nikolai Przhevalsky, a 19th-century explorer of Central Asia. ⊠ *Admiralteisky pr., Admiralteisky* Ⓜ *Nevsky Prospekt.*

Chamber of Art (*Kunstkammer,* **Кунсткамера**). The Chamber of Art, also called the Chamber of Curiosities, is a fine example of the Russian baroque. Painted bright azure with white trim, the building stands out from the surrounding classically designed architecture. It was originally commissioned in 1718 to house Peter the Great's collection of oddities, gathered during his travels. Completed by 1734, the Kunstkammer (from the German *Kunst,* "art," and *Kammer,* "chamber") was destroyed by fire in 1747 and almost entirely rebuilt. Today it houses the **Museum of Anthropology and Ethnography** but still includes a room with Peter's original collection, a truly bizarre assortment ranging from rare precious stones to preserved human organs and fetuses. The museum is enormously popular, so buy your entrance tickets early in the day. ⊠ *3 Universitetskaya nab., Vasilievsky Island* ☎ *812/328–1412* ▒*250R* ⊙ *Tues.–Sun. 11–6, kassa open until 4:45. Closed last Tues. of month* Ⓜ *Vasileostrovskaya.*

Senatskaya Square (*Senatskaya Ploschad,* **Сенатская Площадь**). This square holds one of St. Petersburg's best-known landmarks: the gigantic equestrian statue of Peter the Great. From 1925 through 2008 the square was known as "Decembrists' Square," a reference to the dramatic events that unfolded here on December 14, 1825. Following the death of Tsar Alexander I (1777–1825), a group of aristocrats,

8

some of whom were army officers, staged a rebellion on the square in an attempt to prevent the crowning of Nicholas I (1796–1855) as the new tsar, and perhaps do away with the monarchy altogether. Their coup was suppressed with much bloodshed by troops who were loyal to Nicholas, and those rebels who were not executed were banished to Siberia. Although the Decembrists, as they came to be known, did not bring significant change to Russia in their time, their attempts at liberal reform were often cited by the Soviet regime as proof of deep-rooted revolutionary fervor in Russian society.

In the center of the square is the grand statue called the **Medny Vsadnik** (Bronze Horseman), erected as a memorial from Catherine the Great to her predecessor, Peter the Great. The simple inscription on the base reads, "To Peter the First from Catherine the Second, 1782." Created by the French sculptor Étienne Falconet and his student Marie Collot, the statue depicts the powerful Peter, crowned with a laurel wreath, astride a rearing horse that symbolizes Russia, trampling a serpent representing the forces of evil. The enormous granite rock on which the statue is balanced comes from the Gulf of Finland. Reportedly, Peter liked to stand on it to survey his city from afar. Moving it was a Herculean effort, requiring a special barge and machines and nearly a year's work. The statue was immortalized in a poem of the same name by Alexander Pushkin, who wrote that the tsar "by whose fateful will the city was founded beside the sea, stands here aloft at the very brink of a precipice, having reared up Russia with his iron curb." ⊠ *Senatskaya Ploschad, Admiralteisky* Ⓜ *Sennaya Ploshchad.*

Rostral Columns (*Rostralnyie Kolonny,* **Ростральные Колонны**). Swiss architect Thomas de Thomon designed these columns, which were erected between 1805 and 1810 in honor of the Russian fleet. The monument takes its name from the Latin *rostrum,* meaning "prow." Modeled on similar memorials in ancient Rome, the columns are decorated with ships' prows; sculptures at the base depict Russia's main waterways, the Dnieper, Volga, Volkhov, and Neva rivers. Although the columns originally served as lighthouses—until 1855 this was St. Petersburg's commercial harbor—they are now lit only on special occasions, such as City Day (May 27). The columns were designed to frame the architectural centerpiece of this side of the embankment—the old Stock Exchange, which now holds the Naval Museum. ⊠ *Birzhevaya Pl., Vasilievsky Island* Ⓜ *Vasileostrovskaya.*

Fodor's Choice **St. Isaac's Cathedral** (*Isaakievsky Sobor,* **Исаакиевский Собор**). The
★ grandly proportioned St. Isaac's is the world's third-largest domed cathedral and the first monument you see of the city if you arrive by ship. Its architectural distinction is up for debate; some consider the massive design and highly ornate interior to be excessive, but others revel in its opulence. Tsar Alexander I commissioned the construction of the cathedral in 1818 to celebrate his victory over Napoléon, but it took more than 40 years to actually build it. The French architect Auguste Ricard de Montferrand devoted his life to the project, and died the year the cathedral was finally consecrated, in 1858.

Tickets, which can be bought at the kassa outside, are sold both to the church ("the museum") and to the outer colonnade; the latter affords an excellent view of the city. Follow the signs in English. The interior of the cathedral is lavishly decorated with malachite, lazulite, marble, and other stones and minerals. Gilding the dome required 220 pounds of gold. At one time a Foucault pendulum hung here to demonstrate the axial rotation of the earth, but it was removed in the late 20th century. After the Revolution of 1917 the cathedral was closed to worshippers, and in 1931 was opened as a museum; services have since resumed. St. Isaac's was not altogether returned to the Orthodox Church, but Christmas and Easter are celebrated here (note that Orthodox holidays follow the Julian calendar and fall about 13 days after their Western equivalents).

When the city was blockaded during World War II, the gilded dome was painted black to avoid its being targeted by enemy fire. Despite efforts to protect it, the cathedral nevertheless suffered heavy damage, as bullet holes on the columns on the south side attest.

Opening up in front of the cathedral is **Isaakievskaya Ploshchad** (St. Isaac's Square), which was completed only after the cathedral was built. In its center stands the **Nicholas Statue.** Unveiled in 1859, this statue of Tsar Nicholas I was commissioned by the tsar's wife and three children, whose faces are engraved (in the allegorical forms of Wisdom, Faith, Power, and Justice) on its base. It was designed, like St. Isaac's Cathedral and the Alexander Column, by Montferrand. The statue depicts Nicholas mounted on a rearing horse. Other engravings on the base describe such events of the tsar's reign as the suppression of the Decembrists' uprising and the opening ceremonies of the St. Petersburg–Moscow railway line.

To one side of the cathedral, where the prospekt meets Konnogvardeisky bulvar, is the early-19th-century **Konnogvardeisky Manège,** gracefully designed by Giacomo Quarenghi and decorated with marble statues of the mythological twins Castor and Pollux. This former barracks of the Imperial horse guards is used as an art exhibition hall. Every January it hosts an exhibition of new works by St. Petersburg artists. ⊠ *1 Isaakievskaya Pl., Admiralteisky* ☎ *812/315–9732* ⌨ *Cathedral 200R, colonnade 100R* ⊙ *Cathedral May–Sept., Thurs.–Tues. 10 am–7 pm and 8 pm–10:30 pm; Oct.–Apr., Thurs.–Tues. 11–6 and 7 pm–9:30 pm* Ⓜ *Sennaya Ploshchad.*

WORTH NOTING

Egyptian Sphinxes (*Yegipetskiye Sfinksy,* Египетские Сфинксы). On the landing in front of the Repin Institute, leading down to the Neva, stand two of St. Petersburg's more magnificent landmarks, the famous Egyptian Sphinxes. These twin statues, which date from the 15th century BC, were discovered during an excavation at Thebes in the 1820s. They were apparently created during the era of Pharaoh Amenhotep III, whose features they supposedly bear. It took the Russians more than a year to transport the sphinxes from Thebes. ⊠ *Universitetskaya nab., Vasilievsky Island* Ⓜ *Vasileostrovskaya.*

QUICK BITES

The restaurant **Idiot** (✉ *82 nab. Moika, City Center* ☎ *812/315–1675* Ⓜ *Sennaya Ploshchad*), about 100 meters from St. Isaac's Square along the Moika River in the direction of Yusupov Palace, is a favorite among St. Petersburg expatriates. Its entrance is marked by a discreet white globe with "Idiot" inscribed on it. The cozy café serves hearty vegetarian Russian food, good seafood, and a nice cappuccino. The background music leans heavily on Charles Aznavour, Louis Armstrong, and Ella Fitzgerald. Add occasional art exhibits, chess and backgammon sets, and a small library, and you have several excuses to linger.

Menshikov Palace (*Menshikovsky Dvorets*, Меншиковский Дворец). Alexander Menshikov (1673–1729), St. Petersburg's first governor, was one of Russia's more flamboyant characters. A close friend of Peter the Great (often called his favorite), Menshikov rose from humble beginnings as a street vendor, reportedly getting his start when he sold a cabbage pie to the tsar—or so the legend goes. He eventually became one of Russia's most powerful statesmen, and one famed for his corruption and political maneuvering. He is said to have incited Peter the Great against his son Alexei, and later attempted to take power from Peter II by arranging the young tsar's engagement to his daughter. The marriage did not take place, and the young tsar exiled Menshikov and his family to Siberia.

His palace, the first stone building in St. Petersburg, was, at the time of its completion in 1720, the city's most luxurious building. Although only a portion of the original palace has survived, it easily conveys a sense of Menshikov's inflated ego and love of luxury. Particularly noteworthy are the restored bedrooms: the walls and ceilings are completely covered with handcrafted ceramic tiles. It's said that Peter had them sent home from Delft for himself, but that Menshikov liked them and appropriated them. After Menshikov's exile to Siberia in 1727, his palace was turned over to a military training school and was significantly altered over the years. In June 1917 it served as the site of the First Congress of Russian Soviets. The Menshikov Palace is today a branch of the Hermitage Museum. In addition to the restored living quarters of the Menshikov family, there's an exhibit devoted to early-18th-century Russian culture. ✉ *15 Universitetskaya nab., Vasilievsky Island* ☎ *812/323–1112* ✉ *60R; 780R for two-day multi access ticket to State Hermitage Museum (can be ordered only through the Hermitage's Web site); 1,500R for English- or French-guided tour for up to 15 people: order by phone 1–2 days in advance* ☉ *Tues.–Sun. 10:30–4:30* Ⓜ *Vasileostrovskaya.*

Russian Academy of Sciences (*Rossiiskaya Akademiya Nauk*, Российская Академия Наук). Erected on strictly classical lines between 1783 and 1789, this structure, the original building of the Russian Academy of Sciences, is considered Giacomo Quarenghi's grandest design, with an eight-column portico, a pediment, and a double staircase. The administrative offices of the academy, founded in 1724 by Peter the Great, were transferred to Moscow in 1934. This building, which stands next to the Chamber of Art, now houses the St. Petersburg branch of the Russian

Academy of Sciences and is not open to the public. ⊠ *Universitetskaya nab., Vasilievsky Island* Ⓜ *Vasileostrovskaya.*

St. Nicholas Cathedral (*Nikolsky Sobor,* **Никольский Собор**). This turquoise-and-white extravaganza of a Russian baroque cathedral was designed by S.I. Chevakinsky, a pupil of Bartolomeo Francesco Rastrelli. It's a theatrical showpiece, and its artistic inspiration was in part derived from the 18th-century Italian prints of the Bibiena brothers, known for their opera and theater designs. The church's weddingcake silhouette, marked by a forest of white Corinthian pilasters and columns, closes ulitsa Glinka and makes the area a natural pole of attraction if you find yourself in the vicinity. Canals and green spaces surround the cathedral, which is also flanked by an elegant campanile. Inside are a lower church (low, dark, and warm for the winter) and an upper church (high, airy, and cool for the summer), typical of Russian Orthodox sanctuaries. The interior is no less picturesque than the outside. This is one of the few Orthodox churches that stayed open under Soviet power. It's also of special significance to the Russian navy. If you go during a service, you'll likely hear the beautiful choir. ⊠ *1/3 Nikolskaya Pl., Admiralteisky* ☎ *812/714–6926* ◷ *Daily, usually 7–7; morning services at 7 and 10 am, vespers at 6 pm* Ⓜ *Sennaya Ploshchad.*

St. Petersburg State University (*Sankt-Peterburgskii Gosudarstvenny Universitet,* **Санкт-Петербургский Государственный Университет**). In 1819 Tsar Alexander I founded this university, today one of Russia's leading institutions of higher learning, with an enrollment of more than 20,000. Its campuses date from the time of Peter the Great. The bright-red baroque building on the right (if you're walking west along the embankment) is the **Twelve Colleges Building,** named for the governmental administrative bodies established during Peter's reign. The building, which was designed by Domenico Trezzini and completed in 1741, 16 years after Peter's death, was transferred to the university in 1819 and today houses the university library and administrative offices. It's not officially open to the public, but no one will stop you from looking around.

The next building in the university complex is the **Rector's Wing,** another red building in the yard of the Twelve Colleges Building, where a plaque on the outside wall attests that the great Russian poet Alexander Blok (d. 1921) was born here in 1880. The third building along the embankment is a former **palace** built for Peter II (1715–30), Peter the Great's grandson, who lived and ruled only briefly. Completed in 1761, the building was later given to the university. The palace is connected to the Twelve Colleges Building via a gate and its facade faces the Neva River. It's a three-story rectangular building with two-story wings. The three blocks together with the palace form a large inner courtyard. ⊠ *7 Universitetskaya nab., Vasilievsky Island* Ⓜ *Vasileostrovskaya.*

Siniy most (*Blue Bridge,* **Синий мост**). This bridge spanning the Moika River is so wide (100 meters, about 325 feet) and stubby that it seems not to be a bridge at all but rather a sort of quaint raised footpath on St. Isaac's Square. It's named for the color of the paint on its underside. ⊠ *Admiralteisky* Ⓜ *Sennaya Ploshchad.*

Fodor's Choice
★

Strelka Стрелка. The Strelka ("arrow" or "spit") affords a dazzling view of both the Winter Palace and the Peter and Paul Fortress. This bit of land also reveals the city's triumphant rise from a watery outpost to an elegant metropolis. Seen against the backdrop of the Neva, the brightly colored houses lining the embankment seem like children's toys—the building blocks of a bygone aristocracy. They stand at the water's edge, seemingly supported not by the land beneath them but by the panorama of the city behind them. Gazing here is a great way to appreciate the scope of Peter the Great's vision for his country. The view is also revealing because it makes clear how careful the city's founders were to build

> ## NABOKOV
>
> Vladimir Nabokov was born in St. Petersburg to a rich noble family. The Nabokovs fled Russia soon after the Bolshevik Revolution and would never return. In 1940 they left for the United States, where he began writing his novels and short stories, including *Lolita* (1955), in English. Never forgetting his roots, he once said of himself, "I am an American writer, born in Russia, educated in England, where I studied French literature before moving for 15 years to Germany.... My head speaks English, my heart speaks Russian, and my ear speaks French."

their city not despite the Neva but around and with it. The Strelka is very popular with wedding couples, who traditionally come to visit the sight on their wedding day and often break a bottle of champagne on the ground here. It is a very romantic spot, especially in summer. ⊠ *Vasilevsky Island, at the north end of Dvortsovy Most (Palace Bridge), Vasilievsky Island* Ⓜ *Vasileostrovskaya.*

Vladimir Nabokov Museum-Apartment (*Musei Kvartira Vladimira Nabokova,* **Музей-квартира Владимира Набокова**). Vladimir Nabokov (1899–1977), author of the novel *Lolita,* was born and lived in this apartment until his 18th year. Judging from Nabokov's novels, in which the author often describes his building in detail or at least mentions it, one can say that the writer always kept warm memories about his first home. When in exile, Nabokov lived in hotels or rented apartments in different cities but never had his own house. When asked why he didn't want to buy his own, he would answer, "I already have one in St. Petersburg." Although the museum has not restored interiors of the writer's apartment, it presents family photos; the writer's drawings and various editions of his books; some of his belongings; and his collection of butterflies, which was previously kept at Harvard University. All these exhibits are in one room on the first floor. The museum is very close to the Manège. ⊠ *47 ul. Bolshaya Morskaya, Admiralteisky* ☎ *812/315–4713* 💴 *100R* ☺ *Weekdays Tues.–Fri. 11–6, weekends 12–5* Ⓜ *Sennaya Ploshchad.*

★ **Yusupov Palace** (*Yusupovsky Dvorets,* **Юсуповский Дворец**). On the cold night of December 17, 1916, this elegant yellow palace, which belonged to one of Russia's wealthiest families, the Yusupovs, became the setting for one of history's most melodramatic murders. Prince Yusupov and others loyal to the tsar spent several frustrating and frightening hours trying to kill Grigory Rasputin (1872–1916), who

CLOSE UP

Rasputin the Mystic

Neither a monk nor a priest as commonly believed, Rasputin was a wandering peasant who eventually came to exert great power over Nicholas II, the last Tsar of Imperial Russia. The royal family came under his spell when, claiming to have visions of the future and strange healing powers, they allowed him to see Nicholas's young son, Alexei. Alexei suffered from hemophilia, but when Rasputin prayed over the child, the hemorrhaging mysteriously stopped. The tsarina, Alexandra, soon came to believe that without Rasputin, her son would die. He became a regular palace visitor, though his presence was not always welcome. He was accused of scandalous misdeeds, including rape, and of having too much political control over the royal family. A number of people eventually tired of Rasputin's influence and conspired to murder him. On one cold December night in 1916, the mad healer was lured to the palace of Prince Felix Yusupov, where he was fed cakes and drinks laced with cyanide. To the horror of the conspirators, however, Rasputin was unaffected by their poisons. In desperation, they shot him several times and beat him before dumping him into the icy waters of the Neva River. His body was later found and autopsied; the results purportedly showed that he died of hypothermia, not cyanide or gunshot wounds.

had strongly influenced the tsarina, who in turn influenced the tsar, during the tumultuous years leading up to the Bolshevik Revolution. On display in the palace, which is set on the bank of the Moika River, are the rooms in which Rasputin was (or began to be) killed, as well as a waxworks exhibit of Rasputin and Prince Yusupov (who was forced to flee the country when Rasputin's murder was uncovered). They are visible only on an extended tour given once daily at 1:45 pm. Another tour (scheduled on the hour) takes you through the former reception rooms of the second floor. Both tours are in Russian only. As for the scene where Rasputin was actually poisoned—the palace's underground tunnel—it is ostensibly off-limits, but you may be able to view the tunnel if you can avail yourself of the bathroom facilities on the lower level of the mansion. It's essential that you phone ahead at least a week in advance to arrange an English-language tour. The tour is given only in Russian, Another option is to take an audioguide tour in English, French, German, Italian, Finnish, and Spanish. In that case you'll also need to pay a refundable deposit of 500R for the use of an audio player.

On a lighter note, the showpiece of the palace remains the jewel-like rococo theater, whose stage was once graced by Liszt and Chopin; today, concerts are still presented here, as well as in the palace's august and elegant White-Columns Room (concert tickets usually have to be purchased just before performance time). ⊠ *94 nab. Moika, Admiralteisky* ☎ *812/332–1991; 812/314–8893 tours* ⊒ *500R, tours every hour from 11 am through 5 pm, additional 300R for Rasputin exhibits at 1:45 pm daily* ☉ *Daily 10:45–5; closed 1st Wed. of month* Ⓜ *Sennaya Ploshchad.*

Ⓒ **Zoological Museum** (*Zoologichesky Muzey,* Зоологический Музей). The prize of this zoological museum's unusual collection, which contains more than 40,000 species, is a stuffed mammoth recovered from Siberia in 1901. The museum also has impressive skeletons of whales and large fish, but no dinosaur fossils. The other stuffed animals, posed in natural compositions include tigers, foxes, bears, goats, and many kinds of birds. A few families of penguins seem to proudly pose with their countless funny nestlings on a piece of artificial ice; a moose walks along a fading fall forest. The museum also has a large collection of butterflies and other insects. ✉ *1 Universitetskaya nab., Vasilievsky Island* ☎ *812/328–0112* 🔖 *150R* ◷ *Wed.–Mon. 11–6, kassa open until 4:50* Ⓜ *Vasileostrovskaya.*

THE PETROGRAD SIDE ПЕТРОГРАДСКАЯ СТОРОНА

St. Petersburg was born in the battles of the Northern Wars with Sweden, and it was in this area, on Hare Island (Zayachy Ostrov), that it all began: in 1703 Peter laid the foundation of the first fortress to protect the mainland and to secure Russia's outlet to the sea. Ever since, the small hexagonal island forms, as it were, the hub around which the city revolves. The showpiece of the island is the magnificent Peter and Paul Fortress, the starting point for any tour of this section of the city, which actually consists of a series of islands, and is commonly referred to as the Petrograd Side (Petrogradskaya Storona). Hare Island and the fortress are almost directly across the Neva from the Winter Palace. Cut off from the north by the moatlike Kronverk Canal, the island is connected by a footbridge to Trinity Square (Troitskaya Ploshchad, sometimes still referred to by its Soviet name, Revolution Square) on Petrograd Island (Petrogradsky Ostrov). Along with its famous monuments, this part of the city is also one of its earliest residential areas, and Troitskaya Ploshchad, named for the church that once stood here (demolished in 1934), is the city's oldest square.

GETTING HERE AND AROUND

You can reach the area by walking across the Dvortsovyi (Palace) Bridge (it starts near the Hermitage), passing through the Strelka, and then across the smaller Birzhevoi Bridge. On your right you'll see the Peter and Paul Fortress: the walk will also give you a chance to take in a panorama of the city's grandest sites, including the Hermitage, the Neva River, and the Strelka. You can also take trolley 1 or 7 from Nevsky prospekt, or hire a taxi. Another option is to take the metro to Gorkovskaya station, and from there walk through the park in the direction of the fortress, which remains the major site in the area. The Artillery Museum is across from the Fortress. You'll recognize it at once by the World War II–era cannons.

TOP ATTRACTIONS

Ⓒ **Avrora** (Аврора). This historic cruiser is permanently moored in front of the **Nakhimov Academy of Naval Officers.** Launched in 1903, it fought in the 1904–05 Russo-Japanese War as well as in World War II, but it's best known for its role in the Bolshevik Revolution. At 9:40 pm on November 7, 1917, the cruiser fired the shot that signaled the storming of the Winter Palace. The revolution it launched brought itself under fire in the end. A cherished relic in the Soviet era—it was scuttled during the siege of Leningrad to keep it from being hit by a German shell, and resurfaced later—the *Avrora* was carefully restored in the 1980s and opened as a museum. The cruiser is a favorite with families, and on weekends you may encounter long lines. On display are the crew's quarters and the radio room used to broadcast Lenin's victory address. ⊠ *4 Petrogradskaya nab., Petrograd Side* ☎ *812/230–8440* ⊠ *Free; tours usually 200R per person, price depends on group size* ⊙ *Tues.–Thurs. and weekends 10:30–4, last tour at 3* Ⓜ *Gorkovskaya.*

Fodor's Choice ★ **Peter and Paul Fortress** (*Petropavlovskaya Krepost,* Петропавловская Крепость). The first building in Sankt-Piter-Burkh, as the city was then called, the fortress was erected in just one year, between 1703 and 1704, during the Great Northern War against Sweden. It was never used for its intended purpose, however, as the Russian line of defense quickly moved farther north, and, in fact, the war was won before the fortress was mobilized. Instead, the fortress served mainly as a political prison, primarily under the tsars. The date on which construction began on the fortress is celebrated as the birth of St. Petersburg.

Cross the footbridge and enter the fortress through **St. John's Gate** (Ioannovskyie Vorota), the main entrance to the outer fortifications. Once inside, you'll need to stop at the ticket office, which is inside the outer fortification wall on the right.

Entrance to the inner fortress is through **St. Peter's Gate** (Petrovskiye Vorota). Designed by the Swiss architect Domenico Trezzini, it was built from 1717 to 1718. After you pass through St. Peter's Gate, the first building to your right is the **Artilleriisky Arsenal,** where weaponry was stored. Just to your left is the **Engineer's House** (Inzhenerny Dom), which was built from 1748 to 1749. Now a branch of the Museum of the History of St. Petersburg (as are all exhibits in the fortress), it presents displays about the city's prerevolutionary history.

As you continue to walk down the main center lane, away from St. Peter's Gate, you soon come to the main attraction of the fortress, the **Cathedral of Saints Peter and Paul** (Petropavlovsky Sobor). Constructed between 1712 and 1733 on the site of an earlier wooden church, it was designed by Domenico Trezzini and later embellished by Bartolomeo Rastrelli. It's highly unusual for a Russian Orthodox church. Instead of the characteristic bulbous domes, it's adorned by a single, slender, gilded spire whose height (400 feet, 120 meters) made the church the city's tallest building for over 200 years. The spire is identical to that of the Admiralty across the river, except that it's crowned by an angel bearing a golden cross. The spire remained the city's highest structure—in accordance with Peter the Great's decree—until 1962, when a television tower was erected.

The interior of the cathedral is also atypical. The baroque iconostasis, designed by Ivan Zarudny and built in the 1720s, is adorned by freestanding statues. Another uncommon feature is the pulpit. It's reputed to have been used only once, in 1901, to excommunicate Leo Tolstoy from the Russian Orthodox Church for his denouncing of the

8

institution. You can exit the cathedral through the passageway to the left of the iconostasis. This leads to the adjoining **Grand Ducal Crypt** (Usypalnitsa), built between 1896 and 1908. You can identify Peter the Great's tomb by the tsar's bust on the railing on the far right facing the iconostasis.

As you leave the cathedral, note the small classical structure to your right. This is the **Boathouse** (Botny Domik), built between 1762 and 1766 to house Peter the Great's boyhood boat. The boat has since been moved to the Naval Museum on Vasilievsky Island, and the building is not open to the public.

The long pink-and-white building to your left as you exit the cathedral is the **Commandant's House** (Komendantsky Dom), erected between 1743 and 1746. It once housed the fortress's administration and doubled as a courtroom for political prisoners. The Decembrist revolutionaries were tried here in 1826. The room where the trial took place forms part of the ongoing exhibits, which deal with the history of St. Petersburg from its founding to 1917. Across the cobblestone yard, opposite the entrance to the cathedral, stands the **Mint** (Monetny Dvor), which was first built in 1716; the current structure, however, was erected between 1798 and 1806. The mint is still in operation, producing coins, medals, military decorations, and *znachki* (Russian souvenir pins). The coins that were taken along on Soviet space missions were made here.

Take the pathway to the left of the Commandant's House (as you're facing it), and you'll be headed right for **Neva Gate** (Nevskiye Vorota), built in 1730 and reconstructed in 1787. As you walk through its passageway, note the plaques on the inside walls marking flood levels of the Neva. The gate leads out to the **Commandant's Pier** (Komendantskaya Pristan). Up above to the right is the **Signal Cannon** (Signalnaya Pushka), fired every day at noon. From this side you get a splendid view of St. Petersburg. You may want to step down to the sandy beach, where even in winter hearty swimmers enjoy the Neva's arctic waters. In summer the beach is lined with sunbathers, standing up or leaning against the fortification wall.

As you return to the fortress through the Neva Gate, you'll be following the footsteps of prisoners who passed through this gate on the way to their executions. Several of the fortress's bastions, concentrated at its far western end, were put to use over the years mainly as political prisons. One of them, **Trubetskoi Bastion,** is open to the public as a museum. Aside from a few exhibits of prison garb, the only items on display are the cells themselves, restored to their chilling, prerevolutionary appearance. The first prisoner confined in its dungeons was Peter the Great's own son, Alexei, who was tortured to death in 1718 for treason, allegedly under the tsar's supervision. The prison was enlarged in 1872, when an adjacent one, Alexeivsky Bastion, which held such famous figures as the writers Fyodor Dostoyevsky and Nikolai Chernyshevsky, became overcrowded with dissidents opposed to the tsarist regime. A partial chronology of revolutionaries held here includes some of the People's Will terrorists, who killed Alexander II in 1881; Lenin's elder brother Alexander, who attempted to murder Alexander III (and was executed for his role in the plot); and Leon Trotsky and Maxim Gorky, after taking part in the 1905 revolution. The Bolsheviks themselves imprisoned people here for a short period, starting with members of the Provisional Government who were arrested and "detained for their own safety" for a few days, as well as sailors who mutinied against the Communist regime in Kronshtadt in 1921. They were apparently the last to be held here, and in 1925 a memorial museum (to the prerevolutionary prisoners) was opened instead. Some casemates close to the Neva Gate have been converted into a printing workshop (*pechatnya*), where you can buy good-quality graphic art in a broad range of prices. Origi-

> ## THE BURIAL PLACE OF TSARS
>
> The Cathedral of Saints Peter and Paul is the final resting spot of nearly all the tsars, from Peter the Great on. Nicholas II, who was executed with his family in Yekaterinburg (Siberia) in 1918, was one notable exception. In 1998, what were thought to be the remains of Nicholas II and his family were found and buried here. In July 2007 the remains of the tsarevich Alexei and his sister Maria were found in Yekaterinburg, but there has not yet been any move to have them reburied in the cathedral.

nal late-19th-century presses are used to create lithographs, etchings, and linocuts depicting, most often, urban St. Petersburg landscapes, which make nice alternatives to the usual souvenirs. In the basement, the original foundations were excavated; different layers of the history of the fortress can thus be seen. ✉ *3 Petropavlovskaya Krepost, Petrograd Side* ☎ *812/230–6431; 812/232–9454 excursions* ✆ *Cathedral 140R, cathedral and other sights and exhibitions 250R, audio guide in English, French, German, Spanish, or Italian 250R (purchase guide at the Fortress's Information Center, at Ioanovsky Ravelin; the deposit of 2,000R or a document, such as a passport or driver's license, is required)* ☉ *Thurs.–Tues. 11–6, kassa open until 5 Thurs.–Mon., until 4 on Tues. Cathedral of Sts. Peter and Paul closed Wed., fortress closed last Tues. of month* Ⓜ *Gorkovskaya.*

8

WORTH NOTING

☝ **Artillery Museum** (*Artilleriysky Muzey*, **Артиллерийский Музей**). Formerly the city's arsenal, this building was turned over to the Artillery Museum in 1872. You can't miss it—just look for the hundreds of pieces of artillery on the grounds outside. The museum itself dates from the days of Peter the Great, who sought to present the entire history of weaponry, with a special emphasis on Russia. Today the Artillery Museum is St. Petersburg's main army museum. Like the Naval Museum in the old Stock Exchange, it still has exhibits with a distinctly Soviet feel—if you're interested in circuit boards inside ballistic missiles, for example, this is the place to come. It also contains plenty of military curiosities both modern and ancient. ✉ *7 Alexandrovsky Park, Petrograd Side* ☎ *812/232–0296* ✆ *300R* ☉ *Wed.–Sun. 11–5, kassa open until 5. Closed last Thurs. of month* Ⓜ *Gorkovskaya.*

☝ **LabirintUm Лабиринтум.** Russia's first interactive scientific museum will be most interesting to children. About 60 exhibits of the museum provide visitors with the opportunity to learn the laws of physics, chemistry, and nature in an entertaining way, whether by making lightning, creating an artificial tornado, getting inside a huge bubble, or finding their way through a mirror labyrinth. The museum, which opened in 2010, is a reinvention of sorts of a similar museum that was founded here by the eminent scientist Yakov Perelman in 1935. The museum was destroyed during World War II, and Perelman and his wife starved to death during the Siege of Leningrad. The territory of this private museum includes seven thematic zones, including Children's World, Mirror World, World of Physics Experiments, Black Room, Water World, Workshops, and Laboratorium. Each zone presents the exhibits that illustrate the phenomena of mechanics, optics, dynamics, electricity, and magnetic and various natural phenomena. ⊠, *Petrograd Side* ☎ *812/328–0001* ⊕ *www.labirint-um.ru* ☛ *Mon.–Fri. 200R, Sat.–Sun. 250R* ⊙ *Daily 11–7* Ⓜ *Petrogradskaya.*

Mosque (*Mechet,* **Мечеть**). Built between 1910 and 1914 to serve St. Petersburg's Muslims, the Mosque was designed after the Gur Emir in Samarkand (in modern-day Uzbekistan), where Tamerlane, the 14th-century conqueror, is buried. The huge dome is flanked by two soaring minarets and covered with sky-blue ceramics. In the style of St. Petersburg's northern architecture, the walls of the mosque are lined with rough, dark-gray granite. The inside columns, which support the arches under the dome, are faced with green marble. In the center of the praying hall is a huge chandelier upon which sayings from the Koran are engraved. It's open only during services. ⊠ *7 Kronversky pr., Petrograd Side* ☎ *812/233–9819* ⊙ *Services daily at 2:20* Ⓜ *Gorkovskaya.*

Russian Political History Museum (*Gosudarstvenny Muzey Politicheskoi Istorii Rossii,* **Государственный Музей Политической Истории России**). "From Sublime to Ridiculous," the most popular permanent display at this museum, traces the history of Russia in the 20th century through paintings, posters, flags, and porcelain. Socialist realism is featured prominently in the collections. There are always several theme exhibitions on political figures, spies, and controversial historical personages, such as Rasputin. The elegant art-nouveau house itself, which was built in 1905 by Alexander Goguen, is the former mansion of Mathilda Kshesinskaya, a famous ballerina and the mistress of the last Russian tsar, Nicholas II, before he married Alexandra. She left Russia in 1917 for Paris, where she married a longtime lover, Andrei Vladimirovich, another Romanov. One of Kshesinskaya's pupils was the great English ballerina Margot Fonteyn. The mansion served as Bolshevik committee headquarters in the months leading up to the October Revolution (an exhibit at the museum that reconstructs Lenin's study is a nod to this period). In 1957 it was linked to the adjoining town house by a rather nondescript central wing and turned into the Museum of the Great October Socialist Revolution; in 1991 it was given its current name. All that is left of the original interiors is the reception hall. Call in advance to arrange a guided tour. ⊠ *2/4 ul. Kuybysheva, Petrograd Side* ☎ *812/233–7052* ☛ *200R; 700R with English-speaking guide, per group of up to 5 people or 1,300R per group of 5–15 people* ⊙ *Fri.–Wed. 10–6, kassa open until 5. Closed last Mon. of month* Ⓜ *Gorkovskaya.*

UPPER NEVSKY PROSPEKT AND VLADIMIRSKAYA (LOWER NEVSKY PROSPEKT)
(НЕВСКИЙ ПРОСПЕКТ И ВЛАДИМИРСКАЯ)

"There is nothing finer than Nevsky prospekt, not in St. Petersburg at any rate, for in St. Petersburg it is everything . . ." wrote the great Russian author Nikolai Gogol more than 150 years ago. Today Nevsky prospekt may not be as resplendent as it was in the 1830s, when noblemen and ladies strolled along the elegant avenue or paraded by in horse-drawn carriages, but it's still the main thoroughfare, and remains the pulse of the city. Through the 18th century it was built up with estates and manors of the gentry, most of which still stand as testimony to the city's noble past. The next century saw a boom of mercantile growth that added sections farther south as centers for commerce, finance, and trade. Under the Communists, few new sites were planned on the prospekt. Instead, old structures found new uses, and the bulk of the Soviets' building was directed outside the city center. Today, Nevsky is a retail center, complete with souvenir shops, clubs, neon lights, and young kids sporting some outrageous clothes.

GETTING HERE AND AROUND

You can get to Upper Nevsky Prospekt by taking the metro to Alexander Nevsky Square (Ploschad Aleksandra Nevskogo) station. Alexnder Nevsky Lavra, the monastery, will be in front of you. To reach Lower Nevsky it's better to get off at Ploschad Vosstaniya metro station. Vladimirskaya area is best reached via the Vladimirskaya/Dostoyevskaya metro station.

TIMING

If you want to just see the sights on Nevsky prospekt, you need only plan for a few hours of walking. The top attractions you will most likely want to visit are Kazan Cathedral, Alexander Nevsky Lavra, and Nevsky prospekt. If you want to do some shopping then you may spend another couple of hours at Gostiny Dvor department store. Most of the souvenir shops are on and around Nevsky prospekt.

TOP ATTRACTIONS

Fodor'sChoice **Alexander Nevsky Lavra** (Александро-Невская Лавра). The word *lavra*
★ in Russian is reserved for a monastery of the highest order, of which there are just four in all of Russia and Ukraine. Named in honor of St. Alexander Nevsky, this monastery was founded in 1710 by Peter the Great and given lavra status in 1797. Prince Alexander of Novgorod (1220–63), the great military commander, became a national hero and saint because he halted the relentless eastward drive for Russian territory by the Germans and the Swedes. Peter chose this site for the monastery, thinking that it was the same place where the prince had fought the battle in 1240 that earned him the title Alexander of the Neva (Nevsky); actually, the famous battle took place some 20 km (12 mi) away. Alexander Nevsky had been buried in Vladimir, but in 1724, on Peter's orders, his remains were transferred to the monastery that was founded in his honor.

Entrance to the monastery is through the archway of the elegant **Gate Church** (Tserkovnyye Vorota), built by Ivan Starov between 1783 and 1785. The walled pathway is flanked by two cemeteries—together known as the Necropolis of Masters of Arts—whose entrances are a short walk down the path. To the left lies the older **Lazarus Cemetery** (Lazarevskoye kladbische). The list of famous people buried here reads like a who's who of St. Petersburg architects; it includes Quarenghi, Rossi, de Thomon, and Voronikhin. The cemetery also contains the tombstone of the father of Russian science, Mikhail Lomonosov. The **Tikhvinskoye kladbische**, on the opposite side, is the final resting place of several of St. Petersburg's great literary and musical figures. The grave of Fyodor Dostoyevsky, in the northwestern corner, is easily identified by the tombstone's sculpture, which portrays the writer with his flowing beard. Continuing along the walled path you'll soon reach the composers' corner, where Rimsky-Korsakov, Mussorgsky, Borodin, and Tchaikovsky are buried. The compound includes an exhibition hall with temporary exhibits of "urban sculpture."

> ## WORD OF MOUTH
>
> "I went to the monastery Alexander Nevsky Lavra one day. The monks also sell bread here, which was interesting to see. The cemeteries are also full of famous musicians, novelists, etc. Follow the canal around a bit and get a feel for the solitude."
>
> —Lincasanova

After this look at St. Petersburg's cultural legacy, return to the path and cross the bridge spanning the **Monastyrka River.** As you enter the monastery grounds, the **Church of the Annunciation** (Tserkov Blagovescheniya), greets you on your left. The red-and-white rectangular church was designed by Domenico Trezzini and built between 1717 and 1722. It now houses the Museum of City Sculpture (open daily 9:30–1 and 2–5), which contains models of St. Petersburg's architectural masterpieces as well as gravestones and other fine examples of memorial sculpture. Also in the church are several graves of 18th-century statesmen. The great soldier Generalissimo Alexander Suvorov, who led the Russian army to numerous victories during the Russo-Turkish War (1768–74), is buried here under a simple marble slab that he purportedly designed himself. It reads simply: "Here lies Suvorov." Opposite the church, a shop sells religious items and souvenirs.

Outside the church and continuing along the same path, you'll first pass a millennial monument celebrating 2,000 years of Christianity on your right, before reaching the monastery's main cathedral, the **Trinity Cathedral** (Troitsky Sobor). This was one of the few churches in St. Petersburg allowed to function during the Soviet era. Designed by Ivan Starov and completed at the end of the 18th century, it stands out among the monastery's predominantly baroque architecture for its monumental classical design. Services are held here daily, and the church is open to the public from 6 am until the end of the evening service around 8 pm. The magnificent interior, with its stunning gilded iconostasis, is worth a visit. The large central dome, adorned by frescoes designed by the great architect Quarenghi, seems to soar toward the heavens. The church houses the main relics of Alexander Nevsky.

As you leave the church, walk down the steps and go through the gate on the right. A door on the left bears a simple inscription, written by hand: "Svezhy Khleb" (fresh bread). Here you can buy delicious bread baked on the premises. After the gate comes a courtyard and, at the back of the church, a gate to yet another burial ground: St. Nicholas Cemetery (Nikolskoye Kladbishche), opened in 1863 and one of the most prestigious burial grounds of the time; it's open daily 9–8 (until 7 in winter). In 1927 the cemetery was closed and the remains of prominent people buried here, including novelist Goncharov and composer Rubinstein, were transferred over the course of several years to the Volkovskoye Cemetery and the Necropolis of Masters of Arts. This movement went on until the 1940s, by which time valuable funeral monuments had been lost. As you reach the steps of the little yellow-and-white church in the center (which gave its name to the graveyard), turn right and walk to a derelict chapel of yellow brick, which has been turned into a makeshift **monument to Nicholas II.** Photocopies stand in for photographs of the Imperial family; pro-monarchy white, yellow, and black flags hang from the ceilings; and passionate adherents have added primitive frescoes to the scene. Nearby, in front of Trinity Cathedral, is yet another final resting place on the lavra's grounds—the **Communist Burial Ground** (Kommunisticheskaya Ploshchadka), where, starting in 1919, defenders of Petrograd, victims of the Kronstadt rebellion, old Bolsheviks, and prominent scientists were buried. The last to receive that honor were people who took part in the siege of Leningrad.

Entrance to the monastery grounds is free, although you are asked to make a donation. You must purchase a ticket for the two cemeteries of the Necropolis of Masters of Arts and the museum, and (as with most Russian museums) it costs extra to take photos or use a video camera. There are ticket kiosks outside the two paying cemeteries, after the gate, and inside the Tikhvin Cemetery, on the right side. ⊠ *1 Pl. Alexandra Nevskovo, Vladimirskaya* ☎ *812/274–1612* ⊕ *lavra.spb.ru* ⊠ *60R donation, Museum of City Sculpture 30R, Necropolis of Masters of Arts 200R* ۞ *Fri.–Wed. 9:30–5:30* Ⓜ *Ploshchad Alexandra Nevskovo.*

Anichkov most (*Anichkov bridge*, **Аничков мост**). Each corner of this beautiful bridge spanning the Fontanka River (the name means "fountain") bears an equestrian statue designed by Peter Klodt; the bronze sculpture, erected in 1841, each depict a phase of horse taming. Taken down and buried during World War II, the beautiful monuments were restored to their positions in 1945. The bridge was named for Colonel Mikhail Anichkov, whose regiment had built the first wooden drawbridge here. At that time, early in the 18th century, the bridge marked the city limits, and the job of its night guards was much the same as the guards of today: to carefully screen those entering the city. As you cross the bridge, pause for a moment to look back at No. 41, on the corner of Nevsky and the Fontanka. This was formerly the **Palace of Prince Beloselsky-Belozersky**—a highly ornate, neobaroque pile designed in 1848 by Andrei Stackenschneider, who wanted to replicate Rastrelli's Stroganovsky Dvorets. The facade of blazing red stonework and whipped-cream stucco trim remains the showiest in St. Petersburg.

The lavish building, once opulent inside and out, housed the local Communist Party headquarters during the Soviet era. Today it is the setting for classical music concerts. The interiors have been largely destroyed and are no longer as magnificent as the facades.

Gostiny Dvor Гостиный Двор. Taking up an entire city block, this is St. Petersburg's answer to the GUM department store in Moscow. Initially constructed by Rastrelli in 1757, it was not completed until 1785, by Vallin de la Mothe, who was responsible for the facade with its two tiers of arches. At the time the structure was erected, traveling merchants were routinely put up in guesthouses (called *gostiny dvor*), which, like this one, doubled as places for doing business. This arcade was completely rebuilt in the 19th century, by which time it housed some 200 general-purpose shops that were far less elegant than those in other parts of the Nevsky. It remained a functional bazaar until alterations in the 1950s and 1960s connected most of its separate shops into St. Petersburg's largest department store. Today Gostiny Dvor houses fashionable boutiques, and you can also find currency-exchange kiosks and ATMs here. Virtually across the street, at 48 Nevsky prospekt, is the city's other major "department store," also an arcade, called **Passazh,** built in 1848. ⊠ *35 Nevsky pr., City Center* ☎ *812/710–5408* ⊙ *Daily 10–10* Ⓜ *Gostiny Dvor.*

Kazan Cathedral (*Kazansky Sobor,* **Казанский Собор**). After a visit to Rome, Tsar Paul I (1754–1801) commissioned this magnificent cathedral, wishing to copy—and perhaps present the Orthodox rival to—that city's St. Peter's. It was erected between 1801 and 1811 from a design by Andrei Voronikhin. You approach the huge cathedral through a monumental, semicircular colonnade. Inside and out, the church abounds with sculpture and decoration. On the prospekt side the frontage holds statues of St. John the Baptist and the apostle Andrew as well as such sanctified Russian heroes as Grand Prince Vladimir (who advanced the Christianization of Russia) and Alexander Nevsky. Note the enormous bronze front doors—exact copies of Ghiberti's *Gates of Paradise* in Florence's Baptistery.

In 1932 the cathedral, which was closed right after the revolution, was turned into the Museum of Religion and Atheism, with an emphasis on the latter. Religion was presented from the Marxist point of view, essentially as an archaeological artifact. The museum has since moved to 14 Pochtamtskaya ulitsa, not far from St. Isaac's Cathedral and opposite the main post office (the *pochtamt*). Kazan Cathedral is once again a place of worship.

At each end of the square that forms the cathedral's front lawn are statues of a military leader—at one end, one of Mikhail Barclay de Tolly, at the other, Mikhail Kutuzov. They reflect the value placed in the 19th century on the cathedral as a place of military tribute, especially following Napoléon's invasion in 1812. Kutuzov is buried in the cathedral's northern chapel, where he's supposed to have prayed before taking command of the Russian forces. ⊠ *2 Kazanskaya Pl., City Center* ☎ *812/314–4663* ⊙ *Open daily 8:30–8; services weekdays at 10 am and 6 pm, weekends at 7 and 10 am and 6 pm* Ⓜ *Nevsky Prospekt.*

CLOSE UP

White Nights

St. Petersburg is at 59 degrees north latitude, roughly the same latitude as Oslo, Norway; Stockholm, Sweden; and Anchorage, Alaska. Due to this northerly position, the summer months receive many more hours of sunlight, especially in June and July. The sun's short trip around this part of the earth creates an ethereal glow of twilight into the wee hours. During these White Nights, wrote the poet Joseph Brodsky, "it's hard to fall asleep because it's too light and because any dream will be inferior to this reality. Where a man doesn't cast a shadow, like water." If you are visiting St. Petersburg during this time, you should partake in the many festivals, such as the Mariinsky Theatre's Stars of the White Nights, and spend at least one late night outdoors. Take a walk around the historic center, by Peter and Paul Fortress, St. Isaac's Cathedral, and the State Hermitage Museum which all face the Neva. Stroll along the banks of the river until you come across a bridge such as Dvortsovy most (Palace Bridge) next to the Hermitage and stop to watch the ships pass through the open bridge. Each bridge has its own time schedule, but they begin to open at approximately 1 am and close at about 5 am. If you don't want to stay out all night, be sure to stay on the side of the river that your hotel is on. However, getting trapped on the other side of the city is rather romantic and you'll see couples kissing on the embankment while "waiting" for the bridges to close.

★ **Nevsky prospekt** (Невский проспект). St. Petersburg's Champs-Élysées, Nevsky prospekt was laid out in 1710, making it one of the city's first streets. Just short of 5 km (3 mi) long, beginning and ending at different bends of the Neva River, St. Petersburg's most famous street starts at the foot of the Admiralty building and runs in a perfectly straight line to the Moscow station, where it curves slightly before ending a short distance farther at the Alexander Nevsky Lavra. Because St. Petersburg was once part of the larger lands of Novgorod, the road linking the city to the principality was known as Great Novgorod Road; it was an important route for trade and transportation. By the time Peter the Great built the first Admiralty, however, another major road clearly was needed to connect the Admiralty directly to the shipping hub. Originally this new street was called the Great Perspective Road; later it was called the Nevskaya Perspektiva, and finally Nevsky prospekt.

On the last few blocks of Nevsky prospekt as you head toward the Neva are some buildings of historic importance. No. 18, on the right-hand side, was once a private dwelling before becoming a café called Wulf and Beranger; it's now the **Literary Café**. It was reportedly here that Pushkin ate his last meal before setting off for his fatal duel. **Chicherin's House,** at No. 15, was one of Empress Elizabeth's palaces before it became the Nobles' Assembly and, in 1919, the House of Arts. Farther down, at No. 14, is one of the rare buildings on Nevsky prospekt built *after* the Bolshevik Revolution. The blue sign on the facade dates from World War II and the siege of Leningrad; it warns pedestrians that during

8

air raids the other side of the street is safer. The city was once covered with similar warnings; this one was left in place as a memorial, and on Victory Day (May 9 in Russia) survivors of the siege lay flowers here. ✉ *City Center* Ⓜ *Nevsky Prospekt, Gostinny Dvor, Mayakovskaya, Ploschad Vosstaniya, or Ploshchad Alexandra Nevskovo.*

WORTH NOTING

Anna Akhmatova Literary Museum (*Muzey Anny Akhmatovoy,* **Музей Анны Ахматовой**). This museum occupies the former palace of Count Sheremetyev and is accessible either from 53 Liteiny prospekt or from the Fontanka embankment, through the palace hall and the garden. The famous St. Petersburg poet lived for many years in a communal apartment in a wing of the palace. She was born in 1888 in Odessa and was published for the first time in 1910. Akhmatova did not leave Petrograd after the October Revolution, but remained silent between 1923 and 1940. She died in 1966 and is remembered as one of the greatest successors to Pushkin. Her museum is also the venue for occasional poetry readings, other literary events, and temporary exhibitions—in short, a slice of the old-style Russian intelligentsia. Tours are available in Russian only. ✉ *34 nab. Fontanki or 53 Liteiny pr., City Center* ☎ *812/272–2211 or 812/272–5895* ⊕ *www.akhmatova.spb.ru* ✍ *200R, guided tour an additional 600R for groups up to 10 people; audio guide in English, Finnish, German, or French 150R* ☉ *Tues.–Sun. 10:30–6, kassa open until 5:30* Ⓜ *Nevsky Prospekt.*

> ### THE SONG OF GRIEF
>
> One of Anna Akhmatova's most famous poems is "Requiem," first published in 1963. It is in part about her son, historian Lev Gumilev, who spent many years imprisoned during Stalin's Terror. Akhmatova was asked to describe what was happening by another woman waiting in the visitors' line at the prison. She did just that in the haunting lines: "This happened when only the dead wore smiles— / they rejoiced at being safe from harm. / And Leningrad dangled from its jails / like some unnecessary arm."

QUICK BITES

The Grand Hotel Europe (✉ *1/7 Mikhailovskaya ul., City Center* ☎ *812/329–6000* Ⓜ *Nevsky Prospekt*) has a lovely mezzanine café, where you can enjoy a pot of tea or a glass of champagne, served with bowls of strawberries. Take a peek at the art nouveau lobby, furnished with stained-glass windows and antique furnishings.

City Duma (*Gorodskaya Duma,* **Городская Дума**). This building with a notable red-and-white tower served as the city hall under the tsars. Its clock tower, meant to resemble those in Western European cities, was erected by Ferrari between 1799 and 1804. It was originally equipped with signaling devices that sent messages between the Winter Palace and the royal summer residences. ✉ *1 ul. Dumskaya, City Center* Ⓜ *Nevsky Prospekt.*

Dom Knigi (*House of Books,* **Дом Книги**). This is where you'll find Petersburgers in what's still one of their favorite pursuits: perusing and buying books. The city's largest bookstore, which offers more than

120,000 different books, still goes by its generic Soviet name. You may be pleasantly surprised by the prices for classic Russian literature in the original language. Some books in English and other languages are also sold. The store has several branches around the city, but the main branch is in one of the most exquisite buildings at Nevsky Prospekt. Until 1917 it belonged to the Singer sewing-machine company. Russia was its biggest market after the United States; initially, the company wanted to build a skyscraper similar to the one the company was building at the time in New York City. However, in old St. Petersburg no building other than a cathedral could be built higher than the Winter Palace, which stood at 22 meters (72 feet). To solve this dilemma, Singer's architect erected an elegant tower above the six-story building and topped it with a glass globe nearly 3 meters (10 feet) in diameter. ✉ *28 Nevsky pr., City Center* ☎ *812/448–7888* 🕙 *Daily 9 am–12 am* Ⓜ *Nevsky Prospekt.*

F.M. Dostoyevsky Literary-Memorial Museum (*Literaturno Memorialnyi Muzey Fyodora Dostoyevskovo*, Литературно-мемориальный Музей Ф.М. Достоевского). Here, at the last place in which he lived, Fyodor Dostoyevsky (1821–81) wrote *The Brothers Karamazov*. Dostoyevsky preferred to live in the part of the city inhabited by the ordinary people who populated his novels. He always insisted that the windows of his workroom overlook a church, as they do in this simple little house that has been remodeled to look as it did at the time Dostoyevsky and his family lived here. Perhaps the most interesting section of the museum deals with the writer's stay in prison in the Peter and Paul Fortress, and his commuted execution. ✉ *5/2 Kuznechny per., Vladimirskaya* ☎ *812/571–4031* ⊕ *www.md.spb.ru* 🎫 *150R, 1,550R for English-guided tour for groups of up to 20 people. Call ahead to book tour* 🕙 *Tues.–Sun. 11–6, kassa open until 5:30* Ⓜ *Dostoyevskaya or Vladimirskaya.*

8

QUICK BITES

Abrikosov (✉ *40 Nevsky pr., City Center* ☎ *812/312–2457* Ⓜ *Nevsky Prospekt*), a German venture with a restaurant and a coffee bar, is a soothing place to take a break with a good view of Nevsky prospekt. Coffee, ice cream, and scrumptious cakes are available in the restaurant section, which is no-smoking.

Zhyly-Byly (✉ *52 Nevsky pr., City Center* ☎ *812/314–6230* Ⓜ *Nevsky Prospekt*), a café, takes its name from the phrase used to open every Russian folktale (something like "Once upon a time"). The clean, cool interior displays a smattering of folk-related objects. It's open around the clock, and serves mainly excellent salads, as well as pastries and the most delicious and beautiful cakes. Most surprising is its lengthy wine list.

Ploshchad Vosstaniya (*Insurrection Square*, Площадь Восстания). Originally called Znamenskaya Ploshchad (Square of the Sign) after a church of the same name that stood on it, the plaza was the site of many revolutionary speeches and armed clashes with military and police forces—hence its second name. Like Decembrists' Square, the plaza has reverted to its original name, though people still generally call it Insurrection

Square (the metro station of the same name hasn't changed). The busy Moscow railroad station is here, and this part of Nevsky prospekt is lined with many kinds of shops, including fancy new stores like Stockmann or H&M, as well as art salons, and bookstores. A stroll here is not a casual affair, since Nevsky is almost always teeming with bustling crowds of shoppers and street artists. ✉ *Vladimirskaya* Ⓜ *Ploshchad Vosstaniya.*

Russian National Library (*Rossiiskaya Natsionalnaya Biblioteka,* Российская Национальная Библиотека). Opened in 1814 as the Imperial Public Library, this was Russia's first public library, and today it's still known fondly as the "Publichka." It holds more than 20 million books and claims to have a copy of every book ever printed in Russia. Among its treasures are Voltaire's personal library and the only copy of *Chasovnik* (1565), the second book printed in Russia. The building comprises three sections. The main section, on the corner of Nevsky prospekt and Sadovaya ulitsa, was designed by Yegor Sokolov and built between 1796 and 1801. Another wing, built between 1828 and 1832, was designed by Carlo Rossi as an integral part of Ploshchad Ostrovskovo. The facade is adorned with statues of philosophers and poets, including Homer and Virgil, and the Roman goddess of wisdom, Minerva. You can see the facilities if you bring your passport and ask very nicely. Using the library requires a passport, registration note (a note from a hotel, in the case of tourists), and two photos. ✉ *18 Sadovaya ul., City Center* ☎ *812/310–7137* ☉ *Weekdays 9–9, weekends 11–7. Closed last Tues. of month* Ⓜ *Nevsky Prospekt.*

★ **Smolny** (Смольный). Confusion abounds when you mention the Smolny, because you may be referring to either the beautiful baroque church and convent or the classically designed institute that went down in history as the Bolshevik headquarters in the Revolution of 1917. The two architectural complexes are right next door to each other, on the Neva's left bank. Construction of the Smolny convent and cathedral began under Elizabeth I and continued during the reign of Catherine the Great, who established a school for the daughters of the nobility within its walls. The centerpiece of the convent is the magnificent five-dome **Cathedral of the Resurrection,** which was designed by Bartolomeo Rastrelli and which is, some historians say, his greatest creation. At first glance, the highly ornate blue-and-white cathedral seems to have leaped off the pages of a fairy tale. Its five white onion domes, crowned with gilded globes supporting crosses of gold, convey a sense of magic and power. Begun by Rastrelli in 1748, the cathedral was not completed until the 1830s, by the architect Vasily Stasov. Few traces of the original interior have survived. It's currently used for concerts, notably of Russian sacred music, and rather insignificant exhibits. The cathedral tower affords beautiful views of the city. ✉ *3/1 Pl. Rastrelli, Liteiny/Smolny* ☎ *812/812/400–2437 or 812/577–1422 guided tours; 812/577–1421 box office and information* ✉ *Cathedral 200R, cathedral tower 200R* ☉ *Thurs.–Tues. 10–5* Ⓜ *Chernyshevskaya.*

Piskaryevskoye Cemetery (*Piskaryevskoye Kladbische*, Пискаревское кладбище). The extent of this city's suffering during the 900-day siege by the Nazis between 1941 and 1944 becomes clear after a visit to the sobering Piskaryevskoye Cemetery. On the northeastern outskirts of the city, the field here was used as a mass burial ground for the hundreds of thousands of World War II victims, some of whom died from the shelling, but most of whom died from cold and starvation. The numbingly endless rows of common graves carry simple slabs indicating the year in which those below them died. In all, nearly 500,000 people are buried here. The cemetery, with its memorial monuments and an eternal flame, serves as a deeply moving historical marker. Inscribed on the granite wall at the far end of the cemetery is the famous poem by radio personality Olga Bergholts, which ends with the oft-repeated phrase, "No one is forgotten, nothing is forgotten." The granite pavilions at the entrance house a small museum with photographs and memoirs documenting the siege. (Start with the one on the right side; the pavilions are open until 5 and admission is free.) On display is Tanya Savicheva's diary, scraps of paper on which the young schoolgirl recorded the death of every member of her family. The last entry reads, "May 13. Mother died. Everyone is dead. Only I am left." (Later, she, too, died as a result of the war.) To visit the cemetery go to Ploschad Muzhestva metro station, then take a public bus 123 or 178 to go up Nepokoryonnykh Prospect, and get off at the bus stop marked Piskaryovskoye Kladbische. ⊠ *74 Nepokorennykh, Vyborg Side* ☎ *812/247–5716* ⊠ *Free* ☉ *Daily 10–6* Ⓜ *Ploschad Muzhestva via shuttle from Lesnaya.*

State Museum "Smolny" Государственный Музей «Смольный». The institute, just south of the Cathedral of the Resurrection at Smolny, is a far different structure. Giacomo Quarenghi designed the neoclassical building between 1806 and 1808 in the style of an imposing country manor. It's here where Lenin and his associates planned the overthrow of the Kerensky government in October 1917. Lenin lived at the Smolny for 124 days. The rooms in which he resided and worked are now a memorial museum. The museum also has an exhibit on the Russian Institute of Noble Girls, which was in the building from 1808 through 1917. The school was founded by the decree of Catherine the Great in 1764. It aimed to turn out well-educated women and future mothers, who would go on to raise similarly worthy children. The Institute enrolled girls from noble families from six years of age, who were to graduate it when they turned 18. It was a closed institution with rather intense schedule where girls, aged 6–18 and from noble families, had to get up at 6 am for classes in science, crafts, and the arts. They were allowed to see their parents rarely, and only with special permission. Today the rest of the building houses the offices of the governor of St. Petersburg and can be visited only by special request. To see the museum, make an appointment at least a week in advance. Tours are in Russian only, so you may want to bring an interpreter. ⊠ *1 Proletarskoy Diktatury, Liteiny/Smolny* ☎ *812/576–7461* ⊠ *Museum 250R per person for groups of at least 4 people* ☉ *Museum weekdays 10–5 by appointment* Ⓜ *Chernyshevskaya.*

8

Zodchevo Rossi Ulitsa (*Улица Зодчего Росси*). This thoroughfare, once known as "Theater Street" (because it meets with the Alexandrinsky Theater), has extraordinary proportions: it's bounded by two buildings of exactly the same height, its width (72 feet) equals the height of the buildings, and its length is exactly 10 times its width. It's like a big dancing hall without a roof. A complete view unfolds only at the end of the street, where it meets Lomonosov Ploshchad. The perfect symmetry is reinforced by the identical facades of the two buildings, which are painted the same yellow and decorated with impressive white pillars. One of the buildings here is the legendary **Vaganova Ballet School** (founded in 1738), whose pupils included Karsavina as well as Pavlova, Nijinsky, Ulanova, Baryshnikov, and Nureyev. ⊠ *City Center* Ⓜ *Nevsky Prospekt.*

> ### WORD OF MOUTH
>
> "I thought the mosaics in [the Church of the Savior on Spilled Blood] were the most beautiful that I've ever seen; very colorful and pleasing to the eye. The outside of the church has colorful onion domes, making this destination a must-see. This church abuts a canal, which makes for some pretty pictures with the church in background." —Fluffnfold

OFF NEVSKY PROSPECT, FROM THE SQUARE OF THE ARTS TO THE FIELD OF MARS
ОТ ПЛОЩАДИ ИСКУССТВ ДО МАРСОВА ПОЛЯ

This area introduces you to some of St. Petersburg's prettiest inner streets, squares, and gardens, starting at Ploshchad Iskusstv (Square of the Arts). Along the route are several squares and buildings of historic interest: it was in this part of the city that several extremely important events in Russian history took place, including the murder of tsars Paul I, who was assassinated in the Engineer's Castle by nobles opposed to his rule, and Alexander II, killed when a handmade bomb was lobbed at him by revolutionary terrorists as he was riding in a carriage along Kanal Griboyedova.

GETTING HERE AND AROUND
You can get to this area by taking the metro to Gostinyi Dvor station or by taking trolley 1 or 7, which runs along Nevsky prospect. It's also an easy walk from Nevsky prospekt.

TIMING
Touring this section of the City Center might take between two and three hours, unless you want to linger at the State Museum of Russian Art, in which case you might want to plan an entire day here. Outdoor attractions, such as the Summer Garden, are worth visiting at any time of the year. Note that the Neva is very close here, so it's windy year-round.

TOP ATTRACTIONS
★ **Church of the Savior on Spilled Blood** (*Khram Spasa na Krovi*, **Храм Спаса на Крови**). The highly ornate, old-Russian style of this colorful church seems more Moscow than St. Petersburg, where the architecture is generally more subdued and subtle; indeed, the architect,

Alfred Parland, was consciously aiming to copy Moscow's St. Basil's. The drama of the circumstances leading to the church's inception more than matches the frenzy of its design, however. It was commissioned by Alexander III to memorialize the death of his father, Alexander II, who was killed on the site in 1881 by a terrorist's bomb. The height of the cathedral, 81 meters, symbolizes the year of Alexander II's death.

The church opened in 1907 but was closed by Stalin in the 1930s. It suffered damage over time, especially throughout World War II, but underwent meticulous reconstruction for decades and finally reopened at the end of the 20th century. The interior is as extravagant as the exterior, with glittering stretches of mosaic from floor to ceiling (70,000 square feet in total). Stone carvings and gold leaf adorn the walls, the floors are made of pink Italian marble, and the remarkable altar is constructed entirely of semiprecious gems and supported by four jasper columns. Blinded by all this splendor, you could easily overlook the painted scenes of martyrdom, including one that draws a parallel between the tsar's death and the crucifixion of Christ. Across the road there's an exhibit that takes a compelling look at the life of Alexander II. ✉ *2a Kanal Griboyedova, City Center* ☎ *812/315–1636* ✎ *320R* ☽ *Thurs.–Tues. 11–7, kassa until 6* Ⓜ *Nevsky Prospekt.*

Mikhailovsky (Inzhenernyi) Castle (*Mikhailovsky Zamok,* Инженерный Замок). This orange-hued building belonged to one of Russia's stranger and more pitiful leaders. Paul I grew up in the shadow of his powerful mother, Catherine the Great, whom he despised; no doubt correctly, he held her responsible for his father's death. By the time Paul became tsar, he lived in terror that he, too, would be murdered. He claimed that, shortly after ascending the throne, he was visited in a dream by the Archangel Michael, who instructed him to build a church on the site of his birthplace—hence the name of this landmark: Mikhailovsky Castle. Paul built not just a church but a castle, which he tried to make into an impenetrable fortress. Out of spite toward his mother, he took stones and other materials from castles that she had built. The Fontanka and Moika rivers cut off access from the north and east; and for protection everywhere else, he installed secret passages, moats with drawbridges, and earthen ramparts. All of Paul's intricate planning, however, came to nothing. On March 24, 1801, a month after he began living there, he was suffocated with a pillow in his bed. Historians speculate that his own son Alexander I knew of the murder plot and may even have participated. After Paul's death, the castle stood empty for 20 years, then was turned over to the Military Engineering Academy. One of the school's pupils was Fyodor Dostoyevsky, who may have absorbed something of the castle while he studied here: as a novelist he was preoccupied with themes of murder and greed. The castle is now part of the State Museum of Russian Art; it houses temporary exhibits from the museum, plus an exhibit on the history of the castle. ✉ *2 Sadovaya ul., City Center* ☎ *812/570–5112; tours 812/570–5173* ⊕ *www. rusmuseum.ru* ✎ *300R; 3,000R for group tour in Russian of up to 25 people (you can bring an interpreter along); 1,500R for groups up to 7 people* ☽ *Mon. 10–4, Wed.–Sun. 10–5; tours weekends at 2 and 4* Ⓜ *Nevsky Prospekt.*

8

Ⓒ **Ethnography Museum** (*Etnograficheskii Muzey*, Этнографический Музей). This museum collects applied art, national costumes, weapons, and many sociological displays about peoples of the 19th and 20th centuries, including the various ethnic groups of the former Soviet Union. On Sunday the museum offers Russian crafts workshops where you can learn to paint on wood or clay, model something out of clay or birch bark, or make a folk doll. These activities can be particularly interesting for children. ✉ *4/1 Inzhenernaya ul., City Center* ☎ *812/570–5421* ⊕ *www.ethnomuseum.ru* ✉ *350R, 450R for crafts workshop, tours in English for up to 10 people 1,500R, from 10 to 25 people 2,500R* ☉ *Museum Tues.–Sun. 11–6, kassa open until 5. Closed last Fri. of month. Crafts workshop Sun. 11–5* Ⓜ *Nevsky Prospekt.*

Shostakovich Philharmonia Филармония имени Шостаковича. Once part of the private Nobles' Club, the Philharmonia, or Philharmonia Hall, is now home to the **St. Petersburg Philharmonic.** Its main concert hall, the Bolshoi Zal, with its impressive marble columns, has been the site of many celebrated performances, including the premiere (in 1893) of Tchaikovsky's Sixth (*Pathétique*) Symphony, with the composer conducting. (This was his final masterpiece; he died nine days later.) More recently, in 1942, when Leningrad was completely blockaded, Dmitri Shostakovich's Seventh (*Leningrad*) Symphony premiered here, an event broadcast in the same spirit of defiance against the Germans in which it was written. Later the concert hall was officially named for this composer. A smaller hall, the **Maly Zal** (*Glinka Hall*)(✉ *30 Nevsky pr., City Center* ☎ *812/571–8333 box office, 812/571–4237 information*), around the corner, is also part of the complex. ✉ *2 Milkhailovskaya ul., City Center* ☎ *812/710–4257 kassa; 812/710–4290 directory service* Ⓜ *Nevsky Prospekt.*

Fodor's Choice ★ **State Museum of Russian Art** (*Gosudarstvenny Russky Muzey,* Государственный Русский Музей). In 1898 Nicholas II turned the stupendously majestic neoclassical **Mikhailovsky Palace** (Mikhailovsky Dvorets) into what has become one of the country's most important art galleries. He did so in tribute to his father, Alexander III, who had a special regard for Russian art and regretted, after seeing Moscow's Tretyakov Gallery, that St. Petersburg had nothing like it.

The collection at what's sometimes just called the Russian Museum here is now four times greater the Tretyakov Gallery, with scores of masterpieces on display. Outstanding icons include the 14th-century *Boris and Gleb* and the 15th-century *Angel Miracle of St. George*. Both 17th- and 18th-century paintings are also well represented, especially with portraiture. One of the most famous 18th-century works here is Ivan Nikitin's *The Field Hetman*. By far the most important works are from the 19th century—huge canvases by Repin, many fine portraits by Serov (his beautiful *Countess Orlova* and the equally beautiful, utterly different portrait of the dancer Ida Rubinstein), and Mikhail Vrubel's strange, disturbing *Demon Cast Down*. For many years much of this work was unknown in the West, and it's fascinating to see the stylistic parallels and the incorporation of outside influences into a Russian framework. Painters of the World of Art movement—Bakst, Benois, and Somov—are also here. There are several examples of 20th-century art, with works by Kandinsky and Kazimir Malevich. Natan Altman's striking portrait of the poet Anna Akhmatova is in Room 77. The museum usually has at least one excellent special exhibit in place, and there's a treasure gallery here as well (guided tours only; you need a special ticket that you can only get before noon). The Marble Palace, Engineer's Castle, and Stroganov Palace are all branches of the museum.

The square in front of the palace was originally named Mikhailovsky Ploshchad for Grand Duke Mikhail Pavlovich (1798–1849), the younger brother of Alexander I and Nicholas I and resident of the palace. The square's appearance is the work of Carlo Rossi, who designed

---

HEROIC MUSIC

During Hitler's siege of Leningrad, the conductor Karl Eliasberg managed to put an orchestra together for the premiere of Dmitri Shostakovich's Seventh Symphony ("Leningrad"), despite some of the musicians being too weak from starvation to hold their instruments. The performance went on as scheduled at the Philharmonic on August 9, 1942—the day that Hitler had predicted would mark the success of the German siege. Batteries of loudspeakers were arranged outside the hall and at the edge of the city so it could be heard across German lines.

---

the facade of each building encircling it as well as the Mikhailovsky Palace. Each structure, as well as the plaza itself, was made to complement Mikhail's residence on its north side. The palace, which was built between 1819 and 1825, comprises a principal house and two service wings. The central portico, with eight Corinthian columns, faces a large courtyard now enclosed by a fine art nouveau railing, a late (1903) addition. The statue of Alexander Pushkin in the center of the plaza was designed by Mikhail Anikushin and erected in 1957. ✉ 4/2 *Inzhenernaya ul., City Center* ☎ *812/595–4248* ⊕ *www.rusmuseum.ru* ✎ *350R* ☉ *Mon. 10–5, Wed.–Sun. 10–6, kassa open until 1 hr before closing* Ⓜ *Nevsky Prospekt.*

★ **Summer Garden** (*Letny Sad,* **Летний Сад**). Inspired by Versailles, the Summer Garden was one of Peter the Great's passions. When first laid out in 1704, it was given the regular, geometric style made famous by Louis XIV's gardener, Andre Le Nôtre, and decorated with statues and sculptures as well as with imported trees and plants. Grottoes, pavilions, ponds, fountains, and intricate walkways were placed throughout, and the grounds are bordered on all sides by rivers and canals. In 1777, however, disastrous floods did so much damage (entirely destroying the system of fountains) that the Imperial family stopped using the garden for entertaining. When they decamped for environs farther afield, they left the Summer Garden for use by the upper classes. Today it's a popular park accessible to everyone, but you'll have to imagine the first formal garden, which is long gone. The graceful wrought-iron fence that marks the entrance to the garden was designed in 1779 by Yuri Felten; it's supported by pink granite pillars decorated with vases and urns.

Just inside this southeastern corner is Peter's original **Summer Palace,** Letny Dvorets. Designed by Domenico Trezzini and completed in 1714, the two-story building is quite simple, as most of Peter's dwellings were.

The walls are of brick covered in stucco and painted primrose yellow. Open since 1934 as a museum, it has survived without major alteration. Two other attractive buildings nearby are the **Coffee House** (Kofeinyi Domik), built by Carlo Rossi in 1826, and the **Tea House** (Tchainyi Domik), built by L. I. Charlemagne in 1827. Neither of them serves the beverage they are named for: they're both used for expositions these days. As you walk through the park, take a look at some of its more than 80 statues. *Peace and Abundance,* sculpted in 1722 by Pietro Baratta, is an allegorical depiction of Russia's victory in the war with Sweden. Another statue, just off the main alley, is of Ivan Krylov, a writer known as "Russia's La Fontaine." Peter Klodt, who also did the Anichkov Bridge horse statues, designed this sculpture, which was unveiled in 1855. Scenes from Krylov's fables, including his version of "The Fox and the Grapes," appear on the pedestal. As in many other parks and public places, the sculptures are protected from the harsh weather by wooden covers from early fall to late spring. There's a small admission fee (15R) to the park on weekends in summer. ⊠ *City Center* Ⓜ *Chernyshevskaya or Nevsky Prospekt.*

WORTH NOTING

Mikhailovsky Theater of Opera and Ballet (Михайловский Театр Оперы и Балета имени Мусоргского). This historic theater, built in 1833, is St. Petersburg's second-most-important opera and ballet theater after Mariinsky.The repertoire is conentrated on the most important works of European opera and ballet theater of the 19th and 20th centuries. The theater also pays significant attention to works composed for children. ⊠ *1 Pl. Iskusstv, City Center* ☎ *812/595–4305 or 812/595–4284* ⊕ *www.mikhailovsky.ru* Ⓜ *Nevsky Prospekt.*

Square of the Arts (*Ploshchad Iskusstu*). The magnificent State Museum of Russian Art is at the far end of this square. If you stand in front of the museum and turn to survey the entire square, the first building on your right, with old-fashioned lanterns adorning its doorways, is the Mikhailovsky Theater of Opera and Ballet. Bordering the square's south side, on Mikhailovskaya ulitsa's east corner, is the former Nobles' Club, now the Shostakovich Philharmonia, home to the St. Petersburg Philharmonic. The buildings on the square's remaining side are former residences and school buildings. ⊠ *City Center* Ⓜ *Gostinyi Dvor or Nevsky Prospekt.*

Ⓒ **St. Petersburg Circus** (*Tsirk Sankt-Peterburga,* Цирк Санкт-Петербурга). Though not as famous as the Moscow Circus, the St. Petersburg Circus, dating from 1867, remains a popular treat for children. Avid young circus fans get a kick out of its adjacent **Circus Art Museum** as well, with displays about the world of the circus. ⊠ *3 nab. Fontanki, City Center* ☎ *812/570–5198 circus; 812/313–4413 museum* ☉ *Performances Fri. 7 pm, Sat. 3 and 7 pm, Sun. 1 and 5 pm; museum weekdays noon–5* 🎫 *300R–2,000R* Ⓜ *Gostinyi Dvor or Nevsky Prospekt.*

St. Petersburg
Where to Eat

WORD OF MOUTH

"[The Georgian] style of food is known to be very flavorful, and it didn't disappoint. It was great having someone who speaks Russian order off the menu for us, with a sampling of dumplings, salads, and meats. (By the way, salads are not what you think. They are all a conglomeration of vegetables and marinade. Think potato salad with lots of different stuff in it, like beets, pickles, or cabbage)."
—sdtravels

Updated
by Galina
Stolyarova

The new restaurants and cafés of the burgeoning scene stand in sharp contrast to the traditional, sometimes uninspired, but always inexpensive Russian-style eateries of the former Soviet Union. Although it's certainly worth experiencing Russian-style dining, you have plenty of options.

Hotels often house excellent restaurants and foreign chefs, which have become an integral part of the city's culinary scene. At the restaurants of the Grand Hotel Europe, the Astoria, and the Radisson SAS Royal you will find top-notch service, food, and often good views. The dining sections of *St. Petersburg Times* and *St. Petersburg in Your Pocket* are worth checking out, for both the restaurant reviews and the ads for tempting business lunch-deals, which are typically priced between 300R and 600R.

Homey and jovial budget eateries serving quick, substantial, and good meals for under 250R have mushroomed around the city. Stands selling Russian blini, the hearty Russian cousin of the French crepe, are everywhere, and they make a great pit stop.

A vegetarian section is a rarity in Russian restaurants, and it's pretty much unheard of in restaurants serving traditional Russian cuisine. Those seeking meat-free meals usually head to Italian or Indian restaurants—or else to one of the many pie shops or pancake cafés.

It's not necessary to plan ahead if you want to land a table in a nice establishment on weekdays, but it's generally a good idea to reserve ahead for weekend dining. Ask your hotel or tour guide for help making a reservation. Note that few restaurants in St. Petersburg have no-smoking sections; in fact, some places have cigarettes listed on the menu. Most restaurants stop serving food around 11 pm or midnight, although more and more 24-hour cafés are opening.

WHAT IT COSTS IN RUSSIAN RUBLES					
	¢	$	$$	$$$	$$$$
At Dinner	under 250R	250R–450R	451R–650R	651R–850R	over 850R

Prices are per person for a main course at dinner.

RESTAURANT REVIEWS

Use the coordinate (✛ B2) at the end of each review to locate a property on the Where to Eat in St. Petersburg map.

CITY CENTER

$$$$
FRENCH
✕ **Bellevue.** This hotel restaurant is literally head and shoulders above any other restaurant in St. Petersburg, thanks to its breathtaking, 360-degree panorama. The menu, very expensive but worth every

BEST BETS FOR DINING IN ST. PETERSBURG

With hundreds of restaurants to choose from, how will you decide where to eat? Fodor's writers and editors have selected their favorite restaurants by price, cuisine, and experience in the Best Bets lists below. In the first column, Fodor's Choice properties represent the "best of the best" in every price category. You can also search by neighborhood for excellent eats—just peruse our reviews on the following pages.

Fodor'sChoice★

L'Europe, p. 248
Mechta Molokhovets, p. 259
Restoran $$$, p. 256
Taleon $$$$, p. 252
Terrassa $$, p. 253
Tsar, p. 253

By Price

¢

Chainaya Lozhka, p. 248
Kompot, p. 258
Pirozhkovaya Stolle, p. 254
Teremok, p. 252

$

Da Albertone, p. 248
Bizet, p. 257
Botanika, p. 257
Gavroche, p. 258
Jean-Jacques, p. 260
Kilikia, p. 249
Oliva, p. 249

Tbiliso, p. 260
Teplo, p. 255
Vostochny Ugolok, p. 253

$$

Gastronom, p. 249
Macaroni, p. 258
Mops, p. 259
Tandoor, p. 252
Terrassa, p. 253

$$$

1913, p. 254
Russian Vodka Room No. 1, p. 255

$$$$

Bellevue, p. 246
L'Europe, p. 248
Francesco, p. 258
Mechta Molokhovets, p. 259
Taleon, p. 252
Triton, p. 259
Tsar, p. 253

By Cuisine

RUSSIAN

1913 $$$, p. 254
Chekhov $$, p. 260
Mechta Molokhovets $$$$, p. 259
Restoran $$$, p. 256
Russian Vodka Room No. 1 $$$, p. 255
Tsar $$$$, p. 253

ITALIAN

Francesco $$$$, p. 258
Il Grappolo $$$$, p. 249
Terrassa $$, p. 253

MIDDLE EASTERN

Caravan $$$, p. 254
Kilikia $, p. 249
Tbiliso $, p. 260
Vostochny Ugolok $, p. 253

VEGETARIAN

Botanika $, p. 257
Francesco $$$$, p. 258

Kompot ¢, p. 258
Pirozhkovaya Stolle ¢, p. 254
Tandoor $$, p. 252

By Experience

CHILD-FRIENDLY

Da Albertone $, p. 248
Botanika $, p. 257
Gastronom $$, p. 249
Oliva $, p. 249
Teplo $, p. 255

GREAT VIEW

Bellevue $$$$, p. 246
Bessonnitsa $$$, p. 260
Café Zinger $, p. 248
Palkin $$$$, p. 252
Terrassa $$, p. 253

MOST ROMANTIC

Bellevue $$$$, p. 246
Bessonnitsa $$$, p. 260
Dvoryanskoye Gnezdo $$$$, p. 254
L'Europe $$$$, p. 248
Il Grappolo $$$$, p. 249
Staraya Tamozhnya $$$$, p. 256

MOST AUTHENTIC

Mechta Molokhovets $$$$, p. 256
Oliva $, p. 249
Restoran $$$, p. 256
Tandoor $$, p. 252
Tbiliso $, p. 260
Tsar $$$$, p. 253

9

kopek, fuses Mediterranean classics with traditional Russian dishes, such as beef Stroganoff. For a dessert, there's the coupe Romanoff, an artfully presented concoction of strawberries, vanilla ice cream, and whipped cream. Bellevue welcomes diners who are not guests, including those who just want to stop in for coffee to check out the superb vibe— you can see the golden spire of the Admiralty, the top of the Cathedral of the Spilt Blood, the roof of the Hermitage, and the dome of St. Isaac's Cathedral. ⊠ *Kempinski Hotel, Moika 22, Moika river embankment 22, City Center* ☎ *812/335–9111* ⊕ *www.kempinski-st-petersburg.com* ▭ *AE, DC, MC, V* Ⓜ *Nevsky Prospekt* ✛ *D4.*

$ ✕ **Café Zinger.** This coffee joint is classier and a tad pricier than its
CAFÉ competitors, but the food options are a rung above. They have everything from sandwiches and quiches to cakes, tarts, and ice cream. There is also a choice of traditional Russian dishes, including *pelmeni* (meat dumplings) and borsch. This location, on the second floor of the Dom Knigi bookstore, is one of the best people-watching spots in St. Petersburg. ⊠ *28 Nevsky pr., City Center* ☎ *812/571–8223* ▭ *MC, V* Ⓜ *Nevsky Prospekt* ✛ *E4.*

¢ ✕ **Chainaya Lozhka.** Distinguishable by its white and orange teaspoon
EASTERN logo, this is an extremely cheap and cheerful counter-service blini chain
EUROPEAN with locations all over downtown. You may be put off by the plastic cutlery and the lackadaisical service, but the blini are authentic and filling, and at about 65R each, they're a great deal when you are in a hurry. There is also a popular business lunch deal that buys you a three-course meal, including blinis, at 143R. ⊠ *42 Sadovaya ul., City Center* ☎ *812/310–1315* ⊕ *www.teaspoon.ru* ▭ *No credit cards* Ⓜ *Sadovaya* ✛ *D4* ⊠ *44 Nevsky pr., City Center* ☎ *812/571–4657* Ⓜ *Gostinny Dvor* ✛ *C5.*

¢ ✕ **Coffeehouse.** After settling a legal dispute about the use of its trade-
CAFÉ mark, Starbucks finally opened its first outlet in Russia in 2007. By then, Starbucks clones had sprung up on seemingly every corner, and in St. Petersburg the market leader is Coffeehouse. You can grab a business lunch here for 250R; it includes a salad, sandwich, and coffee or tea. They also serve a full range of not-always-expertly-made coffee drinks. ⊠ *7/9 Nevsky pr., City Center* ☎ *812/570–4774* ⊕ *www. coffeehouse.ru* ▭ *MC, V* Ⓜ *Nevsky Prospekt* ✛ *D4* ⊠ *17 Kanal Griboedova, City Center* ☎ *812/570–6533* ▭ *MC, V* Ⓜ *Nevsky Prospekt* ✛ *D4* ⊠ *3 Malaya Sadovya, City Center* ☎ *812/314–3610* ▭ *MC, V* Ⓜ *Nevsky Prospekt* ✛ *C4.*

$ ✕ **Da Albertone.** Get your cheap and scrumptious pizza here. This cheer-
ITALIAN ful pizzeria serves more than 40 kinds of pizza prepared by Italian cooks who know what they're doing. Other dishes worth looking out for include the osso buco, the risotto Milanese, the baked oysters, or any of the housemade pastas. Though it's busy, the service is friendly and prompt. The children's playroom is an added draw for families. ⊠ *23 Millionnaya ul., City Center* ☎ *812/315–8673* ⊕ *www.daalbertone.ru* ▭ *AE, MC, V* Ⓜ *Nevsky Prospekt* ✛ *C3.*

$$$$ ✕ **L'Europe.** This elegant restaurant with extremely high standards serves
CONTINENTAL fine Russian and Continental cuisine. The breathtaking interior—there's
Fodor's Choice an art nouveau stained-glass roof, shining parquet floors, and private
★

balconies—is fit for a tsar, as are the prices. The mouthwatering menu includes some dishes inspired by authentic royal recipes. Try the venison marinated in vodka and juniper berries, or the lobster, sturgeon, and salmon *à la Russe*. The popular Sunday champagne-and-caviar brunch (4,500R) is the place to see and be seen among the city's high-rollers. Reserve well ahead, particularly in summer. ⊠ *Grand Hotel Europe, 1/7 Mikhailovskaya ul., City Center* ☎ *812/329–6630* ⊕ *www. grandhoteleurope.com* ⚲ *Reservations essential* 🏛 *Jacket and tie* ▤ *AE, DC, MC, V* Ⓜ *Nevsky Prospekt or Gostinny Dvor* ✛ *D4.*

$$ ✕ **Gastronom.** At Gastronom, the dishes taste as if mom cooked. It's a
CONTINENTAL favorite for its relaxed weekend lunches, which can stretch into the late afternoon. The main hall is reminiscent of a classic French kitchen and house, with chunky wooden tables as well as large sofas and wicker chairs with soft cushions. Walls are adorned with rows of dusty wine bottles. There's also a long table along one wall that's half-buried under mounds of cheese, freshly baked bread, grapes, honey, and citrus. Salads, which come in generous sizes, could easily replace a main course. One standout is the reindeer salad, a hearty serving of lightly fried slices of reindeer, with chocolate balsamic vinegar, sautéed strawberries, lingonberries, and arugula. Homemade pastas, such as ravioli with pork and pistachio nuts, or tiger prawns with amaretto, are recommended, as are the beef Stroganoff and the halibut fillet with a porcini sauce. ⊠ *1/7 Naberezhnaya Reki Moiki, City Center* ☎ *812/314–3849* ⊕ *www. gastronom.ru* ▤ *AE, MC, V* Ⓜ *Nevsky Prospekt, Gostinny Dvor* ✛ *D3.*

$$$$ ✕ **Il Grappolo.** The comfortable, elegant Grappolo is one of the city's best
ITALIAN Italian restaurants, a place for people who know and appreciate good food. The chef and owners are knowledgeable and use only the best ingredients available—including true buffalo mozzarella, which helps make the delicious Caprese salad a star here. The menu includes fresh arugula salad, mushroom risotto, veal with mushroom sauce (or just about anything with porcini mushrooms), and an excellent tiramisu. Downstairs at the sister wine bar, Probka, you can order wines by the glass from the well-chosen list and have an authentic Caesar salad. ⊠ *5 ul. Belinskogo, City Center* ☎ *812/273–4904* ⊕ *www.probka.org* ▤ *AE, DC, MC, V* Ⓜ *Gostinny Dvor* ✛ *E4.*

$ ✕ **Kilikia.** A haven for local Armenians, Kilikia, named after an ancient
MIDDLE EASTERN region in modern-day Turkey, has a strong reputation. Sizzling beef stew is a hit, and expertly cooked kebabs are available in tempting variety. There are six halls in this sprawling, dimly lit eatery but seating only expands to them as space is needed. The seemingly endless menu may confuse the uninitiated, but the staff are competent and ready to help. Budget travelers will be thrilled by Kilikia's three-course business lunch, only 140R. ⊠ *26/40 Gorokhovaya ul., City Center* ☎ *812/327–2208* ⊕ ▤ *MC, V* Ⓜ *Sennaya Ploshchad* ✛ *C5.*

$ ✕ **Oliva.** The size of this Greek taverna, seating more than 150 people,
GREEK underscores the confidence of its cooks, and the venue is almost always
☺ full. Feta cheese is delivered directly from Greece, and the house specialties get high marks in the city. Try the *moussaka* (ground meat baked with potatoes and spices) and kefal (a kind of mullet) baked with tarragon. With friendly multilingual servers, it's a great place for

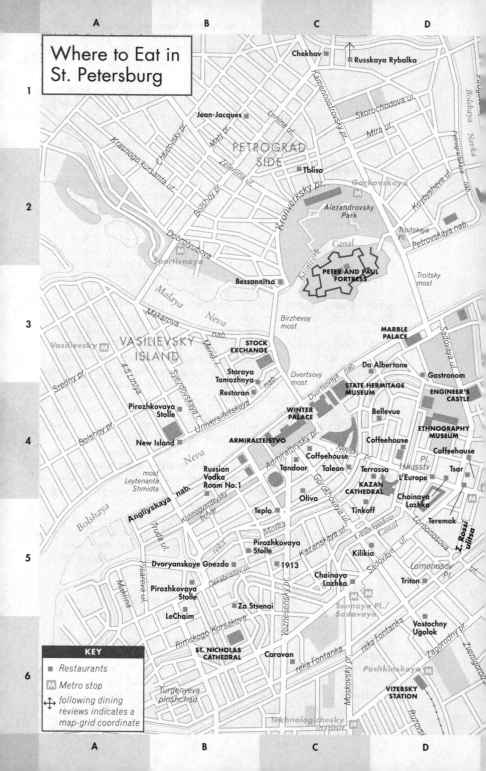

Where to Eat in St. Petersburg

KEY
- ■ Restaurants
- Ⓜ Metro stop
- ↔ following dining reviews indicates a map-grid coordinate

Chekhov
Russkaya Rybalka

Jean-Jacques

PETROGRAD SIDE

Tbliso

Skorochodova ul.
Mira ul.
Kamennoostrovsky pr.
Kronverksky pr.
Gorkovskaya Ⓜ

Alexandrovsky Park

Troitskaya Pl.
Petrovskaya nab.

Canal
Kronverk

Bessonnitsa

PETER AND PAUL FORTRESS

Troitsky most

Sportivnaya

Malaya Neva nab.

Makarova

Birzhevoy most

MARBLE PALACE

Vasilievsky Ⓜ

VASILIEVSKY ISLAND

Sredny pr.
4-5 Liniya
Sverdovskaya l.

STOCK EXCHANGE

Staraya Tamozhnya
Restoran

Da Albertone
Gastronom

Mend. l.

Dvortsovy most

Dvortsovaya nab.

STATE HERMITAGE MUSEUM

ENGINEER'S CASTLE

Sadovaya ul.

Pirozhkovaya Stolle

Universitetskaya

WINTER PALACE

Bellevue

ETHNOGRAPHY MUSEUM

Bolshoy pr.

New Island

ARMIRALTEISTVO

Coffeehouse

Coffeehouse

Neva

Admiralteysky pr.

Coffeehouse

Taleon

Terrassa

Pl. Iskusstv

Coffeehouse

Tsar

most Leytenanta Shmidta

Russian Vodka Room No.1

Tandoor

Gorkhovaya ul.

KAZAN CATHEDRAL

L'Europe

Angliyskaya nab.

Oliva

Chainaya Lozhka

Truda ul.

Konnogvardeysky bulvar

Teplo

Tinkoff

Nevsky pr.

Z. Rossi ulitsa

Teremok

Bolshaya

Moika reka

Pirozhkovaya Stolle

1913

Kazanskaya ul.

Kilikia

Lomonosova

Dvoryanskoye Gnezdo

Dekabristov ul.

Chainaya Lozhka

Griboyedov Canal

Sadovaya ul.

Lomonosov Pl.

Triton

Pirozhkovaya Stolle

Za Stsenoi

LeChaim

Rimskogo-Korsakova

Voznesensky pr.

Sennaya Pl./ Sadovaya Ⓜ

Vostochny Ugolok

Zagorodny pr.

Zvenigorod

Makhna

Psareva ul.

ST. NICHOLAS CATHEDRAL

Caravan

reka Fontanka

Moskovsky pr.

reka Fontanka

Pushkinskaya Ⓜ

Zaraiski

Turgenyeva ploshchad

VITEBSKY STATION

Teknologichesky Institut Ⓜ

lunch, groups, and fans of live folk music, which plays on most nights. ✉ *31 Bolshaya Morskaya ul., City Center* ☎ *812/314–6563* ⊕ *www.tavernaoliva.ru* ⊟ *MC, V* Ⓜ *Nevsky Prospekt* ✛ *C4.*

$$$$
FRENCH

✕ **Palkin.** This grand restaurant evokes the name of a legendary restaurant established on the same spot in 1785. The interior is formal and elegant. You'll be treated like royalty the moment you enter, although the place has become a bit worn around the edges since its Yeltsin-era heyday. Look for chicken with morel sauce, venison with pine nuts–marmalade, fillet of turbot served with pistachio nuts and curry sauce, and a salad of smoked salmon with fresh oysters and beluga caviar. It's worth a visit for the window seats alone, which look out onto bustling Nevsky prospekt. ✉ *47 Nevsky pr., at Vladirmirsky pr., City Center* ☎ *812/703–5371* ⊕ *www.palkin.ru* ⌫ *Reservations essential* ⊟ *AE, MC, V* Ⓜ *Mayakovskaya or Nevsky Prospekt* ✛ *E5.*

> **HEAD FOR A HUB**
>
> Corners of St. Petersburg have recently become dining hubs: a stroll down Rubinshteina ulitsa will reveal high-class Thai, Italian, and Russian options, plus a couple of decent pubs, while the streets around Bolshaya Morskaya teem with cheaper but no less varied eateries.

$$$$
EASTERN
EUROPEAN
Fodor's Choice
★

✕ **Taleon.** Inside an opulent mansion is an upscale restaurant, private club, and casino, all connected with the Yeliseyev Palace Hotel. You'll find the usual array of fun for the bodyguard-protected high-society set—gambling, cigars, cognac—in a glittering setting, with marble fireplaces and gilded ceilings. The Russian and European menus are full of hearty, classic options, including caviar, oven-baked partridge in coriander sauce, veal cutlet with sage sauce, and rack of lamb in rosemary sauce. The Sunday brunch (3,100R) includes black and red caviar as well as lobster and champagne. Be sure to tour the casino, where there's a lush cigar lounge with walnut-covered walls and leather sofas. ✉ *59 nab. Moika, City Center* ☎ *812/324–9911 or 812/324–9944* ⊕ *www.taleon.ru* ⌫ *Reservations essential* 🏛 *Jacket and tie* ⊟ *AE, DC, MC, V* Ⓜ *Nevsky Prospekt* ✛ *C4.*

$$
INDIAN

✕ **Tandoor.** One of the first ethnic restaurants to emerge after the downfall of the USSR, Tandoor has carved out a solid reputation. Every meal is good, and you can trust finding your Indian favorites here. Waiters, dressed in ethnic costumes and soft embroidered shoes, move soundlessly in this comfortable and quiet little place. The restaurant serves a generous business lunch that includes a vegetarian option for 450R. The location, across the street from St. Isaac's Cathedral, is another point in its favor. ✉ *2 Voznesensky pr., City Center* ☎ *812/312–3886* ⊕ *www.tandoor-spb.ru* ⊟ *AE, DC, MC, V* Ⓜ *Sennaya Ploshchad* ✛ *C4.*

¢
CAFÉ

✕ **Teremok.** Don't be intimidated by the café's spartan setting. Teremok's owners penny-pinch only on furnishings and presentation. Cooked in front of your eyes, their famous blini—priced at 40R–300R—are deservedly rated the best in town. Stuffed with mushrooms, ham, pork, grilled chicken, cream, honey, and a dozen other fillings, the blini, rich in flavor and never over- or underdone, taste as if a Russian mom cooked them. A single blini is so rich and hefty, it may leave you stuffed.

Be conservative when you order unless you are absolutely starving. In addition to this café, Teremok also runs a chain of 15 street stands. ⊠ *60 Nevsky pr., City Center* 🕾 *No phone* Ⓜ *Nevsky Prospekt* ✛ *D4.*

$$ ✕ **Terrassa.** This trendy restaurant, on the roof above a fashion boutique, is so close to the Kazan cathedral that it seems as if you could touch its cupola from the open-air terrace. Stylish and glamorous, the restaurant's definitely a place to be seen. Terrassa serves fusion cuisine with mainly Italian and Asian influences. There's a picture of every dish in the menu, where the favorites include duck Chinese style; a beef-fillet sandwich; osso buco; risotto with pumpkin, ricotta, and truffle oil; and spaghetti with clams. Terrassa is one of the more expensive place in the city, but the food, service, and view all make it a sheer pleasure to visit. ⊠ *3 Kazanskaya ul. (6th fl. of Vanity Opera boutique), City Center* 🕾 *812/337–6838* ⊕ *www.terrassa.ru* ⊟ *AE, MC, V* Ⓜ *Nevsky Prospekt or Gostiny Dvor* ✛ *D4.*

ITALIAN
Fodor's Choice
★

$$ ✕ **Tinkoff.** The crowded, loftlike Tinkoff was St. Petersburg's first microbrewery. Trendy people come to enjoy beer and tasty comfort food in a relaxed, club-like dining room. Frequent Western jazz, lounge, and cool pop acts appear at Tinkoff, but when they're here the cover price gets very high, usually around 1,500R. There's a sushi bar, with combos starting from 250R, but you're better off sticking with the beer and burgers. ⊠ *7 Kazanskaya ul., City Center* 🕾 *812/718–5566* ⊕ *www.tinkof.ru* ⊟ *DC, MC, V* Ⓜ *Nevsky Prospekt* ✛ *C5.*

AMERICAN

$$$$ ✕ **Tsar.** With a name that alludes to Nicholas II, the last tsar, this restaurant celebrates Empire style but avoids being kitsch. This restaurant's large, bustling and brightly lit hall seems straight out of *War and Peace,* and oil paintings on the wall commemorate various Romanovs. Tsar provides a royal dining experience in every sense of the word. Try ordering Tsar's quintessential beef Stroganoff, or the Pozharskaya cutlet, served with sizzling-hot potatoes, made in a copper pan. Almost anything you choose from the menu is likely to be good, and that includes the smoked eel, steamed pike-perch, and the layers of herring enclosing a beet vinaigrette. Despite its grand title and the deep-pocketed clientele, Tsar is an inviting and laid-back eatery that manages to avoid seeming intimidating. ⊠ *12 Sadovaya ul., City Center* 🕾 *812/930–0444* ⊕ *www.tsar-project.ru* ⊟ *DC, MC, V* Ⓜ *Nevsky Prospekt* ✛ *D4.*

RUSSIAN
Fodor's Choice
★

$ ✕ **Vostochny Ugolok.** The lamb, herbs, and other ingredients here are laudably fresh, and they ought to be: they're flown in several times a week from Baku, Azerbaijan. It is easy to get lost in the long menu, but much harder to be disappointed in your choice. Juicy kebabs, chops, and *khatchapuri* (cheese bread), one of the venue's stars, are also some of the most affordable options. The portions are vast, and a bowl of soup is a meal in itself. A slight downside is the loud music that comes from the TV sets in each of the three halls, each of which are decorated with oriental carpets, pillows, and pottery. ⊠ *52 Gorokhovaya ul., City Center* 🕾 *812/713–5747* ⊟ *AE, MC, V* Ⓜ *Sadovaya, Sennaya Ploshchad* ✛ *D5.*

MIDDLE EASTERN

9

ADMIRALTEISKY

$$$
RUSSIAN

✕ **1913.** This exclusive restaurant's name recalls Russia's best year in history. Low-key, comfortable elegance combines with a giant menu and giant portions. It's a cozier alternative to the stuffier, more touristy dining options, and it's convenient to the Mariinsky Theatre. The menu's traditional Russian cuisine emphasizes game and fish, and there are more pan-European dishes. Try the mushroom soup or borscht for a starter, followed by sturgeon or salmon. ✉ *13/2 Voznesensky pr., Admiralteisky* ☎ *812/315–5148* ⊕ *www.restaurant-1913.spb.ru* ⌔ *Reservations essential* ⊟ *AE, DC, MC, V* Ⓜ *Sadovaya or Sennaya Ploshchad* ✛ *C5.*

$$$
MIDDLE EASTERN

✕ **Caravan.** The stuffed camel, the Turkish carpets, and food being cooking in the middle of the room leave you in little doubt as to the theme of Caravan, a leading contender for the best Middle-Eastern eatery in town. You can lounge in separate booths at one end of the spacious restaurant, or sit at the more orthodox chairs and tables nearer the entrance. The *kutab,* a lightly fried pocket of dough filled with shrimp, pumpkin, or cheese, makes a good starter. From there move on to any of the more than 30 varieties of kebabs. ✉ *46 Voznesensky pr., Admiralteisky* ☎ *812/310–5678* ⊟ *AE, DC, MC, V* Ⓜ *Sadovaya or Tekhnologichesky Institut* ✛ *C6.*

$$$$
CONTINENTAL

✕ **Dvoryanskoye Gnezdo.** At the Noble Nest, tucked away in the garden pavilion of the Yusupov Palace, the attire of the guests as well as the staff is as formal as the service, decor, and Continental food. There are two set menus: the "Turgenev" is very Russian, and the "Nobleman" is more French. Try the fillet of venison, baked pheasant, or a selection from the small vegetarian menu. The wine list is extensive and includes Lafite, Latour, and Margaux at extraordinary prices, but there are some more reasonable choices. With the Mariinsky Theatre just around the corner, the restaurant attracts a post-theater crowd as well as foreign dignitaries and businesspeople (an expense account helps here). ✉ *21 ul. Dekabristov, Admiralteisky* ☎ *812/3120911 or 812/310–3205* ⊕ *www.dvgnezdo.ru* ⌔ *Reservations essential* ⌂ *Jacket and tie* ⊟ *AE, DC, MC, V* Ⓜ *Sadovaya or Sennaya Ploshchad* ✛ *B5.*

$
KOSHER

✕ **LeChaim.** This spacious, and welcoming kosher restaurant has been a hit with cosmopolitans and a nonreligious crowd since it opened. In a spacious basement of the St. Petersburg Great Choral Synagogue, LeChaim serves generous portions of Jewish cuisine at modest prices. Try chicken schnitzel or trout fillet wrapped in grape leaves. The restaurant can be difficult to find, since its doorway is discreetly marked. It is often booked for weddings and other events that take place in the synagogue, so call ahead. ✉ *2 Lermontovsky pr., Admiralteisky* ☎ *812/972–2774* ⊟ *No credit cards* Ⓜ *Sennaya Ploschad, Sadovaya* ☉ *Closed Sat.* ✛ *B5.*

¢
CAFÉ

✕ **Pirozhkovaya Stolle.** The two branches on the same street combine the best of the old and new: the fashionable surroundings are comfortable, clean, and spacious, while the kitchen turns out fresh pierogi. Choose from sweet or savory fillings, including fish, vegetables, and fruits. The apricot is a must, and the salmon is a dream, but all the pierogi are extremely good. ✉ *19 ul. Dekabristov, Admiralteisky* ☎ *812/315–2383*

⊕ *www.stolle.ru* ▭ *No credit cards* Ⓜ *Sennaya Ploshchad* ⊹ *B4* ✉ *33 ul. Dekabristov, Admiralteisky* ☎ *812/714–2571* ▭ *No credit cards* Ⓜ *Sennaya Ploshchad* ⊹ *B5.*

$$$

RUSSIAN

✕ **Russian Vodka Room No.1.** True to its name, this is the perfect place for a newcomer to try out Russian cuisine. It serves a range of vodkas, home-brewed liqueurs, and fruity alcoholic drinks. The menu blends dishes spanning the centuries, from the time of Peter the Great to today. Fish dishes dominate. A standout starter is the fish platter (790R), with four types of smoked fish—including *omul* (cisco, a kind of whitefish) from Lake Baikal and *sig,* a whitefish from Russia's far east. For the main course, try the Lake Ladoga fried pike-perch with mashed potatoes. Discreet and genteel, this spacious one-room venue could come straight out of one of Chekhov's stories. ✉ *4 ul. Konnogvardeisky bulvar, Admiralteisky* ☎ *812/570–6422* ⊕ *www.vodkaroom.ru* ▭ *AE, MC, V* Ⓜ *Sadovaya, Sennaya Ploshchad* ⊹ *B4.*

$

RUSSIAN

✕ **Teplo.** This is a hot spot—and not just for those who win the plum seats next to its fireplace. Teplo (Russian for "warmth") does indeed make guests feel warm all over, with an interior that resembles a country house (the main dining room has bookshelves, table games, and children's toys.) Try the signature dish, the warm salad: it's a mass of juicy chicken livers and crispy strips of bacon surrounded by salad leaves, cherry tomatoes, and herby croutons. Teplo serves expertly made Russian classics, such as marinated beets, salted herring, pies, and borscht. At 320R, the three-course-plus-a-drink business lunch is and excellent value (a smaller version is also available). Be sure to reserve in advance, especially if you want to sit next to the open fire, which is waiting-list territory. ✉ *45 Bolshaya Morskaya ul., Admiratleisky* ☎ *812/570–1974* ⊕ *www.v-teple.ru* ⌔ *Reservations essential* ▭ *AE, MC, V* Ⓜ *Sadovaya or Sennaya Ploshchad* ⊹ *C5.*

$$$

FUSION

✕ **Wine Bar Grand Cru.** At this molecular gastronomy restaurant, the hits include shrimp carpaccio with orange salt crystals and curry butter, and scallops with foie gras, which arrives under a glass dome filled with smoke. This haven for wine-lovers as well as adventurous eaters has its own wine shop, too. As with the food, the restaurant's decor is not for the timid or introverted, with red lights looming from the ceiling and photos of female nudes bedecking the walls. The portion sizes may be a disappointment, especially if you get there hungry; some main courses are smaller than the starters. ✉ *52 Reki Fontanki nab., Admiralteisky* ☎ *812/363–2511* ▭ *AE, MC, V* Ⓜ *Sadovaya, Sennaya Ploshchad* ⊹ *E5.*

$$$$

CONTINENTAL

✕ **Za Stsenoi.** Steps from the Mariinsky Theatre, with windows overlooking the pretty Kryukova Canal, "Backstage" has a dramatic setting. Its floorboards were taken from the old Mariinsky stage, and the exposed-brick walls display ornate mirrors and theater props. The menu fuses French and Russian influences. Venison carpaccio and crème lobster soup with cognac make good overtures for beluga fillet baked with mushrooms and béchamel sauce or grilled salmon with caviar sauce. A great choice for a post-theater dinner, but be sure to plan ahead as it fills up quickly. ✉ *18/10 Teatralnaya Pl., Admiralteisky* ☎ *812/327–0521* ⊕ *elbagroup.ru/backstage* ⌔ *Reservations essential* ▭ *AE, DC, MC, V* Ⓜ *Sadovaya or Sennaya Ploshchad* ⊹ *B5.*

9

VASILIEVSKY ISLAND

$$$$ ✗**New Island.** In summer this dinner cruise has a stunning view as it
EASTERN sails along the Neva River, past the rows of colorful palaces lining
EUROPEAN its banks. New Island sets sail promptly at 2, 6, 8, and 10:30 pm. A
cruise lasts 90 minutes and is a bargain at 300R (food is extra). In
winter, when the river is frozen, the ship remains docked in the harbor
and serves only prebooked banquets. Inside, all is simple but refined,
including the menu. Try the Kamchatka crab salad as a starter, the veal
Orloff with baked potatoes and dill, or the fried fillet of trout with
almonds—and the various blini are also good. The wine list is extensive
but pricey. ⊠ *Universitetskaya nab., between Lieutenant Schmidt (now
renamed Blagovyeshchensky most) and Palace bridges, Vasilievsky
Island* ☎ *812/320–21100* ⊕ *www.concord-catering.ru* ⚕ *Reservations
essential* ▭ *AE, MC, V* Ⓜ *Vasileostrovskaya* ✦ *B4.*

¢ ✗**Pirozhkovaya Stolle.** This spot, the first of what's now a local chain,
CAFÉ has stylish furnishings resembling a traditional 19th-century Viennese
café. The kitchen turns out fresh pierogi made with fillings that include
seasonal fruit, beef, salmon, cabbage, mushrooms, and rabbit. It makes
an excellent pit stop, given its location next to the Vasileostrovskaya
metro station, the Petrovsky stadium, and Yubileiny Concert Hall. ⊠ *50
1st liniya, Vasilievsky Island* ☎ *812/328–7860* ⊕ *www.stolle.ru* ▭ *No
credit cards* Ⓜ *Vasileostrovskaya* ✦ *B6.*

$$$ ✗**Restoran.** Spacious, with soft lighting and earth tones, Restoran (liter-
RUSSIAN ally "Restaurant") is at once stylish and traditional. The main courses
Fodor's Choice are as minimalist as the decor; try the *sterlet* (sturgeon) baked in fra-
★ grant herbs with horseradish sauce, veal with mashed potatoes and
chanterelles, or the house-made pelmeni (dumplings) filled with lamb,
beef, or potatoes and dill. ⊠ *2 Tamozhenny per., Vasilievsky Island*
☎ *812/327–8979* ⊕ *elbagroup.ru/restoran* ⚕ *Reservations essential*
▭ *AE, DC, MC, V* Ⓜ *Vasileostrovskaya* ✦ *B4.*

$$$$ ✗**Staraya Tamozhnya.** Considered for many years the best restaurant
CONTINENTAL in St. Petersburg, the Old Customs House has been surpassed, but
it's still pretty impressive and a good time. It remains classy without
being snobbish, with open brickwork walls and immaculately presented
tables. Much of the food is exquisitely prepared—and that includes
the duck breast, accompanied by pan-fried foie gras with white beans
and black truffle, or the black-cod fillet on a cushion of saffron and
fennel. The wine list is excellent, and the service is friendly as well as
top-notch. ⊠ *1 Tamozhenny per., Vasilievsky Island* ☎ *812/327–8980*
⊕ *www.concord-catering.ru/restaurants/old-customs* ⚕ *Reservations
essential* ▭ *AE, MC, V* Ⓜ *Nevsky Prospekt or Vasileostrovskaya* ✦ *B3.*

VLADIMIRSKAYA (LOWER NEVSKY PROSPEKT)

$$$ ✗**Bistro Garçon.** This comfortable, Parisian-style bistro on Nevsky pros-
FRENCH pekt may not have the timeworn quality of the real thing, but from the
first bite of baguette, it doesn't matter—the food is the real deal. The
menu changes seasonally, but you can always expect delicious onion
soup, mussels, salad Roquefort, quiche, and crème brûlée. Fresh oysters are flown in from Cancale (in Brittany) on Monday and Thursday.

With omelets starting at 100R, real croissants for 120R, and good coffee, this is one of the best places for breakfast in the city (it opens at 9 am). The excellent Boulangerie Garçon is a few doors down, at 103 Nevsky prospekt. ⊠ *95 Nevsky pr., Vladimirskaya* ☎ *812/717–2467* ⊕ *www.garcon.ru* ⊟ *AE, MC, V* Ⓜ *Ploshchad Vosstania* ✛ *F5.*

$ ✕ **Bizet.** A youngish bohemian
CAFÉ crowd flocks to this cafe for the divine and airy meringues, the free Wi-Fi, and the chatty atmosphere. Furnished in pastel greens and creams, this venue is homey and cutesy, with cuddly rabbits and teddy bears perched on high shelves, a birdcage on the windowsill, and a chunky vintage radio made entirely of marzipan. The Pavlova meringue (120R) reigns supreme. Another hit is the crisp Bizet meringue (120R), with chopped almonds and garnished with fresh raspberries. Try the cupcakes decorated with colorful marzipan (100R). A generous amount of miniature meringues comes with all orders. Also available are some good soups and about a dozen salads, so it's a good bet if you're feeling peckish. ⊠ *41 ul. Zhukovskogo, Vladimirskaya* ☎ *812/702–7738* ⊕ *www.bize.su* ⊟ *AE, MC, V* Ⓜ *Mayakovskaya, Ploshchad Vosstania* ✛ *F4.*

¢ ✕ **Bliny Domik.** This homey, pocket-size place is all about blini. Every-
EASTERN thing served here is tasty, filling, and inexpensive—try the mushroom
EUROPEAN soup, followed by pork, cheese, or jam blini. *Blinchiki* are also available; they differ from blini in that they are wrapped around fillings and sometimes fried. Bliny Domik is no longer the secret it once was, but that also means it's even more foreigner-friendly. You sit at communal picnic tables, giving you a chance to meet other travelers and strike up conversations. ⊠ *8 Kolokolnaya ul., Vladimirskaya* ☎ *812/315–9915* or *812/315–5345* ⌔ *Reservations essential* ⊟ *AE, MC, V* Ⓜ *Vladimirskaya* ✛ *E5.*

$ ✕ **Botanika.** A haven for vegetarians and those seeking lighter dishes, this
VEGETARIAN café serves excellent pumpkin and tomato soups, pastas, sandwiches,
☺ hummus, and ratatouille. Decked out in shades of green, it has an abundance of potted plants and is decorated with arty photographs. Botanika has one main brightly lit dining room, and in summer there are outside tables available on a terrace. Some of the starters come in tiny portions, so if you get there hungry consider a couple of starters or a selection of snacks. Smoking is not permitted in the café, and the only alcohol available is beer. For kids there's a terrific playroom. ⊠ *7 ul. Pestelya, Vladimirskaya* ☎ *812/272–7091* ⊕ *www.cafebotanika.ru* ⊟ *MC, V* Ⓜ *Mayakovskaya* ✛ *E3.*

¢ ✕ **Chainaya Lozhka.** This spacious branch of the counter-service blini
EASTERN restaurant is close to the Galeria and Nevsky Stockmann malls, mak-
EUROPEAN ing it a great alternative to the shopping centers' much pricier cafés. The cheapest blin on the menu is only 29R, and there's an appealing

9

three-course business lunch for 141R. ⊠ *44 Ligovsky pr., Vladimir-skaya* ☏ *812/764–6433* ⊕ *www.teaspoon.ru* Ⓜ *Ploschad Aleksandra Nevskovo* ✛ *D4.*

$$$$ ✕ **Francesco.** With prominent politicians, businesspeople, and television
ITALIAN personalities among its regulars, Francesco thrives as one of the city's busiest and most fashionable venues. Both of its large, charmingly cluttered floors, decorated with display cabinets and birdcages, are almost always packed. With its jolly atmosphere, the place is great for couples and parties. The vast menu is diverse enough to accommodate modestly priced tomato soup, osso buco, and lasagna—all rendered flawlessly by the Italian chef—and more elegant fare, such as risotto with cuttlefish ink, lobster risotto, spaghetti with clams, and mussels in white wine and cherry sauce. The long wine list goes from house wines to vintage relics. ⊠ *47 Suvorovsky pr., Vladimirskaya* ☏ *812/275–0552* ⊕ *www. restoran-francesco.ru* ▭ *AE, MC, V* Ⓜ *Ploshchad Vosstania* ✛ *G4.*

$ ✕ **Gavroche.** One immediately feels at home in this bustling but laid-
FRENCH back bistro. The walls of the single, small room are adorned with retro black-and-white photographs of French film stars and views of Parisian streets. A splendid antique dresser and simple dark wooden tables also emphasize the French feel. This authentic restaurant serves hearty portions of down-home dishes; snails, duck, seafood, and sun-dried tomatoes are among the chef's favorite ingredients. Try the fried chicken with Provençal herbs and Dijon mustard, served with ratatouille, or the hamburger with foie gras and french fries. ⊠ *166 Nevsky pr., Vladimirskaya* ☏ *812/717–1270* ▭ *MC, V* Ⓜ *Ploshchad Alexandra Nevskogo* ✛ *G5.*

¢ ✕ **Kompot.** A glass of *kompot*, an infusion of stewed fruit, is served as
CAFÉ a welcome drink at this funky café that attracts a young crowd. The venue's two halls are furnished with vintage lamps, surrealist paintings, a hammock, bizarre curio items, and walls painted in green. The best bets on the diverse, international vegetable-focused menu include hummus, goat cheese, falafel, curries, and sandwiches. Free Wi-Fi, a breakfast menu available at any hour, and a rapid lunch at a bargain 200R make Kompot an even stronger temptation. ⊠ *10 ul. Zhukovsk-ogo, Vladimirskaya* ☏ *812/719–6542* ▭ *AE, MC, V* Ⓜ *Mayakovskaya, Ploshchad Vosstania* ✛ *E4.*

$$ ✕ **Macaroni.** A sister restaurant of the excellent Il Grappolo (in City
ITALIAN Center), this trattoria serves simple Italian fare, with an emphasis on fresh ingredients. The risotto primavera, pastas, pizzas, and salads are delicious and reasonably priced. As for the interior, its plush booths and muted shades of red, orange, brown, and green set it apart from those of other restaurants in the city. All and all, Macaroni is a comfortable, casual break from the hectic city. A 15% discount is available for weekday dining between noon and 5 pm. ⊠ *23 ul. Rubinshteina, Vladimirskaya* ☏ *812/572–2849* ⊕ *www.probka.org* ▭ *No credit cards* Ⓜ *Dostoevskaya, Vladimirskaya, or Mayakovskaya* ✛ *E5.*

$$ ✕ **Marcelli's.** This friendly, unpretentious spot is a great place for a long,
ITALIAN inexpensive lunch of pasta and salad or as a rendezvous point for a late-night tryst (it's open until midnight). Enjoy the Caeser salad or the satisfying mushroom tortellini with sun-dried tomatoes in a dining room decorated with Italian knickknacks and bare wooden tables. For an

un-Russian shopping experience, you can shop at the retail counter for imported cheeses, cold meats, and coffees. ⊠ *15 Vosstaniya ul., Vladimirskaya* ☏ *812/702–8010* ⊕ *www.marcellis.ru* ▤ *MC, V* Ⓜ *Ploshchad Vosstaniya* ⊹ *F4.*

$$$$
RUSSIAN
Fodor's Choice
★

✕ **Mechta Molokhovets.** A refined restaurant with prerevolutionary flair, "Molokhovets' Dream" has a tantalizing menu based on a famous 19th-century cookbook *A Gift to Young Housewives*, by Yelena Molokhovets. Cooking is elaborate and highly traditional here, and you pay for it, with main courses starting at 1,250R. Try the venison fillet accompanied by baked pears filled with cranberries and soaked in chanterelle sauce, foie gras with hot saffron sauce and iced apples, or pike-perch soaked in a piquant sauce made with red caviar. The restaurant's solid waiters show reverence to the guests, serving them in a pleasantly ceremonial, but not at all artificial, manner. With only six tables, it's an intimate dining experience. ⊠ *23/10 Kovensky per., Vladimirskaya* ☏ *812/929–2247* ⊕ *www.molokhovets.ru* ⌁ *Reservations essential* ▤ *MC, V* Ⓜ *Ploshchad Vosstania* ⊹ *F4.*

$$
ASIAN

✕ **Mops.** Sharing the building (and the name) with the city's finest Thai massage center, Mops serves authentic food prepared by native Thai cooks. The service is top-notch, and the decor is modern black-and-white, with the Asian contribution limited to painted tiger-head lamps that glow with a comforting light. The signature dish here is Bangkok duck. Spring rolls are a must, and the curries are also recommended. But the portions are small, and the spicy dishes are milder than they would be in Thailand. Every month, the chef offers an additional menu with an exotic ingredient, such as shark or truffles. ⊠ *12 ul. Rubinshteina, Vladimirskaya* ☏ *812/572–3834* ⊕ *www.mopscafe.ru* ▤ *AE, MC, V* Ⓜ *Mayakovskaya* ⊹ *E5.*

$$$$
SEAFOOD

✕ **Triton.** This restaurant's clientele is overwhelmingly made up of knowledgeable seafood-lovers. They come in part because of the fame of the chef, Vyacheslav Dmitriev, formerly of Tbiliso. Favorite dishes include sturgeon chateaubriand with braised leeks and creamy morel mushrooms; lobster tail with a spicy Malaysian sambal sauce; and barramundi (sea perch) pavé, a kind of mousse accompanied by ratatouille and a crab sauce with lavender petals. The marine theme is reflected artfully in the sophisticated formal dining hall, which has waterfalls and large aquarium-like windows framed by sea horses. Even the menus are shell-shaped, and the plates are shaped like clams. Triton has an extensive wine list and a knowledgeable sommelier. It's also got a winning location next to the Bolshoi Drama Theater. ⊠ *67 Reki Fontanki nab., Vladimirskaya* ☏ *812/310–9449* ⊕ *www.triton.su* ▤ *MC, V* Ⓜ *Sadovaya, Sennaya Ploshchad* ⊹ *D5.*

$
CAFÉ

✕ **Venezia.** The chocolate ice cream here—bittersweet, smooth, and dizzyingly rich—runs out fastest of all. As for the gooseberry flavor, it's tangy, zesty, and with a sublime pinkish color (and large seeds). There's even tomato ice cream, delicately sweet, with thin bits of peel and a subtle but distinctive aroma. This tiny café (just six tables) is hugely popular with the local Italian community, and reservations are a must, especially on weekends and the evening. When you enter, you face a large glass counter showcasing about 20 different sorts of ice

9

cream, such as tiramisu and kiwi. The flavors rotate every day, and you can taste them all, one by one, for free. Don't be fooled by the fruity titles: these are all velvety ice creams, not sorbets. Venezia also serves soups, snacks and pastas. ⊠ *107 Nevsky Prospekt, Vladimirskaya* ☏ *+7 960/279–0346* ⚏ *Reservations essential* ▭ *No credit cards* Ⓜ *Ploshchad Vosstania* ✛ *F5.*

PETROGRAD SIDE

$$$ ✕ **Bessonnitsa.** At the classy "Insomnia," innovative chefs creatively
ECLECTIC interpret European and Asian dishes. Veal fillet is served with fried grapefruit and blackberry sauce. The *pho* (a Vietnamese noodle soup) arrives sizzling hot, leaving you to put the finishing touches on it by dropping in thin slices of raw meat. Pasta farfalle with mushrooms and cedar nuts is fresh and aromatic. Consider carrot cutlets and the French omelet for breakfast. Beige linen, terra-cotta lamps, and chocolate-color walls make up this comfortable spot, which overlooks the Winter Palace. ⊠ *3 Mytninskaya nab., Petrograd Side* ☏ *812/919–3577* ⚏ *Reservations essential* ▭ *MC, V* Ⓜ *Sportivnaya* ✛ *C3.*

$$ ✕ **Chekhov.** Step into an early-20th-century Russian country house at
RUSSIAN this small family restaurant. Wicker furniture, handwoven napkins, and a birdcage with canaries and finches are some of the charms at this shady backstreet spot. The menu lovingly re-creates Russian recipes of yesteryear, such as grilled quail with fresh dill resting on sweet baked apples stuffed with a mixture of cowberries (lingonberries), pine nuts, and rhubarb; stuffed trout with blini and potatoes; and, as an alternative to vodka, various fruit liqueurs. ⊠ *4 Petropavlovskaya ul., Petrograd Side* ☏ *812/347–6045* ⚏ *Reservations essential* ▭ *MC, V* Ⓜ *Petrogradskaya* ✛ *C1.*

$ ✕ **Jean-Jacques.** This hidden-away gem is full of character and worth
FRENCH seeking out for its authentic bistro ambience—mirrored walls, red and mahogany furnishings, attentive servers, and tables topped with paper for doodling are all part of the charm. With seating for only 25 people, it is advisable to come early or call ahead to enjoy fine wines (about 150R per glass) with hearty comfort-food classics like onion soup, steak and bordelaise sauce, and crème brûlée. Rousseau also offers one of the best Continental breakfast menus in the city, served until 1 pm. ⊠ *2/54 Gatchinskaya ul., Petrograd Side* ☏ *812/232–9981* ⊕ *www.jan-jak.com* ▭ *MC, V* Ⓜ *Chkalovskaya or Petrogradskaya* ✛ *B1.*

$ ✕ **Tbiliso.** A lot of thought was put into refurbishing this busy and
MIDDLE EASTERN authentic Georgian restaurant, which evokes the atmosphere of old Tbilisi, the capital of Russia's southern neighbor. There may be political tensions between the nations these days, but Russians' love affair with Georgian cuisine, from salads such as *lobio* (bean salad) and grilled meat and fish *shashlyks* (shish kebabs) to wonderful breads such as *lavash* (flat bread) and khatchapuri (cheese-filled bread), remains passionate. Tbiliso satisfies this passion and then some, with servers in national costume and a Georgian choir to serenade diners. If you visit only one Georgian restaurant in St. Petersburg, make it this one. ⊠ *10 Sytninskaya ul., Petrograd Side* ☏ *812/232–9391* ⊕ *www.tbiliso.ru* ▭ *MC, V* Ⓜ *Petrogradskaya or Gorkovskaya* ✛ *C2.*

St. Petersburg Where to Stay

WORD OF MOUTH

"I was surprised [by] how many Russian hotels do offer a substantial discount for a single using a double room. They don't seem to do that much in the U.S. or most other places."

—NeoPatrick

Updated
by Galina
Stolyarova
and Irina
Titova

The former imperial capital still captivates, with frequently sumptuous accommodation. Heavy curtains, tapestries, ornate furniture, and deep carpeting grace the interiors of many of the city's top hotels, some of which are set in stately 19th-century mansions. For a much less impressive bill, look into the city's often charming mini-hotels.

In modern Russia, luxury almost always means opulence. Sophisticated minimalist interiors are few and far between. Expect breathtaking vistas, grand designs, and prices to match. One aspect that rarely matches the price, however, is service, which is still the weakest link in the Russian hospitality sector. Unfortunately, a lack of enthusiasm is the order the day in many hotels, and some of the grandest can sometimes suffer from a somewhat haughty staff. That said, the most genial service can often be found in some smaller budget hotels

As in Moscow, there is a big shortage of moderately priced hotels. Economy-class hotels here cost about twice the price than you would pay in almost any other European city. What the city especially lacks are two- and three-star hotels. The best budget options in town are mini-hotels, which are former mansions that became communal apartments during the Soviet era. Much nicer in this reincarnation, these guesthouses are an intimate and often furnished with antiques. Many also have a genial atmosphere and come with home-cooked breakfasts and modern comforts, such as free Wi-Fi.

On an organized tour, you're likely to land in one of the old standbys run by Intourist, the Soviet tourist agency monopoly. Most U.S. and British tour operators take advantage of the discounted rates at the Moskva, the Oktyabrskaya, or the Okhtinskaya-Victoria. The main reason to choose one of these hotels is their lower rates; note that many of them are not convenient to the major attractions.

An expanding number of realty agents like City Realty can organize a suitable and safe apartment rental, usually in the center of the city. The prices for such apartments usually run the level of three-star hotels, but they often have much more space.

WHAT IT COSTS IN RUSSIAN RUBLES					
	¢	$	$$	$$$	$$$$
For two people	under 2,500R	2,500R–5,000R	5,001R–7,500R	7,501R–10,000R	over 10,000R

Prices are for a standard double room in high season, excluding taxes and service charge.

LODGING REVIEWS

Hotel reviews have been abbreviated in this book. For expanded reviews, please visit Fodors.com. Use the coordinate (⊕ B2) at the end of each review to locate a property on the Where to Stay in St. Petersburg map.

CITY CENTER

$–$$ 🖼 **City Realty.** This American-owned company can help you locate a suitable mini-hotel, B&B, or stay in a central apartment (which usually it owns). **Pros:** usually less expensive than the city's central hotels, can choose your own apartment; personalized service; downtown locations; more privacy. **Cons:** fewer services than a hotel; you're staying in a stranger's house. ✉ *2 Muchnoi Pereulok, City Center* ☎ *812/570–6342, 812/570-4709, or 812/310–6477* ⊕ *www.cityrealtyrussia.com* ☉ *Weekdays 9:30–6:30* Ⓜ *Sennaya Ploschad/Sadovaya/Spasskaya.*

$$$$ 🖼 **Grand Hotel Europe.** Combining the elegance of prerevolutionary St. Petersburg with loads of modern amenities, this luxurious landmark from 1875 is one of the finest hotels in town. **Pros:** elegant interiors; prime location; historic building. **Cons:** very expensive. ✉ *1/7 Mikhailovskaya ul., City Center* ☎ *812/329–6000* ⊕ *www.grand-hotel-europe.com* 🛏 *212 rooms, 65 suites.* ♿ *In-room: a/c, Wi-Fi. In-hotel: restaurants, room service, bar, gym, spa, parking, some pets allowed* 🟰 *AE, DC, MC, V* Ⓜ *Nevsky Prospekt or Gostinny Dvor* ⊕ *D4.*

Fodor's Choice
★

$$$$ 🖼 **Kempinski Hotel Moika 22.** This rival to the Grand Hotel is just as elegant, and may be a bit better at service. **Pros:** unbeatable views; unpretentious personal service; next to the Hermitage. **Cons:** some rooms overlook busy restaurant; no pool. ✉ *22 nab. reki Moika, City Center* ☎ *812/335–9111* ⊕ *www.kempinski-st-petersburg.com* 🛏 *197 rooms, 23 suites* ♿ *In-room: a/c, Wi-Fi* ♿ *In-hotel: restaurants, room service, bar, gym, spa, parking, some pets allowed* 🟰 *AE, DC, MC, V* Ⓜ *Nevsky Prospekt* ⊕ *D4.*

Fodor's Choice
★

$ 🖼 **Nevsky Inn 1.** It's a steep climb to the fourth floor of this mini-hotel (there's no elevator), but it is friendly, and it has a quiet, central location that makes it just a two-minute walk to the Hermitage and close to most other attractions. **Pros:** central location; relatively inexpensive; kitchen available for use. **Cons:** no phone in rooms; no elevator. ✉ *2 Kirpichny per., Apt. 19, code 19B, City Center* ☎ *812/315–8836, 812/972–6873* ⊕ *www.nevskyinn.com* 🛏 *7 rooms* ♿ *In-room: a/c, Wi-Fi* 🟰 *MC, V* 🍴 *CP* ⊕ *C4.*

$$ 🖼 **Pushka Inn.** In the heart of the city, this storied hotel is a few minutes' walk from the Hermitage Museum and the Palace Square and also close to Nevsky prospect. **Pros:** central; beautiful views of the canal, good service and friendly staff. **Cons:** expensive, even when compared to similar-quality hotels.

10

> ### WORD OF MOUTH
>
> "We stayed at the Grand Hotel Europe in the City Center. We loved this hotel, and it was five-star all the way! There are myriad choices of restaurants (L'Europe, Caviar, Rossi, Chopsticks, Grand Terrace, Lobby Bar) and shops."
>
> —fluffnfold

BEST BETS FOR ST. PETERSBURG LODGING

Fodor's offers a selective listing of quality lodging experiences in every price range, from the city's best budget beds to its most sophisticated luxury hotels. Here, we've compiled our top recommendations by price and experience. The very best properties—in other words, those that provide a particularly remarkable experience in their price range—are designated in the listings with the Fodor's Choice logo.

Fodor's Choice★

Alexander House, p. 265

Astoria, p. 265

Grand Hotel Europe, p. 263

Kempinski Hotel Moika 22, p. 263

Taleon Imperial Hotel, p. 265

Best By Price

$

Herzen House, p. 268

Hotel Vera, p. 271

Matisov Domik, p. 268

Northern Lights Hotel, p. 268

Okhtinskaya-Victoria, p. 272

$$

Comfort Hotel, p. 268

Courtyard by Marriott St. Petersburg Vasilievsky, p. 270

Petro Palace Hotel, p. 269

Pushka Inn, p. 263

Rossi, p. 265

Tradition, p. 269

$$$

Alexander House, p. 265

Dostoyevsky, p. 270

Novotel St. Petersburg Centre, p. 271

Sokos Hotel Palace Bridge, p. 270

$$$$

Astoria, p. 265

Grand Hotel Europe, p. 263

Kempinski Hotel Moika 22, p. 263

Taleon Imperial Hotel, p. 265

By Experience

BEST SPA

Astoria $$$$, p. 265

Grand Hotel Europe $$$$, p. 263

Sokos Hotel Palace Bridge $$$, p. 270

BEST FOR BUSINESS

Corinthia Hotel St. Petersburg $$$$, p. 270

Courtyard by Marriott St. Petersburg Vasilievsky $–$$, p. 270

Grand Hotel Europe $$$$, p. 263

Novotel St. Petersburg Centre $$$, p. 271

Park Inn Pulkovskaya $$, p. 272

BEST VIEWS

Astoria $$$$, p. 265

Courtyard by Marriott St. Petersburg Vasilievsky $–$$, p. 270

Grand Hotel Europe $$$$, p. 263

Kempinski Hotel Moika 22 $$$$, p. 263

KID-FRIENDLY

Alexander House $$$, p. 265

Ambassador $$$$, p. 265

Corinthia Hotel St. Petersburg $$$$, p. 270

ROMANTIC HOTELS

Alexander House $$$, p. 265

Astoria $$$$, p. 265

Kempinski Hotel Moika 22 $$$$, p. 263

Pushka Inn $$, p. 263

Taleon Imperial Hotel $$$$, p. 265

ECO-FRIENDLY

Alexander House $$$, p. 265

Astoria $$$$, p. 265

BEST DINING

Astoria $$$$, p. 265

Corinthia Hotel St. Petersburg $$$$, p. 270

Grand Hotel Europe $$$$, p. 263

Novotel St. Petersburg Centre $$$, p. 271

Taleon Imperial Hotel $$$$, p. 265

ANTIQUE FURNISHINGS

Astoria $$$$, p. 265

Kempinski Hotel Moika 22 $$$$, p. 263

Old Vienna $$, p. 268

Rachmaninov Yard $–$$, p. 269

✉ *14 nab. reki Moiki, City Center* ☎ *812/312–0913 or 812/312–0957* ⊕ *www.pushka-inn.com* ⇔ *21 rooms, 8 suites, 4 family rooms* ⚄ *In-room: a/c, Wi-Fi. In-hotel: restaurant, room service, parking, some pets allowed* ▤ *DC, MC, V* ⛁ *BP* ⚇ *D3.*

$$ ⊞ **Rossi.** Around the corner from Nevsky Prospekt and the famous Catherine the Great monument, close to the Alexandrinsky theater, this hotel is named for the 19th-century architect Carlo Rossi, whose works grace the historical center, including nearby Rossi Street. **Pros:** great location; good value; great restaurant; last-minute rates available via Web site. **Cons:** some rooms are small, and they can be noisy. ✉ *55 Reki Fontanki embankment, City Center* ☎ *812/635–6333* ⊕ *www.rossihotels.com* ⇔ *46 rooms, 20 suites* ⚄ *In-room: a/c, Wi-Fi. In-hotel: restaurant, room service, laundry facilities, business center, parking, some pets allowed* ▤ *AE, D, DC, MC, V* ⛁ *CP* ⚇ *E5.*

$$$$ ⊞ **Taleon Imperial Hotel.** In the former mansion of the Stepan Eliseev, a
Fodor'sChoice prominent 19th-century banker and arts patron, the hotel still conjures
★ up the romance of that era. **Pros:** splendid interiors; rich breakfast complete with caviar and champagne; vast fitness and spa center. **Cons:** few rooms have views; very expensive; occasional complaints of overbilling. ✉ *59 Moika Embankment, City Center* ☎ *812/324–9911* ⊕ *www. taleonimperialhotel.com* ⇔ *89 rooms, 16 suites* ⚄ *In-room: a/c, Wi-Fi. In-hotel: restaurants, bars, pool, gym, spa, laundry facilities, business center, parking, some pets allowed* ▤ *AE, D, DC, MC, V* ⚇ *C4.*

ADMIRALTEISKY

$$$ ⊞ **Alexander House.** Each of the 19 vast and airy rooms in this grand
☾ cream-color lodge has an original, somewhat quirky design. *27 nab.*
Fodor'sChoice *Kryukova Canala, Admiralteisky* ☎ *812/334–3540* ⊕ *www.a-house.ru*
★ ⇔ *19 rooms* ⚄ *In-room: a/c, Wi-Fi. In-hotel: restaurant, room service, bar, laundry facilities, business center, some pets allowed* ▤ *AE, D, DC, MC, V* ⛁ *BP* ⚇ *E4.*

$$$$ ⊞ **Ambassador.** This nine-story hotel opened in 2005 next to Yusu-
☾ povsky Garden and the over-the-top entrance hall, in bright white and cream, has marble floors, leather sofas, and sparkling Czech glass chandeliers. **Pros:** modern building; quiet location; stylish interiors; kid-friendly. **Cons:** somewhat stark building; not quite central location: a seven-minute walk to the metro and a 20-minute walk to sights; over-the-top interiors. ✉ *5–7 pr. Rimskovo-Korsakova, Admiralteisky* ☎ *812/331–8844* ⊕ *www.ambassador-hotel.ru* ⇔ *251 rooms* ⚄ *In-room: a/c, Wi-Fi. In-hotel: restaurants, room service, bar, pool, gym, children's programs, parking, some pets allowed* ▤ *AE, DC, MC, V* Ⓜ *Sadovaya or Sennaya* ⚇ *C5.*

$$$$ ⊞ **Astoria.** This magnificent, romantic hotel is downtown, next to St.
Fodor'sChoice Isaac's Cathedral and a 10-minute walk from the Hermitage. **Pros:**
★ amazing location; classy dining; stylish rooms. **Cons:** odd-shaped rooms; busy with tour groups; frequent security checks due to VIPs; a bit far from the metro. ✉ *39 Bolshaya Morskaya ul., Admiralteisky* ☎ *812/494–5757* ⊕ *www.roccofortecollection.com* ⇔ *210 rooms, 42 suites* ⚄ *In room: a/c, Internet. In-hotel: restaurant,room service, bar, pool, gym, spa, children's programs* ▤ *AE, MC, V* ⛁ *EP* Ⓜ *Sennaya*

10

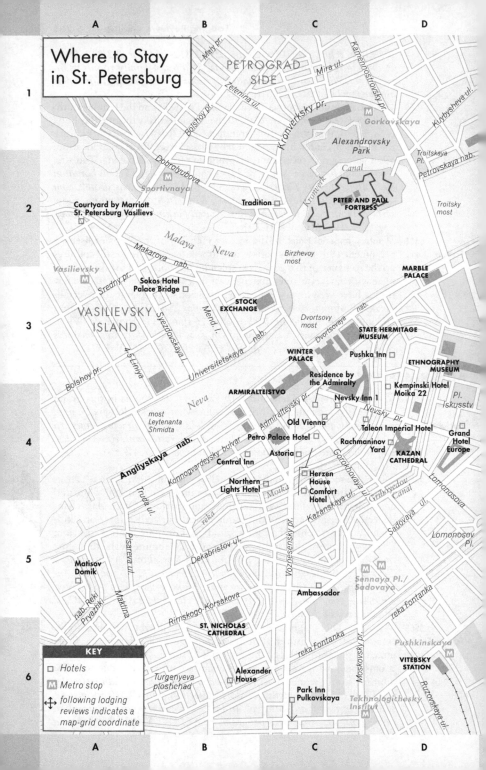

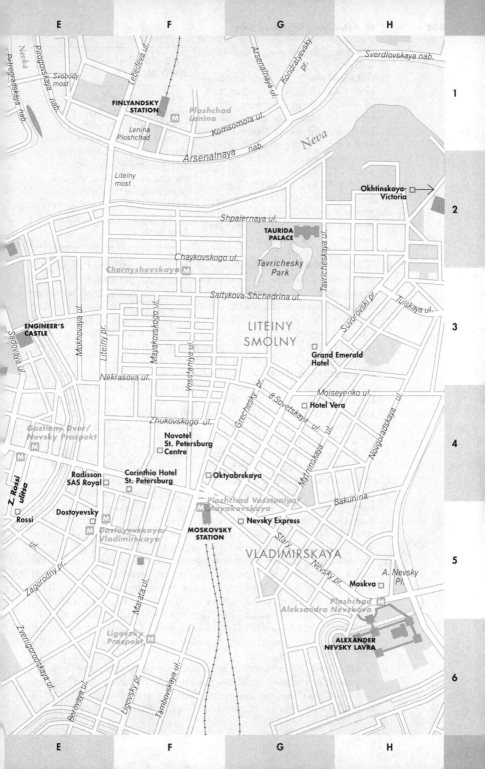

Ploshchad, Spasskaya, or Sadovaya ⊕ *C4.*

$ ⊡**Central Inn.** In a prime location next to St. Isaac's Cathedral, this mini-hotel earns its name. **Pros:** central location; easy to have some meals in your room. **Cons:** rooms aren't very large; slightly expensive, room phones can't call outside hotel. ⊠ *2 ul. Yakubovicha, Admiralteisky* ☎ *812/571–4516* ⊕ *www.central-inn.ru* ⤴ *11 rooms* ⚭ *In-room: a/c (some), no safe (some), Wi-Fi. In-hotel: parking, some pets allowed* ⊟ *AE, D, DC, MC, V* ⦶⦿⫿ *CP* ⊕ *B4.*

> ### THE ASTORIA AND HITLER
>
> Legend has it that Adolf Hitler, on giving the order to lay siege to Leningrad in September 1941, claimed he'd be celebrating New Year's in the Astoria Hotel. The fact that Leningraders held back the Nazis until 1944 at the cost of hundreds of thousands of lives, and that Hitler never got his party in the hotel, is a source of great local pride.

$$ ⊡**Comfort Hotel.** This mini-hotel, on the second and third floors of a 19th-century building, is close to the Admiralty, St. Isaac's Cathedral, the Hermitage, and plenty of good restaurants nearby. **Pros:** very convenient and central location to the major sights. **Cons:** a bit overpriced for what it is; rather small rooms; the street it's on can be noisy; rooms have only showers, not bathtubs. ⊠ *25 ul. Bolshaya Morskaya, Admiralteisky* ☎ *812/570–6700* ⊕ *www.comfort-hotel.ru* ⤴ *18 rooms* ⚭ *In-room: a/c, Wi-Fi. In-hotel: parking* ⊟ *AE, D, DC, MC, V* ⦿⫿ *BP* ⊕ *C4.*

$–$$ ⊡**Herzen House.** This mini-hotel shares the same building (and great location) as the Comfort Hotel. **Pros:** central location; handy amenities. **Cons:** beds and rooms run small. ⊠ *25 ul. Bolshaya Morskaya, Admiralteisky* ☎ *812/571–5098* ⊕ *www.herzenhotel.spb.ru* ⤴ *20 rooms* ⚭ *In-room: a/c, Wi-Fi. In-hotel: children's programs, parking* ⊟ *AE, MC, V* ⦿⫿ *BP* ⊕ *C4.*

$ ⊡**Matisov Domik.** If you're looking for homey accommodations, consider this cozy blue hotel with a tiled roof; most of the rooms overlook the Pryazhka River and a small, pleasant yard with maple and chestnut trees, flowers, and benches. **Pros:** a bit less expensive than more-central hotels; close to the Mariinsky; quiet area. **Cons:** inconvenient to many major sights; no air-conditioning. ⊠ *3/1 nab. Reki Pryazhki, Admiralteisky* ☎ *812/495–0242* ⊕ *www.amaranta.ru* ⤴ *41 rooms* ⚭ *In-room: no a/c, Wi-Fi (some). In-hotel: parking* ⊟ *MC, V* ⦿⫿ *BP* ⊕ *A5.*

$ ⊡**Northern Lights Hotel (Severnoye Siyaniye).** Near St. Isaac's Cathedral and a 10-minute walk from the Hermitage Museum, this mini-hotel is just in front of the Vladimir Nabokov museum. **Pros:** central location; beautiful area; close to sights; welcoming service. **Cons:** a 20-minute walk to the metro. ⊠ *50 ul. Bolshaya Morskaya, Admiralteisky* ☎ *812/571–9199* ⊕ *www.nlightsrussia.com* ⤴ *5 rooms* ⚭ *In-room: a/c (some), no safe (some), Wi-Fi. In-hotel: room service, parking* ⊟ *DC, MC, V* ⦿⫿ *CP* ⊕ *C4.*

$$ ⊡**Old Vienna.** With its stylish art-nouveau interior and some thoughtful amenities, this is a step above most mini-hotels. **Pros:** great location and amenities. **Cons:** on the second floor, and there's no elevator. ⊠ *13 ul. Malaya Morskaya, entrance on Gorokhovaya ul., Admiralteisky*

White Nights = High Rates

St. Peterburg's White Nights, during which the sun hardly sets at all, may be even more popular with hoteliers than it is with everyone else. That's because the period's popularity means that hotels can ask for—and often get—rates that are triple or even quadruple low-season prices. If you're planning on visiting during the general White Nights period, from mid-May through early July, keep in mind that it pays to shop around. Every hotel schedules its "super-high" rates differently, and some may only run them for a couple weeks, while others may have them for as much as two months. In addition, planning your trip immediately before or after the White Nights period can result in significant savings.

Another date to watch out for is mid-June, during which the three- or four-day St. Petersburg Economic Forum is held, bringing with it politicians, business people, and sky-high room rates. Avoid visiting St. Petersburg for pleasure during the forum.

☎ *812/312–9339* ⊕ *www.vena.old-spb.ru* ➳ *14 rooms* ⚓ *In-room: a/c, no safe, Wi-Fi* ▭ *MC, V* ⏍ *CP* ✛ *C4.*

$$ **Petro Palace Hotel.** Staying here puts you in a quiet area that's nevertheless central: a five-minute walk from the Hermitage, near Nevsky prospect, and with lots of good restaurants nearby. **Pros:** central location; quiet and safe area; helpful staff that speaks English. **Cons:** thin walls, windows in some rooms are sealed. ✉ *14 ul. Malaya Morskaya, Admiralteisky* ☎ *812/571–3006* ⊕ *www.petropalacehotel.com* ➳ *194 rooms* ⚓ *In-room: a/c, Internet. In-hotel: restaurant, room service, bar, pool, gym, laundry facilities, parking* ▭ *AE, D, DC, MC, V* ✛ *C4.*

$–$$ **Rachmaninov Yard.** Furnished with antique furniture handpicked by the owners, this elegant hotel has views of Kazan Cathedral and busy Nevsky prospekt. **Pros:** tasteful antique furnishings; art gallery on-site; excellent location. **Cons:** smallish rooms; no restaurant. ✉ *5 Kazanskaya ul., Admiralteisky* ☎ *812/571–7618* ⊕ *www.hotelrachmaninov. com* ➳ *25 rooms* ⚓ *In-room: a/c, no safe, Wi-Fi* ▭ *MC, V* ⏍ *CP* ✛ *D4.*

$ **Residence by the Admiralty.** Popular with Russians, this mini-hotel is oriented toward businesspeople. **Pros:** luxurious furnishings; large bathrooms with big modern tubs. **Cons:** no restaurant; a long walk to the nearest metro. ✉ *8 Gorokhovaya ul., Admiralteisky* ☎ *812/312-7377* ⊕ *www.residencehotels.ru* ➳ *4 rooms* ⚓ *In-room: a/c, no safe, Wi-Fi* ▭ *MC, V* ⏍ *CP* ✛ *C4.*

PETROGRAD SIDE

$$ **Tradition.** If you want peace and quiet after a day of exploring the city, this homespun hotelis a great option. **Pros:** location; comfortable rooms; moderate prices; great river views. **Cons:** rooms facing the street can be noisy; no gym; no bar. ✉ *2 pr. Dobrolyubova, Petrograd Side* ☎ *812/405–8855* ⊕ *www.traditionhotel.ru* ➳ *16 rooms and 1 apartment* ⚓ *In-room: a/c, no safe, Wi-Fi. In-hotel: parking* ▭ *AE, D, DC, MC, V* ⏍ *BP* ✛ *C2.*

10

VASILIEVSKY ISLAND

$–$$ ⊡ **Courtyard by Marriott St. Petersburg Vasilievsky.** In keeping with the businesspeople that make up most of its business, this new hotel on the banks of the Malaya Neva River has a large meeting room and several other spaces for meetings. **Pros:** amazing riverside views; spacious rooms. **Cons:** 20-minute walk away to the nearest metro stop; extras are pricey. ⊠ *61/30, 2 Liniya of Vasilievsky Island, Vasilievsky Island* ☏ *812/380–4011* ⊕ *www.courtyardsaintpetersburg.ru* ↙ *202 rooms, 12 suites* ⟁ *In-room: a/c, Wi-Fi. In-hotel: restaurant, bar, gym, business center, parking* ▭ *AE, D, DC, MC, V* ✢ *A2.*

$$$ ⊡ **Sokos Hotel Palace Bridge.** Part of a Finnish chain, this hotel has one of the city's best spas. **Pros:** comfortable; modern spa and wellness center; good restaurants; close to some historical sights. **Cons:** a bit off the very center of the city; unappealing views of old buildings from some windows. ⊠ *4 Birzhevoi Pereulok, Vasiliyevsky Island* ☏ *812/335–2207* ⊕ *www.sokoshotels.fi/ru/hotels/stpetersburg* ↙ *287 room, 32 suites* ⟁ *In-room: a/c, Wi-Fi. In-hotel: restaurants, room service, bar, pool, gym, spa, children's programs, parking, some pets allowed* ▭ *AE, MC, V* Ⓜ *Vasileostrovskaya* ✢ *B3.*

VLADIMIRSKAYA (LOWER NEVSKY PROSPEKT)

$$$$ ⊡ **Corinthia Hotel St. Petersburg.** This spacious hotel was built from three
 ☾ 19th-century buildings and finished a major expansion in 2009. **Pros:** good location means no time lost in the city's traffic jams; full business services; very efficient. **Cons:** on crowded and loud Nevsky prospekt; bad mobile-phone reception in much of the hotel. ⊠ *57 Nevsky pr., City Center,* ☏ *812/380–2001* ⊕ *www.corinthia.com* ↙ *388 rooms, 43 suites* ⟁ *In-room: a/c, Wi-Fi. In-hotel: restaurants, room service, bar, gym, spa, laundry facilities, business center, parking* ▭ *AE, DC, MC, V* Ⓜ *Mayakovskaya* ✢ *F4.*

$$$ ⊡ **Dostoyevsky.** Fyodor Dostoyevsky did indeed once live near this impressive three-star hotel, inside a discreet building close to several late-19th-century mansions. **Pros:** part of a busy mall; next to a metro station; lots of good restaurants nearby. **Cons:** part of a cheesy mall; next to a traffic-clogged intersection. ⊠ *19 Vladimirsky pr., City Center* ☏ *812/331–3200* ⊕ *www.dostoevsky-hotel.ru* ↙ *207 rooms, 14 suites* ⟁ *In-room: a/c, no safe, Internet. In-hotel: restaurant, room service, bar, gym, spa, parking* ▭ *AE, DC, MC, V* ⦿ *BP* Ⓜ *Vladimirskaya or Dostoyevskaya* ✢ *E4.*

$ ⊡ **Moskva.** The main attraction here is location: this enormous, aging hotel is literally on top of the metro and faces the entrance to the 18th-century Alexander Nevsky Lavra, which is at one end of Nevsky prospekt, but still in the center of town. **Pros:** location, location, location; inexpensive; good services nearby. **Cons:** modest furnishings; hardly any free extras, other than breakfast. ⊠ *2 Pl. Alexandra Nevskogo, City Center* ☏ *812/333–2444 or 812/274–4001* ⊕ *www.hotel-moscow. ru* ↙ *770 rooms, 35 suites* ⟁ *In-room: a/c, no safe, Wi-Fi. In-hotel: restaurants, room service, bars, spa, business center, parking, some pets* *allowed* ⊟ *AE, DC, MC, V* ⦿ *CP* Ⓜ *Ploshchad Alexandra Nevskovo* ✛ *H5.*

$ ⊞ **Nevsky Express.** This small, homey place is centrally located, next to Moscow Railway Station. **Pros:** central location; reasonable prices; kitchen; home-like atmosphere; friendly staff. **Cons:** no elevator; some rooms face noisy Nevsky Prospect (others face the quieter inner courtyard). ⊠ *93 Nevsky Prospect, City Center* ☎ *812/717–1888* ⊕ *www.hon.ru* ⇥ *30 rooms, 1 suite* ⧫ *In-room: a/c, Wi-Fi. In-hotel: room service, parking, some pets allowed* ⊟ *AE, D, DC, MC, V* ⦿ *CP* Ⓜ *Ploschad Vosstaniya* ✛ *G5.*

$$$ ⊞ **Novotel St. Petersburg Centre.** Business travelers like this hotel that's on a quiet street two minutes from Nevsky prospekt. **Pros:** great location; comfortable rooms; good restaurant. **Cons:** some rooms small; crowded lobby; no pool. ⊠ *3a Ulitsa Mayakovskogo, Vladimirskaya* ☎ *812/335–1188* ⊕ *www.novotel.spb.ru* ⇥ *233 rooms, 16 suites* ⧫ *In-room: a/c, Wi-Fi. In-hotel: restaurant, room service, bar, gym, business center, parking, some pets allowed* ⊟ *AE, D, DC, MC, V* ⦿ *BP* ✛ *F4.*

$$ ⊞ **Oktyabrskaya.** It's hard to miss this Soviet-era monolith in the city center, directly opposite the Moscow station, the Oktyabrskaya hits you right between the eyes with its huge sign, "Leningrad–Gorod Geroi" (Leningrad–Hero City), set on top. **Pros:** next to main railway station; in the heart of shopping district; surrounded by restaurants. **Cons:** huge and impersonal; on a noisy intersection; surrounded by litter-strewn streets. ⊠ *10 Ligovsky pr., City Center* ☎ *812/717–6330* ⊕ *www.hoteloktiabrskaya.ru* ⇥ *555 rooms in main hotel, 108 rooms in annex; 87 half-suites, 6 suites, 4 apartments* ⧫ *In-room: a/c, no safe, Internet. In-hotel: restaurant, bars* ⊟ *AE, DC, MC, V* ⦿ *BP* Ⓜ *Ploshchad Vosstaniya* ✛ *F4.*

$$$$ ⊞ **Radisson SAS Royal.** Originally built in 1765, this grand historic structure first became a hotel in 1879; the writer Anton Chekhov stayed here during his first visit to the city. **Pros:** interiors have character; Scandinavian efficiency; centrally located; kids under 18 can stay for free. **Cons:** on Vladimirsky prospekt side, rooms can be dark; on Nevsky prospekt side, noisy. ⊠ *49/2 Nevsky pr., City Center* ☎ *812/322–5000* ⊕ *www.radisson.com* ⇥ *164 rooms, 17 suites* ⧫ *In-room: a/c, Wi-Fi. In-hotel: restaurant, room service, bar, gym, spa, business center* ⊟ *AE, D, DC, MC, V* Ⓜ *Mayakovskaya* ✛ *E4.*

10

LITEINY/SMOLNY

$$$$ ⊞ **Grand Emerald Hotel.** A dark-glass exterior with a modern turret fronts this luxurious, high-tech hotel built in 2003. **Pros:** large rooms; modern building; many amenities. **Cons:** 20-minute walk from downtown; no metro nearby; somewhat generic area; very expensive ⊠ *18 Suvorovsky pr., Liteiny/Smolny* ☎ *812/740–5000* ⊕ *www.grandhotelemerald.com* ⇥ *90 rooms, 31 suites* ⧫ *In-room: a/c, Wi-Fi. In-hotel: restaurants, room service, bar, gym, spa, parking, some pets allowed* ⊟ *AE, DC, MC, V* ⦿ *BP* Ⓜ *Ploschad Vosstaniya or Chernyshevskaya* ✛ *G3.*

$ ⊞ **Hotel Vera.** Although this reasonably priced hotel is inside a portion of a renovated 1903 art nouveau building, the interiors here are modern. **Pros:** reasonable prices; modern interiors; helpful staff. **Cons:** 20-minute walk to a metro station; fairly distant from most major spots; some street noise. ⊠ *25/16 Suvorovsky pr., Liteiny/Smolny* ☎ *812/702–6190; U.S. office 650/969–2939; toll free 866/989–2939* ⊕ *www.hotelvera.ru* ⟲ *69 rooms, 15 suites* ⚹ *In-room: a/c, no safe (some), Internet (some), Wi-Fi (some). In-hotel: room service, bar* ☰ *AE, MC, V* ⦿ *CP* ⊹ *G4.*

VESYOLYI POSYOLOK

$ ⊡ **Okhtinskaya-Victoria.** You get a nice view of Smolny cathedral across the river from some of the rooms of this modern hotel, and though St. Petersburg's main attractions and the metro are some distance away, a hotel shuttle bus runs to Nevsky prospekt and the Moskovsky train station. **Pros:** great value; good views; Nevsky shuttle bus (the schedule is available at the hotel's Web site). **Cons:** cheap-looking fixtures; not in the historical center; Wi-Fi only in rooms on the first and second floors. ⊠ *4 Bolsheokhtinsky pr., Okhta* ☎ *812/380–0038* ⊕ *www.okhtinskaya. com* ⟲ *294 rooms* ⚹ *In-room: a/c, no safe, Wi-Fi (some). In-hotel: restaurants, room service, bar, parking* ☰ *AE, DC, MC, V* ⦿ *BP* Ⓜ *Novocherkasskaya, accessible from hotel by bus* ⊹ *H2.*

SOUTHERN SUBURBS

$$ ⊡ **Park Inn Pulkovskaya.** This attractive, Scandinavian-style hotel, built in 1981, is in decent condition, thanks to timely renovations. **Pros:** quiet residential surroundings; Victory Square museum nearby; handy to airport; good discounts for booking three or more weeks in advance. **Cons:** on a busy intersection; miles from the city center. ⊠ *1 Pobedy Pl., Southern Suburbs* ☎ *812/740–3900* ⊕ *www.pulkovskaya.ru* ⟲ *842 rooms, 27 suites* ⚹ *In-room: a/c, no safe, Wi-Fi. In-hotel: restaurant, bars, pool, gym, spa, parking, some pets allowed* ☰ *AE, DC, MC, V* ⦿ *BP* Ⓜ *Moskovskaya* ⊹ *C6.*

St. Petersburg Nightlife and the Arts

WORD OF MOUTH

"Russia has a two-tiered system for most tickets. There are prices for locals and foreigners. Your ability to buy those tickets depends on how strictly they enforce it and your level of Russian (or being with a Russian guide/friend). However, I've seen firsthand that sometimes even if you buy the 'local' ticket, at the ticket-control the person who's checking tickets may pointedly try to talk to you to determine if you are indeed Russian. If not, they can ask for ID, etc. Worst case, they make you buy a new foreigner ticket."

—lerasp

Updated
by Galina
Stolyarova

St. Petersburg's cultural life is one of its top attractions. The city oozes musical history, and there's a fascinating and thrilling concentration of the brightest names in classical music here. Russian classical ballet was also born in St. Petersburg and you can almost always catch a performance of *Swan Lake* in the summer months.

The city's nightclubs and discos can't compete with Moscow's glamorous establishments in terms of grand scale, pomp, and attitude, but they do offer a more laid-back environment.

Your best source for information about what's going on is the *St. Petersburg Times* (⊕ *www.sptimes.ru*), a free, local, independent English-language weekly that's published on Wednesday. It can be found at Western airline offices, bars, clubs, hotels, cafés, and other places generally patronized by foreigners or students. The publication has a calendar of events in the All About Town section, with theater and concert listings, a club guide, and a restaurant column.

THE ARTS

St. Petersburg may have one of the world's great museums, but it's not known for its contemporary art. Although it was originally designed as a cosmopolitan metropolis, it has become a little insular. Trapped in endless reflection, the city makes it difficult for young, experimental, and unorthodox artists to get exposure, let alone recognition. A new work of art is generally judged according to whether it fits in with the city's venerable artistic traditions. The issue is taken so seriously that the installation of every new monument, especially in the city center, provokes a massive debate. The temptation to preserve the historical center in its original state is so strong that contemporary sculpture is largely absent from the streets of St. Petersburg. However, there is a growing contemporary art scene, with galleries showcasing the work of a range of artists in many styles.

With its 18th-century heritage, St. Petersburg makes the perfect setting to hear Russia's sometimes-overlooked early music. The spiritual presence of Tchaikovsky, Mussorgsky, Prokofiev, and Shostakovich is strong here—they all studied at the St. Petersburg Conservatory. But so far, the city hasn't created a festival or otherwise built up much of a brand around any of its biggest classical names. The Early Music Festival spawned the Catherine the Great Orchestra, Russia's first baroque orchestra, which launched its own recording label and plays year-round at various venues.

Only the St. Petersburg Philharmonic is capable of programming its schedule well in advance, so other places are much more spontaneous. A detailed program of a festival at the Mariinsky is usually available three weeks before the event, while confirmed cast for premieres is normally announced a week prior to the performance. Last-minute changes and cancellations aren't uncommon for any venue. St. Petersburg's concert halls and theaters don't often have Web sites that include info on events more than a month or two out, and you can't usually buy tickets online. Exceptions include the Philharmonic (⊕ *www.philharmonia.spb. ru*) and the Mariinsky (⊕ *www.mariinsky.ru*). You can find information on musical events around town at ⊕ *www.classicalmusic.spb.ru.*

The Imperial Ballet School was founded here on May 4, 1738, by the order of Empress Anna Ioannovna, to be run by Frenchman Jean-Baptiste Lande. French and Italian masters taught the first class of 12 boys and 12 girls. Works of another Frenchman, Marius Petipa, who arrived at the academy in 1847, still dominate the repertoire of the Mariinsky Theatre. Today the school is called the Vaganova Ballet Academy in honor of Agrippina Vaganova, who radically changed the way ballet was taught in Russia. The best students traditionally appear on the venerable Mariinsky stage around Christmas in *The Nutcracker* and then in May and June in graduation performances.

During the high tourist season, *Swan Lake,* a signature production for the Russian classical ballet, appears by the dozen each day on various stages. If purity is important to you, go to either the Mariinsky or Mussorgsky theaters, and beware of the clones: not all stages are fit for such a grand ballet and there's a high risk of being served a brutally cut version, with difficult bits omitted, a few swans missing, and even no live orchestra.

Contemporary dance doesn't really flourish in the cradle of classical tradition but the dance company and school Kannon Dance (⊕ *www. kannondance.ru*) organizes several modern dance festivals during the year.

Russian opera is much less known and much less appreciated abroad. Many potential spectators are frightened merely by the sound of them. There's always a peasant riot, a doomed tsar, much chaos and insanity, and a lack of tuneful heroines. St. Petersburg opera singers, who have long been complaining about a lobby against Russian operas in the West, and who are all convinced that Tchaikovsky's *The Queen of Spades* is the greatest-ever dramatic opera, are eager to make you change your mind. The Mariinsky's artistic director, Valery Gergiev, has declared it the company's policy to perform the obscure masterpieces of Russia's operatic legacy. Opera in Russia is about power, drama, depth, and philosophy. And among those most likely to convert you are the philosophical and spiritual renditions of Rimsky-Korsakov's *The Legend of the Invisible City of Kitezh* or Glinka's *A Life for the Tsar.*

St. Petersburg has some excellent drama theaters; performances are almost exclusively in Russian. But don't except lots of new works: instead, you'll have a choice of multiple productions of such classics as *Antigone,* Gogol's *Marriage,* and Chekhov's *Uncle Vanya,* among others.

There are a number of ways to get the most from St. Petersburg's theater scene if you don't speak Russian. First, stick to English-language authors whose plays you already know. Plays by Shakespeare, Oscar

Wilde, and Tennessee Williams are popular and appear at many of the city's theaters. Then there are Russian classics well-known outside Russia, usually by Chekhov, Dostoyevsky, Gogol, and Tolstoy. The Maly Drama Theater specializes in hosting foreign troupes and puts some effort into welcoming non-Russian-speaking audiences by means of playbills in English and occasionally headsets relaying a translation. The most useful Web site, ⊕ *www.theart.ru*, which features listings and e-ticketing for all St. Petersburg theaters, is in Russian only. You can also purchase tickets online through the Web site ⊕ *www.kassir.ru*. You can arrange for the tickets to be delivered, and if you want to avoid paying with your credit card, you can choose to pay in cash when you get your tickets.

> ## A NOTE ABOUT FESTIVALS
>
> In English, a "festival" usually denotes a special season or group of events, such as the Cannes Film Festival. In Russia, however, the same word is often attached to random or run-of-the-mill presentations or even to a single performance in order to generate interest. Checking ahead to verify that a "festival" you want to see is worthwhile.

Except for the most renowned theaters, tickets are easily available and inexpensive. You can buy them at the box offices of the theaters themselves, at *teatralnaya kassa* (theater kiosks) throughout the city—Central Box Office No. 1 is at 42 Nevsky prospekt (☎ *812/571–3183*) and is open daily from 11 to 7—and at service bureaus in hotels, most of which post performance listings in their main lobby. Note that many venues, including the Hermitage Museum and the Mariinsky theater continue to charge higher prices for foreigners than for Russians. ■**TIP→ If you know a local resident, they can help you to get a ticket at a local price—as much as twice cheaper—although this involves a bit of deception.**

The Mariinsky Theatre sells tickets online through its Web site (⊕ *www.mariinsky.ru*), or at the theater itself, not through other agencies.

Bear in mind that theater tickets purchased through hotels are the priciest of all, as most hotels tend to charge a markup on the foreigner price. All in all, your best option is to go in person to the theater concerned and buy the ticket there.

Most major theaters close down between mid-July and early August and start up again in mid-September or early October. However, summer is also the time for touring companies from other regions in Russia to come to town, so it's a rare day that there are no shows on at all. Sumptuous balls are thrown in the most famous palaces and concert halls in winter; one such event is the Temirkanov Ball, on New Year's Eve.

FESTIVALS

St. Petersburg's premier arts event is the Mariinsky Theatre's **Stars of the White Nights** (☎ *812/714–4344* ⊕ *www.mariinsky.ru*), which stretches from the end of May until the middle of July or longer. The event's founder and driving force is Mariinsky's indefatigable artistic director Valery Gergiev, who brings together a lineup of international stars and orchestras that other Russian festivals can only dream of inviting. It helps that Gergiev, a principal guest conductor with the London Symphony Orchestra, is a regular with the world's most acclaimed orchestras. The festival interweaves opera, ballet, symphonic, and chamber music in almost equal proportions and provides a rare opportunity to see the Mariinsky's most renowned soloists—who spend most of their time between La Scala, Opera Bastille, and the Met—perform on home soil. Don't miss mezzo-soprano Olga Borodina, tenor Vladimir Galuzin, bass Ildar Abdrazakov, baritone Nikolai Putilin, and soprano Anna Netrebko. Prices soar during the festival and may reach 4,000R or more. (In general, price policy ranges wildly at the Mariinsky, depending on the cast, the season, and even the day of the week.)

Every year in July, the Peter and Paul Fortress, also known as the Russian Bastille, hosts the **International Peter & Paul Jazz Festival** (⊕ *www. petrojazz.ru*), three days of performances of bands from Russia and beyond.

Another attractive event is the **Musical Olympus** (⊕ *www.musicalolympus. ru*) festival organized by acclaimed Russian pianist Irina Nikitina at the Philharmonic in May and June. The festival assembles winners and laureates of each year's most respected musical contests from all over the globe. Each musician is handpicked by Nikitina herself or members of the festival's honorary committee. The audiences often get to see the rising talent immediately after they have claimed the fame but haven't yet been booked for years to come.

The Arts Square Winter Festival (⊕ *www.artsquarewinterfest.ru*), brainchild of Yury Temirkanov, artistic director of the St. Petersburg Philharmonic, runs between Western Christmas (December 25) and Russian Orthodox Christmas (January 7) and showcases classical concerts and ballets with top-notch international stars. The State Russian Museum, across Arts Square from the Philharmonic, organizes special exhibitions and hosts receptions for the festival, which includes a luxurious ball in Yusupov Palace on New Year's Eve.

The **Palaces of St. Petersburg** (☏ *812/572–2226* ⊕ *www.palacefest.spb.ru*) festival presents an impressive series of classical concerts in more than two dozen magnificent palaces and mansions year-round. (In the heyday of Imperial Russia, the social season, with its grand balls, masquerades, and concerts, occurred in winter. During the stuffy summers the pillars of high society escaped the heat and dust of the city by heading to their country estates.) A century later, St. Petersburg is trying to restore the glories of the past—minus the serfs.

The **Early Music Festival** (⊕ *www.earlymusic.ru*) attracts international soloists and ensembles; it's usually held late September through early October.

MUSIC GROUPS

Keep an eye out for the **Terem Quartet** (⊕ *www.terem-quartet. ru*), the famous local four who have adapted classic works such as Oginsky's "Polonaise" or Schubert's "Ave Maria" for balalaika, bayan, domra, and alto domra to superb effect. Virtuosi in their instruments, and highly interactive in their performing style, which critics have branded "instrumental theater," they freely mix J.S. Bach's "Toccata and Fugue in D Minor" with Russian folk songs, and make every concert a fun experience.

The marvelous **St. Petersburg Male Choir** (*Peterburgsky Muzhskoi Khor*), led by artistic director Vadim Afanasiev, is a must-see. Their favorite venues are the Capella and Petropavlovsky Cathedral in Peter and Paul Fortress, where the choir performs Orthodox chants and choral works by Russian composers. The sound can be mesmerizing.

The **St. Petersburg Horn Capella** (*Rogovaya Kapella* ⊕ *www. horncapella.ru*) revives the traditions of 18th-century Russian horn music, and is the only ensemble of its kind in Russia. Apart from baroque pieces written specifically for horn, the musicians perform a repertoire of arrangements of well-known classical works.

CITY CENTER

ART GALLERIES

Exhibition Center of the St. Petersburg Artists Union. There's an exhibition hall on the ground floor and works by theatrical artists for sale upstairs. ✉ *38 Bolshaya Morskaya, City Center* ☎ *812/314–4845* Ⓜ *Nevsky Prospekt or Gostinny Dvor.*

Guild of Masters. You'll find paintings, graphics, applied art, and various jewelry items here. ✉ *82 Nevsky pr., City Center* ☎ *812/579–0979* Ⓜ *Nevsky Prospekt or Gostinny Dvor.*

Marina Gysich's Private Art Gallery. One of the best small galleries in St. Petersburg, Marina Gysich hosts local and national Russian artists and exhibitions. ✉ *121 Fontanka, No. 13, City Center* ☎ *812/314–4380* ⊕ *www.gisich.com* Ⓜ *Tekhnologichesky Institute.*

The Russian Icon. This gallery exhibits and sells contemporary Russian Orthodox icons. It's possible to order customized icons. ✉ *15 Bolshaya Konyushennaya ul., City Center* ☎ *812/314–7040* Ⓜ *Nevsky Prospekt.*

MUSIC

CONCERT HALLS

Academic Kapella. One of St. Petersburg's best-kept secrets is also its oldest concert hall, dating to the 1780s. It presents not only choral events but also symphonic, instrumental, and vocal concerts. Many famous musicians, including Glinka and Rimsky-Korsakov, have performed in this elegant space along the Moika, near the Alexander Pushkin Apartment Museum and the Winter Palace. The main entrance and the surrounding courtyards have been beautifully restored. ✉ *20 nab. Moiki, City Center* ☎ *812/314–1153* Ⓜ *Nevsky Prospekt.*

Glinka Hall. For chamber and vocal music, head to this small hall, part of the Shostakovich Philharmonic (it's just around the corner from the Philharmonic). It's also known as the Maly Zal (Small Hall). ✉ *30 Nevsky pr., City Center* ☎ *812/571–8333* Ⓜ *Nevsky Prospekt.*

Hermitage Theater. This glorious and highly unusual theater in the Hermitage mainly hosts the St. Petersburg Camerata, a fine but often overlooked chamber ensemble. The theater doesn't have a box office, so purchase tickets at a theater kiosk or via your concierge. The entrance is reached via the 34 Dvortsovaya embankment. ✉ *32 Dvortsovaya nab., City Center* ☎ *812/571–9025 or 812/710–9030* ⊕ *www.hermitagemuseum.org* Ⓜ *Nevsky Prospekt.*

House of Composers (*Dom Kompozitorov*). Lovers of contemporary classical music flock here for the concerts of music written by its members—look for names such as Sergei Slonimsky, Boris Tishchenko, and Andrey Petrov—and their students at the conservatory. ✉ *45 Bolshaya Morskaya ul., City Center* ☎ *812/571–3548* Ⓜ *Nevsky Prospekt.*

Shostakovich Philharmonic. Two excellent symphony orchestras perform in the Philharmonic's newly refurbished grand concert hall (Bolshoy Zal): the St. Petersburg Philharmonic Orchestra and the Academic Philharmonic (a fine outfit, although it's officially the B-team). Both troupes have long, illustrious histories of collaboration with some of Russia's finest composers, and many famous works have premiered in this hall. ✉ *2 Mikhailovskaya ul., City Center* ☎ *812/312–9871 or 812/710–4290* Ⓜ *Nevsky Prospekt.*

OTHER CLASSICAL MUSIC VENUES
For a relaxing evening of classical music in a prerevolutionary setting, try the concert halls in some of St. Petersburg's museums, mansions, palaces, and churches.

Kochneva's House (*Dom Kochnevoi* ✉ *41 nab. Fontanki, City Center* Ⓜ *Nevsky Prospekt* ☎ *812/710–4062*) offers chamber music in an atmospheric palace. The **Palace of Prince Beloselsky-Belozersky** (*Beloselsky-Belozersky Dvorets* ✉ *41 Nevsky pr., City Center* ☎ *812/315–5236 or 812/319–9790* Ⓜ *Nevsky Prospekt*) is a rose-color art nouveau palace with a large mirrored ball room.

Charming soirees are held in authentic surroundings at the **Samoilov Family Museum** (✉ *8 Stremyannaya ul., entrance from back side of Nevsky Palace Hotel, City Center* ☎ *812/764–1130* ⊕ *www.theatremuseum.ru/eng/expo/sam.html* Ⓜ *Mayakovskaya*). The museum displays memorabilia related to Russia's greatest composers, musicians, conductors, and dancers. Chamber concerts are held in one of the grand rooms of the multifaceted **Sheremetev Palace** (*Sheremetev Dvorets* ✉ *34 nab. Fontanki, City Center* ☎ *812/272–4441* ⊕ *www.theatremuseum.ru/eng/expo/sher.html* Ⓜ *Mayakovskaya*). The museum also houses Russia's national collection of musical instruments.

Many of the concerts organized at St. Petersburg's most historic venues are run by **Peterburg-Concert** (*In Kochneva's House* ✉ *41 nab. Fontanki, City Center* ☎ *812/710–4032* ⊕ *www.petroconcert.spb.ru* Ⓜ *Nevsky Prospekt*). These concerts are not usually of the same high standard found at other musical events in the city, but they are a much better bet than most of the events organized especially for tourist groups. Tickets can be bought right at the Peterburg-Concert offices. The entrance is rather inconspicuous: look for a door on the right side in the passageway at 41 Fontanka.

OPERA AND BALLET

Fodor's Choice **Boris Eifman Ballet Theater.** Psychological drama reigns here. Most of the
★ ballets in the repertoire of this internationally acclaimed troupe—the only professional contemporary ballet company in St. Petersburg—have been inspired by biographies of extraordinary Russians with a tragic fate or are based on Russian literature. A must-see is *Red Giselle,* which tells the story of the great Russian ballerina Olga Spessivtseva, who fled Russia after the Bolshevik Revolution and spent 20 years in a psychiatric ward in New York. Also highly recommended are *Anna Karenina, Tchaikovsky,* and *The Russian Hamlet,* devoted to the doomed life of Russian tsar Paul I, who was murdered in Mikhailovsky Castle. The troupe, founded in the late 1970s, has no permanent home, and spends most of its time abroad. When here, the company usually performs at the Alexander Pushkin Drama Theater, the Mariinsky, or the Mussorgsky. ☎ *812/232–0235.*

Mikhailovsky Theater of Opera and Balley. This lesser-known venue, also known as the Mussorgsky, has productions that at their best rival those at the Mariinsky. As far as opera is concerned, the Russian repertoire is the theater's strong point, but it occasionally strikes gold with Italian works as well. Although the company hosted the world premieres of Shostakovich's *Lady Macbeth of Mtsensk* in 1934 and Prokofiev's *War and Peace* in 1946, the works of these composers are now absent from the repertoire, which focuses heavily on 19th-century classics. Highlights include Mussorgsky's *Boris Godunov,* Rimsky-Korsakov's *The Tsar's Bride,* Borodin's *Prince Igor,* and Tchaikovsky's *Iolanta.*

The company's strong dance division is deservedly rated the second-best in town. The classical fare includes *Swan Lake, Giselle, La Esmeralda,* and *Don Quixote* as well as some jewels of Soviet-era choreography, like Rodion Schedrin's *The Little Humpbacked Horse* and Prokofiev's *Romeo and Juliet.*

The opera season usually opens in early September, traditionally with a gala performance of Mussorgsky's *Boris Godunov.* Ballet and opera are both generally performed September through June or July. ⊠ *1 Pl. Iskusstv, City Center* ☎ *812/595–4319* ⊕ *www.mikhailovsky.ru* Ⓜ *Nevsky Prospekt.*

THEATER

Alexander Pushkin Drama Theater (*Alexandrinsky Teatr*). Russia's oldest theater, opened in 1756, is also one of its most elegant. Its repertoire is dominated by 19th-century classics (and the productions can be as musty as the costumes). With prominent Moscow director Valery Fokin taking the helm in 2004, the company is enjoying a renaissance. Fokin's interpretations of Dostoyevsky's *The Double* and Gogol's *The Government Inspector* are thought-provoking and engaging. ⊠ *2 Pl. Ostrovskovo, City Center* ☎ *812/312–1545 or 812/710–4103* Ⓜ *Gostinny Dvor or Nevsky Prospekt.*

Bolshoi Drama Theatre (*Bolshoi Dramatichesky Teatr*). The legendary Bolshoi is closed for renovation until late 2012. Although the legendary company's best days had seemingly been behind it, the reopening may give its productions some much-needed excitement. ✉ *65 nab. Fontanki, City Center* ☏ *812/310–0401* Ⓜ *Nevsky Prospekt.*

CHILDREN'S THEATER

A passing knowledge of Russian fairy tales, which can differ from other versions, may help children get more out of puppet shows, but the use of music, amusing animals, and stock villains is easy to follow.

The **Marionette Theater** (✉ *52 Nevsky pr., City Center* ☏ *812/310–5879* Ⓜ *Gostinny Dvor*), named in honor of its legendary director of the 1930s, Yevgeny Demeny, revels in an avant-garde and experimental tradition in which works by Shakespeare and Molière are adapted for marionettes. It has a varied repertoire of fairy tales and children's stories.

The **Children's Philharmonic** (✉ *1/3 Dumskaya ul., City Center* ☏ *812/315–7222* Ⓜ *Nevsky Prospekt*) stages children's musicals and even "adult" operas that kids can enjoy.

ADMIRALTEISKY

ART GALLERIES

Matiss Club. Underground art is the main focus of this gallery, which represents a number of well-known local artists. ✉ *6 Nikolskaya Ploshchad, Admiralteisky* ☏ *812/572–5670* ⊕ *www.matissclub.com* Ⓜ *Sadovaya/Sennaya Ploshchad.*

S.P.A.S. This spacious gallery exhibits a good collection of contemporary artists. ✉ *93 nab. Moiki, Admiralteisky* ☏ *812/571–4260* Ⓜ *Sadovaya.*

MUSIC

CONCERT HALLS

Mariinsky Concert Hall. The Mariinsky Theatre's concert hall, built in 2007, is a few hundred meters from the theater itself, on the site of its former warehouse. It's a large-scale, world-class venue for its classical-music performances. ✉ *20 Pisareva ul., Admiralteisky* ☏ *812/714–4344* ⊕ *www.mariinsky.ru* Ⓜ *Sadovaya.*

OPERA AND BALLET

The Rimsky-Korsakov Conservatory. The Conservatory is directly opposite the Mariinsky, but the opera and ballet performances are nothing like the level of its famous neighbor—partly because the Mariinsky is so good at siphoning off the Conservatory's brightest talent. ✉ *3 Teatralnaya Pl., Admiralteisky* ☏ *812/571–8574* Ⓜ *Sadovaya.*

Fodor'sChoice ★ **Mariinsky Theatre of Opera and Ballet** (*Mariinsky Teatr Opery I Balleta*). Once known as the Kirov and still advertised internationally under that brand, the world-renowned Mariinsky is one of Russia's finest artistic institutions, a definite must-see. The names Petipa, Pavlova, Nijinsky, and Nureyev—and countless others associated with the theater and the birth of ballet in St. Petersburg—are enough to lure ballet lovers to an evening here. The Mariinsky is without doubt one of the best ballet companies in the world, with a seemingly inexhaustible supply of stars.

St. Petersburg maintains its reputation as a citadel of classical ballet, but the works of some more modern works do appear on the playbill. However, audiences are slow to change their expectations, and modern ballets almost always perform to a half-empty auditorium. Between February and March, the company runs the impressive **Mariinsky International Ballet Festival,** which has at least one premiere and an array of guest performers from other renowned companies, such as London's Royal Ballet, Opera Bastille, and the American Ballet Theater.

The Mariinsky is also at the forefront of the world's opera companies, thanks largely to the achievements of the Mariinsky's artistic director Valery Gergiev. The company's best operatic repertoire centers on Russian opera: Tchaikovsky's *The Queen of Spades,* Prokofiev's *Semyon Kotko,* Shostakovich's *The Nose,* Rimsky-Korsakov's *The Legend of the Invisible City of Kitezh,* and *The Snow Maiden* are particularly recommended.

Operas are all sung in their original language; Russian operas are all provided with English subtitles, while Russian subtitles are given for foreign operas. Verdi can be hit-or-miss, but Wagner is one of Gergiev's greatest passions, and the company now feels very much at home with the composer. The orchestra's rapport with the conductor is amazing, the sound is nuanced and powerful.

Ballet and opera share the calendar throughout the year; the opera and ballet companies both tour, but at any given time one of the companies is performing in St. Petersburg. A second stage, designed by the renowned Canadian architectural firm Diamond and Schmitt, is set to open in late 2011. ⊠ *1/2 Teatralnaya Pl., Admiralteisky* ☎ *812/714–1211 or 812/326–4143* ⊕ *www.mariinsky.ru/en* Ⓜ *Sadovaya.*

St. Petersburg Chamber Opera (*Opera Sankt Peterburg*). Until 2003 this company, founded in 1987 by former Mariinsky stage director Yuri Alexandrov as an "opera laboratory," had no permanent home. The company is now based in the former mansion of Baron Derviz. The famous theatrical director Vsevolod Meyerhold staged productions here at the end of the 19th century, before it was turned into a concert hall. The company's repertoire is small and dominated by Russian classics and light Italian operas, with occasional experimental performances. ⊠ *33 Galernaya ul., Admiralteisky* ☎ *812/312–3982 or 812/312–6769* ⊕ *www.spbopera.ru* Ⓜ *Sadovaya, Sennaya Ploshchad.*

THEATER

Molodezhny Theater. Although most troupes in town tend to rely heavily on only their most seasoned players, this theater is brave enough to have younger talent figure prominently in the troupe. Shows are bursting with youthful energy and romanticism, yet there's no amateur-student feel to them. Most of the shows are expertly staged by artistic director Semyon Spivak, a professor at the renowned St. Petersburg Academy for Theatre Art. The company's signature show is Alexei Tolstoy's *The*

Swallow. Isaac Babel's *Cries From Odessa* and Alexander Ostrovsky's *Love Lace* are also among its hits. ⊠ *2 Fontanka Embankment, Admiralteisky* ☎ *812/316–6870* Ⓜ *Tekhnologichesky Institute.*

VASILIEVSKY ISLAND

ART GALLERIES

Erarta Museum and Galleries of Contemporary Art. With 2,000 works by nearly 150 Russian artists on display, this mammoth five-floor complex is the country's largest contemporary art exhibition space. Conceived by Marina Varvarina, the widow of a powerful local businessman, Erarta is packed with art works dating from the 1940s to the present day. The gallery has a team of enthusiastic curators who busily tour the country for up-and-coming talent. The place always has the name of an exciting new artist up its sleeve. In addition to the halls, where regular exhibitions are held, there is a gallery where artworks are sold. ⊠ *2 29-ya Liniya of Vasilievsky Island, Vasilievsky Island* ☎ *812/324–0809* ⊕ *www.erarta.com* ⊠ *300R* Ⓜ *Vasileostrovskaya.*

Novy Museum. Emphasizing the work of Soviet artists who opposed the officially approved socialist realism style during the years of the Iron Curtain, this gallery draws from the impressive collection of Aslan Chekhoyev, who purchased his first items several decades ago. He was personally acquainted with many of those at the forefront of Russian nonconformist art. The museum often holds lectures by these artists as well as film screenings and book presentations. ⊠ *29 6-ya Liniya of Vasilievsky Island, Vasilievsky Island* ☎ *812/323–5090* ⊕ *www.novymuseum.ru* ⊠ *100R–200R, depending on event* ⊙ *Closed Mon. and Tues.* Ⓜ *Vasileostrovskaya.*

MUSIC
OTHER CLASSICAL MUSIC VENUES

For a relaxing evening of classical music in a prerevolutionary setting, try the concert halls in some of St. Petersburg's museums, mansions, palaces, and churches. Performances are held regularly at the following venues:

Popular with foreign worshippers, **St. Catherine Lutheran Church** (⊠ *1a Bolshoi pr., Vasilievsky Island* ☎ *812/323–1852* Ⓜ *Vasileostrovskaya*) has an engaging classical concert program that mixes secular and religious music.

VLADIMIRSKAYA (LOWER NEVSKY PROSPEKT)

ART GALLERIES

★ **Loft Project Etagi.** Inside the five floors of what was once a bakery are now a series of galleries, exhibition rooms, and designer boutiques. This arts and cultural center gets attention from the hip for its provocative topics, controversial artists, and unorthodox approches. Exhibitions on themes like urban biking, post-war Italian commercial design, or World Press Photos are displayed among the rough-and-ready painted brick walls, concrete floors, and exposed pipes. There's also a pet adoption market (held every few months) and a bookstore here. On the third floor is a cheap and cheerful café, but the service, like the surroundings, can be patchy. ⊠ *74 Ligovsky Prospeckt, Vladimirskaya* ☎ *812/458–5005* ⊕ *www.loftprojectetagi.ru* ✉ *Free; special events up to 200R* Ⓜ *Ligovsky Prospekt.*

Mitki-VKhUTEMAS. Occupying a spacious attic, the gallery exhibits works of the legendary nonconformist group Mitki, famous for blue-and-white-stripe sailor shirts that they wear and often portray in their artworks. Call to make an appointment. ⊠ *16 ul. Pravdy, Vladimirskaya* ☎ *812/356–7149* Ⓜ *Dostoyevskaya/Vladimirskaya.*

Pushkinskaya-10 Arts Center. Also known as the Free Arts Foundation, this musty maze of studios, galleries, yards, cafés, and performance spaces was once a legendary squat for the pioneering artists of the nonconformist, unofficial, and Neo-Academy art movements that flowered here in the 1980s, as the Soviet Union's grip on cultural life began to loosen. Today the foundation receives state funds, but it has lost none of its thirst for exhibiting modern art that thumbs its nose at the establishment. Pushkinskaya-10 includes, among others, the New Academy Fine Arts Museum, the Museum of Nonconformist Art, the St. Petersburg Archive and Library of Independent Art, FOTOImage, Navicula Artis Gallery, GEZ-21, and Kino-FOT-703. ⊠ *10 Pushkinskaya ul., entrance at 53 Ligovsky pr., through the arch, Vladimirskaya* ☎ *812/764–5371* ⊕ *www.p10. nonmuseum.ru* Ⓜ *Ploshchad Vosstaniya.*

> **RUSSIAN BEATLEMANIA**
>
> The Pushkinskaya-10 Arts Center is known for housing one of Russia's most famous fans of the legendary Beatles, Kolya Vasin. Vasin, who is now in his early 60s, has never worked and never married because, as he says, he only had time for the Beatles. The little apartment-museum he lives in at 10 ulitsa Pushkinskaya is called the "Office of John Lennon's Temple." Vasin dreams of building a temple to John Lennon in St. Petersburg, where thousands of people can worship the Liverpool Four.

THEATER

Ⓒ **Zazerkalye Theater** (*Through the Looking Glass Theater*). This is perhaps the best musical choice for children. Captivating shows masterfully blend dramatic and musical elements and are famous for daring direction experiments. The company is good at winning children over to opera with entertaining versions of serious repertoire such as Donizetti's *L'elisir d'amore*—during which Nemorino sings his famous aria while riding a bike—or Offenbach's *Les contes d'Hoffmann* and Puccini's *La Bohème*. Shows last from roughly 30 minutes to an hour. It's open Friday through Sunday. ⊠ *13 ul. Rubinshteina, Vladimirskaya* ☎ *812/764–1895 or 812/712–5000* Ⓜ *Vladimirskaya or Dostoevskaya.*

Fodor's Choice ★ **Maly Drama Theater** (*Maly Dramatichesky Teatr*). Even if you can't understand the dialogue, any performance at the MDT—home to one of the best theater companies in the city—is well worth seeing. The repertoire includes productions of Chekhov, Dostoyevsky, Shakespeare, and Oscar Wilde. Maly is also one of the few companies in town to continue to stage the finest plays from the Soviet era. Seeing their whole repertoire has been compared to living through the entire 20th-century history of Russia. If you have a whole day to spare and lots of stamina, the nine-hour performance of Dostoyevsky's *The Possessed* makes for an incredible theatrical experience, although it can be a bit hard on the posterior. It takes two consecutive evenings to sit through the company's veteran show, Fyodor Abramov's "Brothers and Sisters," but it's an great experience. Order tickets well in advance, because it's rare that the Maly plays to a less-than-packed house. ⊠ *18 ul. Rubinshteina, Vladimirskaya* ☎ *812/712–2078* ⊕ *www.mdt-dodin.ru* Ⓜ *Vladimirskaya.*

LITEINY/SMOLNY

ART GALLERIES

Borey. On display here are the works of avant-garde and academic artists, including paintings, graphics, and applied art. ⊠ *58 Liteiny pr., Liteiny/Smolny* ☎ *812/273–3693* Ⓜ *Mayakovskaya.*

★ **Sol-Art.** Next to the prestigious Mukhina Academy for Arts and Design and in the same building as the magnificent and crumbling Baron Stieglitz Museum, this gallery exhibits St. Petersburg's young artistic talents. The gallery showcases some of the big names in the local contemporary art scene as well. ⊠ *15 Solyanoy per., Liteiny/Smolny* ☎ *812/327–3082* Ⓜ *Nevsky Prospekt.*

MUSIC

OTHER CLASSICAL MUSIC VENUES

The **Smolny** (⊠ *3/1 Pl. Rastrelli, Liteiny/Smolny* ☎ *812/271–9182* Ⓜ *Chernyshevskaya*) cathedral presents choral music in its beautiful, baroque confines.

THE PETROGRAD SIDE

ART GALLERIES

Krasnoye Znamya (Red Flag) Exhibition Hall. This former textile factory, designed by the German architect Erich Mendelsohn in the early 20th century, was once run-down, but now it has a new lease on life. A local developer is transforming it into an international center for the arts and culture. A former power station here, which Mendelsohn shaped to resemble a ship, is now used for cutting-edge photography exhibitions, fashion shows, and large-scale media installations. Critics have observed that the vast space has a strange quality. On one hand, it can enhance the work of even an indifferent artist. On the other it can overwhelm and swamp the work of the most talented. This venue is a unique space, with tremendous potential, and could host a wealth of arts events, once the full renovation is completed. ⊠ *24 Bolshaya Raznochinnaya ul., Petrograd Side* ☎ *812/965–0659* ⊞ *200–500R* ☺ *Closed Mon. and Tues.* Ⓜ *Chkalovskaya.*

THEATER

Baltiisky Dom Theater-Festival. An umbrella venue for a dozen experimental companies of various genres, Baltiisky Dom holds performances in its large hall and a variety of basements, attics, and backrooms. Once a full-fledged theater, it has turned into a modern art complex, where aspiring directors play with material playwrights like Luigi Pirandello, Ivan Turgenev, and the Presnyakov Brothers. This is the only venue in town staging plays written in the past five years. To get a sense of experimental Russian theater, look for the shows of "Farces" theater and productions directed by Andrei Moguchy as well as one-man shows by local actors. In October the theater hosts an impressive four-week Baltic Theater Festival, attracting the best talent from the Baltic Sea region. ⊠ *4 Alexandrovsky Park, Petrograd Side* ☎ *812/232–3539* Ⓜ *Gorkovskaya.*

NIGHTLIFE

St. Petersburg is hardly hip compared to the major capitals of Europe, but it's waking up to what hip really is. The city's vibrant and evolving club scene is diverse enough to incorporate funky theme clubs, bunker-style techno venues, cozy artsy basements, run-down discos, cool alternative spots, and elegant hedonist establishments to keep the clubbers up all night. There are still several chic nightclubs opened only to members, but more and more elitist venues are canceling memberships, so most of the places are generally accessible. Even popular spots are well hidden and you need to know where to look. At night, the town's quiet and serene historical center has little going on—except during White Nights and public holidays (which seem to occur on a weekly basis).

Russia has adopted the concept of "face control" (a strict door policy) enthusiastically, but in schizophrenic St. Petersburg its rules can either fall to the whim of a zealous doorman or be ignored all together depending on the character of the place. Generally, dirty clothes or men going shirtless will be frowned upon, and in the more glamorous spots designer gear and shows of wealth are required. That said, St. Petersburg's nightclubs are more typically bars or music venues, where just about anything goes. Women are expected to wear feminine clothes, nice shoes—preferably with heels—and makeup. Men can be more relaxed, but Russian men like to wear dark colors, sport coats, and dress shoes. Cover prices vary wildly from nothing at all to hundreds of dollars depending on the type of place, the day of the week, the time of night, and whether there is some sort of act on the bill. However, 500R is a fair average. Drink prices are generally double what they are in a regular bar. Reliable, if pricey, taxis swarm around clubs until chucking-out time. ■TIP➔ **Note that there is no official "last call"—bars and clubs may choose to close anywhere from midnight to 6 am.**

The nightlife scene is ever-changing, so it's always best to consult current listings. The most reliable English-language sources are the free *St. Petersburg Times* (⊕ *www.sptimes.ru*) or the monthly English-language issue of *St. Petersburg in Your Pocket* (⊕ *www.inyourpocket.com*). These publications include excellent unbiased club guides in addition to detailed listings. There are more comprehensive sources in Russian, such as the magazine *Time Out* (⊕ *www.timeout.ru*). A good rule of thumb for tourists with little or no experience in Russia is to stick to the city center, where you have plenty of options: bohemian art clubs,

Bridge Schedules

11

St. Petersburg's mighty Neva River creates some of its most picturesque views, making it easy to forget that it is a working river for transporting many goods and raw materials. During the navigation season (April–November), the Neva is crowded with ships making up for the winter months. However, since its bridges are too low to allow ships to pass and it would cripple the city to lift them frequently during the day, the city's bridges remain raised at night from 1 am to about 5 am. There are published schedules for each bridge, some of which are lowered once during the night, but these are unreliable. If you don't want to get caught on the wrong side of the river from where you are staying and be stuck until morning, think about heading home before 1 am. What at first sounds like a terrific inconvenience for a large, busy city has been turned into something positive by St. Petersburgers: during White Nights the raising of the attractively illuminated bridges has become a crowd-pleasing ritual and "I missed the bridges" has become the perfect excuse to party until dawn.

trendy dance clubs, live-music venues, and simple pubs. Locals in the city center are friendly and more than a few speak English—and foreigners are not the novelty they once were. If you're seeking the company of expats, you'll find them in centrally located Irish and British pubs or at low-key artsy bars such as *Datscha*. The historical center is abundant with expensive strip clubs, but these are meant for deep-pocketed foreign tourists and ravenous Russian beauties hunting for them. The city's red-light district is the part of Nevsky prospekt farther north from Ploshchad Vosstaniya, where prostitutes stand at every other corner and can be rather aggressive. The city's casinos and all other gambling facilities were closed down in 2009 after the Kremlin launched a reform that established four specially designated large gambling zones in the Primorye region, Altai region, Kaliningrad Oblast, and Azov region, all a great distance from St. Petersburg and Moscow. Beware that if you venture to a place beyond the historical center, the risk of being robbed or attacked by one of the city's many skinhead and hooligan gangs increases significantly. ⚠ **During the months when the rivers and canals are not frozen (generally April–November), watch the clock: bridges start to go up around 1:30 am. If you get stuck on the wrong side, you'll have to wait until 5 am or so to cross.**

Unlike much of Europe and North America, Russia has not yet opened up to the idea of gay men and lesbians. The scene in St. Petersburg is in its embryonic stage and the few friendly and unpretentious venues that are available keep a relatively low profile, although St. Petersburg has not seen the levels of official homophobia and violence that have been seen in Moscow. The best starting point into St. Petersburg's scene is ⊕ *www.gay.ru*, which has some English content, including a Traveler's Guide.

Russia's rock movement was born in St. Petersburg, and almost all key names in the country's rock culture come from the city. The first bands emerged in the 1970s, when rock and roll was branded "alien music" and rock culture was repressed by the Soviet culture bosses. Underground musicians and artists refrained from contacts with state-run music organizations. They worked as night guards, boiler-room operators, or street cleaners and expressed their protest in rock ballads, which reached a wider audience only with the arrival of perestroika.

Some of the most famous bands still play regular gigs—look for veteran bands like Akvarium, DDT, and Tequilajazzz. The strongest point of Russian rock ballads are the meaningful lyrics, but even without knowledge of the language, you can still feel the drive.

> **BAR HOPPING**
>
> A small street linking Nevsky prospekt and the Griboyedov canal has recently become the site of a cluster of hip and grungy bars that attract crowds of young people. Dumskaya ulitsa, with its central location, disheveled colonnades, dance-till-you-drop attitude, and two of the city's gay clubs) has been dubbed the city's answer to London's Old Compton Street.

CITY CENTER

BARS

Begemot. A stone statue of a bulky begemot (hippopotamus) decorates the entrance to this loud bar, but despite the name, it's all about glamour here. The slinkily dressed waitresses are immaculate, the interior design is eclectic (wood-covered ceilings, industrial lamps mixed with crystal chandeliers, large, puffy chairs), the crowd fashionable, the cocktails imaginative, and the wine list commendable—all ingredients that have made the bar a favorite with local yuppies. There's also a library, with low lighting, and a karaoke room. During the day Begemot operates as a restaurant serving decent Continental dishes. ⊠ *12 Sadovaya ul., City Center* ☎ *812/925–4000* ⊕ *www.bar-begemot.ru* Ⓜ *Nevsky Prospect.*

Datscha. A tremendously popular haunt of expats, bohemians, students, and night owls, Datscha takes after the merry joints of the Reeper-bahn in Hamburg (the owner is German). The galvanizing spirit of this eclectic art bar is hugely addictive—despite its claustrophobic size, low ceilings, shabby setting, horrific toilets, and lack of food beyond peanuts. The music, mainly rock and ska, is loud enough to make conversation barely possible. Reckless dance parties sometimes get out of hand and spill into the street, where neighborhood bars Fidel and Belgrad are also located. ⊠ *9 Dumskaya ul., City Center* ☎ *No phone* Ⓜ *Nevsky Prospect.*

The Office Pub. Style and elegance characterize the atmosphere of this Irish pub located next to Kazan cathedral. It is frequented by a fash-ionable crowd and is a favorite with the younger adults and local yup-pies. The choice of beers on tap here is one of the widest in the city. ⊠ *5 Kazanskaya ul, City Center* ☎ *812/571–5428* ⊕ *www.mollies.ru* Ⓜ *Nevsky Prospect.*

The Other Side. This comfortable two-room restaurant is run by U.S. expat Douglas Pullar and his capable, informal team. They serve a good range of well-priced drinks and Thai, Mexican, and Middle Eastern food, as well as bagels and cream cheese (not often found in Russia) for 150R. It's understandably popular with foreigners, including Swedes from the nearby Swedish consulate. ⊠ *1 Bolshaya Konnushenaya, City Center* ☎ *812/312–9554* ⊕ *www. theotherside.ru* Ⓜ *Nevsky Prospekt.*

CLUBS

Konyushenny Dvor. It's widely known that foreigners get in free here, and, well, sometimes you get what you pay for. Pop music and strip shows

> **STRIPPED BARE**
>
> St. Petersburg's "adult entertainment" sector promotes itself more vigorously and splashily than any other category of nightlife, particularly to foreign men, who are usually offered discounted entry. These gaudy strip palaces feature shows that range from full-on sex shows down to Moulin Rouge–style "erotic ballets"—often with real ballerinas who didn't quite make the grade. Vulgar, expensive, pushy, and sinister, St. Petersburg's strip clubs increasingly seem like a relic from a different age: the fast and loose 1990s.

are the usual order, and there's no attitude. Also known as Marstall, it's a bit of an institution at this point. ⊠ *5 Kanal Griboyedova, City Center* ☎ *812/315–7607* Ⓜ *Nevsky Prospekt.*

Purga. They literally celebrate the New Year every night here, and it's still as engaging as ever. Whatever season and the weather outside, you get the full holiday package in Purga, complete with decorated Christmas tree, Father Frost, and Snow Maid, champagne, dance party, and festive atmosphere. A thorough collection of season's greetings recordings delivered by Soviet and Russian leaders is broadcast and mocked all through the night. This ritual has become one of St. Petersburg's most memorable nights out. The food and beer is good and inexpensive, and the droll staff is dressed in white rabbit costumes. Each table has its own original design. Be sure to get there and fill your glass before midnight. Purga's clone next door throws wedding parties with the same regularity and similar comic bent. ⊠ *11–13 nab. Reki Fontanki, City Center* ☎ *812/570–5123* Ⓜ *Mayakovskaya.*

GAY AND LESBIAN CLUBS

Central Station. Compared to its Moscow counterpart of the same name, this Central Station is looser and more intimate, but also attracts a youthful, fashionable, mixed crowd. Three floors, each with its own character, are interlinked by a number of dark staircases. There are theme nights, drag shows, multiple lounge areas, and a restaurant. ⊠ *1 Lomonosova ul., City Center* ☎ *812/312–3600* ⊕ *www.centralstation. ru* Ⓜ *Nevsky Prospekt.*

LIVE MUSIC CLUBS

Money Honey Saloon. If rockabilly is your thing, or if you simply want to see a country-western saloon in Russia, head to this always-crowded bar for dancing and lots of fun. The live music usually starts at 8 pm. There's a 40R cover charge. ⊠ *13 Apraksin Dvor, enter courtyard at 28–30*

Sadovaya ul., City Center ☏ *812/310–0549* ⊕ *www.moneyhoney.org* Ⓜ *Gostinny Dvor or Sadovaya.*

ADMIRALTEISKY

BARS

Dickens. A stately slab of Olde Englande kitsch, Dickens is the second pub in a chain after the original opened in Riga, Latvia. There's the best English breakfast in town for 350R. ✉ *108 Nab, Reki Fontanki, Admiralteisky* ☏ *812/380–7888* Ⓜ *Sennaya Ploshchad.*

Kneipe Jager Haus. Designed as a cozy hunting lodge, this German pub is one of the quieter drinking venues in town. It has vaulted brick ceilings, antique bric-a-brac, and stuffed wild animals and game trophies. It's a good bet for a quiet predinner pint and chat with a friend. The spirited and highly herbal Jägermeister digestif pops up in just about every other drink offered here, including the popular Grizli and Jager-Cola cocktails. There's also a sauerkraut-heavy German menu available; a filling three-course business lunch on weekdays is 200R. The pub, open round the clock, also has branches at 17 Ulitsa Pravdy and 64 Srednii Prospekt, on Vasilievsky Island. ✉ *34 Gorokhovaya ul., Admiralteisky* ☏ *812/310–8270* ⊕ *www.jagerhaus.ru* Ⓜ *Sadovaya.*

Fodor's Choice **Shamrock Irish Pub**. A long-standing favorite of local expats, this jolly
★ inn with great pub food, cozy wooden furnishings, and two dozen types of beer stands across the street from the Mariinsky Theatre. The company's younger talent can be often spotted having a quick bite or beers here at any time of day. Live Irish music is played every night, except Tuesday and Friday. ✉ *27 ul. Dekabristov, Admiralteisky* ☏ *812/318–4625* Ⓜ *Sadovaya.*

Stirka. This peculiar hybrid of a bar and a laundromat started life as the graduation project of a German design student. Here you'll find underground rock DJs, international bands, a good sound system, a small bar, and comfortable soft furnishings. Guests are welcome to follow in the footsteps of Led Zeppelin and the Rolling Stones—it's said they made use of the venue's washing machines and dryers while on tour in 2005 and 2007. There are water-pipes to smoke, and free Wi-Fi from 10 am to 4 pm. ✉ *26 Kazanskaya ul., Admiralteisky* ☏ *812/314–5371* ⊕ *www.40gradusov.ru* Ⓜ *Sennaya Ploshchad.*

CLUBS

Zal Ozhidaniya. This modern and minimalist club, whose name means "waiting room," is part of the Varshavsky Express shopping center and entertainment complex, next to the former railway station for trains to Warsaw and beyond. Vast and brightly lit, the club can accommodate up to 1,000 people, making it one of the largest venues of its kind in the city. The bands that perform here are almost always homegrown Russian and cover lots of musical bases, including rock, jazz, pop, and electronic. ✉ *118 Naberezhnaya Obvodnogo Kanala, Admiralteisky* ☏ *812/333–1069* ⊕ *www.clubzal.ru* Ⓜ *Baltiiskaya.*

VLADIMIRSKAYA (LOWER NEVSKY PROSPEKT)

CLUBS

Kitaisky Lyotchik Jao Da. This club, which has a branch of the same name in Moscow, offers a reliable mix of live rock and jazz and some electronic music. A favorite with bohemians and intellectuals, it welcomes both Russian and foreign bands. A good choice of drinks and snacks is available. ✉ 7 *Ulitsa Pestelya, Vladimirskaya* ☎ *812/273–7487* ⊕ *www.spb.jao-da. com* Ⓜ *Nevsky Prospekt.*

Metro. An old standard, Metro is frequented mostly by young teenagers from all over the city and the suburbs. Each of the three floors plays different music. The door policy is very strict. ✉ *174 Ligovsky pr., Vladimirskaya* ☎ *812/766–0204* ⊕ *www.metroclub.ru* Ⓜ *Ligovsky Prospect.*

LIVE MUSIC CLUBS

Fish Fabrique. A favorite haunt of locals and expats who enjoy drinking and listening to local alternative musicians, or who just want to play table football. It's in the Pushkinskaya-10 Arts Centre. ✉ *10 Pushkinskaya ul., entrance through courtyard of 53 Ligovsky pr., Vladimirskaya* ☎ *812/764–4857* Ⓜ *Ploshchad Vosstaniya.*

Griboyedov. The best underground (literally) club in the city, this small former bomb shelter is usually packed with friendly, down-to-earth hipsters. It's owned and operated by a local band. In addition to decent live music, there's a mix of talented DJs spinning house, techno, and funk; check listings for different nights. Upstairs is Griboyedov Hill, or GH, which has a sushi restaurant and stage for poppier music acts. ✉ *2a Voronezhskaya ul., at intersection with ul. Konstantina Zaslonova, Vladimirskaya* ☎ *812/164–4355* ⊕ *www.griboedovclub.ru* Ⓜ *Ligovsky Prospekt.*

Jazz Philharmonic Hall. Russia's top jazz musicians, including the Leningrad Dixieland Band and the David Goloshchokin's Ensemble, regularly appear at this venue in a turn-of-the-20th-century building. ✉ *27 Zagorodny pr., Vladimirskaya* ☎ *812/764–8565* ⊕ *www.jazz-hall.spb. ru* Ⓜ *Dostoyevskaya.*

LITEINY/SMOLNY

CLUBS

Shum. The name means noise—and rightly so. One of the best places for live rock, this beehive of a club has good acoustics; some of the wildest Russian bands play here. Entrance is free on Wednesdays, when the management gives pride of place to up-and-comers as part of its "Noise-Isolation" project, designed to give a leg up to young rock talent. Drinks and snacks, including sandwiches, are available right now, and plans for more food options are in the works. ✉ *45 5-ya Sovietskaya ul., Liteiny/Smolny* ☎ *7921/946–8969* ⊕ *www.shumclub. ru* Ⓜ *Ploshchad Vosstania.*

GAY AND LESBIAN CLUBS

Tri El. Also known as LLL, this the only lesbian club in town. It's also a laid-back, smart venue with a big dance floor. The drinks are cheap, staff helpful, and there are pool tables as well as a room with a small stage for strip shows. ✉ *107–109 Moskovsky Prospekt, Southern Suburbs* ☎ *812/387–1150* ⊕ *www.triel.spb.ru* Ⓜ *Moskovskie Vorota.*

LIVE MUSIC CLUBS

JFC Jazz Club. They know good jazz here. The most popular jazz venue in town, the club attracts top musicians performing all styles of jazz: acid funk, swing and blues, avant-garde, mainstream, improvisation. The only disadvantage is its modest size, so you may want to reserve a seat ahead of time. ✉ *33 ul. Shpalernaya, Liteiny/Smolny* ☎ *812/272–9850* ⊕ *www.jfc.sp.ru* Ⓜ *Chernyshevskaya.*

Sunduk. Head to this intimate and quiet little art café in a British colonial stylefor live jazz, blues, or rock. The menu is varied and good but inexpensive, so Sunduk is a popular eatery during the day as well. The toilet, with its many large decorative but defunct locks, is designed to confuse the guests. ✉ *42 Furshtatskaya ul., Liteiny/Smolny* ☎ *812/272–3100* Ⓜ *Chernyshevskaya.*

SOUTHERN SUBURBS

LIVE MUSIC CLUBS

The Place. Inside an anonymous industrial building in a wasteland far from the center, The Place is still well worth seeking out. Inside, things are cool and sophisticated, decked out in dark woods, chrome and steel fixtures, and clever lighting. There's a modern menu and a lively music program of international art rock, jazz, and experimental acts. ✉ *47 ul. Marshala Govorova, Southern Suburbs* ☎ *812/331–9631* ⊕ *www.placeclub.ru* Ⓜ *Narvskaya or Baltiiskaya.*

VASILIEVSKY ISLAND

BARS

KwakInn. This pint-size Belgian pub—the only one in town—is one of the city's friendliest venues. Within its yellow walls you can get mouthwatering mussels and frites (don't call them french fries here) and a couple of dozen Belgian beers, both draft and bottled. Owned by one of the founding members of a veteran local rock band, KwakInn has a jovial spirit and capitalizes on much of what makes Belgium special. In addition to the beer there are Tin-Tin cartoons and posters recalling Agatha Christie's Hercule Poirot and the charms of Audrey Hepburn, a native of the country. ✉ *37 Bolshoi Prospekt of Vasilievsky Island, Vasileostrovskaya* ☎ *812/493–2639* ⊕ *www.kwakinn.ru* Ⓜ *Vasileostrovskaya.*

St. Petersburg Shopping

WORD OF MOUTH

"I didn't find St. Petersburg to be a shopper's haven, though IMHO your visit isn't complete without perusing the aisles of the Dom Knigi bookstore on Nevsky and checking out the souvenirs in the stalls behind Church [of the Savior] on Spilled Blood (even if you don't buy). Dom Knigi sells amazing postcards of the city and has an English section."

—trsny

Updated
by Galina
Stolyarova

The vast majority of Russians are poor by European or American standards, and the shopping in St. Petersburg reflects that. Official figures suggest that only 10% of Russians earn more than $1,000 a month, but prices always seem to be rising. It's therefore hard to find stores catering to middle-class tastes and budgets.

Instead, there's an awkward juxtaposition. On one hand you have glitzy boutiques adorned with some of the world's finest jewelry and luxury brands. On the other you are faced with vast markets selling cheap, largely Chinese-made goods. These markets are of course where most local people go to buy everything from clothing to electrical goods.

In Russia most Western fashion brands sell for up to twice the price you would expect to pay elsewhere in Europe. Retailers blame outrageous import duties and ridiculously high rents for this situation. Moreover, the collections often appear out of date by one or two seasons. The same goes for English-language books and foreign newspapers, which are only available at exorbitant prices.

Lots of homegrown Russian fashion does exist, however, and to explore it, head to the Baltiysky Fashion Gallery and shops like A.Dress and Tatyana Kotegova. Other Russian designers to look out for include Tatyana Parfyonova, Sultanna Frantsuzova, Leonid Alexeev, and Larissa Pogoretskaya. For the biggest choice of more affordable Western clothes, head to the Galeria shopping mall, which has nearly 300 shops.

People tend to dress conservatively in St. Petersburg, often in plain dark clothes. Fashion as a means of self-expression hardly exists here yet. When it comes to buying clothes, practical considerations hold sway, and that can make for a range of colors that doesn't go much beyond black, white, or gray.

Don't be surprised by the number of supermarkets, pharmacies, and other stores that are now open 24 hours, seven days a week—they are fairly reliable and have emerged because of the hectic lives Russians lead. But if you're buying alcohol, take care: bootleg liquor is a major problem throughout Russia, so buying booze from anywhere other than a specialized wine shop and or Western-brand supermarket is potentially dangerous.

If you want to take presents home, some of the best buys include fine porcelain, carved wooden goods such as toy soldiers or chess sets, and Russian-made silverware and linen. The chain of Serebro (Silver) shops offers a good range of flatware. If you are interested in linen, look out for such brands as Slavyansky Len, Linum, and items made by the Ivanovo factory.

There are also plenty of typical Russian handicrafts, such as *Gzhel* (blue-and-white and majolica pottery), shiny *khokhloma* tablewood (wood painted with flowery ornaments and imitation gilding), *Zhostovo* metal trays (painted with elaborate enamel designs), and electric samovars.

CITY CENTER

DEPARTMENT STORES

Gostiny Dvor. The city's oldest and largest shopping center was built in the mid-18th century. Although it mostly has upscale boutiques, it's still a good place to find souvenirs, such as *matryoshka* (nesting dolls), at some of the best prices in the city (look upstairs). The second floor houses a string of multibrand designer boutiques selling women's and men's clothes from famous European designers. *Gostinka,* as Gostiny Dvor is also known, also has some stores with cheaper prices; it can be a good place to buy winter clothing, such as a fur hat. The store, open daily from 10 until 10, is in the center of town, and is easily reached by the metro—the metro station right outside its doors is named in its honor. ⊠ *35 Nevsky pr., City Center* ☎ *812/710–5408* ⊕ *www.bgd.ru* Ⓜ *Gostiny Dvor.*

Grand Palace. Reigning at the top end of the boutique market and serving shoppers with the deepest pockets, this temple to consumption carries Woolford lingerie, Escada dresses, and Trussardi suits as well as perfume and jewelry at impressively high prices. The café on the ground floor offers irresistible desserts crafted by a sophisticated French chef who knows his art. ⊠ *44 Nevsky pr., City Center* ☎ *812/449–9344* ⊕ *www.grand-palace.ru* Ⓜ *Gostiny Dvor.*

Passazh. Passage, a mid-19th-century shopping arcade across the street from Gostiny Dvor, caters primarily to locals. The souvenir sections, however, are worth visiting, as prices, in rubles, are a bit lower here than in the souvenir shops around hotels and in other areas frequented by tourists. You can also pick up fine table linens at bargain prices. The porcelain section at the far end of the ground floor is worth a look, too, and there's a large supermarket in the basement. ⊠ *48 Nevsky pr., City Center* ☎ *812/312–2210* ⊕ *www.passage.spb.ru* Ⓜ *Gostiny Dvor.*

Stockmann. This Finnish company helped bring some Scandinavian efficiency and style to Russian commerce when branches first opened in the country in 1989. Wares include quality clothes, lingerie, toys, kitchen gadgets, linens, and bathroom goods, mainly by Finnish and Scandinavian producers. ⊠ *25 Nevsky pr., City Center* ☎ *812/326–2637* ⊕ *www.stockmann.ru* Ⓜ *Nevsky Prospekt.*

SPECIALTY STORES

ANTIQUES

Petersburg Antiques Salon. This shop stocks icons, Carl Fabergé jewelry, furniture, and vintage lamps. There is also Soviet propaganda porcelain, such as ashtrays in the shape of an Uzbek man reading a newspaper, or tea sets featuring heroes of the Russian Revolution. Some are collectors' items that once belonged to some of Russia's finest museums. Keep in mind that it's against the law to export any item that's more than 100 years old. In theory, taking out even a rusted nail would be a breach of the law. With any antique purchase you make, you need an export certificate, which can be obtained only at the state-run Board for the Preservation of Cultural Valuables (*see the Art Galleries section of chapter 11 for details*)—and only after an expert assessment that can take up to three days. ⊠ *54 Nevsky pr., City Center* ☎ *812/571–4020* ⊕ *www.salon-petersburg.ru* Ⓜ *Nevsky Prospekt.*

Tertia. All things printed are the specialty of this snug shop, with original Soviet posters, prerevolutionary postcards bearing portraits of Romanov family members, and prints, maps, and books on offer. There is also some silverware and bric-a-brac. The store is popular with both serious collectors and museum researchers, who sometimes manage to fish out rare manuscripts. ⊠ *5 Italyanskaya ul., City Center* ☎ *812/571–8048* ⊕ *tertiaspb.ru* Ⓜ *Nevsky Prospekt.*

BOOKS
Dom Knigi. The city's premiere bookshop is housed in a landmark art nouveau building opposite Kazan Cathedral that is one of the design showpieces of the city. The building, topped by a famous globe, was constructed between 1902 and 1904 as the head Russia office for the Singer Sewing Machine company. Founded in 1919, Dom Knigi was the first bookshop in Soviet Russia. Some of the country's best-known writers, including Mikhail Zoshchenko and Samuil Marshak once worked as salesmen here. Today the store sells lots of art books, history and science tomes, and plenty of fiction and children's books. There's also a large branch at 62 Nevsky prospekt. Nestled on the second floor of the main shop (at 28 Nevsky), there is a café with panoramic windows and great views over Nevsky prospekt and Kanal Griboyedova. ⊠ *28 Nevsky pr., City Center* ☎ *812/448–2355* ⊕ *www.spbdk.ru* Ⓜ *Nevsky Prospekt.*

CRAFTS AND SOUVENIRS
Galereya Stekla. At this glass gallery, the city of St. Petersburg is reflected in carved Easter eggs, stained glass, vases, and candlesticks. Each work is handmade, and many are one-of-a-kind. ⊠ *1/28 ul. Lomonosova, City Center* ☎ *812/312–2214* Ⓜ *Nevsky Prospekt.*

Guild of Masters. Jewelry, ceramics, and other types of Russian traditional art, all made by members of the Russian Union of Artists, are sold here. ⊠ *82 Nevsky pr., City Center* ☎ *812/579–0979* Ⓜ *Mayakovskaya.*

Slavyansky Style. This is a good source for linen goods created in the traditional Russian style of the 19th century. There are several branches throughout the city. ⊠ *151 Nevsky pr., City Center* ☎ *812/717–5164* ⊕ *www.linorusso.ru* Ⓜ *Ploshchad Alexandra Nevskovo* ⊠ *3 Pushkinskaya ul., City Center* ☎ *812/325–8599* Ⓜ *Mayakovskaya.*

Vernisazh. At this open-air market outside the Church of the Savior on Spilled Blood, more than 100 vendors sell nesting dolls, paintings, Soviet icons, and miscellaneous trinkets. It is probably the easiest and quickest market to locate if your time in St. Petersburg is limited; there are sure to be items here that make good gifts and keepsakes. Most vendors speak several languages but the prices can be rather inflated. Don't accept the first price quoted, and try to pay a third or so less than that. ⊠ *1 Kanal Griboyedova, City Center* ☎ *No phone* Ⓜ *Nevsky Prospekt.*

FARMERS' MARKETS

The farmers' markets (*rynok*) in St. Petersburg are lively places in which a colorful collection of goods and foods are sold by individual farmers, often from out of town and sometimes from outside the Russian republic. In addition to the fine cuts of fresh and cured meat, dairy products, and homemade jams and jellies, piles of fruits and vegetables are sold here, even in winter. Try some homemade pickles or pickled garlic, a tasty local favorite. You can also find many welcome surprises such as hand-knit scarves, hats, and mittens. The markets are much cleaner and better lit here than in Moscow, so it can be fun just to visit and browse. In general, the markets are open daily from 8 am to 7 pm (5 pm on Sunday).

12

FARMERS' MARKETS

Apraksin Dvor. St. Petersburg's less wealthy citizens come to this seething bazaar to shop for cheap clothes, shoes, DVDs, household items, and whatever else you can think of. A chaotic relic of the Yeltsin years, and hardly befitting Russia's newfound love affair with Slavic glamour, the city's rulers have decreed that Apraksin Dvor must go, although its very popular with the locals, and the traders are a resourceful bunch who are fighting to remain in place. They are likely to win in the end. ⊠ *28–30 Sadovaya ul., City Center* Ⓜ *Nevsky Prospekt*.

Sennoi Rynok. This may be the cleanest and most organized farmers' market in the city; the entrance is just a short walk from Sennaya Ploshchad. However, like all St. Petersburg's farmers' markets, its existence is becoming increasingly decorative, since right next door there is now a cheaper and more convenient modern supermarket called Perekrostok. ⊠ *4 Moskovsky pr., City Center* Ⓜ *Sadovaya or Sennaya Ploshchad*.

FOOD

Supermarket. Within the Passage shopping arcade, Supermarket sells cheese and fresh fruits and vegetables. It opens daily at 10 (11 on Sunday) and closes at 9. ⊠ *48 Nevsky pr., City Center* ☎ *812/312–4701* Ⓜ *Gostinny Dvor*.

JEWELRY

Jewelry used to be an unlikely reason to come to St. Petersburg, but there are some good places to explore these days, particularly on Nevsky prospekt.

Ananov. Head and shoulders above the jewel meccas in town, this quiet, dim store is owned by former sailor and theater director Andrei Ananov, now famous as a jeweler following in the traditions of the great Peter Fabergé. Ananov is as much a gallery as a shop, and no one here would ever be vulgar enough to list prices; if you have to ask, you probably can't afford it. Rings and necklaces amount to thousands of dollars, although there are cheaper items that start around 6,000R. ✉ 9 *Michurinskaya ul., City Center* ☎ *812/235–4251* Ⓜ *Gostinny Dvor.*

Russian Jewelry House. This is a good bet for jewelry, particularly amber pieces. ✉ *27 Nevsky pr., City Center* ☎ *812/312–8501* Ⓜ *Nevsky Prospekt.*

MUSIC STORES

Kailas. This shop obviously has someone on staff who pays attention to new and interesting music emerging around the world. In addition to an enviable Russian-music section, there's also vast supply or electronica, world music, jazz, and classical music. ✉ *10 ul. Pushkinskaya, City Center* ☎ *812/764–2668* Ⓜ *Mayakovskaya or Ploshchad Vosstaniya.*

SPORTS

Zenit. This shop is devoted to St. Petersburg's hugely popular local soccer team, which has produced international stars that include Andrei Arshavin, currently with London's Arsenal. Merchandise includes printed scarves, sweaters, balls, mugs, bed linen, and wallpaper. There are even jumpsuits and outfits for babies and toddlers emblazoned with the Zenit's light-blue colors. ✉ *54 Nevsky pr., City Center* ☎ *812/606–6516* ⊕ *www.zenit-trade.ru* Ⓜ *Nevsky Prospekt.*

ADMIRALTEISKY

SPECIALTY STORES

CLOTHING

A.Dress. The owner describes this small venue, furnished with antiques, as a "fashion apartment." There are no more than five copies of each design here, and they are placed creatively in cupboards or on shelves— or simply scattered about. You get the feeling that you are visiting a fashion-conscious friend who has been on too many shopping sprees and and is now selling off some of her treasures. A.Dress sells only Russian designers, catering to the decadent, the romantic, and hipsters all at once. It's a shrine that local fashionistas visit regularly. ✉ *5 Gorokhovaya ul., Admiralteisky* ☎ *812/570–4899* ⊕ *www.a-dressspb. ru* Ⓜ *Sennaya Ploshchad.*

JEWELRY

★ **Russkie Samotsvety.** Many items in these collections were inspired by St. Petersburg's architecture, history, literature, and artistic legacy. Jewelers play with familiar visual images, like ballet or shipbuilding, and incorporate city symbols in their designs. ✉ *1-ya Krasnoarmeiskaya ul., Admiralteisky* ☎ *812/316–7646* Ⓜ *Tekhnologichesky Institut.*

MUSIC STORES

Otkryty Mir. For classical music, the choice is surprisingly poor for a city that prides itself on its cultural legacy. Although no one could accuse this CD and DVD store of being overstocked, it does hold the occasional hidden classical delight, particularly when it comes to Russian composers and artists and recordings on the old Melodiya label. Hunt around. ✉ *32 Nevsky pr., Admiralteisky* ☎ *812/315–8222* ⊕ *www.cd-classic. ru* Ⓜ *Nevsky Prospekt.*

VASILIEVSKY ISLAND

SPECIALTY STORES

CLOTHING

Baltiysky Fashion Gallery. The main attraction at this mall is the Russian Fashion gallery. Look out for the boutiques devoted to top Russian designers Larissa Pogoretskaya, Valentin Yudashkin, Kogel, Leonid Alexeyev, and Alexandra Kiaby. The stylish Just Fresh café makes a great pit stop, and the trendily designed atrium has several other cafés. There is free Wi-Fi throughout the gallery. ✉ *68 Bolshoi pr., Vasilievsky Island* ☎ *812/322–6979* ⊕ *www.galeria-spb.ru* Ⓜ *Vasileostrovskaya.*

Rot Front Fur Store. At the large factory shop of this established and respected Russian furrier, founded in 1885, you can get elegant coats, hats, jackets, wraps, and accessories made of mink, polar fox, sheepskin, seal and other furs, all of them from Russia. The prices are lower than in most other fur stores. ✉ *5/7 Reki Smolenki nab., Vasilievsky Island* ☎ *812/321–5726* ⊕ *www.meharf.ru* Ⓜ *Vasileostrovskaya.*

MUSIC STORES

Titanik. Even the best music shops in St. Petersburg have a rather scruffy look about them, not to mention a cavalier attitude toward copyright law. Among the best sources for music is this chain, which sells a motley collection of Western and Russian rock and pop, plus DVDs and videos (the DVDs usually have an English-language option available, and many are without regional-zone coding). ✉ *46 Sredny pr., Vasilievsky Island* ☎ *812/323–1919* ⊕ *www.titanik-spb.ru* Ⓜ *Vasileostrovskaya.*

VLADIMIRSKAYA (LOWER NEVSKY PROSPEKT)

DEPARTMENT STORES

Galeria. This mammoth shopping center contains 290 shops, 24 cafés and restaurants, 10 movie theaters, a supermarket, and even a bowling alley. The fashion-brands are primarily major European labels, such as M&S, Karen Millen and Reiss from Britain, Finland's Lindex and France's Cop. Copine. There is a good children's section, and a wealth of cosmetics shops sell mainly foreign products. ✉ *30a Ligovsky pr., Vladimirskaya* ☎ *812/449–5531* ⊕ *www.galeria-spb.ru* Ⓜ *Ploshchad Vosstania.*

Vladimirsky Passazh. This modern and spacious four-story store, just outside Dostoyevskaya metro station, has numerous small boutiques selling jewelry, clothes, shoes, bags, lingerie, and cosmetics at less than exorbitant prices. The basement houses a large, 24-hour supermarket, and there's a great bakery on the ground floor—an excellent budget choice for a quick refuel. ✉ *19 Vladimirsky pr., Vladimirskaya* ☎ *812/331–3232* ⊕ *www.vpassage.ru* Ⓜ *Dostoyevskaya or Vladimirskaya.*

SECOND SKIN

Westerners are often surprised to see how many people in Russia really do wear fur, perhaps believing the Russian fur hat went the way of the fedora in New York. Although some young people hold anti-fur views, most Russians consider fur coats and hats not only chic but, in winter, eminently practical.

Food Stores in St. Petersburg

For cigarettes, snacks, drinks, and basic foodstuffs like bread, milk and tea, look for a *produkty* shop. They also sell such popular local treats as rye bread, *vatrushka* (a kind of pastry), *pelmeni* (dumplings), smoked salmon, canned salt herring, and pickles. If you want to find a broad range of foreign food, there are well-stocked supermarkets in any large shopping mall. These stores are usually open daily, until at least 8 pm.

Black caviar, which once reigned as the food gift of choice in Russia, is hard to find in the shops these days. Its harvest and sale was banned for several years owing to massive sturgeon poaching. Due to conservation measures, caviar sales are expected to resume only fitfully and with very limited amounts.

Supermarkets with branches all over the city include Pyatyorochka (there's a figure 5 in its logo), Perekryostok ("Crossroads"; look for a cross), Lenta (featuring a daisy), and Diksi (a red disc on a yellow square with "Diksi" written in black). French-style markets include Mega, O'Key, and Giant. There is also a Finnish chain called Prisma (a red-orange-yellow triangle on a green square). If you see a red-and-white logo that reads Maksidom on what appears to be a superstore, don't go in looking for food—it's a home-improvement and furniture chain that competes with IKEA.

Nevsky prospekt itself doesn't have many food shops, but a short walk down its cross streets will usually yield one. Vladimirsky prospekt, which leads to Kuznechny Rynok and Vladimirsky Passage, is a good bet. Large shopping centers around Ploshchad Vosstania have vast food "hypermarkets." As farming in Russia is a very small industry, do not expect to see any private butcher shops, upscale organic fruit shops, or the like.

SPECIALTY STORES
FARMERS' MARKETS
Kuznechny Rynok. This is the best and most expensive of St. Petersburg's farmers' markets. It's just outside the metro station. ⊠ *3 Kuznechny per., Vladimirskaya* Ⓜ *Vladimirskaya.*

FOOD
Vladimirsky Supermarket. In the spacious basement of Vladimirsky Passazh, this good, well-stocked supermarket is open 24 hours a day. ⊠ *19 Vladimirsky pr., Vladimirskaya* ☎ *812/331–3232* Ⓜ *Vladimirskaya.*

LITEINY/SMOLNY

SPECIALTY STORES
CRAFTS AND SOUVENIRS
★ **Armeisky Magazin.** Army surplus—belts, flasks, caps, pins, and marine shirts with Russian and Soviet army symbols—is a much better bargain here, at this state-run store, than in touristy markets. You'll find a huge variety. ⊠ *24 Kirochnaya ul., Liteiny/Smolny* ☎ *812/579–2907* Ⓜ *Chernyshevskaya.*

VYBORG SIDE

SPECIALTY STORES

CLOTHING

Furs of St. Petersburg. Even fur-decorated wedding dresses can be found at this palace of a store that caters to modern-day "tsarinas." The many kinds of fur here include such rarities as lynx, and Russia's famous sable (a type of the weasel-like marten that's found in Siberia). ⊠ *35 ul. Komsomola, Vyborg Side* ☏ *812/591–6448* ⊕ *www.spbmeh.ru* Ⓜ *Ploshchad Lenina.*

CRAFTS AND SOUVENIRS

Farfor. For china and porcelain made at the Lomonosov Porcelain Factory (LFZ), once a purveyor to the tsars, go to this noted porcelain resource. ⊠ *32 Kondratyevsky pr., Vyborg Side* ☏ *812/542–3055* ⊕ *www.farfor.spb.ru* ⊠ *7 Vladimirsky pr., Vladimirskaya* ☏ *812/713–1513* Ⓜ *Vladimirskaya.*

FARMERS' MARKETS

Polyustrovsky Rynok. On the weekend you can find a pet market, with puppies, kittens, chickens, and more. In a possibly surprising twist, the market also boasts an impressive fur department, with some good bargains on things like rabbit winter hats. ⊠ *45 Polyustrovsky pr., Vyborg Side* Ⓜ *Ploshchad Lenina.*

FOOD

Kalinka-Stockmann. If you're looking for a big Western-style supermarket that takes credit cards, try Kalinka-Stockmann. It's open daily 9 am–10 pm. ⊠ *1 Finlandsky pr., Vyborg Side* ☏ *812/542–2297* Ⓜ *Ploshchad Lenina.*

SOUTHERN SUBURBS

SPECIALTY STORES

CRAFTS AND SOUVENIRS

Lomonosov Porcelain Factory. One of the most famous porcelain manufacturers in Russia, the factory was founded in 1744 to serve the imperial family. This is your source for the world-famous hand-painted cobalt-blue china. There is also a porcelain museum here which is part of the Hermitage's holdings. ⊠ *151 Obukhovskoy Oboroni pr., Southern Suburbs* ☏ *812/326–1744* ⊕ *www.ipm.ru* Ⓜ *Lomonosovskaya.*

JEWELRY

Etalon-Jenavi. The detour necessary to get here will be well rewarded: the store has the best costume jewelry in town. It's fashionable, sophisticated, and original, embracing everything from fine replicas of museum artworks to children's collections of enameled pendants in the shapes of insects, toys, and balloons. It certainly won't empty your wallet. ⊠ *172 Moskovsky pr., Southern Suburbs* ☏ *812/371–2722* Ⓜ *Elektrosila.*

SPORTS

Dinamo. This is the factory shop of one of Russia's oldest and largest producers of sports uniforms and sneakers. It supplies many of the country's soccer, basketball, and handball teams. Styles haven't changed much since the Soviet days, and there's also a special retro range that's popular with those with a foot in the past. It's a great place to buy a souvenir, especially given the bargain prices and the durability of the goods. ✉ *140 Leninsky pr., Southern suburbs* ☎ *812/376–9590* ⊕ *www. fsidinamo.org* Ⓜ *Leninsky Prospekt.*

PETROGRAD SIDE

SPECIALTY STORES

CLOTHING

★ **Tatyana Kotegova Fashion House.** Kotegova creates stylish and romantic collections with a note of restraint. Her soaring classical silhouettes capture the essence of St. Petersburg. The designer uses only natural materials, with an emphasis on wool, silk, and cashmere. Kotegova's velvet evening dresses, simple yet exquisite, are the dream of a good half of the local female population. ✉ *44 Bolshoi pr., 2nd fl., Petrograd Side* ☎ *812/346–3467* ⊕ *www.kotegova.com* Ⓜ *Petrogradskaya.*

MUSIC STORES

Titanik. This branch of the music store sells a good selection of Russian as well as international music and films. ✉ *35 Bolshoi pr., Petrograd Side* ☎ *812/235–4885* ⊕ *www.titanik-spb.ru* Ⓜ *Petrogradskaya.*

Side Trips from St. Petersburg

WORD OF MOUTH

"The fountains at Peterhof were amazing! The Grand Cascade is unbelievable! We spent at least two hours walking around the gardens viewing the more than 140 fountains. We loved the Samson and the Lion fountain, Golden Mountain (a smaller version of the Grand Cascade), Chess Mountain (with colorful dragons at the top). . . . Peterhof is a not-to-be-missed sight, in my opinion."
— Fluffnfold

Updated by
Irina Titova

If St. Petersburg is the star of the show, then its suburbs are the supporting cast needed to tell the story. For every aspect of the city's past—the glamour and glory of its Imperial era, the pride and power of its military history, the splendor of its architecture, the beauty of its waterways—there's a park, a palace, a playground of the tsars somewhere outside the city limits with a corresponding tale to tell.

From the dazzling fountains of Peterhof on the shores of the Gulf of Finland, to the tranquil estate of Pavlovsk to the south, to the naval stronghold of Kronshtadt—a quiet town with a turbulent history and a still-Soviet feel (and once completely closed to foreigners)—what surrounds St. Petersburg is as important to its existence and identity as anything on Nevsky prospekt. It might seem odd to tell you to get out of the city almost as soon as you have arrived, but you'll understand why once you have seen the suburbs for yourself, wandered through the palaces imagining what it would be like to call them home, and strolled through the grounds in the footsteps of the aristocrats and officers who made Russia a world power.

Of all the palaces in Russia, the one that generally makes the most distinct and lasting impression on visitors is Peterhof, on the shore of the Baltic Sea, some 29 km (18 mi) west of St. Petersburg. More than a mere summer palace, it's an Imperial playground replete with lush parks, monumental cascades, and gilt fountains. In tsarist times, Tsarskoye Selo, now renamed Pushkin, was a fashionable haunt of members of the aristocracy who were eager to be near the Imperial family and to escape the noxious air and oppressive climate of the capital to the north. After the Revolution of 1905, Nicholas II and his family lived here, more or less permanently. Pavlovsk, the Imperial estate of Paul I, is some 30 km (19 mi) south of St. Petersburg and only 5 km (3 mi) from Pushkin and the magnificent Catherine Palace. Because of the proximity of the two towns, tours to Pavlovsk and Pushkin are often combined. However, it's difficult to do justice to each of these in a one-day visit. If you only have time to visit one of the two, pick Pushkin. The estate of Lomonosov, on the Gulf of Finland, some 40 km (25 mi) west of St. Petersburg and about 9 km (5½ mi) northwest of Peterhof, is perhaps the least commanding of the suburban Imperial palaces. It is, however, the only one to have survived World War II intact.

TOP REASONS TO GO

Peterhof Fountains: The grounds surrounding Peterhof's Great Palace (nicknamed the "Russian Versailles") are filled with whimsical fountains. Don't miss the beautiful Great Cascade fountains or the trick fountains in the Lower Park, where children laugh in delight as they get caught by a burst of water.

The Amber Room: Visit Pushkin (Tsarskoye Selo) to see the famed Amber Room, located in Catherine Palace. The original carved amber panels that once filled this room went missing during World War II and their whereabouts remain a mystery. The panels have been painstakingly re-created and are a wonder to behold.

Ekaterininsky Park: The landscaped park on the grounds of Pushkin (Tsarskoye Selo) contains mirror-effect lakes, vast lawns, and impressive views of Catherine Palace. Enjoy a picnic lunch here in the summer.

Kronshtadt: Experience a Russian navy town and learn about its history, taking in the Baltic Sea air as you tour.

Gatchina Park: The park that offers a lovely walk around Silver Lake is a bit more wild and less pompous than Pushkin's Ekaterininsky Park. It's a charming escape from city fuss. You can see newlyweds there attaching locks to a small bridge—a Russian wedding tradition.

13

ORIENTATION AND PLANNING

GETTING ORIENTED

The area around St. Petersburg is one big monument to its role as Russia's Imperial capital, from the time of Peter the Great (1672–1725) to the ill-fated Nicholas II, whose execution in Ekaterinburg in 1918 brought the Romanov dynasty to an end. Unlike Moscow's Golden Ring, monasteries and churches are not much in evidence, with the exception of Valaam on Lake Ladoga, which is dominated by the 14th-century Transfiguration of the Savior Monastery.

Except for Kronshtadt and Valaam, all of the destinations in this section can be reached by commuter train (*elektrichka*), but the simplest way to see the palaces is to book an excursion (available through any tour company). The cost is reasonable and covers transportation, a guided tour, and admission fees. An organized excursion to any of the suburban palaces will take at least four hours; if you travel on your own, it's likely to take up the entire day. But whichever plan you opt for, you'll enjoy numerous sights filled with splendor and magic.

Note that the sights in this region do not make up one easy circuit. In a few cases—notably Gatchina—you have to return to St. Petersburg to find direct rail transport. Of all the places, the ones that make the most sense to do in tandem would be: Pushkin and Pavlovsk, Peterhof and Lomonosov, Peterhof and Kronshtadt, or Lomonosov and Kronshtadt.

Because this region is so close to St. Petersburg and most people visit on day trips, hotels are few and far between.

Summer Palaces. These status symbols of the royal elite—the Menshikov's Great Palace in Lomonosov, the Great Palace in Peterhof, the Catherine Palace and the Alexander Palace in Pushkin, the Great Palace in Pavlovsk, the Great Palace and Priorat Palace in Gatchina, and the Konstantine Palace in Strelna—are at the heart of any trip outside St. Petersburg. Even Russians who have already visited these tsarist wonders find themselves returning time and time again, drawn back not necessarily by the opulence but by the acres of beautiful parks and gardens, perfect for relaxing.

Kronshtadt and Valaam. The port of Kronshtadt is on an island connected to the city by a dam. Its landmarks include the grandiose Naval Cathedral and numerous forts in the waters around the island. The history of Kronshtadt embraces more than 300 years of Russian navy life. Valaam Island, a national park, is known for its virtually untouched natural surroundings, as well as for its religious history, which includes active monasteries. It is a very popular destination for for Russian Orthodox pilgrims.

PLANNING

WHEN TO GO

To see the palaces and estates to their best advantage, try to time your visits to coincide with spring or summer. Peterhof in particular is best visited in summer, so you can fully appreciate the fountains, statues, monumental cascades, and lush parks. From late September to early June the fountains and cascades are closed down and take on the depressing look of drained pools. Autumn can also be a pleasant time for viewing the palaces. Note also that the waterway along the Neva River and Lake Ladoga to Valaam is only open from the end of May through October.

If you're traveling in the extreme cold of winter or the hottest days of summer, dress carefully, as much of your time will probably be spent outdoors.

GETTING HERE AND AROUND
BUS TRAVEL

Though not as convenient and comfortable as train travel, travel by bus from St. Petersburg can be a good way to go. Buses or minibuses run on direct routes to almost all of the suburbs, as well as to Kronshtadt. Tour companies also operate their own, rather scruffy coaches to Kronshtadt.

Although all the palaces are theoretically within walking distance from their respective train stations, there are often buses linking the two. Bus 1, 5, 7, 431, or 525 will take you to Gatchina from the station for 20R. You can also get to Gatchina Palace taking Bus 18, 18a, or 100 from the city's Moskovsky metro station for 60R. For Pavlovsk, should you for some reason not want to walk through the park to the palace, Bus 370 or 383 will take you directly there for 25R.

Minibuses (called *marshrutka*) from the city to the suburbs are more convenient than commuter trains (called *elektrichka*) because they usually take you directly to the sights. Minibus 299 will take you from St.

GREAT ITINERARIES

IF YOU HAVE 1 OR 2 DAYS
You can take your pick of the suburbs for any day trip, although your choice of destination will be influenced by the time of year. In summer, **Peterhof** is a must. At this time of year, **Pushkin** and **Pavlovsk** are also at their most attractive, and can be seen in a single day or, better still, over two days. If you have to choose, head to Pushkin.

IF YOU HAVE 3 OR 4 DAYS
In summer head to **Peterhof** and **Pushkin** on your first two days. On your third day, take a break from the palaces and visit the unforgettable **Valaam Archipelago**. To get to Valaam, catch the boat on the evening of your second day down the Neva River and up into Lake Ladoga. Spend the third day admiring the secluded monasteries and natural beauty of the islands, and return to the city overnight. On your final day, head for **Gatchina, Lomonosov** or the **Konstantine Palace**. For a destination with a completely different historical feel, head for the naval town of **Kronshtadt**.

13

Petersburg's Moskovskaya metro station to Pavlovsk for 40R. Minibuses 342, 545 can take you to Pushkin for 40R. Yellow double-decker buses marked "Peterhof" and minibus 404 leave from outside St. Petersburg's Baltic station (Baltiisky Vokzal) for Peterhof, charging 50R. From Avtovo metro station you get to Peterhof train station by minibus 424, 300, 224, 424a (for 40R); then take Bus 350, 351, 351a, 352, 353, 354, or 356 to the palace park for 30R. The ride lasts 10 minutes. Minibus 300 will take you to Lomonosov/Oranienbaum from Avtovo metro station as will bus 340 from Baltic station (also Baltiyskaya metro station) for 40R.

To catch a bus to Kronshtadt, take the subway to St. Petersburg's Chernaya Rechka metro station; walk across ulitsa Savushkina to the embankment of the River Chernaya Rechka and catch Bus 405 or 406 for 40R to the very end. Buses leave every 3–5 minutes from 5:40 am through midnight and take about an hour.

HYDROFOIL TRAVEL

From June through roughly the end of September, the *"meteor"-type* hydrofoil is the best way of getting from St. Petersburg to Peterhof, and it's also one of the options for traveling to Kronshtadt. It's possible to buy a ticket on the embankment the day that you would like to travel.

For Kronshtadt, boats depart from a pier at St. Petersburg's Arsenal-naya naberezhnaya in front of Finlyandsky Railway Station and from Lower Hermitage pier (Dvortsovaya Embankment, 38, which is across a defunct entrance to the Hermitage). Keep in mind that the boats to Kronshtadt go infrequently, and their schedules may change. The trip usually takes about an hour. For Peterhof, hydrofoils also depart from the Lower Hermitage pier just outside the State Hermitage Museum in summer; they leave approximately every 30–40 minutes, and the journey time is about a half hour and costs 500R for a one-way ticket. From the end of May through October ferries to the Valaam Archipelago leave from the River Passenger Terminal (Rechnoi Vokzal) at

195 prospekt Obukhovskoy Oborony, not far from Proletarskaya metro station in the south of St. Petersburg. The journey takes about 10 hours.

TAXI TRAVEL

You'll usually have no trouble getting a taxi at a train or bus station in these towns. Most of the towns are small enough to be navigated easily on foot, but a taxi is an alternative to short bus or train trips (e.g., from Pushkin to Pavlovsk). It's also possible to take a taxi all the way back to St. Petersburg from most of these towns (about 1,000R–1,300R), if you speak Russian.

TRAIN TRAVEL

Traveling by *elektrichka* (commuter train) provides a slice of authentic Russian life all on its own, but it's best attempted only if you have at least a little Russian under your belt. Fares are low, and the trip to most suburbs takes less than 45 minutes. Overall, it's worth the minor discomforts of the press of humanity and hard wooden seats. Check with a local travel agent or at the station for schedules. With the exception of traveling by elektrichka at busy times (Friday evening and weekends), you should not have trouble getting a ticket on the same day you wish to travel. For the most part, ticket booths are easy to find; if you don't speak Russian, just say the name of your destination and hold up as many fingers as there are passengers. Bear in mind that there's a lull in departures between 10 am and noon.

The elektrichka to Gatchina leaves from Baltic station (69R); the trip lasts around 45 minutes. For Lomonosov, catch the elektrichka from Baltic station to Oranienbaum-I (not II), approximately one hour from St. Petersburg (60R). For Pavlovsk (39R) and Pushkin (45R), take the elektrichka from Vitebsk station to Detskoye Selo; the trip to Pavlovsk lasts approximately 30 minutes, and it's another 5 minutes to Pushkin (from which you'll have to walk 15–20 minutes to the palace). For Peterhof, take the elektrichka from Baltic station to Novy Peterhof (48R) station, approximately 40 minutes from St. Petersburg; from the station take one of the many buses (number 350, 351, 351a, 352, 353, 354, or 356) to the palace.

RESTAURANTS

Because most of the suburbs are just a short trip from St. Petersburg, there has not been any real demand for tourist-oriented restaurants and cafés. There are some exceptions, notably in Pavlovsk and Pushkin, but on the whole it's best to pack some sandwiches. You will, however, find plenty of beer tents and ice-cream vendors.

WHAT IT COSTS IN RUBLES				
¢	$	$$	$$$	$$$$
under 125R	125R–250R	251R–375R	376R–500R	over 500R

Restaurants

Prices are per person for a main course at dinner.

TOUR OPTIONS

There are several local tour companies operating out of kiosks on St. Petersburg's Nevsky prospect. Usually, it's enough simply to step up and buy a ticket, the price of which includes coach seating and a guided tour in English, but you can also book in advance by visiting or phoning the tour-company offices.

Two of the most reliable excursion companies are MIR Travel and Davranov-Travel. Mir, which specializes in serving foreign tourists, offers excursions to the whole list of St. Petersburg suburbs. For groups of fewer than six people Mir organizes a minivan (for more than six people, a microbus) that will take you to a suburb you choose. For instance, a minivan trip (for up to six people) to Peterhof, which includes excursions and entrance tickets to the palace and park, costs 3,596R per person; an excursion to Lomonosov, 2,065R; Kronshtadt, 4,505R; Pushkin, 3,058R; and Pavlovsk, 2,893R. You can also make a deal if ordering a combined trip to Pushkin and Pavlovsk for 4,505R. The company can also take you to Valaam and even to the old Russian town of Novgorod, known for its fascinating kremlin, and located 200 km (124 mi) from St. Petersburg (for 8,722R). (Keep in mind that if you order a regular bus excursion for 15–25 people the price per person can be almost half as much.) Everything can be organized by phone. Davranov-Travel also offers excursions to all suburbs. You can buy tickets to their travel bus at their kiosk at the corner of Nevsky prospekt and ulitsa Sadovaya (it's outside Gostinni Dvor metro station). Usually they take you on the bus with Russian tourists but provide you with a guide who speaks English. It's less expensive if you're not alone. An excursion to Peterhof for five adult tourists with a guide costs 1,800R, but it's less if you go with more people. Tickets to other suburbs cost about the same. Buses of Davranov-Travel leave four times a day to each suburb from 10 am through 2 pm. There are no buses to Pushkin on Tuesday, to Peterhof and Gatchina on Monday, and to Pavlovsk on Friday because the museums are closed these days.

Tour Contacts MIR Travel (✉ *Office 1, 11 Nevsky prospekt, City Center* ☎ *812/325–2595* ⊕ *mir-travel.com*). **Davranov-Travel** (✉ *17 Italianskaya ul., City Center* ☎ *812/571–8694 or 812/312–4662* ⊕ *www.davranovtravel.ru*).

VISITOR INFORMATION

Any questions about the suburbs should be directed to officials at St. Petersburg's City Tourism Information Center (where operators are very helpful and speak English, French, and German) or private travel agencies and guided-tour companies. St. Petersburg's City Tourism Information Center also has information kiosks at Palace Square, St. Isaac's Square, Moskovsky Railway Station, and Pulkovo airport.

Visitor Information City Tourist Information Center (✉ *14/52 ul. Sadovaya, at Nevsky prospekt and ul. Sadovaya, City Center* ☎ *812/310–2822; 812/310–2231 for information in English; 812/300–3333 tourist helpline [9 am to 11 pm]* ⊕ *eng.ispb.info* Ⓜ *Nevsky Prospekt*).

Summer Palaces
and Historic Islands

THE SUMMER PALACES

A visit to this region takes you through a lavish trail of evidence of the Imperial spirit. These majestic old palaces, estates, and former nobles' residences—all on lovingly tended grounds—are within easy reach of St. Petersburg.

LOMONOSOV (ORANIENBAUM)
ЛОМОНОСОВ (ОРАНИЕНБАУМ)

39 km (24 mi) west of St. Petersburg's city center on the southern shore of the Gulf of Finland.

GETTING HERE AND AROUND

You can get to Lomonosov in an hour by taking a train from Baltiisky railway station and getting off at Oranienbaum-I. From there walk through a public garden down to the white St. Michael's Cathedral. In front of the cathedral you'll see the fence of the palace and its entrance. Minibus 300, which leaves from the Avtovo metro station, is also an option. The trip will cost around 40R. Get off the minibus at the stop called Dvortsovyi Prospekt, cross the road, and walk towards the same cathedral until you see the entrance to the palace grounds. The public bus 200 also leaves from Avtovo metro station and takes you to

Dvortsovyi Prospekt. In this case you won't have to cross the road before walk toward the church.

Lomonosov (Oranienbaum, Ломоносов (Оранниенбаум)). This was the property of Alexander Menshikov (circa 1672–1729), the first governor of St. Petersburg and Peter the Great's favorite, who, following Peter's example, in 1710 began building his own luxurious summer residence on the shores of the Baltic Sea. Before construction was complete, however, Peter died and Menshikov was stripped of his formidable political power and exiled, leaving his summer estate half finished. The palace reverted to the crown and was given to Peter III, the ill-fated husband of Catherine the Great. Most of the buildings on the grounds were erected during his six-month reign, in 1762, or completed later by Catherine.

13

This property was given the German name Oranienbaum after the orangery attached to its palace. A few years after the liberation of Leningrad, Oranienbaum was renamed for the 18th-century scientist Mikhail Lomonosov, who had conducted a number of experiments at his nearby estate. Lomonosov was the only imperial residence to have survived World War II entirely intact. Unfortunately, it's been run-down for some time, and the major sights are now closed for restoration work. They are to reopen in stages, starting with summer 2011.

Menshikov's Great Palace (Bolshoi Menshikovskii Dvorets), the original palace on the property, is also Lomonosov's biggest. It stands on a terrace overlooking the sea. Built between 1710 and 1725, it was designed by the same architects who built Menshikov's grand mansion on St. Petersburg's Vasilievsky Island, Giovanni Fontana and Gottfried Schaedel. The palace hosts annually changing exhibits on everything from the Orthodox Church in St. Petersburg to Japanese artwork. Although the bulk of the palace is closed for restoration, some rooms of the Great Palace are scheduled to reopen their doors in the summer of 2011. Nearby is **Peterstadt Dvorets**, the modest palace that Peter III used. This two-story stone mansion was built between 1756 and 1762 by Arnoldo Rinaldi. Its interior is decorated with handsome lacquered wood paintings. That it seems small, gloomy, and isolated is perhaps appropriate, as it was here, in 1762, that the tsar was arrested, then taken to Ropsha and murdered in the wake of the coup that placed his wife, Catherine the Great, on the throne. The building that most proclaims the estate's Imperial beginnings, however, is unquestionably Catherine's **Chinese Palace** (Kitaisky Dvorets), also designed by Rinaldi. Intended as one of her private summer residences, it is quite an affair—rococo inside, baroque outside. Lavishly decorated, it has ceiling paintings created by Venetian artists, inlaid-wood floors, and elaborate stucco walls. At this writing it is closed for restoration but will reopen some of its rooms in the summer of 2011. The small house outside served as the kitchen. Down the slope to the east of the Great Palace is the curious **Katalnaya Gorka**. All that remains of the slide, which was originally several stories high, is the pavilion that served as the starting point of the ride, where guests of the empress could catch their breath before tobogganing down again. Painted soft blue with white trim, the fanciful, dazzling pavilion looks like a frosted birthday cake; it was, however, closed for extensive (and indefinite) renovations at this writing. Also on the premises, near the pond, is a small amusement park offering carnival rides. When taking a commuter train here, be careful to exit at Oranienbaum-I (not II). ✉ *48 Dvortsovyi prospekt* ☎ *812/422–8016 for tours* ⌨ *Peterstadt Dvorets 140R* ☉ *Estate Tues.–Sun. 11–5.*

PETERHOF (PETRODVORETS) ПЕТЕРГОФ (ПЕТРОДВОРЕЦ)

29 km (18 mi) west of St. Petersburg on the southern shores of the Gulf of Finland.

GETTING HERE AND AROUND

From the city's Baltiisky Railway Station, take minibus 404; from Avtovo metro station take minibus 224, 300, 401, 424, or 424a. The minibuses run from 6 am to midnight and cost 50R. On weekends lines for the bus can be quite long, and it may take a half-hour to board, unless you are will to stand. A trip to Peterhof may take an hour on weekends, although it may take half that on weekdays. When you arrive at Peterhof the bus will stop just next to the entrance to Peterhof's Upper Park. After walking through the park, you'll reach the Grand Palace and its booking offices. There you can buy tickets to the Palace and the Lower Park, site of Peterhof's famous fountains. Another good option for summer season is to take a hydrofoil from the "Baltika" pier, which is just in from of the Hermitage. A one-way ticket for a half-hour journey will cost you 500R. The hydrofoils travel every 15–30 minutes. As you arrive to Peterhof's pier just walk along it, buy entrance tickets in the booking offices, and you'll get to the Lower Park almost immediately.

EXPLORING

ⓒ **Fodor's Choice**
★

Peterhof (Petrodvorets, Петергоф (Петродворец)). It's hard to believe that virtually all of Peterhof and the other palaces were almost completely in ruins toward the end of World War II, when the Germans were finally driven out of the area. Many priceless objects had been removed to safety before the Germans advanced, but a great deal was left behind and was looted. Now, after decades of painstaking work, art historians and craftspeople, have used photographs and other records to return the palaces to their former splendor. Peterhof and its neighboring palaces are so vast, however, that renovation work will continue for many years to come.

The complex of gardens and residences at Peterhof was masterminded by Peter the Great, who personally drew up the original plans, starting around 1720. His motivation was twofold. First, he was proud of the capital city he was creating and wanted its evolving Imperial grandeur showcased with a proper summer palace. Second, he became attached to this spot while erecting the naval fortress of Kronshtadt on a nearby island across the Gulf of Finland; because it lay in easy view, he often stayed here during the fort's construction. When the fort was finished, he had had a series of naval victories (including the Northern War against the Swedes), so he threw himself into establishing many parts of the grounds that would be called Peterhof (Peter's Court). This German name was changed to Petrodvorets after World War II.

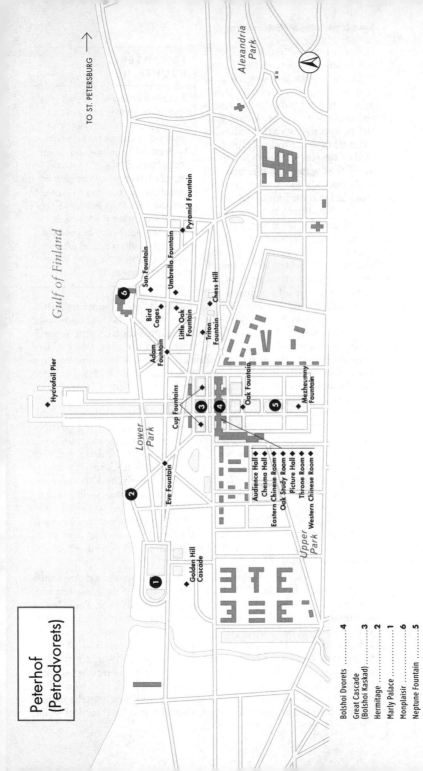

Peterhof (Petrodvorets)

TO ST. PETERSBURG →

Gulf of Finland

Hydrofoil Pier

Lower Park

Eve Fountain

Golden Hill Cascade

Cup Fountains

Adam Fountain

Bird Cages

Sun Fountain

Little Oak Fountain

Umbrella Fountain

Triton Fountain

Chess Hill

Pyramid Fountain

Oak Fountain

Mezheumny Fountain

Upper Park

Alexandria Park

Audience Hall
Chesma Hall
Eastern Chinese Room
Oak Study Room
Picture Hall
Throne Room
Western Chinese Room

Bolshoi Dvorets **4**
Great Cascade
(Bolshoi Kaskad) **3**
Hermitage **2**
Marly Palace **1**
Monplaisir **6**
Neptune Fountain **5**

If you travel by hydrofoil, you'll arrive at the pier of the Lower Park, from which you work your way up to the Great Palace. If you arrive by land, you'll go through the process in reverse. Either way, the perspective always emphasizes the mightiness of water. Half-encircled by the sea, filled with fountains and other water monuments, and with the Marine Canal running straight from the foot of the palace into the bay, Peter's palace was also intended as a tribute to the role of water in the life, and strength, of his city. The **Lower Park** is a formal baroque garden in the French style, adorned with statues and cascades. Peter's playful spirit is still

TRICKSTER'S FOUNTAINS

If you're traveling to Peterhof with small children in the summer, be sure to pack a bathing suit or an extra set of clothes for them and be prepared to get wet. The Lower Park's "trick fountains" are supposedly turned on by stomping on magic stones or pulling on levers, and kids love to try and figure out which one makes the fountains work. You won't want to point out the person sitting nearby who secretly makes them spray at just the right moment.

very much in evidence here. The tsar installed "trick fountains"—hidden water sprays built into trees and tiny plazas. The fountains come with life when staff press hidden mechanisms, much to the surprise of the unsuspecting visitor and the delight of the squealing children who love to race through the resulting showers on hot summer days. Located in the eastern half of Lower Park is the oldest building at Peterhof, **Monplaisir** (literally "My Pleasure"), completed in 1721. This is where Peter the Great lived while overseeing construction of the main Imperial residence. As was typical with Peter, he greatly preferred this modest Dutch-style villa to his later, more extravagant living quarters. The house is open to the public and makes for a pleasant tour. Some of its most interesting rooms are the Lacquered Study, decorated with panels painted in the Chinese style (these are replicas; the originals were destroyed during World War II); Peter's Naval Study; and his bedroom, where some personal effects, such as his nightcap and a quilt made by his wife, are on display. Attached to Peter's villa is the so-called Catherine Wing, built by Rastrelli in the mid-18th century in a completely different style. The future Catherine the Great was staying here at the time of the coup that overthrew her husband and placed her on the throne; the space was later used mainly for balls.

In the western section of the Lower Park is another famous structure, the **Hermitage,** built in 1725. It may be the first of the great Imperial hermitages (the most famous, of course, still stands in St. Petersburg), or retreats, in Russia. This two-story pavilion, which was used primarily as a banqueting hall for special guests, was at one time equipped with a device that would hoist the dining table area—diners and all—from the ground floor to the private dining room above. A slightly different system was put in place after Tsar Paul I's chair broke during one such exercise. The center part of the table could be lifted out, and guests would write down their dinner preferences and then signal for their notes to be lifted away. Shortly thereafter, the separated section would be lowered, complete with the meals everyone had ordered. The only way to the Hermitage was over a drawbridge, so privacy was ensured.

Almost adjacent to the Hermitage is the **Marly Palace,** a modest Peter the Great construction that is more of a country retreat than a palace. As with Monplaisir, there's mostly Peter-related memorabilia on display here. The four ponds around the back were used by Catherine the Great to stock fish.

A walk up the path through the center of the Lower Park (along the Marine Canal) leads you to the famous **Great Cascade** (Bolshoi Kaskad). Running down the steep ridge separating the Lower Park and the Great Palace towering above, the cascade comprises three waterfalls, 64 fountains, and 37 gilt statues. The system of waterworks has remained virtually unchanged since 1721. The ducts and pipes convey water over a distance of some 20 km (12 mi). The centerpiece of the waterfalls is a gilt Samson forcing open the jaws of a lion, out of which a jet of water spurts into the air. The statue represents the 1709 Russian victory over the Swedes at Poltava on St. Samson's day. The present figure is a meticulous replica of the original, which was carried away by the Germans during World War II. A small entrance halfway up the right-hand staircase (as you look at the palace above) leads to the grotto, where you can step out onto a terrace to get a bit closer to Samson before going inside to have a look under the waterworks.

Crowning the ridge above the cascade is the magnificent **Bolshoi Dvorets.** Little remains of Peter's original two-story house, built between 1714 and 1725 under the architects Leblond, Braunstein, and Machetti. The building was considerably altered and enlarged by Peter's daughter, Elizabeth. She entrusted the reconstruction to her favorite architect, Bartolomeo Rastrelli, who transformed the modest residence into a blend of medieval architecture and Russian baroque. Before you begin your tour of the palace interiors, pause for a moment to take in the breathtaking view from the marble terrace. From here a full view of the grounds below unfolds, stretching from the cascades to the Gulf of Finland and on to the city horizon on the shore beyond.

As for the main palace building, the lavish interiors are primarily the work of Rastrelli, although several of the rooms were redesigned during the reign of Catherine the Great to accord with the more classical style that prevailed in her day. Of Peter's original design, only his **Oak Study Room** (Dubovy Kabinet) survived the numerous reconstructions. The fine oak panels (some are originals) lining the walls were designed by the French sculptor Pineau. The entire room and all its furnishings are of wood, with the exception of the white-marble fireplace, above whose mantel hangs a long mirror framed in carved oak.

One of the largest rooms in the palace is the classically designed **Throne Room** (Tronny Zal), which takes up the entire width of the building. This majestic room—once the scene of receptions and ceremonies—has exquisite parquet floors, elaborate stucco ceiling moldings, and dazzling chandeliers. The pale-green and dark-red decor is bathed in light, which pours in through two tiers of windows (28 in all) taking up the long sides of the room. Behind Peter the Great's throne at the eastern end of the room hangs a huge portrait of Catherine the Great. The empress, the epitome of confidence after her successful coup, is shown astride a horse, dressed in the uniform of the guard regiment that supported her bid for power.

Next to the Throne Room is the **Chesma Hall** (Chesmensky Zal), whose interior is dedicated entirely to the Russian naval victory over the Turks in 1770. The walls are covered with 12 huge canvases depicting the battles; they were created for Catherine by the German painter Phillip Hackert. Arguably the most dazzling of the rooms is the **Audience Hall** (Audients Zal). Rastrelli created the definitive baroque interior with this glittering room of white, red, and gold. Gilt baroque bas-reliefs adorn the stark white walls, along which tall mirrors hang, further reflecting the richness of the decor.

> ## FIRE FOR ART'S SAKE
>
> It's said that when Catherine the Great asked the painter Phillip Hackert to depict the naval battles between the Russians and the Turks in 1770, he replied that he could not paint a burning ship since he'd never seen one. The solution: Catherine arranged to have ships blown up for him to use as models.

Other notable rooms include the **Chinese Study Rooms** (Kitaiskye Kabinety), designed by Vallin de la Mothe in the 1760s. Following the European fashion of the time, the rooms are ornately decorated with Chinese motifs. Finely carved black-lacquer panels depict various Chinese scenes. Between the two rooms of the study is the **Picture Hall** (Kartinny Zal), whose walls are paneled with 368 oil paintings by the Italian artist Rotari. The artist used just eight models for these paintings, which depict young women in national dress.

A tour of the palace interiors is offered regularly in English. After this, a stroll through the Upper Park, on the south side of the palace, is in order. This symmetrical formal garden is far less imaginative than the Lower Park. Its focal point is the **Neptune Fountain,** made in Germany in the 17th century and bought by Paul I in 1782. During World War II this three-tier group of bronze sculptures was carried away by the Germans, but it was recovered and reinstalled in 1956.

You can reach the palace by commuter train from St. Petersburg but as long as you're visiting in the summer and there isn't too much fog, the best way to go is by hydrofoil. This way your first view is the panorama of the grand palace overlooking the sea. The lines to get into the palace can be excruciatingly long in summer, and sometimes guided tours get preferential treatment. The ticket office for foreigners is inside the palace, and although admission is more expensive than it is for Russians, the lines are significantly shorter. Some park pavilions are closed Wednesday and others on Thursday; visiting on the weekend is the best chance to see everything.

An integral part of visiting any museum-palace in Russia is encountering the autocratic *babushki* (a colloquial term for museum caretakers, often slightly officious grandmothers). As you enter the palace, you'll be given tattered shoe covers to wear, so as to protect the halls' highly polished floors. ■ **TIP→ On most occasions, flash photography is not allowed, although for a fee, video may be used.** ✉ *2 ul. Razvodnaya* ☎ *812/450–6527; 812/450–6513 kassa (ticket window)* ⊕ *peterhofmuseum.ru* ▨ *Palace 520R, park 350R, separate admission fees (100R–360R) for park pavilions* ⊙ *Great Palace Tues.–Sun. 10:30–5; some park pavilions are closed Wed. and others on Thurs. Closed last Tues. of month.*

WHERE TO EAT

$$$–$$$$

CONTINENTAL

✕ **Bolshaya Oranzhereya.** The best option on the grounds of the palace itself is in the palace's old *oranzhereya*, or garden house. A comfortable, quaint spot for a snack and cup of tea, it also serves prix-fixe Continental meals with various kinds of fish and meat, including venison and duck courses, or traditional Russian options such as borscht (beet soup) or *solyanka* (slightly spicy meat soup with pickles). The restaurant is open from 10 to 6. ✉ *Peterhof palace grounds, near Triton fountain* ☎ *812/450–6106* ⊙ *Closed weekends Oct.–Apr.*

13

KONSTANTINE PALACE КОНСТАНТИНОВСКИЙ ДВОРЕЦ

19 km (12 mi) south of St. Petersburg on the southern shores of the Gulf of Finland.

GETTING HERE AND AROUND

A great option to get to the palace is to join a special tourist bus (labeled "To Konstantine Palace") that leaves from Beloselsky-Belozersky Palace (located at Nevsky prospekt) in St. Petersburg. You can purchase a ticket from any theater box office. The excursion departs weekdays at 2 pm and at 11 am and 3 pm on weekends, and includes a visit to the eastern part of the palace and the return trip. You can also get to the palace by taking public bus 200 or 210 or taking minibus 424 or 424a from the Avtovo metro station. Another option is tram 36, from the same metro station. This is a slower method, and the train stops about 500 yards from the palace. The buses and minibuses stop near an entrance that is unfortunately closed, so you'll have to backtrack a bit to get to a smaller gate. There you'll see a kiosk for an excursion bureau. Buy a ticket here; if you're traveling independently a Russian guide will lead you through a metal detector to reach the palace. Security measures are high here: in addition to being a tourist attraction, the palace is also an official residence of the Russian president.

EXPLORING

Konstantine Palace Константиновский Дворец. Nearly destroyed in World War II, this suburban palace dazzles once again. After years of renovation, based on old photographs and plans, the Italian-baroque, coffee-color palace and grounds reopened in 2003. It's now officially the Palace of Congress and is used to host government functions.

In 1720 Peter the Great commissioned work on this maritime country residence that was to be a "Russian Versailles." Italian architect Nicolo Micketti designed not only the palace, but also beautiful fountains and waterworks meant to draw water from the Gulf of Finland. However, the fountains never worked, and the palace itself underwent several

CLOSE UP

Rostropovich-Vishnevskaya Collection

The Rostropovich-Vishnevskaya collection of some 850 Russian paintings, art, and crafts originally belonged to the Russian cellist Mstislav Rostropovich and his wife, opera star soprano Galina Vishnevskaya. The couple fled the Soviet Union in 1974 under fire for their support of dissident Alexander Solzhenitsyn. After her husband's death, Vishnevskaya decided to auction the collection, saying she didn't have enough money to maintain it and keep it safe. Russian steel magnate Alisher Usmanov preempted a Sotheby's auction by buying the collection outright, reportedly for more than the $40 million it was expected to fetch at auction. He said he chose Konstantine Palace as the collection's home because: "I wanted to obey the will of Galina Vishnevskaya, who would like the collection to find its place in one of the palaces of St. Petersburg. I learned that one of the beautifully and recently rebuilt palaces, the Konstantine Palace, has no collection of its own." The collection includes works by some of Russia's most renowned painters, including Ilya Repin and Boris Grigoryev, as well as furniture, porcelain, silver, and other items.

fires, was redesigned, and had its name changed from Big Strelna Palace to Konstantine Palace.

The palace offers three different tours. One is a regular, 90-minute excursion to the eastern, historical part of the palace and includes narration about the tsar's family and its members who used to live here. The VIP tour covers the western part of the palace, which is used for official occasions and summits. You'll also see a part of the Russian president's apartments and the boudoir of the first lady. The third tour is a 90-minute amble through the vast park, which frankly doesn't have as many attractive sights as the parks of Peterhof and Pushkin.

Of the palace's 50-odd rooms, several are open to the public when no state functions are taking place. Both the VIP and historic tours visit the Marble Hall and Oval Hall. The central **Marble Hall,** used to host official events, lives up to its name, with yellow marble pilasters framed by bluish marble walls. A balcony here affords a breathtaking view of the huge park and canals leading to the Gulf of Finland. Next door is the large, pink **Oval Hall,** also used for official meetings. The VIP tour goes on to visit the **Blue Hall,** opposite the Marble Hall, with blue walls, high mirrors, and gilt ornamentation. A **wine cellar** has been reconstructed; it holds Hungarian Tokay wines, as it did when this was a royal residence.

The third-floor **belvedere** is a new addition. Styled as a ship's hold, it's made of oak, with a spiral staircase leading to an observation deck with lovely views of the grounds. In addition to the rooms themselves, you can see various permanent exhibits, such as Russian state symbols from the Hermitage and naval memorabilia from St. Petersburg's Naval Museum. Also on display is the famed Rostropovich-Vishnevskaya art collection. The grounds themselves are worthwhile, particularly the Upper (English) Park, Big Pond, canals, drawbridges, and the monument to Peter the Great, which stands just in front of the palace.

Before visiting, be sure to call ahead to make sure the palace will not be closed for state functions.

✉ *3 Beryozovaya alleya, Strelna* ☎ *812/438–5360; 812/438–5884 English-language group tours* ⊕ *www.konstantinpalace.ru* ✉ *Eastern palace tour and park: 250R for an excursion with a Russian guide, 2,500R an excursion in English or German for a group of up to 15 people if ordered in advance; VIP tour of western palace 300R; bus excursion from St. Petersburg 600R; excursion to see Rostropovich-Vishnevskaya Collection 350R at 2 pm daily. Buy tickets for it in the city's theater box offices or sometimes at the palace's booking office* ⊙ *Thurs.–Tues. 10–4, ticket office open until 4. Closed for official events (call in advance).*

13

PUSHKIN (TSARSKOYE SELO) ПУШКИН (ЦАРСКОЕ СЕЛО)

Fodor's Choice
★ *24 km (15 mi) south of St. Petersburg's city center via commuter train from the Vitebsk station, 40 km (25 mi) southeast of Peterhof.*

GETTING HERE AND AROUND
From Vitebsky railway station take a suburban train to Deskoye Selo station (in the town of Pushkin), then Bus 371 or 382 or minibus ("marshrutka") 371, 377, or 382 to the Catherine Palace and Park. From Moskovskaya metro station, take minibus 342 or 545 to the Tsarskoye Selo. You can enter the park from the main entrance: there you'll see the magnificent Catherine Palace on your right. The Catherine Park will be on your left. From Moskovskaya metro station, take minibus 342 or 545 to the museum complex.

EXPLORING
Pushkin (Tsarskoye Selo) Пушкин (Царское Село). The town of Pushkin was a summer residence of the Imperial family from the days of Peter the Great to the last years of the Romanov dynasty. Pushkin was initially known as Tsar's Village (Tsarskoye Selo), but the town's name was changed after the Revolution of 1917, first to Children's Village (Detskoye Selo) and then to Pushkin, in honor of the great Russian poet who studied at the lyceum here. During the 18th and 19th centuries, Tsarskoye Selo was a popular summer resort for St. Petersburg's aristocracy and well-to-do citizens. Not only was the royal family close by, but it was here, in 1837, that Russia's first railroad line was opened, running between Tsarskoye Selo and Pavlovsk, to be followed three years later by a line between here and St. Petersburg.

Fodor's Choice
★ Pushkin's main attraction is the dazzling 18th-century **Catherine Palace** (*Ekaterininsky Dvorets*), a perfect example of Russian baroque. The bright-turquoise exterior has row after row of white columns and pilasters with gold baroque moldings running the entire 985 feet of the facade. Although much of the palace's history and its inner architectural design bears Catherine the Great's stamp, it's for Catherine I, Peter the Great's second wife, that the palace is named. Under their daughter, Empress Elizabeth, the original modest stone palace was completely rebuilt. The project was initially entrusted to the Russian architects Kvasov and Chevakinsky, but in 1752 Elizabeth brought in the Italian architect Bartolomeo Rastrelli. Although Catherine the Great had the

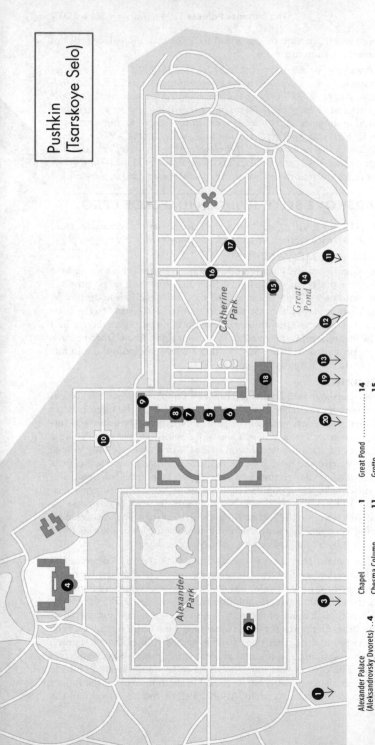

Pushkin
(Tsarskoye Selo)

Alexander Park

Catherine Park

Great Pond

interiors remodeled in the classical style, she left Rastrelli's stunning facade untouched.

You enter the palace grounds through the gilded black-iron gates designed by Rastrelli. The E mounted atop is for Catherine ("Ekaterina" in Russian). To your right, a visual feast unfolds as you walk the length of the long blue-and-gold facade toward the museum entrance. Sparkling above the palace at the northern end are the golden cupolas of the Palace Church. The interiors are just as spectacular, and many of the rooms are famous in their own right. Although little of Rastrelli's original design remains, the many additions and alterations made between 1760 and 1790 under Catherine the Great do; these were carried out by a pair of noted architects, the Scottish Charles Cameron and the Italian Giacomo Quarenghi.

Entering the palace by the main staircase (not added until 1861), you will see displays depicting the extent of the wartime damage and of the subsequent restoration work. Like Peterhof, the palace was almost completely destroyed during World War II. It was used by occupying Nazi forces as an army barracks, and as the Germans retreated, they blew up what remained of the former Imperial residence. Today the exterior of the palace again stands in all its glory, and work on the interior is ongoing.

The largest and arguably most impressive room is the **Great Hall** (Bolshoi Zal), which was used for receptions and balls. The longer sides of the hall are taken up by two tiers of gilt-framed windows. Tall, elaborately carved, gilded mirrors have been placed between them. Light pouring in through the windows bounces off the mirrors and sparkles on the gilt, amplifying the impression of spaciousness and brilliance. The huge ceiling painting, depicting Russian military victories and accomplishments in the sciences and arts, makes the room seem even larger. Here it's easy to imagine the extravagant lifestyle of St. Petersburg's prerevolutionary elite.

On the north side of the State Staircase is one of the palace's most famous rooms, the **Amber Room** (Yantarnaya Komnata), so named for the engraved amber panels that line its walls. The room owes much of its fame to the mysterious disappearance of its amber panels in World War II. In 1979 the Soviet government finally gave up hope of ever retrieving the panels and began the costly work of restoring the room. After 25 years of restoration a nearly exact replica of the room opened in 2003.

CLOSE UP

The Story of the Amber Room

The original Amber Room panels, a masterpiece of amber carving, were presented to Peter the Great in 1716 by Prussian king Friedrich Wilhelm I in exchange for 55 "very tall" Russian soldiers (that was Friedrich's request). The panels were eventually incorporated in one of the numerous halls of Ekaterininsky Dvorets (Catherine Palace) in Tsarskoye Selo. After the Revolution of 1917, Catherine Palace was turned into a museum, and the public had its first chance to see the Amber Room. The Nazis looted the palace in 1941 and moved the contents of the Amber Room to what was then the German town of Königsberg. That town (soon to become the Russian town of Kaliningrad) was captured by the Soviets in 1945, but by the time the Soviet troops entered the city, the amber panels had disappeared.

It's believed that the panels were either destroyed by Allied bombing or were somehow hidden by the Nazis. For obvious reasons, the second theory has held the most appeal, and over the years it has given hope to eager treasure seekers. Some postulated that the amber could have been buried in a silver mine near Berlin, hidden on the shores of the Baltic Sea, or taken as far away as South America. Explorers have searched caves, jails, churches, salt mines, tunnels, bunkers, and ice cellars. For some, the quest was an obsession: Georg Stein, a former German soldier, searched for more than two decades, spent almost all his fortune, and in the end was found mysteriously murdered in a Bavarian forest in 1987. In 1991 the German magazine *Der Spiegel* organized its own archaeological expedition to search for the panels in the ruins of Lochstedt Castle in the Kaliningrad region. It failed to find them.

In 1979 the Soviet government gave up all hope of relocating the panels and initiated the reconstruction of the Amber Room, allocating about $8 million for the project. It would take another $3.5 million donation from the German company Ruhrgas AG in 1999 to complete the restoration work. More than 30 craftspeople worked tirelessly, some dedicating up to 20 years of their lives to the project. Using microscopes to make the tiniest engravings in the amber, many lost their vision over the years or suffered illness from inhaling amber dust. Ironically, most of the amber came from the world's largest deposit of the fossil resin, in Kaliningrad—the very place where the original amber panels had disappeared. After 25 years of work and 6 tons of amber (though 80% of this amber was waste product), the replica of the Amber Room was unveiled in 2003 in time for St. Petersburg's 300th-anniversary celebrations.

Covered with more than a ton of amber, the room embraces you with the warm glow of more than 13 hues of this stone, ranging from butter yellow to dark red. One panel, *Smell and Touch,* is an original, found in Bremen, Germany, in 1997; a German pensioner whose father had fought in the Soviet Union was caught trying to sell the panel. The rest remain a mystery.

Leaving the Amber Room, you'll come to the large **Picture Gallery** (Kartinny Zal), which runs the full width of the palace. The paintings are all from Western Europe and date from the 17th to the early 18th century. Highlights among the other splendid rooms on the north side include the Blue Drawing Room, the Blue Chinese Room, and the Choir Anteroom, all of which face the courtyard. Each has pure-silk wall coverings. The Blue Chinese Room, originally designed by Cameron, has been restored on the basis of the architect's drawings. Despite its name, it's a purely classical interior, and the only thing even remotely Chinese is the Asian motif on the silk fabric. The fine golden-yellow silk now on the walls of the Choir Anteroom is from the same bolt used to decorate the room in the 18th century. When the postwar restoration began, this extra supply of the original silk was discovered tucked away in a storage room of the Hermitage.

13

Having savored the treasures inside the palace, you can now begin exploring the beautiful **Catherine Park** outside, with its marble statues, waterfalls, garden alleys, boating ponds, pavilions, bridges, and quays. The park is split into two sections. The inner, formal section, the French Garden, runs down the terraces in front of the palace's eastern facade. The outer section encloses the Great Pond and is in the less-rigid style of an English garden. If you follow the main path through the French Garden and down the terrace, you'll eventually reach Rastrelli's Hermitage pavilion, which he completed just before turning his attention to the palace itself. Other highlights of the French Garden include the Upper and Lower Bath pavilions (1777–79) and Rastrelli's elaborate blue-domed grotto.

There is much to be seen in the English-style garden, too. A good starting point is the **Cameron Gallery** (Galereya Kamerona), which actually forms a continuation of the palace's park-side frontage. It's off to the right (with your back to the palace). Open only in summer, it contains a museum of 18th- and 19th-century costumes. From its portico you get the best views of the park and its lakes—which is exactly what Cameron had in mind when he designed it in the 1780s. The double-sided staircase leading down to the Great Pond is flanked by two bronze sculptures of Hercules and Flora. From here, descend the stairs to begin your exploration of the park. Just beyond the island in the middle of the artificially created Great Pond stands the Chesma Column, commemorating the Russian naval victory in the Aegean in 1770. At the far end of the pond is Cameron's Pyramid, where Catherine the Great is said to have buried her beloved greyhounds. If you walk around the pond's right side, you'll come to the pretty blue-and-white Marble Bridge, which connects the Great Pond with a series of other ponds and small canals. At this end, you can rent rowboats. Farther along, up to the right, you come to the Ruined Tower. This architectural folly was built in the late 18th century merely to enhance the romantic ambience of these grounds.

Outside the park, just north of the Catherine Palace, stands yet another palace, the **Alexander Palace** (Alexandrovsky Dvorets), a present from Catherine to her favorite grandson, the future Tsar Alexander I, on the occasion of his marriage. Built by Giacomo Quarenghi between 1792 and 1796, the serene and restrained classical structure was the favorite residence of Russia's last tsar, Nicholas II. The left wing of the building is open to the public and hosts topical exhibits. Most of the interior was lost, with the notable exception of Nicholas's cabinet, a fine example of art nouveau furniture and design. A visit is most interesting in the context of the ongoing rehabilitation of Nicholas II's reputation in Russia.

Built in 1791 and originally intended for the education of Catherine the Great's grandchildren, the **Lyceum** later became a school for the nobility. Its most famous student, enrolled the first year it opened, was the beloved poet Alexander Pushkin. The building now serves as a museum; the classroom, library, and Pushkin's bedroom have been restored to their appearance at the time he studied here. In the school's garden is a statue of the poet as a young man, seated on a bench, presumably deep in creative meditation. The building is attached to the Catherine Palace. ⊠ *7 ul. Sadovaya* ☎ *812/465-2024 recorded information in Russian; 812/465-9424* ⌨ *Park 160R, Catherine Palace 550R, Alexander Palace 300R, Alexander Palace 200R, Lyceum 200R* ☉ *Park and palaces Wed.–Mon. 10–5. Catherine Palace closed last Mon. of month, Alexander Palace closed last Wed. of month.*

WHERE TO EAT

$$$–$$$$
EASTERN
EUROPEAN
✕ **Admiralteistvo.** This charming little restaurant is on the second floor of an old redbrick pavilion across the lake from the Catherine Palace. Its nostalgic, interiors are furnished with antique furniture and a number of partially enclosed seating areas that give you some isolation for a private dinner. The restaurant specializes in European and excellent Russian cuisine. For a genuine Russian dish, go for fish such as baked sturgeon or sterlet, which was very popular at the tsars' tables. You can also try traditional Russian homemade pelmeni or different kinds of *kotleta,* a stuffed and breaded meat dish (also known as Kiev). ⊠ *7 Sadovaya ul., in Ekaterininsky Park* ☎ *812/465-3549.*

$$$–$$$$
EASTERN
EUROPEAN
✕ **Staraya Bashnya.** Inside a clutch of buildings known as the Fyodorovsky Gorodok (a short walk north of Alexander Palace) is the Old Tower, a tiny restaurant that serves Russian and European cuisine. The European dishes are more expensive than they should be, so stick to Russian items such as the *pelmeni* (meat dumplings) with garlic or beef Stroganoff. The portions are very generous. ⊠ *14 Akademichesky per.* ☎ *812/466-6698* ⌨ *Reservations essential.*

PAVLOVSK ПАВЛОВСК

30 km (19 mi) south of St. Petersburg's city center, a 5-min train journey from Tsarskoye Selo, 6 km (4 mi) south of Pushkin.

★ GETTING HERE AND AROUND

From the Moskovskaya metro station take minibus (marshrutka) 299, which will take you directly to the palace in Pavlovsk. After passing the palace stop, the minibus continues, so make sure to get off at the palace (it's an obvious stop). From Kupchino metro station take minibus 286, which also takes you directly to the palace. This is the most convenient way to get to Pavlovsk, and seeing the palace and its surroundings first helps explain why the park was designed the way it is. A less preferable option is to take a commuter train from Vitebsky Railway station, which takes about 40 minutes. But if you don't speak Russian you may feel a bit lost at the station, and as you arrive at Pavlovsk Railway Station you'll either have to walk through the museum's park for about half an hour to get to the palace or take minibus 513, 299, 286, or 521 to get there. If you reach the park first, buy tickets from a kiosk and enter it through a small iron gate. First walk straight, and then head a bit right to head to the palace grounds. The park has rather thick forest and many lanes, but few signs, so you can get a bit lost. Don't hesitate to ask other tourists for directions to the palace.

13

EXPLORING

Pavlovsk Павловск. The grounds of Pavlovsk had always been the royal hunting grounds, but in 1777 Catherine the Great awarded them to her son, Paul I, upon the birth of his first son, the future Tsar Alexander I. (Pavlovsk comes from "Pavel," the Russian word for Paul.) Construction of the first wooden buildings started immediately, and in 1782 Catherine's Scottish architect Charles Cameron began work on the Great Palace and the landscaped park. In contrast to the dramatically baroque palaces of Pushkin and Peterhof, Pavlovsk is a tribute to the reserved beauty of classicism. Paul's intense dislike of his mother apparently manifested itself in determinedly doing exactly what she wouldn't—with, most visitors agree, gratifying results. The place is popular with St. Petersburg residents, who come to stroll through its beautiful 1,500-acre park, full of woods, ponds, tree-lined alleys, and pavilions.

Begin a tour of Pavlovsk with the golden yellow **Great Palace** (Bolshoi Dvorets), which stands on a high bluff overlooking the river and dominates the surrounding park. (If you walk the grandiose park first, you risk being too tired or too late for touring the palace, whose rooms begin closing after 4 pm.) Built between 1782 and 1786 as the summer residence of Paul and his wife, Maria Fyodorovna, the stone palace was designed in imitation of a Roman villa. The architect Vincenzo Brenna enlarged the palace between 1796 and 1799 with the addition of a second story to the galleries and side pavilions. Despite a devastating fire in 1803 and further reconstruction by Andrei Voronikhin in the early 19th century, Cameron's basic design survives. The building is crowned with a green dome supported by 64 small white columns. In front of the palace stands a statue of the snub-nosed Paul I, a copy of the statue at Gatchina, Paul's other summer residence.

Many rooms are open for viewing, and you may start on either the first or the second floor. The splendid interiors, with their parquet floors, marble pillars, and gilt ceilings, were created by some of Russia's most outstanding architects. Besides Cameron, Brenna, and Voronikhin, the roll call includes Quarenghi, who designed the interiors of five rooms on the first floor, and Carlo Rossi, who was responsible for the library, built in 1824. The state apartments on the first floor include the pink-and-blue **Ballroom;** the formal **Dining Hall,** where the full dinner service for special occasions is set out; and the lovely **Corner Room,** with walls of lilac marble and doors of Karelian birch. On the first floor, on the way from the central part of the palace to the southern section, are the **Dowager Empress Rooms** (Komnaty Vdovstvuyuschei Imperatritsy), six rooms that were designed for Maria Fyodorovna after the death of Paul I. The most impressive of these is the Small Lamp Study (Kabinet Fonarik), a light-green room that overlooks the Tsar's Little Garden. The empress's library and other belongings are on display here.

Among the lavishly decorated state rooms on the second floor is the famous **Greek Hall,** with a layout like that of an ancient temple. Its rich green Corinthian columns stand out against the white of the faux-marble walls. The hall, which also served as a small ballroom, linked the state chambers of Paul I to those of his wife, Maria. The last room on his side, leading to the Greek Hall, was the **Hall of War.** Maria's **Hall of Peace** was designed to correspond to it. The gilt stucco wall moldings of her suite are decorated with flowers, baskets of fruit, musical instruments, and other symbols of peace. Beyond Maria's apartments is the light-filled **Picture Gallery,** with floor-length windows and an eclectic collection of paintings. From the gallery, via a small, pink, marble waiting room, you reach the palace's largest chamber, **Throne Hall.** It once held the throne of Paul I, which was removed for a victory party after Napoléon's defeat and somehow never returned.

Like the palace, the design of the park was shared by the leading architects of the day—Brenna, Cameron, Voronikhin, and Rossi. The park differs greatly from park designs of other Imperial palaces, where the strict rules of geometrical design were followed; at Pavlovsk nature was left much less controlled.

The combined length of the park's paths and lanes is said to equal the distance between St. Petersburg and Moscow (656 km [407 mi]). Because you can't possibly cover the entire territory in one day anyway, you might just want to just wander a bit. If you walk down the slope just behind the palace to the **Tsar's Little Garden** (Sobstvenny Sadik), you can see the Three Graces Pavilion, created by Cameron. The 16-column pavilion encloses a statue of Joy, Flowering, and Brilliance. Directly behind the palace, a stone staircase, decorated with lions, will take you to the Slavyanka Canal. On the canal's other side, down to the left, is the graceful **Apollo Colonnade,** built in 1783. Its feeling of ruin isn't just due to time: it was struck by lightning in 1817 and never restored. If you bear right at the end of the stairs, you come to the **Temple of Friendship,** meant to betoken the friendship between Empress Maria and her mother-in-law, Catherine the Great. Beyond it is a monument from Maria to her own parents; the center urn's medallion bears their likenesses. Of the other noteworthy pavilions and memorials dotting the park, the farthest one up the bank is the **Mausoleum of Paul I,** set apart on a remote and overgrown hillside toward the center of the park. Maria had the mausoleum built for her husband after he was murdered in a palace coup. Paul was never interred here, however, and though Maria is portrayed as inconsolable in a statue here, historical evidence indicates that she was well aware of the plot to kill her husband. ⊠ *20 ul. Revolutsii* ☎ *812/470–2156; tours 812/452–1536* ⊕ *www.pavlovskmuseum.ru* ⊠ *Palace and grounds 500R, park 150R,* *additional 120R for Dowager Empress Rooms, Sobstvennyi Sadik 100R* ☉ *Sat.–Thurs. 10–5. Closed 1st Mon. of month.*

WHERE TO EAT

$$$–$$$$
EASTERN
EUROPEAN

✕ **Podvoriye.** This is one of St. Petersburg's most popular restaurants for traditional Russian food, and it's best to make a reservation. Past guests at this wooden restaurant built in the *terem* (folk or fairy tale) style include the former presidents of France and Russia as well as luminaries of Hollywood and fashion, including Michael Douglas and Georgio Armani. Inside, a stuffed bear greets you with samples of vodka. Traditional Russian fare includes pickled garlic and mushrooms, excellent sturgeon dishes, and cutlets of wild boar, bear, or elk. Among the less expensive mains are pelmeni and *golubtsy* (a mixture of rice and meat wrapped in cabbage or grape leaves). Drinks to try are *kvas* (a sweet, lightly fermented drink made from bread or grains) and *mors* (a sour-sweet cranberry juice). The delicious kids' menu has all kinds of pancakes and dozens of different jams—most of them are made of berries that grow at the restaurant owner's dacha in the Crimea Peninsula of Ukraine. ⊠ *16 Filtrovskoye shosse* ☏ *812/465–1399* ⊕ *www. podvorye.ru.*

$$$
EASTERN
EUROPEAN

✕ **Grand Column Hall.** The former servants' quarters inside Pavlovsk Palace now house this Russian restaurant with both cafeteria-style and full-menu service. The European offerings include different kinds of salads and well-prepared trout and pike perch. If you want to go Russian, you can order traditional national dishes, such as pancakes with caviar, or fish or meat in aspic, by phone beforehand. You can also order picnic items here to eat on the palace's extensive grounds. Keep in mind that the restaurant closes by 6 pm, and it is closed on Fridays. ⊠ *Pavlovsk Palace* ☏ *812/452–3809.*

GATCHINA ГАТЧИНА

45 km (28 mi) southwest of St. Petersburg's city center.

GETTING HERE AND AROUND

From the city's Moskovskaya metro station take minibus ("marshrutka") 18A. It will take you just next to the palace and its park. Get off in front of the palace and walk towards its central entrance to buy tickets. From Baltiisky railway station take a commuter train to Gatchina Baltiiskaya station. If the train brings you to the first platform, exit the train and towards the palace grounds, which are visible from there—it's a five-minute walk. If the train brings you to the second platform, head through the underground passage; as you exit you'll see the palace.

EXPLORING

Gatchina Гатчина. The main attractions of Gatchina, the most distant of St. Petersburg's palace suburbs, are an expansive park with a network of bridges for island-hopping, and a grim-looking palace—resembling a feudal English castle—that has unfortunately deteriorated over the years. Probably because Gatchina lacks the splendor that's available in excess at the other suburban palaces, it's usually not included in prearranged tours, and thus is rarely visited by foreign tourists. Because it does offer a chance to escape from the crowds for a while, however, it's worth a visit. Keep in mind that few restaurants are available, so be sure to bring along a lunch that you can enjoy on the shores of Silver Lake. The name Gatchina is a bit of a mystery. One popular suggestion is that it comes from the Russian expression *gat chinit,* meaning "to repair the road." Others believe it comes from the German phrase *hat schöne,* meaning "it is beautiful." In its current state, both expressions could apply. Gatchina, which is the name of both the city and the park-palace complex, dates to the

> ### COUNT ORLOV
>
> Count Grigory Orlov, young and handsome, was a favorite of Catherine the Great, and the feeling was mutual. Ready and willing to do anything for her, he headed the coup against Catherine's husband, Peter III, in 1762, which allowed Catherine to take the thrown. Orlov was also supposedly the father of Catherine's illegitimate son Alexei.

15th century, when it was a small Russian village. In 1712, following the final conquest of the area by Russia, Peter I gave Gatchina to his sister, the tsarevna Natalya Alexeyevna. The land changed hands several times over the years, eventually ending up as a possession of Catherine the Great. She gave it to one of her favorites, Count Grigory Orlov, in 1765. It was during this period that the architect Antonio Rinaldi designed and built the Grand Palace and laid out the park, which was eventually decorated with obelisks and monuments in honor of the Orlovs.

In 1783 Orlov died, and Gatchina passed to Catherine's son, Paul I, and his wife. At various times, Gatchina Palace was a residence of Nicholas I, Alexander II, and Alexander III, and it bears witness to many important historic events, as well as the political and personal secrets of the Romanov dynasty.

In contrast to the pastel colors and flashiness of the palaces of Pushkin and Peterhof, Gatchina Palace has the austere look of a military institution, with a restrained limestone facade and a blocky structure with little ornamentation. The palace, which is built on a ridge, is also surrounded by a deep moat, which emphasizes the castle design of the facade. Its northern side faces a green forest stretching for some distance. The southern facade opens up to the main parade grounds, which were once used for military displays. Along the outer edge of the parade grounds runs a short bastion with parapets cut out with openings for firing weapons. The palace is also accentuated by two five-sided, five-story towers, the Clock Tower, and the Signal Tower.

Construction on the palace was carried out in three main phases. The first period began in 1766 under the guidance of Rinaldi. He built the three-story central part of the palace, as well as the service wings and the inner courtyards, known as the Kitchen Block and the Stable Block (later called the Arsenal Block). The second stage of construction began in 1783, when Brenna made the side blocks level with the galleries and installed cannons, adding to the palace's image as a feudal castle. Brenna also integrated new palatial halls, thus turning Rinaldi's chamberlike interiors into ceremonial rooms.

The third stage took place under Nicholas I. He hired the architect Roman Kuzmin to reconstruct both side blocks between 1845 and 1856. He also built a new chapel, and living rooms were arranged in the Arsenal Block. Kuzmin's work also eventually led to the restoration of the 18th-century rooms, the construction of a new main staircase in the central section, and the reshaping of the bastion wall in front of the palace.

The palace was badly damaged during World War II, and restoration is still underway. Fortunately, a collection of watercolors by the artists Luigi Premazzi and Edward Hau survived. Painted during the 1870s, these watercolors have been a helpful guide for restoring the palace to its prewar condition. Within the palace you can see some partially restored rooms and exhibits of 19th-century arms and clothing. Some rooms are now restored to the appearance they had when they belonged to the family of Alexander III. ✉ *1 Krasnoarmeisky pr.* ☎ *813/712–1509 directory, 813/719–3492 tours Gatchina Palac* ⬚ *Gatchina Palace and park 220R; Alexander III exposition 120R* ☉ *Tues.–Sun. 10–5. Closed 1st Tues. of month.*

> **ECHO**
>
> It was during Count Orlov's control of the complex that a subterranean passage was created between Silver Lake and the halls of the Grand Palace. The 130-yard passage was built to emphasize echoes, repeating up to four words. Today visitors of the palace stand at the start of the passage, and guides ask them to speak a few special questions. The last word in the question becomes the echo's "answer." For example, after asking "Kto boitsya moroza?" (Who is afraid of frost?), the echo answers: "rosa" (rose).

13

Prioratsky Palace. A 10-minute walk from Gatchina Palace bring you to Black Lake and this white palace, a unique construction made of rammed earth (compressed clay, sand, and gravel, and other materials). It was built at the end of the 18th century by architect Nikolai Lvov, the first person in Russia to introduce cheap, fireproof, construction of this type. The palace was meant for the great French prior Prince Condé (though he never lived here). The southern part of the palace resembles a Gothic chapel, but the rest resembles a fortification. On the first floor are exposed samples of the rammed earth; the second floor has displays on the palace's construction. To reach the palace directly, you can take minibus 18 or 18a and get off at the bus stop for Ulitsa Chkalova. ✉ *Ul. Chkalova, Prioratsky Park* ☎ *813/712–1509 directory; 813/717–6467 Prioratsky Palace* ⬚ *120R* ☉ *Tues.–Sun. 10–5. Closed 1st Tues. of month.*

English Landscape Gardens (Angliiskiye Sady). After touring the palaces here, you may want to head down to the lakes for a little relaxation. Rowboats and catamarans are available at a cost of 100R for 30 minutes—look for the bare-chested, tattooed men standing along the lake (you may be asked to provide your passport as a deposit, to make sure you actually return the boat instead of fleeing to Finland). The Gatchina park is laid out around a series of lakes occupying about one-third of its entire area. The English Landscape Gardens, one of the largest in the park, was built around the White and Silver lakes. On a clear day the mirrorlike water reflects the palace facade and pavilions. The park is dotted with little bridges, gates, and pavilions, among which several are dedicated to the state and military deeds of the Orlov brothers. These include the Eagle (Orliny) Pavilion, built in 1792 on the shores of the Long Island, and the so-called Chesma Column, built by Rinaldi in honor of the Orlovs' military deeds. Keep in mind that the signs in the park are in Russian and point to eventual destinations, such as Berlin, but if you keep to the lakeshore, you shouldn't have any trouble. ✉ *1 Krasnoarmeisky pr.* ☏ *813/712–1509 directory* ✉ *Gatchina Palace and park 220R* ⊙ *Tues.–Sun. 10–5. Closed 1st Tues. of month.*

KRONSHTADT AND VALAAM

Two islands, one to the west and one to the northeast of St. Petersburg, set a different tone than the palace suburbs but are still of historic significance. The town of Kronshtadt, on Kotlin Island, has a long and proud naval tradition, while the monasteries of Valaam Archipelago date back to the earliest days of Christianity, more than a millennium ago.

KRONSHTADT КРОНШТАДТ

30 km (19 mi) west of St. Petersburg.

GETTING HERE AND AROUND

Take minibus 405 from the Chyornaya Rechka metro station (as you exit the metro station go to your left, cross the road, and you'll see the row of various minibuses). From Prospekt Prosvescheniya metro station, take minibus 407. The cost of the trip will be approximately 60R and takes about 40 minutes. Get off at the stop next to the Naval Cathedral (Morskoi Sobor) which is being renovated until at least 2013. If you'd rather skip the Cathedral, head by the same minibus to Kronshtadt's embankment, another attraction here. In summer you can also take a hydrofoil or an aquabus (a water taxi) from the pier at Arsenalnaya Embankment, in front of Finlyandsky Railway Station (Finlyandsky metro station) or from the pier at Lower Hermitage (Dvortsovaya Embankement 38, in front of the major exit from the Hermitage Museum). The trip costs 96R. Keep in mind that the hydrofoils travel infrequently (usually at 10am, 1 pm, and 7 pm) and the schedule for an aquabus can change yearly (check the schedule at ⊕ *www.vodohodneva.ru*). There can be long lines, especially in good weather. There's also a tour to Kronshtadt using a similar boat that takes 4 to 5 hours round-trip. This leaves from Lower Hermitage pier at 10:45 am. The tour costs 500R.

Arriving by boat, you arrive a pier near a number of military ships. From the pier walk straight for about 10–15 minutes to reach the Naval Cathedral. (You may need to ask directions on the way). The simplest method to reach Kronshtadt is a bus tour. Tickets are sold at the excursion kiosks at the corner of Nevsky prospekt and ulitsa Sadovaya (near the Gostinni Dvor metro station), and buses depart from a location nearby.

Hydrofoils: Ships on Wings

Hydrofoils, or *meteory*, are a popular mode of transport in St. Petersburg, especially for visiting the city suburbs of Peterhof and Kronshtadt near the Gulf of Finland. A hydrofoil is essentially a ship that works on underwater wings, or hydrofoils, below the hull. As the ship picks up speed, the hull lifts off the water, creating less drag and allowing for even greater speed—they can go as fast as 80 kph (about 43 knots). Travel by hydrofoil from St.

Petersburg to Peterhof takes about half an hour. By car, the same trip may take up to an hour and a half to two hours with traffic. Hydrofoils are only available in the summer months, as the Neva River freezes in winter.

13

EXPLORING

Kronshtadt Кронштадт. Kronshtadt (Kotlin Island), to the west of St. Petersburg, was built between 1703 and 1704 by Peter the Great as a base from which to defend St. Petersburg and to attack the long-standing enemy of the Russian empire, the Swedish navy. For a long time it was the only military harbor of the empire, which is why it was off-limits to all but its permanent residents; visitors were stopped at special checkpoints as late as 1996. Today anyone can visit, either by taking a "Meteor" hydrofoil, which departs from St. Petersburg, or by taking an excursion from one of the agencies on St. Petersburg's Nevsky prospekt (between Gostinny Dvor and the old City Duma).

In the first half of the 20th century the Kronshtadt Commune aimed to break the monopoly of the Communist Party and to give back to peasants the right to use their land freely; the revolt lasted two weeks, seriously jeopardizing Lenin's hold on power, but was finally bloodily repressed. The streets of Kronshtadt are still named after Marx and Lenin, and the town still seems to live in the past, as if to hold on to the mighty era of the Soviet military machine. Despite being in dire condition, Kronshtadt is proud of its naval pedigree. Its significance was gradually diminished by the development of St. Petersburg throughout the 19th century, but there are still military and scientific vessels using its harbors. Off the shore of Kotlin Island are several forts that were constructed during the Crimean War (1853–56). The most interesting of these is **Fort Aleksandr,** which in the 19th century was turned into a laboratory to research the bubonic plague. These days it's a favorite stop-off point for yachters sailing either from Kotlin Island or St. Petersburg; it also hosts the occasional evening dance in summer. One of Kronshtadt's highlights is its **Naval Cathedral** (Morskoi Sobor), built between 1902 and 1913 by Vassili Kosyakov—the finest example of neo-Byzantine architecture in Russia. It is currently under major reconstruction and it due to re-open in 2013, in time for its centennial. Other sights include the Gostinny Dvor (one of Kronshtadt's first build-

ings and now a department store in need of renovation), the Summer
Garden, and the Menshikov Palace, now a club for the island's sailors.

VALAAM ARCHIPELAGO ВАЛААМСКИЙ АРХИПЕЛАГ

★ *170 km (105 mi) north of St. Petersburg, east along the Neva River,
and up into Lake Ladoga.*

GETTING HERE AND AROUND

From the end of May through October, ferries to the Valaam Archipelago leave from Rechnoi Vokzal (River Passenger Station) at 195
prospekt Obukhovskoy Oborony, near Proletarskaya metro station in
the south of St. Petersburg. The journey takes around 10 hours. Usually ferries leave at 9 pm and arrive by 8 am. You can contact a tourist
agent, such as MIR, to order a tour to Valaam. When the ferry pulls
into Valaam Island, follow the crowd and you'll reach the monastery.

EXPLORING

Valaam Archipelago Валаамский Архипелаг. An overnight trip by boat
from St. Petersburg delivers you out of the bustle of the city and into
the Republic of Karelia. The republic is one of the 88 federal subjects
of the Russian Federation; though its language is Russian, it has close
cultural ties to its neighbor, Finland. One of its most tranquil and beautiful settings is Valaam, a cluster of islands in the northwestern part of
Lake Ladoga, Europe's largest freshwater lake. The southern part of
the lake borders Russia. The archipelago consists of Valaam Island and
about 50 other isles.

Valaam Island is the site of an ancient monastery said to have been
started by Saints Sergey and German, missionaries who came to the
region (probably from Greece) sometime in the second half of the 10th
century—perhaps even before the "official" conversion of the land of
the Rus' to Christianity. The next 1,000 years are a sorry story of
Valaam and its monks battling to survive a regular series of catastrophes—including plague, fire, invasion, and pillage—only to bounce
back and build (and rebuild) Valaam's religious buildings and way of
life. In 1611 the monastery was attacked and razed by the Swedes;
it languished for a century until Peter the Great ordered it rebuilt in
1715. Valaam was also to pass into the hands of Finland on more than
one occasion, the longest period being from the end of World War I
to 1940. After World War II, during which the islands were evacuated
and then occupied by Finnish and German troops, the monasteries fell
into almost total disrepair, and it was only in 1989 that monks returned
to Valaam.

A guided tour of Valaam takes about six hours, although with a break
for lunch this is not at all as arduous as it might sound. You can also
buy a map of the island (easy to find at any of the many tourist shops
here) and strike out on your own. But the tour guides, most of whom
live on the island throughout the summer, have an enormous amount
of interesting information to impart about Valaam (most, however,
don't speak English). The guides also know where the best shady spots
to sit and relax are, and while you catch your breath they will tell you
everything about Valaam's history, prehistory, wildlife, geology and

geography, religious life, and gradual renaissance as a monastic center. The island's beauty has also inspired the work of many Russian and foreign artists, composers, and writers; the second movement of Tchaikovsky's First Symphony is said to be a musical portrait of the island, and you will hear it played over loudspeakers as your ferry departs.

Most tours to Valaam spend the first half day on a small selection of the *skity,* a monastery in seclusion. Only four skity are currently used as places of worship, and some of them are in the archipelago's most remote areas. Closest to where the ferries dock is the **Voskresensky (Resurrection) Monastery,** consecrated in 1906. In the upper church, you can hear a performance of Russian liturgical music (for an extra 20R) performed by a male quartet. Another monastery within easy walking distance is the **Getsemanskii (Gethsemene) monastyr,** consisting of a wooden chapel and church built in a typically Russian style, and monastic cells, which are inaccessible to the public. The squat construction next door is a hostel for pilgrims, some of whom you may see draped in long robes on your walk.

After lunch, buy a ticket (100R for round-trip) for the ferry that will take you to the 14th-century **Spaso-Preobrazhensky Valaamskii (Transfiguration of the Savior) Monastyr,** the heart of the island's religious life. You can walk the 6 km (4 mi) from the harbor in either direction, but if you choose to walk back from the monastery, make sure you give yourself enough time to catch the ferry back to St. Petersburg (about 1¼ hours should be enough time to walk back). As you reach the monastery, you'll see tourist stands and beer kiosks—something the monks themselves have mixed feelings about. The walk up the hill past the bric-a-brac, however, is well worth it, as you reach the splendid Valaamskii Monastyr cathedral (under ongoing restoration). The cathedral's lower floor is the **Church of St. Sergius and St. German,** finished in 1892, and is in the best condition. It's a living place of worship, as you'll see from the reverence of visitors before the large icon depicting Sergey and German kneeling before Christ. The upper **Church of the Transfiguration of the Savior,** consecrated in 1896, is still in a terrible state, although the cavernous interior, crumbling iconostasis, and remaining frescoes are still impressive in their own right.

■**TIP→** Although drinking and smoking are permitted in most areas of the island, you'll be asked to refrain while on the territory of the monasteries. Visitors are also required to observe the dress code on the grounds of the cathedral: women must wear a long skirt and cover their heads (scarves and inelegant black aprons are provided at the entrance for those who need appropriate garb), and men must leave their heads uncovered and wear long trousers—shorts are forbidden.

You can visit Valaam only from June through September or early October, when the waterway along the Neva River and Lake Ladoga is open. The 10-hour ferry journey to Valaam is not luxurious—you'll be witnessing a real throwback to the Soviet era. The rooms are clean, if spartan, and are perfectly manageable for two nights' sleep. In any case, you can spend much of the journey sitting on the sundeck; watch the industrial south of St. Petersburg give way to the rural setting of the lower Neva, before you pass the ancient fort of Petrakrepost on your right as the ferry sails into Lake Ladoga. The return journey is just as magical, as the golden spires and cupolas of the monasteries poke out of the tree line and glint in the setting sun.

■ TIP→ Take some food with you for your trip to Valaam. Although three meals are included in the price of most tours, they are best avoided. Instead, pack some sandwiches, fresh fruit, and perhaps some wine. You might want to poke your head into the rather severe bar on the island, but you are unlikely to want to linger. ⊕ *www.valaam.ru.*

UNDERSTANDING
MOSCOW AND
ST. PETERSBURG

RUSSIA AT A GLANCE

ENGLISH–RUSSIAN
VOCABULARY

RUSSIA AT A GLANCE

FAST FACTS

Type of government: Federation
Capital: Moscow
Administrative divisions: 89 administrative regions, broken down into 46 *oblastey* (districts), 21 *respubliky* (republics), 4 *avtonomnykh okrugov* (autonomous regions), 9 *krayev* (regions), 2 *goroda* (federal cities), 1 *avtonomnaya oblast* (autonomous oblast)
Independence: August 24, 1991 (following the collapse of the Soviet Union)

"I cannot forecast to you the action of Russia. It is a riddle wrapped in a mystery inside an enigma."
— Winston Churchill, 1939

Constitution: December 12, 1993
Legal system: Based on civil law, with judicial review of legislative acts
Legislature: Bicameral parliament: Duma (lower house) and Federation Council (upper house)
Population: 139,390,205 (est. July 2010)
Fertility rate: 1.41 children per woman
Language: Russian is the official state language; other languages are spoken by limited numbers of ethnic minorities, including Bashkir, Tatar, Yevnik (Evenk), Chuvash, Buryat, and numerous languages in the Caucasus.
Ethnic groups: Russian 79.8%, Tatar 3.8%, Ukrainian 2%, Bashkir 1.2%, Chuvash 1.1%, other 12.1% (2002 Census)
Life expectancy: Female 73, male 59
Literacy: Total population 99.4%; male 99.7%, female 99.2% (2002 Census)
Religion: Russian Orthodox 15%–20%, Muslim 10%–15%, Other Christian 2%
Inventions: Ice slide (precursor to the roller coaster, 17th century), periodic table (invented by Dmitry Mendeleev, 1869), Kalashnikov assault rifle (AK-47; invented by Mikhail Kalashnikov, 1947), magnetohydrodynamic power generator (1972)

ECONOMY

The Soviet Union is a long-forgotten memory for Russia's capitalists as the country's economy continues to surge ahead. The economy is largely dependent on commodities exports—mostly oil and natural gas.

"To believe that Russia has got rid of the evils of capitalism takes a special kind of mind. It is the same kind of mind that believes that a Holy Roller has got rid of sin."
— Henry Louis Mencken, mid-20th century

Annual growth: 4% in 2010
Inflation: 6.7% in 2010
Unemployment: 7.6% in 2010
Per capita income: $15,900
GDP: $2.229 trillion
Services: 62%
Agriculture: 4.2%
Industry: 33.8%
Work force: 75.55 million; agriculture 10%, industry 31.9%, services 58.1%
Currency: Ruble
Exchange rate: 30 rubles per U.S. dollar
Major industries: Petroleum, natural gas, coal, chemicals, steel, mining, lumber, transportation equipment (aircraft, ships, railways), communications equipment, medical and scientific instruments, consumer goods, textiles
Agricultural products: Wheat, potatoes, livestock, sugar beets
Exports: $376.7 billion in 2010
Major export products: Crude oil and refined oil products, natural gas, wood and wood products, metals, chemicals, military equipment
Export partners: Netherlands 10.62%, Italy 6.46%, Germany 6.24%, China 5.69%, Turkey 4.3%, Ukraine 4.01%
Imports: $237.3 billion in 2010

Major import products: Machinery, medicine, meat, sugar, consumer goods, metal products
Import partners: Germany 14.39%, China 13.98%, Ukraine 5.48%, Italy 4.84%, United States 4.46%

POLITICAL CLIMATE

A guerilla conflict with militants in the Chechen Republic continues to dominate headlines, despite government claims that the situation is under control. Other unresolved conflicts include a dispute with Japan over the Kuril Islands south of Sakhalin in the Pacific Ocean. The biggest dispute between Russia and the European Union is over travel and visa regulations for Kaliningrad residents (Kaliningrad, formerly Konigsberg, was captured from Germany by the Soviet Union in World War II). A 1990 maritime boundary agreement between the United States and the Soviet Union regarding the Bering Sea has yet to be ratified by Russia.

"A Russian is wise after the event."
—Russian proverb

DID YOU KNOW?

■ Russia contains the greatest mineral reserves of any country in the world.

■ The world's only freshwater seals live in Russia, at Lake Baikal in Siberia.

■ Russia's population density is a mere eight people per square mile.

■ More than 100 languages are spoken in Russia.

■ In the Soviet Union, the richest 10% of the population earned only four times more than the poorest 10%. By the mid-1990s, the richest 10% earned as much as 15 times more than the poorest 10%.

■ More than 20 million Russian civilians died as a result of World War II.

THE RUSSIAN ALPHABET AND SOUNDS

LETTER	SOUND	SOUND IN ENGLISH WORD
А а	ah	father
Б б	b	boy
В в	v	voice
Г г	g	go
Д д	d	day
Е е	yeh, eh	yet, keg
Ё ё	yo	yolk
Ж ж	zh	measure
З з	z	zero
И и	ee, e	feel, me
Й й	y	boy
К к	k	kit
Л л	l	lamp
М м	m	map
Н н	n	now
О о	oh	folk
П п	p	pan
Р р	r, rr (rolled)	roll
С с	s	see
Т т	t	top
У у	oo	boot
Ф ф	f	fun
Х х	kh, h	hush
Ц ц	ts	cats
Ч ч	ch	chair
Ш ш	sh	shut
Щ щ	shch	fresh
ъ	hard sign a consonant	short pause after
ы	y	it
ь	soft sign	often preceding consonant
Э э	eh	elk
Ю ю	yoo	Yule
Я я	yah	yacht

Adapted from "The Russian Alphabet and Sounds" table in Living Language: Ultimate Russian Beginner-Intermediate.

RUSSIAN VOCABULARY

ENGLISH	CYRILLIC	TRANSLITERATION

COMMON GREETINGS

Hello!	Здравствуйте!	**Zdrahst**-vooy-tyeh!
Good morning!	Доброе утро!	**Dohb**-rah-yeh **oot**-rah!
Good afternoon!	Добрый день!	**Dohb**-ree **dyehn**!
Good evening!	Добрый вечер!	**Dohb**-ree **vyeh**-cherr!
Good bye.	До свидания.	**Dah** svee-**dah**-nya.
Pleased to meet you!	Очень рад с вами познакомиться!	**Oh**-chen **rahd** s **vah**-mee pah-znah-**koh**-meet-sah!
How are you?	Как дела?	**Kahk** dee-**lah**?
Fine, thanks.	Хорошо, спасибо.	Hah-rah-**shoh**, spah-**see**-bah.
What is your name?	Как вас зовут?	**Kahk vahs** zah-**voot**?
My name is ...	Меня зовут ...	Men-**yah** zah-**voot** ...
Nice to meet you.	Очень приятно.	**Oh**-chen pree-**yaht**-nah!
I'll see you later.	До встречи.	**Dah fstreh**-chee.

POLITE EXPRESSIONS

Please / You're welcome	пожалуйста	pah-**zhah**-loos-tah
Thank you	спасибо	spah-**see**-bah
Yes	да	**dah**
No	нет	**nyet**
Perhaps	может быть	**moh**-zhet **bweet**
I do not understand.	Я не понимаю.	**Yah nee** pah-nee-**mah**-yoo.
I am from USA (America, Britain).	Я из США (Америки, Англии).	**Yah** is **Seh Sheh Ah** (Ah-**myeh**-ree-kee, **Ahn**-glee-ee).
I speak only English.	Я говорю только по-английски.	**Yah** gah-vah-**ryoo tol'**-kah pah-ahn-**glees**-kee.
Do you speak English?	Вы говорите по-английски?	**Vwee** gah-vah-**ree**-tee pah-ahn-**glees**-kee?
Please, show (explain, translate)	Пожалуйста, покажите (объясните, переведите)	Pah-**zhah**-loos-tah, pah-kah-**zhee**-tee (ahb-yas-**nee**-tee, pee-ree-vee-**dee**-tee)

| Excuse my poor pronunciation. | Извините меня за плохое произношение. | Eez-vee-**nee**-tee men-**yah zah** plah-**hoh**-ye prah-eez-nah-**sheh**-nye. |
| I don't know. | Я не знаю. | **Yah nee znah**-yoo. |

QUESTIONS

Who?	Кто?	**Ktoh?**
What?	Что?	**Shtoh?**
Where?	Где?	**Gdyeh?**
When?	Когда?	Kahg-**dah?**
Why?	Почему?	Pah-chee-**moo?**
How do you say ... in Russian?	Как по-русски ...?	**Kahk** pah-**roos**-kee ...?
Do you understand?	Вы понимаете?	**Vwee** pah-nee-**mah**-ee-tye?
Please speak slowly.	Пожалуйста, говорите медленно.	Pah-**zhah**-loos-tah, gah-vah-**reet**-ye **myed**-lee-nah.
Please write it down.	Пожалуйста, напишите.	Pah-**zhah**-loos-tah, nah-pee-**shee**-tee.
Can you please repeat?	Повторите, пожалуйста.	Pahf-tah-**ree**-tee, pah-**zhah**-loos-tah

DIRECTIONS

Where is...	Где ...	**Gdyeh ...**
... the metro station?	... метро (станция метро)?	... meet-**roh** (**stahn**-tsee-yah meet-**roh**)?
... the restroom?	... туалет?	... too-ahl-**yet?**
... the Internet café?	... Интернет-кафе?	... In-terr-**net** café?
... the ... hotel?	... гостиница?	... gahs-**tee**-nee-tsah ...?
... restaurant?	... ресторан?	... rees-tah-**rahn?**
Here/there	тут/там	**toot/tahm**
Left/right	налево/направо	nah-**lyeh**-vah/ nah-**prah**-vah
Straight ahead	прямо	**pryah**-mah
Forward	вперед	**fpee-ryod**
Back	назад	nah-**zahd**

Turn right	поверните направо	pah-verr-**nee**-tee nah-**prah**-vah
Turn left	поверните налево	pah-verr-**nee**-tee nah-**lyeh**-vah
Turn around	развернитесь	rahz-verr-**nee**-tyes
Around the corner	за углом	**zah** oog-**lohm**
Is it near/far?	Это близко/далеко?	**Eht**-tah **blees**-kah/ dah-lee-**koh**?

AT THE HOTEL

I would like a room...	Мне нужен номер ...	Men-**yeh noo**-zhen **noh**-mehr ...
for one person.	... на одного.	... nah ahd-nah-**voh**.
for two people.	... на двоих.	... nah dvah-**eekh**.
for tonight.	... на сутки.	... nah **soot**-kee.
for two nights.	... на двое суток/на два дня.	... nah **dvoh**-ye **soo**-tok/nah **dvah dnyah**.
How much does it cost?	Сколько стоит?	**Skohl**-kah **stoh**-eet?
Do you have another room?	У вас есть другой номер?	Oo **vahs yest** droo-**goy noh**-mehr?
with a private bathroom?	... с ванной и туалетом?	... s **vah**-noy **ee** too-ahl-**yeh**-tahm?
Is there a larger room?	Есть номер побольше?	**Yest noh**-mehr pah-**bohl**-she?

MEALS

breakfast	завтрак	**zahft**-rahk
lunch	обед	ah-**byehd**
dinner	ужин	**oo**-zheen
appetizers	закуски	zah-**koos**-kee
dessert	десерт	dee-**sehrt**
bar	бар	**barr**
café	кафе	kah-**fé**
restaurant	ресторан	rees-tah-**rahn**
menu	меню	men-**yoo**

The menu, please.	Меню, пожалуйста.	Men-**yoo**, pah-**zhah**-loos-tah.
I would like to order.	Примите заказ.	Pree-**mee**-tee zah-**kahz**.
Do you have a vegetarian dish?	У вас есть вегетарианские блюда?	Oo **vahs yest** veh-geh-tah-**ryahn**-skee **blyoo**-dah?
The check, please.	Счет, пожалуйста.	**Schyot**, pah-**zhah**-loos-tah.
To your health!	За ваше здоровье!	Zah **vah**-she zdah-**rohv**-yeh!

TOURING

tourist	турист	too-**reest**
guide	гид	**geed**
museum	музей	moo-**zay**
church	церковь	**tsair**-kahv
monestary	монастырь	mah-nah-**styrr**
palace	дворец	**dvah**-ryehts
open	открыто	aht-**kree**-tah
closed	закрыто	zah-**kree**-tah
admission fee	плата за вход	**plah**-tah zah **fhoht**

DAYS OF THE WEEK

Monday	понедельник	pah-nee-**dyel**-neek
Tuesday	вторник	**ftorr**-neek
Wednesday	среда	sree-**dah**
Thursday	четверг	chet-**vyerk**
Friday	пятница	**pyaht**-neet-sah
Saturday	суббота	soo-**boh**-tah
Sunday	воскресенье	vahs-kree-**syeh**-nye
Holiday, feast	праздник	**prahz**-neek
Today	сегодня	see-**vohd**-nyah
Tomorrow	завтра	**zahf**-trah
Yesterday	вчера	fchee-**rah**

NUMBERS

How many?	Сколько?	**Skohl**-kah?
1	один	ah-**deen**
2	два	**dvah**
3	три	**tree**
4	четыре	che-**teer**-ee
5	пять	**pyaht**
6	шесть	**shest**
7	семь	**syem**
8	восемь	**voh**-syem
9	девять	**dehv**-yat
10	десять	**dehs**-yat
11	одиннадцать	ah-**dee**-nah-tset
12	двенадцать	dvee-**nah**-tset
13	тринадцать	tree-**nah**-tset
14	четырнадцать	che-**teer**-nah-tset
15	пятнадцать	pyat-**nah**-tset
16	шестнадцать	shest-**nah**-tset
17	семнадцать	seem-**nah**-tset
18	восемнадцать	vah-seem-**nah**-tset
19	девятнадцать	dee-vet-**nah**-tset
20	двадцать	**dvah**-tset
30	тридцать	**tree**-tset
40	сорок	**soh**-rahk
50	пятьдесят	pyat-dee-**syaht**
60	шестьдесят	shest-dee-**syaht**
70	семьдесят	**syem**-dee-syaht
80	восемьдесят	**voh**-syem-dee-syaht
90	девяносто	dee-vee-**noh**-stah
100	сто	**stoh**
1000	тысяча	**tee**-se-chah

SIGNS

Toilet (Gentelmen) (Ladies)	Туалет (М), (Ж)	too-ahl-**yeht** (M), (Zh)
No smoking!	Не курить!	**Nee** koo-**reet**!
Taxi stand	стоянка такси	stah-**yahn**-kah tahk-**see**
Entrance	вход	**fhohd**
Exit	выход	**vwee**-hahd
No exit	нет выхода	nyet **vwee**-hah-dah
Emergency exit	запасной выход	zah-pahs-**noy vwee**-hahd
Stop!	Стоп!	**Stohp!**

DRINKS

beverages	напитки	nah-**peet**-kee
cold water	холодная вода	hah-**lohd**-nah-ya vah-**dah**
mineral water	минеральная вода	mee-nee-**rahl**-nah-ya vah-**dah**
grape, tomato, orange juice	виноградный, томатный, апельсиновый сок	vee-nahg-**rahd**-nee, tah-**maht**-nee, ah-peel-see-nah-vee **sohk**
whisky, vodka	виски, водка	**vees**-kee, **voht**-kah
liqueur	ликер	lee-**kyorr**
lemonade	лимонад	lee-mah-**nahd**
beer	пиво	**pee**-vah
tea, coffee, cocoa	чай, кофе, какао	**chai, koh**-fe, kah-**kah**-oh
with sugar/without sugar	с сахаром/без сахара	s **sah**-khah-rahm/**behs sah**-kha-rah
milk, skim	молоко, обезжиренное	mah-lah-**koh**, ah-be-**zzhee**-re-nah-ye
fruit juice	сок	**sohk**
ice	лед	**lyod**

MEAT

meat	мясо	**myah**-sah
steak	стейк	**steak**
roast beef	ростбиф	**rohst**-beef
veal	телятина	teel-**yah**-tee-nah
pork	свинина	svee-**nee**-nah
ham	ветчина	veet-chee-**nah**
sausage	колбаса	kahl-bah-**sah**

POULTRY

chicken	курица	**koo**-reet-sah
hazel-grouse	рябчик	**ryahp**-cheek
partridge	куропатка	koo-rah-**paht**-kah
duck	утка	**oot**-kah

FISH

fish	рыба	**rwee**-bah
red caviar	красная икра	**krahs**-nah-yah eek-**rah**
black caviar	черная икра	**chyorr**-nah-yah eek-**rah**
salmon	лосось, лососина	lah-**sohs**, lah-sah-**see**-nah
sturgeon	осетр, осетрина	ahs-**yotr**, ah-see-**tree**-nah

VEGETABLES

vegetables	овощи	**oh**-vah-schee
green peas	горошек	gah-**roh**-shek
radishes	редиска	ree-**dees**-kah
tomatoes	помидоры	pah-mee-**doh**-rwee
potatoes	картошка	kahrr-**tohsh**-kah
cucumbers	огурцы	ah-goorr-**tsee**
onions	лук	**look**
salad	салат	sah-**laht**

DESSERTS

desserts	десерт	dee-**syert**
cake	торт	**tohrrt**
fruit	фрукты	**frook**-te
apple	яблоко	**yahb**-lah-kah
orange	апельсин	ah-peel-**seen**
pear	груша	**groo**-shah
tangerine	мандарин	mahn-dah-**reen**
grapes	виноград	vee-nahg-**raht**
banana	банан	bah-**nahn**
rye bread	черный хлеб	**chyorr**-nee **khlehp**
white bread	белый хлеб	**beh**-lee **khlehp**
butter	масло	**mahs**-lah
cheese	сыр	**seer**
fried eggs	яичница	ya-**eesh**-nee-tsah
omelet	омлет	ahm-**let**
yogurt	йогурт	**yo**-gurrt

SHOPPING

shopping	шопинг	**shoh**-ping
good	хороший	hah-**roh**-shee
bad	плохой	plah-**hoy**
beautiful	красивый	krah-**see**-vee
dear	дорогой	dah-rah-**goy**
cheap	дешевый	dee-**shoh**-vee
old	старый	**stah**-ree
new	новый	**noh**-vee
How much is it?	Сколько стоит?	**Skohl**-kah **stoh**-eet?
It's expensive/cheap	Это дорого/дешево.	**Eht**-tah **doh**-rah-gah/ **dyo**-she-vah.
I would like this.	Вот это, пожалуйста.	**Voht eht**-tah, pah-**zhah**-loos-tah.

I'd like to pay by credit card.	Я заплачу кредитной картой.	**Yah** zah-**plah-choo** kree-**deet**-noy **kahrr**-toy.
Bakery	булочная	**boo**-lahch-nah-yah
Supermarket	супермаркет	**soo**-perr-**marr**-ket
Store	магазин	mah-gah-**zeen**
Market	рынок, базар	**ree**-nahk, bah-**zaar**
Bookstore	книжный магазин	**kneezh**-nee mah-gah-**zeen**
Drugstore	аптека	ahp-**tyeh**-kah
Wine and Spirits	вино-водочный магазин	**vee**-nah **voh**-dah-chnee mah-gah-**zeen**
Fruit and Vegetables	фрукты и овощи	**frook**-te ee **oh**-vah-schee

EMERGENCIES

Can you help me?	Помогите мне, пожалуйста?	Pah-mah-**geet**-ye men-**yeh**, pah-**zhah**-loos-tah?
I've lost my baggage.	Мой багаж потерялся.	**Moy** bah-**gahzh** pah-teer-**yahl**-syah.
I've lost my wallet.	Я потерял бумажник.	**Yah** pah-teer-**yahl** boo-**mahzh**-neek.
Help!	Помогите!	Pah-mah-**geet**-ye!
Police!	Милиция!	Mee-**lee**-tsee-yah!
Fire!	Пожар!	Pah-**zhahrr**!
I've been robbed.	Меня ограбили.	Men-**yah** ahg-**rah**-bee-lee.
I'm hurt.	Мне больно.	Men-**yeh bohl**-nah.
I need a doctor.	Мне нужен доктор.	Men-**yeh noo**-zhin dohk-torr.

Travel Smart
Moscow and
St. Petersburg

WORD OF MOUTH

"From my former trips to Russia, I remember cumbersome immigration procedures, with declaring all currencies, X-raying bags and even body-searching. This time, it was a breeze. Domodedovo Airport (DME) is a contemporary, state-of-the-art international airport with efficient service. I just left the plane, walked to the baggage claim area, where I waited not more than a minute for my bag, and went through immigration. Practically no lines, I just flashed my passport (with visa), got a couple of stamps, and that was it."

—Echnaton

GETTING HERE AND AROUND

■ AIR TRAVEL

Major U.S. and European carriers have a number of nonstop flights to Russia, making flying here a lot more convenient than it used to be. Two Russian airlines, Aeroflot and Transaero, also make nonstop flights from North America and Europe. Flying time to Moscow is 9½ hours from New York, 10 hours from Washington D.C., 11–13 hours from Chicago, 10½ hours from Atlanta, 12½ hours from Los Angeles, and 11 hours from Miami. From Europe, it's 4 hours from London and 3 hours to Frankfurt. Moscow is 24–30 hours from Sydney, depending on which airline you choose.

Nonstop flights from the United States to Moscow originate in New York; Atlanta; Washington, D.C.; Miami; and Los Angeles. To St. Petersburg from the U.S., your options are either a direct flight, which requires at least one stop (usually in Moscow), or a connecting flight, which requires a change of airplanes. Some flights, especially those that are nonstop, may be scheduled only on certain days of the week. Depending on your destination and the originating city, you may need to make more than one connection. Your best bet is to use Helsinki or Frankfurt, which have the greatest number of connecting flights. Helsinki is less than an hour by air from St. Petersburg and less than two hours from Moscow.

Two airlines may operate a connecting flight jointly, so ask whether your airline operates every segment of the trip; you may find that the carrier you prefer flies you only part of the way. To find more booking tips and to check prices and make online flight reservations, log on to ⊕ www.fodors.com.

If you're flying as an independent traveler within the CIS (Commonwealth of Independent States, a quasi-confederation of states that includes most of the former Soviet Union), it's best to purchase your ticket with a credit card via an agent in your home country or a reputable one in Russia. This will allow you the best chance for refunds if your flight is canceled. Russian airlines have a habit of permitting refunds only at the office at which the ticket was purchased. If you book from abroad, you should reconfirm your reservation in person as soon as you arrive in the country.

Note that in Russia, check-in officially ends 40 minutes before departure, and if you arrive late you may need to do some serious begging to be allowed onto the plane. At St. Petersburg's Pulkovo I, there is a separate check-in for flights to Moscow—take the entrance on the right-hand side of the upper floor of the building.

Smoking is prohibited on all international flights, but some of the smaller Russian carriers may have designated smoking areas partitions off by a curtain on some of their domestic flights. Ask your carrier about its policy.

Within Russia, you do not normally need to reconfirm your outbound flight or intra-destination flights.

Airlines and Airports Airline and Airport Links.com (⊕ www.airlineandairportlinks.com) has links to many of the world's airlines and airports.

Airline Security Issues Transportation Security Administration (⊕ www.tsa.gov) has answers for almost every question that might come up.

AIRPORTS

The major international airports are Sheremetyevo II Airport (airport code SVO), which also handles some domestic flights, and Domodedovo (DME) in Moscow. Pulkovo II Airport (LED) is the international airport in St. Petersburg.

For domestic travel, Moscow has three airports in addition to Sheremetyevo II:

Sheremetyevo I (for flights to the north and west), Domodedovo (for eastern destinations and for the carriers British Airways, United Airlines, and Transaero), and Vnukovo (VKO) (for southern destinations). In St. Petersburg, there's one airport other than Pulkovo II: Pulkovo I, which handles domestic flights. Even though the departing or arriving airport may be printed on your ticket, double-check this information with your local travel agent.

Airport Information **Domodedovo Airport** (☎ 495/933–6666 ⊕ www.domodedovo. ru). **Pulkovo I Airport** (☎ 812/704–3822 ⊕ www.pulkovoairport.ru). **Pulkovo II Airport** (☎ 812/704–3444). **Sheremetyevo I Airport** (☎ 495/232–6565 ⊕ www.sheremetyevo-airport.ru). **Sheremetyevo II Airport** (☎ 495/956–4666 or 495/578–9101). **Vnukovo Airport** (☎ 495/436–2813).

GROUND TRANSPORTATION
(For information on getting to Moscow and St. Petersburg from the airport, ⇨ Transfers sections in Chapter 2 for Moscow and Chapter 8 for St. Petersburg.)

FLIGHTS
When flying internationally, you must usually choose among a domestic carrier, the national flag carrier of the country you are visiting (Aeroflot-Russian International Airlines), and a foreign carrier from a third country. National flag carriers have the greatest number of nonstop flights. Domestic carriers may have better connections to your hometown and serve a greater number of gateway cities. Third-party carriers may have a price advantage.

Within Russia, in addition to Aeroflot, there are several smaller, regional airlines (sometimes called "babyflots"). Aeroflot offers good international service between Russia and some 140 destinations, and it also flies several domestic routes. The babyflots are slowly bringing their service up to international standards, and service to and from St. Petersburg and Moscow is far better than that between smaller cities. Although the older Russian aircraft are

being phased out in favor of Boeing and Airbus planes, they're still much in use. On the better airlines, this is nothing to worry about, but the state of the cabin may be shabbier than what you're used to.

Two airlines that stand head and shoulders above the rest are Transaero, which flies to several destinations in Europe and the CIS, and has internal flights to major Russian cities; and Rossiya (formerly known as Pulkovo), which also has a number of international flights as well as good domestic service. Both have established partnerships with international airlines in order to increase their reach—Transaero has links to the United States with Continental, Virgin, and Lufthansa, for example. A third domestic airline that will take you into the heart of Siberia (and elsewhere) is S7 (formerly known as Sibir), which coordinates some of its routes with Aeroflot and the One World group of airlines.

Delays and cancellations are more frequent in winter, particularly in those places where the climate is severe. The farther east you go from Moscow, the more unreliable air travel can be. If possible, stick to the airlines mentioned above.

Airline Contacts **Aeroflot-Russian International Airlines** (✉ *10 Rockefeller Plaza, Suite 1015, New York, NY* ☎ *888/340–6400 or 212/944–2300 in U.S., 495/223–5555 in Moscow, 812/718–5555 in St. Petersburg* ⊕ *www.aeroflot.ru/cms/en).* **Air France** (☎ *800/237–2747 in U.S., 495/937–3839 in Moscow, 812/336–2900 in St. Petersburg* ⊕ *www.airfrance.com).* **British Airways** (☎ *800/247–9297 in U.S., 495/363–2525 in Moscow, 812/380–0626 in St. Petersburg* ⊕ *www.britishairways.com).* **Czech Airlines** (☎ *212/765–6545 in U.S., 495/973–1847 in Moscow* ⊕ *www.csa.cz).* **Delta Airlines** (☎ *800/221–1212 for U.S. reservations, 800/241–4141 for international reservations, 495/937–9090 in Moscow, 812/571–5820 or 812/571–5819 in St. Petersburg* ⊕ *www.delta.com).* **Finnair** (☎ *800/950–5000 in U.S., 495/933–0056 in Moscow, 812/303–9898 in St. Petersburg* ⊕ *www.finnair.com).* **KLM**

(☎ 800/374-7747 in U.S., 495/258-3600 in Moscow, 812/346-6868 in St. Petersburg ⊕ www.klm.com). **Lufthansa** (☎ 800/645-3880 in U.S., 495/980-9999 in Moscow, 812/320-1000 in St. Petersburg ⊕ www.lufthansa.com). **SAS** (☎ 800/221-2350 in U.S., 495/775-4747 in Moscow, 812/326-2600 in St. Petersburg ⊕ www.flysas.com). **United Airlines** (☎ 800/864-8331 for U.S. reservations, 800/538-2929 for international reservations ⊕ www.united.com).

Within Russia **Rossiya (formerly known as Pulkovo)** (☎ 812/704-3428 international flights, 495/995-2025 in Moscow, 812/333-2222 in St. Petersburg for domestic flights ⊕ www.rossiya-airlines.com). **S7 (formerly known as Sibir)** (☎ 495/777-9999 in Moscow, 812/718-6876 in St. Petersburg ⊕ www.s7.ru). **Transaero** (☎ 877/747-1191 in U.S., 495/788-8080 in Moscow or 800/200-2376 toll free throughout Russia ⊕ www.transaero.ru).

▌ BOAT TRAVEL

Moscow has a river-taxi service that runs from Kiev train station to the Southern River Terminal from April to October, with stops at Gorky Park and the bottom of Sparrow Hills. The open-top boats are more of a tourist attraction than a form of commuter transport, although they can beat the traffic snarls. Tickets cost 300R for adults and 150R for children, and the timetable can be found at the ferry stops. Trips last about 1½ hours, and it's possible to buy drinks and snacks on board. The same company organizes longer tours in and around Moscow. In St. Petersburg, canal tours are offered at several locations in the city center. Look for the signs near the bridges and along the Fontanka. There are also pleasure cruises from St. Petersburg that pass by some of the summer palaces, and trips to Valaam Island, Kizhi Island, and Moscow. *(For more information on river cruises, ⇨ Boat and Ferry Travel in Chapter 2 for Moscow and Chapter 8 for St. Petersburg.)*

Boat Info **Capital Shipping Company** (☎ 495/225-6070 ⊕ www.cck-ship.ru/cck).

CRUISES

All the major cruise lines listed below visit Russia, but they only dock at St. Petersburg, and it's making a brief stop-off. Crystal Cruises has tours that go between Copenhagen and Stockholm and between London and Stockholm with three days in St. Petersburg. Cunard has a Russian Rendezvous tour that goes from Southampton and stops off in St. Petersburg for two days. It also visits Poland and Estonia. Princess Cruises sails a round-trip from Copenhagen that stops off in Berlin and spends two days in St. Petersburg. Regent Seven Seas has a tour from Stockholm to Copenhagen. Its visit to St. Petersburg includes a day spent at the Hermitage and its restoration workshops and an onboard lecture from a Russian art expert.

International cruise lines offering tours to Russia usually disembark in St. Petersburg and continue to Moscow by land. Some cruises follow the Volga River between Moscow and St. Petersburg on a journey of up to two weeks. It's also possible to take longer trips calling at destinations such as the southern cities of Volgograd and Astrakhan and east to Kazan. (⇨ Moscow and St. Petersburg chapters for more information.)

Cruise Lines **Celebrity Cruises** (☎ 800/647-2251 ⊕ www.celebrity.com). **Costa Cruises** (☎ 954/266-5600 or 800/462-6782 ⊕ www.costacruise.com). **Crystal Cruises** (☎ 310/785-9300 or 800/446-6620 ⊕ www.crystalcruises.com). **Cunard Line** (☎ 661/753-1000 or 800/728-6273 ⊕ www.cunard.com). **Holland America Line** (☎ 206/281-3535 or 877/932-4259 ⊕ www.hollandamerica.com). **Mediterranean Shipping Cruises** (☎ 212/764-4800 or 800/666-9333 ⊕ www.msccruises.com). **Norwegian Cruise Line** (☎ 305/436-4000 or 800/327-7030 ⊕ www.ncl.com). **Oceania Cruises** (☎ 305/514-2300 or 800/531-5658 ⊕ www.oceaniacruises.com). **Princess Cruises** (☎ 661/753-0000 or 800/774-6237 ⊕ www.princess.com). **Regent Seven Seas Cruises** (☎ 954/776-6123 or 800/477-7500 ⊕ www.rssc.com). **Royal Caribbean International** (☎ 305/539-6000 or

800/327–6700 ⊕ www.royalcaribbean.com).
Seabourn Cruise Line (☎ 305/463–3000 or
800/929–9391 ⊕ www.seabourn.com). **Silver-
sea Cruises** (☎ 954/522–4477 or 800/722–
9955 ⊕ www.silversea.com).

River Cruises Amadeus Waterways
(✉ 21625 Prairie St., Chatsworth, CA
☎ 800/626–0126 ⊕ www.amadeuswaterways.
com). **GlobalQuest** (✉ 185 Willis Ave.,
2nd fl., Mineola, NY ☎ 516/739–3690 or
800/221–3254 🖷 516/739–8022 ⊕ www.
globalquesttravel.com). **Infoflot** (✉ 28 Shchep-
kina ul., Moscow ☎ 495/684–9188 ⊕ www.
infoflot.com). **Orthodox Cruise Company**
(✉ 5 ul. Alabyana, Moscow ☎ 495/943–8560
or 495/943–8561 🖷 495/198–1101 ⊕ www.
cruise.ru). **Smithsonian Journeys** (✍ Box
23293, Washington, DC 20026 ☎ 877/338–or
800/338–8687 🖷 202/633–6088 ⊕ www.
smithsonianjourneys.org). **Uniworld** (✉ 17323
Ventura Blvd., Encino, CA 91316 ☎ 818/382–
7820 or 800/733–7820 🖷 818/382–7829
⊕ www.uniworld.com). **Viking River Cruises**
(✉ 5700 Canooga Ave., Suite 200, Woodland
Hills, CA 91367 ☎ 800/304–9616 or 818/227–
1234 ⊕ www.vikingrivers.com).

∎ BUS TRAVEL

Traveling by bus can be daunting in Russia if you do not speak the language.
When you can, you should travel by train
or suburban train (*elektrichka*). But for
some smaller towns and suburban destinations, this may be the only way to
travel.

Ticket offices tend to have long hours of
operation, and you can typically purchase
your bus ticket ahead of time at the city
avtovokzal, or bus station. Payment is
accepted only in rubles.

If you have any contact who will help
negotiate the purchase for you, avail yourself of him or her. Handwritten seating
charts and tickets are the norm, but tickets are sold even when there are no seats
left (even for longer rides). This leads to
some very crowded conditions (and, on
hot days, quite stuffy situations, as these

buses, although reasonably comfortable,
do not have air-conditioning and only
sometimes do their windows open). It's
recommended that you buy advance tickets for peak long-distance travel days—
Friday, Saturday, and Sunday.

There are long-distance international
buses to the Baltic States, several CIS
countries and some points in Europe
including Helsinki, Berlin, and Warsaw.
The trips are long and often require extensive waiting times at the border.

∎ CAR TRAVEL

Driving in Russia is not for the faint-
hearted. You must first be comfortable
driving on roads marked only with Cyrillic
and/or international symbols; you must be
willing to deal with the bribe-hungry traffic inspectors; and you must be prepared
for poor and sometimes even dangerous
road conditions. Even the main highways
have potholes and are in poor condition.
Repair stations are few and far between,
and many places sell poor-quality gasoline. In addition, you should not underestimate the risk of crime: highway robbery
and car theft are common, and foreign
drivers are often targets. Do not stop to
help motorists whose cars appear to have
broken down, even if they wave at you for
help—this is a classic ambush technique.
Never leave anything of value inside your
car. In light of these concerns, you may
wish to hire a car and driver rather than
driving yourself (⇨ Car Rental).

If you do choose to drive, note that your
own driver's license is not acceptable in
Russia. You'll need an International Driver's Permit and, if traveling into the country by car, an international certificate of
registration of the car in the country of
departure. You'll also need a certificate
of obligation (which should be registered
with customs at the point of entry; consult
your rental company about this) if you
have plans for driving a rental car in over
the border. International Driving Permits
(IDPs) are available from the American

and Canadian automobile associations and, in the United Kingdom, from the Automobile Association and Royal Automobile Club. All of these documents will need to have a certified Russian translation, which you can obtain at a Russian consulate or embassy before you leave.

GASOLINE

More and more stations bearing the names of major oil companies have opened, and it's easy to find somewhere to fill up, even outside of major towns. However, you may not be able to pay with a credit card. Always ask for a *chek*, or receipt. Gas prices are comparable to those in the United States. It's also fairly easy to find unleaded gasoline; for leaded gas, foreign cars should be filled only with 95-octane gas. Russian-made cars run on 92-octane. Gas is sold by the liter. Some stations provide full service, while at others you pump your own gas.

PARKING

Moscow has some off-the-street parking in the big shopping malls. Often, random sections of curb will be cordoned off and you will be expected to pay a guard—who may or may not be acting in an official capacity—to park there. The "official" city parking guards should wear uniforms with the parking price—currently 50R per hour in the city center—printed on the back. There are no parking meters. Cars parked illegally run the risk of being towed away. The driver then has to spend hours filling in official documents and pay a fine. Expect to see stricter parking rules in Moscow as the current mayor, Sergey Sobyanin, has made improving transportation in the capital a top priority.

ROAD CONDITIONS

Around Moscow and St. Petersburg, most of the country roads have been paved with asphalt. Nonetheless, driving in winter can be dangerously slippery, and the spring thaw can turn roadways into lakes. Driving in snowy conditions in the cities is only for the experienced—Russian drivers see fallen snow as an obstacle to be overcome, not as a reason to take the metro.

ROADSIDE EMERGENCIES

Because service stations are few and poorly stocked, it's recommended that for long distances you carry a complete emergency repair kit, including a set of tools, a towing cable, a pressure gauge, a pump, a spare tire, a repair outfit for tubeless tires, a good jack and one or two tire levers, a gasoline can, a spare fan belt, spare windshield-wiper blades, and spark plugs. You should also have a set of headlight bulbs and fuses, a set of contact-breaker points for the ignition distributor, a spare condenser, a box of tire valve interiors, and a roll of insulating tape. There's no national emergency service to call, but if you're in the Moscow area, consider joining the Angel Club, an autoclub that offers some emergency services Angel Club (☏ 495/747–0022 ⊕ *angelclub.ru*).

RULES OF THE ROAD

Driving regulations are strict, but they're often broken by local drivers; a good rule of thumb is to drive defensively. Traffic keeps to the right. The speed limit on highways is 90 kph (56 mph); in towns and populated areas it's 60 kph (37 mph), although on the wide streets of Moscow few people observe this rule. It's illegal to use a mobile phone while driving, but again you are likely to see many drivers on their phones. You can proceed at traffic intersections only when the light is green—this includes left and right turns. You must wait for a signal—an arrow—permitting the turn, and give way to pedestrians crossing. Wearing front seat belts is compulsory; driving while intoxicated carries very heavy fines, including imprisonment. Do not consume any alcohol at all if you plan to drive. You should also keep your car clean—you can be fined for having a dirty car.

Traffic control in Russia is exercised by traffic inspectors (GIBDD, but still commonly known as GAI), who are stationed all over cities and at permanent posts out of town; they also patrol in cars and on motorcycles and like to sit in ambush. They may stop you for no apparent reason other than to check your documentation. In this event, you're not required to exit your vehicle. Do not ignore attempts by a traffic cop—known colloquially as *gaishnik*—to flag you over. Remember that the GIBDD is regarded as a confounded nuisance by most Russians, and the friendly cop who will provide directions to gas stations or garages is rare. Traffic cops are also good at finding *something* wrong with your documentation and/or your driving; this may be nothing more than an attempt to secure a bribe.

CAR RENTAL

If you don't speak Russian and don't have local knowledge, don't drive in Russia, particularly around Moscow and St. Petersburg. The poor roads, dangerous drivers, and unwanted police attention all make doing so dangerous. To explore parts that are off the beaten path, or visit nearby towns in warmer weather, a car is certainly convenient, but can be very expensive. Some hotels will make car-rental arrangements for you. Otherwise, several international car-rental agencies have offices in Moscow; be sure to reserve at least three days in advance.

Car-rental rates are all over the map in Russia, but if you shop around you should be able to get rates from the major chains for as low as $60 a day for a Russian car (manual, no air) with at least 100 free km (60 mi) per day. If you want a foreign car, automatic transmission, or air-conditioning, they will cost you more. These prices usually include the tax on car rentals, which is 18%. Insurance is mandatory (Russian rentals usually include the cost of insurance).

All agencies require advance reservations (at least two to three days is a good idea), and you'll have to show your driver's license, an International Driving Permit (IDP), and a credit card.

Children's car seats aren't mandatory in Russia, but agencies are able to provide them. Ask for one when you book your

---

> **WORD OF MOUTH**
>
> "The primary reason for the train is the experience of it. You can choose which type of train according to your interests. As for the snow season, there is nothing like Russia in the winter, and an overnight train journey is even better." —Odin

---

car. You'll pay about 125R per day for a seat.

If you're returning a car to Sheremetyevo II, bear in mind that the Leningradskoye shosse leading to the airport is notoriously slow. Allow two hours for the drive from the center.

If you would rather hire a car with driver—and we think it's a way to avoid a lot of potential hassle—you can do so for about 375R–875R per hour. Major hotels will arrange this service for their guests. Some local tour companies, such as Patriarshy Dom Tours, or Western travel agents specializing in independent travel, such as Mir Corporation, can arrange daily-rate car-and-driver options, which are less expensive.

Car and Driver Hire Mir Corporation (☎ 800/424–7289 in U.S. ⊕ www.mircorp.com). **Patriarshy Dom Tours** (☎ 495/795–0927 in Moscow, 650/678–7076 in the U.S. ⊕ www. russiatravel-pdtours.netfirms.com).

▌ TRAIN TRAVEL

In Russia trains are the most reliable, convenient, and comfortable form of transportation. Remarkably, most trains leave exactly on time; there's a broadcast warning five minutes before departure, but no whistle or "all aboard!" call, so be careful not to be left behind.

There are numerous day and overnight trains between St. Petersburg and Moscow. The new Sapsan express train makes the trip in just over four hours and has several departures a day from each city. The Siemens-built trains travel at speeds of 150 mph. Other fast day trains include the *Avrora* and *Nevsky Express,* which take around four hours, 30 minutes and also have comfortable compartments. The *Grand Express,* which runs overnight, has showers in the compartments of the higher classes, and hand basins in lower classes, as well as satellite television and other amenities.

Train travel in Russia offers an unrivaled opportunity to glimpse the Russian countryside, which is dotted in places with colorful wooden cottages. If you're traveling by overnight train, set your alarm and get up an hour or so before arrival so that you can watch at close hand the workers going about their morning rounds in the rural areas just outside the cities.

To make your train trip more comfortable, be sure to bring along bottled water, both for drinking and brushing your teeth on longer journeys. Vendors run up and down train cars at and between stops, selling drinks and sandwiches. You may, however, want to bring a packed meal; most Russians do so, and your compartment mates may offer to share (beware of offers of vodka, however; poison bootleg vodka is a big problem in Russia). The communal bathrooms at both ends of each car can be dirty, so bring premoistened cleansing tissues for washing up. You may want to pack toilet paper just to be on the safe side, although it's rare now for train bathrooms to be without it. Also be sure to pack a heavy sweater. The cars are often overheated and toasty warm, but sometimes they're not heated at all, so in winter it can get very cold, especially in the smoking areas between cars. (Note: smoking in the cars is not acceptable, but smokers will find plenty of company in between cars.)

Train travel to most major cities inside Russia is fairly painless, but you should stick to the usual precautions when it comes to security. If you're traveling alone on an overnight train, you should take extra security precautions. You may want to buy out the entire compartment so as not to risk your luck with unknown compartment-mates. Conductors who find out you have done this will often insist this is not permissible, and threaten to put a cabin-mate in with you. Do not allow this. Show the tickets to all the berths, and be firm. To be on the safe side you should stow your luggage in the bin under the lower bunk, and you should sleep with your money, passport, and other important items.

On the more expensive trains (the lower the train number, the faster and more expensive the journey), you're likely to share compartments with businessmen or families. Many travelers to Russia say their trips on overnight trains have proven to be some of their most memorable experiences. For many, it is a chance to get to know real Russians, despite language barriers.

Trains are divided into four classes. The highest class, "deluxe," is usually available only on trains traveling international routes. The deluxe class offers two-berth compartments with soft seats and private washrooms; the other classes have washrooms at the end of the cars. First-class service—the highest class for domestic routes—is called "soft-seat," with spring-cushion berths (two berths to a compartment). When buying your ticket, ask for "SV."

There's rarely segregation of the sexes (although this has been introduced as an experiment on a few train services), and no matter what class of service you choose, you could end up sharing a compartment with someone of the opposite sex. Never fear. There is an unspoken system on Russian trains that allows each passenger to change into comfortable train clothes in privacy. Your traveling partner will most likely signal this by exiting the compartment for you to change. When he or she returns 15 minutes later, consider that your signal to do the same.

Second-class service, or "hard-seat" service—ask for *coupé*—has a cushion on wooden berths, with four berths to a compartment. The third class—wooden berths without compartments—is not the most comfortable choice but sometimes necessary. Known in Russian as *platskart,* this class entails an almost complete surrender of privacy in an open compartment. If you have to travel in this class, be sure to keep your valuables on you at all times.

Most compartments have a small table, limited room for baggage (including under the seats), and a radio that can be turned down, but not off. In soft-seat compartments there are also table lamps. The price of the ticket may or may not include use of bedding; sometimes this fee (which will not be much more than 150R) is collected by the conductor.

All of the cars are also equipped with samovars. Back in the days of Communism, the conductor would offer tea to passengers before bedtime. It's not uncommon in soft-seat class to be offered tea in the evening and morning, plus a small boxed meal. For second- or third-class travel, you may want to bring some tea bags or instant coffee and a mug, since you can take hot water from the samovar at any time.

Russian Railways is experimenting with online ticket purchases. At this writing, this can only be done easily if you have Russian language skills, although an English booking site is in the works. In the meantime, there are several online services, such as Way To Russia, Visit Russia, and Russian Passport, who will buy the tickets for you for a nominal service fee. Tickets go on sale 45 days prior to departure, and for popular routes during peak travel times (summer and winter holidays), it's advisable to buy them as far in advance as possible. Note that you must show your passport or a photocopy when purchasing train tickets. Your best bet is to go to Moscow or St. Petersburg's central booking office, although you can buy tickets for any destination at any mainline train station. Telephone inquiries for train services usually involve poor lines and clerks who speak only Russian. Try to get your hotel, a Russian acquaintance, or an independent travel agency to help you book tickets. A one-way ticket between Moscow and St. Petersburg on the Sapsan express train start at 2,350R. The Grand Express overnight train starts at 4,380R for the luxury class. *For more information,* ⇨ *Train Travel in Chapter 2 for Moscow and Chapter 8 for St. Petersburg.*

Train Info Russian Railways (☎ *800/775– 0000 toll free in Russia* ⊕ *rzd.ru*).

Train Travel and Visa Support Russian Passport (⊕ *www.russia-rail.com*). **Visit Russia** (⊕ *www.visitrussia.com*). **Way to Russia** (⊕ *www.waytorussia.net*).

ESSENTIALS

■ COMMUNICATIONS

INTERNET

Checking your email or surfing the Web can often be done in the business centers of major hotels, which usually charge an hourly rate. Web access is also available at many fax and copy centers, many of which are open 24 hours and on weekends. The easiest way to get online in Moscow and St. Petersburg is to visit one of the plentiful cafés, many of which offer free Wi-Fi. Some require you to pay an hourly rate, which can run from about 60R, or $2, per hour and up.

PHONES

The good news is that you can now make a direct-dial telephone call from virtually any point on earth. The bad news? You can't always do so cheaply. Calling from a hotel is almost always the most expensive option; hotels usually add huge surcharges to all calls, particularly international ones. In some countries you can phone from call centers or even the post office. Calling cards usually keep costs to a minimum, but only if you purchase them locally. And then there are mobile phones (⇨ *below*), which are sometimes more prevalent—particularly in the developing world—than landlines; as expensive as mobile phone calls can be, they are still usually a much cheaper option than calling from your hotel.

The country code for Russia is 7. Moscow has two city codes, 495 and 499; St. Petersburg's is 812. When dialing a Russian number from abroad, drop the initial 0 from the local area code.

The country code is 1 for the United States and Canada, 61 for Australia, 64 for New Zealand, and 44 for the United Kingdom.

CALLING WITHIN RUSSIA

Direct dialing is the only way to go. Russian phone numbers have 10 digits (including the area code). To use your North American cell phone in Russia, it must be tri or quad band. If it's an unlocked GSM cell phone, purchase and install a SIM card so that you'll be charged Russian rates for usage while there.

Throughout the country you can dial 09 for directory assistance. However, because directory workers and operators are underpaid, overworked, and speak only Russian, you probably have a better chance of getting telephone information from your hotel concierge or a friendly assistant at a business center.

Public phones, which are similar to those found in most other European countries, can be harder to find these days, as most Russians have mobile phones. The modern public phones are all card-operated, and the line tends to be atrocious. You can buy cards at kiosks.

City centers have telephone centers handy for making all sorts of calls: in Moscow, try the Central Telegraph office at 7 Tverskaya ulitsa, and St. Petersburg has one located at 2 Bolshaya Morskaya ulitsa.

For long-distance calls within Russia, simply dial 8, wait for another dial tone, and then dial the rest of the number as listed.

CALLING OUTSIDE RUSSIA

The country code for the United States is 1.

Most hotels have satellite telephone booths where, for several dollars a minute, you can make an international call in a matter of seconds. If you want to economize, you can visit the main post or telegraph office and order a call for rubles (but you'll still pay about a dollar or two a minute). From your hotel room or from a private residence, you can dial direct. To place your call, dial 8, wait for the dial tone, then dial 10, then the country code (1 for the United States) followed by the number you're trying to reach. In the Western-managed hotels, rooms are usually equipped with international, direct-dial (via satellite) telephones, but beware that the rates are hefty.

LOCAL DO'S AND TABOOS

CUSTOMS OF THE COUNTRY

In general, there's no such thing as being overdressed in Russia. Bring some nice, urban, dressy clothes. Russians believe that keeping shoes clean is particularly important, even when the weather conditions make this difficult.

SIGHTSEEING

Russia is far stricter about enforcing dress codes at religious sites than are most similar places in Europe. Men are expected to remove their hats, and women are required to wear below-knee-length skirts or slacks (*never* shorts) and bring something to cover their heads. It's considered disrespectful to put your hands inside your pockets when visiting an Orthodox church.

OUT ON THE TOWN

When entering a restaurant, you will be asked to leave your coat in a cloakroom. This is virtually compulsory in more formal, upscale establishments. To hail a male waiter, catch his eye and say *molodoi cholovik*; to attract a waitress, say *devushka*. To ask for the check, say *Chek, pozhaluista*. Most restaurants allow smoking, although a few have token nonsmoking areas. Diners usually dress smartly, although it's rare for a restaurant to insist on a jacket and tie.

At a dinner, usually a carafe or bottle of vodka will be ordered for the whole table and shots will be gulped down whole (not sipped) after repeated toasts throughout the meal. Shots will usually be poured for women even if they don't want any. Although it's quite acceptable for a woman to not drink vodka and to have wine or champagne instead, men are obliged. It's not good form to drink vodka without food.

If you're invited to a home, be ready to remove your shoes and put on some of the household's communal slippers.

If you meet any Russians socially, chances are they'll give you something; Russians tend to give small gifts even on short acquaintance. You may want to be prepared to reciprocate with souvenirs from your hometown or state, such as postcards, pens, or decorative pins. One of the great taboos, however, is to present someone with a gift, shake hands, or kiss across the threshold or doorway. Wait until you're inside. If the hosts have children, it's appropriate to bring them some small sweets or trinkets.

DOING BUSINESS

Gift-giving is also the norm in business relations—as is drinking. Personal trust and personal relations are more important in Russian business than in the West, so businesspeople should be willing to take part in all sorts of bonding sessions, from vodka drinking to visiting the *banya*, or Russian-style sauna. That said, vodka-drinking sessions with strangers should be avoided, especially on trains.

LANGUAGE

Try to learn a little of the local language. You need not strive for fluency; even just mastering a few basic words and terms is bound to make chatting with the locals more rewarding.

If you make an effort to learn the Russian (Cyrillic) alphabet, you'll be able to decipher many words; a rudimentary knowledge of the alphabet can help you to navigate the streets and subways on your own. Hotel staff almost always speak good English. If you need to find an English-speaking person on the street, the younger generation tends to speak more English than the older.

The following terms pop up in this book and may help you in your travels: *dom*, or house; *dvor*, or courtyard; *dvorets*, or palace; *khram*, or church; *monastyr*, or monastery or convent; *muzey*, or museum; *palata*, or palace; *passazh*, or arcade; *sobor*, or cathedral; *stantsiya*, or metro station; *teatr*, or theater; *tserkov*, or church; *vokzal*, or train/bus station; and *vorota*, or gateway.

If you want to save money, computer applications such as Skype and Google's voice and video chat are both good ways to stay in contact with people back home. If you didn't bring your computer with you, such services are also frequently available in Internet cafés. Another option is to set up an international call-back account in the United States before you go. These services can often save you as much as half off the rates of the big carriers. To use the call-back account, you must dial a preestablished number in the United States from any phone in Moscow or St. Petersburg, let the call ring a few times, then hang up. In a few minutes, a computer calls you back and makes a connection, giving you a U.S. dial tone, from which you dial any number in the United States.

ACCESS CODES

AT&T Direct (☎ 8/755–5042 from Moscow to U.S., 8/10–800–110–1011 or 8/10–800–120–1011 from within other cities in Russia). **MCI WorldPhone** (☎ 747–3320 or 747–3322, when dialing from Moscow use city code 495; use 812 from St. Petersburg). **Sprint International Access** (☎ 8/10–800–120–2011 from Russia to U.S).

Callback Company Kallback (☎ 877/777–5242 ⊕ www.kallback.com).

CALLING CARDS

Phone cards can be bought at street kiosks that also sell cards for dial-up Internet access. You stick the card in the pay phone (there's a picture showing you the right way) and wait for the dial tone. Then press 8 and wait for another dial tone, then dial the number. A number will flash on the screen showing you how many units you have left; as you speak, units are subtracted from your total.

MOBILE PHONES

If you have a multiband phone (some countries use different frequencies from those used in the United States) and your service provider uses the world-standard GSM network (as do T-Mobile, AT&T, and Verizon), you can probably use your phone abroad. Roaming fees can be steep, however. When overseas you normally pay the toll charges for incoming calls. It's almost always cheaper to send a text message than to make a call, since text messages have a very low set fee (often 15¢).

If you just want to make local calls, consider buying a new SIM card (note that your provider may have to unlock your phone for you to use a different SIM card) and a prepaid service plan in the destination. You'll then have a local number and can make local calls at local rates. If your trip is extensive, you could also simply buy a new cell phone in your destination, as the initial cost will be offset over time.

■**TIP➔** If you travel internationally frequently, save one of your old mobile phones or buy a cheap one on the Internet; ask your cell phone company to unlock it for you, and take it with you as a travel phone, buying a new SIM card with pay-as-you-go service in each destination.

To get around the problem of unlocking a U.S. cell phone, you could buy a cell phone in Russia. The country has embraced cell phones with enthusiasm, and you can buy them in stores on every corner. Basic models can be found for less than $50. Handsets are not usually sold as a package with a service provider, so you simply choose which network you want to join. Offices for the main providers, Beeline, MTS, and Megafon, are ubiquitous. They may ask to see your registration card and passport before signing you up. The country uses GSM.

Contacts Cellular Abroad (☎ 800/287–5072 ⊕ www.cellularabroad.com) rents and sells GSM phones and sells SIM cards that work in many countries. **Mobal** (☎ 888/888–9162 ⊕ www.mobalrental.com) rents mobiles and sells GSM phones (starting at $49) that will operate in 140 countries. Per-call rates vary throughout the world. **Planet Fone** (☎ 888/988–4777 ⊕ www.planetfone.com) rents cell phones, but the per-minute rates are expensive.

■ CUSTOMS AND DUTIES

You're always allowed to bring goods of a certain value back home without having to pay any duty or import tax. But there's a limit on the amount of tobacco and liquor you can bring back duty-free, and some countries have separate limits for perfumes; for exact figures, check with your customs department. The values of so-called duty-free goods are included in these amounts. When you shop abroad, save all your receipts, as customs inspectors may ask to see them as well as the items you purchased. If the total value of your goods is more than the duty-free limit, you'll have to pay a tax (most often a flat percentage) on the value of everything beyond that limit.

Upon arrival in Russia, you first pass through passport control, where a border guard will carefully examine your passport and visa.

It's very important that you fill out a migration card and get it stamped while passing though passport control. These white cards are automatically issued on some flights, but not all. It's possible to enter the country without one, but lack of a card can cause all manner of headaches, from hotel registration problems to document checks by police. If you're not given a card, ask for one (*migratsionnaya karta* for one, *migratsionnye karty* for several) or look for them on stands in the arrivals hall.

If you haven't been given a customs form on the plane, look for the forms on a table or stand at customs after retrieving your luggage. You must keep it until your departure, when you'll be asked to present it again (along with a second, identical form noting any changes). You may import free of duty and without special license any articles intended for personal use, including clothing, food, tobacco, up to 200 cigarettes, two liters of alcoholic drinks, perfume, sports equipment, and camera equipment. One video camera and one laptop computer per person are allowed. Importing weapons and ammunition, as well as opium, hashish, and pipes for smoking them, is prohibited. The punishment for carrying illegal substances is severe. You are allowed to bring up to $10,000 in cash without declaring it. It's important to include any valuable items, such as musical instruments, and the like, on the customs form to ensure that you'll be allowed to take them back with you out of Russia (note that you're expected to take them with you, so you cannot leave them behind as gifts). If an item included on your customs form is stolen, you should obtain a police report to avoid being questioned upon departure. Technically you're allowed to bring into the country only up to $3,000 of consumer items for personal use and gifts. But customs agents at the airport have been enforcing this rule sporadically at best, and will not likely challenge you on this front unless you have an excessive amount of luggage. For information about bringing domestic animals in and out of Russia, see ⊕ *www.moscowanimals.org*.

Anything that is likely to be considered valuable art or an antique (this could include coins, manuscripts or icons) by customs officials requires a receipt from the Committee for Culture showing that you have paid a special tax on it. Art and antique dealers usually have updated information about this, but for more details call ☎ *495/244–7675* in Moscow and ⊕ *812/311–5196* in St. Petersburg.

INFORMATION IN RUSSIA

The **Russian Federal Customs Service** (⊕ *www.customs.ru/en*) has some information in English.

U.S. Information **U.S. Customs and Border Protection** (⊕ *www.cbp.gov*).

■ EATING OUT

MEALS AND MEALTIMES

At traditional Russian restaurants, the main meal of the day is served in midafternoon and consists of a starter, soup, and a main course. Russian soups, which are excellent, include borscht, *shchi* (cabbage soup), and *solyanka*, a spicy, thick stew made with vegetables and meat or fish. Delicious and filling main courses include Siberian *pelmeni* (tender dumplings, usually filled with minced pork and beef, and sometimes also lamb) or beef Stroganoff. If you're looking for Russian delicacies, try the excellent smoked salmon, blini with caviar, or the famous *kotlety po-Kievski* (chicken Kiev), a garlic-and-butter-filled chicken breast encased in a crispy crust. Consider ordering a shot of vodka or a glass of local beer to accompany your meal.

Restaurants are typically open from noon until midnight, and late at night many nightclubs serve good food. There are also several 24-hour restaurants in both cities. During the week, many restaurants are nearly empty, but there's no hard and fast rule about this—an ordinary Wednesday can find even an off-the-beaten-path eatery packed, because more and more Russians eat out regularly.

Unless otherwise noted, the restaurants listed in this guide are open daily for lunch and dinner.

PAYING

Restaurants are now required by law to list their prices in rubles. There are some restaurants that cater to tourists that still list their prices in "conditional units" (YE in Cyrillic), which are pegged to an exchange rate of their own devising (usually the dollar or euro). They are required to also list the ruble equivalent, as payment can only be accepted in rubles. Many restaurants accept credit cards, though you should always double-check with the staff, even if the restaurant has a sign indicating that it accepts cards.

Also see Tipping, below.

RESERVATIONS AND DRESS

For the trendiest restaurants, it's a good idea to book in advance, particularly for groups of four or more. Regardless of where you are, it's a good idea to make a reservation if you can. In some places, it's expected. We only mention reservations specifically when they are essential (there's no other way you'll ever get a table) or when they are not accepted. We mention dress only when men are required to wear a jacket or a jacket and tie. In general, reservations are always a good idea.

WINES, BEER, AND SPIRITS

Drinks are normally ordered by milliliters (50, 100, or 200) or by the bottle. In upscale establishments you'll often find an impressive wine list with imported wine and foreign liquors. Most hotel restaurants and smaller restaurants have some imported wines, as well as cheaper wines from Moldova and Eastern Europe. Even the less-expensive restaurants can serve a bewildering array of vodkas and other spirits. Make any non-restaurant alcohol purchases from a proper shop, as wine and spirits counterfeiting is a problem. In Moscow, you won't be able to buy hard liquor after 10 pm, but beer and wine can still be purchased.

In the past few years, sales of beer have really taken off. Perhaps the most famous national brand is Baltika, which produces numbered beers—0 being the lightest, and 9 being difficult to distinguish from rocket fuel. But there are dozens of other companies producing ales, lagers, porters, and flavored and unfiltered beers, making it a drink that's become almost as ubiquitous as vodka.

Note that public intoxication is strictly punished. It's okay to become inebriated within an establishment as long as you don't fall over or become aggressive. However, if you walk along the streets in a drunken state, you'll be a target for police document checks and could possibly be arrested for public drunkenness. It is also technically illegal to drink alcoholic beverages on the street or in the metro. Although many people do this, you risk being fined by police.

■ ELECTRICITY

The electrical current in Russia is 220 volts, 50 cycles alternating current (AC); wall outlets take Continental-type plugs, with two round prongs.

Consider making a small investment in a universal adapter, which has several types of plugs in one lightweight, compact unit. Most laptops and mobile phone chargers are dual voltage (i.e., they operate equally well on 110 and 220 volts), so they require only an adapter. These days the same is true of small appliances such as hair dryers. Always check labels and manufacturer instructions to be sure. Don't use 110-volt outlets marked "for shavers only" for high-wattage appliances such as hair dryers.

Contacts Steve Kropla's Help for World Traveler's (⊕ *www.kropla.com*) has information on electrical and telephone plugs around the world. **Walkabout Travel Gear** (⊕ *www. walkabouttravelgear.com*) has a good coverage of electricity under "adapters."

■ EMERGENCIES

In case of emergency, the U.S. and U.K. consulates have consular officers on call at all times. This can be useful if a shakedown on the part of the local police goes too far, and—heaven forbid—if you land in jail. Insist on your right to call your consulate. There's a Canadian consulate in St. Petersburg; Australians and New Zealanders should check with the U.K. consulate first and the Canadian one if that doesn't work. A word of warning: phone lines to the U.S. consulate are constantly busy. It may take hours of persistent dialing to get through. In Moscow, unless you have official business or are met by embassy personnel or a compound resident, the U.S. embassy is off-limits, even to Americans.

FOREIGN EMBASSIES IN MOSCOW

Contact Canada (✉ *23 Starokonyushenny per., Kropotkinsky District* ☎ *495/105–6000* ⊕ www.russia.gc.ca Ⓜ *Kropotkinskaya*). **United Kingdom** (✉ *10 Smolenskaya nab., Arbat* ☎ *495/956–7200* ⊕ *ukinrussia.fco. gov.uk* Ⓜ *Smolenskaya*). **United States** (✉ *19/23 Novinsky bulvar, Bolshaya Nikitskaya* ☎ *495/728–5000* ⊕ *moscow.usembassy.gov* Ⓜ *Barrikadnaya*).

FOREIGN EMBASSIES IN ST. PETERSBURG

Contact Canada (✉ *32 Malodetskoselsky pr., Vladimirskaya* ☎ *812/325–8448* 🖷 *812/325– 8393* ⊕ *www.dfait.gc.ca* Ⓜ *Tekhnologichesky Institut*). **United Kingdom** (✉ *5 Pl. Proletarskoi Diktatury, Liteiny/Smolny* ☎ *812/320–3200* 🖷 *812/325–3211* ⊕ *ukinrussia.fco.gov.uk* Ⓜ *Ploshchad Vosstaniya*). **United States** (✉ *15 Furstadtskaya ul., Liteiny/Smolny* ☎ *812/331– 2600 or 812/274–8689, 812/271–6455 off-hours emergencies* 🖷 *812/331–2852* ⊕ *www.stpetersburg-usconsulate.ru* Ⓜ *Chernyshevskaya*).

GENERAL EMERGENCY CONTACTS

Ambulance (☎ *03*). **Fire** (☎ *01*). **Police** (☎ *02*).

■ HEALTH

The most common types of illnesses are caused by contaminated food and water. Especially in developing countries, and this includes Russia, drink only bottled, boiled, or purified water and drinks; don't drink from public fountains or use ice. You should even consider using bottled water to brush your teeth. Make sure food has been thoroughly cooked and is served to you fresh and hot; avoid vegetables and fruits that you haven't washed (in bottled or purified water) or peeled yourself. If you have problems, mild cases of traveler's diarrhea may respond to Imodium (known generically as loperamide) or Pepto-Bismol. Be sure to drink plenty of fluids; if you can't keep fluids down, seek medical help immediately.

SPECIFIC ISSUES IN MOSCOW AND ST. PETERSBURG

A visit to Russia poses no special health risk, but the country's medical system is far below world standards, a fact you should consider if you have chronic medical conditions that may require treatment during your visit. There are, however, Western-style clinics in Moscow and St. Petersburg. Bear in mind that treatment at these clinics will be expensive unless you have traveler's health insurance. You should also purchase insurance that covers medical evacuation. Sometimes even minor conditions cannot be treated adequately because of the severe and chronic shortage of basic medicines and medical equipment. Tuberculosis is a serious problem in Russian prisons, but the short-term visitor to Russia needn't worry about infection.

You should drink only boiled or bottled water. The water supply in St. Petersburg contains giardia, an intestinal parasite that can cause diarrhea, stomach cramps, and nausea. The gestation period is two to three weeks, so symptoms usually develop after an infected traveler has already returned home. The condition is easily treatable, but be sure to let your doctor know that you may have been exposed to this parasite. Avoid ice cubes and use bottled water to brush your teeth, particularly in St. Petersburg. In Moscow and St. Petersburg, imported and domestic bottled water is widely available in shops. It's a good idea to buy a liter of this water whenever you can. Hotel floor attendants always have a samovar in their offices and will provide boiled water if asked. Many top-end hotels filter their water, but it's best to double-check with reception. Mild cases of traveler's diarrhea may respond to Imodium (known generically as loperamide) or Pepto-Bismol, both of which can be purchased over the counter. Drink plenty of purified water or tea—chamomile is a good folk remedy. In severe cases, rehydrate yourself with a salt-sugar solution—½ teaspoon salt and 4 tablespoons sugar per quart of water.

Fruits and vegetables served in restaurants are generally washed with purified water and are thus safe to eat. However, food poisoning is common in Russia, so be wary of dairy products and ice cream that may not be fresh. The *pierogi* (meat- or cabbage-filled pies) sold everywhere on the streets are cheap and tasty, but they can give you a nasty stomachache.

SHOTS AND MEDICATION

Foreigners traveling to Russia are often advised to get vaccinated against diphtheria—in the early 1990s, both Moscow and St. Petersburg had outbreaks of this disease, and cholera is not unknown either. These outbreaks are now rare, but in particular, children should be immunized against diphtheria, measles, mumps, rubella, and polio, as well as hepatitis A and typhus. A flu shot is also recommended for winter travel for people of all ages.

■ TIP→ **If you travel a lot internationally— particularly to developing nations—refer to the CDC's** *Health Information for International Travel* **(aka Traveler's Health Yellow Book). Info from it is posted on the CDC Web site (⊕** *www.cdc.gov/travel/yb*)**, or you can buy a copy from a bookstore for $24.95.**

Health Warnings National Centers for Disease Control & Prevention (*CDC* ☎ *877/394–8747 international travelers' health line* ⊕ *www.cdc.gov/travel*). **World Health Organization** (*WHO* ⊕ *www.who.int*).

OVER-THE-COUNTER REMEDIES

Just about everything is available in pharmacies without a prescription, and many pharmacies stock Western painkillers and cold medicines, which mostly come from Germany and France. If you can't find your favorite brand, just ask for either aspirin or Panadol, which is another brand name for acetaminophen, the active ingredient in Tylenol. However, there's a good chance of buying a counterfeit medicine as well. According to official statistics, up to 30% of the most popular drugs in Russian pharmacies are fake or made illegally with inadequate technology. Large chains—including 36.6, PetroFarm, Natur Produkt, Pharmacy Doctor, and Pervaya Pomoshch—as well as the pharmacies of international clinics are believed to be free of such fakes. The chains are also more likely to stock Western brands.

▮ HOURS OF OPERATION

General hours for most businesses and banks are from 10 am to 6 pm. They are usually closed on weekends, and many take an hour off for lunch. In Moscow, there are many 24-hour shops, grocery stores, and restaurants.

Consulates, government offices, ticket agencies, and exchange offices tend to close for an hour in the afternoon for lunch. Nothing stands between Russian businesses and public holidays, and the major holidays often involve a break of at least two days—three if they coincide with a weekend. *See Holidays, below, for national holidays and Mail and Shipping for post office hours.*

Most gas stations are open 24 hours.

Museum hours vary, but many are closed on Monday. Many museums close for one extra day (on which they'd normally be open) at the end of the month.

In general, pharmacies are open from 9 am or 10 until 9 pm. There are, however, some 24-hour pharmacies in the major cities—check with the staff at your hotel to find those that are closest. Most shops and department stores are open from 10 am until 7 pm or even as late as 9 pm seven days a week. Fewer and fewer break for lunch for an hour in the afternoon. Restaurants and shopping arcades and malls are rarely closed at that time.

HOLIDAYS

Below is a list of Russia's major holidays, most of which entail closures of many businesses; note that religious holidays like Christmas and Easter are celebrated according to the Russian Orthodox calendar. In addition, from May 1 through May 9 and from December 31 through January 13, the entire country shuts down. These are major holiday periods when absolutely nobody does anything: even medical clinics close. These weeks can pose a real problem for visitors, so try not to travel to Russia during these special holiday periods. Be aware, too, that on the day before a public holiday, everything tends to close early.

January 1–5 (New Year's), January 7 (Russian Orthodox Christmas), February 23 (Defenders of the Fatherland Day), March 8 (International Women's Day), May 1 (Day of Spring and Labor), May 9 (Victory Day), June 12 (Russia Day), November 4 (Day of Reconciliation and Agreement).

▮ MAIL

The Russian postal system's service is more reliable than it once was, and many travelers report letters, postcards, and even packages arriving safe and sound abroad within a reasonable time. Post offices or *pochta* are open approximately from 8:30 am to 7 pm and mailboxes are painted blue. WestPost in St. Petersburg, which whisks mail off to Finland and sends it from there using European postal service, is another option if you don't want to risk it with the Russian post. There are also DHL and Federal Express offices in Moscow and St. Petersburg.

You can buy international envelopes and postcards at post offices and in hotel-lobby kiosks.

Sending mail from Russia to the United States, Europe, or Australia starts at 20R for a postcard or letter and is priced according to weight.

Mail from outside Russia takes approximately four weeks to arrive, sometimes longer, and sometimes it never arrives at all. The postal service will often open large packages and envelopes to inspect them, and sometimes things go missing.

Contacts DHL (⊠ *11 [1st] Pervaya-Yamskaya ul., Tverskaya, Moscow* ☎ *495/956-1000* ⊕ *www.dhl.ru* Ⓜ *Mayakovskaya*). **Federal Express** (⊠ *17 Gogolevsky bulvar, Kropotkinsky District, Moscow* ☎ *495/788-8881* ⊕ *www.fedex.com/ru* Ⓜ *Kropotkinskaya*). **WestPost** (⊠ *86 Nevsky pr., City Center, St. Petersburg* ☎ *812/275-0784* ⊕ *www.westpost.ru*).

SHIPPING PACKAGES

Stores don't offer shipping, so you should use DHL, Federal Express, or another mailing service. Don't attempt to send a work of art without the correct accompanying documents from the store where you bought it, proving that you are allowed to take it out of the country.

▌ MONEY

Today the ruble is reasonably stable at around 30R to the dollar. Talk of a growing middle class aside, the majority of Russians can only dream of buying Western-made cars and clothes, dining out, and traveling abroad for their holidays.

Goods and services aimed at foreigners are as expensive as anywhere in Western Europe. Public transport is cheap; a ride on the metro costs about 26R one-way. Taxi rates are generally low, but as soon as the driver realizes that you're a foreigner, the rate goes up. Some museums and theaters, such as the Armory Palace in the Moscow Kremlin and the Hermitage Museum in St. Petersburg, have instituted special, higher fees for foreign

tourists, whereas tickets for Russians are incredibly inexpensive. For example, a "foreign ticket" for an opera or ballet at the Mariinsky (Kirov) Theater costs around 3,400R, whereas a Russian can get a seat for a tenth of that, or even less. Expect to pay higher prices at any of the major cultural institutions—only foreigners who can prove they live in Russia can get "Russian" tickets.

ITEM	AVERAGE COST
Cup of Coffee	150R
Glass of Wine	300R
Glass of Beer	200R
Sandwich	300R
One-Mile Taxi Ride in Capital City	150R–200R
Museum Admission	50R–750R

Prices throughout this guide are given for adults. Substantially reduced fees are almost always available for children, students, and senior citizens.

■ **TIP→** Banks never have every foreign currency on hand, and it may take as long as a week for them to get it. If you're planning to exchange funds before leaving home, don't wait until the last minute.

ATMS AND BANKS

Your own bank will probably charge a fee for using ATMs abroad; the foreign bank you use may also charge a fee. Nevertheless, you'll usually get a better rate of exchange at an ATM than you will at a currency-exchange office or even when changing money in a bank. And extracting funds as you need them is a safer option than carrying around a large amount of cash.

■ **TIP→** PIN codes with more than four digits are not recognized at ATMs in Russia. If yours has five or more, remember to change it before you leave.

Bankomaty (bank machines) have cropped up all over the place in Moscow and St. Petersburg, and in the city centers they are not difficult to find: hotels and banks are the most obvious (and safest) places to look, but there are some on the streets as well. In addition, many metro stations now have them—but have a partner watch your back when you take money out, and remember what that pickpockets often hang around such places.

ATM Locations Cirrus (☎ 800/424–7787). **Plus** (☎ 800/843–7587).

CREDIT CARDS
Throughout this guide, the following abbreviations are used: **AE,** American Express; **DC,** Diners Club; **MC,** Master-Card; and **V,** Visa.

It's a good idea to inform your credit-card company before you travel, especially if you're going abroad and don't travel internationally very often. Otherwise, the credit-card company might put a hold on your card owing to unusual activity—not a good thing halfway through your trip. Record all your credit-card numbers—as well as the phone numbers to call if your cards are lost or stolen—in a safe place, so you're prepared should something go wrong. Both MasterCard and Visa have general numbers you can call (collect if you're abroad) if your card is lost, but you're better off calling the number of your issuing bank, since Master-Card and Visa usually just transfer you to your bank; your bank's number is usually printed on your card.

If you plan to use your credit card for cash advances, you'll need to apply for a PIN at least two weeks before your trip. Although it's usually cheaper (and safer) to use a credit card abroad for large purchases, note that some credit-card companies *and* the banks that issue them add substantial percentages to all foreign transactions, whether they're in a foreign currency or not. Check on these fees before leaving home, so there won't be any surprises when you get the bill.

Many shops, restaurants, and hotels within Moscow and St. Petersburg accept credit cards, though you should always double-check with the staff, despite any

signs you may see. If you can use your credit card or a debit card, the benefits are several. A credit card allows you to delay payment and gives you certain rights as a consumer. Establishments outside the cities are less likely to accept credit cards.

To report lost or stolen credit cards, the U.S. Embassy in Russia advises that you call your credit-card company collect through AT&T Direct. From Moscow, dial ☎ 755–5042; from St. Petersburg, dial ☎ 325–5042.

When you use your credit card to make travel purchases you may get free travel-accident insurance, collision-damage insurance, and medical or legal assistance, depending on the card and the bank that issued it. American Express, MasterCard, and Visa provide one or more of these services, so get a copy of your credit card's travel-benefits policy. If you're a member of an auto club, always ask hotel and car-rental reservations agents about auto-club discounts. Some clubs offer additional discounts on tours, cruises, and admission to attractions.

Reporting Lost Cards American Express (☎ 800/528–4800 in the U.S. or 336/393–1111 collect from abroad ⊕ www.americanexpress. com). **Diners Club** (☎ 800/234–6377 in the U.S. or 303/799–1504 collect from abroad ⊕ www.dinersclub.com). **MasterCard** (☎ 800/627–8372 in the U.S. or 636/722–7111 collect from abroad ⊕ www.mastercard. com). **Visa** (☎ 800/847–2911 in the U.S. or 410/581–9994 collect from abroad ⊕ www. visa.com).

CURRENCY AND EXCHANGE
The national currency in Russia is the ruble (R). There are paper notes of 10, 50, 100, 500, 1,000, and 5,000, and there are 1-, 2-, 5-, and 10-ruble coins. There are 100 kopeks in a ruble and there are coins for 1, 5, 10, and 50 kopeks.

Russians and resident expats have gotten used to thinking in both rubles and dollars—that is, talking in rubles but mentally pegging prices to the dollar. This can create a certain amount of confusion for the tourist, so bear the following in mind. First, remember that payment, by law, can only be made in rubles or by credit card. Nonetheless, some stores, restaurants, travel agencies, and retailers list prices in dollars, or "conditional units" (*uslovnye yedinitsy*, often marked on menus and price lists as *YE*), a euphemism for the dollar (or in some cases the euro). This practice is thankfully diminishing and you will most often see prices in rubles. In this book prices are listed in rubles for everything, including sights, attractions, hotels, and restaurants. Bear in mind that the sum in rubles will be high for hotels especially, it may be helpful to carry around a small pocket calculator for conversions that are difficult to do in your head.

At this writing one U.S. dollar equaled 31 rubles; one euro equaled 41 rubles; one U.K. pound equaled 50 rubles; one Canadian dollar equaled 30 rubles; one Australian dollar equaled 30 rubles; and one New Zealand dollar equaled 23 rubles.

Rubles can rarely be obtained at banks outside Russia, but if you somehow acquire them (through friends or acquaintances) it's legal to import or export them. There's no limit on the amount of foreign currency you may bring in with you, but you have to declare more than $10,000. ATMs are the way to go, but traveler's checks are a better option than bringing lots of currency. You should have at least $100 in cash (in 10s and 20s). If you don't mind the risk of theft or loss, bring more; you're bound to need it. For the most favorable rates, change money through banks. Although ATM transaction fees may be higher abroad than at home, ATM rates are excellent because they're based on wholesale rates offered only by major banks. You can also exchange foreign currency for rubles (and vice versa) at state-run exchange offices—where you'll get the worst rate—or at any of the numerous currency-exchange booths (*obmen valyuty*). Try to bring newer bills with you to Russia, as older versions (as well as worn or torn foreign bills) are frequently rejected by exchange offices. On your way out of Russia you can change excess rubles back into dollars at any bank or at the airport. For this you will need your passport.

■ TIP→ **Even if a currency-exchange booth has a sign promising no commission, rest assured that there's some kind of huge, hidden fee. (Oh . . . that's right. The sign didn't say no *fee*.) And as for rates, you're almost always better off getting foreign currency at an ATM or exchanging money at a bank.**

EXCHANGE RATES

Google does currency conversion. Just type in the amount you want to convert and an explanation of how you want it converted (e.g., "14 Swiss francs in dollars"), and then voilà. **Oanda.com** also allows you to print out a handy table with the current day's conversion rates. **XE.com** is another good currency conversion Web site.

Conversion sites Google (⊕ *www.google.com*). **Oanda.com** (⊕ *www.oanda.com*). **XE.com** (⊕ *www.xe.com*).

TRAVELER'S CHECKS

Some consider this the currency of the caveman, and it's true that fewer establishments accept traveler's checks these days. Using an ATM is preferable, but traveler's checks remain a cheap and secure way to carry extra money, particularly on trips to urban areas. Both Citibank (under the Visa brand) and American Express issue traveler's checks in the United States, but Amex is better known and more widely accepted; you can also avoid hefty surcharges by cashing Amex checks at Amex offices. Whatever you do, keep track of all the serial numbers in case the checks are lost or stolen.

Traveler's checks can be cashed at the state-run offices, at private banks, and at most major hotels within the cities (note that some exchange counters and many stores will not accept traveler's checks). If you're going to rural areas and small towns, convert your traveler's checks to rubles before you go. Lost or stolen checks can usually be replaced within 24 hours. To ensure a speedy refund, buy your own traveler's checks—don't let someone else pay for them: irregularities like this can cause delays. The person who bought the checks should make the call to request a refund.

Contacts **American Express** (✆ *888/412–6945 in the U.S., 801/945–9450 collect outside of the U.S. to add value or speak to customer service* ⊕ *www.americanexpress.com*).

■ PACKING

No matter what time of year you visit, bring a sweater. St. Petersburg especially can be unexpectedly cold in summer. A raincoat and fold-up umbrella are also musts. You'll probably be doing a lot of walking outdoors, so bring warm, comfortable clothing, and be sure to pack a pair of sturdy walking shoes.

Russians favor fashion over variety in their wardrobes, and it's perfectly acceptable to wear the same outfit several days in a row. Be sure to pack one outfit for dress-up occasions, such as the theater. The layer system works well in the unpredictable weather of fall and spring; wear a light coat with a sweater that you can put on and take off as the weather changes. In winter, bring heavy sweaters, warm boots, a wool hat, a scarf and mittens, and a heavy coat. Woolen tights or long underwear are essential during the coldest months. Russian central heating can be overly efficient, so again, use the layer system to avoid sweltering in an overheated building or train.

Russian pharmacies, supermarkets, and hotels all have reasonable stocks of the essential toiletries and personal hygiene products, but bring your own supplies of medicines and prescription drugs you take regularly. Although some well-known Western brands are easily available, you may not recognize the Russian equivalent of certain medicines. Consider whether you might want to bring along any items that can be difficult to find in Russia, such as insect repellent (in summer and fall mosquitoes can be a serious problem), camera batteries, laxatives, anti-diarrhea pills, travel-sickness medicine, and the like.

Toilet paper is plentiful in hotels but less so in public buildings, so bring small packages of tissues to carry around with you. Premoistened cleansing tissues will also come in handy, especially if you're traveling by train. A small flashlight may also prove useful, particularly if visiting someone's apartment—stairwells are often dimly lit.

Within Russia, the rules regulating carry-on luggage are strict but often disregarded. Checked luggage is frequently lost and/or pilfered, so pack as much as you can in your carry-on, including all of your valuables, for internal flights.

■ PASSPORTS AND VISAS

You must have a valid passport and visa to enter Russia. Within Russia you should carry your passport, visa, migration card, and registration card at all times. ■ TIP→ Make two photocopies of the data page of your passport (one for someone at home and another for you, carried separately from your passport). If you lose your passport, promptly call the nearest embassy or consulate and the local police.

PASSPORTS

U.S. citizens, even infants, need a valid passport to enter Russia for stays of any length, plus a visa. The passport should be valid for at least six months after the date you apply for the visa and must have at least two clear pages. U.S. passports are valid for 10 years. You must apply in person if you're getting a passport for the first time; if your previous passport was lost, stolen, or damaged; or if your previous passport has expired and was issued more than 15 years ago or when you were under 16. All children under 18 must appear in person to apply for or renew a passport. Both parents must accompany any child under 14 (or send a notarized statement with their permission) and provide proof of their relationship to the child.

There are 13 regional passport offices, as well as 7,000 passport acceptance facilities in post offices, public libraries, and other governmental offices. If you're renewing a passport, you can do so by mail. Forms are available at passport acceptance facilities and online.

The cost to apply for a new passport is $110 for adults, $80 for children under 16; renewals for adults are $110. Allow six weeks for processing, both for first-time passports and renewals. For an expediting fee of $60 you can reduce this time to about two weeks. If your trip is less than two weeks away, you can get a passport even more rapidly by going to a passport office with the necessary documentation. Private expediters can get things done in as little as 48 hours, but charge hefty fees for their services.

VISAS

You must have a valid visa to enter Russia for any length of time. Visa application procedures change frequently, so check the Russian Consulate's Web site for the latest information. At this writing, visa applicants must submit the following items to the Russian Consulate at least 21 days before departure: a completed visa application, your passport, two passport photos, confirmation letters and official itineraries from a Russian travel agency, hotel, or cruise line you'll be using (to prove that you have confirmed reservations) or a properly endorsed business invitation from a host organization, a self-addressed stamped envelope, and the application fee (between $140 and $450 for U.S. citizens, depending on what kind of visa—tourist, business, or multi-entry). The fee is higher if you need a faster turnaround time. Requirements vary slightly if you'll be staying as a guest in a private home or if you're traveling on business. Travel agencies have ways of getting around the advance hotel reservations requirement, but usually you must pay for at least one night's accommodation.

Go To Russia (⊕ *www.gotorussia.net*) is a useful resource for obtaining a visa.

Once in Russia, you will need to register your visa within 72 hours (three days) of your arrival (excluding weekends and official holidays). If you are staying at a hotel, they can register your visa for a small fee, usually around 300R, but they may charge up to 1,000R. If you are staying in an apartment, your visa must be registered by your landlord. The landlord will need to fill out a notification form indicating your passport and migration card details and present his or her passport registered at the same apartment to the local police precinct (in Moscow) or FMS office (commonly known as OVIR) in other cities. ⚠ **If you don't register your visa, you may be detained by police, fined on departure, and possibly even prevented from boarding your plane.** Citizens of Australia, Canada, and the United Kingdom must also obtain a visa to enter Russia. The procedures are similar to those outlined above for American citizens.

U.S. Passport Information U.S. Department of State (☎ 877/487–2778 ⊕ *travel.state.gov/ passport*).

U.S. Passport and Visa Expediters A. Briggs Passport & Visa Expeditors (☎ 800/806–0581 or 202/338–0111 ⊕ *www. abriggs.com*). **American Passport Express** (☎ 800/455–5166 or 800/841–6778 ⊕ *www. americanpassport.com*). **Passport Express** (☎ 800/362–8196 ⊕ *www.passportexpress. com*). **Travel Document Systems** (☎ 800/874–5100 or 202/638–3800 ⊕ *www. traveldocs.com*). **Travel the World Visas** (☎ 866/886–8472 or 301/495–7700 ⊕ *www. world-visa.com*).

Russian Consulates General Australia (✉ 7–9 Fullerton St., Woollahra, NSW, Australia ☎ 2/9326–1188 or 2/9326–1866). **Canada** (✉ 3685 ave. du Musée, Montréal, QC, Canada ☎ 514/843–5901). **New Zealand** (✉ 57 Messines Rd., Karori, Wellington, New Zealand ☎ 4/476–6742 or 4/381–3101). **U.K.** (✉ Kensington Palace Gardens, London, UK ☎ 020/7229–6412 ⊕ *ru.vfsglobal.co.uk*) *visa* applications). **U.S.** (✉ 9 E. 91st St., New York, NY, United States ☏ 212/348–0926 or 800/634–4296 ⊕ www.ruscon.org).

▌RESTROOMS

Public restrooms do exist, but they're mostly poorly marked and difficult to spot, and many are crumbling and not up to Western standards of hygiene. Blue chemical toilets on the street have no wash basin, and toilets in train stations and other public buildings are often the squat type. Your best bet is to buy a snack in a café or bar and avail yourself of its facilities. With the exception of some restrooms in stores, you always have to pay to use the facilities, usually around 10R. The attendant sometimes has a dish for tips. It's also a good idea to carry a package of tissues with you into public restrooms.

▌SAFETY

Travel to Russia is fraught with many unusual challenges, in addition to the normal safety and security issues you would associate with travel to any large city. Terrorist acts such as bombings have occurred in large Russian cities. In January 2011, a suicide bomber set off an explosion in the arrival's hall of Moscow's Domodedovo Airport, killing 35 people. A year before, some 40 people died after two bombs exploded on the capital's Metro system during rush hour. Russian authorities have attributed such attacks to an increase in the Islamist insurgency in Russia's troubled North Caucasus region. Be alert for any unusual behavior or packages left unattended in public. Consult government-issued travel advisories (⇨ *Visitor Information*) before your trip.

Never change money on the street; as with con artists everywhere, counterfeit money, sleights of hand, and the old folded-note trick are practiced by people standing outside official exchange offices. When using money-exchange booths, thoroughly check that you have received the full amount. As well as avoiding taxis that already have occupants and avoiding gypsy cabs, never allow your driver to stop to take an extra passenger after you have gotten in. It's possible that this is indeed a random passerby; it's also possible that he is an accomplice of the driver who has been waiting around the corner. If your driver attempts to take another fare, say *"nyet"* (no) and/or *"nye nado"* (literally "not necessary," meaning here "I'd rather not"). Better still, team up with a fellow lone traveler and split the fare.

Tourists are a common target for thieves in Moscow and St. Petersburg, so stay alert, particularly in places commonly frequented by visitors (outside hotels, for example, and at bars). If you get in trouble, don't expect much help from the police, who are often called *bandity* (gangsters) by natives.

Although police in the West are usually considered keepers of the peace, those in uniform do not enjoy this image in Russia. The reason is partly because of their habit of shaking people down to supplement their meager salaries. The Russian government is attempting to improve relations between the police and the public, and there is talk of a future name change from militsia to politsia. Pay special attention when leaving a nightclub—the cops know that these are hangouts for foreigners and have been known to lie in wait to extract "fines" for alleged drunken behavior. If you find yourself in any tricky situations with the police, be prepared to show your passport, migration card, registration card, and visa. In all situations, be polite, allow the police to search you if they require, and stay cool. This is by no means the way all Russian police act, but it happens too frequently to be dismissed as the actions of a minority.

Exercise the same precautions you would in any major city. If you are catching a night train, avoid waiting on the street outside the train station. In the metro, avoid very crowded cars where you could get your pocket picked. If you go to a street market, keep an expensive camera or phone out of sight. In cafés, don't hang your bag on the back of your chair where you can't see it. Moscow has well-lit central streets, and many stores, clubs, and cafés are open 24 hours, so as long as you avoid deserted areas, you should be fine. It's best to stick with a companion if you're out at night.

■ TIP→ **Distribute your cash, credit cards, IDs, and other valuables between a deep front pocket, an inside jacket or vest pocket, and a hidden money pouch. Don't reach for the money pouch when you're in public.**

GOVERNMENT INFORMATION AND ADVISORIES

Advisories U.S. Department of State (⊕ *travel.state.gov*).

Safety Transportation Security Administration (*TSA* ⊕ *www.tsa.gov*).

■ TAXES

Airport departure taxes are almost always included in the price of the airline ticket. Hotels charge an 18% value-added tax if you pay in cash or by credit card upon arrival; if you pay in advance, then you don't get charged these taxes (at least that's the general rule). Moscow hotels add an additional 1% tax to your bill.

Russia's 18% value-added tax (V.A.T.) is charged on most everything and refundable on almost nothing (interestingly, the V.A.T. law specifically says the V.A.T. does not apply to exported goods, but there's no mechanism worked out for handling refunds at the airport, nor do stores have V.A.T. refund forms). Goods bought at duty-free shops in the airport are free of V.A.T.

■ TIME

Russia, the largest country in the world, has 11 time zones. Moscow and St. Petersburg share one and are both three hours ahead of London, eight hours ahead of New York City, 11 hours ahead of Los Angeles, and six to eight hours behind Sydney, depending on daylight saving. Daylight saving time is in sync with the rest of the Northern Hemisphere.

TIPPING GUIDELINES FOR MOSCOW AND ST. PETERSBURG	
Bartender	50R, or round up the bill on simple orders; leave more for larger or special orders
Bellhop	100R per bag, depending on the level of the hotel
Hotel Concierge	150R to 300R or more, if he or she performs a service for you
Hotel Doorman	50R to 100R if he helps you get a cab
Hotel Maid	100R per day (either daily or at the end of your stay, in cash)
Hotel Room-Service Waiter	10%–15% per delivery, even if a service charge has been added
Porter at Airport or Train Station	100R per bag
Tour Guide	10% of the cost of the tour
Waiter	15%–20%, with 20% being the norm at high-end restaurants; nothing additional if a service charge is added to the bill
Restroom and coat-check attendants	Restroom attendants in more expensive restaurants expect some small change. Tip coat-check personnel at least 100R per item checked unless there is a fee, then nothing.

■ TIPPING

Tipping is the norm in Russia. Waiters and porters will all expect a tip, and cloakroom and restroom attendants will appreciate them. A tour guide may be given a tip by the group as a whole after an excursion, although depending on the situation, it may be more appropriate to give a small souvenir. Whether you should tip the bartender depends on the establishment, but it's not the norm. Add an extra 10% to 15% to a restaurant bill. If you have negotiated a taxi fare ahead of time, there is no need to tip on top of that payment. Some restaurants add a service charge to the bill automatically, so double-check before you leave a big tip. If you're paying by credit card, leave the tip in cash—the waiter is less likely to see it if you add it to the credit-card charge. Moreover, some restaurants actively refuse to allow tips being added on to the bill by credit card. The only places with bellhops who carry your bags are Moscow and St. Petersburg's five-star hotels; in such establishments, a 100R tip—more if you have many heavy bags—is a decent thank you.

▮ TOURS

GUIDED TOURS

Among companies that sell tours to Moscow and St. Petersburg, the following are nationally known, have a proven reputation, and offer plenty of options. The classifications used below represent different price categories, and you'll probably encounter these terms when talking to a travel agent or tour operator. The key difference is usually in accommodations, which run from budget to better, and better-yet to best.

CONTACTS

Budget Cosmos (⇨ Globus in Deluxe). **ITS Tours & Travel** (✉ 707 Texas Ave., Suite 101A, College Station, TX ☎ 800/533-8688 🖷 979/693-9673 ⊕ supersavertours.com).

First-Class Brendan Tours (✉ 21625 Prairie St., Chatsworth, CA ☎ 818/428-6000 or 800/421-8446 🖷 818/772-6492 ⊕ www.brendantours.com). **General Tours** (✉ 53 Summer St., Keene, NH ☎ 603/357-5033 or 800/221-2216 🖷 603/357-4548 ⊕ www.generaltours.com). **Insight International Tours** (✉ 801 Katella Ave., Anaheim, CA ☎ 800/582-8380 🖷 714/935-2570 ⊕ www.insightvacations.com). **Intourist** (⊕ www.intourist.com). **Isram World of Travel** (✉ 630

3rd Ave., New York, NY ☎ 212/661-1193 or 800/223-7460 🖷 212/370-1477 ⊕ www.isram.com). **Mir Corporation** (✉ 85 S. Washington St., Suite 210, Seattle, WA ☎ 206/624-7289 or 800/424-7289 🖷 206/624-7360 ⊕ www.mircorp.com). **Trafalgar Tours** (✉ 11 E. 26th St., New York, NY ☎ 800/854-0103 🖷 800/457-6644 ⊕ www.trafalgartours.com).

Deluxe Exeter International (✉ 25 Davis Blvd., Tampa, FL ☎ 813/251-5355 or 800/633-1008 🖷 813/251-6685 ⊕ www.exeterinternational.com). **Globus** (✉ 5301 S. Federal Circle, Littleton, CO ☎ 866/755-8581 🖷 303/347-2080 ⊕ www.globusandcosmos.com). **Maupintour** (✉ 10650 W. Charleston Blvd., Summerlin, NV ☎ 800/255-4266 🖷 702/260-3787 ⊕ www.maupintour.com).

Super-Deluxe Abercrombie & Kent (✉ 1520 Kensington Rd., Suite 212, Oak Brook, IL ☎ 630/954-2944 or 800/554-7016 🖷 630/954-3324 ⊕ www.abercrombiekent.com). **Travcoa** (✉ Box 2630, 2350 S.E. Bristol St., Suite 310, Newport Beach, CA 92660 ☎ 946/476-2800 or 800/992-2003 🖷 946/476-2538 ⊕ www.travcoa.com).

▮ TRIP INSURANCE

Comprehensive trip insurance is valuable if you're booking a very expensive or complicated trip (particularly to an isolated region) or if you're booking far in advance. Comprehensive policies typically cover trip cancellation and interruption, letting you cancel or cut your trip short because of illness, or, in some cases, acts of terrorism in your destination. Such policies might also cover evacuation and medical care. (For trips abroad you should have at least medical-only coverage. *See Medical Insurance and Assistance under Health.*) Some also cover you for trip delays because of bad weather or mechanical problems as well as for lost or delayed luggage.

Another type of coverage to consider is financial default—that is, when your trip is disrupted because a tour operator, airline, or cruise line goes out of business.

Generally you must buy this when you book your trip or shortly thereafter, and it's available to you only if your operator isn't on a list of excluded companies.

Always read the fine print of your policy to make sure that you're covered for the risks that most concern you. Compare several policies to be sure you're getting the best price and range of coverage available.

Insurance Comparison Info **Insure My Trip** (☎ 800/487–4722 ⊕ www.insuremytrip.com). **Square Mouth** (☎ 800/240–0369 ⊕ www. squaremouth.com).

Comprehensive Insurers **Access America** (☎ 800/284–8300 ⊕ www.accessamerica.com). **AIG Travel Guard** (☎ 800/826–4919 ⊕ www. travelguard.com). **CSA Travel Protection** (☎ 800/873–9855 ⊕ www.csatravelprotection. com). **Travel Insured International** (☎ 800/243–3174 ⊕ www.travelinsured. com). **Travelex Insurance** (☎ 888/228–9792 ⊕ www.travelex-insurance.com).

▌ VISITOR INFORMATION

Russia does not have major tourism board offices in Moscow and St. Petersburg or abroad, but many commercial travel agencies can help you plan your trip. The Moscow Committee for Tourism has an office in Moscow. Their Web site is in Russian, but you can access an English version by

> ### WORD OF MOUTH
>
> After your trip, be sure to rate the places you visited and share your experiences and travel tips with us and other Fodorites in Travel Ratings and Talk on www.fodors.com.

clicking the first option on the left-hand sidebar, which is unhelpfully only sign-posted in Russian. St. Petersburg's general tourist information is available at Travel. SPB.Ru.

Contacts **The Moscow Committee for Tourism** (☎ 495/232–5657 ⊕ www.moscow-city. ru). **Travel.SPB.Ru** (⊕ www.travel.spb.ru).

ONLINE TRAVEL TOOLS

Media **Johnson's Russia List** (⊕ www.cdi.org/ russia/johnson). **The Moscow Times** (⊕ www. themoscowtimes.com). **Radio Free Europe** (⊕ www.rferl.org). **Russia!** (⊕ www.readrussia. com). **RT** (⊕ www.rt.com). **The St. Petersburg Times** (⊕ www.sptimes.ru).

Other Resources The following Web sites give provide interesting historical background as well as current statistics about Russia and its language. **Bucknell Russian Program** (⊕ www.departments.bucknell.edu/russian). **CIA World Factbook** (⊕ www.cia.gov/library/ publications/the-world-factbook). **Way to Russia** (⊕ www.waytorussia.net).

INDEX

PHOTO CREDITS

NOTES

ABOUT OUR WRITERS

Sabra Ayres is a journalist who has spent more than seven years working in the former Soviet Union. She was based in Moscow for four years as a correspondent for the Cox Newspapers. Her articles on Russia and beyond have appeared in the *International Herald Tribune, The Baltimore Sun, Newsweek Japan,* ABCnews.com, and the *Economist Intelligence Unit.* Before becoming a journalist, Sabra spent two years as a U.S. Peace Corps volunteer in Ukraine. She worked on the Experience Moscow and St. Petersburg and Travel Smart chapters.

Anna Coppola, a native of Russia has spent over four years in the United States. A professional journalist and media producer she holds a master's degree in media arts from Emerson College, Boston, and has extensive experience reporting and writing in Russia and abroad. Since 2007 she has been working as a Culture Fluent for the global market research publication *Iconoculture,* where she literally and figuratively translates cultural differences of the Russian consumer market for American marketing professionals. She is also a contributing writer of Moscow's business magazine *Kompania* and a self-proclaimed tour guide for her visiting foreign friends and family in Moscow and St. Petersburg. She updated the Moscow Shopping and Understanding Moscow and St. Petersburg chapters this edition.

Tom Parfitt has lived and worked as a journalist in Moscow since 2002, contributing to *The Guardian, The Sunday Times, Foreign Policy, The Boston Globe,* and other international publications. Prior to moving to Russia, Tom studied politics and security at the University of London's School of Slavonic and East European Studies. Tom's particular interest is the North Caucasus region of southern Russia. In 2008 he completed a four-month trek from the Black Sea to the Caspian across the region; a trip which was sponsored by the Royal Geographical Society (UK). He has also travelled to the Arctic, Siberia, and the Russian Far East. He updated the Moscow Nightlife and the Arts and Side Trips from Moscow chapters.

Ezekiel Pfeifer is a freelance writer and journalist living in Moscow. He worked for the city's most respected English-language newspaper, *The Moscow Times,* from 2007–2009 writing mostly about culture and food. He worked on the Moscow Exploring, Moscow Where to Eat, and Moscow Where to Stay chapters this edition.

Galina Stolyarova is the chief reporter of *The St. Petersburg Times,* covering the arts, culture, and travel. She has traveled extensively in Europe, Latin America, and the United States and has written travel features and reports from São Paulo, Orlando, Abu-Dhabi, St. Moritz, Vienna, and other places. She also writes regularly about travel, arts, fashion, health, and beauty for *Life Style Magazine,* a supplement to *Vedomosti* newspaper. Galina is also a columnist with the award-winning English-language analytical Internet magazine *Transitions Online.* She updated St. Petersburg Where to Eat, St. Petersburg Where to Stay, St. Petersburg Nightlife and the Arts, and St. Petersburg Shopping chapters this edition.

A reporter at the *St. Petersburg Times,* **Irina Titova** has written everything from daily-news articles to unusual feature stories. She also studied for a year at St. Michael's College in Vermont, which first introduced her to American journalism. Irina worked on Exploring St. Petersburg, St. Petersburg Where to Stay, and Side Trips from St. Petersburg this edition.